Creative Minds in Contemporary Theology

Edited by
Philip Edgcumbe Hughes

This symposium, now revised and updated, is designed to provide an introduction to the thought of some of the religious thinkers who have made an impact on Christian theology in the twentieth century. Fifteen major "creative minds" are treated — Karl Barth, G. C. Berkouwer, Dietrich Bonhoeffer, Emil Brunner, Rudolf Bultmann, Oscar Cullman, James Denney, C. H. Dodd, Herman Dooyeweerd, P. T. Forsyth, Charles Gore, Reinhold Niebuhr, Pierre Teilhard de Chardin, William Temple, and Paul Tillich.

A separate chapter is devoted to each of these thinkers. Each chapter is made up of four sections: (I) a biographical sketch, which places the man in his national and cultural setting; (II) an exposition, which explicates the governing concepts and main contributions in his thought and writings; (III) an evaluation, which assesses the man's thought as measured against the biblical revelation and as viewed from within the perspective of historic evangelical theology; (IV) a bibliography.

These essays have been written by scholars who in each case are thoroughly familiar with the works of the men about whom they write. Each essay is characterized by clarity of style and arrangement, and depth of understanding is conveyed with simplicity of

(Continued on back flap)

well as to ministers and thoughtful laymen.

*Creative Minds in
Contemporary Theology*

Creative Minds in Contemporary Theology

*A guidebook to the principal teachings of
Karl Barth, G. C. Berkouwer, Dietrich Bonhoeffer,
Emil Brunner, Rudolf Bultmann, Oscar Cullmann,
James Denney, C. H. Dodd, Herman Dooyeweerd,
P. T. Forsyth, Charles Gore, Reinhold Niebuhr,
Pierre Teilhard de Chardin, and Paul Tillich*

—EDITED BY PHILIP EDGCUMBE HUGHES
TH.D., D.LITT

Second, Revised Edition WITHDRAWN

Wm. B. Eerdmans Publishing Co., Grand Rapids, Michigan

Quotations from the following works by Dietrich Bonhoeffer reprinted
with permission of The Macmillan Company: *Letters and Papers from
Prison* (Copyright by The Macmillan Company 1953. © by SCM Press
Ltd., 1967), *Ethics* (© SCM Press Ltd., 1955), and *The Cost of Discipleship* (© SCM Press Ltd., 1959).

Editor's Preface

This volume is designed as a guidebook for the serious reader who desires a summary introduction to the principal teaching of some of the religious thinkers who have made an impact on contemporary theology. Its purpose is both expository and critical; but it will not do the reader's thinking for him. An adequate acquaintance with and understanding of the minds of these men will be achieved only by the study at first hand of their writings. The chapters that follow have, however, been prepared by scholars who in each case have a thorough knowledge of the works of the men about whom they write. Their exposition of the thought of these "creative minds" (all men who have been active during this twentieth century) is factual and objective; their evaluations are intended to be helpful and critically constructive.

It will be readily apparent that the "contemporary theology" of the title does not mean "modernistic" theology or some particular brand of theology to which the prefix "neo" may be attached, but the theology of our twentieth century in its great variety of manifestations — Reformed, liberal, evolutionistic, and so on. The epithet "creative," too, is used in a general sense. The reader will be able to decide for himself the extent to which the theologians discussed in this book deserve to be described as creative in the sense of that term as defined in the opening chapter on "The Creative Task of Theology."

The unitive feature of this volume is to be found in the fact that all the contributors are scholars of evangelical conviction who place themselves under the authority of Holy Scripture, wishing to bring every thought into captivity to the obedience of Christ. They have, of course, enjoyed complete freedom in the composition of their respective chapters.

Inevitably, regarding a book of this nature, some will feel that important theological figures of our day are missing who ought to have a place in such a collection. This no doubt is true. A selection had to be made, however, and certain limits set. But the desirability of preparing a further volume which will augment the range of this present one by giving a second collection of studies of modern theological thinkers is under consideration.

PHILIP EDGCUMBE HUGHES

5

Preface to the Second Edition

It is gratifying that this volume has been so well received that a second edition is now called for. Apart from a number of smaller adjustments and corrections, two major changes have been introduced. A chapter on Dietrich Bonhoeffer from the pen of Professor Kenneth Hamilton has been added; and a new chapter on Teilhard de Chardin, written by the Rev. Richard Acworth, has been substituted for the one that appeared in the first edition. Rev. Acworth, who is a specialist in philosophy and has recently completed advanced studies in Paris, was until recently a Jesuit priest, and is particularly well qualified to write on Teilhard de Chardin. These changes, it is hoped, will extend and enhance the usefulness of this volume.

P. E. H.

Contents

1 PHILIP E. HUGHES

The Creative Task of Theology

Creativity, properly speaking, is the faculty or process of making something out of nothing. Given this definition, the cynic might be tempted to observe that the overwhelming flood of elucubrations that now pour forth from the religious publishing houses indicates that there is an astonishing number of theological technicians with a facility for fabricating intricate patterns out of nonexistent or insubstantial premises. Inventiveness, however, rather than creativity, is the category to which industry of this kind belongs. Its exponents seem intent on producing or reproducing nothing old: for them whatever is not new is dismissed as archaic and irrelevant. At the other end of the spectrum are those who seem intent on producing nothing new: for them, whatever is not old is suspect and threatening. They deal in prefabricated blocks of theological concrete. Creativity is not for them. But there is a mean between these two extremes, for we have it on good authority that the theologian who is well instructed in the kingdom of heaven is "like a householder who can produce from his store both the new and the old" (Matt. 13:52).

Both the new and the old: this is the framework of theology that is truly creative. But it is important that we should understand clearly what we mean by creativity in this connection. To produce half a hundred massive volumes of divinity is in itself not necessarily creative, except (almost certainly) of fatigue and boredom. Nor is the most brilliant human theorizing in the ultimate issue creative. The creative function, in its absolute sense, belongs to God, not to man. God alone is the Creator of all that exists. "By faith we understand that the world was created by the Word of God" (Heb. 11:3). This is the first of the old things that the wise theologian brings out from his storehouse. Man himself is God's creature, and he is this before he can even begin

Dr. Philip Edgcumbe Hughes is Professor of Historical Theology and Chairman of the Department of Theology at Conwell School of Theology in Philadelphia. He is the author, translator, and editor of numerous theological works.

to think about being in any sense creative himself. It follows that if we are to speak about creativity in relation to man and his powers the term can be used only in a secondary or derivative sense. Indeed, the creative faculty, which is one of the glories of man, is a significant aspect of the image of God in which man has been made.

The Creator's mandate to man to "subdue" the earth and to "have dominion" over the created order is in itself essentially creative (Gen. 1:28). It is an invitation to man to realize and bring to expression the creative potentialities that reside within him. Man alone of all God's creatures has the power to think, to discuss, to plan, to explore and harness the limitless forces of nature, to adapt, to build, to civilize — in short, to be a cultural being. He has been given the logical capacity to investigate, systematically and scientifically, the logic of the universe, which itself is the imprint of the logic of the Divine Mind. It is the basic rationalty of things which not only explains the fact that the world is a *cosmos* and a *universe,* that is, an ordered whole, but also alone makes possible the function of the scientist and the philosopher, so that, as one fact or truth leads on to another, man the thinker can penetrate ever more deeply and creatively into the logical structure of the world to which he belongs. But the exercise of the faculty of creativity, if it is to be consistently meaningful and progressive, must be fulfilled by man in constant recognition of his own creatureliness: in other words, in acknowledgment that as a finite creature he has capacities that are limited, that he is ever dependent on and indebted to his Creator for all that he is and has, and therefore that in all that he does his ambition should be to glorify and be grateful to God. Man is not God. He does not and cannot work from nothing. He works from the fundamental *datum* of an ordered universe which is stamped with the logic and the goodness of the divine character.

But there is a second "old" thing which the wise theologian brings out of his storehouse, and that is the lamentable fact that man is a *fallen* creature. With incredible folly he has allowed himself to be drawn by an enemy into rebellion against his beneficent Creator, in the empty expectation that by doing so, by asserting his own self-adequacy, he will become as God. But man can never cease to be what he essentially is, a creature (and all that that implies), any more than the Creator can cease to be what He essentially is, God. How could man's willful attempt to overturn the true order of things have any effect other than to bring a curse on the expression of his creativity? By his self-esteem and self-inversion he has introduced a dark shadow of chaos into the universe. The nemesis of frustration dogs his steps. There is evil mixed with the good of even his highest achievements. The perversion of society, which is the rotten core of every civilization, is the bitter harvest of human sinfulness. Despite all the remarkable cultural, scientific, and philanthropic advances of the centuries, man shows

10

a malign propensity (which certainly has not decreased with the increase of knowledge) to employ his great faculties neither to the glory of God nor for the benefit of his fellow men, but for the creation of falsehood and hatred and injustice and destruction. The advance of technology has not been matched by an advance of morality and magnanimity.

By persuading himself, against all reason, that the image of God is the same thing as the being of God, that the reflection or imprint is identical with the reality, or, to put it in more recent language, that God is the ultimate depth of all his being, man seeks to destroy the "image" with its implications of dependence and creatureliness and shuts his eyes to the inescapable truth, so emphatically expounded by Christ, that it is precisely from the depths of his fallen nature that all the things which defile him proceed (Mark 7:21). Unable, however, to gainsay the defilement of society (of which he is part) by greed, lust, lying, and violence, he attempts to cover over his guilt by blaming forces over which he has no control — heredity, environment, sickness, mental black-out — and pleads for consolation, not punishment. This, of course, is an appalling abnegation of the proper dignity of man. It warns us that the suppression of the image of God, in which man's true dignity resides, so far from exalting man to God-like heights, plunges him into an abyss of human futility. He is conscious of the amazing creative faculties within himself; yet, instead of using them consistently and purposefully and with gratitude to the glory of God, whose image he bears, he finds himself, through his own folly, increasingly in the grip of frustration and meaninglessness. How could it be otherwise when the true order of things, which alone can give coherence and meaning to existence, is met with denial and rebellion?

This predicament of man is, of course, the setting for the Gospel. Redemption is essential if man is to be made whole once again. And the Good News is precisely this: that "God was in Christ reconciling the world to Himself" (II Cor. 5:19); that through Christ's offering of Himself in man's stead the work of atonement has been achieved, so that the new man in Christ Jesus is one in whom the divine image is renewed, his dignity restored, and his personality reintegrated. Now at last such a man begins to live creatively and purposefully to the glory of God and the benefit of his fellow men. And this stupendous truth — that, thanks entirely to the divine initiative on man's behalf, the grace and mercy and power of God are freely available — is the third "old" thing that the wise theologian brings out of his storehouse. It is a *datum,* a constant, ever true and ever relevant

"Know thyself" was the Socratic principle of wisdom; but Socrates' interpretation of this principle was vitiated by the dualistic concept of the world which governed his thought. The dilemma he faced could be surmounted only by the abandonment of the true humanity of man, by tearing man asunder in an irreconcilable dichotomy of soul and body.

11

The Christian understanding of man alone enables him to know himself in a manner which is free from the crippling conflicts of a dualistic world-view. While it is true that, inasmuch as he is a creature, man cannot have that completeness of knowledge which belongs to the Creator, yet the man-in-Christ has a knowledge of himself which is true and coherent, and indeed he looks forward to the consummation of his redemption when he will know even as he is known (I Cor. 13:12). And to know oneself truly is also to know oneself creatively, because it is to know oneself as constituted in the image of God, which, for the believer, is reintegrated in Christ. The man-in-Christ is set free to live in joyful creativity to the glory of God. Furthermore, as the whole man is redeemed by Christ, body as well as soul, so this applies to man's being in its entirety, in every one of his activities and relationships. In no sphere, surely, does it apply more obviously than in the sphere of theology.

The proper task of theology, then, is a creative task. But the theologian does not fashion his system out of thin air. Just as the scientist works with and from the given substance of the cosmos, and just as the sculptor shapes his forms from a given substance such as marble, so the theologian has a given "substance" with which to work. This "substance" is the Word of God. The Word of God is indeed the creative force of the universe. The world itself is the effect of that dynamic word (cf. Heb. 11:3 already cited) and vibrates with its creative potentialities. Nor is the substance of the cosmos a mere static mass. The basis of all matter, as we know today, is energy. In every minute particle there is an unimaginable potential of dynamic force. In every structure, small and great, there is an amazing logic. The more we learn about our universe, the more conscious we become of how little we really know of the wonders of its structure and operation. Despite the spectacular advances of our day and the preceding centuries of intensive research, thinkers, scientists, and artists are aware that they have advanced but a short distance into the vast ocean of creativity that lies before them. The increase of man's horizon of knowledge and perception leads, indeed, not to the diminishment but to the expansion of the creative task. In this sense at least it may be affirmed that ours is an ever-expanding universe.

The scientist does not find that his creative faculties are inhibited by having to work with the given substance of the world. On the contrary, he is ever discovering that the treasures and potencies of the cosmos are inexhaustive and that his task becomes ever more demanding and exciting. So, too, the creative faculties of the theologian are not inhibited by having to work with the *datum* of the Word of God, but are unfailingly stretched and challenged by the inexhaustible treasures and potencies that belong to it.

But what exactly is this Word of God with and from which the theologian has to work. It is, for all practical purposes, the Word of God written, that is, the Bible. This by itself is a blunt statement, and open to misunderstanding. It must not be taken to imply, as some have supposed it to imply, the supplanting of the authority of the Living Word of God, Jesus Christ our Lord, by the authority of an inanimate document of paper and print. The authority of Scripture and the authority of Christ are not in fact in conflict; for it is precisely the Bible that bears unequivocal testimony to the supreme Lordship of Christ. The central focus of the scriptural revelation is the person of Jesus Christ and His redeeming work. Within the framework of God's dealings in creation, judgment, and redemption with His creatures, man is placed in his world in the perspective of eternity. The Bible, indeed, in that it conveys the knowledge of God's saving deeds in Christ, plays an integral role in the divine purpose of redemption. The treasures creatively quarried from Holy Scripture are not the treasures of an inanimate object but the riches of Him who is the living Lord. The Written Word ever points us to the Living Word "in whom are hid all the treasures of wisdom and knowledge" (Col. 2:3).

The authority of the Bible, moreover, rests on the fact that it bears the imprimatur of Christ our supreme authority. So plainly is this the case, that there can be no question of the authority of Christ being dependent on the word of the Bible: it is in fact the authority of the Bible which is dependent on the word of Christ. And this is true not only of the authority of the Old Testament. The crucial factor is certainly the authority of the New Testament, for the authority of the Old Testament, seen in the Christian perspective of fulfillment and consummation, stands or falls with the authority of the New Testament. How, then, is the authority of the New Testament to be established? The answer, already indicated, must be: only by the supremely authoritative word of Christ. And this particular word has been preserved for us in the pages of the New Testament itself.

St. John tells us how, during those sacred hours in the upper room prior to His betrayal and crucifixion, our Lord assured His apostles that after His departure the Holy Spirit, who is the very Spirit of truth, would not only be sent, but would actually dwell in them; that He would bear witness to Christ, and glorify Him, taking the things of Christ and declaring them to them; and that He would bring to their remembrance all that He had taught them (John 14:16f., 26; 15:26; 16:13ff.). This explains the transformation in the apostles after the day of Pentecost, as seen in the Acts and the Epistles, compared with what they were before Pentecost, as seen in the Gospels. The privileged but uncomprehending years at the feet of Christ were not wasted: what before they had failed to grasp they now understood and expounded with assurance. Their teaching was not their own; it was Christ's, under the guidance of the Holy Spirit. It is customary to speak of

13

the doctrine of the New Testament as apostolical; but it is something more than this, for, in the true and ultimate analysis, it is dominical: it is the doctrine of the Lord Himself.

These promises of Christ, then, and their Pentecostal fulfillment constitute the veritable charter of the New Testament. The teachings of its pages carry the authentic ring of the voice of the Master Himself. Christ continues to instruct His Church through the writings of His apostles, who themselves were under the control of the Holy Spirit. This means, inevitably, that if the Church is to obey the authority of the Living Word it must submit itself to the authority of the Written Word. This the Church appreciated from the beginning. Hence the careful sifting out of the spurious from the genuine apostolic writings. And hence the most significant development in the history of the post-apostolic Church, namely, the ecumenical acknowledgment of the canon of the New Testament. So far from placing itself above Scripture, the Church thereby placed itself under Scripture, saying in effect: This is the rule and standard to which the faith and conduct of the Church must conform if it is to remain genuinely Christian. The fixing of the canon was of crucial and abiding importance because it was the acknowledgment of the dominical authenticity of the New Testament. It was a clear and fully conscious marking out of the boundary line beyond which the Church was not to wander. As Oscar Cullmann has written:

> The fixing of the Christian canon of Scripture signifies precisely that *the Church herself* at a given moment traced a clear and firm line of demarcation between the period of the apostles and the period of the Church. . . , in other words, between apostolic tradition and ecclesiastical tradition. If this was not the significance of the formation of the canon the event would be meaningless. By establishing the *principle* of a canon, the Church recognized in this very act that *from that moment* tradition was no longer a criterion of truth. She drew a line under the apostolic tradition. She declared implicitly that from that moment every subsequent tradition must be submitted to the *control* of the apostolic tradition. In other terms, she declared: here is the tradition which *constituted* the Church, which imposed itself on her.[1]

This being so, it is undoubtedly true, as Emil Brunner has observed, that the fate of the Bible is the fate of Christianity. Christ sternly rebuked the traditionalists of His day for rejecting the commandment of God in order to keep their tradition and thus making void the Word of God (Mark 7:9ff.). And it has been amply demonstrated in the history of the Church that when the Bible has been lost from sight, overlaid with the traditions of men, Christianity has languished and sunk

---

[1] "Scripture and Tradition," *Scottish Journal of Theology*, Vol. 6, No. 2, June 1953, pp. 126f.

into ineffectiveness; but when the Bible has been restored to its rightful place then too the Church has recovered its vitality and authority and sense of purpose.

It cannot be too strongly emphasized, however, that the phenomenon of Holy Scripture is *a mystery*. The temptation at all times is to seek, even with the best of motives, to explain this mystery — which can only have the effect of explaining the mystery *away* and reducing the phenomenon to a category where it does not belong. The mystery in this case consists in the paradox that a book composed of the writings of human authors can yet at the same time be designated the Word of God. As with every Christian paradox, the truth lies, and only lies, in the retention and combination of its two poles. "Explanation" of the paradox solely in terms of one of its poles is nothing other than rationalization. To dissolve a mystery in this way is not to solve it. But this is what is constantly being done. Either the Bible is explained as entirely the work of God, the human writers being no more than the pens which God used, so to speak, or it is explained as merely the work of men. In either case the "solution" is neatly parcelled up in accordance with a particular predisposition, and the mystery of the paradox has been ignored. But nothing has been gained. Indeed, the character of the phenomenon has been violated and we are now confronted, not with a dynamic paradox, but with the static either/or of a contradiction.

It was attempts to explain the mystery of the person of the Incarnate Son, by stressing either the pole of His divinity or the pole of His humanity, that gave rise to the heresies which threatened the survival of the early Church. But the frailty of His body, which was apparent in hunger and fatigue and above all in His sufferings and death on the cross, was not in fact a contradiction of His divine sovereignty. Similarly (though, of course, the analogy does not belong to the realm of ontology) the frailty inherent in Scripture as the word of man does not invalidate it as being truly at the same time the Word of God. Like a body, the Bible in its own particular category of revelation is an organic whole. Every part has its proper place and function. The removal of a part disturbs the balance and integrity of the whole. Yet all the parts are not equally important. Just as certain parts of the human body, such as the head and the heart and the lungs, are vital and indispensable, whereas other parts are dispensable in the sense that the body can survive their loss, albeit in a maimed condition; so too some parts of Scripture are vital and indispensable, while others have a humbler function and are relatively dispensable.

There is another phenomenon which is familiar to the Christian experience, namely, that to the eye of unbelief the Bible may be dull and dry-as-dust, or it may perhaps be of academic and literary interest, but

15

it is not seen as the dynamic and authoritative Word of God. To the eye of faith, however, it comes alive. Suddenly, when a man comes to faith in Christ, the Bible becomes a necessity for him. The book that before he found closed and remote he now studies with eagerness and delight. The explanation is what the Reformers used to call the internal witness of the Holy Spirit: the Spirit of God bearing testimony to the Word of God in the believing heart. The reintegration, in Christ, of the image of God leads at once to a hunger for the Word of God, a strong desire for a knowledge of the things of God, which is the knowledge of absolute truth. This is what Paul is talking about when he says that "no one comprehends the thoughts of God except the Spirit of God," and that as believers "we have received not the spirit of the world, but the Spirit which is from God, that we might understand the gifts bestowed on us by God." Indeed, through this inner working of the Holy Spirit "we have the mind of Christ" (I Cor. 2:11ff.). Helmut Thielicke speaks of this phenomenon in the following terms:

> Our deliverance lies in Him who opens our deaf ears and blind eyes that we may see Him at the vanishing point of every biblical perspective. In this sense we are always setting out toward someone who has already overtaken us and from whom we came in the first place. For, as Augustine said, we would not be able to seek Him if He had not already found us. . . . Therefore if there is to be such a thing as theological knowledge, an understanding of the Word and the mighty acts of God, then the analogy to God which men have given up must be restored in a new act of creation. The divine Word must create its own hearers. (For there are no longer any hearers who would understand it 'naturally'.) The theological locus in which this creative function of the Word — or if you will — this 'creation of the hearer', is dealt with is the doctrine of the Holy Spirit. For this doctrine declares that we are called to share in God's self-knowledge and thus to be put into the proper analogy. The Holy Spirit, who enlightens us, is none other than God Himself. In Him and through Him we become partakers of that which God Himself knows about Himself. For the Spirit (not man's reason, but *this* Spirit, the *Holy* Spirit) 'searches everything, even the depths of God'.[2]

Scripture, indeed, belongs to the Holy Spirit. It is He, the Lord and Life-Giver, who makes real in the hearts of men the redemption procured by Christ, thereby and at the same time authenticating the genuineness of the testimony of the biblical authors; for, as the creed declares, He it is "who spake by the prophets." Should not the creed be a constant reminder to us that the mystery of Scripture belongs to the realm of faith and therefore is accessible only to faith? I question very much whether it is right for us to propound and defend notions

---

[2] *Between Heaven and Earth* (New York, 1965), pp. 38, 42.

concerning the mechanics of inspiration. To do so is to transpose, however unintentionally, the Bible from the area of faith to the area of reason, and in this respect to place it under man instead of under God. Just at this point, it seems to me, fundamentalists have developed a somewhat frenetic rationalism of their own and tend, all unwittingly, to conduct their warfare from the same ground as the radicals whom they oppose. Not, however, that the radicals are models of consistency, for, though they are avowedly rationalistic in their approach, yet it is their custom to seek support by quoting passages from the Bible, as though from the authoritative Word of God, when it suits them to do so.

If the Church has placed itself under Scripture, which, as we have seen, is the significance of the acceptance of the canon of Scripture, then it must approve and preserve the teaching of the Bible concerning itself. As Hermann Sasse has said:

> It is the Bible itself which tells me that the Scriptures are written under the inspiration of the Holy Spirit and are therefore the Word of God. This and nothing else is taught concerning the Inspiration in the written Word of God. This, therefore, is the dogma of the Church, to be accepted by faith, just as we accept the dogma of the Incarnation or any of the great doctrines confessed in the Creed. We shall never know in this world how the Virgin Birth of Christ or His bodily resurrection was possible. So we shall never understand in this life the inscrutable miracle which is expressed in the words "according to the Scriptures," "who spake by the prophets."[3]

But if, conversely, theologians and others now wish to supplant the teaching of Scripture with their own ideas and "insights," they must resist the temptation to use the Bible as a prop for their positions.

In academic circles today the Bible is largely a discredited book. To all intents and purposes biblical studies have become a branch of technology, so much so that the electronic computer is the latest authority to make a pronouncement on questions of authenticity and authorship. All too commonly Scripture is treated anatomically, like a corpse in pickle to be dissected. It has become the preserve of the expert in the laboratory. Warned that trespassing is prohibited, the ordinary man is advised that he is not competent to understand and interpret the meaning of the Bible. No one will question the necessity for an analytical approach to the text of Scripture and the immense contribution which contemporary scholarship is making to our knowledge of the semantics and linguistics of the Bible and its historical provenance. What is to be deplored is the loss of the sense of the mystery of Holy Scripture as dynamic and God-given, and therefore vital, and the removal of the Bible from the hands of the ordinary

---

[3] "Concerning the Nature of Inspiration," *The Reformed Theological Review* (Australia), Vol. XXIII, No. 2, June 1964, p. 41.

Christian who can make no claims to theological or technological expertise. As Alan Richardson has written:

> There were losses as well as gains amongst the consequences of what we may call the new historical control of biblical exegesis. Amongst the losses must be reckoned the gradual decay of the ordinary Christian's sense that he can read the Bible for himself without an interpreter and discover its unambiguous meaning. One factor at least in the decline of Bible reading on the part of individual Christians must surely be that the Bible came to be regarded as a book for experts, requiring an elaborate training in linguistic and historical disciplines before it could be properly understood; if it needed expert knowledge before it could be read, it was best to leave the Bible to the experts, like so many other things in a world of specialization. The layman would be satisfied if, every now and then, some expert would bring him up to date in the conclusions which the research workers had reached; he could thus be spared the trouble of reading the Bible for himself, since he would be unlikely to profit by his own inexpert flounderings.[4]

This is indeed a grievous loss, and it cannot be viewed with complacency, for the survival of a whole civilization built on the foundation of Scripture is at stake. While we agree that "both spiritual insight and historical understanding are necessary for the accomplishment of sound biblical exegesis," we dispute the assertion that "today the modern reader knows that he cannot understand what Jeremiah or St. Paul is talking about because he does not know enough about the historical background."[5] Over and over again in the past, and still today in the present, the experience of any humble man or woman with the spiritual insight of faith proves that through the pages of the Bible Jeremiah and St. Paul speak the message of God with power and meaning to the believing heart. In other words, spiritual insight is essential for the apprehension of the message of Scripture; it does not wait on the acquisition of historical understanding, much though the latter is to be prized as an adjunct of the former.

The impression given by Richardson at this point seems, however, to be corrected later in the same essay when he declares, in words with which we entirely concur:

> . . . it is of course agreed that the prophetic and apostolic understanding of the meaning of the events of the biblical history is entirely due to the revealing action of God. Revelation is a mystery, like all the miraculous works of God. It is God alone who can open the eyes

[4] "The Rise of Modern Biblical Scholarship," chapter VIII in *The Cambridge History of the Bible: The West, from the Reformation to the Present Day* (Cambridge, 1963), p. 301.

[5] *Loc. cit.*

of faith, whether of the prophets and apostles of old or of those who read or hear the biblical message in subsequent generations.[6]

The message of Scripture is addressed to everyman, and its focus is the person and work of Christ, who came into the world to save sinners (I Tim. 1:15). No finer or more memorable explanation has been given of the purpose of the Bible than that which was given by that great master of Holy Scripture, William Tyndale: "The Scripture," he wrote, "is that wherewith God draweth us unto Him. The Scriptures sprang out of God, and flow unto Christ, and were given to lead us to Christ. Thou must therefore go along by the Scripture as by a line, until thou come at Christ, which is the way's end and resting-place."[7]

The sum of the situation is this: that biblical scholarship is not an end in itself; it belongs to the precincts, not to the sanctuary; in isolation, it will never arrive at the heart of the matter. The scholar should be combined with the preacher; the study should never be divorced from the pulpit. Thus Bishop Stephen Neill has said:

> The New Testament is concerned with *proclamation.* It is a *Kerygma,* the loud cry of a herald authorized by a king to proclaim his will and purpose to his subjects. It is *Euangelion,* good news, sent to those who are in distress with the promise of deliverance. It is the Word of the Lord — and in the East a word is no mere vibration in the atmosphere, it is a living power sent forth to accomplish that for which it is sent. When the New Testament scholar has done his utmost in his sphere, his work remains lifeless, until it is transformed into the living voice of proclamation. The scholar may say, as many have done, that this is none of his business; he will scientifically make known the facts, and it will be the task of others to do with them as they will. But . . . we have seen that many of the giants reached out beyond the study to the pulpit, believing that the two are most intimately linked, and that any truth gained by the intense application of labour in the study will find its way out in living proclamation as the Word of God to men. And so, in fact, from generation to generation, the New Testament has taken on new life, as the ancient words have asserted their relevance in every changing scene of human existence, have clothed themselves afresh in human understanding, and have come home to the heart and conscience as challenge, enlightenment and consolation.[8]

Mere scholarship, however able and however worthy it may be, is not creative; seen as a Christian function, it is analytical and subservient. It is in the proclamation of the scriptural message as the Word of the

---

[6] *Op. cit.,* p. 333.

[7] *Works,* Vol. I (Parker Society edition, Cambridge, 1848), p. 317.

[8] *The Interpretation of the New Testament, 1861-1961* (London, 1964), pp. 347f.

Living God that the creative task of theology finds achievement, and that note of proclamation should inform the theological tome as well as the pronouncement from the pulpit.

If faith is an essential ingredient of that spiritual insight which is able to understand and appropriate the message of the Bible, it is important to emphasize that faith is not something which exists antecedently or in independence. Faith cannot exist or be engendered in a vacuum; for faith is response, and in particular it is response to the message of Scripture. The object of faith is the Christ to whom Scripture bears witness. To quote Emil Brunner: "The Bible is the precondition of all faith, that which alone makes it possible. And the whole Bible at that."[9]

That is why evangelical proclamation is so indispensable an element in the fulfillment of the creative task of theology. We need, more than ever, to be reminded today, as P. T. Forsyth had to remind his generation, that "the first value of the Bible is not to historical science but to evangelical faith, not to the historian but to the gospeller," and that the theologian "should first be not a philosopher but a saved man, with eternal life working in him."[10] And the following admonition, uttered by the same author, is still valid and salutary:

> The authority of the Bible speaks not to the critical faculty that handles evidence but to the soul that makes response. The Bible witness of salvation in Christ is felt immediately to have authority by every soul pining for redemption. It is not so much food for the rationally healthy, but it is medicine for the sick, and life for the dead. Even historical criticism, which is a real part of theology, should be pursued on that basis. . . . It is only knowledge with a soul of faith that grasps the full scope of revelationary history.[11]

Since the focal point of the biblical message is the figure of Jesus Christ, the divine Redeemer of the world, the repudiation of the authenticity of the biblical witness leads inevitably to the repudiation of the authenticity of Jesus Christ as Saviour and Lord. This was amply demonstrated by the consequences of the destructive criticism which flourished in Germany during the last century and which today again is being advocated within the Church on a geographical scale far surpassing that of the nineteenth century. The radicals of our century and the last have this in common, that they adopt as a fundamental premise the inadmissibility of the supernatural on the ground that it is unacceptable to the modern mind. The application of this principle to

[9] *The Christian Doctrine of the Church, Faith, and the Consummation*, Dogmatics Vol. III (London, 1962), p. 249.

[10] *Positive Preaching and Modern Mind* (London, 1907), pp. 13, 305.

[11] *The Person and Place of Jesus Christ* (London, 1909), pp. 178f.

Scripture can only result in the banishment of God from His world and the rejection of such cardinal doctrines of the Christian faith as the deity and the resurrection of Jesus Christ. The radicals of last century sought to dismiss the authenticity of the New Testament by relegating its writings to the second century, and thereby assigning them to the category of spurious fabrications. That, however, it was the scholarship of these radical critics and their followers which was spurious was proved with devastating conclusiveness by a theologian of such intellectual repute as George Salmon, whose learning and judgment caused him to speak with scorn of the critical speculations and manipulations as

> these German dreams retailed as sober truth by sceptical writers in this country, many of whom imagine that it would be a confession of inability to keep pace with the progress of critical science if they ventured to test, by English common sense, the successive schemes by which German aspirants after fame seek to gain a reputation for their ingenuity. . . ."[12]

and by that prince of biblical scholars, Bishop J. B. Lightfoot, who composed his massively erudite work on the Apostolic Fathers with the express purpose of demonstrating the untenability of the position propounded by the Tübingen radicals:

> To the disciples of Baur [he wrote] the rejection of the Ignatian Epistles is an absolute necessity of their theological position. The ground would otherwise be withdrawn from under them, and their reconstructions of early Christian history would fall in ruins on their heads. On the other hand, those who adopt the traditional views of the origin of Christianity and of the history of the Church as substantially correct, may look with comparative calmness on the result. The loss of the Ignatian Epistles would be the loss of one buttress to their fabric but the withdrawal would not materially affect the stability of the fabric itself. . . . I have been reproached by my friends for allowing myself to be diverted from the more congenial task of commenting on S. Paul's Epistles; but the importance of the position seemed to me to justify the expenditure of much time and labour in 'repairing a breach' not indeed in 'the House of the Lord' itself, but in the immediately outlying buildings.[13]

Lightfoot's attitude is summarized in the Preface to his *Essays on the Work entitled 'Supernatural Religion,'* a crushing rejoinder to an anonymous "sceptical writer" of his day, where he says: "I cannot pretend to be indifferent about the veracity of the records which pro-

[12] *A Historical Introduction to the Study of the Books of the New Testament* (London, 1892), p. 15.
[13] *The Apostolic Fathers,* Part II, Vol. I (second edition, London, 1889), pp. xif., xv.

21

fess to reveal Him, whom I believe to be not only the very Truth, but the very Life."

It is this same issue, only in an intensified form, with which the Church is confronted today. The radicals of our age, however, no longer, for the most part, seek to depreciate the New Testament writings as forgeries of a post-apostolic period. Their method, rather, is to contend that the portrait of Jesus and the sayings attributed to him in the New Testament are the products of the imagination or wishful thinking of the early Christian community, which, in the years following Calvary, gradually built up an idealized picture of the one who had been their leader and teacher. In the determination of what portions of the story may be original and authentic, the criteria applied are arbitrary and subjective in character. The conclusions reached are predetermined by the predilections and prejudices of each individual. Novelty allied with an abstruse kind of linguistic ingenuity or an inventive historical "reconstruction" is almost always assured of academic applause. The Holy Spirit has been ushered off the stage and the human spirit dominates the scene. To the degree in which theology affirms the self-adequacy of man, or, in other words, denies man's creaturely dependence on God and asserts the human spirit in opposition to the Holy Spirit — to that degree it will disallow both the nature and the necessity of Holy Scripture as the Word of God, and to that degree also it will incapacitate itself for its distinctively creative task; for, as we have previously explained, the creative task of theology inheres in the capacity of man as, in the first place, created in the image of God, and now in Christ re-created in that image, to work constructively with and from the given "substance" of the revelation of God's Word. The affirmation of human self-adequacy is but the repetition of the primeval heresy that man in himself is "as God." Like all heresy, it is not constructive (though it may wish to be) but subversive of the true nature and capacity of man, entangling him in a web of contradiction and frustration of his own making.

The sickness of theology in our modern age is attributable to the increasing extent to which it is becoming infected with the arrogance of human self-sufficiency. In many academic institutions theology has degenerated into a department of the humanities. Those who utter a word of protest are blandly assured that "man has now come of age" — though this, in fact, was precisely the cry of eighteenth-century rationalism! The conclusion we are invited to draw is that twentieth-century man must be set free from the doctrinal and ethical absolutes of Scripture, that to require belief in the supernatural is an insult to *homo sapiens,* that the objective otherness of God must go because God is but a synonym for man's ultimate concern, or, put in other terms, God is only a way of expressing a human value-judgment, and that the only legitimate scandal of Christianity is that Jesus Christ was a mere ordinary mortal man no different from all other human beings. This situation has elicited the following comment from Paul H. Holmer of Yale Divinity School:

> This complaint about the church's outmoded theology must not be taken lightly. It creates the conviction that the whole world would like to become Christian if only the theologians would become modern. Of course, the price is a little high: resurrection, atonement, the virgin birth, the last judgment, lately God and a few other things must go, but everything else, and especially the meaning of these, can be kept! This is what happens when the responsibility is laid unequivocally on the church and the theologians — the only possible way to make Christianity palatable is to strip everything from it and make its meanings coextensive with what people will discern for themselves and believe anyway.[14]

In complete contrast to J. A. Froude's venerable father who believed, a hundred years ago, that "the way to heaven was to turn to the right and go straight on," the temper of the radical theology of our day is to move in the diametrically opposite direction. The anguished disillusionment of the last generation of left-wing liberals has quickly been forgotten, though it was vividly described by able men who had personally experienced it. Thus Richard Niebuhr has written:

> The romantic conception of the kingdom of God involved no discontinuities, no crises, no tragedies or sacrifices, no loss of all things, no cross and resurrection. In ethics it reconciled the interests of the individual with those of society by means of faith in a natural identity of interests or in the benevolent, altruistic character of man. In politics and economics it slurred over national and class divisions, seeing only growth of unity and ignoring the increase of self-assertion and exploitation. In religion it reconciled God and man by deifying the latter and humanizing the former. . . . For an Edwards divine sovereignty had been a hard truth to which he had slowly learned to adjust his thought and life; for liberalism it was an untruth. It established continuity between God and man by adjusting God to man.
>
> Since no reconciliation to the divine sovereign was necessary the reign of Christ, in the new interpretation, involved no revolutionary events in history or the life of individuals. Christ the Redeemer became Jesus the teacher or the spiritual genius in whom the religious capacities of mankind were fully developed. Moreover the radical revolution at the centre of life for which dynamic Protestantism and Evangelicalism had contended seemed unnecessary to a liberalism which objected not only to the identification of this revolution with mechanical conversion but also to the belief that life had been corrupted. The

[14] "Contra the New Theologies," *The Christian Century,* 17 March 1965, p. 331.

23

renovation of which it spoke was not so much the restoration of health to a diseased body as the clearing out of the accumulated rubbish of traditional beliefs or customs. Evolution, growth, development, the culture of the religious life, the nurture of the kindly sentiments, the extension of humanitarian ideals and the progress of civilization took the place of the Christian revolution. . . .

A God without wrath brought men without sin into a kingdom without judgment through the ministration of a Christ without a cross.[15]

Unbiblical humanism, which denies the sovereignty and the otherness of God and affirms the adequacy and the centrality of man, is always present because it is the expression of original sin. And its main threat to the Church of Christ is *from within*. (It is far more menacing than the militant humanistic atheism which assails the Church from without and is so easily recognizable for what it is.) It is no new thing, but is as old as sin itself; and it is adept at ignoring the lessons of even recent history. In the fifteenth century the humanism of the Renaissance panegyrized man as the complete being, the crown of the cosmos and the key to its understanding, and proudly declared that the dignity of man was so sublime that, even if he had not sinned, the Son of God would still have become incarnate in token of man's supreme excellence. It remained for the Reformation, in the following century, by its rediscovery of the Word of God and the message of redemption by grace alone, to recover the proper dignity and humanity of man and at the same time enthusiastically to dedicate itself to the creative task of theology. The benefits of that dynamic restitution are still present with us today. Of particular significance is the development by Herman Dooyeweerd of a system of Christian philosophy — a work of immense erudition — constructed in loyalty to the principles of the biblical revelation which are also the principles of Reformed thought. (Dooyeweerd will frown at finding himself placed among the theologians in this volume; but his philosophy is erected upon a genuinely theological foundation.) His purpose has been to construct a philosophy which, being authentically Christian, penetrates to every sphere of human life and activity. In doing so, however, he has engaged in a transcendental critique of philosophy as a science in its specific manifestations throughout the centuries and has shown how the only system which is not incapacitated by insoluble inner contradictions is that which is founded on the creation-fall-redemption ground-motive of the biblical revelation. Herman Dooyeweerd has given a notable lead as with singleness of purpose and intellectual integrity he has devoted himself to the creative task of the Christian thinker.

In the historical perspective, indeed, it is the theology of the Reforma-

---

15 *The Kingdom of God in America* (Chicago, 1937), pp. 191ff.

tion which has most faithfully applied the scriptural principles relating to both God and man. With its evangelical emphasis, its reverence for the Word of God, and its dynamic doctrine of the Holy Spirit, it has helped to restore the right balance between the supreme honor of God and the dependent dignity of man; it has demonstrated the creative interrelationship between the grace of God and the responsibility of man; and it has pointed man to the realization of the fullness of his potentialities by the union of both mind and heart, both intellect and emotion, in the service of his fellow men and to the praise of Almighty God. On either side of the Reformed tradition, the theological process may be simplified as a see-saw between the Enlightenment and Romanticism, or between rationalistic and pietistic currents of thought, the former advocating the supremacy of human reason and the latter the supremacy of human feeling or experience. Both movements have this in common, however, that they are humanistic, in the sense that their approach is fundamentally anthropocentric, assigning ultimacy either to man's reason or to his sentiment.[16]

The creative task of theology is, first of all, the task of the redeemed who, through the prior grace of God, have returned to the Father by the Son, and through the inner working of the Holy Spirit have been put into tune with the mind of Christ. The creative task of theology must be performed with the given "material" of the Word of God written, from whose pages the same Holy Spirit causes the truth to beam forth with inexhaustible wonder and beauty, so that it is always an unfinished task, and always a task with limitless possibilities ahead. And, finally, the creative task of theology is related to mankind, indeed to the whole world in which we live. The truth has to be applied once it is known, and it has to be applied in relevant and comprehensible terms. This would be impossible if the truth were something inert and static; for history is not motionless and mankind is not an undifferentiated mass. Just as no two fingerprints are identical, so every single personality is different and sacrosanct, and every single human situation has a quality of uniqueness about it. What endless scope there is for creativity here! The truth is constant; but it is not static: it is dynamic. That is why the glorious Gospel of Jesus Christ is always old, yet ever new, and must be proclaimed afresh in every generation with the creative power of God the Holy Spirit.

[16] A penetrating study, historical and theological, will be found in Karl Barth, *From Rousseau to Ritschl* (London, 1959); cf. also A. R. Vidler, *The Church in an Age of Revolution: 1789 to the Present Day* (London, 1962).

2 G. W. BROMILEY

Karl Barth

I. BIOGRAPHY

KARL BARTH was born in Basel on May 10, 1886. His Swiss nationality is worth noting. From a practical standpoint it gave him a position of strength in his ecclesiastical opposition to the Hitler régime. The worst that National Socialism could do was to deport him to the Swiss side of the Rhine. More deeply, it accounts for many of his political and social attitudes, his basic attachment to democracy, his no less profound conservatism regarding many aspects of modern life, his fear of power blocs, and perhaps his tendency toward a certain neutrality as between Russia and America.

Born into Swiss Protestantism, he received his first Christian instruction in the Swiss Reformed Church. For all his later movements, this has left an abiding impress on his dogmatic work. The majestic phrases of the *Heidelberg Catechism* resound through the *Dogmatics*.[1] He still maintains a preference for praise of God in the unaccompanied human voice.[2] He even recalls the dialect hymns of Abel Burckhardt, second pastor at Basel Minster, who wrote for children a collection of songs which admirably presented the historicity of the great events of the Gospel and the influence of which was "calculated to carry one relatively unscathed through all the serried ranks of historicism and anti-historicism, mysticism and rationalism, etc., and to bring one back some day to the matter itself."[3]

Dr. Geoffrey W. Bromiley, tranlator and editor of Barth's *Church Dogmatics,* translator and editor of Kittel's *Theological Dictionary of the New Testament,* is Professor of Church History and Historical Theology at Fuller Theological Seminary.

1 E.g., *Church Dogmatics*, I/2 (1956), pp. 9f., 76, 168, 216f.
2 *Ibid.*, IV/3 (1961-62), p. 867.
3 *Ibid.*, IV/2 (1958), pp. 112f.

The atmosphere in the Barth home was theological, Fritz Barth, the father, being an eminent New Testament scholar and professor. It was natural, then, that Barth should move towards the pastorate with a strong interest in theological study. His father stood for a more orthodox position against developing liberalism, but Barth himself came under the powerful influence of Harnack and Hermann during his student days at Marburg and Berlin, and when he became pastor of Safenwil in Aargau in 1911, he had little message to preach except the Christianized culture so well expressed in Harnack's *What is Christianity?*

Experience in the pastorate quickly produced a sense of incongruity between commission and performance. Liberal platitudes answered neither the demands of his calling nor actual problems in his parish. As he said later, "I found myself . . . being forced back at every point more and more upon the specific minister's problem, the sermon."[4] His early disquietude was intensified by the outbreak of war in 1914, and especially by the support given to the Kaiser by 93 leading German intellectuals, including his own theological mentors. In his own words, this was a *dies ater* for him personally.[5] The new situation necessitated intense reappraisal.

It is typical of Barth that, unlike many of his fellow pastors, he recognized the crisis as primarily theological. Historical events and the liberal failure were in a sense contingent and incidental. To deal with the root of the problem theological measures were necessary. The war years (1914-1918) thus proved to be most formative in shaping Barth's future course. New influences began to assert themselves: on the outer edge critical voices like those of Feuerbach and Nietzsche; more powerfully the prophetic utterances of Dostoevski and especially Kierkegaard and philosophical existentialism; of greater lasting significance the work of Kohlbrügge and the two Blumhardts; above all these the great Reformers; and supremely, of course, the Bible itself, which Barth now began to read with eyes no longer blinkered by liberal reinterpretation.

The result was the epoch-making *Epistle to the Romans,* first published in 1918 and then revised and re-issued in 1921 and many successive editions. Barth himself has said that when he wrote this work he was like a man climbing a dark tower who grasped a rope for guidance and awakened the whole countryside with the sound of a great bell. Less kindly, but with some truth, others have said that it is more of a commentary on Barth than on Paul. Theologically, however, *Romans* proved a turning-point both in Protestant theology generally and in Barth's own development in particular.

A first and more superficial influence was to introduce a new vocabu-

---

[4] *The Word of God and the Word of Man* (1928), p. 100.
[5] *Die protestantische Theologie im 19. Jahrhundert* (1947), p. 6.

lary which is still to some extent with us — the vocabulary of the tangent and the mathematical point, of the wholly other and the infinite qualitative distinction, of paradox and singularity, of the dialectical and the existential.[6] Behind the new terminology, however, lay the reintroduction of old themes — the divine transcendence, grace, historicity, justification by faith, miracle. Barth himself would now disown many of the terms and concepts of 1921.[7] Even at the time he allowed that many of them were only marginal corrections, with the implication that they were fragmentary and perhaps exaggerated. Even where they seem to be along the lines of biblical orthodoxy, there is often doubt whether the underlying thought is really the same. There can be no doubt, however, that they represented a direct and conscious rejection of the prevailing liberalism. There can also be no doubt that they evoked a widespread and influential response.

For Barth himself *Romans* had four results. It opened up a period of unceasing literary activity. *Romans* was followed at once, not merely by articles in the newly formed journal *Zwischen den Zeiten,* but also by the sermons *Come Holy Spirit* (1924), by *The Resurrection of the Dead* (1924), *The Word of God and the Word of Man* (1924), *Philippians* (1927), and the projected *Christian Dogmatics* (1927). Again, Barth was brought into touch with like-minded younger thinkers such as Gogarten, Brunner, Merz, and Bultmann, who constituted a loose kind of school or movement known as the dialectical theology or the theology of crisis. Furthermore, Barth was diverted to an academic rather than a pastoral ministry, for in 1921 he was called to be Professor of Systematic Theology at Göttingen, and subsequently taught at Münster and Bonn before returning to Basel. Finally, he was reoriented to dogmatic theology. *Romans* was theology and had to be read as such.[8] He had recovered from the childish ailment of being ashamed of theology.[9] With his call to Göttingen, however, he had to go further and tackle systematics. He soon found that his training had given him little guidance. At this hour of need he turned to Heppe's *Reformed Dogmatics,* which might seem "out of date, dusty, unattractive, almost like a table of logarithms, dreary to read, stiff and eccentric,"[10] but which gave him a vision of what dogmatics should be and has left its mark on all his own discussions in the *Church Dogmatics.*

The reorientation to dogmatics was to be more significant than the association with Brunner and Bultmann, for it pointed the way forward

[6] Cf. the humorous comments in *The Humanity of God* (1960), p. 35.
[7] *Church Dogmatics,* I/1 (1936), Preface.
[8] *Der Römerbrief* (1922), Preface to 2nd edition.
[9] *Das Wort Gottes und die Theologie* (1924), p. 99.
[10] Heppe, *Reformed Dogmatics* (1950), Foreword.

from original mistakes and extravagancies. The way was slow, perhaps, but it was sure and steady. Already in 1927, Barth could publish the first volume of his *Christian Dogmatics in Outline*. Yet even before he could continue, Barth saw the inadequacy of this beginning. For one thing, it was too short. Again, it suffered from the influence of an existentialist framework. More basically, it did not express the basic insight which Barth was now learning from his study of Anselm.[11] The publication of the book on Anselm in 1931 (*Fides quaerens intellectum*) marked the direction in which his real dogmatic work was to lie, and it was followed at once, not by a new edition of the *Christian Dogmatics,* but by a completely new beginning in the first half of Volume I of the *Church Dogmatics* (1932).

As Barth foresaw, this marked the end of the so-called dialectical theology and its school. The new work does not claim to represent any movement. It is not a dogmatics of dialectical theology but of the Word of God. The decisive break with Brunner followed at once. It focused on natural theology, but the basic issue is probably the larger conception of theology itself and of theological basis and method. Even more radical was the ultimate break with Bultmann, in whom Barth perhaps sees a caricature and yet also the logical end of his dialectical errors. Of the former group only his long-standing friend and associate, Thurneysen, remained in constant theological affinity.

The accession to power of Adolf Hitler, and the National Socialist attempt to push through a Germanization of the Church, brought Barth into a new conflict which finally resulted in his expulsion from Germany in 1935. By this time, however, Barth had helped to give theological content to the resistance in the famous Barmen *Declaration* (1934) with its insistence that Jesus Christ is the one Lord whom we must trust and obey in life and in death.[12] Barth is perhaps a little hard in claiming that "German Christianity" is the ultimate end of Neo-Protestantism[13] (as papal infallibility is of Romanism), but he again sees clearly that the political and ecclesiastical aspects of the struggle rest on the theological and that success can be achieved only as a sound theology is established and put into effect.

Barth's deportation from Germany brought him back to his native land and city, and from 1935 to 1961 he pursued his literary and teaching work at the University of Basel, enjoying a special extension beyond the normal retiring age of 70. During the later period of the German Church conflict, he continued to give encouragement from

[11] *Church Dogmatics,* I/1 (1936), Preface; III/4 (1961), Preface.
[12] *Ibid.,* II/1 (1957), pp. 172ff.
[13] *Loc. cit.*

across the Rhine. Two shorter dogmatics works appeared in 1935 (*Credo*) and 1938 (*The Knowledge of God and the Service of God*). During the war years he bore the additional burden of military service against possible invasion. Immediately after the Second World War he played an important, though not direct or perhaps decisive, part in the shaping of the ecumenical movement, his distinctive contribution at Amsterdam being a theological examination of Christian unity. He also contributed several essays on political matters, and his advice to church leaders in Communist lands has proved particularly controversial. Of smaller postwar works we might mention especially his *Dogmatics in Outline* (1949), his *Shorter Commentary on Romans* (1956), *Protestant Thought from Rousseau to Ritschl* (1947), and several important essays — for example, *Rudolf Bultmann* and *The Humanity of God,* in the series *Theologische Existenz Heute.* Increasingly, however, Barth has concentrated his time and energy on *Church Dogmatics,* which seems to have increased in scope with each successive part. Since the war years he has lived constantly under the sense that life is in the hands of God[14] and that every ounce of time and strength will be needed if he is to reach his discussion of the last things before he is called to their reality. The final picture of Barth is thus one of happy and reverent, but strong and purposeful, concentration upon the dogmatic task.

II. EXPOSITION

Barth has expressed the desire that he should be judged theologically by the *Church Dogmatics* rather than by earlier writings. This does not mean that the latter are unimportant. Nor does it mean that many of the earlier themes are not present in the *Dogmatics.* It might be argued that the *Dogmatics* can be understood only in the light of *Romans.* Yet there is a difference in assumptions, emphases, and basic understanding. Hence one must look to the *Dogmatics* for a proper view of Barth's teaching.

As regards the nature of the *Church Dogmatics,* it must be noted that during the period 1927-1932 Barth saw that dogmatic utterance must rest on thorough exegetical and historical work, that there is a need to make this foundation explicit, and that dogmatics must also comprehend ethics. Thus in the *Dogmatics* we have not merely a work of dogmatic theology, but much exegesis, an incidental history of doctrine and a full-scale ethical treatise. The exegetical and historical portions are grouped in small print, but they are essential foundations

---

14 Cf. *ibid.,* II/2 (1957), Preface, p. x.

and not just supplementary buttresses. The ethical discussions are closely related to the dogmatic development by the inclusion of a special ethical chapter in each main volume (Vols. II-V).

As regards the structure of the *Dogmatics,* Barth takes this very seriously. When he rejects systematization, he has in view the forcing of the material under a philosophical view or a ruling dogmatic principle. He does not mean that there should not be order or coherence.[15] True order will derive from revelation itself. But revelation is the revelation of the triune God. Hence dogmatics will fall naturally into five main divisions, as Barth sees it. The first is that of revelation, which gives us a volume of prolegomena on the doctrine of the Word of God. The second is that of the one God — the second volume on the doctrine of God. The third, fourth and fifth are those of the three persons of Father, Son, and Holy Spirit — Vols. III, IV, and V on the doctrine of God the Creator, God the Reconciler, and God the Redeemer. It is within this general scheme that Barth treats the detailed dogmatic and ethical themes. He selects the individual order with great care. Yet he is always aware that there is some arbitrariness in method and that the themes are so closely interrelated that they are constantly seen from new aspects with the unfolding of the whole. This accounts for much of the apparent repetitiveness of the *Dogmatics.*

THE DOCTRINE OF THE WORD OF GOD

Theology (Introduction)

Certain initial definitions are important. Theology is for Barth "the scientific self-examination of the Christian Church with respect to its speech about God."[16] It is a science like others, yet strictly it includes all sciences and it must not let itself be subjected to others, for example, history or philosophy, in an attempt to commend itself. The special task of prolegomena is not to provide a philosophical substructure, nor to clear the ground in a negative operation, but to mark off the starting-point and method of true theology from heresy — that is, Roman Catholicism and Neo-Protestantism.[17] Theology is not an end in itself; it exists in the context of the whole ministry of the Church to scrutinize, purify, and inform the Church's preaching and teaching.[18]

[15] *Ibid.,* I/2 (1956), pp. 853ff.
[16] I/1 (1936), p. 3.
[17] I/1 (1936), § 2, 1.
[18] I/1 (1936), § 3.

The Word of God (Chapter I)

The basis of true theology is the Word of God in its three forms: as the Word proclaimed, the Word written, and the Word revealed. Though it takes these three forms, the Word itself is one, so that here is an analogy to the divine trinity.[19] The Word is God's speech to man. It is spiritual, personal, and purposeful; sovereign, necessary, and declaratory. As God's speech, it is no empty word but an active Word, contemporaneous, dominant, and imposing decision. Yet if it is God's act, it is also God's mystery. This is seen in its involvement in history, in its absolute quality and in its relation to the Holy Spirit.[20] It may be known by man, not in virtue of an inherent human capacity, but in virtue of its self-communicable power in the Spirit. Knowledge is through acknowledgment, and it is thus the knowledge of faith.[21] The Anselmic principle of *fides quaerens intellectum* is the key to a true understanding of dogmatics.

The Revelation of God (Chapter II)

The Triune God. The Word is God Himself in His self-revelation. But the God thus self-revealed is the triune God. Hence the primary theme of Christian dogmatics is the doctrine of the Trinity, to which there correspond the three aspects of revelation as revealer, thing revealed, and act of revelation. The doctrine of the Trinity must be placed thus early in dogmatics because the all-important question is who is the self-revealing God. God's sovereign self-revelation is what Barth calls the root of the doctrine.[22] This is known, not from vestiges in nature, history, the constitution of man, etc., nor even from direct biblical texts, but from revelation itself.[23] The Trinity means that God is one and the same in indestructible unity and yet also that He is one and the same thrice in indestructible differentiation. Father, Son, and Holy Ghost are the one God in unity of essence, and the one God is Father, Son, and Holy Ghost in distinction of persons.[24] The Trinity does not mean tritheism or a tripartite God, for there is only one divine essence. It means that God is the one God in threefold repetition.[25] On the other hand, the unity of God is not solitariness. It includes a distinction or order of three persons, or three modes of being, who, if they are not personalities in the modern sense, are also

---

[19] I/1 (1936), § 4, 1-3.
[20] I/1 (1936), § 5, 4.
[21] I/1 (1936), § 6.
[22] I/1 (1936), § 8, 2.
[23] I/1 (1936), § 8, 3.
[24] I/1 (1936), § 8, 2 (p. 324).
[25] I/1 (1936), § 9, 1.

not mere emanations or parts or manifestations of Deity.[26] The problem of mathematical triunity is a false problem, since we are here dealing, not with our world, but with God, in relation to whom we are wholly dependent on what God has revealed concerning Himself. In God's dealings with us, His triunity means that we know Him in threefold manner as the Creator, the Reconciler, and the Redeemer.[27] Against modalism, however, Barth insists that this threefoldness corresponds to an essential being of God as Father, Son, and Holy Spirit. He also insists that all three persons are equally engaged in each of the specific works of creation, reconciliation, and redemption.[28]

The Incarnation of the Word. Having asked who is the God of self-revelation, we must then ask what He does for us. The answer is to be found in the Incarnation. The Incarnation is the objective reality of the revelation of the free God.[29] As such — and the order here is all-important — it is also its objective possibility. The divine revelation has taken place in the event of the presence of Jesus Christ. It has taken place in time, and this means that God has time for us.[30] This time of God, being that of the Lord of time, is fulfilled time, expected in the prophetic witness of the Old Testament and recollected in the apostolic witness of the New.[31] The event which has taken place in time is the miracle of God's coming into the world by the assumption of human nature to oneness with the eternal Word. This poses the problem of Christology — that is, of God's oneness with man in Jesus Christ, very God and very man. In the Bible this is expressed supremely in John 1:14: "The Word became flesh." The subject here is the Word. The act is thus one of divine freedom and the statement is irreversible — one cannot say that flesh became the Word. Yet the act is so real that in a strictly christological context — carefully marked off from a false Mariology — one may rightly call Mary the "mother of God." The object of the statement is flesh. This means that the Word became participant in humanity as a specific man. This man exists only in appropriation to the Word. As man He stands in full solidarity with all men, yet with the dissimilarity of sinlessness. The becoming does not mean that the Word ceased to be the Word. It was an act of assumption. It was also a single act, not a process. It implied no infringement on the divine freedom and therefore no exclusive concentration of the life of the Logos on the human and historical existence of

26 I/1 (1936), § 9, 2.
27 I/1 (1936), § 9, 3; also § § 10-12.
28 I/1 (1936), § 9, 4; also § 10, 2; 11, 2; 12, 2.
29 I/2 (1956), § 13, 1.
30 I/2 (1956), § 13, 2.
31 I/2 (1956), § 14, 1-3.

Jesus (the famous *extra Calvinisticum*).[32] The concrete sign of this mystery is the miracle of Christmas, that is, the Virgin Birth. Born of the Virgin implies the sovereign initiative of God, the genuine humanity of Christ, and the exclusion of active human initiative or co-operation. Conceived of the Holy Ghost denotes, not the Spirit's fatherhood of the human Jesus, but the direct action of God in the fulfillment of revelation and the establishment of communion between God and man.[33]

The Outpouring of the Holy Spirit. A final question in relation to the divine self-revelation concerns what God does in us. The answer lies in the outpouring of the Holy Spirit by which man is enlightened to knowledge of the Word. This outpouring is the subjective reality and therefore the subjective possibility of revelation which makes man free for God as God is free for him.[34] It is itself revelation, and by actualizing this revelation in men it establishes Christians as the children of God on the basis of the Incarnation, in a common life for Christ's sake which is a life of fellowship, divine and human, eternal and temporal, invisible and visible.[35] Revelation in the outpouring of the Holy Spirit is a judgment on merely human religion. Even in a nominally Christian form, this is basically unbelief, since it does not start with God's self-revelation and it opposes self-reliance to God. Its ultimate tendency is along a twofold road of atheism and mysticism which is basically one.[36] Yet subjective revelation does not only judge. It also restores, and therefore it establishes true religion, that is, the religion of repentance and faith in response to the Word and in the power of the Spirit. Life on this basis is one of doing the Word, and it is characterized by the love of God and by the praise of God through love for one's neighbors.[37]

Holy Scripture (Chapter III)

From the Word revealed Barth now turns to a fuller discussion of the written Word under three headings: (1) the Word of God for the Church, (2) authority in the Church, and (3) freedom in the Church.[38] His first main point is that Scripture is revelation, not directly, but as witness to the revealed Word. In this secondary sense it may itself be called revelation. Though it is human in form, its theme is the divine revelation and God Himself speaks through its witness.[39] Secondly,

---

[32] I/2 (1956), § 15, 1-2.
[33] I/2 (1956), § 15, 3.
[34] I/2 (1956), § 16, 1-2.
[35] I/2 (1956), § 16, 1 (p. 219).
[36] I/2 (1956), § 17, 1-2.
[37] I/2 (1956), § 17, 3; § 18, 1-3.
[38] I/2 (1956), § § 19-21.
[39] I/2 (1956), § 19, 1.

he argues that as God's Word it is distinct from all other books. This gives rise to the concept of the canon, which is necessarily closed from the divine standpoint though always open in principle from the human.[40] Thirdly, Holy Scripture is the Word of God in both form and content. It has, however, an enduring humanity in virtue of which it is fallible. It thus depends constantly on the miracle of the Holy Spirit and by this miracle the fallible human word has been and will be again the Word of God.[41] Fourthly, the inspiration of the Bible is not to be regarded as a static attribute which places the Bible under human control. It is a dynamic moving of the Spirit which cannot be taken for granted but holds us subject to the divine sovereignty.[42] Fifthly, the Bible imposes recognition that it is God's Word by the fact that it is, and in virtue of this fact it alone has direct, absolute, and material authority in the Church as distinct from the indirect, relative, and formal authority of the ecclesiastical canon, the fathers, and confessions, whose authority is only under that of Holy Scripture. This true doctrine needs to be asserted supremely against the false authoritarianism of Rome.[43] Finally, the Bible as God's Word alone enjoys direct, absolute, and material freedom in the Church as distinct from the indirect, relative, and formal freedom of the Church's interpretation in the threefold sense of exposition, meditation, and application, which must always take place under Holy Scripture. This true doctrine of freedom is to be affirmed specifically against the false freedom of Neo-Protestantism.[44]

The Proclamation of the Church (Chapter IV)

Barth now moves on from the second form of the Word of God to the third. In a very real, though subsidiary sense the preached word of man is also the Word of God.[45] This cannot be regarded as self-evident. But it is a truth in so far as God Himself commissions and empowers men to preach in His name. The human impossibility is made possible by God. This means that proclamation must always be undertaken in prayer. It also means, however, that it must be undertaken in responsibility and with a readiness to work at knowledge of God's Word. Nor is this merely a matter of human scholarship. To have true proclamation of the Word of God there must be self-proclamation of the Word. But self-proclamation cannnot be expected where there is falsity to the revealed and written Word and the mere construction of human theory.

[40] I/2 (1956), § 19, 2 (pp. 473ff.).
[41] I/2 (1956), § 19, 2 (pp. 502ff.).
[42] I/2 (1956), § 19, 2 (pp. 506ff., esp. 514ff.).
[43] I/2 (1956), § 20, 1-2.
[44] I/2 (1956), § 21, 1-2.
[45] I/2 (1956), § 22, 1.

Hence a definite task of obedience is imposed on the Church's proclamation, and in this field obedience means concern for the purity of doctrine, that is, of the teaching given and received in the Church.[46] The final test of purity in doctrine and preaching is whether it creates obedience to the Word in those who hear. Here again the primary demand is for prayer that God Himself may graciously purify our teaching and create this response. But here again human effort is also required, and it is here that dogmatics acquires its specific function in the Church and its ministry.[47] Dogmatics is the pursuit of purity of doctrine. It operates at the sensitive point between exposition and application, that is, at the point of meditation, where there is the particular danger that other voices will make themselves heard. Its specific task is to ensure that there will be good preaching and therefore right knowledge.[48] But dogmatics also includes ethics, since preaching is with a view to action as well as knowledge, and those who receive the Word are called to be doers as well as hearers.[49] In this comprehensive sense dogmatics has the formal task of summoning the teaching Church to hear again the Word of God, and in so doing it remembers that it is itself part of the hearing Church and it therefore places itself under the same norm of the revealed and written Word, and of subsidiary authorities under this Word.[50] Dogmatics has also the material task of summoning the hearing Church to take up again the work of proclamation, and in so doing it remembers that it is itself part of the teaching Church and that it must therefore offer example and guidance in its own dogmatic method.[51]

THE DOCTRINE OF GOD

The Knowledge of God (Chapter V)

The first issue in the doctrine of God is that of the knowledge of God. Here again Barth begins with the fact rather than the possibility. God is knowable because He is known as His Word is fulfilled by the Holy Spirit and received in faith and obedience. This knowledge is objective and certain, but with a secondary objectivity through the signs of other objects, so that it is the knowledge of faith. Since the objectivity is that of the Creator, the resultant knowledge is obviously that of grace, and man enters the picture only in obedience.[52] From man's

[46] I/2 (1956), § 22, 2.
[47] I/2 (1956), § 22, 2 (pp. 766ff.).
[48] I/2 (1956), § 22, 2 (p. 767).
[49] I/2 (1956), § 22, 3.
[50] I/2 (1956), § 23, 1-2.
[51] I/2 (1956), § 24, 1-2.
[52] II/1 (1957), § 25, 1.

standpoint the knowledge is a divine enablement to love God and to
fear Him above all things on the basis of a revelation in which God is
known both in perfect clarity and for this very reason in mystery — that
is, through creaturely events — in a Thou-He relationship and in temporal succession.[53] The knowability of God derives from both God and
man. It derives from God in the sense that as the Truth He is ready to
make Himself known according to the mystery of His good-pleasure.
There is no basic way from man to God, though this is argued by
natural theology with a persistence which has its origin in a dubious
pragmatic claim, a supposed pedagogic necessity and a questionable
biblical authorization.[54] It derives from man as man in the Word and
by the Spirit becomes an object of the divine good-pleasure. The readiness of man is not to be construed from an anthropocentric standpoint.
The ultimate power and error of natural theology is the assumption of
another basis, and finally the only basis, in man himself. This readiness
is neither anthropological nor ecclesiological; it is christological. It is
the readiness of Jesus Christ as the Incarnate Lord, and it may be ours
because Jesus Christ is eternally for us and because in the Spirit we
may share it by faith. In the light of this christological fact of man's
readiness, natural theology is not merely opposed; it is excluded. It
may certainly be understood and described in Christian theology, but
it can have no integral place, not even as an alternative to be discussed
and discarded. It cannot even lay claim to consideration once the true
readiness of man is seen in Jesus Christ.[55] But how far can we be
sure that our knowledge of God is authentic knowledge? In so far as
God is known by God we may have certainty. Yet human cognition
can only be in terms of views and concepts, and we must unquestion-
ably admit that our views and concepts are inadequate in face of this
object. The fact is that knowledge of God begins with knowledge of
God's hiddenness. Faith itself shows us that God is inapprehensible.
But when this confession of God's inapprehensibility truly derives from
revelation and is uttered in faith, it belongs to real knowledge. And
from this knowledge we also learn that God is willing and able to make
Himself apprehensible. He does this through creaturely witnesses which
we can view and conceive.[56] Even though our views and concepts may
still be imperfect, we know that our attempt to view and conceive of
God in this way is successful and authentic because by God's grace
we are really dealing with God. The veracity of our knowledge is that
of His revelation in its claim on us and in its enabling of us to meet

[53] II/1 (1957), § 25, 2.
[54] II/1 (1957), § 26, 1.
[55] II/1 (1957), § 26, 2.
[56] II/1 (1957), § 27, 1.

38

the claim. Our knowledge shares in this veracity as an act of obedience, joy, gratitude, and wonder. Between the revelation and our views and concepts there is still disparity as well as parity, and therefore we can speak only in terms of analogy. But in true analogy, as distinct from that of natural theology, the object is the original, and our views and concepts are the partial likeness, not in the quantitative sense of partial, but according to a teleologically ordered dialectic. Since this whole movement is from knowledge to knowledge, objection may be made that it is circular. This circle, however, is the legitimate circle of truth established by the divine reality of Jesus Christ, and we may move in it confidently under the peculiar assault and with the distinctive comfort of faith.[57]

The Reality of God (Chapter VI)

From the knowledge of God we naturally turn to the being of the God thus revealed and known. God is. But what does this imply? Barth's first answer is that He is in His act, that He is the living God, that He engages in His own distinctive and self-motivated action.[58] But this God in His act is also He who loves, the loving God. His act is the loving act of seeking fellowship for its own sake, irrespective of the worth of the other, with no ulterior motive and under the necessity of inner compulsion. This loving act is personal and it thus reminds us that, though God is absolute being, He is also absolute person.[59] But this loving act is also God's own act. God in His act is the free God. He lives and lives in freedom. This specific freedom means that God does not need even His own being to be, that He is in no way grounded in or moved by anything else, that He cannot be classified among other beings, that even His distinctiveness is unique, that He may reveal Himself to what is not God, that He can both create and also indwell what He has created, and that He is capable of infinite though ordered variation in respect of the creature.[60] The perfections of God — Barth prefers this term to attributes or properties — are distinct and individual forms of His one perfect life. Since the plural raises a problem, Barth insists that each is perfect both in itself and in combination with any or all others. Each is indeed God Himself. Since love and freedom are basic features in the being of God, Barth thinks it legitimate that two series should be listed with reference to these two, though he is adamant that there is no antithesis, that no epistemological conclusions are to be drawn, and that the right order should be observed, that

[57] II/1 (1957), § 27, 2.
[58] II/1 (1957), § 28, 1.
[59] II/1 (1957), § 28, 2.
[60] II/1 (1957), § 28, 3.

is, from the more specific love to the more general freedom.[61] It is along these lines that he discusses the individual perfections, though to keep in view the unity of God's being in love and freedom he carefully arranges his two series in such a way that in each there are three pairs, the perfection of love being always accompanied by one which reminds us of freedom, and the perfection of freedom by one which reminds us of love. Thus under the perfections of the divine love are the successive pairs grace and holiness, mercy and righteousness, patience and wisdom,[62] and under the perfections of the divine freedom, with a reversal of order, the successive pairs unity and omnipresence, constancy and omnipotence, eternity and glory.[63] Interesting points of detail are the discussion of the divine spatiality,[64] the distinction of omnipotence from omnicausality,[65] the understanding of eternity in terms of pre-temporality, supra-temporality, and post-temporality,[66] and the fine passage on the beauty of God, with the resultant demand that theology be the most beautiful of all the sciences.[67]

The Election of God (Chapter VII)

To the doctrine of God belongs the discussion not only of the knowledge of God and the being of God but also of the election of God. The election is an election of grace in Jesus Christ. Despite the shadow which it casts, it is thus the sum of the Gospel. In it our concern is with God's free, mysterious, and righteous decision which frees, assures and justifies man.[68] The basis of the doctrine is to be sought, not in tradition, pragmatic considerations, experience, or an abstract doctrine of the divine will, but in Jesus Christ as attested in Holy Scripture.[69] It belongs to the doctrine of God because it is the doctrine of God's being and action for us in Jesus Christ.[70] It is primarily the election of Jesus Christ in both the subjective and the objective sense. Actively Jesus Christ is the electing God. In Him God determines Himself for us. Passively He is elected man. In Him God determines man for Himself. Since God's election of Jesus Christ is His eternal will, a reconstructed supralapsarianism naturally follows.[71] It also follows that God's will

[61] II/1 (1957), § 29.
[62] II/1 (1957), § 30, 1-3.
[63] II/1 (1957), § 31, 1-3.
[64] II/1 (1957), pp. 468ff.
[65] II/1 (1957), pp. 528ff.
[66] II/1 (1957), pp. 619ff.
[67] II/1 (1957), pp. 654ff.
[68] II/2 (1957), § 32, 1.
[69] II/2 (1957), § 32, 2.
[70] II/2 (1957), § 32, 3.
[71] II/2 (1957), § 33, 1.

is a revealed will and not an inscrutable decree. Yet it is a will to reject as well as elect, for in Jesus Christ God elected rejection for Himself. This is not the rejection of man. It is the rejection of the Son in man's stead and with a view to man's election. Identical with the election of Jesus Christ, the will of God is a divine activity in the form of a history. It is thus dynamic, not static. It is the living act of the living God.[72] Implied in the election of Jesus Christ is that of the community by which witness to Jesus Christ is to be given in the world. This is the one community of Scripture in the form of Israel in the Old Testament and the Church in the New.[73] In the form of Israel it represents the divine judgment and the hearing of the promise. This is the passing form. In the form of the Church it represents the divine mercy and the believing of the promise. This is the coming form.[74] Finally, within the election of Jesus Christ there is also the election of individuals. The elect are those who accept and attest the truth of election in Jesus Christ, while the reprobate are those who in a perverse and empty choice deny this truth, though involuntarily bearing witness to Jesus Christ as the Rejected by whom their choice is invalidated.[75] The elect are ordained to be objects of God's love and therewith to blessedness and to the reponse of gratitude and service.[76] The reprobate are ordained to an improper existence in the shadow of the elect according to the divine "non-willing." In this existence they portray man in need of election, attest the false choice of man, and manifest the hopelessness of life outside God's saving will. Their true determination is always to hear and believe the truth and thus to become direct and willing instead of involuntary witnesses.[77]

The Command of God (Chapter VIII)

Within the doctrine of God is to be placed the divine command, as well as the divine election. Ethics, too, has its basis in the doctrine of God. For the election is only one side of the covenant of grace in Jesus Christ. God has a purpose for His elected partner, and since this partner is originally Jesus Christ this purpose, too, goes back to the beginning with God. The holy God is the One who sanctifies man. His will is expressed in His command, which is the Gospel in the form of Law. Ethics, then, is a special task of dogmatics. In this sense theological ethics is to be distinguished from philosophical ethics, in respect of which there can be neither synthesis, friendly demarcation, nor co-

[72] II/2 (1957), § 33, 2.
[73] II/2 (1957), § 34, 1.
[74] II/2 (1957), § 34, 1-3.
[75] II/2 (1957), § 35, 1-2.
[76] II/2 (1957), § 35, 3.
[77] II/2 (1957), § 35, 4.

ordination.[78] This ethics is objectively referred to the Word of God and to responsibility to God's command.[79] The command takes three forms. It is the claim of God, grounded in the election, finding its content in conformity with Jesus Christ and taking the form of a liberation which impels and an impulsion which liberates.[80] It is also the decision of God which is sovereign, enforcing total responsibility, which is definite, leaving us no option but obedience or disobedience, and which is good, having an inner unity by which it unifies men and gives them inward unity.[81] Finally, it is the judgment of God, based upon the fact that He gives us Himself and treats us as His own in Jesus Christ, executed as the condemnation of our sin in the death of Jesus Christ and yet also in the declaration of our righteousness in His resurrection, and designed to give us the freedom of everlasting life, of sanctification, by faith in Jesus Christ and in the power of the Holy Spirit.[82]

THE DOCTRINE OF CREATION

The Work of Creation (Chapter IX)

The first work of God in fulfillment of election is His work as Creator. Like God Himself, creation — that is, the derivation from God of all reality distinct from Him — is known only by faith responding to God's self-witness in Holy Scripture. It is thus known only by faith in Jesus Christ, in whom we see God as Creator, man as creature, and the bond between them. Faith in Him is life in the presence of the Creator and recognition of His power, right, and goodness in respect of creation.[83] Creation is the beginning of all reality distinct from God. Embracing the beginnning of historical time, it eludes normal observation and description and is thus recorded only in the form of saga. It really happened, but in a way which defies ordinary documentation.[84] Biblical saga, however, has theological content. From it we learn that creation is not merely for its own sake. It is the work of the triune God in fulfillment of the election of grace. Its purpose is thus to make possible the history of the covenant which has its beginning, center, and culmination in Jesus Christ. As may be seen specifically from the first creation story in Genesis 1, creation is the external basis of the cove-

---

78 II/2 (1957), § 36, 1.
79 II/2 (1957), § 36, 2.
80 II/2 (1957), § 37, 1-3.
81 II/2 (1957), § 38, 1-3.
82 II/2 (1957), § 39, 1-3.
83 III/1 (1958), § 40.
84 III/1 (1958), § 41, 1.

nant, providing the necessary setting for its enactment.[85]   But we can put this the other way round, as in Genesis 2, and say that the covenant is the internal basis of creation, its *raison d'être*. If the covenant rests on creation, it is also the goal of creation, and its outlines may already be discerned within it — for example, in the history of man as male and female.[86] Thus understood, creation is unconditionally a divine benefit.[87] It is so because it has been actualized.[88] Existence within the limits of the creaturely is real, and it forms a real basis for the fulfillment of the covenant. Again, it is so because it is good.[89] This goodness does not rest on facile optimism, nor is it undermined by pessimism or neutralism. It is the goodness manifested in the divine self-revelation which confirms and yet also transcends the contradictions in creaturely life by displaying the final purpose of grace which underlies it.

The Creature (Chapter X)

The central object of creation is man. Though firmly set in the cosmos, man alone is the object of God's revelation. Hence theological cosmology cannot expand into a world view, but narrows down to anthropology.[90] Based on the Word of God, this must be a theological anthropology as distinct from one which is illegitimately speculative or restrictedly scientific. But it must also be christological, for it is in Christ that God's relationship to man is disclosed and in Christ that we see true man rather than the false and perverted man of ordinary observation. Though there can be no direct transition from Him to us in view of His unlikeness as well as likeness, our human nature is to be inferred from His nature. This is done in four main areas of man's relationship, namely, to God, to his fellows, to himself, and to time.[91] In Jesus Christ we see man related to God, delivered by Him, and responding to Him. Hence real man is to be found, not in natural, ethical, or existential accounts which at best deal only with indications, but in his calling by God and his responsibility to Him.[92] Again, in Jesus Christ we see man referred to other men, in and with and for them in genuine encounter and solidarity. This means that the basic form of humanity is fellow humanity, or being in encounter, in an I-Thou relation. The fact of sex imposes this form on man, and in this respect

85 III/1 (1958), § 41, 2.
86 III/1 (1958), § 41, 3.
87 III/1 (1958), § 42, 1.
88 III/1 (1958), § 42, 2.
89 III/1 (1958), § 42, 3.
90 III/2 (1960), § 43, 1.
91 III/2 (1960), § 43, 2.
92 III/2 (1960), § 44, 1-3.

humanity is a likeness of the divine being which nurtures hope in God.[93] Again, Jesus is whole man, both soul and body in ordered unity. This means that man, existing because he has spirit, is the soul of his body. He is wholly and simultaneously both in a unity which cannot be dissolved (as against dualism or monism), yet in an ineffaceable distinction of perception and action and in a rational order in which, within the one man, the soul rules and the body serves.[94] Finally, Jesus is the Lord of time. He has His life history, but He also has His Easter history, and therefore in the three dimensions of past, present, and future His time is God's time for us.[95] For man in his time this means that time is willed and given by God and that it is therefore real in present, past, and future.[96] It also means that each man's time is beneficially allotted by the God from whom we come and to whom we return.[97] It means finally that this allotted time begins and ends with the gracious God, so that the mystery of birth is resolved and the terror of death, of the unnatural end which is also a sign of divine judgment, yields to confident hope.[98]

The Creator and His Creature (Chapter XI)

Having spoken of Creator, creation, and creature, Barth now expounds the history of the creature under the guidance of the Creator. This is providence, which deals with the continuation of the relationship begun in creation. Providence means that God is faithful to His creation.[99] It is known from God's Word and believed in faith in God and Jesus Christ.[100] Its theme is God's preservation and overruling of all history as the external basis of the history of the covenant.[101] It implies God's fatherly lordship in terms of the divine preserving, accompanying, and ruling of the course of earthly existence.[102] The Christian perceives this in the triune movement of faith, obedience, and prayer.[103] The threat to world occurrence as thus divinely controlled is that of what Barth calls nothingness. This is known from the divine self-revelation in Jesus Christ. It is not to be confused with the dark side of creation. Nor is its reality to be denied. It exists as an impossible possibility in virtue of the divine non-willing. Yet it exists

[93] III/2 (1960), § 45, 1-3.
[94] III/2 (1960), § 46, 1-5.
[95] III/2 (1960), § 47, 1.
[96] III/2 (1960), § 47, 2.
[97] III/2 (1960), § 47, 3.
[98] III/2 (1960), § 47, 4-5.
[99] III/3 (1960), § 48, 1.
[100] III/3 (1960), § 48, 2.
[101] III/3 (1960), § 48, 3.
[102] III/3 (1960), § 49, 1-3.
[103] III/3 (1960), § 49, 4.

only in opposition, and even before the final manifestation of its defeat by God it is controlled by Him and forced to serve His Word and work.[104] The thought of God's rule includes the concept of the Kingdom of heaven and therefore of angels (and demons). Understood from Holy Scripture alone and in the strict context of faith, with no speculation, philosophizing, or scepticism, the Kingdom of heaven is God's lordship over the mysterious upper world which is the counterpart of earth and the place where God is and acts for man and from which His lordship comes to earth.[105] Heaven has its own creatures, the angels, who constitute God's entourage and who engage in a ministry of pure witness, not as mediators, co-workers, or vicegerents, but as ambassadors whose presence and action are indirectly the presence and action of God. Alongside heaven and the angels is the kingdom of evil with its demons. These are a false and insubstantial but powerful copy of God's true work, and part of the ministry of angels is to bear counterwitness to the falsity of this kingdom and the triumphant truth of God by which it is overthrown.[106]

The Command of God the Creator (Chapter XII)

The special task of ethics is to pose the command, not in terms of casuistry or orders, but in terms of the commanding God and the man commanded.[107] In relation to creation this means that the command of the one gracious God is to be discussed as the command of the Creator addressed to man the creature, and that the implied sanctification is that of man's creaturely action.[108] Barth proceeds to work this out in respect of man as he is known in Jesus Christ (III, 2) and therefore in the four areas of man's relationship to God, to fellow men, to self, and to time. Responsibility to God involves free and joyful keeping of His day, confession to God in the heart and with the lips, and the prayer of common and confident petition.[109] Being in encounter involves the right relationship of man and woman, of parents and children, and of near and distant neighbors, with the implied problems of sex, parental discipline, birth control, and nationalism.[110] Individual life demands respect for one's own life and for that of others as a loan from God. Negatively, this means that life is to be protected, and, positively, that it is to be a life of active service. Under this head fall the many ethical problems of asceticism, treatment of animals, health

104 III/3 (1960), § 50, 1-4.
105 III/3 (1960), § 51, 1-2.
106 III/3 (1960), § 51, 3.
107 III/4 (1961), § 52, 1.
108 III/4 (1961), § 52, 2.
109 III/4 (1961), § 53, 1-3.
110 III/4 (1961), § 54, 1-3.

and sickness, power, suicide, abortion, euthanasia, killing in self-defense capital punishment, war, work, and recreation.[111] Finally, the limitation of life requires that man should seize the unique opportunity of his allotted span with application and urgency, that he should fulfill his vocation in the sense of his place of responsibility — for example, in age, historical situation, aptitude, or sphere of activity, and that he should thus enjoy in the divinely appointed form the honor which is his in obedience to the divine command and acceptance of the divine gift. To this whole sphere belong such questions as hedonism, fear of death, youth and age, choice of profession, fame, and the proper defense of honor.[112]

THE DOCTRINE OF RECONCILIATION

The Work of God the Reconciler (Chapter XIII)

Barth introduces his theology of reconciliation with a brief characterization of the Reconciler in terms of Emmanuel[113] and of His work as the fulfillment of the broken covenant.[114] The sections on the covenant firmly link the volume to the purpose of God in Vol. II and the creation-covenant relationship in Vol. III. Reconciliation is the form which fulfillment takes in the face of the episode of human sin. In a preparatory survey of the doctrine Barth then points out: (1) that this divine work is still grace; (2) that it is not part of a higher dialect; (3) that it cannot be deduced; (4) that it is sovereign; and (5) that it is a fact in Jesus Christ.[115] Nevertheless, its sovereignty does not rule out man, since reconciliation introduces a new being of man in faith, love, and hope.[116] Jesus Christ the Reconciler is the middle point between reconciling God and reconciled man, and it is in Him as true God, true man, and the God-man that the event of reconciliation was accomplished.[117] The work is now expounded in three counterbalancing forms according to these three christological affirmations and to the threefold office of Christ as Priest, King, and Prophet.[118]

Jesus Christ, the Lord as Servant (Chapter XIV)

In a first form of the doctrine, Jesus Christ the Son of God is represented as the Lord who became a servant in fulfillment of His

[111] III/4 (1961), § 55, 1-3.
[112] III/4 (1961), § 56, 1-3.
[113] IV/1 (1956), § 57, 1.
[114] IV/1 (1956), § 57, 2-3.
[115] IV/1 (1956), § 58, 1.
[116] IV/1 (1956), § 58, 2.
[117] IV/1 (1956), § 58, 3.
[118] IV/1 (1956), § 58, 4.

priestly work. He manifested His lordship in obedience and self-humiliation, that is, in a decision to be God in an alien as well as in His proper form. This is a divine possibility, and on a true understanding of the order of Father and Son within the Trinity even obedience raises no problem.[119] The purpose of this act of condescension is that the true Judge is judged for us in the judgment of His passion, by which the justice of God is fulfilled.[120] The verdict of the Father is expressed in the new act of the resurrection, by which transition is made from the objective fact to its historical outworking in us.[121] In the light of this work the sin of man may be considered. As Barth believes, sin is known only in Jesus Christ in whom it is here disclosed to be rebellion against God, fratricide, and self-destruction.[122] Its specific form in the light of the divine self-humiliation is the pride of desiring to be one's own God, judge, lord, and helper.[123] Sin involves the fall in the three senses of hopeless, total, and comprehensive sin.[124] To this the answer of the divine work is justification.[125] If the divine judgment in Christ accuses man, it also acquits him in virtue of his replacement by Jesus Christ, electing God and elected man. Though he is still a sinner, man's past is over.[126] Instituted to a new right as the child of God, he may live in hope.[127] From this standpoint justification is by faith alone, though it must be understood that faith is an empty hand and that its exclusiveness is that of Christ alone as its ontic and noetic principle.[128] In the Church, the outworking of justification involves the gathering of the Church, which in being is one, holy, catholic, and apostolic and which lives in the intervening time between Christ's coming in the resurrection and His final coming.[129] For the individual, it involves faith in its threefold form as acknowledgment, recognition, and confession.[130]

Jesus Christ, the Servant as Lord (Chapter XV)

In a second form of the doctrine, Jesus Christ the Son of Man is represented as the servant who becomes Lord in fulfillment of His

119 IV/1 (1956), § 59, 1.
120 IV/1 (1956), § 59, 2.
121 IV/1 (1956), § 59, 3.
122 IV/1 (1956), § 60, 1.
123 IV/1 (1956), § 60, 2.
124 IV/1 (1956), § 60, 3.
125 IV/1 (1956), § 61, 1.
126 IV/1 (1956), § 61, 2.
127 IV/1 (1956), § 61, 3.
128 IV/1 (1956), § 61, 4.
129 IV/1 (1956), § 62, 1-3.
130 IV/1 (1956), § 63, 1-2.

kingly work. To the self-humiliation of God corresponds the exaltation of man.[131] This is rooted in the fact that Jesus Christ is also very man, elected as well as electing. God the Son became also man and thus assumed human essence to union with His deity in terms of the *anhypostasis,* the *unio hypostatica,* the *communio naturarum,* and the *communicatio idiomatum.* By the self-witness of the Risen Lord, through the testimony of the Spirit, it may be known that this is the real truth concerning Jesus.[132] In this light the man Jesus, even in His apparently inconspicuous though unusual course, appears before us as the royal man whose person, words, and acts can only be those of God. In the light of Easter even His cross can be viewed only as His coronation. His kingliness is that of the incomparable exaltation of His humanity, not for Himself, but for us.[133] Through the Holy Spirit transition is made from Him to us by the direction of the Son whereby He shows us where to begin, warns us against false alternatives, and gives us instruction.[134] Against this background the sin of man is lit up in a way which puts us to shame.[135] For viewed against the kingliness of Jesus Christ, it is the sin of sloth in its various forms as folly, inhumanity, dissipation, and enervating care.[136] The end of sin in this form is misery.[137] But against it the direction of the Son has a positive influence in man's sanctification. This rests on, and is the goal of, justification.[138] It is achieved exclusively, but effectively, in Jesus Christ, the Holy One.[139] It finds expression in the call to discipleship, awakening to salvation, the praise of works, and the dignity of the Cross.[140] In the Church, the outworking of sanctification is the upbuilding of the Church, by the quickening of the Spirit, as a provisional representation of the sanctification of all men in Christ.[141] The Church's growth is expansion, but it is also integration.[142] Protection is afforded against the complementary dangers of secularization and sacralization.[143] The required order of the Church must be the law of service, liturgical law (that is, law centered in worship), living or dynamic law, and exemplary law.[144]

[131] IV/2 (1958), § 64, 1.
[132] IV/2 (1958), § 64, 2.
[133] IV/2 (1958), § 64, 3.
[134] IV/2 (1958), § 64, 4.
[135] IV/2 (1958), § 65, 1.
[136] IV/2 (1958), § 65, 2.
[137] IV/2 (1958), § 65, 3.
[138] IV/2 (1958), § 66, 1.
[139] IV/2 (1958), § 66, 2.
[140] IV/2 (1958), § 66, 3-6.
[141] IV/2 (1958), § 67, 1.
[142] IV/2 (1958), § 67, 2.
[143] IV/2 (1958), § 67, 3.
[144] IV/2 (1958), § 67, 4.

In the individual, the outworking is in a life of true love.[145] Distinct from *eros,* this has its basis in the love of God,[146] consists in love for God and for Christians and enemies,[147] and is characterized by the fact that it alone counts and conquers and abides.[148]

Jesus Christ, the True Witness (Chapter XVI)

In a third form of the doctrine, Jesus Christ the God-man is represented as the true Witness in fulfillment of His prophetic work. There is here no material addition to the objective work of reconciliation, but a self-declaration of what is accomplished.[149] On this declaratory side of reconciliation Jesus Christ is the Light of life in a history, in an active Word, in a living presence, for which the only biblical parallel is the history of Old Testament Israel. Jesus Christ is factually and exclusively light, so that all other lights and truths can be so only in relation to Him. Divine truth in Him is binding, total, and definitive, claiming, relativizing, and integrating all others.[150] This prophetic work is the action of a victorious conflict in the stages of mediation of knowledge, emergence of opposition, the impinging of knowledge and defeat of the contradiction.[151] The promise of the Spirit as a third form of Christ's second coming between His resurrection and His return is the mode by which transition is made from the christological to the anthropological sphere.[152] In the light of this work sin is the opposition of man to Jesus Christ as the true Witness in this indirect and puzzling form.[153] From this angle sin is falsehood, whether as direct denial, rival belief, or transformation of divine truth into principles and platitudes.[154] The falsehood of man results in his condemnation, his nailing to the lie. The lie cannot overthrow the truth, but God may finally condemn the liar to live in it.[155] But against this the prophetic work of Jesus Christ has a positive side in vocation. The basis of vocation is the calling of all men in Jesus Christ.[156] Vocation itself, however, is a real event consisting decisively in

---

145 IV/2 (1958), § 68, 1.
146 IV/2 (1958), § 68, 2.
147 IV/2 (1958), § 68, 3.
148 IV/2 (1958), § 68, 4.
149 IV/3 (1961-62), § 69, 1.
150 IV/3 (1961-62), § 69, 2.
151 IV/3 (1961-62), § 69, 3.
152 IV/3 (1961-62), § 69, 4.
153 IV/3 (1961-62), § 70, 1.
154 IV/3 (1961-62), § 70, 2.
155 IV/3 (1961-62), § 70, 3.
156 IV/3 (1961-62), § 71, 1.

illumination and awakening.[157] Simply to be a Christian — not a minister, missionary, or monk — is its goal. To be a Christian consists in discipleship, in attachment and supremely in union with Christ.[158] Yet the essence of the Christian life is not the enjoyment of salvation. It is endowment with the task of witness, that is, union with Christ in His prophetic work.[159] This carries with it the affliction of a forward movement,[160] but also liberation to fellowship, to concentration on the one necessary thing, to the sphere of the human, to receiving, to action, to forgiveness, and to prayer.[161] In the Church, this implies the sending of the community into a world of human confusion and divine disposing to attest the new reality of Jesus Christ.[162] Knowing the world and its own solidarity with it, the Church is for the world.[163] Its task is to declare the divine acceptance to needy man as its object.[164] In the discharge of this task its ministry takes the two main forms of speech and action.[165] In individual life, vocation means life in hope. Living in the intervening time, the Christian has powerful and certain hope in Christ.[166] Looking for His return, he lives representatively in the context of hope for the world, actively in the hope of provisional fulfillments and constantly in prayer for the Holy Spirit as the free God who makes man free in hope.[167]

III. EVALUATION

Barth covers so wide a field in his *Church Dogmatics,* and his material is so closely interrelated, that evaluation is extremely difficult. In the last analysis, it is necessary to work through the exegetical and historical matter in detail before there can be confident judgment on his statements. A thorough knowledge of the whole *Dogmatics* is also required, for the various themes may appear in different connections and there is even an element of emendation or retractation. To try to proceed only in terms of broader points of censure or commendation is to run a high risk of facile and misleading generalization.

There is also a problem of approach. Some men's works are so ob-

---

[157] IV/3 (1961-62), § 71, 2.
[158] IV/3 (1961-62), § 71, 3.
[159] IV/3 (1961-62), § 71, 4.
[160] IV/3 (1961-62), § 71, 5.
[161] IV/3 (1961-62), § 71, 6.
[162] IV/3 (1961-62), § 72, 1.
[163] IV/3 (1961-62), § 72, 2.
[164] IV/3 (1961-62), § 72, 3.
[165] IV/3 (1961-62), § 72, 4.
[166] IV/3 (1961-62), § 73, 1.
[167] IV/3 (1961-62), § 73, 2.

viously biblical or unbiblical in the orthodox sense that a clear-cut position may be taken regarding them. Barth, however, attempts a biblical and evangelical dogmatics which cuts across established orthodoxy at many points. This makes a definite attitude more difficult. Almost all readers will find things they approve and things they suspect or condemn. But how then is a final assessment to be made? Is the good to be interpreted in terms of the bad and discounted? Is the bad to be exculpated by reason of the good? Even in an objective statement of defects and qualities much may depend upon the emphasis. A semi-Pelagian may be the same, but not sound the same, as a semi-Augustinian. The stress and even the order may be enough to tip the scales.

Finally, Barth deliberately seeks a new language in which to state the Gospel and to fashion its proclamation in the modern age. This may be sound in principle, but it raises its own problems. The language is often difficult. It makes old truths sound strange. Does it also make them different? It carries overtones of current philosophies. Does it also introduce their assumptions and concepts? Even if not, does it do any good? Is not ambiguity or confusion introduced? Can one ever be sure of Barth's real meaning no matter how he tries to explain himself? This is, of course, a general problem of communication. In Barth's case, however, it is intensified by the novelty of presentation, and assessment is correspondingly more difficult.

The best that can be done, therefore, in a short and general statement is to present what seem to be the main defects and qualities. For this purpose such formal aspects as vocabulary, style, and arrangement will be ignored. Detailed demonstration at the exegetical and historical level will be left for expert treatment in monographs. The criterion will be that which Barth himself acknowledges with the Reformation, namely, the Word of God in Holy Scripture. There will be no attempt at final judgment, but we shall respect Barth's own desire that dogmatics should serve a positive purpose of purifying preaching and teaching by the sifting out of the bad and the strengthening of the good.

DEFECTS

Some writers have suspected in the *Dogmatics* a basic principle which is erroneous and which thus vitiates the whole. For example, Van Til in *The New Modernism* and in *Christianity and Barthianism* describes an ultimate Neo-Protestant presupposition, and Berkouwer in a more discerning study, *The Triumph of Grace in the Theology of Karl Barth,* finds an overruling concept in the idea of triumphant grace. There has even been complaint of a dangerous Christomonism resulting from excessive concentration on Christology. The question arises, therefore, whether we should not begin with some such comprehensive error that casts its shadow over all the rest.

The possibility cannot be ruled out. Barth himself now sets Kierkegaard in the liberal tradition for similar reasons, and he finds a theologically "pre-Copernican" attitude in Brunner and Bultmann. Why should there not be something of the same in his *Dogmatics,* as there fairly obviously is in the *Romans?* Yet Van Til's study is so strained that Barth has apparently seen in it almost a willful caricature, and Berkouwer's criticism, though more thoughtful, runs contrary to the plain attempt of Barth to find his basis and center, not in an abstraction like the triumph of grace, but in the person of Jesus Christ.[168] Christomonism is perhaps a more valid description, but this falls rather wide of the mark in view of the ultimate Trinitarianism of the *Dogmatics* and the lofty New Testament view of Christ. A master key to Barth's weaknesses might resolve many problems, but it is hard to feel much confidence in those suggested.

Nevertheless, there are real defects, not merely in lesser matters, but at points of major significance. A first group concerns the doctrine of Holy Scripture.[169] Barth accepts the Bible's absolute authority. He allows that it is revelation. He endorses its uniqueness. He makes no artificial distinction between word and content. But he also advances some extraordinary propositions which are poorly supported in Scripture and which open the door wide to liberal approaches. Thus he finds the inspiration of Scripture predominantly in its present use by the Spirit. In terms of a historicist criterion of errancy, he attributes all kinds of errors to the Bible. In a curious application of the concepts of offense and sovereignty, he even argues the necessity of a fallible Bible. His handling of Scripture is in many ways the weakest and most disappointing part of the whole *Dogmatics,* and his safeguards against subjectivism here are very flimsy.

A second group of defects relates to the doctrine of God. The charge of modalism, usually advanced for linguistic reasons or by those who tend toward tri-theism, can be discounted. Barth clearly rejects modalism and espouses an essential Trinity. More serious is the rather arbitrary grouping of the divine perfections under the two master concepts of freedom and love. The resultant counterbalancing is not wholly wrong. Nor is there difficulty in the thought of sovereign love or loving sovereignty. Nor is the importance of these attributes in question. The problem is whether they can be legitimately exalted in this way. The scheme is formally satisfying but it lacks material

[168] Cf. Barth's reply, *Ibid.* IV/3 (1961-62), § 69, 3.
[169] I/2 (1956), § 19.

justification.[170] Again, there is the problem of God's election. It could be asked whether this belongs in any case to the doctrine of God. But if it does, Barth's view seems to bring some disruption into the Godhead. God's manifest purpose in Christ is to save, but under the sovereignty of the Spirit some might not be saved. The question is whether the Christological reference finally helps or matters very much. Is not the ultimate decision still taken apart from the revealed election — that is, not in the prior counsel of the Father but in the inscrutable operation of the Spirit? In other words, the decision regarding individuals is simply removed from the inscrutability of sovereign predetermination to the inscrutability of sovereign calling.[171]

The doctrine of creation also has its weaknesses. The first is linked with the doctrine of Scripture. Barth stresses the historicity of creation as event. He points out that this is not the kind of event which can be put in ordinary historical writing. With this there need be little quarrel. But he then introduces the dubious and unbiblical genre of saga to describe this special type of narration. Though Barth works hard to distinguish this from fairy story and especially myth, there is no doubt that the word saga is quite unsatisfactory and even misleading in this connection.[172] Applied similarly to the event of the fall, it leaves us in a world of equivocal historicity. Even theologically, Barth seems to have little place for a real fall. It is true that for him the world is fallen, but, since he seems to see its goodness only in terms of reconciliation in Christ, it may be asked whether there is ever a real fall from a real goodness in creation. Granted that this goodness no longer concerns either us or the main part of the Bible, should we not still say that God is justified in the initially perfect work of creation which He accomplished by Christ as well as in the reconciliation of this creation by Christ? It is true enough that, as things are, creation and reconciliation cannot be artificially sundered. But theological unity is no reason for dissipating historical distinction.[173]

Along the same lines two other dubious features arise in respect of the doctrine of creation, namely, in the conception of the *imago Dei* and in the whole presentation of evil or nothingness. It may be granted, of course, that both these are difficult questions in any theology. It may also be granted that in the one Barth offers a view which cannot be called incorrect and that in the other he follows substantially such classical conceptions as that of Augustine. Yet, as regards the *imago,* we may ask whether he is right to link it so

[170] II/1 (1957), § 29.
[171] II/2 (1957), § § 32-34.
[171] II/2 (1957), §§ 32-34.
[172] III/1 (1958), § 41, 1.
[173] III/1 (1958), § 42, 1ff.

closely with bisexuality and to conceive of it so exclusively in terms of relationship.[174] And as regards evil, we must protest that the whole discussion is very speculative, that the paradoxical definitions are not solidly supported, that the differentiation between evil and the dark side of creation is hazardous, that reckoning natural death with this dark side demands better biblical justification, and that the presentation as a whole leaves an impression of the negativeness of evil which Barth's protestation of its reality cannot wholly dispel.[175]

In the sphere of reconciliation many detailed points demand investigation. Among these is his rejection of Christ's humiliation and exaltation as successive states, his insistence that the doctrine of sin must be brought into this sphere, his specific characterization of sin, his interpretation of Law and Gospel, his description of faith, and his underlying supralapsarianism. Yet these topics are all open to clarification and discussion both in relation to what Barth says and to its bearing on biblical and historical teaching. There remains, however, one outstanding weakness which may be the defect of a quality but which does in fact cast its shadow over the whole understanding of reconciliation. This is the trend toward an ultimate universalism.

We must be clear on three points. The universalist trend derives from Barth's excellent objectivism in opposition to Bultmann. Again, Barth is not an express universalist. Thirdly, universalism in the sense of the salvation of all individuals is not a necessary implicate of Barth's christological universalism. Barth is not speaking at random when he resists those who say that he should logically be a universalist. So far as individuals go, he sees the position in terms of a shifting line of evangelism (his deep-rooted activism) under the Spirit's sovereignty. If we cannot reject the possibility that all will be saved, we cannot say that they must be.[176] The reservation is good, but it is not really adequate. What Barth fails to see is that to deny the possibility of the salvation of all is no infringement of the divine sovereignty if God Himself has made it plain that all will not be saved. But on any reading this is surely the Bible's teaching. We may not know who will be saved, or how many, but we do know that there will be the lost as well as the saved. Hence the divine sovereignty cannot be invoked in favor of a state of suspense on this matter. Unless Barth is persuaded, and can show, that the biblical data are different, his hesitation here is a violation of his own Scripture principle. To use an admittedly biblical doctrine of divine freedom to contradict

---

[174] III/1 (1958), § 41, 2-3; III/2 (1960), § 45, 3.
[175] III/3 (1960), § 50.
[176] Cf. II/2 (1957), § 35, 1-4; IV/3 (1961-62), § 70, 3.

evident biblical data is an illustration of the arbitrary and illegitimate dogmatic thinking which elsewhere Barth rightly deplores. And it casts a sinister shadow over what is from many angles an admirable and forceful statement of the divine reconciliation in and through Jesus Christ.

QUALITIES

The fact that there are errors in the *Dogmatics* does not force us to deny all points of value. It is rather a reminder of human fallibility and of the need for the biblical norm and for discrimination in its exercise. Even the presence of what is wrong does not necessarily vitiate what is right, as though the wrong were a principle by which to weigh and condemn the right. Good and useful things may still be found in plenty in the *Church Dogmatics*.

Within the Proiegomena, for instance, the doctrine of the Trinity is basically orthodox,[177] as is also the assertion of the Virgin Birth, in relation to which Barth contributes illuminating theological implications and a fine criticism of Mariology.[178] The emphasis on the place and role of the Holy Spirit is also timely and healthy. Indeed, the whole conception of a trinitarian and christological theology is good in distinction from the anthropological and ecclesiological aberrations of the two dominant heresies of the day. No less sound is Barth's fundamental understanding of the nature and norm of dogmatics. He is surely right in his insistence that dogmatics must be an objective science drawing on the data, not of human religion and philosophy, but of the self-revelation of the Triune God.[179] He is also right to insist that, if this is so, the only absolute norm of theology, as of Christian preaching and action, is the divinely established record of revelation in the prophetic and apostolic testimony of the Bible. Indeed, in his section on authority with its clear distinction between absolute authority and relative authorities Barth has made one of the most solid and significant contributions to perhaps the most critical issue in the whole doctrine of Scripture.[180] For this alone, as for his perspicacious study of papalism and his wise words on hermeneutics, one must be grateful to Barth in spite of his poor handling of inspiration.

Barth's uncompromising rejection of natural theology is variously assessed. Perhaps the greatest weakness here is the failure to make a clear distinction between natural revelation and natural theology. But

[177] I/1 (1936), Chapter II, Part 1.
[178] I/2 (1956), § 15, 3.
[179] I/1 (1936), Chapter I.
[180] I/2 (1956), § 20.

55

when it is seen that Barth's reference is to the natural theology of fallen man, and that he does not deny that there may be partial lights and words and truths even outside special revelation, it is hard to maintain that he is not basically right in his understanding, that he does not give a more correct account of, for example, Romans 1-2 (as well as I Corinthians 1) than many who try to see here a foundation of knowledge rather than of guilt, and that his examination of natural theology is not amongst the most acute and helpful in this whole area. That the true God is known only in terms of Himself as both subject and object, that He is known only as the living God and not as a posited object of human thought, fancy, or emotion, is a truth which needs the vigorous statement which it receives in the *Dogmatics* and by which some of our overphilosophized orthodox dogmatics might profit.[181]

The christological concentration of Barth appears at its greatest strength in his discussions of election, creation, and anthropology. Attention has been drawn already to defects in these fields. These should not blind us, however, to the real elements of strength. The closer linking of Christ with election as both Elector and Elect, while it does not solve all problems, certainly lights up the doctrine, safeguards it from speculativeness, introduces a strong doctrine of substitution, and provides a powerful basis for assurance.[182] Similarly, the christological theodicy of Barth is intrinsically true, for even in its initial goodness by creation the world is surely made in and through and for Him. Nor can creation be separated in fact from reconciliation. This is plain enough in the Bible, and it is well brought out in all great theology from Irenaeus and Athanasius to the Reformers. Even fallen creation is also justified when seen with reference to the divine work of reconciliation according to God's eternal counsel fulfilled in Christ.[183] The christological anthropology of Barth is admittedly tentative and it opens up the possibility of speculative divergence along the lines of archetypal man. But the primary thesis that Adam is image rather than original, and that Christ is the original, is not so perverse as some critics depict it. Furthermore, the true humanity of Christ surely implies more than that Christ is really man. If He is really man, we see true humanity in Him. It is thus with reference to Him and not to observations concerning ourselves that a dogmatic anthropology is to be constructed. Whether this is correctly worked out in detail in Barth's four areas may be questioned, but here, too, there are illuminating

[181] II/1 (1957), § 26, 1-2.
[182] II/2 (1957), § 33, 1.
[183] III/1 (1958), § 42, 3.

56

elements in the discussion of the man-woman relationship, of the problem of body, soul, and spirit, and of the mystery and fulfillment of time.[184]

Also deserving of mention is the solidity of much of Barth's work in the field of reconciliation. If the christological framework verges on the artificial, especially in its relation to the parallel schema of prophet, priest, and king, it shows an acute sense of the interrelatedness of Christ's person and work, and the detailed christological teaching is penetrating, scholarly, and substantially Chalcedonian and Reformed.[185] The understanding of justification and sanctification is equally sound, and, profiting by recent biblical study, Barth contributes a far more satisfying account of vocation than in most past and present discussions.[186] Above all, however, Barth emphasizes the objective reality of the finished work of Christ in death and resurrection and the substitutionary nature of this work of Christ for us.[187] Notwithstanding the dangers implicit in his outworking, these are magnificent emphases which are only too often obscured even in evangelical preaching and teaching. No less magnificent in Barth is the stress on the fact that Christ's work, though finished in the sense that atonement has been made, continues by the Holy Spirit in the proclamation of the Gospel.[188] Here, as so often, Barth makes full allowance for the role, presence, and power of the Holy Spirit. Even in relation to Scripture his concern for the present work of the Spirit through Scripture is in itself wholly biblical and Reformed. But in the area of reconciliation it gains added strength through the linking of this present work in us with the past work for us, that is, with the objective event of the finished work.

In addition to these main elements of value there are many matters of detail on which, positively or provocatively, Barth has valuable things to say. His historical surveys are always useful, and along with more purely dogmatic material they include powerful evaluations of Descartes,[189] Leibnitz,[190] Fichte,[191] Nietzsche,[192] and the Existentialists,[193] and interesting encounters with Brunner[194] and Bultmann.[195]

---

184 III/2 (1960), § 43, 2.
185 IV/2 (1958), § 64, 2.
186 IV/3 (1960), § 71.
187 Esp., *Ibid.*, IV/1 (1956), cf. the Preface.
188 Cf. esp., *Ibid.*, IV/3 (1961-62).
189 III/1 (1958), pp. 350ff.
190 III/1 (1958), pp. 388ff.
191 III/2 (1960), pp. 96ff.
192 III/2 (1960), pp. 231ff.
193 III/3 (1960), pp. 334ff.
194 III/2 (1960), pp. 128ff.
195 III/2 (1960), pp. 443ff.

Ironical retractations should also be noted — for example, his dismissal of the Wholly Other as idolatry,[196] his relegation of paradox to the realm of the demonic,[197] and his discovery of supreme Pharisaism in the despair of Kierkegaard.[198] Incidental discussions of such diverse topics as the pace of modern life,[199] the dangers of monkish theology,[200] and subjectivist trends in evangelical hymnology[201] all demand consideration. Fine treatment is given to themes like providence,[202] angels,[203] apostolicity,[204] anti-Semitism,[205] union with Christ,[206] the second coming, and even the rapture.[207] The biblical expositions, if naturally uneven, contain some good word studies,[208] much solid development,[209] fine homiletical application,[210] challenging if rather fanciful typology,[211] and beautiful passages like the commentary on I Corinthians 13 at the end of IV, 2.[212] Nor should one overlook the profound and acute handling of ethical problems — the Lord's Day, feminine emancipation, war, suicide, patriotism, economic issues — in the great ethical chapter in III, 4. Indeed, even if one rejects his conception of dynamic ethics and disputes his individual judgments, there can be no objection to his basic principle that a true Christian ethics must be rooted in Christian theology. Thus he undoubtedly provides a stimulating model of true ethical method.

This opens up the way to the only possible conclusion. Without some measure of improper partisanship, it is difficult to strike a balance between the more dubious and the more solid aspects. It is possible, however, to bring out certain more general features of Barth's *Dogmatics* which are commendable and exemplary even though they may be applied here in a bad cause. There is, for instance, his steadfast refusal to allow an intellectual and academic abstraction of theology and his determination to relate it strongly and positively to the whole

196 IV/1 (1956), p. 186.
197 IV/3 (1961-62), p. 178; cf. IV/2 (1958), p. 348.
198 Cf. IV/1 (1956), pp. 150, 689, 741.
199 III/4 (1961), pp. 555ff.
200 III/2 (1960), pp. 289f.
201 I/2 (1956), pp. 252ff.
202 III/3 (1960), § 49, 1-3.
203 III/3 (1960), § 51, 2-3.
204 IV/1 (1956), § 62, 2.
205 Cf. esp. *Ibid.*, III/3 (1960), pp. 210ff.
206 IV/3 (1961-62), § 71, 3.
207 IV/3 (1961-62), § 73, 1.
208 E.g., *Ibid.*, 11/2 (1957), pp. 480ff.; III/4 (1961), pp. 600ff.
209 E.g., *Ibid.*, II/2 (1957), pp. 202ff.; 213ff.; etc.
210 E.g., *Ibid.*, IV/2 (1958), pp. 424ff.; 445ff.; 464ff.
211 E.g., *Ibid.*, II/2 (1958), pp. 354ff.; 366ff.
212 IV/2 (1958), § 68, 4.

task of Christian ministry. There is also his acceptance in principle of the bondage of the theologian to the divine Word and his condemnation of free speculation. Again, there is his high sense of the joyousness and beauty of theology in accordance with the ultimate joyousness and beauty of its theme. Finally, there are the deeply spiritual qualities of reverence and humility and wonder which give to many pages, and ultimately to the whole work, a devotional power and evangelical fervor that we often seek in vain in more orthodox but more abstruse and barren compositions. Here is a dogmatics which seeks its starting-point in faith, which depends for its strength on prayer, which consciously orientates itself to the Lord, and which finds its true climaxes in praise. Reverence is, of course, no substitute for truth; yet the truth is not honored without reverence. Hence these are qualities in Barth's theology which we cannot fail to respect, which we may seek to emulate even in our criticisms and which we should covet earnestly for all theological endeavor.

IV. BIBLIOGRAPHY

WORKS BY KARL BARTH

Anselm: *Fides Quaerens Intellectum (Faith in Search of Understanding).* Richmond, 1961 (*Fides Quaerens Intellectum. Anselms Beweis der Existenz Gottes.* Zollikon-Zürich, 2nd ed., 1958).

Call for Christ. London, 1967.

Christ and Adam. Edinburgh, 1956 (*Christus und Adam nach Römer 5.* Zollikon-Zürich, 1952).

Christmas. Edinburgh, 1959 (*Weihnacht.* Göttingen, 2nd ed., 1957).

Church Dogmatics. Vol. I, Part 1, *The Doctrine of the Word of God.* Edinburgh, 1936 (*Die Kirchliche Dogmatik,* Erster Band, erster Teil, *Die Lehre vom Wort Gottes.* München, 1932).

Vol. I, Part 2, *The Doctrine of the Word of God.* Edinburgh, 1956 (Erster Band, zweiter Teil, *Die Lehre vom Wort Gottes.* Zollikon-Zürich, 1938).

Vol. II, Part 1, *The Doctrine of God.* Edinburgh, 1957 (Zweiter Band, erster Teil, *Die Lehre von Gott.* Zollikon-Zürich, 1940).

Vol. II, Part 2, *The Doctrine of God.* Edinburgh, 1957 (Zweiter Band, zweiter Teil, *Die Lehre von Gott.* Zollikon-Zürich, 1942).

Vol. III, Part 1, *The Doctrine of Creation.* Edinburgh, 1958 (Dritter Band, erster Teil, *Die Lehre von der Schöpfung.* Zollikon-Zürich, 1945).

Vol. III, Part 2, *The Doctrine of Creation.* Edinburgh, 1960 (Dritter Band, erster Teil, *Die Lehre von der Schöpfung.* Zollikon-Zürich, 1948).

Vol. III, Part 3, *The Doctrine of Creation.* Edinburgh, 1960 (Dritter Band, dritter Teil, *Die Lehre von der Schöpfung.* Zollikon-Zürich, 1950).

Vol. III, Part 4, *The Doctrine of Creation.* Edinburgh, 1961 (Dritter Band, vierter Teil, *Die Lehre von der Schöpfung.* Zollikon-Zürich, 1951).

Vol. IV, Part 1, *The Doctrine of Reconciliation.* Edinburgh, 1956 (Vierter Band, erster Teil, *Die Lehre von der Versöhnung.* Zollikon-Zürich, 1953).

Vol. IV, Part 2, *The Doctrine of Reconciliation.* Edinburgh,

1958 (Vieter Band, zweiter Teil, *Die Lehre von der Versöhnung.* Zollikon-Zürich, 1955).

Vol. IV, Part 3, first half, *The Doctrine of Reconciliation.* Edinburgh, 1961 (Vierter Band, dritter Teil, erste Hälfte, *Die Lehre von der Versöhnung.* Zollikon-Zürich, 1959).

Vol. IV, Part 3, second half, *The Doctrine of Reconciliation.* Edinburgh, 1962 (Vierter Band, dritter Teil, zweite Hälfte, *Die Lehre von der Versöhnung.* Zollikon-Zürich, 1959).

Vol. IV, Part 4, Fragment, *The Doctrine of Reconciliation.* Edinburgh, 1968 (Vierter Band, vierter Teil, Fragment, *Die Lehre von der Versöhnung.* Zollikon-Zürich, 1967.

Come, Holy Spirit! New York, 1933 (*Komm, Schöpfer Geist!* — Predigtsammlung von K. Barth und E. Thurneysen. München, 1924).

Credo. New York, 1962 (München, 1935).

Deliverance to the Captives. New York, 1961 (*Den Gefangenen Befreiung.* Zollikon-Zürich, 1959).

Dogmatics in Outline. New York, 1949 (*Dogmatik im Grundriss.* Zollikon-Zürich, 1947).

Epistle to the Philippians. London, Richmond, 1962 (*Erklärung des Philipperbriefs.* Zollikon-Zürich, 6th ed., 1947).

Epistle to the Romans. London, 6th ed., 1933 (*Der Römerbrief.* Bern, 1919).

Evangelical Theology, an Introduction. New York, 1963 (*Einführung in die evangelische Theologie.* Zollikon-Zürich, 1962).

The Faith of the Church: Apostles' Creed. New York, 1958.

From Rousseau to Ritschl. London, 1959 (*Die protestantische Theologie im 19. Jahrhundert.* Zollikon-Zürich, 1957).

God, Grace and Gospel, three essays. Edinburgh, 1959 (*Evangelium und Gesetz.* München, 1956, *Die Menschlichkeit Gottes.* Zollikon-Zürich, 1956; *Evangelische Theologie im 19. Jahrhundert.* Zollikon-Zürich, 1957).

God's Search for Man. New York, 1935 (*Die Grosse Barmherzigkeit* — Predigtsammlung von K. Barth und E. Thurneysen. München, 1935).

The Humanity of God, three essays. Richmond, 1960 (*Evangelische Theologie im 19. Jahrhundert.* Zollikon-Zürich, 1957; *Die Menschlichkeit Gottes.* Zollikon-Zürich, 1956; *Das Geschenk der Freiheit.* Zollikon-Zürich, 1956).

The Knowledge of God and the Service of God. London, 1938 (*Gotteserkenntnis und Gottesdienst nach reformatorische Lehre.* Zollikon-Zürich, 1938).

Prayer According to the Catechisms of the Reformation. Philadelphia, 1952 (a stenographic record of three seminars at Neuchâtel, January 1947, January 1948, September 1949, adapted by A. Poulin).

A Shorter Commentary on the Romans. London, 1959 (*Kurze Erklärung des Römerbriefes.* München, 1956).

The Teaching of the Church Regarding Baptism. London, 2nd ed., 1956 (*Die Kirchliche Lehre von der Taufe.* Zollikon-Zürich, 1943).

Theology and Church. New York, 1962 (*Die Theologie und die Kirche.* München, 1928).

This Christian Cause. New York, 1941 (*A Letter to Great Britain from Switzerland.* London, 1941).

The Word of God and the Word of Man. New York, 1928 (*Das Wort Gottes und die Theologie.* München, 1924).

WORKS ON KARL BARTH

Balthasar, Hans Urs von. *Karl Barth, Darstellung und Deutung seiner Theologie.* Köln, 1951.

Berkouwer, G. C. *De Triomf der Genade in de Theologie van Karl Barth.* Kampen, 1955 (*The Triumph of Grace in the Theology of Karl Barth.* Grand Rapids, 1956).

Bouillard, H. *Karl Barth, Genèse et Evolution de la Théologie Dialectique,* vols. I-III. Paris, 1957.

Brown, Colin. *Karl Barth and the Christian Message.* London, 1967.

Camfield, F. W., ed. *Reformation Old and New.* London, 1947.

Küng, Hans. *Rechtfertigung, Die Lehre Karl Barths und eine katholische Besinnung.* Einsiedeln, 1957.

Parker, T. H. L., ed. *Essays in Christology for Karl Barth.* London, 1956.

Runia, Klaas. *Karl Barth's Doctrine of Holy Scripture.* Grand Rapids, 1962.

Torrance, T. F. *Karl Barth: An Introduction to His Early Theology, 1910-1930.* London, 1962.

Van Til, Cornelius, *The New Modernism,* Philadelphia, 1947; *Christianity and Barthianism,* Philadelphia, 1962.

Weber, Otto, ed. *K. Barths kirchliche Dogmatik. Ein einführender Bericht.* Neukirchen, 1950, 1952 (*Karl Barth's Church Dogmatics. An Introductory Report.* Philadelphia, 1954).

Wolf, E., ed. *Antwort.* Zollikon-Zürich, 1956.

3 LEWIS B. SMEDES

G. C. Berkouwer

I. BIOGRAPHY

G ERRIT CORNELIS BERKOUWER is the son of a devoutly Reformed home and a devoutly Reformed church. Born in 1903, he was reared in the kind of Calvinistic atmosphere that combined a deep commitment to the Reformed religion with a profound respect for humane learning. His father, a teacher in Holland's classical preparatory schools, seems to have affected him with the sober piety married to cultural concern that is the genius of Dutch Calvinism. Berkouwer has always been at home in the confessional and the cultural life of the Reformed community. There is no hint of a theological crisis in his life like that found in the careers of contemporary European theologians who had their weaning on Ritschl and Harnack. While there must have been tensions within the thinking of a man so congenially committed to Reformed confessionalism and at the same time so involved in the ecumenical concerns of theology as Berkouwer has been, we find no trace of a radical theological conversion, an agonized break with a theological past. Whatever movement has taken place in Berkouwer's thought has gone on within the single-minded commitment of his earliest days to the Reformed confessional theology.

Berkouwer was educated in the classics at the Christian Gymnasium, in theology at the Free University of Amsterdam, the university born in Abraham Kuyper's grand idea of a Calvinistic academy free from Church and free from State. Most of his theological education at the Free University was received under the tutelage of Valentinus Hepp, a

Dr. Lewis Benedict Smedes is Professor of Religion and Theology at Calvin College, Grand Rapids, Michigan. He is the author of *The Incarnation in Modern Anglican Thought*.

genuine Reformed scholastic, whose theological method left no imprint on Berkouwer, but who, as it turned out, had to accept Berkouwer as his own successor in the chair of dogmatics. Leaving the university in 1927, Berkouwer went to the northern province of Friesland to be pastor to the Reformed villagers of Oudehorne. From the flatlands of the north, he was called to the metropolis of Amsterdam, where he served as pastor until 1945. Perhaps it was these years in the pulpit, perhaps a more independent conviction, that affected him, but Berkouwer left the pastorate with a stubborn conviction that theology, if it was to be meaningful outside the function of academic exercise, had to be a theology directed to the pulpit. He has always considered himself to be first and always a pastor, a *dominee,* of the Church, and secondly, and in an auxiliary sense, a professional theologian. He still preaches; almost every Sunday finds him in one of the many pulpits in and around Amsterdam, and always attracting a large following.

During his pastoral period in Amsterdam, Berkouwer published his doctoral dissertation on the problem of revelation in contemporary German theology, and was given a doctor's degree *cum laude* at the Free University in 1934. During the latter years of Hepp, Berkouwer was appointed as part-time lecturer in theology, and when Hepp retired in 1945 he was elected to the chair of dogmatics, standing in a line drawn through the lives of Kuyper, Bavinck, and Hepp. Lecturing in the stately and antiquated residence hall on the Keizersgracht, where the university had its birth and where theology still is taught along with philosophy and law, Berkouwer began lecturing to capacity student audiences. A new and fresh theological wind had begun to blow along the Keizersgracht, and the evangelical world, along with the world of theology from Basel to Rome, was soon going to catch its drafts.

Almost at once, Berkouwer prepared an ambitious agenda of theological writing. But what was he to write? The systematic theology of Bavinck, the unofficial *doctor theologicus* of the Dutch Reformed churches, still stood in its respected place on every dominee's book shelf. It would have been presumptuous and, perhaps, untimely to embark on a course leading to a new dogmatics in the systematic style of eighteenth and nineteenth-century Reformed theology. At any rate, Berkouwer chose the way of the dogmatic studies in monograph. Timed to appear every other year, the dogmatic studies turned out to be learned and highly relevant treatises on whatever subject appeared to be most crucially at the center of discussion at the time. There has never been a logical order to their publication; for instance, the doctrine of sin followed election and in turn was followed by eschatology. Besides the dogmatics, there have been many other books, two of them taking their place among the most effective polemical theology of the era. There have been weekly topical pieces for the Dutch newspaper *Trouw,* weekly articles for the Reformed church journal *Gereformeerde Weekblad,* and articles for theological journals. In addition, Berkouwer has involved himself almost continuously in the theological dialogues that are so much more common in Europe than in America: there have been dialogues with theologians of the Hervormde Kerk (the largest Protestant group in Holland, and the established church from which Berkouwer's communion, the Gereformeerde Kerken, had separated in the previous century) and with others of the Roman Catholic Church. In 1961 he was invited, on the basis of his polemics with Rome, to be an official observer at the Second Vatican Council. He is a member of the Royal Academy of Science, the first orthodox theologian since Bavinck to be elected to the Academy. Berkouwer shows no sign of slackening his pace. He is still supervising the graduate work of a large number of Dutch and foreign students, he is still writing his monographs, still absorbed in the practical affairs of the Church, still pastor to the pastors, and looking to the Lord "from whence cometh our help" for whatever labors the future directs him to undertake.

II. EXPOSITION

THE GUIDING PRINCIPLE: CO-RELATION

Berkouwer does not set out his methodological guide lines in any formal prolegomena to his theology, but they are not hard to ferret out of his various volumes. They can be summed up in his word "co-relationship." Though he uses the term frequently, he gives it no systematic explanation. It indicates that theology does not work according to its own inner-evolved principles, nor according to self-selected norms, nor for its own sake. Theology is in constant and dynamic relationship with faith and, hence, with the Word of God, on the one hand, and with the Church and the pulpit on the other. Only as it lives and works at the center of this double polarity can theology be meaningful and relevant.

Theology is a work of faith, and all of its statements must be such as the believer can recognize as objects of faith. This is perhaps the single most influential principle in Berkouwer's theology. It means that the object of theology is never the construction of a logically coherent system. Theology is not finished when it has produced abstract and profound thoughts about God that the simple believer can well dismiss from his own life of faith. Only those matters that the believer can and ought to confess as his personal faith and which the Church can proclaim as the faith of the Gospel are the proper conclusions of theology. The theologian knows no more and nothing other than what the prostrate penitent at the Cross knows when he, in confession of sin and reception of grace, discovers the God of Jesus Christ. And the end of theology must always be a doxology to the grace of the God of salvation.[1]

Theology, then, lives in faith and for this reason works in creative response to the Word. Berkouwer says that this relation of theology to the Word means that all theology is relative. In an early dogmatic study, he explains what he means.

> This relativity, needless to say, is quite another thing than philosophical relativism; it refers simply to the relation of a thing to something other than itself. Theology is relative to the Word of God. This relativity is decisive for the method and significance of theology. It means that theology is occupied in continuous and obedient listening to the Word. And since listening, unlike remembering, is always a thing of the present moment, theological questions must have relevance and timeliness. Theology is not a complex system constructed for their own entertainment by scholars in the quiet retreat of their ivory towers. It must have significance for the unquiet times; but it can achieve its proper relevance only in obedient attentiveness, not to the times first of all, but to the Word.[2]

This means that a genuinely biblical theology is not simply a theology buttressed with proper proof texts, but one done in responsive and believing listening to the Word, one done, moreover, by getting inside the perspective and genius of the biblical writers. And, most importantly, it is done with a constant understanding that the key to everything, theological as well as practical, is the revelation of God's grace in the Cross of Christ. Nothing that is not implied in the Cross and Resurrection of Christ is the proper material of theology. "Theology," writes Berkouwer in one place, "is not an excursion into the stratosphere that lies beyond scriptural speech in time; it may not travel beyond the borders of faith's perspective. Beyond the word of Scripture we dare not go, in speech or in theological reflection; *for it is in*

[1] "This, too, is the joy of all theologians, that they know no more than the simple believers know, that they may serve, want to serve, and can serve that Church of God for which Christ died outside the gates of Jerusalem" (*The Triumph of Grace in the Theology of Karl Barth* [1956, 1954], p. 393). The reader will note that there are two dates given in parentheses following the English titles of G. C. Berkouwer's works cited in the footnotes of this essay. In each of these instances the first date given is the publication date of the English translation, whereas the second is the publication date of the original Dutch edition.

[2] *Faith and Justification* (1945, 1949), p. 9.

the Word that God's love in Jesus Christ is revealed. There is nothing beyond that."[3]

When Berkouwer insists that the material of theology is confined to the revelation of the grace of God that was revealed in Christ, he does not line up behind Karl Barth's principle of the exclusivity of revelation in Christ. Barth's principle involves him not only in a rejection of natural theology and general revelation, but in a rejection of revelation in the strictest sense anywhere — including the prophets and the apostles — outside of the person and work of Jesus. Berkouwer respects Barth's motive: the rejection of any so-called knowledge of God that is other than a knowledge of the God of grace. For this reason, Berkouwer too rejects natural theology. But both general revelation and revelation in the Scripture through the prophets and apostles are something else again. He discerns in Barth a capitulation to an unbiblical deduction from an *a priori* notion of how revelation from a Person to persons *must* take place. Moreover, he suspects Barth of making an illicit jump from the correct understanding of exclusive redemption in Christ to an incorrect notion of exclusive revelation in Christ. Revelation, insists Berkouwer, always involves God coming to man with a message concerning His gracious will for men. And God came through the Incarnation in a way that surpasses and fulfills all other comings. But the Incarnation does not render the other comings unreal. Nor do His other comings reduce the unique significance of His coming personally in Jesus Christ. "The fact that every speech of God points to Christ and that the light of God's revelation fully arose in Him, is something entirely different from revelation commencing with Him."[4] The Christomonists, in Berkouwer's view, are guilty of schematizing the divine mode of revelation and making one doctrine (the kenosis) the key to the divine method of revelation.

We have seen that for Berkouwer theology is done in constant corelation with the Word of God. But Berkouwer is also a committed confessional theologian. And to be a confessional theologian involves an understanding that the creeds of the Church are but the Church's human articulation of the message of the Bible, defined as to character and form by the situation in which they were first uttered. The question is whether one's commitment to the creeds of his church compromises in any way his boundness to the Word. What is the meaning of one's churchly commitment to the confessions?

Berkouwer is aware that it is tempting for confessional churches to absolutize their creeds. On the other hand, any reader of the history of many confessional churches knows that under the pretext of a

---

[3] *Ibid.,* p. 160.
[4] *General Revelation* (1955, 1951), p. 106.

distinction between the spirit and the letter of the creeds theologians have been known to violate the very heart of the creeds of their church. How can a church, for the sake of the Gospel, insist on adherence to the creeds without elevating them to the authority of revelation? And how can a theologian be true to his commitment to the creeds without being bound to the creeds in a way that subverts his unique bondage to the Word of God?

Berkouwer calls for the Church and its theologians to "seek for the deepest intent of the confessions."[5] Biblical fidelity to the confessions can be achieved only when the Church keeps asking what the creeds, in their human and fallible form and content, intended to teach regarding the Gospel. This means that the Church must keep alert to the priority of the Gospel over the creeds. The Church's demand for loyalty to the creeds must basically be a demand for loyalty to the kerygma. Creeds function only for the purpose of guiding the Church in its preaching of the Word. And they can fulfill this function only as they are read, studied, and proclaimed in a living relationship with the Gospel. When the creeds are faithfully maintained, they will be maintained as human documents, subject to the touchstone of the Word. And they will be used and understood in their human character by each generation anew in order to get at what the Church in other generations understood to be the message of the Word of God.[6]

It is in this sense that Berkouwer all along has intended his theology to be a confessional theology. In every point of doctrine he subjects himself to a careful consideration of the ecumenical and Reformed creeds, not for historical interest, but as a point of orientation. On the other hand, he makes it clear that theology is not to be bound by or limited to even the most classic creedal terminology. We must never, he insists, assume that no new light can be shed by the Word beyond the creeds. The Word can break through every situation with new light for new generations. Hence, theology, operating out of faith, is a co-relative to the creeds only within the framework of a more basic co-relation with the Word.

No confession, then, may be looked on as the terminal point for theological discussion. In his work on the person of Christ, for instance, Berkouwer asks whether we are bound forever to the terms of the definition of Chalcedon. Warning that new words can sometimes smuggle in new content, Berkouwer also has this to say:

> Theology must not be intent on continually saying new things because they are new; but because from age to age it is confronted

[5] "Vragen Rondom de Belijdenis," *Gereformeerde Theologische Tijdschrift,* February, 1963, p. 19.
[6] *Ibid.,* pp. 21f.

by new situations — situations, too, implying an acute threat to the Gospel — the Church must be ready each time to formulate the truth anew. It does not then propose a new dogma, but tries to understand the truth of God in the new situation. Through conflict, and under the guidance of the Word and Spirit, the Church often becomes more clearly aware of the riches of the salvation . . . . And so there is no reason to make the pronouncement of Chalcedon a final mile-post in the history of the Church . . . . For the Scriptures are richer than any pronouncement of the Church, no matter how excellent it be and how faithfully it has been formulated in subjection to the Word of God. To acknowledge this fact is not to have a relativistic view of dogma but to have a right sense of proportion: the place of dogma is in the Church, which in turn is subject in all of its expressions to the Word of God.[7]

Theology also lives in co-relation to the pulpit of the Church. It stands between the Word as its life and the pulpit as its goal. Its only genuine vocation is to keep the message of the Word straight for the sake of the preacher. Theology must be preachable. This is the reason for Berkouwer's persistent shunning of abstractions: they cannot comfort or challenge the man in the pew. This is why he declines the temptation to let deduction and inference determine theological conclusions: the demand for faith, not the dictates of logic, must characterize the kerygma. Those matters that are truly objects of faith are the material of theology, for only they are the content of the Gospel. The work of theology must be climaxed, not with the satisfaction of having solved an intellectual problem, but with a doxology to the God of grace: theology and liturgy alike must end in a *soli Deo gloria,* the glory of God's majestic grace. The theologian is the servant of the Church, the proclaiming, listening, and believing Church. And this service is the joy of doing theology.[8]

This leads us to say something more about Berkouwer as a polemical theologian. He has been called a theologian of confrontation, with the suggestion that he does theology by way of response to encounter with the *vox theologica* of the day. This is a correct characterization only if understood within the context of what has been said about the more basic relationships of theology. Nonetheless, it is true that the two most widely read and acknowledged works of Berkouwer are his polemical sorties on Karl Barth and Roman Catholic

7 *The Person of Christ* (1954, 1952), p. 91.

8 Almost all of his criticisms of other theologians are made in terms of what their positions do to the preaching of the Gospel. Cf. the following passages: *The Work of Christ* (1965), pp. 289ff.; *Faith and Justification* (1954, 1949), pp. 11, 12; *ibid.,* pp. 198ff.; *The Triumph of Grace in the Theology of Karl Barth* (1956, 1954), pp. 268-275; *ibid.,* p. 393.

theology.[9] It is also true that his dogmatic studies are throughout dialogues with the spokesmen for theology of all ages. Berkouwer's polemics are significant for evangelical theology in that he carries on a true dialogue with others. He never uses them as a foil for his own contrary assertions. He never yields to the temptation to strike out at the weakest link in his opponents' armor. He meets his opponents, Roman and Barthian, on their own platform. For instance, he insists on taking Barth seriously for what Barth insists on teaching, a theology of the grace of God. It is clear, he writes, that "Barth's main concern is to speak of the all-conquering grace of God in Christ Jesus."[10] A judgment on Barth, therefore, must be a judgment on whether Barth consistently maintains the whole biblical perspective of grace, including man's relationship to it and the possibility of man's rejecting it. He declines the gambit offered by the presuppositional method of criticism, the method that discerns certain philosophical presuppositions in a thinker and then deduces the results to which those presuppositions ought to lead. "Whoever leads a person out of particular assumptions to an absurd position seems to be a sharp critic. But at bottom such criticism is weak and cannot in the long run hold its own against exhaustive analysis."[11]

Wherever the Word of God breaks through, Berkouwer insists, we must recognize it and be thankful for it. He is sure that this occurs in Barth's theology.[12] Still, where the kerygma is affected, he offers severe criticism of Barth. The weakness of Barth's doctrine of sin is seen to lie in its inability to do justice to urgent pastoral warnings against it.[13] When Barth's view of the christological basis for creation, election, and ultimate cosmic redemption is considered, Berkouwer wonders whether it really allows for anything truly significant to happen in history. Do not even the Cross and the Resurrection become revealers of an absolutely fixed state of affairs against which nothing, not even man's sin and apostasy, can genuinely militate? What comes, then, of a victory of grace where there is really nothing to oppose it? What comes of the urgency of preaching? What comes of the life-and-death crisis

---

[9] *The Triumph of Grace in the Theology of Karl Barth* (1956, 1954); *The Conflict with Rome* (1957, 1948).

[10] *Triumph of Grace* (1956, 1954), p. 392.

[11] *Ibid.,* p. 389.

[12] *Ibid.,* p. 388.

[13] Cf. *De Zonde,* II (1960), p. 56, where in a note, Berkouwer elaborates on the criticism he made of Barth's view of sin in *The Triumph of Grace.* In this note Berkouwer points out that his critique of Barth on this point was not based on a theoretical judgment as to an inadequacy in Barth's doctrine of the essence of sin as "das nihil," but on the question of whether the relationship between the power of sin and the grace of God *in preaching* was adequately maintained.

of belief and unbelief?[14] Even while raising such basic questions, Berkouwer does not leave the false impression that Barth is unaware of them and has no answer to them. But he persists in pressing the point because he is sure that Barth's position — in spite of all Barth so magnificently says about the kerygma — does not allow room for the preaching of the Gospel to play its crucially relevant role in the working of grace.

THE DOCTRINE OF GOD

The God of Providence

The doctrine of providence, as does the doctrine of any other act of God, centers on and finds its exclusive key in the salvation brought to the world by Jesus Christ. "He who searches outside this salvation, into the inscrutability of the origin, continuation, and future of the natural world will never understand the Church's confession of God's upholding all things."[15] The subject of providence, then, is not preliminary to the consideration of the grace of God in Christ. It falls within the biblical message of the redemption in Christ. For this reason, a consistent doctrine of providence has nothing at all to do with a choice for a kind of determinism and against indeterminism. There is no more affinity between the Christian notion of providence and determinism (even when God is said to be doing the determining) than there is between providence and indeterminism (even in the form of atheistic existentialism).[16] The doctrine of God's providence should not be confused with the notion that things happen as they do because of a predetermined ordination or an inescapable necessity. The God of providence is known only when He is believed within the context of the revelation of Christ and, so, within the sphere of grace.[17]

Berkouwer's rejection of a natural theology of providence affects his entire treatment of the significance of the doctrine. He refuses to use such terminology as First Cause, Ultimate Cause, and the like because they always involve us in non-biblical problematics. Such problems as the freedom of man in view of a determined course of events, human freedom as over against natural necessity, are not the same as the problem of human freedom and divine providence. The biblical problem of freedom is the problem of man's free resistance to God's grace and command. Moreover, Berkouwer not only rules out a natural

14 Cf. the chapters on "The Nature of the Triumph" and "The Universality of the Triumph" in *The Triumph of Grace* (1956, 1954).

15 *The Providence of God* (1952, 1950), p. 39.

16 *Ibid.*, p. 147.

17 "The only conclusion is that in the doctrine of Providence we have a specific Christian confession exclusively possible through a true faith in Jesus Christ" (*ibid.*, p. 45).

theology in general terms but warns against natural theology in the guise of an attempt to *interpret* providence in the concrete events of history. Biblical faith in the God of providence brings the assurance that behind the shadows of tragedy and within the light of prosperity, the God of all grace is mysteriously working out His benevolent purpose. This provides the courage to accept all things as challenges to believe and carry on in patience and gratitude. It does not, however, offer a rational key to the understanding of God's will in particular events. Faith in providence means that concrete events are accepted as challenges to further faith and to courageous living, but it provides no intellectual explanations of the will and intent of God.[18]

The providential work of God is traditionally discussed via a three-fold distinction: sustenance, government, and concurrence.

Sustenance. The Christian confession that God sustains the world in being is not a quasi-philosophical concept of a transcendent power providing continuous substance to existent being, nor is it a pseudo-scientific idea of God as the unexplained link between causes and their effects in nature. What theology has to say about the preservation of the world and the continuation of human history can be said only within the belief that God's redemptive purpose for the world is moving forward to its consummation.[19] On the other hand, God's preservation of the world and history must not be thought of as a neutral and graceless employment of nature and culture for the purpose of redeeming men *out* of the world. The very preservation of the world for the purpose of grace is an act of grace *to* the world. That God should allow sinful and rebellious human history to continue must be understood biblically as an act of grace and patience to the world, and the time of history must be viewed as a time of challenge and opportunity given to the world to hear and receive the Gospel of grace. "He who knows God in His grace and forbearance with the world knows that the confession of sustenance is not a theological refinement, but a call to preach."[20]

Government. In biblically oriented thought, God's government of world events is also always related to the accomplishment of His redemptive purpose.[21] God is the Governor whose servants include even the most pretentiously self-governing men, and who employs all His servants in the mysterious design of bringing salvation to men. This relates providence to Christ, and sweeps even the state into the picture. In modern theology, much has been said about the christological foundation of

18 *Ibid.,* pp. 159ff.
19 *Ibid.,* pp. 67ff.
20 *Ibid.,* p. 82.
21 *Ibid.,* p. 98.

the State. Berkouwer finds the notion of a christological foundation of the State speculative, but this does not prevent him from insisting that, theologically considered, the State is God's servant for the sake of His Kingdom in Christ. The State "makes the path of the Kingdom of Christ through the world a path through an ordered world." And no State, regardless of its godless pretentions, can shake itself free from this servitude. All things, including the modern State, are set within the royal Lordship of Jesus Christ.[22] The christological view of the State, however, is not discernible through the methods of a political science; it is known only as one knows the Sovereign Lord through faith.

Concurrence. The doctrine of concurrence is an attempt to indicate that the acts of God and the acts of men coincide in a way that takes nothing from the seriousness of human decision and takes nothing from the certainty of the divine decision. It is a way of preserving the real significance of human decision within the overarching providence of God. Berkouwer has no objections to the distinction, except that it is useless and misleading when it is posed as an explanation of the relationship between divine and human acts. Its ineffectiveness is illustrated most pointedly when it is applied to sinful acts. Here the notion of concurrence always tends to suggest that God is a partner to human evil.[23]

But if concurrence does not offer a rational solution to the problem of human evil and divine providence, can theology say anything to reduce the tension between these two apparently irreconcilable notions? At this point, Berkouwer entrenches himself in the consistent conviction of the Church that *Deus non causa peccati est.* In no sense may God ever be suggested as the cause of sin. And if there is a philosophical *lacuna* in our understanding of how God can be universally the God of providence and yet in no way the origin or the cause of sin, so be it. Berkouwer refuses to take seriously the most refined solution if it casts a shadow over the Johannine assertion that "God is light and in him is no darkness at all." He rejects out of hand the suggestion that, while God is not the direct or immediate cause of sin, He may be called its ultimate cause.[24] He also declines to use the very familiar (to Reformed theology) distinction between the hidden and revealed will of God. To suggest that in His hidden will God somehow wills evil, though in His revealed will He is against it, is to impugn the trustworthiness of revelation. And this is the most serious charge that a theologian of the Word can bring against a theological distinction.[25]

[22] *Ibid.,* pp. 119, 120.
[23] *Ibid.,* p. 129.
[24] *De Zonde,* I (1959), pp. 55ff.
[25] Cf. *ibid.,* pp. 51, 53ff.; *The Providence of God* (1952, 1950), pp. 132ff.

A rational theology may insist that when two such theological assertions are made as (1) that God governs all things, and (2) that some things are evil, theology is also responsible for making some sort of synthesis between them. Berkouwer responds, in effect, by saying that the doctrine of providence is a religious confession, not a philosophical conclusion, and that as a religious confession it is very ready to acknowledge an area of mystery. But the crucial issue is where the mystery is allowed to lie. This issue is crucial, not only for the intellect, but also for preaching. Theology may not say anything that would put the mystery of evil somewhere within the will of God. To do this would be, no matter how subtly, to explain away human responsibility for moral evil. Every time a causal relationship is suggested between human evil and God, there are overtones of self-excuse and self-justification. The mystery cannot be set in the dialectic according to which God on the one hand does not want man to sin and on the other hand does will his sin. As far as God is concerned there is no mystery and no ambiguity: He is only light, with not even a hint of shadow. The mystery lies in the desperately irrational, wholly dark, exclusively destructive, and yet very powerful character of evil.[62]

The God of Election

Two fundamental theses dominate Berkouwer's important discussion of divine election and enable him to break through the scholastic methodology with which the doctrine has been burdened. The first thesis is that divine election is identical with the grace of God that was revealed in Jesus Christ. It is therefore not to be confused with a notion of an arbitrary, graceless decree of a purely Sovereign Deity.[27] The second thesis is that divine election can be known only by faith, the very faith by which one knows God as the God of grace through Christ crucified. The comforting assurance of election by grace cannot be obtained by way of logical deduction from another theological premise, however con-

---

These passages are interesting because in them Berkouwer criticizes his mentors Bavinck and Kuyper in their efforts to find a place for sin in the will of God and yet avoid making God the ultimate cause of sin.

[26] *De Zonde,* I (1959), pp. 124ff.

[27] "Scripture shows us that in the doctrine of God's election, the issue is not a *decretum absolutum* abstracted from Jesus Christ, neither a *necessitas rerum* which cannot be changed under any circumstances, nor a dark and irrational power of the *potentia absoluta.* Rather Scripture points in its doxologies and songs of praise of the free election of God to the deep, unfathomable source of salvation in Jesus Christ" (*Divine Election* [1960, 1955], p. 172; cf. also p. 149).

vincing the deduction may be to reason.[28] The comfort and the whole reality of election is known only where *grace* is revealed — in Jesus Christ — and hence only in faith. For this reason Berkouwer insists that election is the heart of the Gospel and is meant to be preached. But it may not be preached as a speculative idea apart from the Gospel of the Cross. It may be preached only as it woos us into a resounding doxology. Indeed, asserts Berkouwer, the singing of the doxology is the *only* proper context for election. But no hidden decree of an arbitrary Sovereign has ever compelled anyone to break out in a Hallelujah. Only a doctrine of election that is identical with the revelation of God's grace carries the overtones of Christmas joy and Easter jubilation.

Berkouwer is eager also to rescue the doctrine of election from the caricatures often made of it. One of the caricatures of election is the notion that it is a hidden decree of God, lurking behind the shadows of the revelation of grace. If election were a hidden matter, unknowable to faith, the ultimate personal question of assurance would be unanswerable. We would have to say with the Council of Trent: "No one can know with certainty that he belongs to those that are destined to be saved." Moreover, the very reliability of revelation in Christ is destroyed if we throw up a smoke screen of hidden election behind the light of revelation. Two objectionable implications lie within the notion of a hidden decree of election. One is that election is prior to and separate from grace, that while grace is revealed in Christ, the more decisive and ultimate decision of God is set in the abyss of an impenetrable eternity. The second is that a person while believing in Jesus Christ is left in the dark as to the ultimate and prior question of his election.[29] Berkouwer

28 *Ibid.*, p. 161. Election, Berkouwer insists, is not a matter of an objective, fixed state of affairs as is suggested by the bare notion of a brute decree of a merely sovereign Deity. But, he adds, "we can only escape this fixedness and rigidity if it becomes clear that insight into the mirror of election is possible only in the way of faith. No theological reflection can by itself lead to this insight" (cf. pp. 22ff.). To get an idea of how real is Berkouwer's break with a hard core of logical deduction in the consideration and proof of divine election, one need only consult such a work as L. Boettner's *The Reformed Doctrine of Predestination,* where we read: "If the doctrine of total inability or original sin be admitted, the doctrine of unconditional election follows *by the most inescapable logic"* (p. 95; cf. also pp. 83ff.). A similar method of getting at divine election is followed by L. Berkhof in his *Systematic Theology,* where he includes divine election as a logically inferred corollary of the doctrine of divine decrees (cf. p. 109).

29 A person wondering about election may be told that he should be content to believe in Christ, but this admonition can be understood "as a well-meant attempt to still the storm of questions and doubts, but at bottom nothing but an impotent pastoral device, an effort to compensate for the 'high tension' of the hidden election" (*Divine Election* [1960, 1955], p. 109).

agrees that the fact of divine election is a hidden truth in a sense, but it is hidden to those who in pride are offended by the grace of God. It is hidden from the Pharisee, who interprets election as divine proof of his own self-righteousness. It is hidden from the worldly wise, who in their wisdom refuse to know God and crucify the Lord of Glory. But it is revealed to those who humbly accept their need of grace at the foot of the Cross.[30]

The Bible, Berkouwer knows, makes it clear that God is a hidden God. But His hiddenness is not in contrast to His revelation of Himself. He reveals Himself as the hidden God. We meet God in the cloud of revelation as the God who is hidden from corrupt eyes, from the proud and disdainful, but revealed to those who in confession of sin and receptive faith are open to His grace. This is quite another concept than that of the God who teasingly lets just enough be known of Himself to throw men into despair of ever knowing the real, hidden God. "Such a completely unbiblical concept of God separates the God of revelation from our lives and mitigates the absolute trustworthiness and sufficiency of that revelation."[31]

Another caricature of divine election is that it is an arbitrary selection of some to be saved and others to be damned. With this, we get the picture of a powerful Sovereign who, simply because He is sovereign, has the right and power to select some yet-to-be-created persons for one destiny and some for another. The suggestion of arbitrariness is part and parcel of the notion of an absolute sovereign Deity, for selection is a purely formal sovereign decision. It is obvious that this caricature separates both election and the God of election from the revelation of grace. In it God arbitrarily selects some to whom He thereupon determines to be gracious. The correction of this caricature may not be found, however, in a rejection of divine sovereignty. "One may not limit the divine sovereignty or violate the immutability of the council of God, but neither may one detach the counsel of God from the connections which Scripture repeatedly points out to us, and which find their point of concentration in the love of God."[32]

---

[30] Berkouwer's rejection of election as a hidden decree is of a piece with his rejection of the distinction between a hidden and a revealed will of God in regard to sin and command. The distinction between an "actual will" of God by which He does will evil and an "unactual will" by which He prohibits evil is both unbiblical and treacherous. It can only lead, practically, to an excusing of evil as ultimately the will of God (*Divine Election* [1960, 1955], pp. 115ff.; cf. *De Zonde,* I [1959], pp. 53f.).

[31] *Divine Election* (1960, 1955), p. 125.

[32] *Ibid.,* p. 153. Familiar scriptural images have sometimes been taken to suggest an arbitrary sovereign power to which men must blindly bow. The image of the potter and the clay could be understood as meaning that the sovereign God does anything He arbitrarily decides to do with His creatures;

The thesis that election is identical with grace and, in particular, with the grace of God in Christ brings Berkouwer into a confrontation with Barth's doctrine that Christ is the ontological foundation of election. Berkouwer knows that the Synod of Dort rejected the Arminian notion of Christ as the foundation of election, but he wants to show why Dort rejected it. In effect, the Remonstrants were rejecting a divinely effective decision to save when they said that Christ, as it were, persuaded God to elect those who believed and as they believed. Berkouwer, of course, has no temptation to follow the Arminian path. On the other hand, he cannot accept the notion that a decree to elect was made prior to and apart from the decree to send Jesus Christ to save, as though Christ were merely the executor of a graceless decree. This would separate election from grace and from the revelation in Christ. He insists, not only that Christ is the basis for our knowledge of election in a pastoral sense, but that the "very structure of election is revealed in Christ."[33]

Barth has also reacted against the notion of Jesus Christ as an "executor" of a divine election made in the hidden counsels of an arbitrary God. He has taught that the historical Christ is the foundation of election, the Elect One in whom we are all elect, and the Electing One as well. Berkouwer agrees with Barth that election must be inseparable from grace in our thought.[34] Christ is indeed, as Calvin said, "the mirror of our election." However, Berkouwer thinks that Barth's notion of the historical Jesus Christ as the "Electing One" is the product of speculation. Moreover, the implications in Barth's doctrine that point in the direction of a universal election required by the very nature of grace are, for Berkouwer, both unbiblical as such and incompatible with the biblical nature of preaching as an urgent life-and-death summons to believe.[35] The point is sufficiently made for Berkouwer if we say that divine election is of grace, the grace revealed in

---

but it really means that God is free and sovereign in the exercise of His *gracious purpose.* The "good pleasure of God" according to which we are chosen in Christ is sometimes taken to mean that God simply does anything that He arbitrarily decides, whereas the "good pleasure of God" is His gracious purpose to save: Christ is the revelation of His "good pleasure." The phrase "before the foundation of the world" is sometimes taken to indicate that election is eternal, and so separate from God's revelation of grace in history, whereas it refers to the "decisive depth-aspect of salvation," the fact that salvation is "free from what we know in the world to be arbitrary and precarious" (*ibid.,* pp. 150f.).

[33] *Ibid.,* p. 149.

[34] "We must listen to Barth's warning not to separate God's sovereignty from His love, and His election from Jesus Christ" (*ibid.,* p. 161).

[35] *Ibid.,* pp. 240ff., and *Triumph of Grace* (1956, 1954), pp. 262ff.

Christ, that it is knowable, not through logical deduction, but by the faith that bows before the Christ of the Cross. When a man comes in faith to know Jesus Christ, he has seen his election, and has seen all there is to see. There are no secrets since Calvary, except to those who will not believe.

Lurking in the background of this treatment, however, is the doctrine of reprobation, the negative and distressing face of election. Perhaps the most significant contribution that Berkouwer has made to the doctrine of election is his rescue of it from the doctrine of reprobation as its logical corollary. The notion of reprobation as a logical consequence of election is inescapable, as long as election is viewed as an arbitrary selection of individuals.[36] To Berkouwer this is as objectionable as it is logical. But it is also an inevitable result of viewing election as a graceless decree. According to the Bible, election is the fountain of all good. Reprobation or rejection is the divine response to human evil. God is the source of election. Man is the cause of his reprobation. This means that in our view of the relationship between election and reprobation there is an essential asymmetry. The two are not balanced as two equally ultimate decrees of God. They are, biblically seen, inherently unlike each other. Election is sovereign grace and reprobation is divine response to sin.[37] Berkouwer is not embarrassed by the strongly worded Canons of Dort concerning reprobation. He underscores his agreement with the "Conclusions" of the Canons, which emphatically reject that "in the same manner in which election is the foundation of faith and good works, reprobation is the cause of unbelief and impiety." Reprobation, then, cannot be viewed as a logical corollary of election.

Rejecting the view that election and reprobation of individuals to heaven and hell are logical corollaries, Berkouwer also rejects another kind of symmetry in this matter, the doctrine of universal election taught by Barth. When Barth says that all men are reprobate in Christ and therefore elect in Christ, Berkouwer responds by insisting that this notion violates the earnestness of preaching. Divine election is never portrayed in the Bible as the announcement of a state of affairs involving all men irrespective of their response to it. The kerygma comes as a summons with dire consequences pointed out for all who

---

[36] This kind of logic is demonstrated by L. Berkhof when he writes: "The doctrine of reprobation *naturally follows from the logic of the situation* [italics mine]. The decree of election inevitably implies the decree of reprobation. If the all-wise God, possessed of infinite knowledge, has eternally purposed to save some, then He, *ipso facto*, also purposed not to save others. If He has chosen or elected some, then He has by that very fact also rejected others" (*Systematic Theology*, pp. 117f.).

[37] *Divine Election* (1960, 1955), p. 202.

78

do not heed it. For those who do heed it, and only for those who do, the meaning of election is the jubilation of a man who has discovered that his life is truly hidden with Christ in God's love.[38]

Berkouwer's pastoral intent in his whole treatment of election is to secure the simple Christian believer against intimidation by it. No one need think of election as a matter hidden in eternity. Nor need he be set to trembling by the thought of an arbitrary deity perhaps decreeing his damnation, in spite of all his faith and works. As long as the doctrine of election is taught as an arbitrary decree, a graceless selection of individuals, a decision that lies apart from the grace of God in Christ Jesus, the doctrine will continue to cast a shadow over the Gospel of grace for many people. But where election is proclaimed as the very sovereign grace of God revealed at Calvary, which can be known by theologian and peasant alike only in faith, it will be the deep source of comfort and joy that it was to St. Paul. Seen in biblical perspective, it will bring believers to their feet in a Hallelujah to the God of sovereign grace. And never will it be the occasion for the greatest misconception of all, that "my election" must mean my superiority over the non-elect. Only the person who knows himself as the "chief of sinners" and the "justified by grace," knows anything at all about election.[39]

The God of Wrath

The wrath of God, according to Berkouwer, is the instrument of His grace. It is God's response to sin, the cauterizing instrument in His hand to burn away all that obstructs the purpose of grace.[40] Only in this manner can the Cross be seen in faith as a revelation both of the grace and the wrath of God. The Cross is not the scene of a duel between divine wrath and divine grace, with grace winning over wrath. The Cross is the scene of His wrath serving the purpose of His grace. It is the decisive act by which God cleanses the world of that which stands in the way of grace and in the way of the fellowship between God and man that grace intends to restore.[41]

With this said, it is clear that Berkouwer does not intend to teach the reality of divine wrath as an inherent characteristic of God, coordinate with His love. Wrath and grace do not form two parallel and somehow equally ultimate ingredients of the divine being. Nor on the

---

[38] "Barth's solution of the universalism of the triumph of election unavoidably brought him into difficulty with the meaningfulness of the hortatory *kerygma* and of the human decision in the area of history" (*The Triumph of Grace* [1956, 1954], p. 296).

[39] *Divine Election* (1960, 1955), pp. 307ff.

[40] *De Zonde*, II (1960), 138.

[41] *Ibid.*, pp. 138, 180.

other hand is the notion of divine wrath only a human misunderstanding that God removed by showing in Christ the kind of loving being He really is. Berkouwer does not react to a scholastic balancing of wrath and grace by leaning toward a Marcion or a Schleiermacher. Wrath is very real; but its blazing destructiveness is God's striking out against all that would keep His grace from fulfilling its purpose.

God is the unchanging Merciful One. When, in biblical history, He appears as the One who at one time shows His wrath and then His love, He is shown in wrath as the God of grace clearing the way for a restoration of fellowship with His people. "In the depths of her faith, Israel knew that God, in turning from wrath to mercy, was being the Unchangeable One."[42] The suggestion of God's turning from wrath to mercy brings up the old problem of the so-called *Umstimmung*, the turning about, of God because of the propitiation offered by Christ. Berkouwer recalls, on the one hand, that the mercy of forgiveness is based upon an event in history: "without shedding of blood, there is no remission of sins." He recalls, on the other hand, that the Cross does not cause God to hold back His wrath to let mercy through. For the Cross reveals the awful exercise of wrath. The wrath of God is not turned away by the Cross, but revealed at the Cross as the wrath that is against *ungodliness*.

Moreover, grace is not revealed *in spite of* wrath, or *after* a demonstration of wrath, but *in* the exercise of it. "It is not as though God's mercy was revealed only because and after His righteousness was satisfied, as though mercy was possible only because and after His righteousness was taken care of. . . . The Gospel reveals the righteousness of God as wrath against and judgment upon sin. . . . And *in* this intolerance of sin, the act of His mercy is revealed."[43] For God's wrath is the extended arm of His grace, cleansing away in judgment the obstacles that human sin placed in its way. Returning to a basic motif, Berkouwer adds that this relationship is knowable, not by deduction or intuition, but in faith that discovers at the Cross that God's wrath is against everything in him that kept him from God's love. In faith alone, we see that the wrath of God is the hot instrument of His love.[44]

God in Christ

The reality of God in Christ is a mystery known only to faith, known to faith precisely as a mystery, and known to faith only within the large reality of His reconciliation of the world to Himself. Theology has no mandate to explain the mystery; its task is only to help the Church

[42] *Ibid.,* p. 164.
[43] *Ibid.,* p. 189.
[44] *Ibid.,* p. 203.

understand where the mystery lies and where it does not lie. The New Testament proclaims God in Christ as the mystery of godliness, and theology, with no pretense of having insights unavailable to simple believers, can only help make clear the proclamation.

> It is the proclamation of the "truly God and truly man": and the Church did not attempt (at Chalcedon) to make this mystery transparent, but rather preached in the scriptural contexts of reconciliation. Only by faith can the unity of Christ . . . be understood. And this understanding is not a comprehension of the great mystery, but rather a life of communion with him . . . . And one can reverence the mystery only by faith in Him, whom to know is eternal life.[45]

What is clear from this passage is that we have not finished with christology when we have kept the two natures, divine and human, distinct. Nor have we a christology complete when we have discussed the person of Christ apart from His work of salvation. The starting point for theology must be the total witness to what Christ was and did. So, though he writes two separate volumes on the person and work of Christ, respectively, Berkouwer really is much involved with both aspects in each volume.[46]

Berkouwer insists that the Church's confession of the deity of Christ is a response to revelation and not a projection of its own faith.[47] From the beginning he sets himself against those who interpret christology according to what is scientifically feasible for modern man. But he also has a warning for those who abstract the deity of Christ from His humanity. The Church never speaks of the *vere deus* apart from the *vere homo*. The deity of Christ has significance in the kerygma only if it is constantly kept in view as God in the flesh.[48] The same is true of His humanity. It is a mistake to assume that while the confession of Christ's deity calls for faith, His humanity is apparent to common sense. The humanity of the Savior, in its theological significance, is knowable only to faith. For Christ is never merely a man, but *the* man, the man under judgment, the man through whom grace comes to men, and the man in whom the Godhead is revealed.[49]

After both the deity and the humanity of Christ are confessed, we face the problem of the unity of the two, unconfused and unseparated,

---

45 *The Person of Christ* (1954, 1952), p. 326.
46 Cf. *ibid.*, p. 106, and *The Work of Christ* (1965), pp. 10ff. On this point, Berkouwer disagrees with Emil Brunner's insistence that we can know the person of Christ only by way of His work. (Cf. E. Brunner, *Dogmatik*, II, 317.) Berkouwer considers this arbitrary and too closely related to an *a priori* theory of revelation as occuring only in act (*The Person of Christ*, p. 105).
47 *The Person of Christ* (1954, 1952), pp. 178f.
48 *Ibid.*, pp. 191f.
49 *Ibid.*, p. 234.

in Christ. Berkouwer is far less interested in speaking of a communication of attributes than he is in maintaining a unity of action. He does not pretend to solve any problems this way, but feels that this is the way in which the Bible speaks and the way in which the Church can most confidently speak without fear either of Nestorianism or Theopaschitism (the theory of the suffering God). It can avoid the artificial manner often employed of dividing the works of Christ into human and divine acts. Even in speaking of the Cross, we need not hesitate to speak of the whole Christ suffering and dying. "For at stake here is the unique mystery of the one Christ in the singleness of the person. He is the subject of all His deeds. And He is the object of our praise and worship as the One who performed His work in the absolute unity of and faithfulness to His office."[50]

To Berkouwer there is no way to clarify the mystery of the union of God and man in Christ. There are no analogies to it.[51] With this, Berkouwer implicitly rejects all attempts to make the Incarnation the keystone of a philosophy of life. He has no sympathy at all for the efforts of Anglo-Saxon thinkers to construct an incarnational philosophy. To him, the great mystery cannot be fitted into a general pattern of universal life of which the Incarnation is the God-given realization and fulfillment. In this same line of thought, he also rejects the notion found in many Christian philosophical thinkers, that the Incarnation is a necessity inherent in the creation. From Origen through Osiander and to nineteenth-century idealists and contemporary Anglo-Catholics, we find the Incarnation presented as the crowning act of God upon creation, the making up of what was lacking in humanity, either by the "elevation of mankind into God" or the "self-emptying of God into mankind." Berkouwer insists that God became man for ethical or religious, not metaphysical reasons. Man's created essence is manifest in his relationship with God. The purpose of the Incarnation is to restore *that* essence. The Incarnation is not a means of elevating man to his destined metaphysical level, but a means of restoring man's essential being-in-fellowship.[52]

Finally, we may note Berkouwer's response to the notion of the paradox in Christology. Since Kierkegaard, the idea has prevailed that the infinite qualitative difference between God and man makes a paradox of the faith that God can be made known through a man. Brunner took this theme up in *The Mediator,* where he insisted that there can be no direct, obvious revelation of God anywhere, certainly not in the human Jesus. This is why there is always an element of the

[50] *Ibid.*, p. 294.
[51] *Ibid.*, p. 299ff.
[52] *The Work of Christ* (1965), p. 34.

incognito in the Christ revelation. And this is why the notion of a revelation of God in Christ is an offense to man. His mind can find no direct route to the knowledge of God in Christ, so the thought that it is available there offends him. Berkouwer agrees that concealment does play a part in the revelation. But the Bible does not construe this hiddenness as a result of the infinite qualitative difference between God and man. It ascribes the hiddenness of God to the refusal of man, or the prideful inability of man, to recognize God on the pathway of suffering toward man's redemption. Not paradox, but pride keeps man from seeing the Father in Jesus. "In Him we are confronted, not just with the knotty problem of how it is possible that this man should claim to be the Son of God, but with the decision to believe or not to believe the revealed Word of God."[53] With a touch of irony, Berkouwer accuses the theologians of paradox of failing to think concretely. The notion that paradox is the offense of Christ to man stems from a desire to apply a general notion of paradox to the uniqueness of Christ and to define Him in those terms. Theirs is a kind of inverted natural theology. And, in fact, most people are not offended at the abstract thought of a God-man combination. Most people, even Greek philosophers, are offended at the Christ because He exposes their need to be died for.

MAN

Man as God's Image

The essence of man, theologically speaking, is seen only in his indestructible relatedness to God and his fellow man.[54] The Bible, says Berkouwer, gives us no material with which to construct a philosophical anthropology. The Bible is concentrated on the whole of man as he exists concretely in relationship with God and neighbor, in his apostasy from God and in his alienation from neighbor, and in his restoration by grace to them both. Theology's concern is to make that relationship intelligible in systematic terms. It is not to construct a concept of man as such. "Without thereby in any sense," Berkouwer writes, "detracting from the full creaturely reality of being human, we may say that we never encounter in the Bible an independently existing, abstract, ontological structural interest in man. In the Bible, man is indeed analyzed, but in a very special sort of analysis, a basic sort which exposes man in his evil and apostasy, in his mortality and rebellion, his sin and guilt. It deals fully with the actuality of humanness, but it is an actuality before God."[55]

[53] *Ibid.*, p. 356.
[54] *Man, the Image of God* (1962, 1957), pp. 139ff.
[55] *Ibid.*, p. 196.

As to the distinction between the body and the soul, Berkouwer insists that even where the Bible speaks clearly of man's soul in distinction from his body (as in Heb. 4:12 and I Thess. 5:23) and where the confessions speak of a "reasonable soul" and body, neither is intending to give to a scientific anthropology the status of church doctrine or biblical teaching. They only wish to underscore man's inescapable Godward orientation, to say that man is more than the chemical components of his flesh.[56] Man as he is constituted, as he exists in himself abstracted from his relationship to God, does not interest the Bible and therefore is not the proper object of theological concern. "We may say without much fear of contradiction that the most striking thing in the biblical portrayal of man lies in this, that it never asks attention for man in himself, but demands our fullest attention for man in his relation to God."[57]

Berkouwer acknowledges the Church's wisdom in rejecting a trichotomy of substances in man, but thinks it achieved nothing at all by teaching a dichotomy. Indeed, he suspects that even dichotomy has the danger of making the soul the valuable and God-like part of man while the body is that which drags the soul down to sin and corruption. As to the soul's origin, he sees point in rejecting traducianism in its classic form, but sees just as much point in rejecting creationism. The creationist-traducianist argument was wholly unproductive of shedding any biblical light on man. The question of man's origin must be one, not of the origin of a given part, but of the origin of man as a whole, a question that can be considered biblically only in the light of man's restoration to community with God and man by grace.[58]

The rejection of the notion of the human soul as an integral part of theological study runs hard against the pious belief that at death the soul departs to be "with the Lord." Modern theology has recently been at great pains to deal with this subject in the light of modern psychology and the modern world-view. But Berkouwer does not deal with it as a demythologizing theologian. He insists that we must think of the future of man, not in terms of the part of man that is with Christ, but in terms of the victory of Christ over sin and death, of total resurrection, of the glorious acts of God still awaited in the coming of Christ to establish the New Earth. The state of man in the "between times" we must leave as one of the hidden things. Scripture itself "gives us no help in a search for an analyzable anthropological solution."[59]

Berkouwer does not mean to deny that after death man in some

---

[56] *Ibid.,* pp. 200ff., 210, 212ff.
[57] *Ibid.,* p. 195.
[58] *Ibid.,* pp. 299ff.
[59] *Ibid.,* p. 264.

sense is with the Lord. But the outlook for the Christian provided by the Bible is not that of an immortal soul, but the coming of the Kingdom in all its glory where we shall as complete men be in communion with God and with each other. "And this reality, so full of comfort, surely can hardly be expressed clearly through an anthropological 'division' within man; and if we are not satisfied with the New Testament description, and wish to achieve more reality by postulating the 'substantiality' of a part of man, the 'ego' or the 'heart' or the 'person,' we contribute nothing to a deeper understanding of salvation."[60]

The subject of man as the image of God has to include some account of the state of that image in fallen man. The Reformed Confessions speak of a vestigial remnant of man's original condition, but Berkouwer explains that the confessions never intended to suggest that a certain area in human nature is left untouched by the corruption that has invaded other parts of man. Parallel with the notion of a remnant of the image, theologians have frequently employed the distinction between the image of God in a narrower and a broader sense: the narrower referring to man in his moral and religious condition, the broader referring to the possession by man of a rational soul and volition. Man, being still man and not beast, retains the image of God in the broader sense. Being separated from fellowship with God, man has lost the image of God in the narrower sense. Berkouwer finds this distinction basically unhelpful because of its concentration on man as such, man in the structural sense, a concentration Berkouwer has already said is not at all shared by the Bible.

Rather than speaking of the preservation of the image of God, Berkouwer speaks of the preservation of a basic humanness, a humanness construed, of course, in terms of man's relatedness. Man's relationship with God is never absolutely eradicated: God still impinges upon him everywhere and man still responds, though antithetically, to God. Moreover, man is never alone. Threatened always, at the precipice of destruction often, the community in which man's being is found is never wholly annihilated. Not even his total depravity can force man into a totally solipsistic self-concentration. The tendency toward egoistic disregard of fellow men, toward self-exaltation at the expense of others, is never allowed to destroy community altogether. And the fact of man's indestructible relatedness coming to expression in noble efforts to restore some form of genuine community is evidence and manifestation of the fact that man, despite the fall, is still human. And since Berkouwer has defined the image in terms of relatedness, we may gather that he intends us to understand that man is, in this sense, a perverted and tenuous, yet real, reflection of the image of God. Since

[60] *Ibid.*, p. 265.

this is the gift of God's grace, it should not be despised or minimized, even though it is totally unable to lead to the genuine restoration looked forward to in the Kingdom of God's grace.[61]

Man as Sinner

Moral evil is a mystery in its origin and essence. Revelation cannot clear up the mystery of iniquity; revelation only exposes it as mystery. Faith cannot dispel the mystery; faith alone recognizes it as mystery. Berkouwer means that human evil is mysterious in the sense that it is without meaning, without rationale, without any reason for being. Faith recognizes it as not belonging to created reality, as being senseless, nihilistic, and under judgment, bound for the burning. But the relationship between faith and moral evil is such that a man recognizes the nature of evil as mystery only as he recognizes his personal involvement in and guilt for it. To know that evil is a mystery *means* to know oneself as guilty of it. "Confession of guilt is the corollary of the inexplicability of sin."[62]

Moral evil, as the Christian knows it, is not merely a violation of an ideal. Nor is it illuminating theologically to speak of evil in terms of its effect on an abstraction like "human reason" or "human will." Sin has affected these things, but from the biblical viewpoint moral evil is seen only in terms of its violation and contradiction of man's *relationship* with God. The heart of moral evil must be seen in terms of man's lost fellowship with God and man.[63] Sin is the violation of love. For this reason, love being the total dynamic communion between God and man, sin cannot be defined. It can only be portrayed in all of its dynamic destructiveness. Sin, in the Bible, rises before us in *act*: in hostility, hatred, murder, loneliness, transgression — the acts that break the fellowship with God. As man's essence is known only with respect to a dynamic relationship, man's evil is known only in terms of the disruption of this relationship.

Berkouwer's handling of the doctrine of original sin is of a piece with his insistence that knowing evil means confessing sin, a personal awareness of self-involvement in an evil that is judged by God. The profound insight behind the phrase "original sin" is that human evil is not gauged by this and that discrete act, but by the radical sinfulness of man. The question is one of how the corruption and the guilt of the original sinner, Adam, are passed on to the rest of the human race, and what the relationship is between the inheritance of the corruption to the fact of guilt. Reformed theology, since Cocceius, has adopted

[61] *Ibid.,* pp. 148ff.
[62] *De Zonde,* I (1959), p. 131.
[63] *De Zonde,* II (1960), p. 48.

the so-called federal theory that Adam represented mankind in a covenant of works and that his failure incurred an imputed guilt for all
mankind. The objection to this theory (which, Berkouwer believes,
has never adequately been answered) is that it sets up a fictional situation in which God imputed to all men a guilt for something they had
not yet done.[64]

The weakness of the federal theory lies in its treatment of the problem apart from Christology. The broad context of Romans 5:12 (where
Paul says: "as sin came into the world through one man and death
through sin, and so death spread to all men because all sinned") is
not Adam's sin, but Christ's victory. Adam and human sin are viewed
in the light of Christ: Adam is brought in to show the darkness into
which the great light shone. A mistake has been perpetuated in dogmatics by allowing the Adam/human race relationship to define the
Christ/believer relationship rather than the other way around. And this
tended not only to discolor the Adam/human race relationship, but
the Christ/believer relationship as well. For when Adam's guilt was
seen as *simply* imputed to the human race, Christ's righteousness was
also seen as *simply* imputed to the believer. Both the sinful human
race and the body of believers seemed to be imputed with a guilt, on
the one hand, and a righteousness, on the other, which were truly alien
to them.[65]

No theory of the inheritance of original sin will really suffice if it
leaves the impression that man is accounted guilty for a sin other than
his own. Do we find a satisfactory theory in Berkouwer? The answer
is that we find no theory at all. He insists that a theological knowledge of universal guilt is gained only by a personal knowledge of
personal guilt. From the low vantage point of my own confession, I
perceive that the divine judgment of guilt is not a judgment on me for
Adam's (and not my) sin. Divine judgment is levelled against my
real sin. And in my guilt I perceive my solidarity with mankind. "In
confession of guilt we do not neglect our solidarity with the human race
in guilt: we recognize our own guilt *in* our solidarity with humanity,
and in this recognition the doors to forgiveness are flung open."[66]

Once again, we find Berkouwer shaking himself free from dependence
on causal relationships to explain spiritual realities. He avoids pitting
one explanation against the other, realism against federalism, when he
thinks that neither really does justice to the realities it attempts to
explain. He goes back to his basic thesis that the material of dogmatics
is always the material of faith. And here, too, in the matter of impu-

[64] *Ibid.*, p. 242; cf. p. 210.
[65] *Ibid.*, p. 281.
[66] *Ibid.*, p. 317.

tation of guilt, sin and guilt are known for what they are only by faith in Christ. For it is within faith that repentance is real. And only as repentance is real does knowledge of sin and guilt become real.

Man in Grace

The Co-relation of Faith and Grace

The co-relation between grace and faith determines Berkouwer's doctrine of the life of man in grace. Grace, to Berkouwer, is an attribute of God, never a quality of the believer. When we speak of grace we speak of God; we do not speak of man. Grace is not a substantial quality added to man's natural life. Nor is there ever more or less grace. Man never gets to the point in the holy life where he needs less grace. Even the saint is the man who lives at the mercy of God, in the freedom of His love, and the joy of His forgiveness. For grace is God moving into human life to create a fellowship of love and service between Himself and man.[67] Faith, on the other hand, is man's response to grace. Faith is not creative of the fellowship; it is not even a contributing factor. Nor is it one step along the way to salvation. Faith is decisive and indispensable in salvation, but always, all along the way of the saved life, as a response to grace.[68] For this reason, faith has no value *per se* and is of no interest to the theologian as a psychological phenomenon. It has an expendable value and is of great interest only as the subjective pole of a dynamic relationship with the grace of God. "The mystery of the way of salvation exists in the call to the faith which expects everything and rests its all in divine grace."[69]

Within the co-relation of grace and faith, there is no room at all for the Roman Catholic description of faith as one in a series of discrete steps on the way to the terminal of justifying grace. But neither does Berkouwer find congenial the traditional *ordo salutis* that was developed in post-Reformation dogmatics.[70] Besides exaggerating the importance of the proper logical sequence, and suggesting that the order of logic is the order of life, it makes of faith a discrete item distinct from and on the same line with such realities of grace as justification and sanctification.[71] If we must speak of an order of salvation of any sort, let

[67] *Faith and Justification* (1954, 1949), pp. 34, 112, 191.
[68] *Ibid.*, pp. 171ff.
[69] *Ibid.*, p. 200.
[70] Cf. L. Berkhof, *op. cit.*, pp. 415f.: "The *ordo salutis* describes the process by which the work of salvation . . . is subjectively realized in the hearts and lives of sinners. It aims at describing in their logical order and also in their interrelationships, the various moments of the Holy Spirit in the application of the work of redemption."
[71] *Faith and Justification* (1954, 1949), pp. 25ff.

88

us say, with Christ, that *He* is the *Way* of Salvation, and that faith is man's response to Him and acknowledgment of Him as the only Way from rebirth to glorification. Faith, says Berkouwer, "is not added as a second, independent ingredient which makes its own contribution to justification in Christ. On the contrary, faith does nothing but accept, or come to rest in the sovereignty of His benefit. . . . To walk the way of faith is simply to admit that Christ is the Way."[72]

Justification and Sanctification

The Reformation manifesto of salvation by grace alone does not devalue faith and works. *Sola fide* is the other face of *sola gratia,* and justification by grace alone destroys, not the necessity of works, but only the pretensions of the works of the law. Justification by grace alone opened up the true role of faith as the vital response of man to God's amazing grace, the only way in which men enter the relationship created by grace.[73] And the pathway of Christian works is one that winds through the valley of grace in which we walk by faith.

If, then, justification is wholly without regard to works and if not even faith is the basis for our justification, if the believer is *simul peccator et justus,* is not God involved in the moral contradiction of calling the sinner good, calling black white?[74] Berkouwer's answer to this question is basically that the situation in which man discovers the grace of justification is the one in which he specifically recognizes the just severity of God's wrath against and intolerance of sin. At the Cross of Christ, the believer recognizes that God never calls white black or a sinner good in a game of make-believe, but that He judges sin and punishes it so that the way may be cleared for grace.[75]

Justification is, however, inseparable from sanctification in a way that Reformed dogmaticians have not always made clear. Justification is sometimes described in a way that makes it a finished deed, accomplished once in time, and then made the starting point from which the justified sinner goes on to the life-long process of sanctification.[76] Berkouwer brings the entire life of man in grace into constant relationship with faith, intending to say that we are always, at every point on the way, being justified, sanctified, and preserved in and

---

[72] *Ibid.,* p. 43.
[73] *Ibid.,* p. 92.
[74] "A man outwardly justified, but inwardly a sinner would be a moral monster, and Almighty God would be guilty of an intrinsic contradiction were He to regard and treat such a one as just" (Pohle-Preuss, *Grace Habitual and Actual,* p. 321). This is a typical Roman Catholic indictment of the Reformed doctrine of justification by grace alone.
[75] *Faith and Justification* (1954, 1949), pp. 92 and 183.
[76] For an example of this type of distinction, see L. Berkhof, *op. cit.,* pp. 513ff.

through faith. "The moment sanctification is ejected from the temple of faith, and hence of justification, that moment justification by faith has become an initial state on the pilgrim journey, a supply station which later becomes a pleasant memory." [77]

Sanctification is not a process by which the saved sinner is increasingly renewed and therefore decreasingly in need of grace. It is not a quantitatively measurable change in man that bit by bit renders him less and less in need of forgiving grace. Man is a whole, and the whole man is in need of justification by grace alone at the end as at the beginning of his Christian pilgrimage. In sanctification as well as in justification, man stands at the foot of the Cross, pleading only divine mercy. There is, of course, growth in grace, but this is the kind of growth that leads the man in grace to confession of guilt, to constant prayer, to a deepening sense of dependence on the faithful mercies of God. And faith's relationship to sanctification is not that of a creative act by which fresh power is constantly gained to climb the ladder of self-improvement until finally the top is reached where one no longer need stand in the shadow of the Cross.[78] Sanctification is a kind of progress, not from justification, but within justification, and a progress not quite like any other we can discover in life. Berkouwer writes:

> This progress is not an automatic, causal development from first-fruits to full harvest, but a progress in faith, prayer, meekness, and confession of guilt . . . . The progress of sanctification then is a progress comparable with no other process . . . . For progress in sanctification never meant working out one's own salvation under one's own auspices; on the contrary, it ,meant working out one's salvation with a rising sense of dependence on God's grace . . . . Thus we can understand that progress in sanctification can never consist in building ourselves up in morality. Litanies of guilt are spoken on the way of salvation, not only during the first stage of conversion, but, as Christ becomes more wonderful to us, in crescendo.[79]

Berkouwer does not mean to minimize, certainly not to exclude, the value of moral activity, nor enthusiasm, nor even ascetic practices rightly undertaken. What he is trying to emphasize is that man never leaves the atmosphere of forgiveness as grace. And sanctification is horribly distorted if it is portrayed as a process by which we gradually rise to the heights where we are weightless as far as the burden of repentance and the need for grace are concerned. Sanctification "as increased immersion in the grace and knowledge of Christ must result

[77] *Faith and Sanctification* (1952, 1949), p. 21.
[78] *Ibid.*, pp. 28, 78, 42.
[79] *Ibid.*, p. 112.

in a deeper sense of unworthiness" — and, Berkouwer would add, a corresponding fortissimo in doxology.[80]

The co-relation between faith and grace becomes especially meaningful in Berkouwer's treatment of the perseverance of believers. For one who believes in divine election and justification by grace alone, an intrinsic logic may lead to a doctrine of perseverance that is necessarily implied by the state of affairs as God has created them.[81] For one who thinks of grace as an infused quality of the human soul, on the other hand, the pressures of temptation and the weakness of faith may lead to a denial of the certainty of perseverance.[82] Berkouwer, believing in perseverance, seeks to rescue the doctrine from its treatment as an objective, inherently necessary conclusion from the premise of election on the one hand, and seeks to preserve it from the subjective, inherently uncertain type of salvation found in Roman and Pelagian theologians on the other. The co-relation between faith and perseverance that Berkouwer finds in Scripture is the way he takes.

The doctrine of perseverance is an assurance gained only in faith, in the faith that finds its way to assurance through doubt and temptation, in the faith that is directed only to Christ.[83] The faith that looks to Christ realizes that grace has priority over his doubts and weakness. Our duty to persevere is oriented to God's preservation. And we find confidence in God's preservation of us only when we see His powerful grace at the Cross. Assurance is not the prerogative of the person who can reason inferentially from a doctrine of election. Assurance is the gift that everyone finds who finds God at the Cross.[84] The admonitions of Scripture to persevere lest we fall, the temptation to disbelieve, and the weakness of human will, are the ways along which faith comes to rest in the reliability of grace. For these, within the Christian life of faith, are goads to drive us to the Cross, the only place where the faith-certainty of perseverance is found.

III. EVALUATION

An assessment of the theological work of G. C. Berkouwer must finally be made much later, when he has finished his task and when history gives us a perspective of the total effect of his work. Whenever such an assessment is made, however, it will have to take seriously

---

[80] *Ibid.,* p. 129.

[81] A good example of this is found in L. Berkhof, *op. cit.,* p. 547, where he lists a series of inferential proofs for the doctrine.

[82] A good example of this is the official doctrine of the Roman Church as expressed at the Council of Trent in its section on justification (cf. Trent, VI/9).

[83] *Faith and Perseverance* (1958, 1949), p. 78.

[84] *Ibid.,* p. 105; *De Zonde,* II (1960), p. 343.

the fact that Berkouwer is a confessionally committed theologian. The confessions of the Church are, to him, not historical documents that one must rise above in personal creativity. They are expressions of the Gospel in which the theologian must find his starting point and within which he must serve the Church whose confessions they are. For Berkouwer, then, it was impossible to be a creative theologian in any basically original sense. He could not, within his own premise of faith, be the founder of a school or, as it was said of Schleiermacher, of an epoch. All he has permitted himself is the task of serving the Church by helping to make the Gospel clear.

It is within his relationship to the confessions of the Church, however, that he has made a lasting contribution to confessional theology. He has become the modern-day example of a biblical theologian within the scope of ecclesiastical confessionalism. For he has tried to get at the *message* of the confessions, and in doing so he has freed theology from the letter of the confessions. Likewise, in working within the framework of a church with a theological tradition, he has, in adhering to that tradition, at the same time set it free from bondage to dogmatic distinctions that had received almost canonical status. Or, we may say, he has released theology from the tyranny of logic and set it within the freedom of faith.

We need only call to mind his putting election back into the faith of the simple believer and rescuing reprobation from the questionable status of an eternally set decree of God with no real relationship to human guilt. We may recall also his re-establishment of the co-relationship between justification and sanctification, the dislodging of the doctrine of a substantial soul from the biblical doctrine of man, and the whole doctrine of man from such irrelevant and uninteresting questions as those of the soul's origin. Berkouwer has shaken his own theology — and, he dares hope, the Church's proclamation of the Gospel — free from many traditional deductions and distinctions in theological thought by taking what he is sure is a biblically rooted stance.

The primary material facet of his theology that has contributed to his freedom from traditional deductive theology within the confines of confessional theology is his establishment of all theological material as the material of faith. What could sound like a theological bromide for evangelicals is actually a basic principle for theological reflection that evangelical Protestant theology has too often forgotten. The truth of theology is known to faith. It is always a thing to be believed. And specifically, it is believed with the same faith by which one acknowledges Christ as Savior and Lord. This means that the matter of theology is always part of the good news of grace. Election, after this, can never be a sterile and rather nasty notion of an arbitrary decree of a graceless Sovereign. Sin can never be a matter of philosophical speculation: it is truly known only by the faith that recognizes God's judgment of sin at Calvary. And theologians can never again suppose that they are privy to secrets unknown to simple believers. All theologians can do is to help the simple believer articulate his faith.

Perhaps one of the most important immediate contributions that Berkouwer has made to evangelical theology is the example he has given of Christian and responsible polemic confrontation. Berkouwer's polemics are meant to be servants of grace, for the theology he is criticizing, for the preachers of the Church. There is a style of polemics that is revealed in the motives of the man engaging in it. A loveless polemics is possible, a polemics with a design to refute without a desire to serve. An irresponsible polemics is possible, and evangelical theology is no stranger to it, a polemics that is eager only to find the weak spot in the armor of one's opponent, eager, that is, for victory and not for truth. After Berkouwer, evangelical theology ought have no excuse to revert to the uncreative and loveless style of polemics of which it has too often been guilty.

One could wish for Berkouwer to do many things he does not do. One could wish that he would, now and then, develop a line of thought more concisely, more pointedly than he does. An Anglo-Saxon may be forgiven for wanting at times less circumlocution and more succinctness than he finds in European theologians.

It is possible to ask some questions that will have to be included in some final assessment of Berkouwer's theology. Has he, in his understandable zeal to set sanctification within the right relationship to divine mercy, done justice to sanctification as the life of Christ *in* the believer? It is true that the believer lives by faith, a faith directed to God's mercy. But is it not true that, by faith, Christ dwells in the heart of the believer? Has Berkouwer found a real place for the mystic reality of *Christus in nobis?* Could he not, indeed, profit by leaning more heavily just at this point? Calvin finds no embarrassment in emphasizing the reality of the very life of Jesus Christ taking root in our lives. Communion with Christ is not, after all, quite parallel with the communion between individual persons. For we not only bow before the grace of God in Christ; the life we live is in reality Christ *in* us. It has seemed to this writer that Berkouwer's truly powerful treatment of the inseparable unity of justification and sanctification leans too heavily on justification and not enough on the subjective reality of sanctification through the indwelling of the Christ.

Again, on the profoundly difficult subject of man, has Berkouwer adequately faced the question of whether, after all, his quarrel is not with

93

an antiquated psychology, and whether therefore it may be unnecessary to reject the old ontology of body and soul once it is separated from the old psychology? Even granted that the Bible does not specifically teach an anthropology, and that we need not assume that its mention of soul and body means a biblical doctrine of a substantial soul — even granted this, is it not possible that the classic ontological distinction between soul and body still best fits the religious and redemptive portrayal of man? It is very clear in Berkouwer that he is not finding fault with an obsolete psychology, with its unreal separation of the functions of soul and body, but is rejecting the ontological distinction between them. But, given the fact that man, after death, is at home with the Lord while his body is rotting in the grave, and given the fact that the Bible speaks of a separation of the soul from the body, is it not possible that the older notion best fits both pious hope and biblical suggestion? And, after we clear our minds of the expendable psychology that was appended to the body-soul distinction, what would be wrong with assuming that man is a substantial soul, and that the man with whom the Bible is concerned is the whole man, body and soul, in their mysterious but indivisible unity? Berkouwer insists that the "unmixed and unconfused" natures of Christ do not impede their genuine unity in the One Christ. Why should not man be a unity — a different kind and level than that of Christ's unity, indeed — between two distinct ontological realities? Could we not have both, the "whole man" in dynamic relationship with God *and* the whole man in a unity of ontologically distinct entities, body and soul?

The co-relationship between faith and theology could be the single most significant feature of Berkouwer's theological contribution. We called it the guiding principle of his theological method. But it dominates the material as well. It is significant because with it Berkouwer frees himself from the penchant that orthodox Reformed theology has often displayed for making theological statements equivalent to metaphysical statements. That is, orthodox Reformed theology has tended often to do theology by deducing propositions from objective truths given by revelation. The difference between theological truths and, let us say, mathematical truths lay in their source: the former were derived from divine revelation and the latter from natural reason. Faith entered, only at the beginning of the enterprise, as an assent to the truthfulness of the statements. Thus, theology did not do *all* of its work guided, limited, and determined constantly by the obedience of faith. Berkouwer has insisted that theology, each step of the way, be in dynamic and determinative relationship to faith.

This means, in effect, that Berkouwer insists that theology be shaped and formed by the nature of the thing it talks about—the Gospel of

Jesus Christ. The Gospel comes to man as an urgent summons and merciful invitation to enter into a grateful relationship with God the Father through Christ. It does not come as a matter-of-fact disclosure of a set of objective, abstract truths about the state of affairs beyond man. Faith, therefore, is a life response of the total person, at the depths of his being, to the summons and opportunity of the Gospel. Faith is not an assent to the objective truth of things as they are outside of man. The truth of the Gospel, therefore, is known and understood only within the total context of *both* revelation *and* the obedience of faith. Theology, whose task is to restate that truth, is determined in its methods and limited in its conclusions by the nature of the Gospel as it is heard and obeyed in faith.

Another way of saying this is that Berkouwer has allowed his theology to be informed throughout by the subjective factor of faith. This is why, incidentally, one looks in vain for a separate book about faith; faith is not a discrete item in the Christian complex of truths, but the subjective correlate of the whole of it. Berkouwer rejects the naive modernistic notion that faith creates theological truth. But he does recognize that truth is Christian truth only within the framework of faith. The objective reality of God and Christ, the objective reality of grace and salvation, is the Christian truth, not in isolation, not abstracted from, but in relationship to faith. Theological truth, therefore, is not a set of general propositions about "things as they are," like mathematical formulas, valid for everyone and open to discussion by everyone. Theological truths are true only as believed and obeyed truths. This is the case with theology because it is the case with the Gospel. And for this reason, theology *always* ought to be done, and in every part, in co-relationship with faith.

We have noted some of the implications of co-relationship for specific doctrines. The most notable example, within Reformed theology, was perhaps that of the doctrine of election. If we were able to take the sentence, "God elects men to salvation," and treat it as a general, abstract truth about God, we would readily turn it into a fantastic metaphysics. Together with an atheist, we could define the words and agree upon the meaning of the sentence. We could agree that it means something like this: the Supreme Being selects some men to be given salvation and, by the same token, rejects others. The atheist would say: "I understand this and reject it." The believer would say: "I understand it just as the atheist does, but I affirm it." Both would have done theology. But one accepts and the other rejects the truth. Berkouwer disavows this as a proper way of doing theology.

The doctrine of election is part of the Gospel. The Gospel is a proclamation of salvation in Christ. No part of it is a general, universally valid and universally understandable truth. Therefore, when we say, "God elects men to salvation" we are not simply uttering a metaphysical truth. Rather, we are responding in grateful acknowledgment to the prevenient grace of God. We are making a confession. And theology has no business turning a confession of faith into a general and abstract truth from which all kinds of fatalistic deductions can be drawn. Faith is a response to the urgent summons to man that he should bow before the sovereign love of God in Christ. The statement about election is made as part of his response. And this is the framework within which theology must talk about election, and about all other doctrines.

Berkouwer has called orthodox Reformed theology away from its love affair with metaphysics. In doing so, he has called it back to its proper and humble service as hand-maid to the *preaching* of the Gospel.

IV. BIBLIOGRAPHY

WORKS BY G. C. BERKOUWER

Studies in Dogmatics

Geloof en Rechtvaardiging. Kampen, 1949* (*Faith and Justification.* Grand Rapids, 1954).
Geloof en Heiliging, 1949 (*Faith and Sanctification.* Grand Rapids, 1952).
Geloof en Volharding, 1949 (*Faith and Perseverance.* Grand Rapids, 1958).
De Voorzienigheid Gods, 1950 (*The Providence of God.* Grand Rapids, 1952).
De Algemeene Openbaring, 1951 (*General Revelation.* Grand Rapids, 1955).
De Persoon van Christus, 1952 (*The Person of Christ.* Grand Rapids, 1954).
Het Werk van Christus, 1953 (*The Work of Christ.* Grand Rapids, 1965).
De Sacramenten, 1954 (*The Sacraments.* Grand Rapids, 1968).
De Verkiezing Gods, 1955 (*Divine Election.* Grand Rapids, 1960).
De Mens Het Beeld Gods, 1957 (*Man, the Image of God.* Grand Rapids, 1962).
De Zonde, Vol. I, 1959; Vol. II, 1960.
De Wederkomst van Christus. Vol. I, 1961; Vol. II, 1963.
De Heilige Schrift, Vol. I, 1965; Vol. II, 1967.

Other Works

Geloof en Openbaring in de Nieuwe Duitse Theologie, 1934.
Karl Barth, 1937.
Het Probleem der Schriftkritiek, 1938.
Toelichting op het Synode-besluit tot Schortsing van Prof. K. Schilder, n.d.
Barthianisme en Katholicisme, 1940.
Wereld Oorlog en Theologie, 1945.
Gevaren en Perspectieven voor ons Kerkelijk Leven, 1946.

Karl Barth en de Kinderdoop, 1947.

Het Conflict met Rome, 1948 (*The Conflict with Rome.* Grand Rapids, 1957).

Het Dogma der Kerk (edited by Berkouwer), 1949.

Augustinus over het Credo (with A. Sizoo), n.d.

Op de Tweesprong, 1951.

"Ex Operato," *Gereformeerde Theologisch Tijdschrift,* No. 1, 1953.

Modern Uncertainty and the Christian Faith. Grand Rapids, 1953.

De Triomf der Genade in de Theologie van Karl Barth, 1954 (*The Triumph of Grace in the Theology of Karl Barth.* Grand Rapids, 1956).

"De Kritische Functie van het sola fide," *Gereformeerde Theologisch Tijdschrift,* No. 4/5, 1957.

Verdienste of Genade, 1958.

Recent Developments in Roman Catholic Thought. Grand Rapids, 1958.

Het Licht der Wereld, 1960.

"Vragen Rondom het Belijdenis," *Gerefomeerde Theologisch Tijdschrift,* No. 1, 1963.

Het Tweede Vaticaanse Councilie en het Nieuwe Theologie, 1964 (*The Second Vatican Council and the New Catholicism,* 1965).

* All of Berkouwer's books in Dutch are published by Kok, Kampen.

4 PAUL G. SCHROTENBOER

Emil Brunner

I. BIOGRAPHY

HEINRICH EMIL BRUNNER was born on December 23, 1889, in Winterthur, Switzerland. While the greater part of his life was spent in his homeland, he also lived in other parts of the Continent as well as in England, the United States, and Japan.

Brunner received his academic training in the Gymnasium in Zürich, from which he matriculated in 1908, and later studied theology in Zürich, Berlin, and Union Theological Seminary in New York City. He received a Th.D. degree from the University of Zürich in 1913 and was later granted honorary degrees from several institutions on the Continent, in Edinburgh, and the United States. From 1924 until his death in 1966, he was professor of theology in Zürich.

Brunner may be called a pioneer theologian of the twentieth century. Reinhold Niebuhr has called him a seminal theologian. He has been a planter of great seed thoughts. Together with Karl Barth, he has stood in the vanguard of theological discussion since the days of the First World War.

He stands between the worlds of the waning old liberalism and the advancing new liberalism, between the decline of the old orthodoxy and the forward march of neo-orthodoxy. He broke with the traditional theology (liberal and orthodox both) in order to become a dialectical theologian. He took issue with the advocates of impersonal dogmas in order to engage man in the existential encounter of personal

Dr. Paul G. Schrotenboer, a minister in the Christian Reformed Church, is Executive Director of the Association for Reformed Scientific Studies. He is also the author of *Faith and Its Problems* and *A New Apologetics: An Analysis and Appraisal of the Eristic Theology of Emil Brunner.*

99

truth. He will perhaps be remembered most for the impact he gave to theology by his stress upon dialecticism and personal correspondence. His feet stand upon the shoulders of such men as G. J. Hamaan, S. Kierkegaard, E. Griesbach, Ferdinand Ebner, and Martin Buber. A host of thinkers in turn have taken him as their teacher and guide.

Among the theologians of the present century, Brunner also stands out as being one of the most cosmopolitan. The impact of his teaching is undoubtedly greater beyond the borders of his native land than in Switzerland itself. This cosmopolitanism revealed itself early — when he went to New York to study (1913) and later when he taught languages in England (1914). These early excursions made it easier for him later to make inroads into the English-speaking world with his teaching. All along he enjoyed the advantage of having his major works, written mostly in German, translated into English at a relatively early date.

Besides teaching theology in Zürich, where he was professor from 1924 on, Brunner lectured at Princeton Theological Seminary (1938-1939) and in the Christian University of Japan (1953-1955). In each place he enjoyed popularity as a teacher and lecturer. As a result of these extended periods of lecturing away from his home in Zürich, his influence has been felt both in the orient and the occident.

Brunner has indeed upon occasion received great recognition. In 1952 there appeared a *Festschrift* (Zwingli-Verlag, Zürich) dedicated to him on occasion of his sixtieth birthday and later, in 1962, the Macmillan Company published *The Theology of Emil Brunner* in *The Library of Living Theology*. This volume contains essays written by Paul Tillich, Reinhold Niebuhr, and others and an intellectual autobiography by Brunner himself.

Besides being a pioneering spirit and a cosmopolitan figure, Emil Brunner showed himself to be a man of many interests. Throughout he was a pastor and theologian first of all. But in the age of specialization he did not fall prey to the evil of overspecializing. He showed interest not only in fields other than theology, but more especially to the relationship of his field of study to others. His thought constantly dwelt on the relationship of theology and philosophy. His own theology is both apologetical and missionary. For years he lectured in pastoral psychology. His mind often reflected upon the relationship of faith and science. He wrote great tomes on ethics and social problems. Everything he wrote confronts the reader with a challenge.

Brunner's views on politics were almost as outspoken as those of his contemporary Karl Barth. Their difference in opinion concerning reason and apologetics has been emphasized since the early thirties. Their difference in attitude towards Communism is no less pronounced. Barth wrote in his open letter to the German Christians: "One can, after all, preach Christianity, believe Christianity, and live Christianity under a Communistic regime." In reply to this Brunner wrote in 1961 in an article that appeared in the *Neue Zuricher Zeitung:* "And so the poison which paralyses the will to resist — is becoming virulent. Thus the church, without at all being Communist, is unwittingly doing the work of Communism." In this exchange it was Brunner who said "No!"

Emil Brunner died in Zürich on April 6, 1966. Much has been written about Brunner's works but little about his life. One is puzzled somewhat that the life history of a theologian who over a period of forty years taught and produced great theological works has not become the object of a thorough study. The few preceding notes only stress the need for a comprehensive biography. This awaited biography might well portray the major trends in the thinking and living of the Western world, for Emil Brunner is one of the minds that have set a stamp upon the twentieth century.

II. EXPOSITION

GOVERNING IDEAS

A writer should always be permitted to interpret his own writing. In the event of his doing so, an exposition of his writing by another should conform, as much as possible, to the author's own analysis of his works. Such an exposition should then reproduce the governing ideas so that the author can recognize his thoughts even after they are recast in the expositor's mold.

If the author has accurately characterized his writings, he has thereby provided a good basis for their evaluation. Although it would be hazardous to accept uncritically an author's analysis of his own work, it must be admitted that, if it is possible to use his self-analysis, we have common ground for a basic confrontation in the appraisal of the writings. In any case we may use the author's self-appraisal as a point of departure. Let us look at Brunner's characterization of his own writings.

Brunner has called his theology a theology of the Word. With all possible emphasis he pitted his position against that of the consciousness theologians in his book *Die Mystik und Das Wort* (1924). That which constitutes man, he then said, is that he has been given the Word (p. 5). The Word is divine revelation, which must take priority over human knowledge and reason.

Brunner has called his theology dialectical. Dialectical theology, he

101

informs us, portrays the contradiction.[1] Dialectical theology must be set off against orthodox theology. Orthodoxy stands for direct revelation; dialecticism, indirect. God's Word, says Brunner, is broken or refracted in the elements of the world like a rod submerged in troubled water. "Just as the Christ could only reveal the glory of God through the form of a servant, so all speech concerning God, if in the sense of this revelation, is necessarily 'paradoxical.' It is only by means of the contradiction between two ideas — God and man, grace and responsibility, holiness and love — that we can apprehend the contradictory truth that the eternal God enters time, or that the sinful man is declared just. Dialectical theology is the mode of thinking which defends this paradoxical character, belonging to faith-knowledge, from the nonparadoxical speculations of reason, and vindicates it as against the other."[2] "Since the Word of God confronts man in revolt, it must itself be 'in revolt.' "[3]

As in revelation, so in faith: "If faith simply means that human thought and will finally capitulate to the truth and the will of God, then theology can never be anything other than an attempt, in some way or other to transcribe the controversy between the Word of God and the thought of man. Hence all genuine theology is dialectical and not orthodox."[4] In short, theology must be dialectical because it should portray the true paradox which is the real content of the Christian faith. "The paradox is nothing else than the deliberate expression of the fact that God is portrayed as the one who posits Himself, and that he cannot be posited by us."[5]

In *Der Mensch im Widerspruch* (1941), Brunner said that since 1925 the abiding central point of his theology had been the dialectic of law and gospel (p. 531). As he works this dialectic out, it means that the Gospel both annuls law and fulfills law. The law is both the herald of Christ and His enemy. It both reveals (impersonally, that is) and conceals the will of God.

In his most recent major writings, the *Dogmatik,* Brunner characterizes his work as the promulgation of "personal correspondence." He believes that the progress in his thinking has been in the direction of a more consistent application of his personalism gained from the insights of Ferdinand Ebner and Martin Buber.[6]

These characteristics: the priority of revelation, the dialectical re-

[1] *Die andere Aufgabe der Theologie* (1929), p. 226.
[2] *The Word and the World* (1931), pp. 6f.
[3] *Die andere Aufgabe der Theologie* (1929), p. 226.
[4] *Der Mensch im Widerspruch* (1941), p. viii.
[5] *Theologie und Ontologie* (1931), p. 118.
[6] *Dogmatik,* III (1960), p. 252.

lationship, the gospel-law motif, and personal correspondence run through the full spectrum of Brunner's theology. We shall not rightly understand his teaching on any subject unless we see these structural motifs functioning in the theological exercise.

Brunner's theology is a theology of correlativity and may be called a theology of the conjunction. Various titles of his works bear this out: *Die Mystik und das Wort* (1924), *Philosophie und Offenbarung* (1925), *Gott und Mensch* (1930), *Das Gebot und die Ordnungen* (1933), *Natur und Gnade* (1934), *Das Wort Gottes und der Moderne Mensch* (1936), *Offenbarung und Vernunft* (1941), *Christianity and Civilization* (1948), *Eros und Liebe* (1952). In each instance Brunner proceeds from the correlation of the two parts which the conjunction joins. In his work on Christology Brunner explains that there is basically no immediate relationship of man to God, but only a mediate. Between man and God there is a third party which both separates and binds the two. He is the Mediator.[7] In his anthropology[8] (*Man in Revolt*) Brunner defines man as a responsible being, that is, man in response. Man's revolt indicates that his response has been wrong. But as with Christology, so with the doctrine of man: he is defined in his relationship to God. In his important little book on epistemology (*Wahrheit als Begegnung*) Brunner explains that truth is not objective but personal. Revelation is not doctrine, not the disclosure of this fact or that, but God's once-for-all unique disclosure of Himself.[9]

In his work on eschatology[10] Brunner says that Scripture gives us no reliable information about the future, but in presenting mutually contradictory doctrines, such as the final judgment of the world and universal salvation, it snatches from man the possibility of being in any sense an observer and makes him decide in response to revelation.

Brunner's three-volume *Dogmatik* is not a departure from the correlatively he displayed in earlier years but is, as he says, a more consistent explication of the truth he stated earlier in his *Wahrheit als Begegnung*.[11] The conjunction has not been weakened in the later works but is rather intensified. This may be seen, for instance, in the way he develops the idea of God's encounter with man under the dual terms of *Anspruch* (claim) and *Zuspruch* (address), a distinction, he admits, he did not make in his earlier writings.[12]

---

7 *Der Mittler* (1927), p. 11.
8 *Der Mensch im Widerspruch* (1941).
9 *Wahrheit als Begegnung* (1938), pp. 80ff.
10 *Das Ewige als Zukunft und Gegenwart* (1953), p. 201.
11 *Dogmatik*, II (1950), vii.
12 *Dogmatik*, III (1960), 170, 176.

REVELATION[13]

Brunner titled his major work on revelation *Offenbarung und Vernunft*. In the foreword he wrote that he deliberately chose this order of the words because he wanted to start with revelation and proceed to reason, not vice versa. This emphasis has characterized his teaching on revelation throughout: at every point it takes priority over human reason and science. But just as surely as revelation comes before reason, it cannot do without reason. The problem of the relationship of relevation to reason is, Brunner said, the ground problem of all theology (p. vii).

The following summary of Brunner's view on revelation is taken from his *Dogmatik*, I, pp. 16-58, which is his own summary of his work on revelation mentioned above.

God's essence, says Brunner, defies human conceptualization, for He is not some "thing" about which men speak; He is Absolute Subject. Man cannot master the knowledge of God, for all that which man masters is world (p. 16).

Human knowledge of God exists only in so far as God has disclosed and communicated Himself. Man's doctrine of God is legitimate and can claim validity only to the extent that he accords to divine revelation its rightful place. All Christian doctrine, which points to what God has spoken about Himself, points to an entity outside itself. This the Bible calls "witness." Revelation therefore is not only the ground and the content of the apostolic doctrine, but also the basis for its legitimacy (p. 17).

Central to the New Testament witness of revelation is the historical event of Jesus Christ. That the Word became flesh is the center of the divine self-disclosure. Jesus Christ, Himself the Word, is incommensurable with every human word, that is, human speech about Him. Revelation's center is both a decisive event and a person. God has revealed Himself in the once-for-all event of the Incarnation and the person of Jesus Christ.

Around this revelation center are clustered the witnessings of both the Old and the New Testaments. The Old Testament was provisional because the God who spoke in it had not yet revealed Himself in personal confrontation. This anticipatory witness spoke of a primal revelation that antedates and is presupposed by human sin (p. 19).

After the Christ event of revelation came the witnessing reports of the apostles and their doctrine. This too was historical. The Church has called this witness itself the Word of God, but in so doing it reverted to an Old Testament or Jewish standpoint. The apostolic wit-

[13] Cf. Paul King Jewett, *Emil Brunner's Concept of Revelation* (1954).

ness may be called the Word of God only in the sense that it is the normative form of revelation from which the revelation in Christ cannot be separated and which recognizes and makes valid the revelation in Christ.

The Church has been the agency that has made known to us the witness of the apostles. The Christian congregation does not in the first instance live from the Bible, and the Christian religion is not a religion of a book but of the living Word of the Church which testifies to us of the living Presence. Preaching is one of the forms of revelation and even the Church's doctrine is a bearer of revelation (p. 22).

Revelation, Brunner continues, is not mere communication of doctrine but life-dispensing and life-transforming fellowship. Revelation, in the final analysis, is Immanuel: God with us. In Christ, God's Son, the believer will in the consummation see God face to face. Jesus Christ is both the Speaker and the Actor of revelation (p. 27). He Himself, not His Words, is real revelation. This is the force of the Prologue of John. Jesus is not, like a prophet's message, a word about life, but the Word of life. The appearance of Christ in human flesh reduced the word of human communication to second place (p. 30).

Revelation is a person and person is not speech, nor can speech designate the content of the new manner in which God revealed Himself in Christ. The Word of God, when it is put into the form of human speech, is revelation only in an indirect sense, as a witness to Jesus Christ (p. 32). As Brunner wrote in *Natur und Gnade* (p. 36), direct revelation is heathenism. The insight that revelation is indirect will keep the Church from the intellectualism of the identification of the word of the Bible with the Word of God, as in the theory of verbal inspiration, and of the conception of revelation as revealed doctrine.

Revelation is indirect, but in the testimony of the Holy Spirit there is an identity of revelation of Christ and the word of human speech. By this testimony of the Spirit Brunner means the Spirit-given understanding of the word of Scripture, the deposit of the apostolic witness. Over this witness man has no power of disposal, and it is of Christ only (p. 36).

Revelation is not an object in itself but a transitive process. The witness of the apostles, accordingly, is not the ground or object of our faith, but only the means. Faith in Jesus Christ does not rest on an antecedent faith in Scripture, that is, on a blind faith that believes ahead of time, but solely on the testimony of the Spirit which is the same for us as for the apostles. Scripture, as Luther said, is the cradle in which Christ lies. Although it is inspired by the Spirit of God, it is also a human word and therefore is afflicted with all the deficiency and incompleteness of all that is human (p. 40).

105

The Christian message, which is not first of all doctrine but reporting, is nevertheless inseparably joined to doctrine. The Gospels are not neutral accounts, not photographs of Christ either, but portraits. Revelation is contained, not in the words of the witness, but in the One witnessed (p. 42). Here Brunner brings in his "reason" motif. He points out that in the teaching of doctrine the Church turns from facing God to face the world. The Church no longer speaks now in personal address, but impersonally. Doctrine is not spontaneous, is not a personal answer of prayer to God's Word, but is a reflective speaking about God. Doctrine therefore leaves one dimension of existence (the personal) in order to enter another dimension (the impersonal). God is no longer the Speaker, but the One spoken about. Men, not God, are addressed (p. 45).

Between revelation and doctrine there is a relation of degrees of nearness. Some doctrine is farther removed from personal revelation than other. The more the witness of revelation reflects upon revelation the less revelation his reflection contains. In the New Testament this reflection is minimal (p. 46). Furthermore, the confessional witness of the apostles demands faith. In the name of God the apostles said: We beseech you in Christ's stead, be ye reconciled to God. Theirs was a personal address, albeit to man. But the more dogmatics expands, the more impersonal it becomes (p. 47).

Scripture, says Brunner, is the norm of doctrine. It is authoritative because it is the primary witness of the revelation of God in Jesus Christ. Its witness has normative power for us. That which bears Christ is apostolic. The superiority of the apostles is not absolutely and sharply discernable, but their doctrine is the primary medium through which the revelation comes to us.

The priority of Scripture (by virtue of its being the primary witness) involves *per se* the relativity of its normativity. Both its historical reports and the theological doctrine of the apostles about Jesus Christ depend on critical evaluation. Jesus Christ alone has unconditional authority. This denies to us both the axiomatic authority of orthodox Protestantism and the infallible papal authority of the Roman Catholic Church. We must test Scripture; only, in so doing we must limit ourselves to Scripture, not, however, as the authority, but as the source of the knowledge that does have unconditional authority (p. 55). Scripture speaks about both Christ and the world. To the extent that it speaks about the world, it has no doctrinal authority. Its world image is subject to demythologization.[14] Concerning all worldly knowledge contained in the Bible, rational-scientific criticism must have free play (p. 57).

[14] *Dogmatik,* III (1960), 248.

Besides speaking about revelation in the first volume of his *Dogmatik*, Brunner has written about it also in the third volume.[15] Here, while he reiterates his earlier stand, he stresses even more the personal character of revelation. The word of the Bible is the Word of God only if God Himself speaks to us (p. 274). To claim that we must believe all that the Bible contains is to change the character of faith as encounter into a universal law and faith becomes faith in a book (p. 275). Brunner contends that the dual construction of faith, that is, faith both in Christ and in Scriptures, fails to honor the basic dimensional distinction in human existence.

What we need, says Brunner, is a new formulation of a true scriptural principle, not that we must believe in it as well as in Christ, but in the sense that it is the only place in which God speaks to us, acquits us from judgment and communicates to us His bestowing love by which He renews us (p. 275). In advocating a verbal inspiration of Scripture, Protestantism, he says, has returned to the legalistic Jewish conception of revelation. In fact, the Second Letter to Timothy (which Brunner claims is a second-century pseudonymous writing) teaches, he also states, the formal legalistic Jewish conception of inspiration (3:16) and led the Church into its legalistic train of thought (pp. 220 f.). At the same time, Brunner stresses repeatedly that II Corinthians 3:6 ("the letter killeth but the spirit maketh alive") teaches that faith in the letter of Scripture and spirit-worked faith are mutually contradictory (p. 284).

In Brunner's view both the "legal Jewish" and the "personal" are contained in Scripture, and the theologian has to choose the one and reject the other. The reason he chooses for the "personal" and against a "formal" authoritative Scripture is due to the application of his dialectical principle of the incommensurability of personal truths of revelation and faith with the rational, scientific, impersonal truths of the world. In his most recent books Brunner does not stress the dialectical contradictory character of the relationship of the personal and the impersonal quite as much as in previous years, but he emphasizes more than ever the character of relevation as "personal correspondence" and the correlation between the two dimensions.

THE DOCTRINE OF GOD

Brunner's teaching concerning God, like the rest of his theology, is determined by his personalistic penchant. God, He says, is the Absolute Person and the Absolute Subject. Therefore God is known by revelation only, not by human reason. Therefore He is the free Lord,

---

[15] *The Christian Doctrine of the Church, Faith, and the Consummation* (1962).

transcending man's thought. Since what man thinks, he masters,[16] if God is to remain Lord, He cannot be thought. Because God is the Absolute Person, He is mystery, even after He has been revealed. As we shall indicate, Brunner construes the various attributes of God in line with his personalistic view of reality.

God's absolute personality, His being always Subject, never Object, is the dominant theme of Brunner's "theology." God is wholly other. For this reason Brunner stresses always the disparity between the God of revelation and the God of philosophy. The philosopher's God, he complains, was a product of man's thought, a corrollary of the world, and was really therefore only an idea. The God of the Bible cannot be known as an idea, but only in His historical self-revelation (*ibid.,* p. 12). Brunner never tires of repeating the words of Pascal: "the God of Abraham, Isaac and Jacob — not the God of the Philosophers."[17] He rejects with fervor the possibility of a natural theology.

At the same time, in the doctrine of God, as elsewhere, one finds the evidence of the dialectic. This is apparent already in man's knowledge of God, for the better we learn to know Him through His revelation, the more we realize that He is an impenetrable secret.[18] The dialectic, the view of God *sub contraria specie,* not only underscores the personality of God, but it also brings us to the subordinate theme of Brunner's doctrine, namely, that there is continuity between God and the world; and man's reason, while it cannot reach God, can nevertheless approach Him. Let us trace this through Brunner's teaching on the doctrine of God, the Trinity, and a number of the attributes of God. We shall limit the references to the *Dogmatik, I.*

Brunner finds a problem right in the very question of how man can in any sense teach concerning God, for "whoever teaches concerning God, neglects precisely that of which he wants to teach" (p. 121). God is incomparable and we simply cannot know Him. But to know that we cannot know Him is in part to know God. The teaching about God that comes closest to the truth is that which most strongly stresses the mystery. This is the constitutive qualification of the God of biblical revelation (p. 122).

The personal God is known only through the disclosure of His name. He is not an "It" but a "Thou." Therefore, although a man may know something of God apart from the disclosure of His name, he does not know Him in a way that leads to communion. The failure of the philosophical thought of God is that it does not lead to fellowship with Him (p. 126). A truly personal God cannot be the object

16 *Gott und Mensch* (1930), p. 15.
17 *Dogmatik,* I (1946), 258.
18 *Ibid.,* p. 122.

of thought, but intrudes from outside into the circle of my thought and experience by telling me His name. This revelation marks the end of man's "I-loneliness" (p. 131).

The Being of this God who is altogether removed from man's thought, however, is His self-communicating will. Only in the presence of His revelation is He knowable as He is. He is knowable, moreover, only as He is "for" us, as He discloses Himself as a person (p. 133).

Scripture reveals God to us as a God of holiness and of love. These now are opposites. God's holiness sets Him off as the wholly other and is the characteristic which distinguishes God from everything else (p. 163). In His holiness God maintains His distance. At the same time, in His Love God establishes fellowship (p. 196). In God, therefore, there is a unity of opposites. Holiness and love must be placed in contradiction to each other, and yet at the same time love completes holiness and is fully love only in the completion of holiness (p. 198). The unity and at the same time the non-identity of holiness and love mark the decisive character of revelation's thought about God (p. 303).

God's wrath means that God takes His holiness seriously. The biblical message contains a dialectical tension between wrath and mercy, between the holiness which is identical with love and the holiness that stands in opposition to us as the wrath of God (p. 250). This dialectic cannot be resolved. In the course of history, theologians' attempts to solve this have resulted on the one hand in the Calvinistic doctrine of a double decree and on the other hand in the doctrine of universal salvation. Both doctrines err, for God has only one decree (in Christ) and there is no universal salvation, for there is an area outside of Christ (*ibid.*).

The dialectic manifests itself not only in Brunner's construction of one divine attribute in comparison with another, such as the comparison between God's holiness (wrath) and love, but even manifests itself within the several attributes. Accordingly, Brunner speaks of God's holiness not only in terms of God's maintaining the distance between Himself and creation, but also in terms of a transitive holiness. It belongs to the essence of God that He be accepted by the creature (pp. 170f.). God's essence, says Brunner, is identical with His revelation. He is not only far removed from human thought, but He is in correlation with the world; in fact, He is identical with the correlation, that is, the revelation.

The God of holiness and love reveals Himself in the three names: Father, Son, and Holy Spirit. These three names are signs of God-in-communication in an unchangeable order: from the Father, through the Son, to the Holy Spirit (p. 228). The three names do not stand in an order of under and over, but of before and behind. The trinitarian doctrine sets forth the unity of God's essence and revelation (p. 232). The Trinity reveals the tri-personality of God.

The Trinity is the deepest mystery, but it is not a logical mystery. "That there are three divine persons whose mutual relation and paradoxical unity is incomprehensible to us, is a thought which arose in no apostle's heart" (p. 239). The traditional doctrine of the Church (one substance and three persons) is therefore suspect. But the value of the Church's doctrine is that every formulation of this mystery that violates or annuls the identity of the Revealer and the revelation and of the revelation and the essence of God endangers the decisive biblical message (p. 235).

In its trinitarian doctrine, the Church sought to synthesize biblical thought and anti-biblical philosophical speculation. The doctrine of the *"una substantia"* was especially destructive. To think of God as a substance is in sharpest contradiction to the Bible's thought of Him as the Absolute Subject. A substance is an object and it was a great misfortune that the substance concept found a place in the creed (p. 254).

Brunner speaks of a dialectic in the very essence of revelation in connection with the Trinity. The revelation of God discloses the mystery and reveals to us the heart of God. But this God who has revealed Himself in His Son leads to an ineffable, impenetrably mysterious existence (p. 239).

Since space does not permit us to deal with Brunner's treatment of each divine attribute separately, we shall limit ourselves further to what he says about the righteousness of God. God's righteousness is scarcely distinguishable from His faithfulness. It indicates the constancy of His will (p. 297). The righteousness of God is His seeking to attain His goal in the gracious acts of Jesus Christ (p. 298). In His righteousness, God takes His law, which is grounded in His lordship, seriously. He therefore punishes the sinner. God's righteousness is His holiness as He applies it to the creature which He has made unto freedom (pp. 300f.). If God did not take His law seriously, there would be no constancy in His will or command. He therefore judges without respect of persons.

This aspect of the divine will which is designated by righteousness is the rational element of the doctrine of God. God created reason, and the rational is according to law (p. 302). But in distinction from this, God's freedom means that God is not law and the law is not God, but God has posited the law. God therefore stands over His law and manifests His freedom in acquitting the sinner. When He wills,

God can set His law aside (pp. 303f.). According to the Apostle Paul, says Brunner, the Cross does not resolve the conflict of righteousness and mercy, but establishes their identity. Orthodox Protestantism has failed to understand the biblical doctrine of the righteousness of God, for it has placed the stress upon the rational element of the retributive correspondence between God's will and His law. While this rational element is not lacking, and it comes to expression especially in God's punishment of the impenitent sinner, this is only a minor refrain of the symphony of revelation (p. 322).

In the righteousness of God, Brunner naturally stresses the continuity between God and the world, for righteousness has to do with law. But this attribute of God must become subordinate to His freedom, because the continuity motif always functions in the service of discontinuity. Since God maintains His lordship in setting the law aside when He chooses, and the freedom of God means the discontinuity of all our thinking with the Word of God, the doctrine of the righteousness of God, which, due to the influence of natural theology, played too large a role in Protestant dogmatics, must be relegated to second place.

Priority must be given to the relation of personal correspondence. This means that God's relation changes according to His relation to man. Precisely herein is the living God distinguished from the godhead of abstract thought (p. 289).

It has become apparent that Brunner's construction of the doctrine of God is formulated with the idea of philosophical theism in mind. This is the chief polemic: either the God of Plato or the God of biblical revelation (p. 137). Nevertheless, although Plato's philosophical idea of God is nearly as far removed from the Christian as is the Aristotelian, we should not summarily negate the philosophical doctrine of God, for it does strive for God. Theism shows that even in the working of sinful reason the original revelation of God is still active. Though from a distance, it still follows the revelation of God. It does not recognize the Creator in the biblical sense, but it is the closest approximation to the thought of a creator which reason left to itself can reach (pp. 159, 161).

Although God cannot be grasped by rational categories, there is no conflict between God and reason, for reason has its ground and right to exist in God (p. 306). What is considered by man on earth to be thought and decided by valid reason is considered valid in heaven also. The laws of logic are the emanation of the divine thought and will. Truths of reason participate in the much greater truth of God. Creation is not rational, but rationable (p. 307).

111

THE DOCTRINE OF MAN[19]

Brunner has developed a "theological" understanding of man. By this he means that the proper understanding of man requires that he be understood in his relation to God. The essence of man is his God-relatedness. "Man is a 'theological' being, that is, his ground, his goal, his norm, and the possiblity of understanding his own nature are all in God."[20] God is *actus absolutus*; man is *actus relativus*.[21]

As the God-related creature, man is a responsible being. "Man is not first of all a human being and then responsible; but his human existence consists in responsibilty. And man is not first of all responsible and then in addition he possesses a relation to God; but his relation to God is the same as his responsibility."[22] Man's responsibility must not be conceived of so much morally as in the sense of his having his existence in the Word of God. Man must hear God's Word in order to exist.[23] Man is a "verbicompetent" being.

Even as man owes his present existence to the Word of God, so he also owes his creation to the Word. The understanding of man as a creature of God is not a theory, but an existential expression. Creation is not a cosmic event, nor was man created on a particular day. "It is not some human being who happened to live in the far-off dim ages of pre-history who is the Adam created in the image of God; it is you and I and everybody."[24] Creation has nothing to do with causality and did not bring anything into being; Man was created in the Word of God's personal address to man.[25]

It will become apparent here that Brunner constructs his anthropology by an empirical consideration of man. He has no use for a prelapsarian man and pays scant attention to the *post mortem* state. There is no resurrection of the body.[26] As in the doctrine of creation, so in the teaching of man: we must take our starting point in the Prologue of John, not in Genesis.[27] Psalm 139 is for him the *locus classicus* of the creation of man. It will be necessary to bear in mind throughout that Brunner accepts man as he now is in the fallen state as normative for the understanding of man.

[19] For a more extensive exposition of Brunner's anthropology, see Paul G. Schrotenboer, *A New Apologetics, an Analysis and Appraisal of the Eristic Theology of Emil Brunner* (1955), pp. 60-95.
[20] *The Christian Understanding of Man* (1938), pp. 159f.
[21] *Ibid.*
[22] *Ibid.*, p. 159.
[23] *Das Wort Gottes und der Moderne Mensch* (1937), p. 21.
[24] *Der Mensch im Widerspruch* (1941), p. 102.
[25] *Ibid.*, p. 87.
[26] *Das Ewige als Zukunft und Gegenwart* (1953), p. 164.
[27] *Dogmatik*, II (1950), 61.

Man, says Brunner, is the image of God.[28] In developing this doctrine of the image he resorts to the well-used distinction of the formal and the material image. But whether one looks at the image as a material something or as merely formal, in either case it is relational. In the image of God in man the structural and the relational are identified. The formal aspect of the image constitutes his humanity and is that permanent quality which distinguishes man from the animals. It is identical with man's responsibility.[29] The material image is man's responsive love. Man is intended for participation in the love of God.[30] Neither formally nor materially may man be considered a substance which is in the slightest degree dissociated from God.

After his revolt against God, sinful man still knows himself as answerable. Only he now conceives of it in the legal sense of "Thou shalt" (*Du sollst*).[31] Legalism is the very essence of sin. Love does not demand, but gives. However, the point of greatest distance is also the point of greatest nearness. Having rejected the Romish doctrine of the distinction between the image and the likeness as well as the Reformers' doctrine of a relic in man which is not affected by sin, Brunner construes the image of God in an activistic, personalistic sense so that man is always a theological being, always related to God.[32]

Man is not only the image of God; he is also a sinner.[33] Man's likeness to God and his sinfulness are his basic determinations as he now exists. Sin is man's opposition against the flawless creation and the image of God.

Sin is neither to be restricted to separate acts of the will, nor does it belong to the nature of man. The traditional view of the Church destroys the unity of responsibility and necessity. Sin is a personal transaction. It cannot be pinpointed in time and space. "We can no more localize personal transactions between God and man in the world of time and space than we can localize the spirit of man in the brain."[34] The fall of man was not an historical event. The possibility of sin must be seen in man's being constituted a free, responsible being. Sin means that man misunderstands and misuses his freedom.[35] Sin is act, never state; it does not become a quality or a sub-

---

28 Cf. Hermann Volk, *Emil Brunners Lehre von der Ursprünglichen Gottebenbildlichkeit des Menschen* (1939).

29 *Dogmatik*, II (1950), 67.

30 *The Christian Understanding of Man* (1938), pp. 159f.

31 *Das Wort Gottes und der Moderne Mensch* (1937), p. 23.

32 *Der Mensch im Widerspruch* (1941), p. 96.

33 Cf. Hermann Volk, *Emil Brunners Lehre von der Sünder* (1950).

34 *The Christian Understanding of Man* (1938), p. 63.

35 *Der Mensch im Widerspruch* (1941), p. 277.

stance.[36] Since man is a God-responsible being and true responsibility is identical with love, sin is the denial of this responsibility.[37] Thus sin should not be oriented to law, for law is oriented to sin. That the law is written on the heart does not mean the unity of man's desire with God's command, but indicates that man's legal self-understanding pervades man to his very center.

Sin is irrational, mysterious, unexplainable. *Per definitionem* it defies comprehension by theory. It can be grasped only by faith. Apart from faith there is some knowledge of sin (consider the Kantian doctrine of radical evil) and this experiential knowledge apart from faith does not conflict with the knowledge of sin in faith. What faith does is not to give exclusive knowledge of sin, but exclusively to give correct knowledge of sin.[38]

In dealing with the effect of sin upon human reason, knowledge, and science, Brunner applies his personalistic motif and works this out in the distinction between God-truths and world-truths. Since sin is a personal relation of man to God, its effect is most devastating in those areas of life where the God-relation is dominant. As a rule of thumb, in worldly things, both in science and practice, reason is adequate, but not in matters of faith. Sin does not prevent man from knowing the things of the world, natural laws, natural facts, and man in his natural cultural and historical manifestations.[39]

The distinction between the two realms of God and the world may not be rigidly drawn, however. To the contrary, the principle of the degrees of nearness must be applied. "The nearer anything lies to that center of existence where we are concerned with the whole, that is with man's relation to God and the being of the person, the greater is the disturbance of rational knowledge by sin; the farther anything lies from this center, the less is the disturbance felt and the less difference is there between knowing as a believer or as an unbeliever. This disturbance reaches its maximum in theology and its minimum in the sphere of the formal."[40] There can then be a conflict between reason and sin, especially in the areas of life which are most personal. Here revelation must supplement reason. But, in line with the dialectical motif, the relation of reason and revelation is not one of supplementation only, but of supplementation *and* correction.

The correction that revelation must give to reason is due to the arrogance of reason against faith. Reason claims too much. It wants

---

[36] *Ibid.,* p. 142.
[37] *Ibid.,* p. 150.
[38] *The Scandal of Christianity* (1951), p. 68.
[39] *Dogmatik,* II (1950), 33f.
[40] *Offenbarung und Vernunft* (1941), p. 398.

to be the last court of appeal, the supreme judge of truth. The conflict is not caused by the right use but by the misuse of reason.[41]

Reason, for Brunner, is a dual concept: it is the power of ideation (*Das Vermogen der Idee*), a tool of world mastery, and it is also the receiver of the Word. In the realm of world-truths, reason must master and control. In the realm of God-truths it must humbly receive what it is given. Man's autonomy is legitimate in the world, but is illegitimate in dealing with God. Moreover, there is no neat separation between God and the world, but rather a dialectical relation. Man cannot be expected to understand sin from outside of himself, and he cannot be held responsible for an historical fall into sin.

Before leaving Brunner's doctrine of sin, we should recall that he said that one of its direct effects is that it makes the Ego lonely. Sin has no place for community. But it should be noted that Brunner says the same of reason. What is rational, man can understand by himself, without the aid of any other person. The ideal of reason is independence.[42] But Brunner does not draw the conclusion that reason is therefore wrong; he rather affirms that it is fully legitimate in its proper sphere. This does mean, however, that if sin is the lack of community, then, in the formal sphere, sin is legitimate. If Brunner were to apply his personalistic motif with rigid consistency to all reality, he would deprive the world of its rational aspect. His theology, however, seeks to keep the rational and the personal in solution.

THE CHURCH

The Church, says Brunner, is the organ, the bearer of the proclamation of the Gospel. It is the proclaiming existence (*verkundigende Existenz*) as the historical continuum of revelation.[43] The Church is every form of historical existence that has its origin in Jesus Christ and recognizes in Him its ground and highest norm.[44]

The Church and faith are joined essentially. Man is a believer only by means of his membership in the body of Christ in the Church and nowhere else.[45] In the New Testament the Church is considered exclusively as a fellowship of believers in Christ, never as an institution. To be in Christ through faith and to be in the fellowship of the Church are one and the same.[46] Faith now is communicating ex-

41 *Ibid.*, p. 57.
42 *Das Grundproblem der Ethik* (1931), p. 11.
43 *Dogmatik*, III (1960), p. 17.
44 *Ibid.*, p. 19.
45 *Ibid.*, p. 35.
46 *Ibid.*, p. 36.

istence (*kommunizierende Existenz*) and faith goes through communication to communion.[47]

The three classic definitions of the Church (the *coetus electorum,* the *corpus Christi,* and the *communio sanctorum*) all indicate different aspects of the ground of the Church. Election reveals the transcendent aspect; the body of Christ, the historical; the communion of the saints, the spiritual-subjective.[48]

The dual concept of the Church as being both visible and invisible is foreign to the New Testament.[49] The Church is throughout a non-cultic, non-sacral spiritual brotherhood which lives in trusting obedience to Jesus Christ and in love with the brethren.[50]

Baptism makes visible what occurs invisibly through the Word and faith. But that which becomes visible in society is not an institution. The Apostle Paul knew of no presbyterial or episcopal orders. The Spirit does not create offices, but service. Out of faith in Christ has arisen a fellowship of life, the ecclesia, but not an institution or church.[51] The ecclesia of the New Testament is not an organization, but a unified, living cosmos of free, spiritual gifts.[52]

Brunner maintains that, while this is the truly Pauline teaching of the Church, this is not the teaching of the pastoral epistles. In the pastoral epistles the Church is not considered spiritually but juridically. Here the office of bishop is pictured and praised in a way that would be impossible in a truly Pauline congregation. Thus there is no unified doctrine of the Church in the New Testament and the divergent views presented are not unifiable. The essence of the Church is in contradiction to the essence of polity (*Rechts*). The Pauline ecclesiology excludes radically the idea of polity from the essence of the Church.[53]

The existence of the ecclesia is essentially and necessarily grounded upon the apostolate. The early Church recognized the apostles as the primal form of the apostolic authority, but the apostles had no other authority than that of the primal witnesses of Christ and the Holy Spirit.[54] For this reason the authority of the apostles was non-transferable, and after the death of the apostles this authority took the form of a fixed tradition put into Scriptural form.[55]

[47] *Ibid.,* p. 42.
[48] *Ibid.,* p. 43.
[49] *Ibid.,* p. 45.
[50] *Ibid.,* p. 49.
[51] *Ibid.,* p. 61.
[52] *Ibid.,* p. 62.
[53] *Ibid.,* p. 65.
[54] *Ibid.,* p. 67.
[55] *Ibid.,* pp. 68f.

116

Whoever takes the Pauline personalism seriously will make no allowance for sacramental thought. Brunner admits that there are indeed expressions in the Pauline writings which are sacramental, but these, he holds, are remnants of Hellenistic thought. The Pauline teaching of baptism is irreconcilable with the doctrine of infant baptism.[56] Brunner's objection to the Catholic doctrine of baptism is that it makes the event the vehicle of redemption without making a personal claim upon man.[57]

The ecclesia of the New Testament developed historically into the Roman Catholic Church. Brunner's thesis is that this regrettable development was caused by the sacramental misunderstanding of redemption and the validation of formal-legal authority.[58] Personalism leaves room neither for sacraments which work automatically, nor for formal authority which makes no direct claim upon the person, nor yet for the authority of office. The Charisma did not create an order, nor a power of command, nor yet a right of obedience.[59]

No church today can be identified with the Church of the New Testament. The organized Church is only the vessel of the ecclesia. The institutional form of the Church does not belong to the essence of the Church. The task of the ecumenical movement is to build a Church which is the true ecclesia.[60] The Church is the fellowship in faith and love of those who believe in Jesus Christ and is therefore the presupposition of faith.[61]

FAITH[62]

Faith, says Brunner, always exists within the Church. A Christian individualism is therefore a contradiction in terms. And even as Brunner depreciates the institution of the Church, together with its offices and authority, by making it a dwelling to house the true ecclesia, so too he rejects the idea of a heteronomous faith. The Christian should not be required to believe the word of the Bible.[63] Faith is not based upon doctrine, but upon testimony.

Faith is a kind of human existence in which man says he is not his own but belongs to Jesus his Lord. Faith is the decision that says: Thou art Lord, I belong not to myself but to Thee. It is an inner overpowering. Faith is not thinking, for by thinking I establish my

---

[56] *Ibid.*, p. 72.
[57] *Ibid.*
[58] *Ibid.*, p. 78.
[59] *Ibid.*, p. 85.
[60] *Ibid.*, p. 154.
[61] *Ibid.*, p. 159.
[62] Cf. Lorenz Volken, *Der Glaube bei Emil Brunner* (1947).
[63] *Dogmatik*, III (1960), 64.

self-sovereignty. I am master of my own thoughts and so long as I remain by myself I remain unchallenged and undisturbed. And to the extent that I remain with myself I am excluded from reality.[64]

In developing the idea of faith, Brunner in his *Dogmatik* stresses the obedience of faith. He recognizes an advance in his thinking here over that in *Offenbarung und Vernunft* in that he now distinguishes between God's claim upon man (*Anspruch*) and his address to man (*Zuspruch*).[65]

Unbelief always tries to leave the realm of the personal, where faith functions, in order to enter the realm of the impersonal, where there are objective truths (It-truths). But in objective truth there is no Lord who places his claim upon me and addresses me. When a man conceives of God as an objective truth, he has made Him a piece of the world.[66]

New Testament faith is not directed to doctrine but to Christ. Faith is the obedient and trusting acceptance of God's address in which God takes man into His own existence and then for the first time makes man belong to Him.[67] Faith and Christ are synonyms, at least in the sense that to have Christ and to believe are one and the same thing.[68]

After rejecting doctrine as the object of faith, Brunner next makes room for doctrine. It explains who Jesus was, namely, the Son of God in His earthly, pre-Easter existence. Doctrine has no basis in itself, but is a pointer to Him.[69] The kerygma of the New Testament is not a reporting, and yet it contains reports. It is not doctrine, and yet it contains doctrine. It is not authoritative and therefore is not a word that must be believed, but still it is the word of rightful witness.[70]

A fatal displacement has taken place in the Church. The witness of Jesus Christ has been construed as the reporting of facts which must be believed as such. We may call this misunderstanding of faith a faith in facts.[71] Together with faith in doctrine this has become an aprioristic faith in the Bible.[72]

It is significant that Brunner, in castigating orthodox Protestantism because it has made the Bible a paper Pope, admits that II Timothy 3:16 apparently gives apostolic approbation to this view. But he judges that this letter dates from the second century, and he finds it

---

[64] *Ibid.*, p. 169.
[65] *Ibid.*, pp. 170, 176.
[66] *Ibid.*, p. 173.
[67] *Ibid.*, pp. 199f.
[68] *Ibid.*, p. 203.
[69] *Ibid.*, p. 212.
[70] *Ibid.*, p. 216.
[71] *Ibid.*
[72] *Ibid.*, p. 219.

118

highly significant that the same letter which sets forth an episcopal conception of the Church also presents the Judaistic, legalistic conception of Scripture. Both the formal authority of the Church and the formal authority of the Bible stem from the same source: legalistic thinking.[73] Aprioristic faith in the Bible is not biblical but originated from this Jewish legalistic thinking which overpowered the true justifying faith.[74]

We would close this short and admittedly incomplete exposition of Brunner's theology by quoting from the section on "The Consummation" in Vol. III of his *Dogmatik*. Here he deals with the problem of demythologizing and divine communication in eternity. It is typical and indicative of his entire theology. "The result of our considerations up to this point is this: while on the one hand we agree that the decisive kerygma of the self-communication of God in Jesus Christ is mythical, we deny most decisively that from this lack of correspondence would follow the dispensability of the specific biblical form of thought, since we should rather see in it the only possibility of bringing to expression that upon which faith comes to us and which distinguishes faith from the philosophy of the loneliness of the Ego. The mythical form of expression is nothing less that the necessary consequence of the incommensurability of Creator and creature, which we hope to overcome only in the coming revelation at the End, which is the object of our faith. 'For we know in part . . . but when that which is perfect is come, then that which is in part shall be done away' " (p. 454).

III. EVALUATION

We recall that Brunner's theology is built around a framework that partitions reality into two realms or dimensions of existence, namely, law and Gospel or, the impersonal and the personal, world-truths and God-truths. This may also be called nature and grace.[75] In seeking to relate these two dimensions of existence to each other he gives priority to the realm of the personal and therefore calls his theology a "biblical personalism." Here his irrational penchant, which does not annul man's power of reason but devaluates it to a secondary place, becomes apparent. This permits him at every point to make room for the freedom of man.

Brunner's theology must be seen as an amazingly consistent attempt to explain reality and Scripture in accordance with this motif of the priority of the personal over the impersonal. In seeking to delineate the exact relationship between the two he makes use of the principle

[73] *Ibid.,* p. 221.
[74] *Ibid.*
[75] Cf. H. G. Hubbeling, *Natuur en Genade bij Emil Brunner* (1956).

of the degrees of nearness. That is, in the realm of world-truths there are grades of proximity to the personal.[76] In theology the influence of faith and sin (both are personal characterizations of human existence) is maximal. In the strictly formal areas of thought and reality the effect of sin and faith is nil.

However, in working out the relationship between the two basic areas of reality Brunner resorts to the dialectic that connects them to each other by the relation of *incommensurability* (contradiction) and *supplementation* (preparation). And these two also assume a specific order. The relation of incommensurability takes uncontested priority, and therefore the relation of supplementation assumes a subordinate place. This, in short, is the structural framework of Brunner's "biblical personalism!"

It may be helpful to point out in barest outline how Brunner's personalism and his devaluation of reason and law affect various doctrines. In his view of revelation this is seen in his claim that the I-Thou revelation of God stands above and outside all normativity of thought.[77] In his Christology it has resulted in an interpretation of Christ as "truth that became." Christ is the fulfillment of the law in the sense that He reveals its meaning. He did not destroy law itself, but the impersonal abstractness of the law and the false direction of legality or work-righteousness.[78] In his view of faith it is seen in his claim that faith does not have doctrine or teaching as its object but only Christ. Faith has to do only with a Thou-word, not an It-word. In justification this is seen in his view that God's justification of the sinner is actually unjust, for God puts the law aside.[79] In the same vein he claims that regeneration is not a natural event, but an I-Thou word.[80] For the same reason too, in speaking of conversion, he rejects the doctrine of divine monergism.[81] In dealing with sanctification he rejects moralism because the Spirit who places us in the immediate presence of God knows nothing of any law.[82]

In his ethics his personalism has resulted in a devaluation of law and also in the distinction between *Gebot* and *Gesetz*. Everyone can understand the law, but only the man to whom God speaks knows the love-command. The love-command, moreover, does not say what man should do and cannot be known beforehand.[83]

---

[76] See p. 106.
[77] *Dogmatik,* III (1960), 346.
[78] *Der Mittler* (1927), p. 565.
[79] *The Scandal of Christianity* (1951), pp. 43ff.
[80] *Dogmatik,* III (1960), 305.
[81] *Ibid.,* p. 314.
[82] *Ibid.,* p. 339.
[83] *Das Gebot und die Ordnungen* (1932), p. 97.

In describing the true Church (ecclesia), his personalism results in the rejection of the Church as an officialdom, for an institution is not a community.[84] In the Church, sacramentarianism should be rejected too because a magic rite is not a personal event.[85] In his teaching on missions he denies the need of a special command, for the love of Christ must constrain us.[86] Finally, his personalism results in his elevating the New Testament above the Old, for only in the New is the Word of God an event, and within the New Testament it means his rejection of the genuineness of II Timothy because, he contends, in its teaching both of Scripture and of the Church it represents a return to the legalistic Jewish view.

Brunner's theology is a grand attempt to synthesize an irrational (reason-devaluating) personalism and the biblical message. Our evaluation of his theology will concern the legitimacy and degree of success of this attempt. The central question is: *Can Brunner bring his personalism and the biblical data into a harmonious unity?* While a discussion is required at the level of each specific doctrine, we cannot begin to do that here. We must be satisfied with a consideration of the central structural motifs. This is needed in any case for a correct appraisal of the individual doctrines. Here we only consider his claim that the unification of truth and community is the ground phenomenon of the biblical message.[87]

It must be admitted that many of Brunner's goals are praiseworthy. He would at all costs pluck man from his pose of complacency and get him involved personally at the center of his being with the Gospel of Jesus Christ. He emphasizes the lordship of Christ, man's relationship to God, the obedience of faith, and the need of personal encounter. He would snatch from man the last vestige of his hope of remaining on the sidelines without becoming entangled in the life-and-death struggle of human existence.

It must be seen, however, that the deepest stratum of Brunner's theology is situational, rather than biblical. The consideration of concrete existing man is constitutive for his theology; the consideration of man in the prelapsarian and post-mortem states is only additive. The latter are limiting concepts which assist man in explaining himself as he is today. Brunner finds man's responsibility more important than his creatureliness. Moreover, creation is not a cosmic or *causal* event, but an act of God's address. Every man is his own Adam and must be understood from his existential situation.

---

[84] *Ibid.*, p. 311.
[85] *Ibid.*
[86] *Ibid.*, p. 240.
[87] *Dogmatik*, III (1960), 10.

There need be no conflict, of course, between a kind of personalism and Christianity, but then the personalism must be based upon Scripture, and must truly accord, as Brunner claims, with the biblical message.

In seeking to answer the question concerning this true synthesis, it will not do just to set one interpretation of Scripture against another. While this must be done, it must be preceded by the attempt to penetrate behind the interpretation to the religious attitude toward the Word of God.

We may agree with Brunner that this attitude should be *the obedience of faith.* Man should respond to God's Word in trust and obedience. Faith is man's basic religious relation.[88] But does Brunner's religious motive actually accord with what he claims it should be? It will be admitted by all that Brunner has consistently stressed that Scripture does not give us direct revelation of God. Scripture does not reveal this or that, but testifies to God's personal self-revelation. With Kierkegaard, he has equated direct revelation with heathenism. Revelation is not direct, not doctrinal (neither biblical nor dogmatic), but personal and incommensurable with man's thought. But now, when the question is asked: Is this idea of revelation derived from Scripture or from some other source? the only answer is that Scripture cannot teach that revelation is indirect, for this would itself constitute a direct revelation, and would be a contradiction in terms.

Our evaluation should not rest exclusively on an *a priori* consideration, however, but should be substantiated by an analysis of the various doctrines and the exegetical labor by which Brunner seeks to buttress his system.

We saw that the construction given to revelation itself reveals a religious attitude toward Scripture and the Word of God. This attitude toward Scripture, however, is intimately related to the attitude toward God Himself, for in the Bible the expressions "Scripture says" and "God says" are used interchangeably.[89] But here too, it is not enough to set against Brunner's free criticism of Scripture the obedience of faith, for he too lauds obedience as the essential for true belief. He has a view that not only makes room for criticism, inasmuch as it touches only the alphabet, not the essence, of the Word of God, but advocates criticism because it helps man effect that personal encounter. The legitimacy of biblical criticism, Brunner claims, stems from his division of reality into world-truths and God-truths. Jesus

[88] *Ibid.,* p. 179.
[89] Cf. Synod of the Christian Reformed Church, 1961, *Decision on Infallibility and Inspiration,* pp. 8-16.

Christ is not dependent upon the results of a critical investigation.[90]
Thanks to the new research of Scripture we have learned that it is
impossible to believe in an inerrant Scripture.[91] Faith, he would
teach, is dependent, to this extent at least, upon scientific investigation.
So then, the obedience of faith, in Brunner's view, must be united with
a view which warrants sitting in judgment upon Scripture in all that
it contains of world-truths and even claiming it was not written the way
it should have been. Whatever else the import of the charge of errancy may be, this much is unavoidable: it says Scripture is not as it
should be and needs correction.

The priority Brunner gives to revelation does not mean that he
accepts scriptural authority as commonly understood; for he insists
that it was the formal, legalistic view of the authority of the Bible
that led to the writing of the Second Letter to Timothy and resulted
in the doctrine of the "paper pope." Scripture has authority only
because it is the primal witness to the event of Jesus Christ.

Brunner's attitude toward Scripture (the cradle in which Christ lies),
would safeguard the freedom of man and affirm the right of man to
judge all that which by his critical analysis he thinks belongs to world-
truths (what man thinks he masters) and to reject that which does
not accord with the biblical kerygma. This, Brunner claims, is the
theme of his entire third volume of his *Dogmatik*: the personal correspondence which completes itself in the self-communication of God and
the faith of man.[92] Brunner advocates the obedience of faith ($\dot{v}\pi\alpha\kappa o\grave{\eta}$
$\pi\iota\sigma\tau\epsilon\omega s$), but he follows a path of peace by means of dialectical segre-
gation between reason with its mastery of the world and faith with its
ineffable capitulation. Faith for Brunner becomes the coincidence of
divine self-communication and human self-understanding.[93]

As Brunner has said: the point of greatest nearness is also the
point of greatest distance. We may apply this now to his view that
the biblical message is personal correspondence.

With all emphasis it should be said that Scripture effects a personal
confrontation of God and man. This is both the purpose and the result of the truly biblical message. Here we seem ready to join hands
with Brunner. But when we ask whether this divine-human encounter
requires the devaluation of the scriptural word to a pointer or sacrament,
whether the Word conceals as well as reveals, whether the encounter
requires a revelation that defies conceptualization, even if it is directed
and disclosed by the Spirit of God, and whether it demands precisely

90 *Dogmatik*, III (1960), 386.
91 *Ibid.*, p. 213.
92 *Ibid.*, p. 325.
93 *Ibid.*, p. 237.

that we do not believe Scripture just because it is Scripture — then the ways diverge sharply.

Let us consider the obedience of faith. But then let us consider faith, not as it has been remolded according to the demands of modern irrationalistic thought, but as it is presented in Scripture in the non-scientific idiom and language of everyday experience. Let us seek to penetrate to the meaning of Scripture, not by means of a scientific investigation of Scripture which seeks to judge the Book according to the canons of judging any other book of comparable literature, but by listening obediently to the message of the living Word of dynamic power that lives and discerns the thoughts and motivations of the heart. If faith is for every man who wills to believe, it must come in a way that is not limited to those who supposedly have gained the insights of modern personalistic philosophy.

So too, when we consider the dialectic of law and Gospel, we find much with which we can agree in the dogmatics of Brunner. There is most surely a conflict between law and Gospel in this sinful human situation. Man is corrupted, is estranged from God, and lives under the curse. Legalism is always a bane. But is the present sinful situation in which man is in revolt normative for the dialectic? Should we absolutize existence here and now, with its criss-crossing streams of sin and redemption? Or should we take the position of faith upon the Word of God that rises above the existence of man in his present state on the basis of the time-transcending Word, accepting it as being both reliable and authoritative communication *and* a communion-establishing address?

Scripture, the Word of God written, is not in its essence a collection of stories and propositions, a mixture of world-truths and truths about God. Rather, in instructing us of God, ourselves, and the world, it is the dynamic Word of power that sets us in the truth which is Christ and is the key to the understanding of all reality. As such it is most assuredly direct, predicational revelation.

The redeemed sinner who has learned to love the law of God has overcome in principle the contradiction between law and Gospel. He has been reconciled in Christ, who fulfilled the law, and he is on the way back to a state of rectitude where there is perfect harmony both in God, between His demand and His gift, and in man, between his obedience to the law and his response of love.

Over against Brunner's personalistic theology, we should affirm the need both of the formal and of the material authority of Scripture. We need this, not by way of compromising the personal encounter, but in order to effect a *total, all-embracing* engagement. Brunner has said

124

that legalism is the same as deciding by principle.[94] He has also said that God's I-Thou revelation stands above all normativity of thought (*Denkgesetzlichkeit*). But it should be seen clearly that in the name of personalism Brunner has withdrawn a very large part of reality from the area of personal encounter. He cannot bring it back until he has made peace between personal encounter and the authority of the Word of God in its scriptural form, the permanent embodiment of eternal truth. Then the way will have been opened for an encounter with God at every point, in basic thinking as well as in the commitment of faith, in truths concerning the world and man, as well as in truths concerning God. Then even the inanimate world will have become a valley of decision. Basic to every personal engagement is God's established Order.

There is indeed a conflict between law and love, but the Gospel message is that the Word of God breaks the conflict and brings peace. In this resultant peace the law is written on the heart (cf. Heb. 8:10; II Cor. 3:3). How far removed Brunner's theology is from the central biblical message can be seen in a comparison of the new covenant of peace, the highest expression of communion between the believer and God, and Brunner's statement that the writing of the law upon the heart means that man's legal understanding of himself reaches to his center. This shows the extreme misconstruction of Scripture to which his personalism leads.

Even as Brunner's view of revelation in effect downgrades the truly personal encounter, so his construction of faith also violates the total personal relationship between man and God. Brunner claims that faith is not the acceptance of doctrine, either dogmatic or biblical, but personal encounter with Christ. The Church has said that true faith is the acceptance for truth of all the Bible contains and a hearty confidence in Jesus Christ that sins are forgiven.[95] Between these which the Church has joined together Brunner posits the relation of incommensurability.[96]

Here the question is not whether the acceptance of biblical teaching is the whole of faith, but whether it is agreeable with and necessary for hearty confidence or trust and the assurance of belonging to Christ. Is faith in Christ of a piece with the acceptance of His and His apostles' *didache?* It must be said that Brunner here has once again done violence to the personal relation between God and man's responsibility to God. We may sympathize with his emphasis upon man's responsibility. We may rejoice in his call for personal involvement, but if it

---

[94] *Das Gebot und die Ordnungen* (1932), p. 69.
[95] *Heidelberg Catechism*, 21.
[96] *Dogmatik,* III (1960), p. 219.

is true, as he claims, that involvement requires the logical contradiction, he, instead of safeguarding the responsibility of man, deprives
man of that to which he must respond: the *authoritative Word* and
its claim that will not be set aside. His view eliminates the theonomy
of the written Word in which God confronts man. God's law is not
the enemy of encounter, but the indispensable instrument.

In still another way Brunner has severely damaged the truly personal encounter between God and man: namely, by his rejection of
the Church as an officialdom and an institution. He claims that the
only authority the apostles had was their primal witnesses. Once
again, his view is situational, rather than biblical. He looks at the
situation of the apostles, rather than at the *assignment* which Christ
gave them. Brunner's theology has little place for representatives. In
fact, his personalism has virtually no room for office at all.

In reaction to Brunner, we do well not to choose the official instead of the personal. To the contrary, we must maintain that in
order to effect encounter, God instituted the offices in the Church so
that, as Jesus said, "he that receiveth you, receiveth me and he that
receiveth me receiveth him that sent me" (Matt. 10:40). The true
view of the Christian's office in the world would deliver life from
the bane of impersonalism if men would only see the special *place* and
assignment that God has given them. To consider the implications of
the idea of office for a theology of biblical personalism would take us
too far afield. We would, however, point out that the influence of
personalistic philosophy upon Brunner's thinking, instead of helping
him construct a "biblical personalism," leads him to misconstrue
seriously at crucial places the personal encounter between God and
man.

Because of the synthetic character of Brunner's theology, our view
of it should be bifocal. That is, since he has made a grandiose attempt
to understand Christianity, revelation, God, Christ, man, the Church,
and faith in terms of the law-Gospel dialectic and "biblical personalism,"
we can neither accept it uncritically in its entirety, nor reject it outright as a whole. Because this structural motif is not derived from
Christianity, nor from Scripture, but from an extra-biblical personalism,
one must conclude that the attempt to harmonize it with the scriptural
message is misdirected from the start. To the extent that Brunner suc-
ceeds in subordinating the revelational data and the Christian faith to
this motif, to that extent he misconstrues them. Our first assessment
must be critical and cautious.

But Brunner does not fully succeed. He cannot fit revelation and
faith into his Procrustean bed. He deals with power too great for his
motif. The Word of God is not bound by his construction of it. His

126

zeal for the lordship of God does not do justice to God's lordship. The power and truth of the Word shine through every attempt to synthesize it with conflicting motifs. One sees the Gospel in Brunner's writings as though refracted through a prism: it is discolored and distorted, but not blacked out. Although the Gospel cannot be brought into harmonious unity with personalistic philosophy, nevertheless Brunner maintains the priority of the Gospel and, in spite of all the deficiencies of his theology, the biblical and Christian message does somehow and in part shine through.

Brunner has done the Church a great service in dealing with crucial issues. His writings warrant careful study. Some of his insights are penetrating and will continue to exert great influence upon theology. But he has failed to produce a harmonious unity between his extra-scriptural motifs and the biblical message. We therefore suggest that the Church should not seek to build upon the structural framework he has proposed, but upon the scriptural message which puts all systems of thought in the balance and finds wanting all those which do not accord with its dynamic, directing power and its authoritative revelation.

IV. BIBLIOGRAPHY

WORKS BY EMIL BRUNNER

(For a complete list of Brunner's works, see *Das Menschenbild im Lichte des Evangeliums, Festschrift, zum* 60. *Geburtstag von Prof. Dr. Emil Brunner.* Zürich: Zwingli-Verlag, 1950, pp. 171-185.)

Das Symbolische in der religiösen Erkenntnis. Beitrage zu einer Theorie des religiösen Erkennens. Tübingen, 1914.

Die Grenzen der Humanität. Tübingen, 1922.

Erlebnis, Erkenntnis, und Glaube. Tübingen, 1923.

Die Mystik und das Wort. Tübingen, 1924 (2nd ed., 1928).

"Das Grundproblem der Philosophie bei Kant und Kierkegaard," *Zwischen den Zeiten,* 1924.

Philosophie und Offenbarung. Tübingen, 1925.

"Gesetz und Offenbarung," *Theologische Blätter,* 1925.

Die Absolutheit Jesu. Berlin, 1926.

Der Mittler. Tübingen, 1927 (*The Mediator.* Philadelphia, 1947).

Religionsphilosophie protestantischer Theologie. Munich, 1927 (*Philosophy of Religion.* London, 1937).

"Der Zorn Gottes und die Versöhnung durch Christus," *Zwischen den Zeiten,* 1927.

"Griesbachs Angriff auf die Theologie," *Zwischen den Zeiten,* 1928.

The Theology of Crisis. New York, 1929.

"Die andere Aufgabe der Theologie," *Zwischen den Zeiten,* 1929.

Gott und Mensch. Tübingen, 1930 (*God and Man.* London, 1936).

"Secularism as a Problem for the Church," *The International Review of Missions,* Vol. XIX, 1930.

"Die Botschaft Soren Kierkegaards," *Neue Schweizer Rundschau,* 1930.

"Die Bedeutung des Alten Testament für unsern Glauben," *Zwischen den Zeiten,* 1930.

"Theologie und Ontologie — oder die Theologie am Scheidewege," *Seitschrift für Theologie und Kirche,* 1931.

The Word and the World. London, 1931.

Das Gebot und die Ordnungen. Tübingen, 1932 (*The Divine Imperative.* Philadelphia, 1947).

128

Emil Brunner

"Die Frage nach dem 'Anknupfungspunkt' als Problem der Theologie,"
    Zwischen den Zeiten, 1932.
"Eros und Liebe," *Neue Schweizer Rundschau,* 1933.
Natur und Gnade, Gespräch mit Karl Barth. Tübingen, 1934 (*Natural
    Theology,* comprising *Nature and Grace,* by Professor Dr. Emil
    Brunner, and the reply *No!* by Dr. Karl Barth. London, 1946).
"Imago Dei," *Neue Schweizer Rundschau,* 1934.
Unser Glaube. Bern, 1935 (*Our Faith.* New York, 1936).
Das Wort Gottes und der moderne Mensch. Berlin, 1937.
Der Mensch im Widerspruch. Berlin, 1937 (*Man in Revolt.* Philadel-
    phia, 1947).
Wahrheit als Begegnung. Berlin, 1938 (*The Divine-Human Encounter.*
    Philadelphia, 1943).
"Schicksal und Freiheit in christlicher Sicht," *Neue Schweizer Rund-
    schau,* 1938.
Saat und Frucht. Berlin, 1938.
"The Christian Understanding of Man," *Church, Community and
    State,* Vol. II (pp. 139-178). London, 1938.
Ich glaube an den lebendigen Gott. Zürich, 1940.
"Die Christusbotschaft und der Staat," *Der Grundriss,* 1940.
Offenbarung und Vernunft. Zürich, 1941 (*Revelation and Reason.*
    Philadelphia, 1946).
Glaube und Forschung. Festrede des Rektors, geh. an der 110. *Stift-
    ungsfeier der Universität Zürich,* am 29. April 1943. *In Jahr-
    esbericht 1942/43.*
*Gerechtigkeit. Eine Lehre von der Grundgesetzen der Gesellschafts-
    ordnung.* Zürich, 1943 (*Justice and the Social Order.* New
    York, 1945).
"Wissenschaft und Glaube, Vertrag anl. der Generalversammlung des
    Technischen Vereins Winterthurer." *Neues Winterthurer Tag-
    blatt,* 1944.
Die Lehre vom heiligen Geist. Luzern, 1944.
Die christliche Lehre von Gott, Dogmatik, I. Zürich, 1946 (*The
    Christian Doctrine of God, Dogmatics,* I. Philadelphia, 1950).
Christianity and Civilization, Vol. I, *Foundations* (Gifford Lectures,
    delivered at the University of St. Andrew's). London, 1947.
Christianity and Civilization, Vol. II, *Specific Problems.* London, 1948.
Die christliche Lehre von Schöpfung und Erlösung, Dogmatik, II.
    Zürich, 1950 (*The Christian Doctrine of Creation and Re-
    demption, Dogmatics,* II. Philadelphia, 1952).
The Scandal of Christianity. Philadelphia, 1951.
"The Christian Understanding of Time," *Scottish Journal of Theology,*
    Vol. IV, 1951, pp. 1-12.

"The New Barth," *Scottish Journal of Theology,* Vol. IV, 1951, pp. 123-135.

Das Ewige als Zukunft und Gegenwart. Zürich, 1953 (*Eternal Hope.* London, 1954).

Fraumunster Predigten. Zürich, 1953.

Die Lehre von der Kirche von Glauben und von der Vollendung, Dogmatik, III. Zürich, 1960 (*The Christian Doctrine of the Church, Faith, and the Consummation, Dogmatics,* III. Philadelphia, 1962).

WORKS ON EMIL BRUNNER

Hubbeling, H. G. *Natuur en Genade bij Emil Brunner.* Assen, 1956.

Jewett, Paul King. *Emil Brunner's Concept of Revelation.* London, 1954.

Schrotenboer, Paul G. *A New Apologetics, an Analysis and Appraisal of the Eristic Theology of Emil Brunner.* Kampen, 1955.

Volk, Hermann. *Emil Brunners Lehre von der Ursprungliche Gottebenbildlichkeit des Menschen.* Emsdetten, 1939.

———— *Emil Brunners Lehre von der Sünder.* Munster, 1950.

Volken, Lorenz. *Der Glaube bei Emil Brunner.* Freiburg in der Schweiz, 1947.

5 ROBERT D. KNUDSEN

Rudolf Bultmann

I. BIOGRAPHY[1]

RUDOLF KARL BULTMANN was born on August 20, 1884, in Wiefelstede, in what was then the grand Duchy of Oldenburg. The eldest son of the Evangelical Lutheran minister, Arthur Bultmann, and his wife Helene (née Stern), he came from a family which was close to the Church. On his father's side, his grandfather was a missionary. His grandfather on his mother's side was a pastor in Baden.

Bultmann's early years were spent in the country. From 1892 to 1895 he attended the elementary school in Rastede, the town to which his father had been transferred. From 1895 to 1903 he was a student at the humanistic gymnasium (classical high school) of Oldenburg. There, after 1897, his father was the pastor of the Lamberti church. During his high-school years what especially interested Bultmann, in addition to the study of religion, was the instruction in Greek and the history of German literature. He also eagerly attended the theater and the concerts.

After passing the final examination at the gymnasium in 1903, Bultmann began the study of theology at the University of Tübingen. Upon completing three semesters there, he studied in Berlin for two semesters and finally in Marburg for yet two more. In addition to

Dr. Robert Donald Knudsen is Assistant Professor of Apologetics, Westminster Theological Seminary, Philadelphia. He is the author of *Symbol and Myth in Contemporary Theology*.

1 Bultmann's own short biographical reflections are found in Schubert M. Ogden, ed., *Existence and Faith*: *Shorter Writings of Rudolf Bultmann* (1960).

studying theology, he followed lectures in philosophy and the history of philosophy. In Berlin also he greatly enjoyed the theater, the concerts, and the museums. He himself lists the theological professors to whom he was particularly indebted: at Tübingen, the church historian Karl Müller; at Berlin, the Old Testament scholar Hermann Gunkel and the great historian of Christian dogma Adolf Harnack; at Marburg, the New Testament scholars Adolf Jülicher and Johannes Weiss, and the systematic theologian Wilhelm Herrmann. It was Johannes Weiss who encouraged him to prepare for the doctorate and to qualify as a lecturer in New Testament.

In 1907, however, before entering upon his studies for the doctor's degree, he passed his first theological examination, under the High Consistory in Oldenburg. Here he was a teacher for a year (1906-1907) in the gymnasium. In the summer of 1907 he received a scholarship to Marburg, which made it possible for him to proceed to work toward his degree and his goal of becoming a lecturer in the field of New Testament.

In 1910 Bultmann was awarded the degree of licentiate in theology after writing on a theme proposed by Johannes Weiss, namely, "The Style of Pauline Preaching and the Cynic-Stoic Diatribe." In 1912, upon completion of a research thesis, "The Exegesis of Theodore of Mopsuestia," he qualified as a lecturer in New Testament at Marburg. There he taught as a *Privat-dozent* (roughly the equivalent of an instructor) until the autumn of 1916.

At this time he was called as a *professor extraordinarius* (an assistant professor) to Breslau, where he remained until 1920. Here he was married and had two daughters. Here also he wrote what is probably his most significant work, *The History of the Synoptic Tradition,* which was published in 1921.

In the autumn of 1920 Bultmann was called to Giessen as a full professor, succeeding the famous Wilhelm Bousset. Although he was satisfied with his position, he accepted in 1921 an invitation to return as a full professor to Marburg, the university he regarded as his scientific home. As the successor of his former teacher, Heitmüller, he now received the title of Professor of New Testament and Early Christian History. From this time he remained at Marburg, becoming emeritus in 1951.

At Marburg there was a considerable exchange of ideas among the professors. Marked differences of opinion were expressed within the faculty and by visiting lecturers. Bultmann speaks of the tension between himself and the philosopher of religion Rudolf Otto, who had succeeded Wilhelm Herrmann and who represented a position which Bultmann considered to be irrationalistic. There was also lively discussion during the visits of outside lecturers. Bultmann was strongly attracted to the new so-called dialectical theology. He agreed with it that Christianity was not simply one religion among others but was the response to the Word of God as it encounters man. He himself contributed toward its advancement and shared many of its positions. Although he continued to feel close to Gogarten, he became, as time passed, more and more estranged from Karl Barth, and a visit of Barth to Marburg would stir up excited discussion. Within the Marburg faculty itself there was a lively interchange between the theologians and the philosophers. This, Bultmann writes, was particularly true when the philosopher Martin Heidegger taught at Marburg from 1922 to 1928. Bultmann entered into a particularly close relationship with him and began to draw heavily upon his ideas. It seemed to him that Heidegger's philosophy had a special relevance to the study of the New Testament. Together with Bultmann's professor, Wilhelm Herrmann, Heidegger has had a decisive influence upon Bultmann's thought.

In addition, Bultmann has also drawn heavily from the thought of Søren Kierkegaard. Although he occupies his own distinctive place in theology, Bultmann is within that circle of theologians who, like Barth, Brunner, Niebuhr, Tillich, and Gogarten, are the spiritual heirs of the reaction to idealistic liberalism which was prepared by the literary effort of Kierkegaard in the nineteenth century and which gained a hearing during the Kierkegaard renaissance between the first and the second world wars.

More particularly in his own field of New Testament, Bultmann has been one of the foremost representatives in Germany of the scientific, radical criticism of the Bible. Coming out of the historical-critical school, he co-operated in developing a distinctive approach to the New Testament which is called "form criticism." He has an intimate acquaintance with the New Testament and also with classical literature. He has intensely pursued the study of primitive Christianity, examining its relationship to the Old Testament and Judaism as well as to the religions of its contemporary world.

II. EXPOSITION

THE PROGRAM OF DEMYTHOLOGIZATION

The name of Bultmann is most often linked with his famous program of demythologization. Itself much older, this program began to receive widespread attention during the second world war, when Bultmann published his article, "New Testament and Mythology."[2]

2 This article, which appeared first in 1941, was based on an address delivered

This writing provoked widespread discussion, and the program it set forth has been a focal point of attention, particularly on the European continent. Some believe that this program is indispensable if the Church is to speak to the contemporary world; others hold that it means the destruction of the Christian message. What is this program and what does it entail?

According to Bultmann the message of the New Testament is expressed in mythological terms. Its materials are drawn from the myths of Jewish apocalyptic literature and from the Gnostic myths of redemption. Naturally sharing the world view current in their time, the New Testament writers thought in the framework of a three-level cosmology, a heaven above, an earth beneath, and a hell under the earth. This view takes for granted that nature and human life are influenced by supernatural agents (Satan, demons, angels, God), which can invade and affect the course of nature and history. The New Testament regards history as the battlefield of these super-mundane powers. Its Gospel is also couched in mythological terms. The drama of human salvation unfolds against the background of a celestial history. Salvation is conceived and planned in the eternal counsels of the pre-existent God. A heavenly being is sent to earth in order to accomplish man's salvation. He influences nature, performing miracles which attest and authenticate His heavenly origin. In a sacrificial death, a substitutionary atonement, He overcomes the powers of the demons. In a final triumph He rises from the dead and ascends into heaven. The early Church expected His imminent return on the clouds of heaven. The New Testament views history as proceeding to a literal, cosmic end, an event of the same order as the events of our daily lives, though of much greater proportions. According to Bultmann all these teachings of the Bible and the Church are mythical.

Bultmann's criticism is not piecemeal. It involves the entire framework of the biblical message. The world view of the Bible is mythological and is as such impossible for the modern man honestly to believe.

As a type of thinking characteristic of primitive peoples, mythology has been displaced as a whole by the modern scientific world view. Whatever specific form this modern view may take, it does not allow for the possibility that our world can be invaded by supernatural powers. Worldly processes are controlled by purely immanent forces

---

in the same year at Alpirsbach, Germany, before the Society for Evangelical Theology. The article has been republished as the leading selection in Hans-Werner Bartsch, ed., *Kerygma und Mythos,* I (1948).

and operate according to law. It is impossible for man to assume the uniformity of nature by using modern apparatus like the radio and methods like that of modern medicine and yet honestly to believe in the biblical world view.

Bultmann's negative criticisms arise in part out of his concern with what the Church is to preach to our time. He wants to avoid coming to our generation with the demand that it accept what he believes is an outworn view of the world in which the biblical message has been encapsulated. To demand this belief of it is forced and unnatural. Modern man can accept the biblical world view only by a sacrifice of the intellect.

When one views Bultmann's program of demythologization, however, one must see it in its positive as well as its negative aspects. Bultmann holds that there is a biblical message (*kerygma*) which need not be jettisoned along with the framework in which it is expressed. It can be removed from its mythological setting.

By this Bultmann does not mean that certain mythological accretions should be pared off, leaving as the gospel message a hard core of rational or moral truths. His program does not mean a simple elimination of the thought-world of the New Testament. His program depends upon the idea that there is an alternative to demanding the literal acceptance of the biblical world view or rejecting it out of hand for another world view. The key, he thinks, is to view the New Testament literature, which is thoroughly impregnated with myth, with an eye for the self-understanding of the primitive Christian community expressed in it. This self-understanding is supposed to express the true intent of the biblical writers behind their mythological pattern of thought. The demythologization program has the purpose of setting free this biblical message, which is able to speak to man as he understands himself today.

Bultmann, however, does not regard demythologization as his own private undertaking nor even as something recent. It has been carried out, he thinks, in all so-called periods of enlightenment, in the criticism of myth among the Greeks and more particularly in modern times with the rise of science and the ascendancy of a naturalistic attitude to the world. Even within the myths themselves there is the beginning of demythologization.

With regard to the latter point the thought-world of the New Testament is no exception. The tensions within it give rise to criticism. Bultmann discovers such a contradiction between the ideas of the Virgin Birth and the pre-existence of Christ. Especially significant, he thinks, is the contradiction he discovers between the sovereignty of God and the appeal for human decision.

135

Demythologization within the New Testament appears to some extent in the writings of Paul and thoroughly in the writings of John. The decisive step was taken, Bultmann avers, when Paul declared that the transition from perdition to salvation was not reserved for the time of a final catastrophe but had already taken place in the coming of Jesus Christ. A concern with a literal end is transmuted into the concern for the meaning of the event of Jesus Christ here and now.

Within the mythological framework itself of the New Testament there is, therefore, the suggestion that the true meaning of the myths is not found in their literal (what he calls their "objective") form. This point is of the greatest importance for Bultmann. Myths reflect man's understanding of himself in his world.

Critique of Liberal Demythologization

The twofold orientation of Bultmann's program of demythologization is reflected in his attitude toward the older liberalism. Although his theology has arisen in reaction to liberalism, it is not a return to orthodoxy. Bultmann appreciates the critical spirit which inspired liberalism's own demythologization program. What he criticizes is liberalism's view of the Gospel message.

Liberalism sought to reinterpret the Christian faith, in order to square it with the modern, humanistic view of the world stemming from the Renaissance and the Enlightenment. In a long history of Bible criticism it tried to remove the husk of a primitive, mythological world view in order to retrieve the kernel of moral truth which comprised the message of the historical Jesus. Bultmann does not at all object to these criticisms. On the contrary, he welcomes them as being indispensable to honesty and clarity. If anything, his caveats are even more radical than those of the majority of the liberals. Although it is not the whole of his program, criticism is one of its major pillars.

Bultmann objects, however, to the positive interpretation of the Christian faith which liberalism sought to rescue from the critical flames. In its various forms liberalism believed that it could penetrate beyond the picture of Jesus given by the primitive Church to the real Jesus, the Jesus of history. The religious liberals viewed Jesus as the prophet of a kingdom of moral righteousness. He was the teacher of general human values. His impact upon history was ascribed to the strength of His towering personality. This reconstruction of the Christian message, though difficult, was carried on with the confidence that the methods of modern critical research would eventually bear fruit.

Even within the older liberalism itself Bultmann discovers tendencies which led to its dissolution. One example is the contribution of the New Testament scholar Johannes Weiss. His research convinced him that a purely "historical" Jesus, the teacher of moral truths, could not be disengaged from the supposedly mythological and more particularly the eschatological elements in the Bible. Far from being a disposable wrapper, they belonged essentially to Jesus' teachings. After the labors of Johannes Weiss, Bultmann concludes, it was no longer possible to think of Jesus' message as the expression of general human truths. Jesus' teaching focused on the expectation of a future coming of the Kingdom of God, not by the moral efforts of man but by a "supernatural" incursion of the power of God.

The shift away from the older liberalism cannot be understood, however, in terms of one or another single person or influence. The change of theological insights depended upon a change of mood which resulted in the breakdown of the idealistic philosophy upon which liberalism depended. The older liberalism fell when the general truths in which it thought it could find a transcendent key to the meaning of human existence were declared to be "human, all too human." On this background it is possible to understand why the dialectical theology entered the scene with a definite "no" to everything general. No longer able to discover the key here, it had to look beyond.

Bultmann is confronted on one side by a vanquished idealism. On the other side is a victorious philosophic realism, which brought the transcendent ideals to earth, viewing them as the projection of material human needs. Bultmann acknowledges this victory. He does not attempt to reverse it. Instead, his approach is to disqualify both idealism and realism. They are, he says, both "general." Idealism is general because it finds the key to man's life in general ideals. Realism is general, because it finds the explanation of man's life in general terms, as the expression of some specifiable motivations. Bultmann's answer, like that of the existentialists, is that the key cannot be found in anything general. That is to say, it cannot be located in anything that can be set over against one's self and viewed from outside. The ultimate is not anything general nor anything that can be understood in general. Everything falling within this scope is immanent. The transcendent is beyond.

The repudiation of the older liberalism must be seen therefore against the background of a shift in the idea of transcendence itself, which is most sharply expressed in the transition from idealistic to existentialistic philosophy.

We have now reached the vantage point from which the critique by Bultmann of liberal demythologization can be understood. While

137

he agrees completely with liberalism's negative attitude toward the biblical world view, he objects that the older liberalism failed to rise above what is general. It sought to replace the mythological world view of the Bible with another world view, with an interpretation in general terms of the meaning of man's life. Such a program conflicts, he says, with the contemporary self-understanding of man. Here Bultmann is completely in line with existentialism. With it he maintains that any such general or "cosmical" interest only veils the true nature of man and of the human predicament. The critique extends not only to the interpretation of human existence but also to the interpretation of Jesus Christ. Bultmann's major criticism is that liberalism, remaining on the level of generality, has missed or at least has seriously distorted the biblical message (*kerygma*), which centers in the once-for-all event of Jesus Christ. This is the crux of his often-repeated attack.

A good illustration of Bultmann's position is his attitude toward his former professor, Wilhelm Herrmann. He discovers tendencies in this liberal theologian which go beyond liberalism. These he has taken up into his own theology. Herrmann is lauded for his idea of the purity of faith. Faith is not a state which can be described from outside, nor is it founded on anything outside of itself. Faith is inherently a directedness (an intention) toward something beyond it. Nevertheless, Bultmann thinks, Herrmann has fallen short of his own view; he has not entirely abandoned the standpoint of the older liberalism. He still regards faith as being anchored in something which can be viewed apart from faith. According to Herrmann, Bultmann writes, faith is respect and trust in moral goodness and power. What redeems us is the impressiveness of the person of Jesus. He is the embodiment of personal goodness who impresses man as being a revelation and who induces him to trust in the power of the good over the stubborn realities of life. This moral goodness and power, Bultmann retorts, is a general human possibility. Herrmann has not risen in the last analaysis above the level of general human goodness. With the older liberalism therefore he cannot see the true profile of the once-for-all (*einmalig*) event in Jesus Christ.

GENERAL HISTORY AND TRUE HISTORY

Bultmann's rejection of the older liberalism for having stayed on the level of generality has a positive goal in mind. It is to affirm that the focus of Christian faith is the once-for-all event of Jesus Christ, the act of God which encounters man in the moment of decision. What this positive side of Bultmann's program means, however, depends upon the important distinction between general history and true history. This distinction, a legacy of Kierkegaard's view of time, pervades contemporary theology. It is regarded as a means of criticizing the older liberalism without falling back into what is thought to be an outworn, myth-ridden orthodoxy. This distinction is most important for Bultmann. Here the many strands of his thinking come together. What he once said about the theology of Barth and Gogarten could also be applied to his own thought. What the slogan "dialectical theology" means, he wrote, is, briefly stated, the insight into the true historicality of human existence.[3]

Bultmann uses the word "history" (*Historie*) to refer to the science of history or to the events on the ordinary level of history, which are as such open to investigation by the scientific historian. In the fashion of the modern naturalistic historian, Bultmann views history as a drama of human interaction, the product of human planning and accomplishment, without the intervention of any supernatural agency. It is the domain of the all-penetrating historical understanding, which seeks to grasp the course of events in a neutral, objective way. Any hope of obtaining an over-all view of history, which could disclose its direction and meaning, is however abandoned. Ordinary history is not a source of ultimate values and meanings.

In answer to the ultimate meaninglessness of history, Bultmann does not appeal, as Lessing did, to a super-historical source of meaning, a "timeless truth." Together with the existentialists, Bultmann would regard such an appeal as a disengagement, a flight out of existence. Instead, he vigorously sets forth the existentialistic idea of true historicality (*Geschichtlichkeit*).

Geschichte refers to a level of true occurrence, a decisive time or time of decision. It can be understood only by distinguishing it carefully from both the particular event (on a certain calendar date) of ordinary history and the timeless principle or meaning which is supposed to be above history. For Bultmann, both of these are general, because they are in principle available to anyone provided he can satisfy the proper conditions. Their truth is "objective," true apart from the riskful commitment of the self. Man's existence, on the contrary, is true or concrete history. It is not established beforehand, in effect already decided. It is not given in general, not anywhere and everywhere available. Instead, man is always involved in projecting his possibilities in terms of a particular understanding of himself and his world. What he is depends upon his decisions, in which he may either gain himself or lose himself.

With the existentialists, Bultmann does not wish to discover his final reference point in anything general, that is, in anything that can

---

[3] Rudolph Bultmann, *Glauben und Verstehen*, I (1933), 118.

be set over against the subject and be viewed by it. That was the thrust of his criticism of Herrmann, that the ultimate was found in something that was objectifiable. What can be objectified is for a subject. And the subject can also be viewed from outside. Both subject and object, Bultmann claims, are general. As such they must be distinguished from the true selfhood of man.

In true history, one does not set his world, himself, and the other as objects over against himself as a subject. In the spirit of Martin Heidegger, Bultmann seeks to go beyond this distinction of subject and object. Heidegger has said that the very possibility of making this distinction is dependent upon something more fundamental, one's being-in-the-world. In brief, I do not *have* my being, which I then relate to my world; my being is itself being-in-the-world. I do not exist as an isolated self, which is then related to the other; my being is being-for-the-other. Bultmann has applied this existential thinking to his theology. At the heart of his criticism of generalizing thought is the idea that I am not related to myself as to something outside of myself, for example, an ideal to be attained for a true explanation or understanding of myself; I am myself only in relation to what is absolutely and completely concrete-historical, even as my being is also exhaustively concrete-historical.

Only in the context of this existentialist-inspired battle against generalizing thought can one understand adequately Bultmann's repudiation of the supposedly mythical framework of the proclamation of the New Testament. It is his intent to interpret all of the objectifying, non-concrete-historical elements in the Scriptures, discovering behind them their true intent, the existential self-understanding which is itself part of man's concrete-historical existence.

This struggle has also the positive goal of disclosing the message of the Gospel as Bultmann understands it. As we have pointed out, this message has to do with an event, an event of the peculiar kind that we have described. It is not an event of general history but the once-for-all event of Jesus Christ. To this event, Bultmann says, one is related not by generalizing thought but in faith.

KERYGMA AND FAITH

For Bultmann, as for Kierkegaard, the final reference point for the Christian is what is ultimately concrete-historical, the invasion of the eternal into time in the moment. The proclamation of this event, and not of any true statements about it, is the biblical message which is to be disengaged from the mythical framework which envelopes it.

The event of Jesus Christ is not open to the neutral historical

140

investigator; it is only for faith. What this means for Bultmann cannot be altogether clear at this point. An implication, however, is that the event itself cannot be separated from the reception of the event by the believing individual, but primarily by the believing community, the Church. The Gospels witness more to the faith of the early Church than to any historically verifiable events.

The fact that Bultmann regards the Gospels as a witness to the faith of the early Christian community does not prevent him from asserting that there is a primary stratum of history in the Gospels which biblical criticism should seek to recover. There is now an adequate method, he claims, to distinguish the early strata of tradition concerning Jesus from the later ones. Besides being famed for his program of demythologization, Bultmann is also renowned for his contribution to the development of this method, known as form criticism.

The method of form criticism claims to be able to distinguish certain stylized forms which the primitive Christian community employed in expressing its faith in Jesus Christ. Applying carefully worked-out criteria of development, form criticism believes that it has an adequate means of distinguishing earlier from later Gospel traditions. In this way it uncovers a thin stratum of tradition which it believes is very close to the actual sayings of Jesus, if it is not identical with them.

Whatever historical stratum can be discovered in the biblical writings is, however, of secondary importance to Bultmann. In the entire body of the New Testament, he thinks, it is only an insignificant part. He agrees with Wrede that the Gospels may not be taken seriously as historical records of Christ. Together with Wellhausen, he regards them as the expression of the faith of the early Christian community. So far are they from the historical Jesus that they do not even reflect primarily the faith of the Palestinian church. They are for the greater part the expression of the preaching of the Hellenistic church, which was the earliest preaching to represent Christ as a cult deity whose death and resurrection are the basis of salvation. The message of the Gospels is that of the Christ-myth. Matthew and Luke are more mythical than Mark. In John the mythical has prevailed.

Bultmann is not dismayed at this scepticism. It is not necessary, as the liberal theology supposed, to reconstruct a life of Jesus. He is ready, he says, to let the entire edifice of the quest of the historical Jesus burn down quietly. All that is burned is the imaginative picture drawn by a theology which believed it could base faith upon history. Such reconstructions can let us know only a Christ after the flesh. Concerning such a Christ he has little or no interest.

Bultmann's unconcern rests upon his conviction that it is the faith of the Christian Church and not historical tradition or knowledge that brings it into contact with the saving event in Jesus Christ. What little we can salvage of historical value concerning the life of Jesus portrays him only as a rabbi and a prophet who made certain ethical and eschatological statements. It is faith that sees the event of Jesus Christ in its saving significance.

For Bultmann, this awareness — that the Christ event is for faith — is more important than any calculation of the proportion of historical to non-historical elements in the Scriptures. In fact, on the background of Bultmann's view of *Geschichte,* the entire question of the historical *(historisch)* and the non-historical *(unhistorisch)* becomes of secondary importance. The kerygma indeed refers to an event, but not to an event on the level of ordinary event. The message itself is made up of a tightly knit composite of historical and non-historical elements, so tightly knit that it is irrelevant for faith to discriminate between them.

Part of this message, for instance, concerns the historical event of the crucifixion of Christ. This event is not part of the kerygma, because it occurred on a calendar date of history. As a simple historical event it was, he says, repugnant to the early disciples. It was a scandal. It was only as the historical event of the death of Christ was joined with the triumphant faith in the non-historical resurrection of Christ from the dead that it attained its status as part of the kerygma. In its kerygmatic significance, having to do with man's salvation, it is only for faith. For faith the kerygma is that Jesus has died and is risen again. Bultmann is certain that it is an actual historical occurrence that Jesus was crucified. He is just as sure that Jesus did not rise actually from the dead. In the kerygma there is the intertwining of the historical and the unhistorical. They are both present in what is the object of faith.

The center of attention therefore is the correlation of faith and the kerygma of the saving event in Jesus Christ. In this correlation it is quite impossible to distinguish what is the foundation and what is the superstructure. As there is no objective (subjective) basis for the Christ event, either in a (general) eternal truth or a (general) individual fact, so there is no objective (subjective) ground for faith. Both are concrete-historical. Faith is a total orientation of man's being toward salvation in Christ. At the same time the Christ event is unthinkable apart from the faith of the believing community. It is just as possible to say that the faith produces the event as it is to say that the event produces the faith. The faith and the event are in strict correlation.

Nevertheless, Bultmann wishes to give the event in Christ a kind of priority. Within the correlation it is faith that is oriented to the event of Christ, and not the event to faith. Bultmann expresses this relationship in various ways. He says that faith is possible only from the "time" of Jesus Christ. He also says that the event of Jesus Christ is always coming, always impinging upon the believing community from beyond. He says that faith is openness to Christ.[4]

When Bultmann says that the event is coming and that it is on the boundary, he expresses its eschatological character. His eschatology, however, is also demythologized.

It is clear that no simple event in the past is theologically relevant. It is relevant only as it is taken up in faith. The same is true of the simple event in the future. A known event of the future is as irrelevant to faith as a known event of the past. Simple occurrences in the future or the past, even though they be of overwhelming magnitude, are equally indifferent theologically. To think of the end as a literal event on the plane of ordinary occurrence is itself mythological. Even as there must be a demythologized view of faith, there must also be a demythologized view of eschatology.

ESCHATOLOGY

Bultmann agrees with the New Testament scholars who came to regard eschatology, the doctrine of the last things, as at the heart of Jesus' teachings. Jesus looked to the future. He expected the Kingdom of God to come as a literal end of world history in a cosmic catastrophe.

As we have indicated, however, Bultmann holds that this literal expectation of Jesus and of the primitive Church began very early to be demythologized. This occurred in the thought of Paul and especially in that of John. For Paul the Kingdom was not only a future occurrence but also a present reality. In John the demythologization process has been carried on much further. The Kingdom is regarded even more strongly to be a present reality in the believer's life of faith.

What we have observed about the foundations of Bultmann's thought applies in a telling way to his views on eschatology. It too must be demythologized. For modern man it is impossible to think of the end of the world as Jesus and the primitive Church thought of it. They viewed it in mythological terms as an end catastrophe resulting from the incursion of supernatural powers. Indeed, modern

---

[4] Cf. Rudolf Bultmann, "Neues Testament und Mythologie," *Kerygma und Mythos,* I (1954), 29, 31.

man is more inclined to think of a possible end of the world, especially since the invention of the atom bomb. If he does so, however, this end is the result of purely immanent causes, perhaps the result of an atomic chain reaction or the leveling off of usable energy. Such events would be purely contingent, without any reference to man's eternal destiny.

Demythologized eschatology does not refer to a future supernatural invasion of time nor even to a simple occurrence in the future with a decisive meaning. The idea of the end has become demythologized when it has lost its supposedly objective character altogether and has become contemporaneous, referring to the here and now. Demythologized eschatology is completely existential, having to do with the ultimate meaning of one's existence. It is that which confronts man from beyond himself, bringing him to a decision. It regards the end not as a *finis* but as a horizon of human life which gives it its final perspective.

From what we have said it is clear that Bultmann's distinction between the historical (*Historie*) and the concrete-historical (*Geschichte*) is more basic than any distinction between the past and the future in ordinary time. To speak of the last things as literal events in history which bear upon one's eternal destiny is mythological. It is an objectivizing manner of expression. Eschatology does not have to do with something that will come sometime. Even to speak of the event of Jesus Christ as a simple event of the past is also objectivizing. Together with Herrmann and Kierkegaard, Bultmann holds that the event of Christ must be contemporaneous. Hence the event of Christ is not a simple event in the empirical world; it is eschatological, bearing upon our existence here and now and establishing a horizon of meaning for our entire lives. For Bultmann therefore the simple event of the past or future, even though it be of the greatest magnitude, can have no decisive significance for one's self. Only as it relates concretely to one's decision, only as it is contemporaneous, is it theologically significant.

In his interpretation of the eschatological expectations of Jesus, therefore, Bultmann must distinguish between the outward, objectivizing expression and the inner meaning or intent. Like the liberals of the old school, he must distinguish the kernel from the husk. The difference is that the older liberal thought he could extricate rational and moral truths from the husk of mythical expression. On his part, Bultmann interprets the mythical itself for the concrete-historical, existential truth behind it. In spite of their differences both methods demand a demythologization and reinterpretation of Jesus' sayings.

144

Although Jesus believed that there would be a literal end of history, Bultmann claims that this was not His true intent. According to Jesus, he says, the present has meaning not because there will be an imminent world catastrophe and judgment. Instead, the objectivizing idea of a literal end of history arose because the present was regarded to be filled with meaning. The present was of decisive significance. It was a time of decision.

As we have said, Bultmann regards the event of Jesus Christ to be eschatological because it is decisive. It is transforming. It sets man before a decision. The moment of the appearance of eternity in time is the eschatological "now" because in it falls the decision between life and death. The Church is regarded as the eschatological community because it has its being only in relationship to the once-for-all event of Jesus Christ and the new life which comes to it through him. In the eschatological present one is set before the decision whether to continue in his natural, fallen existence or (what is not within the scope of his own powers) whether he is to be truly open to the future.

SIN

To be in the eschatological present is to be faced with the most basic decision. This is, Bultmann says, not a decision of the will. Such a decision is on the surface of one's life. The intended decision is a basic decision that underlies all other decisions. This is the decision between sin and salvation.

What these distinctions mean can be grasped only in terms of Bultmann's understanding of the New Testament view of man. Here, he says, man is described in terms of body (σῶμα), soul (ψυχή), spirit (πνεῦμα), and flesh (σάρξ). These distinctions do not refer to parts or levels of his make-up. Bultmann rejects a dichotomy (body and soul) or a trichotomy (body, the feeling soul, and the thinking spirit). Instead, each of these terms refers in its own way to man in the totality of his being. Man is body as he exists in a relation, either normal or abnormal, to himself. He is related to himself either in harmony or in inner conflict. He is soul as the specifically human state of being alive, which inheres in him as a striving, willing, and purposing self. *Psyche* refers to the full human life, the natural life of earthly man. As purposefully active he is also one who knows and judges (νοῦς) and one who has conscience (συνείδησις)[5]

All the above designations have a neutral coloring that is replaced by a dark hue in Paul's use of "flesh." Again "flesh" does not refer

[5] See *Theology of the New Testament*, Vol. I (1951), pp. 190ff.

to a part or a layer of man's being. It designates a total orientation, a total self-understanding, of man as a concrete-historical being. It is what is most characteristic of man as he exists in the world. As "flesh" man's entire being is conditioned by his having chosen a false direction and having fallen short of his own true self. In Pauline usage "flesh" has become nearly synonymous with "sin."

In terms of his anthropology Bultmann believes that he can attain a view of human sin and salvation that is deeper than that either of the older liberalism or orthodoxy. That is because his idea of human sinful existence, like the other aspects of his thought, is dominated by the idea of concrete-historicality. One is not a sinner because he has a sinful human nature or because he has committed an act of transgression. Man's sinfulness is a total orientation. His existence before faith is qualified entirely by being a sinner, by being fallen on the world.

The latter expression indicates that Bultmann, like the existentialists in general, ties in the idea of sin with that of objectification. At its heart, sin is the attempt of man to escape his concrete-historicality by seeking objective guarantees. As concrete-historical, one's being is not pre-established. It must always be decided. Sin is the human attempt to escape the uncertainty of one's being by reliance upon what is at hand, upon what is at one's disposal. Man seeks to pre-establish his own life and its values. As such he is oriented to the past. His life is already decided.

This state is a fallen one, because in seeking guarantees man takes himself to be what he really is not. His sinful existence is a veiling of his true selfhood.

The state of being fallen Bultmann takes to be a possibility for man. At the same time it is the elimination of possibility, because one considers his existence in effect to be already completed. One who is fallen can say only that he *has* possibility, not that he, in truly concrete-historical fashion, *is* possibility.

The above is the description of human fallenness as Bultmann conceives it, disengaged from the supposedly mythical conceptions which have surrounded it. It views man in a total self-understanding, a total dependence upon his past. In Bultmann's thinking the past is identical with what is at hand and at one's disposal. In this sense the past can even include the future, insofar as it falls within the scope of human knowing and intending. For as known it is already pre-established and at one's disposal.

Completely mythological, however, is the idea of the fall as a lapse at a certain calendar date of ordinary history. Mythological

146

also is the idea of the fall as the transgression of the law of God. In his natural existence man is already fallen.

Dependent upon his past, man becomes dependent upon the powers of the world. It is these powers which it is possible for him to represent in an objectivizing, mythological way. As powers they are subject to the mythical imagination. They become represented as objectivized, mythological entities. Since they are temporal and transitory, one who is under their sway is fallen on what is ephemeral, on death and anxiety.

It is from this veiling of his true selfhood and from the attempt to establish his own value and worth that man must be saved. It is, Bultmann says, possible for man to gain insight into his condition of being fallen. But of himself he cannot overcome this bondage to the world. The more he seeks to establish his own righteousness, the more he is involved in sinful pretension. Man can overcome the world only from a source that is beyond himself. Salvation is not within the limits of what is at man's disposal; it is a salvation by grace.

SALVATION

What is impossible for man of his own volition becomes actual in an encounter with God's forgiving grace in Jesus Christ. In this encounter one breaks with his dependence upon the past — that is, upon that which is at his disposal — and becomes open to the future. That is, he becomes open to his true self, not as one who has possibilities but as one who *is* the possibility of being and who is always set before decision.

It is only faith that can orient us to the future. Salvation is an attitude of faith. Authentic life is that which lives out of the unseen, that which is not at man's disposal. It gives up all of its self-created securities.

Bultmann does not intend, however, to absolutize faith. Faith is always directed toward the object of faith. Apart from this orientation it would be no faith at all. It is only as one listens to the revelation of the Word of grace that faith exists and the possibility of the future is opened up. The life of salvation is possible in faith in God's grace, that is, in the faith that precisely the invisible, that which comes to man from beyond the scope of his powers of command, means for him not death but life. This grace is forgiving grace; it frees man from the past which holds him in bondage. This faith is faith in Jesus Christ, through whom is made possible the obedience in love which allows one to live authentically in the present.

Openness to the future does not mean that the past is eliminated.

147

Indeed, the past is sinful. It can be in the authentic present, however, as forgiven. Openness to the future means that man is free from the temporality and the ephemerality which imprison him. He is free from death and anxiety. He no longer seeks to establish himself and guarantee his existence.

Authentic life is a complete devotedness. One is completely committed to the forgiving love in Jesus Christ. Devotion to Christ, however, cannot be produced. Faith is not a work. Devotion of faith is possible only in an encounter with God's own devoting love. Only the one who is already loved can love.

The life of faith is not a state or a condition. The encounter with the forgiving grace of Christ is concrete-historical. It must continually be renewed. One is always set afresh before the decision whether he is to be saved or lost, whether he is to be fallen in the world or whether he will grasp the new life of faith in Jesus Christ.

Considering the unbreakable connection which Bultmann sees between faith and the event of Jesus Christ, it is not surprising that this ever-newness also applies to it. Faith in Jesus Christ is not faith in an event that is simply past and finished. The event of Jesus Christ is ever coming, ever impinging upon our present. It is, to use Bultmann's expression, a truly eschatological event. This ever-recurring encounter takes place in the obedient listening to the preaching of the Church, which is the eschatological community.

PROCLAMATION AND THE CHURCH

Bultmann's program of demythologization has one of its roots in his concern for the proclamation of the Church. He was concerned how the witness of the Gospel could relate to contemporary man with his modern self-understanding. There are, however, other and more theological reasons why preaching and the Church are central in Bultmann's thinking. The Church is regarded by him to be the eschatological community. The eschatological event happens within the Church as the Word is preached. Where this moment occurs in the Church there is salvation.

Bultmann's position here again dovetails with what we have observed about concrete history. The Word of God has not come as a once-for-all-event on a particular calendar date of history. It is not an event whose significance touches us as it is passed down by memory and tradition to later generations. It is a continuing thing. There is nothing to stop Bultmann from saying that the event of Jesus Christ, His death and resurrection, happens over and over again in the life of the Church. In fact, this is exactly his position. The event of Christ is event in the preaching of the Church. In preaching,

Jesus comes again. It is as faith is awakened in the Church that Jesus rises from the dead. What has happened in the resurrection occurs in all who believe.

The following are identical: the eschatological proclamation of the Word impinging on the Church, the saving act of Christ, and the resurrection of Christ. The Church is part of the resurrection.

Is there then a true proclamation of the once-for-all events, the life, death, and resurrection of Jesus Christ? Or have these unique events become reflections of the ongoing life of the believing community?

Bultmann certainly does not believe that his position dissolves the events of holy history into the subjective life of the Church. He says that as the content of faith (*quae creditur*) is preached, the event of revelation and salvation occurs. He says, further, that this eschatological event, the presence in the Church of judgment and of life, is not at the Church's disposal but is present only by the revelation of the Spirit of God.

It is important to remember, however, that Bultmann's rejoinder to the charge of subjectivism depends entirely upon his particular view of the structure of faith. Faith is intention. That is, faith is directed to the object of faith and is impossible apart from this directedness. Within the correlation of faith and the event in Jesus Christ, the accent must be on the event.

Whatever truth there may be in this general description of the nature of faith, it is undeniable that Bultmann gives a creative role to the faith of the community and that he regards the Christ event as concrete-historical, in the eschatological present. So great is the place he gives to the believing community that it is possible for him to say that it is not the resurrection which engenders the belief of the early Church but the belief of the Church which gives being to the resurrection. Further, the only event having significance for salvation is the ever-recurring event of Christ in the proclamation of the Church.

Bultmann has not dissolved the Christian faith into supposedly timeless ideal values. He has nevertheless dissolved the once-for-all event of Jesus Christ into a recurring, paradoxical contemporaneity of Jesus Christ in the preaching of the Church. This is indeed a different kind of dissolution but just as effective.

III. EVALUATION

The majority of contemporary theologians view revelation as event. Revelation is a holy history, centering in the event of Jesus Christ. They attack the older liberalism not only for eliminating the once-

149

for-all-ness of the event in Christ but also for denying its true nature as event.

In some respects this emphasis is a wholesome corrective. It is true that God's plan of salvation depends upon a series of events which may be called a holy history. Salvation is not attained by way of a mystical withdrawal into oneself, away from the outside world. Whether in anticipation or in retrospect, faith is oriented to Jesus Christ, who lived, died, and rose again from the dead. It is also true that there is a once-for-all-ness to this revelation. Salvation is the issue of faith in the finished work of Christ. Christ is once for all delivered for our sins, the Just for the unjust, that He might bring us to God. Salvation is not anywhere and everywhere available to all. There is also a "too late," a passing of the day of God's call to the sinner. It is perfectly acceptable to speak of God's revelation thus in dynamic fashion.

As we have observed, however, Bultmann does not simply emphasize revelation as event. His view of revelation depends on a particular view of what a real event is. This understanding, in turn, depends upon the distinction between the historical and the concrete-historical. This distinction, finally, is a legacy of Søren Kierkegaard's idea of the moment filled with eternity. The paramount question is whether the saving event in Jesus Christ is truly understood in these terms or whether they distort it by pressing it into a false mold.

THE CORRELATION OF FAITH AND THE CHRIST EVENT

In Bultmann's thought the correlation of faith and the saving event in Jesus Christ is sharply set in contrast to the ordinary event in history, which is as such open to the historian. That is, the meaning of the saving event in Jesus Christ, in its correlation with faith, is not itself dependent upon an historical foundation. This certainly implies that faith and the Christ event cannot have an adequate ground in history, as the result of a neutral historical investigation. Technically put, they cannot find their legitimation in history. It is clear, however, that Bultmann's position involves more than this. It implies that the saving truths should not be dependent upon genetic questions — for example, concerning the origins of belief in the resurrection of Jesus Christ. The resurrection has meaning for Bultmann only within the correlation of event and faith in the kerygma. In contrast, the event occurring on the purely historical level is contingent. It may not be regarded as having cosmic significance. That is, it may not be thought of as having significance for the "eternal" destiny of man.

Bultmann's framework of thought demands that the correlation of faith and saving event be strictly distinguished from the level of history. A close look at his thinking discloses, however, that his view of the kerygma has embarrassing historical consequences.

Bultmann's Christology appears to be an improvement over that of the older liberalism in important respects. As we have seen, he has helped to form the attitude of the newer biblical criticism, which has more of an eye for the unity of the biblical message. He sees that a supposedly human teacher of ethical truths cannot be disengaged from the portrayal of the supernatural Savior of the world. It is artificial and wrong to attempt to separate out a kernel of moral truth in Jesus' teaching from the husk of an outworn mythical world view. These are bound up with each other, so that more particularly the eschatological teachings of the New Testament have been found to belong essentially to its message.

As we have observed, however, Bultmann holds that there was never a literal fulfillment of whatever kind of these expectations and that there will never be one. Under the pressure of the continued postponement of the end, the Church resorted to a demythologization, which related the future expectations more and more to the eschatological present. Christ was now thought to have come already, being present in the Church in the person of the Holy Spirit.

On the purely historical level, the creative role which Bultmann ascribes to the Christian community runs into difficulty. In an exceedingly short while after the death of Jesus there is supposed to have arisen in the consciousness of the primitive Church a picture of Jesus that was a blend of historical reports and mythological elements drawn from Jewish apocalyptic and Hellenistic cults. The time lapse is, however, far too short to allow for the memory of the Church to be molded by its spiritual environment, in whose thought-forms it is supposed to have expressed its sense of the importance of Jesus. Furthermore, it is difficult to discount the influence of the immediate disciples of Jesus. It has been said that if the method of form criticism were correct the disciples would have had to be translated into heaven immediately after the crucifixion.

In terms of Bultmann's theory the problems surrounding the resurrection of Christ are particularly difficult. As he himself recognizes, the resurrection is most certainly a part of holy history as understood by the Scriptures. Jesus Christ was delivered for our offenses and was raised again for our justification (Rom. 4:25). If the resurrection had not occurred, Paul argues, the witness of the Christians would have become meaningless and they would have been proved to be liars (I Cor. 15:14). The good news of the resurrection of Christ was at the heart of the preaching of the early Church.

What has happened to the resurrection in Bultmann's theology?

Because it would mean an interruption of the natural course of events, a breaking of the chain of cause and effect, a literal resurrection could not have happened. Even if it had occurred as a simple event in the past, it would have no significance of a saving kind for our lives at present. As a simple event, the resurrection would be purely contingent, altogether removed from the sphere of what is relevant to us. The resurrection becomes tied into the proclamation of the early Church as an expression of the constant awakening in its midst of the new life of salvation. It has significance only in terms of the faith of this primitive community. As we have seen, it is the faith of the early Church that gave rise to the resurrection and not the resurrection to the faith of the Church.

Even stressing as he does the creative power of the Church's faith, Bultmann cannot escape the problem of how this central and powerful belief originated. If Christ did not truly rise from the dead and if the story of the resurrection is a myth, how did this myth originate? It would have had to come into being a very short while, perhaps only a few days, after the death of Jesus Christ. This would have involved a very radical change in the thoughts and attitudes of the disciples to their dead master. As Herman Ridderbos says: "To think of this as the mythical formation of the significance (*Bedeutsamkeit*) which the disciples abruptly ascribed to Jesus' crucifixion without any new fact as its basis, a fact which originated outside of themselves, is a postulate which is dictated by Bultmann's concept of reality but which is at the same time absolutely unintelligible from an historical point of view. It is especially incomprehensible if one remembers that this resurrection witness, in the primary sense of an eye witness (compare Acts 1:21, 22ff.), was the starting point and center of the Christian proclamation and formed the foundation of Christian certainty."[6]

From a somewhat different point of view the historical consequences of Bultmann's position are equally puzzling. In terms of his comparative-religions method, one would expect that there would be a foundation in the Jewish or the Greek milieu for the belief in the resurrection. It is precisely at this point, however, that Bultmann's theory runs into profound difficulty. The disciples were Jews; but, as Ridderbos says, " . . . it is an undeniable fact that to Judaism the figure of the dying and resurrected Messiah was entirely alien."[7] There is no point of contact in the current Jewish ideas in which to discover the origin of the belief in Jesus' return from death to life. Yet, some point of contact is required by Bultmann's presuppositions and method.

[6] Herman Ridderbos, *Bultmann* (1960), p. 34 (altered).
[7] *Ibid.*, p. 35.

Such a point might be sought in the Greek conceptions of the dying and rising gods. It is clear, however, that the faith of the Jerusalem Church could not have had its origin in such myths. Before any such invasion of outside influences could have occurred, the early Church was living in the faith that Christ had risen from the dead.

There is a further problem of a psychological nature. If one grants that there was a change of attitude on the part of the disciples from profound discouragement to assurance, how could this new faith have taken the form of a belief in the resurrection? This so-called "myth" is related to an historical person whose death had been experienced three days before. If it is denied that an actual resurrection took place, it is not enough to point by way of explanation to the supposed gullibility of men of this time or to the inadequacy of their conception of the world. It would be necessary to explain the origin of this belief in terms of profound psychological impressions, perhaps hallucinations. It is a psychological puzzle how the Christian proclamation could have been built upon such a foundation.

There are also considerations of a theological nature which relate to Bultmann's view of the correlation of faith and the event in Jesus Christ. Viewed from within the framework of his own theology, these questions far outreach the genetic problems we have already mentioned.

There is indeed a great difficulty in accounting psychologically for the subjective belief of the primitive Church in the resurrection if no actual bodily resurrection took place. It must also be observed that the certainty and power with which the early disciples preached the Gospel of the resurrection depended upon their subjective belief that it had occurred as a matter of fact, as an event of history with a before and an after, involving an empty tomb, various appearances, and eyewitnesses to these appearances. These disciples could not have preached with assurance and yet have delivered up the object of their faith to a view of nature and history that would rule out the possibility of the resurrection's having occurred. It can be objected, of course, that this anomalous situation could not have been that of the disciples, since in their mythological way of thinking they did not yet distinguish between the realm of faith and that of scientific understanding. However proper such a rejoinder might be from within the framework of Bultmann's thought, the same antinomy must apply to anyone who, like Bultmann himself, does make confession of the resurrection while denying from a critical, historical point of view that it ever occurred. This antinomy threatens what Bultmann should be very interested in retaining, the intentional directedness of faith.

Faith depends upon the conviction of the truth of that to which it is directed. It need not be argued at this point whether faith is based upon adequate evidence. The relationship of faith to evidence is complex. All we must ascertain at this juncture is that faith cannot exist side by side with the awareness of the untruth of that in which it is vested. With reference to Bultmann's position, it can be said that faith cannot be maintained in Jesus Christ if at the same time there is the awareness that what his faith refers to is explainable in purely immanent terms, perhaps as the result of profound psychological impressions or even hallucinations. It is not sufficient to object that faith is directed to the truth but not to truth of an objective kind. Such a rebuttal does not at all diminish the force of the observation that in such a dialectical situation the commitment of faith is impossible.

Contemporary theology is not unaware of this problem. It recognizes the fact that the so-called neutral understanding dissolves faith. It is sometimes said that it "de-divinizes" the world. In the thought of some theologians this antinomy is taken up into the structure of faith itself, when the claim is made that faith depends upon a constant purification by the acids of criticism if it is not to be objectified.

Equally difficult problems attach also to Bultmann's view of the saving event in Jesus Christ, particularly with regard to its uniqueness. It is not sufficient to say that Bultmann regards holy history as a chain of events in history which do not have historical analogies as do other historical events. Bultmann agrees with Ernst Troeltsch that the mere recital of events of the past is not history. Historical facts must be seen in an historical nexus. Any fact of history has at least possible historical analogies. It also has a possible immanent historical explanation. If this is the case, the historical fact is purely contingent, having as historical fact no possible relationship to man's eternal destiny. The implication is clear. Even though Bultmann should accept the historicity of the resurrection of Christ and of other biblical miracles, they would, as contingent events of history, still have no cosmic significance. That is to say, they would have no significance for our present life of salvation. They would be swallowed up in the unrelatedness of the brute facts of history.

We must conclude that, in the context of the neutral understanding of history, the event of Jesus Christ is lost in the abyss of the unrelated. Indeed, this unrelatedness need not imply that it, as an historical event, would have no relationship to other events. Any historical event, as we have seen, has at least possible analogies with other events. It would be unrelated in the sense that it could not relate to the center of man's being, to his self. It would have no significance for his here and now except insofar as its historical consequences might figure as an irrational quantity in his situation.

Bultmann rejects the attempt to overcome this contingency by seeking a trans-historical source of meaning and value in a timeless ideal.

He likewise rejects a "historistic" position, which would discover ultimate meaning within the historical process itself. Such a view would be fundamentally mythical. As we have seen, Bultmann attempts a solution in terms of the concrete-historical event of Jesus Christ occurring in the eschatological present. Here, in an antinomic fashion, the uniqueness which is denied as such to any (general) historical event is supposed to characterize the encounter with the saving event in Christ. At the same time, however, this "once-for-all" event is anomalously thought of as recurring in the life of the Church. It occurs again and again in the preaching of the Word and its reception by the believing community.

Indeed, the Church takes a most important place in Bultmann's thinking. It has been said that all of the powers that Bultmann takes from Jesus Christ he gives to the primitive Church, so that its faith is even constitutive of the Gospel message. In his thought the fulcrum has shifted from the events of holy history, rightly conceived, to events in the consciousness of the Church. In reply to the charge of subjectivism Bultmann might point to his effort to maintain the priority of the event in Jesus Christ. It is eschatological, impinging from beyond on the present life of the believer. No one can produce salvation; it is a gift. Nevertheless, Bultmann's position must always provoke the question, whether the events of holy history have not become symbols of the existential experience of the believing community. If so, they have lost their uniqueness and Bultmann has been unmasked as a liberal, with no true place for the saving acts of God.

The above discussion uncovers a dilemma that is acutely felt by contemporary theology. It is involved in the contemporary view of *Geschichte* itself, which tends to disintegrate in either of the two directions it has been devised to avoid. The attempt, on the one hand, to express the significance of Jesus Christ tends to reduce Him to the symbol of something else, either of a timeless ideal or of a human existential experience. The attempt, on the other hand, to do justice to the uniqueness of Christ tends to make him sink into the abyss of the unrelated. To avoid this dilemma, we think, it is necessary to take an altogether different standpoint, forsaking the distinction between history and concrete history and listening more closely to the witness of the Scriptures to Jesus Christ.

THE REVELATION OF JESUS CHRIST

The most sensitive nerve of any theology is its answer to Christ's question, "Who do you say I am?" If Bultmann's answer in terms of the idea of *Geschichte* is inadequate, how can the true profile of Christ be allowed to appear?

Any adequate approach to the question of the identity of Jesus Christ must take into consideration the ongoing revelation of God, and more particularly the witness of Christ Himself. The Bible recognizes the importance of this testimony. Any claim to speak for God, for instance, must be authenticated. In the Old Testament the true prophet is sharply distinguished from the false by the fact that he has received his message from Jehovah. This is authenticated by his prophecy's coming true and by the agreement of his words with the Divine revelation which has been given before (cf. Jer. 28:9 and Deut. 18:21f.). Any event of divine revelation has to be seen in the context of the divine revelation concerning the event.

Jesus thought of Himself as being anticipated in prophecy and confirmed by it. To the Pharisees He gave the advice to search the Scriptures, because they testified of Him (John 5:39). The early Church was also convinced of this connection. It was conscious of preaching nothing else than Moses and the prophets had said (Acts 26:22). Christ chided the Jews for seeking a sign. No sign would be given them, He said, other than the sign of the prophet Jonah. The Son of man would be three days in the bowels of the earth and would rise again (Matt. 12:39f.).

Within the framework of his idea of *Geschichte* Bultmann allows for a correlation of revelation and event. The event of Jesus Christ is identical with the revelation of the significance of the event. At the same time, however, this history is sharply distinguished from the level of ordinary occurrence. Here there is no such correlation. Any event supposed to witness immediately to God is rejected as being mythical and a faith-producing miracle. Under the attack of criticism this gives way to a neutral, secular history where no miracle is possible and where no event can witness to God. In the context of the neutral view there is no God and no revelation.

The effect is sharply to set off event from revelation. Instead of the idea that the events of holy history — for example, the death and resurrection of Christ — have their meaning proclaimed and confirmed in divine prophecy, the events on the level of *Historie* become altogether ambiguous. Christ comes *incognito*. The death of Jesus becomes a complete surd, a brutal end to His disciples' illusions. It comes into the orbit of revelation only paradoxically, by being joined to the unhistorical idea of the resurrection in the faith and proclamation of the early Church. Instead of being interpreted as the shock and discouragement of the disciples, the result of their having misunderstood and forgotten what Christ Himself prophesied concerning His death and resurrection, the death of Jesus is wrenched entirely out of the context of prophetic interpretation and becomes a brute fact, an irrational shattering of the disciples' expectations.

The central issue is whether anything in the life of Christ, of the nature of ordinary or extraordinary event, can be considered in isolation from the witness which the Scriptures give of Him and from His own witness to Himself. It is only in the context of divine prophetic interpretation that the events surrounding Christ were brought into focus. It is useless to consider these facts "in themselves" and to declare that they themselves are ambiguous. They have their place and their meaning in the context of God's revelation, and to see them otherwise is to distort this meaning in unbelief. It is likewise useless to denature these facts by giving them over to a neutral, critical understanding of history and then paradoxically to incorporate them in a holy history within the life of a believing community. The events surrounding Christ, including His miracles, have their meaning in the light of what they were disclosed to be by divine revelation. They establish the identity of Christ as Savior and point to His saving work only in the context of the revelation of what that saving work is.

Indeed, it is true that the Christian faith is not the conclusion of a process of reasoning. It is not the end product of historical research, let us say, faith in a reconstructed Jesus of history. Christianity is indeed a faith; but it is a faith that may not be divorced from the events of holy history culminating in Christ and from the prophetic witness to the meaning of those events. It is only in terms of this prophetic witness, of the Scriptures as a whole and of Christ to Himself, that the true identity and uniqueness of Christ can be understood.

What Moses and the prophets said was that Christ would suffer and that He would be the first to rise from the dead (Acts 26:23). "And without controversy great is the mystery of godliness: God was manifest in the flesh, justified in the Spirit, seen of angels, preached unto the Gentiles, believed on in the world, received up into glory" (I Tim. 3:16).

Whatever mysteries remain in the Word of the Gospel, the ultimate question is whether the Church receives the witness of Christ or puts stumbling blocks in the way by a false confidence in a supposedly neutral science. A most central question is that of ultimate authority.

THE QUESTION OF AUTHORITY

It might be objected that our very method of approach indicates that we have misunderstood Bultmann. According to our interpretation, his theology is dominated by the idea of *Geschichte*. Our approach itself, it might be objected, is abstract and generalizing. Does not Bultmann want to avoid interpreting the Bible in terms of a general principle? Does he not want to let the New Testament speak for itself? Is not his interest theological instead of philosophical?

Bultmann's viewpoint, however, rests upon a specific view of the relationship between philosophy and theology. His idea of concrete, true historical events depends upon a particular view of what an event is. To see the concrete-historical nature of the biblical message one must revise completely his natural way of understanding. This does not mean that a natural, childlike attitude must be regained after having been spoiled by abstract scientific or theological reasoning. What he means is that our ordinary way of looking at things is objectivizing. The natural attitude must be transcended by grace.

The implication of this position is that Bultmann's concrete-historical view of the saving event in Christ and of the *kerygma* cannot be reached or understood apart from a wide sweep of the critical broom to clear the way. His positive program depends upon the negative impact of demythologization. That is recognized by commentators. Bultmann, as we have observed, criticizes the biblical world view in terms of the modern one. Indeed, he does not advocate the modern world view for its own sake. Myths themselves are supposed to indicate in a pre-critical way man's awareness that his world is bounded by powers that are not at his disposal. Nevertheless, as Heinrich Ott correctly observes, Bultmann gives the modern world view a critical function.[3] It is, Bultmann judges, incompatible with this world view for one to believe in any literal way in a host of biblical doctrines.

Anything that is an invasion of the supernatural or anything that "confuses" the saving activity of God with a literal event either past or future is eliminated as being mythological. The result is the denial of an entire list of historic Christian doctrines. Rejected as mythological are the pre-existence of Christ, the sinlessness of Christ, the idea of a sacrificial atonement, the resurrection, the ascension into heaven, the intercession of the exalted Christ, the coming judgment of God, and many other cardinal truths. "Mythological" becomes in this fashion little more than another term for "supernatural."

The evangelical critic of Bultmann must be careful not to criticize him simply in this or that respect — for example, with respect to his denial of the substitutionary atonement — while he lets him go uncriticized with respect to the general structure of his thinking. Bultmann's acceptance or rejection of particular doctrines of the Christian faith is controlled by the general principles with which he works. These involve such a basic transformation of the biblical message that what Bultmann emerges with may not rightly be called Christianity.

[8] Heinrich Ott, *Geschichte und Heilsgeschichte in der Theologie Rudolf Bultmanns* (1955), pp. 36, 115.

His thought is a total reinterpretation of the Gospel in terms of an existentialist-inspired philosophy.

When one enters into discussion with such a theology, the issues are broad and inclusive. Involved is nothing less than the acceptance or rejection of the authority of the Word of God. One cannot have both the Bible and the theology of Bultmann, because Bultmann places the critical reason of man next to the Scriptures. He does not see them truly through the eyes of faith but through the spectacles of rationalistic and naturalistic commitment.

The once-for-all of the Scriptures is altogether different from that of Bultmann. Bultmann holds paradoxically that the once-for-all event of Jesus Christ is an eschatological event happening again and again in the life of the Church. According to the New Testament, the Church is built upon the foundation of the apostles and prophets, Jesus Christ being the chief cornerstone.

IV. BIBLIOGRAPHY

(A nearly complete bibliography of Bultmann's writings to August 1, 1954, may be found in "Veröffentlichungen von Rudolf Bultmann," *Theologische Rundschau,* XXII [1954], 3-20. A supplementary list of German works, of writings available in English, and of books and articles dealing with Bultmann's theology is found in Schubert M. Ogden [ed.], *Existence and Faith: Shorter Writings of Rudolf Bultmann* [Cleveland and New York, 1960, pp. 317-320].)

WORKS BY RUDOLF BULTMANN

Der Stil der paulinischen Predigt und die Kynisch-Stoische Diatribe. Göttingen, 1910.

Die Geschichte der synoptischen Tradition. Göttingen, 1921, 1931[2], 1957[3] (*History of the Synoptic Tradition.* New York and Evanston, 1963).

Jesus (in the collection *Die Unsterblichen*). Berlin, 1926, 1929[2] (*Jesus and the Word.* New York, 1934, 1958[2]).

Glauben und Verstehen. Tübingen: I, 1933; II, 1952 (*Essays, Philosophical and Theological.* London, 1954); III, 1960.

Das Evangelium des Johannes. Göttingen, 1941, 1950[2].

Theologie des Neuen Testaments. Tübingen: I, 1948; II, 1951; III, 1953 (*Theology of the New Testament.* New York: I, 1951; II, 1955).

Das Urchristentum im Rahmen der antiken Religionen. Zürich, 1949 (*Primitive Christianity in Its Contemporary Setting.* London, 1956).

The Presence of Eternity: History and Eschatology. New York, 1957.

Jesus Christ and Mythology. New York, 1958.

Existence and Faith: Shorter Writings of Rudolf Bultmann (edited by Schubert M. Ogden). Cleveland and New York, 1960.

"Gnosis," *Theological Dictionary of the New Testament,* Vol. 1 (edited by Gerhard Kittel). Grand Rapids, 1964.

160

Rudolf Bultmann

Works on and Relating to Rudolf Bultmann

Barth, Karl. *Rudolf Bultmann: Ein Versuch ihn zu Verstehen. Theologische Studien,* Heft 34. Zollikon-Zürich, 1952, 1953[2].

Bartsch, Hans-Werner (ed.). *Kerygma und Mythos.* Hamburg-Volksdorf: I, *Ein theologisches Gespräch,* 1948, 1951[2], 1954[3] (*Kerygma and Myth: A Theological Debate* [a partial translation of *Kerygma und Mythos,* I]. London, 1953); II, *Diskussionen und Stimmen des In- und Auslandes,* 1952; III, *Das Gespräch mit der Philosophie,* 1954; IV, *Die Oekumenische Diskussion,* 1955; V, *Die Diskussion innerhalb der katholischen Theologie,* 1955. (Bultmann contributed essays to Vols. I, II, and III of this work.)

Berkouwer, G. C. *De Algemeene Openbaring.* Kampen, 1951 (*General Revelation.* Grand Rapids, 1955).

Brown, James. *Subject and Object in Modern Theology.* London, 1955.

Brunner, Emil. *Die christliche Lehre von Schöpfung und Erlösung, Dogmatik,* II. Zürich, 1950 (*The Christian Doctrine of Creation and Redemption, Dogmatics,* II. Philadelphia, 1952),

Gogarten, Friedrich. *Demythologizing and History.* London, 1955.

Hartlich, Christian (with Walter Sachs). *Der Ursprung des Mythosbegriffes in der modernen Bibelwissenschaft.* Tübingen, 1952.

Hughes, Philip Edgcumbe. "Myth," *Baker's Dictionary of Theology* (edited by Everett F. Harrison). Grand Rapids, 1960.

———— *Scripture and Myth: An Examination of Rudolf Bultmann's Plea for Demythologization.* London, 1956.

Jaspers, Karl (with Rudolf Bultmann). *Myth and Christianity: An Inquiry into the Possibility of Religion Without Myth.* New York, 1958.

Knudsen, Robert D. *Symbol and Myth in Contemporary Theology, with Special Reference to the Thought of Paul Tillich, Reinhold Niebuhr, and Nicolas Berdyaev.* Unpublished dissertation for the Union Theological Seminary, New York, 1952, 1963[2]

Macquarrie, John. *An Existentialist Theology: A Comparison of Heidegger and Bultmann.* London, 1955, 1960[2].

———— *The Scope of Demythologizing: Bultmann and His Critics.* London, 1960.

Malevez, Leopold. *Le message chrétien et le mythe.* Brussels, 1954. (*The Christian Message and Myth: The Theology of Rudolf Bultmann.* London, 1958).

Marlé, René. *Bultmann et l'interprétation du Nouveau Testament.* Paris, n.d.

Miegge, Giovanni. *Gospel and Myth in the Thought of Rudolf Bultmann.* Richmond, 1960.

Niebuhr, Richard R. *Resurrection and Historical Reason: A Study of Theological Method.* New York, 1957.

Noller, Gerhard. *Sein und Existenz: Die Überwindung des Subjekt-Objectschemas in der Philosophie Heideggers und in der Theologie der Entmythologisierung.* München, 1962.

Ott, Heinrich. *Geschichte und Heilsgeschichte in der Theologie Rudolf Bultmanns.* Tübingen, 1955.

Ridderbos, Herman. *Bultmann (Modern Thinkers Series,* edited by David H. Freeman). Philadelphia, 1960.

———— *Heilsgeschiedenis en Heilige Schrift van het Nieuwe Testament: het gezag van het Nieuwe Testament.* Kampen, 1955.

———— *Paul and Jesus: Origin and General Characteristics of Paul's Preaching of Christ.* Philadelphia, 1958.

Robinson, James M. (with John B. Cobb, Jr.). *The Later Heidegger and Theology. New Frontiers in Theology: Discussions among German and American Theologians,* I. New York and Evanston, 1963.

———— *A New Quest of the Historical Jesus.* Naperville (Illinois), 1959.

Schnübbe, Otto, *Der Existenzbegriff in der Theologie Rudolf Bultmanns.* Göttingen, 1959.

Stonehouse, Ned B. *Origins of the Synoptic Gospels: Some Basic Questions.* Grand Rapids, 1963.

———— "Rudolf Bultmann's Jesus," *Paul Before the Areopagus and Other New Testament Studies.* London, 1957.

Theunis, Franz. *Offenbarung und Glaube bei Rudolf Bultmann. Ergänzung zu Kerygma und Mythos V.* Hamburg-Volksdorf, 1960.

Wingren, Gustaf. *Theology in Conflict: Nygren — Barth — Bultmann.* Philadelphia, 1958.

162

6 DAVID H. WALLACE

Oscar Cullmann

I. BIOGRAPHY

Oscar Cullmann was born on February 25, 1902, at a critical juncture of theological eras, for the turn of the century witnessed the full flowering of classical German liberalism which was to be followed after two shattering wars by a radical shift in the cultural and theological tides of this century. This prominent New Testament exegete, theologian, and historian of the early Church was to play a significant role in the change in the theological scene, for in him there is seen the evolution from liberalism to the present prestige which biblical theology enjoys.

Strasbourg, the city of his birth and early years, is a magnificent cathedral and university center of Alsace which at the time, even though it lies to the west of the Rhine, belonged to Germany. Although Strasbourg had come under German political control in 1871, it retained its basic French character, a fact which affected the decision to return Alsace to French sovereignty in 1919. Cullmann's home was in lower (northern) Alsace, which is about half Protestant in religious loyalties, whereas upper Alsace is predominantly Roman Catholic. About 70 per cent of the inhabitants of Alsace speak French, and an Alsatian dialect is also spoken which is not greatly different from the German spoken in Basel, some ninety miles to the south. In this context Cullmann grew up speaking both French and German as his native tongues. The Protestant tradition in Alsace provides the back-

Dr. David H. Wallace is Professor of Biblical Theology, California Baptist Theological Seminary, Covina, California. His writings include a commentary on the Epistle of Jude.

ground for his Lutheran theology, and it may partially explain his interest in ecumenicity.

Cullmann's early schooling was received in Strasbourg, which then was under the influence of German· theological teachers who were from Württemberg.[1] When he was only sixteen he read Schleiermacher's famous *Addresses on Religion,* which served to confirm in him the current theological liberalism of his day.

Having more interest in theology as an academic discipline than in the parish ministry, Cullmann enrolled in the University of Strasbourg (founded in 1566) to study theology and classical philology. In the course of his studies the young theological student came under the teaching influence of W. Baldensperger, and during this time he also read A. Schweitzer's *The Quest of the Historical Jesus,* which exposed, to him, the failure both of the old orthodoxy and the "prevailing currents of philosophy" as reliable interpretative schemes for understanding the New Testament.[2] At Strasbourg he began to develop an interest in form criticism (*Formgeschichte*) as a highly useful method of reconstruction of New Testament history, and in 1925 he wrote his first published article on this problem.[3] Now he saw that a part of liberalism's weakness lay in demanding that the New Testament be understood in the language and thought patterns of a dominant philosophy, a method which inevitably led to the suppression or distortion of the spontaneous message of the New Testament.

Following his graduation from Strasbourg, with a baccalaureate degree in theology, in 1924, Cullmann went on to become an instructor in Greek and German at the École des Batignolles in Paris, and he concurrently took up studies at the Sorbonne under M. Goguel, A. Lods, and C. Guignebert, along with work under A. Loisy at the École des Hautes-Études. "That year in this extremely stimulating intellectual center was the most fruitful in my whole apprenticeship."[4] While these men of great learning did not share Cullmann's enthusiasm for form criticism, he nevertheless learned much from them.

Cullmann returned to Strasbourg in 1926 to become director of studies at the theological seminary (Thomasstift) and also soon thereafter taught Greek in the university; one of his predecessors in this position was Albert Schweitzer. During this period of his life he

---

[1] O. Cullmann, "An Autobiographical Sketch" (translated by T. N. Rice from *Lehre und Forschung an der Universität Basel zur Zeit der Feier ihres fünfhundertjährigen bestehens* [1960], pp. ˙24-28), *Scottish Journal of Theology,* Vol. XIV, No. 3 (Sept., 1961), pp. 228f., hereinafter cited as "Sketch."

[2] *Ibid.,* p. 229.

[3] "Les récentes études sur la formation de la tradition évangélique," *Revue d'histoire et de philosophie religieuses,* Vol. V (1925), pp. 459-477, 564-579.

[4] "Sketch," p. 230.

launched into an investigation of the Pseudo-Clementine literature, an interest which eventually led to the publication of an important book.[5] This research was to bear fruit in many of his subsequent books and articles, and the conclusions he reached have been supported by the texts of the Dead Sea Scrolls. In these early years he had also given consideration to the exegetical method of Karl Barth, whose significance in the field of Christian dogmatics was already being recognized. Cullmann's success as a teacher and scholar at Strasbourg was crowned by his appointment as Professor of New Testament in 1930. In this post he was a colleague of Jean Héring and W. Seston, and he enlarged his field of inquiry in patristic studies and history of dogma so that he took over the chair of Ancient Church History when Seston departed for Paris.

Because of his established competence in the two fields of New Testament and early church history, Cullmann was called in 1938 to Basel as successor to E. Vischer. He states that it was difficult to leave his native city of Strasbourg, but the appeal of a new and vigorous theological and academic climate was sufficient to draw him to the ancient university at Basel.[6] This move signaled the beginning of his productive and lengthy Basel career in the combined chairs of New Testament and church history, a post he fills to the present with great erudition and distinction. In large measure because of his reputation, Basel University has become a center of theological research, not only for European scholars, but for British and American students as well.

Basel was attractive to Cullmann not only because of the unusual arrangement of his chair of New Testament and patristics, but also because of the geographical benefits which lay to hand. Being in the center of Western Europe, Basel is close to Germany, France, Italy, and Austria, and even Scandinavia and Britain are not remote. This mixture of ideas and traditions is enhanced by Basel's long-standing humanist heritage. It was inevitable that Cullmann and Barth should find much in common, especially in view of their unified opposition to Bultmann and the existentialist school in Germany.

While maintaining his work at Basel, Cullmann was concurrently invited to be the successor to his illustrious teachers at the École des Hautes-Études in Paris, a post which brought him into useful contact with many Roman Catholic theologians. In Paris he holds three academic posts. In 1949 he was appointed Professor of the History of

---

[5] *Le problème littéraire et historique du roman pseudo-clémentin. Étude sur le rapport entre le gnosticisme et le judéochristianisme — Études d'histoire et de philosophie religieuses*, 23 (1930).

[6] "Sketch," p. 231.

Early Christianity in the École des Hautes-Études, and in 1950 he was made Professor of New Testament in the Faculté Libre de Théologie Protestant, and finally in 1953 was named Professor of Early Christianity in the philosophy faculty of the Sorbonne. In subsequent years he has also been lecturer at the Waldensian Seminary in Rome, thereby extending his academic influence in three main cities of Europe. In 1954, 1959, and again in 1964 he came to the United States, where he lectured at many leading seminaries and universities. In 1962 and 1964 he participated as a Protestant observer at the Second Vatican Council in Rome. He regarded this Council's activities as fruitful for eventual Christian unity, but also warned against illusory expectations.

The esteem, respect, and affection in which Professor Cullmann is held by his New Testament colleagues on both sides of the Atlantic is indicated by the publication of a *Freundesgabe,* edited by W. C. van Unnik, and entitled *Neotestamentica et Patristica.* Containing 29 technical articles on New Testament and patristic subjects, written by Protestants and Roman Catholics, French, German, Swiss, British, Dutch, Scandinavian, and American scholars, it was dedicated to Professor Cullmann upon the occasion of his 60th birthday in 1962.[7]

Professor Cullmann's theological writings commenced in 1925 and grew in an increasing volume of articles, monographs, and books covering an amazing variety of New Testament and patristic studies. His works are to be found in French, German, English, Italian, Spanish, Dutch, Japanese, Icelandic, Hungarian, and Swedish, a fact which gives evidence of his influence not only in contemporary Western theology, but also in the rapidly developing Christian theological interest in the Orient. For purposes of classification and analysis Cullmann's contributions will be reduced to four categories as follows: Biblical Theology, Patristics, Biblical Criticism, and Ecumenics. These four areas reckon with all his major monographs and books as well as numerous journal articles. It is readily apparent that this classification is quite arbitrary, for many of his writings could be placed in two or more of these categories. Moreover, this arrangement is not exhaustive of all his writings; he has written articles and short commentaries which stand apart from these four fields. Limitations of space preclude a discussion of his research on the Dead Sea manuscripts, the new Egyptian Gnostic Gospel discoveries, and other matters.

---

[7] In addition a *Programmschrift,* entitled *Oikonomia: Heilsgeschichte als Thema der Theologie,* edited by Felix Christ, was published in 1967 honoring Cullmann's 65th birthday.

II. EXPOSITION

BIBLICAL THEOLOGY

It is a commonplace in contemporary theology to associate the concept of the "history of salvation" (*Heilsgeschichte*) with the work of Oscar Cullmann. Although neither the idea nor the expression is directly traceable to Cullmann,[8] he is responsible for elaborating upon the studies of Hofmann and Schlatter so as to elevate and fix this as a ruling principle of interpretation of the New Testament. In 1941 he wrote on the problem of the Lordship of Christ and the Church,[9] and the same year saw the publication of an essay on eschatology and its relationship to the Christian mission.[10] These two writings were followed in 1943 by two more publications, one taking up the theology of the Parousia, a subject which would not have received so favorable a hearing fifty years earlier,[11] and another a monograph on primitive Christian confessions.[12] In these articles there appears a basic theological principle of the history of divine salvation, a principle which was worked out in great exegetical and theological detail in his important book *Christus und die Zeit*,[13] which was published in 1946. The impact of this book is of such magnitude that A. M. Hunter speaks for many if not most contemporary scholars when he classes it with the six most important books in recent decades,[14] and it seems reasonable to assert that his judgment still stands today.

Christ and Time is an examination of the underlying basis of the

[8] Cf. K. G. Steck, "Die Idee der Heilsgeschichte. Hofmann-Schlatter-Cullmann," *Theologische Studien*, 56 (1959).

[9] "Königsherrschaft Christi und Kirche im Neuen Testament," *Theologische Studien* 10 (1941). The English translation by S. Godman appears in *The Early Church* (1956), pp. 103-137.

[10] "Eschatologie und Mission im Neuen Testament," *Evangelisches Missionsmagazin*, 85, pp. 98-108. This appeared in English as "Eschatology and Missions in the New Testament" (translated by O. Wyon) in *The Background of the New Testament and its Eschatology*, edited by W. D. Davies and D. Daube (1956), pp. 409-421, and also in *The Theology of the Christian Mission*, edited by G. H. Anderson (1961), pp. 42-54.

[11] "Die Hoffnung der Kirche auf die Wiederkunft Christi," *Verhandlungen des Schweizerischen Reformierten Pfarrervereins*, pp. 26-50. An English translation was made by S. Godman which appeared in *The Early Church*, edited by A. J. B. Higgins (1956), pp. 141-162.

[12] "Les premières confessions de foi chrétiennes," *Cahiers de la Revue d'histoire et de philosophie religieuses*, 30. J. K. S. Reid prepared an English translation of this work under the title *The Earliest Christian Confessions* (1949).

[13] The English translation was made by F. V. Filson and published as *Christ and Time* in 1951. In 1962 a third edition was published with a new introductory chapter.

[14] *Interpreting the New Testament* 1900-1950 (1951), pp. 126f.

theology of the New Testament, indeed of the entire Bible, and this positive effort was shaped by the theological influences which prevailed at the turn of this century. Albert Schweitzer, Rudolf Bultmann, and Karl Barth are the three principal theologians who affected Cullmann's movement of thought. Schweitzer is correct in restoring eschatology to its rightful place in the *kerygma,* a truth not grasped by the classical liberalism of Harnack. Bultmann's pioneer work in form criticism is acknowledged as an attempt to reconstruct the historical situation of the primitive Church, and Barth's emphasis upon a Christocentric dogmatic understanding of the New Testament is indispensable. But Cullmann claims that these three men have allowed alien philosophical notions to corrupt their grasp of the spontaneous and independent message of the New Testament. The impulse to distinguish between the accidental and essential elements of the message of the New Testament is arbitrary and naive because it prejudices the ability of the New Testament to be understood on its own terms.

Proceeding upon the assumption that history and time are "of the essence" of the New Testament message, a position directly opposed to that of Bultmann and the existentialist school, Cullmann commences his case by an examination of the key words expressive of time: day, hour, season, time, age, now, today. Of special significance are the words καιρός, a point of time, and αἰών, a duration or extent of time, and out of these facts emerges a biblical concept of time and history. Whereas in Greek thought time was considered to be cyclical, the Bible presents time as both linear and telic. History begins with creation, moves through a succession of redemptively decisive events (καιροί), and is to conclude with the eventual consummation of all things. Therefore history is central to the biblical idea of salvation, for time is the arena where God acts to accomplish man's redemption. The succession of individual saving-events constitutes the biblical time line, or pattern of *Heilsgeschichte,* which might also be called the "history of revelation" (*Offenbarungsgeschichte*).

Implicit in this understanding of time is the rejection of the distinction between time and eternity, and it is over this question that Cullmann challenges Barth, in whose writings he finds "the last traces of a philosophical and non-biblical statement."[15] Eternity is not a qualitatively different entity, but is rather simply unending time, or an infinite series of ages (αἰῶνες τῶν αἰώνων). God is not timeless, nor does He exist in some kind of metaphysically paralyzed state, but the biblical emphasis is rather upon His sovereignty over time which is God's creation and possession.

[15] *Christ and Time* (1951), p. 60, n. 14.

168

The specifically Christian understanding of time and history exhibited in the New Testament is defined by the place of Jesus Christ in redemptive history. Without hestitation the New Testament affirms that the Incarnation or "Christ event" is the midpoint, qualitatively considered, of the ages of history. Even the Jew looked to the coming of a Messiah as signaling the center of history after which the glories of the "Age to Come" would be introduced. Christianity affirmed that the Messiah was Jesus of Nazareth and that in Him the New Age did in fact begin. It is here that Cullmann re-examines the temporal implications of eschatology. Traditionally, eschatology has been assigned to those events and doctrines which relate to the Parousia, but Cullmann understands it to embrace all saving events beginning with the Incarnation and concluding with the Parousia. Seen thus, all New Testament events and all subsequent church history are by definition eschatological. In Cullmann's well-known D-Day analogy, Christ is shown to have marked the beginning of the end.

Contrary to the Judaistic pattern of eschatology, the Christian pattern shows that the blessings of the Age to Come are introduced and are seminally present in the Advent of Christ, but their completion and consummation await the Parousia when the Kingdom of God will be fully present with all its power and glory. This means that the Church exists in an interim period in the final phase of the divine plan of redemption. "The hope of the final victory is so much the more vivid because of the unshakably firm conviction that the battle that decides the victory has already taken place."[16]

So this view of redemptive history conceives of a narrow stream within the confines and movement of the larger stream of total history. Redemptive history is distinct but inseparable from total general history. However, there is no empirical proof of this notion of history apart from the consistent witness of the Bible, and therefore it is an article of faith and not logic or metaphysics. To a Roman soldier the crucifixion of Jesus of Nazareth meant the death of a troublesome Jewish prophet, but to the eyes of faith it marks the climax of God's redemptive actions in history for mankind. Faith therefore is imperative for a faithful exegesis of the New Testament. Cullmann's insistence upon time as essential to the New Testament kerygma separates his thought from that of Bultmann, who insists that time is only a framework or an element of myth which must be dismissed in order to ascertain the inner truth of the Gospel. Moreover, Cullmann's exegesis is to be distinguished from that of A. Schweitzer and his followers, Martin Werner, W. Michaelis, and Fritz Buri, in that New Testament eschatology is to be reckoned in terms of the historical centrality of

---

[16] *Ibid.,* p. 87.

Christ. That is, the Kingdom did come in the Christ-event, whereas the Schweitzer school casts it wholly into the future. Lastly, Cullmann's book serves more as a corrective to Barth's Hellenistic ideas of time rather than as an attack.

It could be argued that Cullmann's work on the biblical idea of time and history was penultimate to his real goal, which is the New Testament idea of Christ. The appearance of his very important *Die Christologie des Neuen Testaments*[17] in 1957 was preceded by numerous articles in learned European journals touching on various aspects of the subject. This work gathers together the text of the New Testament and the scheme of *Heilsgeschichte*. The work is defended as primarily an exegetical study which implies adherence to the philological-historical method. By implication this is a rejection of Bultmann's attempt to explain Christology in the language of Heidegger.

Cullmann opens his subject by posing the christological problem of the New Testament. Simply stated it is "Who is Jesus Christ?" The New Testament addresses itself to this fundamental and intensely practical question by reflecting the self-estimate of Christ and the estimate of Him in and by the primitive Christian community. This reflection is kerygmatic and confessional rather than formal and metaphysical. The answer to the question is seen in the collection of titles which Jesus either took to himself or which were assigned to him by the apostolic churches. Form criticism is deliberately adopted as the method by which the author uncovers "layers" or strata of tradition about these confessions. The competent New Testament scholar does not have to be motivated by historical skepticism, but he proceeds with the assumption that the New Testament documents are both confessional *and* historical.

The titles of Jesus are regarded as theologically freighted statements which contain no conscious distinction between person and work. That is, they proceeded from a dynamic, not a philosophically analytical, situation in the mind of Jesus and the early Church. Cullmann argues with great cogency that the Gospels disclose the mind of Jesus, details of his self-consciousness and sense of mission — an idea which is anathema to the existentialist form critics of the Bultmann school. Since these titles contemplate the work of Christ as powerfully as His person, it follows that the theology of the Atonement resides implicitly in some of them. Many other aspects of the work of Christ are involved in these titles: prophecy, intercession, creation, rule, and redemption are apparent implicitly or explicitly.

Cullmann discriminates among all the names and titles ascribed to

---

[17] This was published in an English translation (S. C. Guthrie and C. A. M. Hall) in 1959 with the title *The Christology of the New Testament*.

Jesus Christ in the New Testament in order to select only those which address themselves in specific answer to the fundamental question: Who is Jesus Christ? Thus, for example, the title "physician" is not considered for the simple reason that there were other healers in Judah; the same principle affects rabbi, judge, shepherd, *et al.* Out of all these titles Cullmann selects ten which uniquely and specifically answer the christological question, and he classifies them into four categories: (1) titles relating to the earthly work of Christ include Prophet, Servant of the Lord, and High Priest; (2) those relating to the future work of Jesus are Messiah and Son of Man; (3) those which point to his present work are Lord and Savior; (4) titles referring to his pre-existence are Word, Son of God, and God.

His conclusion to this study is that *Heilsgeschichte* exposes the development of the Christology of the early Church, and the older approach of imposing a dogmatic scheme upon the data of the New Testament is deficient.[18]

In 1948 Cullmann's essay on Christian baptism was published[19] and it proved so vigorous a statement of this vexatious issue that it was translated into French, English, Swedish, and Icelandic in that same year. The English translation by J. K. S. Reid became the first monograph in the well known "Studies in Biblical Theology" series currently edited by C. F. D. Moule, J. Barr, F. V. Filson, and G. E. Wright.

As in the case of other monographs and books, Cullmann's essay on baptism was preceded by several articles in European journals. The occasion for writing this work on baptism was to defend pedobaptism in the face of an attack against it by Karl Barth.[20] Cullmann points out that baptism did not originate with Jesus, but its distinctively Christian meaning is attributed to Him. However, Christian baptism became possible only after the death and resurrection of Jesus, for His baptism at the hands of John was anticipatory of the Cross. Cullmann refers to the Cross as the occasion of Jesus' "general" baptism,[21] by which he means that the passion of Christ is for all people; Jesus' solidarity with His whole people is demonstrated in this baptism through death and resurrection.

Cullmann stresses that Jesus' Servant role is cognate with this general baptism in that Jesus' baptism is for all men, and its validity exists

---

18 "Therefore all Christology is *Heilsgeschichte,* and all *Heilsgeschichte* is Christology," *ibid., * p. 326.

19 *Die Tauflehre des Neuen Testaments — Erwachsenen und Kindertaufe.*

20 Cf. K. Barth, *Die Kirchliche Lehre von der Taufe;* see for a similarly developed thesis F. J. Leenhardt, *Le baptême chrétien, son origine, sa signification.*

21 *Baptism in the New Testament (Studies in Biblical Theology, * 1 [1950]), pp. 19f.

independently of individual responses of faith. Barth's position is contrary to this, for he says that faith is the necessary precondition to baptism. According to Cullmann, Christ's baptism affects all men, but he preserves the necessity of individual baptism by understanding it as the external sign of the individual's participation in the body of Christ, and an analogy is adduced in the case of a child who acquires citizenship in a given country even though his parents are foreign-born. Faith follows and does not precede baptism, and this justifies baptism of infants who are not conscious of its meaning

Finally, Cullmann understands Colossians 2:11ff. to mean that baptism is the fulfillment and replacement of the Old Testament rite of circumcision, and that after Pentecost baptism expressed acceptance into the Covenant people (circumcision) and cleansing from sin (proselyte baptism). He concludes this study by affirming that both infant and adult baptism have equal biblical attestation, but "the baptism of adults, whose parents at their birth were already believing Christians, is not demonstrable."[22]

The year 1956 witnessed the publication of two further contributions to contemporary biblical theology: *Der Staat im Neuen Testament,*[23] and an article, written for the *Festschrift* in celebration of Barth's seventieth birthday and entitled *Unsterblichkeit der Seele und Auferstehung der Toten: Das Zeugnis des Neuen Testaments,* which also was translated into several languages.[24] Cullmann's treatise on the nature of the secular state grew out of the welter of Church-State relations in Europe at the time of the Second World War, coupled with the larger concern for understanding the doctrine of the New Testament as it applies to every Christian in every age. A tension exists in the relationship between the Church and the world; the Church is an eschatological community which happens also to live in this present age. This tension is traceable to the ministry of Jesus Himself, who came to introduce the Kingdom of God into a world colored by the resistance of zealot Jews against the Roman State. Thus a problem emerges in the mission of Jesus which is classical and typical for all generations of the Church.

The civil State as a part of the present age is therefore distinct from the coming Kingdom which is future in its consummation. Jesus

---

[22] *Ibid.,* p. 70.

[23] This was translated into French, Swedish, Italian and English; the English translation was done by F. V. Filson under the title *The State in the New Testament* (1961).

[24] The English version was given by Prof. Cullmann as the Ingersoll Lectureship at Harvard Divinity School and was published under the title *Immortality of the Soul and Resurrection of the Dead? The Witness of the New Testament* (1958).

taught that His followers have a duty to render to the State its due, and they are not to oppose the State unless it deifies itself by requiring what rightfully belongs to God alone. Jesus made no precise definitions concerning what is specifically Caesar's and what is God's. He acknowledged the rightness of much Jewish feeling against the Roman State, for it could never be a substitute for the reign of God, but He opposed the temper of the zealots on the ground that their program called for a new totalitarianism which was potentially even more venal than the Roman State because the zealots readily identified the aim of their vision with the Kingdom of God. The Kingdom of God, according to Jesus, cannot coincide with the zealot's scheme for two reasons: the Kingdom is of divine, not human, origin, and it is future and not wholly realizable in the present.

Having extracted the teaching of Jesus on this issue, Cullmann analyzes how Paul and the Apocalypse treat the subject. The thought of Paul in Romans 13 is critical, and I Corinthians 6:1ff. and 2:8 fill in details, all of which "taken together, furnish a uniform picture, which coincides astonishingly with Jesus' conception of the State."[25] The state is not a divine instrument, but it is an element of God's provisional arrangement, and Christians are therefore subject to it. The Apocalypse addresses one side of this issue: the self-apotheosis of the State. Emperor-worship stands in unequivocal and direct conflict with the Christian's duty to God, and the Christian must oppose it even upon pain of death. This opposition is not expressed by means of the sword, but rather by perseverance in proclaiming the Gospel, and by persistent refusal to worship anyone but God. Cullmann's study closes with an appended excursus on the ἐξουσίαι in Romans 13:1 in which he argues that the word ambivalently points to angelic powers and to the civil State. This he concedes as only an hypothesis, but invokes philology, Jewish ideas, and general New Testament theology in support.

Just as Greek ideas about time and eternity need to be expunged in order to recover the thought of the primitive Christian community, so also does the New Testament idea of resurrection need to be freed from the shackles which Plato has placed on much current Christian thought. Cullmann took the occasion of the Ingersoll Lectureship on the Immortality of Man at Harvard University (April, 1955) to pursue this theme which he subsequently restated in the Barth *Festschrift*.[26] Much sentimentalism and religious philosophy have combined with Greek idealism on this subject of life after death with the result that the Christian message has been submerged. "I Corinthians has been

[25] *The State in the New Testament* (1961), p. 64.
[26] Cf. "Unsterblichkeit der Seele und Auferstehung der Toten. Das Zeugnis des Neuen Testaments," *Theologische Zeitschrift,* 12 (March-April, 1956), 126f.

sacrificed for the *Phaedo*,"[27] and the solution must be a recovery of Christian theology and faith by exegesis of the text of the New Testament.

To Socrates, death was a friendly door to the continuing life of the soul, which does not perish; but to Jesus Christ death is the last enemy of man and as such is real, and to be dreaded, for it has its sting. However, without death there can be no triumph over death, and no subsequent resurrection, for resurrection does not mean continuation of life in the absence of death, but rather it points to a positive recreation of life after death. It is because of sin universally present in the race that death comes to all men. Both sin and death are contrary to the intention of God who wills life for us. In the resurrection of Christ, God defeated death and opened up the possibility of life in the New Age, and the resurrection body is a sign and part of the new creation. This truth rests upon the biblical idea of man as body-soul, and specifically rejects the Hellenistic notion of the immortality of the soul and the inherently evil nature of the material body.

Cullmann concludes that Christians who die participate in the victory of Christ over death, but they must await the End Time in order to receive their full inheritance, which includes a recreated spiritual body. Such persons are asleep, but they also, because of the Holy Spirit, enjoy a "special proximity" to Christ who will clothe their "nakedness" at the Last Day with a body like His own.

PATRISTICS

Cullmann's early interest in patristics led him to an investigation of the Pseudo-Clementine literature, which is in two parts, and is basically a form of Christian romance or novel. *The Ten Books of Recognitions,* which are extant in a Latin translation by Rufinus, contain the story of the family affairs of Clement, who is alleged to be the son of an imperial Roman family. Owing to misfortunes the family is scattered, but the burden of the work is really the sermons of Peter, who is responsible for reuniting the family of Clement. The second main part of this literature is the *Twenty Homilies* which relate the discourses of Peter while he accompanied Clement; these sermons are cast in the form of debates of Peter with Simon Magus, and it is the doctrines in these sermons that are the center of interest in the literature.

Despite the obvious pseudonymity of these documents, they are of interest to patristic scholars because they reveal the developments of thought in the third and fourth centuries among certain heretical

---

[27] "Immortality of the Soul or Resurrection of the Dead?" (1955), p. 8.

sects within the larger confines of Christianity. In this instance a small group of Judaistic Christians is in view, a sect which espoused the dogmas of the Ebionites, who declared that Christianity was nothing more than a purged form of Judaism. Great emphasis was laid upon the office of prophet, and it was taught that God reveals Himself through the true prophet who appears as Adam, Moses, and finally as Christ, who is identified as the Son of God, but is not called Savior. Cullmann laid the foundation for his later studies in Christology in this research into the Pseudo-Clementines, for in this sect there is evidence of the evanescent influence of a small wing of Jewish Christianity. This group focused its attention on prophetism, but because of its preoccupation with Gnosticism and its failure to account for the uniqueness of Christ's prophetic office, it disappeared in the sands of history. The Pseudo-Clementines had no Christology, but only a prophetology. Cullmann makes the interesting suggestion that this one-sided emphasis on prophetism after the Christian era survives in the faith of Islam.[28]

The detailed analysis of the Pseudo-Clementines in 1930 was followed six years later by the publication of an article on the Eucharist in primitive Christianity.[29] As the term is used, "primitive Christianity" embraces both apostolic and post-apostolic times in the first century and therefore belongs in the earliest stage of the patristic tradition. At the outset Cullmann accepts Lietzmann's hypothesis of two primitive strands of tradition about the Eucharist: the liturgy of Hippolytus which is concerned with the death of Christ, and the old Egyptian liturgy which stressed the Parousia and table fellowship. Lietzmann, however, assumed that there was no continuity between the Last Supper and the primitive celebration of the Eucharist, and it is at this point that Cullmann disagrees and proposes to demonstrate that pre-Pauline and Pauline traditions are dominated by recollection of Jesus' Last Supper and its overtones of impending death.

Noting that the early Christians celebrated breaking bread with joy (Acts 2:46), Cullmann argues that if Lietzmann were correct, the word joy should have been nostalgia. But in fact simple recollection will not explain this joy; the explanation lies in the conviction that they had eaten with the risen Lord. Thus the Eucharist embraced both the Last Supper and Easter.

Paul's statement (I Cor. 11:23f.) does not modify the practices

---

[28] Cf. *The Christology of the New Testament* (1959), pp. 49, 50.

[29] "La signification de la Sainte Cène dans le christianisme primitif," *Revue d'histoire et de philosophie religieuses* 16 (1936). J. G. Davies made an English translation entitled "The Meaning of the Lord's Supper in Primitive Christianity" for the series *Essays on the Lord's Supper, Ecumenical Studies in Worship*, no. 1 (1958).

described in Acts, but only carries forward the conviction of a theological relationship between the celebration of the Eucharist and the Passion of Jesus. The Pauline understanding of the Eucharist is marked by at least three features: the establishment of a new covenant, the assurance of forgiveness of sins, and a heightened sense of participation in the Body of Christ, the Church. When the Eucharist is eaten under the prayer "Maranatha" the Church today will eat not only in recollection, but also in the presence of Christ at the sacred meal, and in the sure hope of Christ's eventual return.

In 1943 Cullmann's *Les premières confessions de foi Chrétiennes*[30] made another contribution to the field of patristics by posing four central questions: (1) Why were confessional formulae needed in addition to sacred Scripture? (2) How did this need emerge? (3) What is the composition of the earliest confessions and how did they take form? (4) What is the essential content of the Christian faith as these formulae state it?

These primitive confessions were drawn up to provide terse and concise affirmations of Christian belief; the New Testament was too lengthy to serve this purpose. They were, then, summaries of Christian doctrine. Secondly, the need for them emerged in view of five factors which characterized the *Sitz im Leben* of partristic times: baptism and catechumenism, the liturgy and preaching found in regular worship, exorcism of demons, confession of Christ in the face of persecution, and polemic statements against heretics. Thirdly, "proclamation of Christ is the *starting-point of every Christian confession*,"[31] and the later creeds added statements about God the Father and the Holy Spirit. The primitive Church practice of baptism led to the tripartite form of the confessions, but the essence of Christianity is implied in the creeds to be faith in Jesus Christ the Lord. In this simple credo was implied a belief in God the Father, in God the Holy Spirit, in the resurrection and the eschatological work of Christ.

Urchristentum und Gottesdienst was published in 1950, and was subsequently chosen as the tenth monograph in the "Studies in Biblical Theology" series.[32] The first chapter treats the basic features of early Christian worship, and the second takes up the relationship of the Fourth Gospel to primitive worship. Thus the two chapters stand somewhat independent of each other. Cullmann takes as his sources for studying primitive Christian worship the New Testament, the *Didache,* Justin Martyr's *First Apology,* and Pliny's letter to Trajan,

[30] Cahiers de la *Revue d'histoire et de philosophie religieuses,* 30. See J. K. S. Reid's English translation entitled *The Earliest Christian Confessions* (1949).
[31] *The Earliest Christian Confessions* (1949), p. 39.
[32] Translated by A. S. Todd and J. B. Torrance and entitled *Early Christian Worship* (1953).

which embraces literary materials up to 150 A.D. The temple and private homes were the earliest meeting places, and Sunday was the time, a day chosen in recognition of the Resurrection. Elements of worship were preaching, doxological and free prayers, the celebration of the Eucharist, and baptism. Cullmann declares that the purpose of all early worship with all its constituent parts came to focus in the building up of the Body of Christ. The genius of the worship pattern in primitive times lay in the harmonious balance between freedom of the Spirit (tongues, prophecy) and elements of liturgical order. Such a felicitous union of tendencies liberated the Church from fanaticism on one hand, and the moribund effect of liturgy simply for its own sake on the other hand. The specifically Christian character of early worship was vouchsafed by the conscious intention of building up the Body of Christ through breaking of bread, reading of Scripture, preaching, confession, prayer, doxology, blessing, hymns, and prophecies, and by the awareness of the presence of the Holy Spirit who is the divine Agent in *Heilsgeschichte*.

The second chapter is an attempt to understand the Johannine literature in terms of liturgical and doxological purpose. The Fourth Gospel and the Apocalypse are saturated with allusions to Christian worship; indeed, both books might be called heavily sacramental. The Johannine corpus should be re-read and re-evaluated from this fresh and fruitful perspective.

The Early Church is an anthology of Cullmann's articles which were written across several years, published in numerous European theological journals, and collected in English translation by A. J. B. Higgins. These articles are devoted to New Testament exegesis and theology, and to patristic studies. Of special concern to early Christian thought is the discussion of the origin of Christmas, in which Cullmann takes up the problem of the date of Jesus' birth and the several pagan festivals with which it has been identified. For three centuries in the rise of the Church there was no concern to celebrate Jesus' birth by notice of any special day. December 25 and January 6 were later chosen as His birthday, but for quite fanciful reasons. The conclusion of this study is that Christmas is celebrated not for historically accurate reasons, but simply for the theological fact of the Incarnation. The Roman festive days of December 25 and January 6 were chosen as appropriate times for Christian celebration, and no pagan overtones were implied in this arbitrary choice of a date.

"The Plurality of the Gospels as a Theological Problem in Antiquity" is taken up as a concern of both theology and patristics. In the primitive Church the sheer fact of the multiplicity of Gospels implied that no one Gospel narrative was deemed adequate to reflect the life of Jesus Christ and to meet the needs of the Church. Luke himself in

177

his prologue suggests that a need existed to improve upon prior accounts of Jesus' life, and so he added his contribution to the rest. These Gospels after Mark were not written to displace Mark, but simply to add data which Mark had omitted, and which were regarded as useful by the Evangelists. The fact of a future canon played no part in their decisions to write other Gospels.

In time the fourfold Gospel became an ecclesiastical embarrassment, and efforts were made to write or recognize one authoritative Gospel. Several attempts at one Gospel were made before Tatian, but his *Diatessaron* easily became the most famous in post-apostolic times. The *Diatessaron* was not consciously a new Gospel, but a literary conflation of the fourfold Gospel, and it came to be widely used for a while. However, it eventually fell into disuse because of Tatian's failure to see that "Gospels are intended not simply to state historical facts, but to proclaim a revealed religious truth based on historical facts."[33] Thus the whole Church, ancient and modern, has accepted the historical fact of a fourfold Gospel structure which emerged, not out of some mystical respect for the number four, but out of the dynamic situation of the first generation of the Church. Matthew, Mark, Luke, and John all wrote their own records of the one Gospel which is indelibly associated with the person and work of Jesus of Nazareth. They are not competitive biographies, but rather complementary testimonies to their faith, and the Church has accepted and used them on that spiritual basis.

"Early Christianity and Civilization" is Cullmann's assessment of the relationship of the Church to the world in the first two centuries. Since the New Testament devotes so little attention to the specific problem of the Church and civilization, primitive Church history is of importance to ascertain how the Church reacted. First, Cullmann points out that the earliest generation of Christians stood aloof from culture and civilization in general because of its persuasion of the imminence of the Parousia. The present world and all its structure are transitory, and therefore have no ultimate value. Final loyalty was given only to Christ. Whenever a question of practice arose, the interests of the Kingdom were transcendent, and these interests were applied in settling any given question. However, this pristine spiritual attitude suffered erosion in the second century, for sometimes the New Testament (that is, first-century) principle was upheld, and sometimes it was abandoned. The second-century Church continued Paul's attitude toward the State, that it would support the State insofar as it did not infringe upon the Church's allegiance to Christ. In maintaining its loyalty to Christ the Church actually modified civilization, and in

[33] *The Early Church* (1956), p. 50.

178

some respects it created new elements of civilization such as the Gospel as a literary genre, and the establishment of Christian theology as a Spirit-energized discipline. In the face of second-century heresy and syncretism, two unfortunate reactions took place in the Church. Clement of Alexandria on the one hand taught the Stoic idea of moderation in all ethical questions; his approach was not basically eschatological, but casuistical, and so it was a moralistic, not a spiritual reaction. On the other hand, Tertullian and the Montanists solved the problem of the Church and the world by advocating separatism and asceticism. This solution is contrary to the New Testament which urges a Christian resolution of conflicts, whereas Tertullian urged flight from the world itself. The Epistle of Diognetus has the correct counsel: live in the world, but as strangers; live as strangers, but in the world.

BIBLICAL CRITICISM

Cullmann has written of his early reaction to form criticism[34] which he came to regard as a "liberation" from the attempt to impose various philosophies upon the New Testament. His first published article[35] was a discussion of this new method of biblical investigation, and the result was that Bultmann regarded him as an "ally." At Basel, Cullmann's colleague K. L. Schmidt was a pioneer, along with Bultmann and M. Dibelius, in the development of this kind of biblical criticism which takes for its province the relationship between the oral and written tradition of the New Testament. An examination of the strata of the Gospel tradition (*Gesetze*) is an essential part of this discipline so that the connection between the historical Jesus and the life and thought of the primitive Christian community may be traced.

That form criticism as an instrument and method of historically examining the New Testament is theologically neutral is dramatically demonstrated in the way that Cullmann and Bultmann use it in studying the rise of early Christianity. Bultmann the form critic concludes that the Gospel narratives are virtually useless in reconstructing the events of the historical Jesus, for they are radically colored by the theological bias of the Evangelists and the early Church.[36] On the other hand, Cullmann the form critic sees the usefulness of this technique as "establishing the deviation of the early Christian community from Jesus as its object, but as also designed to help

[34] Cf. "Sketch," pp. 229f.
[35] "Les récentes études sur la formation de la tradition évangélique," *Revue d'histoire et de philosophie religieuses* (1925), pp. 459-477; 564-579.
[36] Cf. R. Bultmann, *Jesus and the Word* (1935), pp. 8f.

us draw nearer to the historical Jesus."[37] It is only accidental that many form critics are animated by a severe historical skepticism concerning the reliability and credibility of the Gospel narratives, but Cullmann and others (for example, V. Taylor) have shown that this discipline of discriminating between strata of tradition leads to, and not away from, the historical Jesus, and even to contact with Jesus' self-consciousness. This use of form criticism is especially evident in Cullmann's treatment of Christology, where repeatedly he identifies the kerygma of the Church with the prior historical fact of Jesus' self-estimate and self-knowledge.

Bultmann's historically sceptical *a priori* combined with his existentialist reinterpretation of the New Testament symbolize the perpetuation of the error of Harnack, Schleiermacher, and others who felt that a distinction must be drawn between "the kernel and the husk." In the case of Bultmann the dispensable husk is the mythical content of Gospel history, and the kernel is the kerygma which calls for decision. To Cullmann, this is a gravely dangerous trifling with salvation history, which is in fact essential to the Gospel, and he specifically rejects Bultmann's metaphysical reinterpretation of eschatology as "our permanent availability for existential decision (Bultmann)."[38] So although these two form critics seemed allies in the 1920's it soon appeared that they were to take seriously divergent paths, and now these two men head up the two dominant positions in New Testament scholarship in Europe today.

In his article "Rudolf Bultmann's Concept of Myth and the New Testament"[39] Cullmann draws out some of the implications of dismissing *Heilsgeschichte* as myth. Bultmann's program of demythologizing the New Testament yields results very much like those of the early Gnostics and Docetists who were impatient with a truly historical Jesus. Secondly, Bultmann is guilty of special pleading in his persistence in retaining the death of Christ as the sole historical datum about Jesus in the Gospels. The Cross must stand as God's invitation to man to abandon his meaningless and inauthentic existence and make an existential decision for God. But *which* cross contains this invitation? Thirdly, Cullmann asks whether this existentialist reinterpretation was the attitude of the apostles and the early Church toward the Cross. The answer lies in the kerygma emphasis upon the objectively unique character of the Cross of Christ. It stands in judgment over us apart from any human response, whereas Bultmann completely subjectivizes the Cross and requires it to be re-experienced

---

[37] "Sketch," p. 233.
[38] *The Early Church* (1956), p. 144.
[39] *Concordia Theological Monthly,* 27, 1 (Jan., 1956), 13-24.

in every man. It is undeniable that early Christians came into a new mode of existence, but this experience was understood to rest upon the objective fact of the Cross. In sum, Cullmann urges that modern scientific technological truths have not displaced or invalidated the eternal and ineradicable "foolishness" of the New Testament, that God has decisively intervened in history in the person of Jesus Christ in order to accomplish our salvation.

Again in 1961 Cullmann pressed the attack against the Bultmann school by taking issue with its handling of the historical-Jesus problem.[40] He accuses this school of perpetuating the mistake of classical liberalism in requiring the New Testament to reflect a current philosopical motif, for it approaches the kerygma with a notion about Jesus which inevitably prejudices the results of its research. Bultmann and his disciples have contaminated their objectivity by a deliberate fusion of the methodology of form criticism with the existentialist philosophy of Heidegger, and, to Cullmann, the results are disastrous for the message of the New Testament. The historical Jesus declared to be uncovered by the Bultmann school "owes more to existentialist exegesis than to its alleged basis, form criticism."[41] In fact, the union of these two ideas of form criticism and existentialism tends sharply to neutralize and overturn the positive contributions of form criticism, and sound historical research is sacrificed to a philosophy. Thus the Bultmann school is guilty of a *petitio principii* in that it arrives at a judgment about Jesus' eschatology which is "introduced already at the beginning of the analysis, at the stage when one is establishing the Church's witness. One may appeal to the inevitability of a circle."[42] So the philosopher-exegete has spoken his word before the New Testament speaks its word.

Cullmann contests the existentialists' assumption that any New Testament witness to Jesus' self-consciousness must be understood as *Gemeindetheologie*. "How does one know that the Church's tendency on this point introduced an idea foreign to Jesus himself?"[43] Wrede's thesis about "the messianic secret" in Mark has been raised to unchallenged dogmatic status in the Bultmann school, and the possibility that the Gospels may reveal something of the original and spontaneous mind of Jesus is excluded as a part of the analysis of the problem. The conclusion of the issue is that the existentialists' bridge between the Jesus of history and the Christ of the Church is inadequate be-

---

[40] "Out of Season Remarks on the 'Historical Jesus' of the Bultmann School," *Union Seminary Quarterly Review,* 16 (1961), 131-148.

[41] *Ibid.,* p. 134.

[42] *Ibid.,* p. 139.

[43] *Ibid.,* p. 144.

cause it rests upon the foundation of existentialist philosophy and not history and exegesis.

In a brilliant article on higher criticism[44] Cullmann pointed out the connection between historical criticism and theology. He commences by defending the intrinsic dignity of revelation apart from psychological or cultural explanations, for the truth of revelation can be known only on its own terms. However, our present understanding of that revelation rests in a significant way upon the undeniable gains made in the field of literary, philological, and historical criticism in the nineteenth century, irrespective of how misguided those "historicist" scholars may have been.

Cullmann next proceeds to demonstrate that higher criticism has a theological basis in the fact that the Bible has as its central theme *Heilsgeschichte*. God has acted in history for our salvation, and therefore historical analysis and examination of these acts is both inevitable and necessary. This truth points up the error of the allegorical and existentialist interpretations of the New Testament, for neither takes history as essential to God's dealings with man.

The function of higher criticism is seen in three ways. First, because biblical theology is primarily concerned with the history of salvation, the Bible scholar must apply canons of historical investigation of the text in order to trace out the theological relationships of past, present, and future. Second, it is imperative to ascertain the *Sitz im Leben,* the total milieu, of the provenance of the several books of the New Testament. Because the truth of God is transmitted in human speech and in historical circumstances, it is necessary to evaluate all these factors as closely as the philological-historical method allows. Third, the role of the higher critic is to dismiss irrelevant and frivolous ideas from the proper theological interpretation of the text. This role demands both skill in controlling his evidences and a humility before them. The philological-historical method is not preliminary to the theological analysis of the text, but "It must rather accompany exegesis from its beginning to its end."[45]

ECUMENICS

Protestant and Roman Catholic relations have long been a serious concern of Professor Cullmann, and he has given both exegetical and practical suggestions toward partial solutions of this centuries-old

---

[44] "La nécessité et la fonction de l'exégèse philologique et historique de la Bible," *Verbum Caro,* 3 (1949); an English translation was prepared by D. Macie under the title "The Necessity and Function of Higher Criticism," for *The Student World,* 42, pp. 117-133. This was included in *The Early Church* (1956), edited by A. J. B. Higgins (1949), pp. 1-16.

[45] *Op. cit.* (English translation), p. 16.

rift in Christendom. His reputation as a theologian led him to participate in the Roman Catholic council, Vatican II, in Rome in 1962 and also in 1964 and 1965 as an accredited Protestant observer.

The year 1952 saw the publication of one of Professor Cullmann's major contributions to contemporary theological and ecclesiastical discourse in his book *Petrus — Junger, Apostel, Martyrer: Das Historische und das theologische Petrusprobleme.*[46] This study amply demonstrates Cullmann's power as an historian of the early Church and as an exegete and theologian. Although it is historical and theological, Dr. Filson is correct in pointing out that "his book is thus an important contribution to the ecumenical discussion of our time,"[47] and it is therefore classed among his ecumenical studies. Cullmann declares in his foreword[48] that the book is intended to augment knowledge in the history of primitive Christianity, but the greatest detectable impact is made upon the ecumenical question.

Two main sections comprise this study, the first being a treatment of the historical problem of Peter as a disciple, apostle, and martyr, and the second an analysis of the exegetical and theological issues which take their rise from Peter's history. The source of the Church's knowledge of Peter is the Gospels; the apocryphal materials have no historical value for understanding him. It is clear from an examination of all four gospel narratives that Peter occupied a prime place of representation among the disciples of Jesus. His representative leadership as a disciple laid the foundation for his apostolic responsibility in heading up the Jewish Christian mission, whereas Paul assumed the initiative in the mission to the Gentiles. Cullmann holds that Peter's responsibility is traceable to Jesus' designation of him as *Petros,* rock, and to the commission from the risen Lord (John 21:16ff.). It is an illegitimate inference to assume that because Peter and Paul were charged with different mission sectors, and because they had at one time a conflict over Christian practice, their theologies therefore diverged. Rather, Peter in fact stands closer to Paul's position than any of the other apostles. Cullmann identifies the universal character of the Gospel offer and servant Christology as predominating elements in Peter's theology.

Since the martyrdom of Peter is not discussed in the New Testament, appeal to extra-biblical sources must be made. In a lengthy chapter Cullmann reviews all the extra-biblical evidences, literary, liturgical, and archeological, and concludes that the *First Epistle of Clement* and the *Letter of Ignatius of Antioch to the Romans* render it highly

[46] This was published in an English translation by F. V. Filson as *Peter — Disciple, Apostle, Martyr. A Historical and Theological Study* (1952).
[47] *Ibid.,* p. 7.
[48] *Ibid.,* pp. 12, 13.

probable that Peter visited Rome and was martyred there. However, this conclusion is ventured with caution, for the evidences are not absolutely decisive. Moreover, Cullmann is reluctant to accredit the recent and continuing claims of Roman Catholics to have found the tomb of Peter under the Vatican. "In order to prove that the bones of Peter really rested in the supposed grave under the present dome, we would need more certain indications than have been produced by the most recent excavations."[49]

The second section of the book is addressed to the exegetical and theological overtones of the place of Peter in the early Church. Matthew 16:17ff. is the point at issue because the interpretation of this highly disputed passage of Scripture divides Christendom into its two main camps. The treatment of the exegesis of this passage is thorough and exhaustive, taking into consideration the history of interpretation from patristic through modern times. Cullmann doubts whether the setting of the confession as Matthew reports it is correct, and he goes on to hypothesize that the saying is to be associated with the passion narrative.[50] But in any case, he affirms the historicity of the confession — contrary to much contemporary thought, especially in the Bultmann tradition. The general conclusion of Cullmann's exegesis is that Jesus promised Peter that he would be the foundation for the earthly people of God, and this would eventuate in the Kingdom of God. Peter is to assume leadership in missions and basic organization of the people of God. However, this special position and power expires with Peter's own death: ". . . what is said of Peter as the Rock refers only to him, the historical apostle . . . ."[51]

Last, Cullmann reviews the theological implications of this passage for the later Church, and he sets forth a fundamental principle of consideration: "on the one hand, the significance of the saying (i.e., Matt. 16:17ff.) for the present may not be seen in the *repetition* of a function, if this is *basically* unique; and on the other hand, the application may not be arbitrarily *restricted*."[52] Following the application of this principle Cullmann concludes that Peter the Apostle was given the promise of primacy in the early Church, but this was a unique and unrepeatable promise, and it was not addressed to a

---

[49] *Ibid.*, p. 150.

[50] See the second edition (1962), p. 191, where he says that the statement about the Church is more intelligible in the passion context than in Matthew's narrative. Cf. also Cullmann's article "L'apôtre Pierre instrument du diable et instrument de Dieu: la place de Matt. 16:16-19 dans la tradition primitive," *New Testament Essays* (ed. A. J. B. Higgins, 1959), pp. 94-105 where this theme is followed out.

[51] *Peter — Disciple, Apostle, Martyr* (1952), p. 212.

[52] *Ibid.*, p. 214.

bishop. As to continuing leadership, it is evident that the reference to the keys means a continuing office of leaders, but it is an illegitimate inference to take this to imply a repetition of the unique position of Peter. Peter was, in any case, the chief figure, not of the Church in Rome, but of Jerusalem, and even this leadership was temporal and unduplicated in the apostolic sense. Therefore, the Roman Catholic position can maintain itself only by appeal to its own tradition and private scheme of support, but this support cannot be derived from strict philological-historical exegesis of Matthew 16:17ff.

The year of appearance of Cullmann's work on Peter saw also the publication of two articles touching on the problem of Scripture and tradition. Inevitably a subject of this nature involved him in yet further debate with Roman Catholic theologians. In 1952 he read a paper before a group of Protestant and Roman Catholic theologians,[53] and again a year later he expanded on the question of tradition in a larger article[54] which embodies the substance of the earlier and shorter article. Cullmann commences by a minute examination of the idea of tradition (*paradosis*) in the New Testament; in the Gospels, Jesus rejects the "traditions of men" (Mark 7:8), whereas in the Epistles exhortations appear to "hold the traditions" (II Thess. 2:15). In the former case Jesus specifically rejects the rabbinic tradition which had become an accretion around the "commandment of God" in such a way as to supersede it in authority. However, the use of παράδοσις in the Epistles looks not to the rabbinic tradition, but rather to the new tradition which is traceable to the exalted Christ who is the fulfillment of the Torah. This is to say that "the exalted Christ Himself stands as transmitter behind the apostles who transmit His word and words,"[55] and the agent in this process of perpetuating the new *Kyrios-paradosis* is the Holy Spirit who replaces the tradition of the Torah in the Old Covenant. The Holy Spirit is essential to the communication of the Christian tradition in that tradition is dynamically related to him, whereas in the rabbinic pattern the perpetuation of tradition was mechanical and lifeless. Thus the originator of Christian tradition is the risen Christ, who commits the revelation of Himself to eyewitnesses (that is, apostles), and who secures this tradition to the Church through His Holy Spirit. Since the Lord originates and controls this tradition through His apostles, it may be said that apostolic tradition and direct revelation from Christ are coterminous expressions.

Next, Cullmann examines the distinguishing marks of the apostolate

---

53 Cf. *Dieu vivant*, 23, pp. 47f. See also D. H. C. Read's English translation, "Scripture and Tradition," *Scottish Journal of Theology*, 6 (1953), 113-135.

54 Cf. *La Tradition* (1953). A. J. B. Higgins's English translation is found in *The Early Church* (1956), pp. 57-99.

55 *Ibid.*, p. 69.

as opposed to the continuing office of bishop. The uniqueness of the apostolic office resides in the time in which it was instituted, the time being the critical period which includes the totality of Christ's events upon earth and the life of the early Church to the death of the last apostle. To be an apostle in the strict theological sense was to be an eyewitness of the risen Jesus. Since this is the criterion for an apostle, it follows that a bishop is not a synonym for apostle, for the simple reason that they exist on different levels of history and authority. Apostles appointed bishops to perpetuate and transmit apostolic truth, but this appointment is not a commission to create new doctrine, for direct revelation is limited to the apostolic age. This distinction between apostles and subsequent bishops has become blurred in Roman Catholic theology, and the result has been the recapitulation in the Christian era of precisely the error of rabbinism and its developing tradition. The "tradition of men" has interposed itself between the authentic authoritative written Word and the believer. The critically unique apostolic office has been diluted by the infallible teaching office of the Church, and while the Church does not in principle claim to supplant the apostolic office, practically considered this is the effect of the Church's official dogmatic interpretation of the apostolic record. Thus the ecclesiastical interpretation is elevated to equal authority with Scripture itself, and a new tradition is established which is not subordinated at every point to Scripture, but thrives in competition with it.

Last, Cullmann directs attention to the importance of the establishment of the canon by the second-century Church as it relates to Scripture and tradition. The sheer fact of the beginnings of the formation of the canon in the second century is a witness to *Heilsgeschichte,* for it in principle demonstrated that the Church was concerned to discriminate between authentic and inauthentic traditions, or between apostolic and solely ecclesiastical traditions. What transpired in the apostolic era, and what was transmitted by the apostles themselves about those events, were deemed to be both anterior and superior to other traditions already taking their rise in the early part of the second century. Simply stated, the apostolic age and its report were unique because they were revelatory, whereas other traditions which were later did not and could not bear this authentic imprimatur.

Because of the proliferation of ecclesiastical traditions as early as the second century, the Church found it mandatory to recover and confirm its apostolic norm (hence "canon") which served to judge other traditions about Jesus. It was decided that since only the apostles were eyewitnesses of the events of Jesus, their testimony alone was authentic and revelatory, and traditions which did not reflect and preserve these truths were rejected. Thus, as early as the second century a principle of discrimination between apostolic and church tradition was recognized so that the latter was clearly subordinated to the former. Once the canon was articulated and acknowledged, it became the primary norm for truth, and other traditions were eclipsed. "To fix a canon was to say: henceforth we give up regarding as a norm other traditions that are not fixed by the apostles in writing."[56]

To regard the canon as normative does not mean the abolition of the Church's office as teacher, but it does mean that the Church is only a teacher of apostolic truth — but not an expander of it, for what was laid down by the apostles is binding on the Church of all ages as finally and uniquely authoritative. Therefore, the second-century Church is not a special Church arrogating to itself a special privilege in canonizing the apostolic heritage; rather it simply acknowledged what every age of the Church must acknowledge, that in view of *Heilsgeschichte,* the apostolic age and its testimony are definitive and irreversible for the entire age of the Church.

In the light of these evidences, it is apparent that the Roman Catholic position on the relationship of Scripture and tradition is at fundamental variance, not only with the apostolic consciousness, but also with the episcopal consciousness of the second century. It is conceded that the Church recognized the canon, but the Church also placed itself under the authority of the apostolic tradition to the specific exclusion of all competing ecclesiastical traditions, for in the apostolic tradition alone is to be heard the continuing voice of the risen *Kyrios* of the Church.

Because of his interest in ecumenicity, Cullmann was invited to give an address on the occasion of the ecumenical week of prayer in January, 1957, at Zurich.[57] In this address he proceeds from the situation of the early Church and draws four lessons which may apply to the current Protestant-Roman Catholic controversy. Just as the temple was the evident sign of Judaic unity, so was the apostolic collection for the poor in Jerusalem the clear indication of the unity of the early Church. Thus the collection served as a practical confessional standard of the unity of all Christians under the Lordship of Christ. Admitting that the schisms in the early Church were not as radical as the present one, Cullmann none the less feels that the first-century response is instructive for today. First, the earliest Christians were constant in their conviction of the unity of the Church, and that unity was not affected by the various dispositions of the

[56] *Ibid.,* p. 90.
[57] This address was published in *Kirchenblatt für die reformierte Schweiz* (21 Feb., 1957), pp. 50f. It appeared in an English translation by F. T. Kingston as "The Early Church and the Ecumenical Problem," *Anglican Theological Review,* 40 (1958), 181-189; 294-300.

several elements in the Church. Second, Paul moved against schisms which arose out of personalities, for exaggerated allegiance to a man is a denial of the Gospel and the unity of the Church. Third, Paul urged Christians to make concessions to "weaker brethren," so long as this was possible without sacrificing an essential truth of the Gospel. And fourth, differences of liturgy or early Christian practice did not prevent their uniting in the common task of taking up a collection for the impoverished members of the Jerusalem Church.

This last point Cullmann suggests as a practical and immediately available expression of Christian unity and service, and he urges that Protestants and Roman Catholics unite in receiving an offering for the poor of today. Catholics could give to Protestants, and Protestants to Catholics. Such an action could be taken in full recognition of the dogmatic differences which divide Christendom, but this action would provide an expression of common devotion without either side conceding any dogma.

In 1957 this same thesis was set forth at ecumenical meetings in Paris and Rome, and in 1958 Cullmann expanded his lecture into a small book in which he carries forward his suggestion in greater detail.[58] The fourth chapter is especially interesting because of the recording of responses to his proposal of a yearly offering among Protestants and Catholics. At the close of the book he lists six objections which have been made against this proposal. (1) The receiving of an offering implies some kind of formal recognition by one side or the other. The answer is that the offering is only an expression of Christian concern of people for one another, and does not carry with it official dogmatic recognition on either side. (2) Such an offering veils differences between the two sides. Cullmann urges that it does not minimize doctrinal differences, but only the polemical spirit which so often accompanies doctrinal debates. (3) It is objected that similar co-operative programs are already in force between Protestants and Catholics. The reply is that no other effort has as its conscious goal a practical demonstration of transconfessional solidarity. (4) Giving to the poor is a vague program which is an inadequate objective. Cullmann's response is that the same objection can be leveled against any collection for the poor *within* a given congregation. (5) It is objected that inequality of needs in a given area would benefit one side at the expense of the other. Cullmann's answer to this is that donations should not be published, but that a mixed commission should keep all details of income and distribution secret. (6) The question is

---

[58] *Katholischen und Protestanten. Ein Vorschlag zur Verwirklichung christlicher Solidarität.* The English translation by J. A. Burgess was published under the title, *A Message to Catholics and Protestants.*

188

asked how such a yearly offering can be given so much importance. Here the reply is that the importance lies in the sober and firm expectation that these offerings would alter the atmosphere in which Roman Catholic and Protestant debate and discourse are carried out, and if this is the result, all the effort is eminently justified.

III. EVALUATION

Since the 1930s there has been a remarkable renascence of the discipline of biblical theology, and Professor Cullmann's name belongs in the forefront of the contributors to this development. Of primary concern to the biblical theologians in the last three decades has been a recovery and restatement of the essential unity of the Bible, for the liberal movement in theology tended to be excessively analytical so that the Bible came to be regarded as a compendium of religious ideas of Jews and Christians. Further, the work of the *religionsge-schichtliche Schule* Hellenized the New Testament to the extent that its Hebraic element was almost wholly overlooked. The meager results of such excessive criticism gave rise to a renewed interest in biblical theology and its positive affirmations. Concurrent with the synthetic view of the Bible is a strong emphasis upon the essentially Hebraic character of the New Testament so that the Greek language is but the clothing of the Semitic body.

Cullmann has been brought under attack by James Barr, whose concern is that enthusiasm for biblical theology has been sustained at the expense of good linguistics,[59] a weakness he finds ubiquitous in Kittel's great theological dictionary. Barr's objection focuses on Cullmann's "concept method" which he claims is imprecise and tends toward large blurred generalizations which allegedly support a given theological assumption. He criticizes Cullmann severely for failing to reckon with word uses which do not accord with his program, for in fact words may exhibit a multiple meaning (polysemy) which undercuts Cullmann's selective word choice. This criticism springs from a linguistic philosophy which is quite analytical and nominalistic, whereas Cullmann, along with T. Boman and many contributors to Kittel's dictionary, is more idealistic in his linguistic theory. Barr's analytical approach conceives of words as counters or units almost in a mathematical sense, and he consc.̣ ntly scorns the "concept method" for its inaccuracies. On the other hand, Cullmann's approach takes words as vehicles or signs of concepts which bear overtones or colors of meaning. This does not preclude other usages of the given word. Rather, words are signs surrounded by concentric circles of semantic

---

[59] Cf. James Barr, *The Semantics of Biblical Language* (1961); *Biblical Words for Time, Studies in Biblical Theology,* 33 (1962), esp. pp. 47-81.

value, an idea opposed by Barr, who takes words only as counters or ciphers.

In view of this difference of linguistic philosophy much of Barr's criticism of Cullmann fails to register. His accusation that Cullmann has neglected other word uses of καιρός, for example, ignores the fact that Cullmann is consciously selective of this word. That is, Cullmann deliberately seizes upon those instances of καιρός in which there is a clustering or bunching of concepts in a word which is theologically suggestive. It is inconceivable that Cullmann could be guilty of failing to do his basic concordance work as he assessed these words for time, and he would probably regard Barr's criticisms as examples of trivializing.[60] Barr rebukes Cullmann for implying that his exegesis of these key words for time is exhaustive and exclusive, but this criticism is wide of the mark for the simple reason that Cullmann directs attention only to those uses and passages which are theologically significant. So Cullmann is admittedly selective of his evidences, but this does not undercut his position, for he makes no claim to an exhaustive analysis of these words in the New Testament.[61]

Barr further rejects Cullmann's assertion that a succession of *kairoi,* or distinctive moments in salvation history, provide the materials of the redemptive time-line,[62] and he particularly disagrees with Cullmann's exegesis of I Timothy 2:6 in support of the thesis. Affirming that his understanding of the passage is "precarious," he then offers a criticism which merely states that Cullmann's view is "implicitly contradicted by many works of reference," but cites only Bultmann, Bauer, and himself. This is not only a weak attack, but it proposes no positive evaluation of the passage. Barr's atomizing critique of Cullmann may expose a weakness in lexicography from time to time, but it does not disestablish the general validity of his program of *Heilsgeschichte,* for it rests upon a much larger foundation than the exegesis of some of the words for time.

In his text on Christology Cullmann makes a statement which has provoked critical comment. He says that "early Christian theology is

[60] For a highly critical and sometimes fierce analysis of Barr himself, see T. Boman's review of Barr's works in the *Scottish Journal of Theology,* 15, 3 (Sept., 1962), pp. 319-324. N. Snaith accurately states that " . . . words do not stand for pinpoints of expression, but for large circles, and the nearer we get to the circumference, the more the particular significance gets blurred," *Distinctive Ideas of the Old Testament,* p. 144; see also his discussion on pp. 21f.

[61] A frequent note in the reviews of Barr's books is his own failure to offer a constructive and positive alternative. His efforts are largely critical in the negative sense, and this is necessary and useful, but inadequate. This criticism does not, of course, either confirm or remove Cullmann's exegesis.

[62] Cf. Barr's *Biblical Words for Time,* pp. 61f.

in reality almost exclusively Christology."[63] This assertion is challenged by E. Fascher in a lengthy article entitled "Christologie oder Theologie?"[64] Asking the question "Ist das richtig gesehen?", Fascher proceeds to adduce numerous passages from the New Testament, such as Romans 8:31-39, John 1:18, and Romans 1:7, along with many others, in demonstration of the primacy of the person of God the Father in early Christian thinking. His criticism is somewhat compelling insofar as Cullmann has overstated his case for the centrality of Christ; II Corinthians 13:13 and similar passages in which Christ is named before God do not necessarily point to a suppression of theology in favor of Christology as a universal phenomenon in the primitive Church, for other doxologies and introductions clearly assign primacy to God the Father, as is clear in I Corinthians 15:28. Therefore, it might be more acceptable to affirm that the early Church indeed had a theology — that is, a doctrine of God — but it was richly informed and colored by Christology. Such a correction of Cullmann's statement[65] does not damage his main thesis, and does free it from misunderstanding by overstatement.

Whereas nineteenth-century biblical criticism in the *religionsgeschichtliche Schule* tended to Hellenize the New Testament, biblical theologians have recently attempted to restore the basic Hebraic perspective of the New Testament. Cullmann vigorously follows this course, so much so that he purges the New Testament of almost any Greek influence.[66] The effect is to take an opposite pole so that the New Testament is "Hebraicized," and this tendency is seen in two ways in his work on Christology: (1) a strong preference for "function" as over against any concern for "being," and (2) his exegesis of certain words such as μορφή (form or being) in Philippians 2:6.

"When it is asked in the New Testament 'Who is Christ?', the

---

[63] *Christology,* pp. 2, 3. See also his *The Earliest Christian Confessions* (1949), p. 39.

[64] *Theologische Literaturzeitung* 12 (December, 1962), 881-910.

[65] In German Cullmann's statement reads: " . . . die urchristliche Theologie in Wirklichkeit fast ausschliesslich Christologie ist."

[66] Cf. James Barr's statement that Cullmann "is so active in repudiating what he holds to be Hellenic conceptions of time that he is not likely to invoke classical senses as a guide to the relation of time and eternity in the New Testament" (*Biblical Words for Time,* pp. 71, 72). Speaking of the rare instances in the New Testament where there is concern for the "natures" of Christ, Cullmann says, "The dogmatic theologian can deal with it (i.e., the question of the essence of Christ), but never the New Testament exegete" (*Christ and Time,* 3rd ed., p. xxvii). It is not clear why the New Testament exegete must regard such questions as virtually forbidden territory, especially in view of Cullmann's admission that there are at least a few passages which touch on this issue. It might have been better to say that the exegete leaves such questions to the dogmaticians except where the New Testament itself expresses an interest.

191

question never means exclusively, or even primarily, 'What is his nature?', but first of all, 'What is his function?' "[67] With this assertion Cullmann sets the tone for much of what is to follow in the book, and there is little ground for disagreement with this statement as it stands. However, as the thesis is developed, Cullmann means by it that the New Testament, being at heart a Hebraically oriented series of documents, has almost no interest in any questions of ontology, nature, or being. He argues that any exegesis of the New Testament which pretends to discover truths about the "nature" of Christ reflects in fact an intrusion of Hellenistic ideas into the sense of the text, and is therefore irrelevant.[68] A typical statement, "Jesus himself *is* what he *does*,"[69] suffers the danger of a one-sided emphasis. There can be little doubt that the Gospels are primarily given to narratives of the "mighty deeds" of Jesus, and naturally little will be found on the nature of Jesus.[70] However, as the early Church advanced, and the person and passion of Christ became the objects of kerygmatic reflection, it is natural to expect statements about the person of Christ as well as his work. It must be admitted that Paul and John and the *Auctor ad Hebreos* were not metaphysicians, but it is useful to remember that they spoke Greek, were familiar with its cultural heritage, and did not hesitate to use the language of abstraction. Therefore to affirm that the New Testament has scant metaphysical or ontological interest is to prejudice the exegesis of words and passages which may in fact contain a spontaneous, native, and therefore legitimate assertion about the being of Christ. Moreover, to find in Paul an ontological statement does not qualify him as a Hellenistic metaphysician, but rather it indicates only that as a Greek-speaking and thinking Hebrew Christian he found a word which usefully connoted something he had to say about the person of Christ. Thus it is possible to go behind Chalcedon to the New Testament with questions about the "nature" of Jesus Christ. This fact does not deny the basic truth of Cullmann's thesis, but corrects it to the obvious linguistic evidences which he himself recognizes in at least one instance.

This position of Cullmann's has exposed him to criticism by both Protestant and Roman Catholic scholars. J. S. Arrieta speaks for many Roman Catholics when he suggests that the logical result of this

[67] *Christology*, pp. 3, 4.
[68] Cf. *Ibid.*, pp. 234, 247, 261, 266, 293 *et passim*.
[69] *Ibid.*, p. 261.
[70] It is most interesting to observe one place where Cullmann abandons his position, for in the discussion of the *Logos* he says, "Nevertheless we do have here one of the few New Testament passages which speak in this sense of the 'being' of the pre-existent Word" (p. 265). Thus it is plain that the principle which he urges is not uniformly applicable.

view is a denial of the true inherent deity of Jesus Christ.[71] This accusation is in itself a gratuitous overstatement, but the fact that Cullmann replied to defend himself in a special article on this issue indicates that a potential danger lay in this view.[72] In this article he modifies some statements, clarifies others, and suggests that his readers have read him too hastily. His confessed concern is to free the New Testament from the restrictions imposed upon our understanding by the later creeds so that we today do not make an equation between the creeds and the New Testament itself. However, he claims that his *a posteriori* arguments demonstrate that "the dogma formulated by this council [Chalcedon] corresponds to what the Christology of the New Testament presupposes."[73] In view of this statement and others in his response it is clear that the charge of heresy is ill-chosen and specious. But on the other hand this response strengthens the case for genuine New Testament expressions about the person of Christ anterior to and distinguishable from His work.

Cullmann's strong preference for Hebraic motifs appears in his exegesis of μορφή (form, being) as it appears in Philippians 2:6ff.[74] He follows J. Héring who says that the meaning of this word is really "image" rather than form in the sense of essence or nature,[75] and it is also theologically cognate with the idea of glory (δόξα). The other pole of interpretation is propounded by J. B. Lightfoot,[76] who conceives of μορφή in the classical and formal sense of "essence" or "being," a position which he defends from classical Greek sources. So these become the two basic treatments of this word; the one is characterized by its sharp dependence upon Hebraic antecedents supported by appeal to the Septuagint, and the other formally conditioned by Plato and Aristotle.[77] Cullmann's position, stimulated by Héring, is provocative, but on balance unconvincing, not because of its alleged support from Hebraic considerations, but because it does not sufficiently account for the genuine Greek semantic character of the word in itself. This can be shown by an examination of μορφή in its compounded forms in the

---

[71] *La Iglesia Del Intervalo*: *Aspecto Escatológico Del Tiempo De La Iglesia En Oscar Cullmann* (1959). See also J. Frisque, *Oscar Cullmann*: *Une Théologie de l'Histoire du Salut* (1960).

[72] Cf. "La Response du Professor Cullmann," *Choisir*, 9-10 (1960). This appeared in an English translation by R. P. Meye in the *Scottish Journal of Theology*, 15, 1 (March, 1962), 36-43.

[73] *Ibid.*, E. T., p. 43.

[74] Cf. *Christology*, pp. 176ff.

[75] *Le royaume de Dieu et sa venue*, pp. 159-167.

[76] *St. Paul's Epistle to the Philippians*, pp. 125-131.

[77] For a thorough analysis not only of this word but the contemporary exegetical scene on Philippians 2:6-11, see R. P. Martin, *An Early Christian Confession* (1960).

New Testament (Rom. 12:2; II Cor. 3:18) and by comparing the phrase "form of God" and "form of a servant," so that if μορφή means image and glory in Philippians 2:6, it ought to mean approximately the same thing in the following verse. But in fact such a reading breaks down the movement of thought, for little sense attaches to the phrase "image of a servant." The sum of the matter is that it is not doubted that Lightfoot's exegesis of this word is excessively informed by formal Greek metaphysical distinctions, and it needed the corrective initiated by Héring and others to restore a strong Hebraic flavor to the word. However, again there exists a case of over-Hebraicizing the New Testament when a resident and clear Greek metaphysical sense present in a word is suppressed in favor of the Semitic element.[78] A sounder exegesis would recognize both aspects in Paul's use of the word here, for it is not impossible that he set up a calculated semantic ambivalence in this instance.

Upon few biblical themes is it so difficult to be dispassionate as upon the theme of baptism, for confessional and traditional loyalties becloud this issue almost to the point of preclusion of hearing any opposing exegesis. The pedobaptists will commend Cullmann for an excellent piece of historical and theological scholarship in his treatment on baptism, and baptistic groups will rejoice to claim Karl Barth as an outstanding theologian who has seen the light. At the end of his study of the subject Cullmann makes two significant observations. He asserts that "proof of infant baptism is at best indirectly demonstrable from observable indications,"[79] thereby indicating his sensitivity to the absence of any clear word in support of pedobaptism in the New Testament: its case must therefore be inferential. Secondly, Cullmann takes a softer position on both modes than many Reformed theologians do when he says that ". . . both adult and infant baptism are to be regarded as equally biblical."[80] But in so saying he affirms that those who are children of first-generation Christians should not be baptized

---

[78] In private correspondence Professor Cullman indicates that his preference for the "semitischen Sprachhintergrund" has to do with his basic procedure in handling the New Testament. This approach is above dispute, of course, for it is well established that the primitive Palestinian Church was essentially Hebraic in character and theology. Moreover, I do not dispute that *morphe* has some roots in the Genesis account about Adam. My sole disagreement in the exegesis of *morphe* in Philippians 2:6 is that the Hebraic character of Cullmann's exegesis appears to exclude the native Hellenistic semantic quality of the word in question. On this issue Professor Cullmann graciously notes: "Denn es wurde dabei ja auch nicht um Korrekturen, sondern um eine Diskussion zwischen Ihnen und mir gehen."

[79] *Baptism in the New Testament* (1950), p. 70.

[80] *Ibid.*

because they may be regarded as Christians without baptism. It is a safe prediction that this debate will continue into the indefinite future.[81]

Although he has demonstrated high scholastic competence in patristics, biblical criticism, and ecumenics, Cullmann's signal importance and reputation rest upon his power as an exegetical theologian of the Word. And this reputation is particularly associated with his theology of *Heilsgeschichte,* for more than any living theologian Cullmann has established and expanded this concept so that, drawing upon the assured results of philological and historical science, he has made it the principle of interpretation, not only of the New Testament, but the entire history of God's redemptive activity. Out of this theological understanding of history has emerged a fresh and dynamic reassessment of the biblical doctrine of eschatology, and New Testament scholarship will be enriched by Cullmann's forthcoming book, *Heil als Geschichte.*

As a theologian of the Word, Cullmann makes frequent and unqualified reference to "direct revelation," an idea which has not always found itself at home in some contemporary theological circles. Especially in his treatment of tradition he places the "direct revelation" of the risen Christ to Paul above the objective historical grounds of his apostleship.[82] Although such an understanding of the text is anathema to the Bultmann school, it is none the less central to Cullmann's analysis of the formation of primitive Christian tradition. Because he so regards the text of the New Testament, he is often criticized by the radical scholars as being "biblicist," and therefore uninformed and naive. Cullmann's answer to this charge is: "I have at least made the attempt to avoid being influenced in my exegesis by theological or philosophical schools. The labels 'critical' and 'uncritical' are greatly misused today, especially by the youngest followers of Bultmann."[83] Similarly, in his study on Christology he confesses that he knows no system of interpretation other than the proved philological-historical method of exegesis, and by this mild statement he disposes of Bultmann's severely existential method.[84] Only seldom does Cullmann engage in direct debate with Bultmann, but the implied differences in methods constitute the wide gulf which separates them in European theology today. Cullmann's early determination, activated by his studies in form-criticism, to liberate the New Testament from the shackles of any dominant philosophy has been a consistent principle of his exegetical method. It is necessary for the scholar to listen primarily to what the

[81] For a scholarly and yet irenic critique of Cullmann's view see G. R. Beasley-Murray, *Baptism in the New Testament* (1962), esp. pp. 49f., *et passim.*
[82] Cf. *The Early Church* (1956), pp. 62f.
[83] *Union Seminary Quarterly Review,* 16 (1961), 134.
[84] Cf. *Christology,* p. xiv.

New Testament says to him before he states what he thinks about its message. He well notes that "Albert Schweitzer's *Quest of the Historical Jesus* was written in vain if the 'liberal' portrait of Jesus, which corresponds to the idealistic philosophy of the nineteenth century, disappeared only in order to make room for the existentialist portrait which corresponds to the existentialist philosophy of the twentieth century."[85] Exegetical theology, if it is to be soberly responsive to its object and method, must never be bound by any transient philosophy, irrespective of how provocative it may be or how many valuable insights it may afford the Church.

In a time when it is fashionable to draw superficial distinctions between "theoretical" and "practical" understandings of the Christian faith, it often happens that a pragmatic society will place the higher value upon the "practical." Many churchmen regard the theological enterprise as a kind of bagatelle, an interesting but rather ornamental fixture of the Church. Cullmann repudiates this as a cheap and basically harmful notion, for revelation and Christian theology, because they are involved with truth, lie at the very center of all that takes place in the life and reflection and activity of the Church[86]

Cullmann, although primarily a theologian, has demonstrated his practical churchmanship by his contributions to the current ecumenical dialogue and by his interestingly practical suggestion that Protestants and Roman Catholics take annual offerings for each other as a minimal sign of their unity in Christ. Such a proposal serves notice that Cullmann's interests lie beyond his study and the classroom. It is a practical idea in the best sense in that it strives for limited and yet useful objectives which are realistic in view of the hiatus between these two branches of Christendom. There is in Cullmann none of the woolly-thinking visionary and the unrealistic dreamer which too often is the vocal element in the ecumenical movement. He admits that a *rapprochement* is not now possible at the dogmatic level for this would call for surrender in principle by one side or the other, and the prospects are dark. But at the practical level he discerns hopeful signs of at least a kind of drawing together of Protestants and Roman Catholics, and the effect can only be beneficial. Continued discussions and church actions, if they are to be fruitful, must be carried out in a spirit of utter candor, fully displaying those things which divide us, and out of such an environment will emerge a profitable "interchange of views among the Christian communions."[87]

---

[85] *Union Seminary Querterly Review,* 16 (1961), 132.
[86] Cf. *Message to Catholics and Protestants,* pp. 49, 50.
[87] *The Early Church* (1956), p. 99; see also "The Early Church and the Ecumenical Problem," *Anglican Theological Review,* 40 (1958), 183; *Peter,* p. 12.

Cullmann the theologian has not only successfully related theology and practical life of the Church, but he has also indicated in a compelling manner that faith is the *sine qua non* of theology. Christian theology cannot be engaged in from a detached and uncommitted viewpoint because this violates the true character of revelation. It is noteworthy that whereas form criticism has led so many scholars away from any contact with the historical Jesus, it is precisely this method which Cullmann finds so helpful in recovering, not merely church theology about Jesus, but the actual self-consciousness of Jesus Himself. The final truth of the Christian kerygma is grasped by faith and not only by scientific historical research, and Cullmann points this out in an impressive way in these words: "Only when we ourselves become 'sons' by accepting in faith Jesus Christ's witness to His own sonship, and by doing His divine will, can we know that Jesus is *the* Son."[88] This spirit of great learning united with a sense of genuine Christian devotion is found again at the conclusion of his article on the Parousia, when he affirms: "Following the example of the Church of the New Testament we *preach* Christ who was *crucified in the past,* we *acknowledge* courageously that Christ is the *Kyrios* who *now reigns* hidden from our eyes, we *pray* in truth to the Christ who *is to return*: Maranatha![89]

If the task of the theologian is to bless the Church, then one may conclude that the Church today and in future years has been enriched in a most significant and powerful way by Professor Cullmann. Long after contemporary theological and philosophical fads have spent themselves and taken their place in the theological museum of *curiosa,* Cullmann's work will still provide useful exegetical and theological insight. This is, and will be, true for the simple reason that as a theologian of the Word he has not been fettered by any alien scheme of explaining the New Testament, but instead attempts only to hear its message and communicate its meaning.

[88] *Christology,* p. 303.
[89] *The Early Church* (1956), p. 162.

IV. BIBLIOGRAPHY

This bibliography contains a partial listing of Cullmann's articles, monographs, and books in chronological order of publication from 1925 to about the end of 1962. The reader is referred to *Neotestamentica et Patristica,* pp. x-xix, for a complete listing of all languages in which his works have been translated and published. There is appended to the present bibliography the titles of important critical analyses of Professor Cullmann's writings and theology.

ABBREVIATIONS USED IN THIS BIBLIOGRAPHY

BZNW	*Beihefte zur Zeitschrift für die neutestamentliche Wissenschaft und die Kunde der älteren Kirche*
EMM	*Evangelisches Missionsmagazin*
ET	*Expository Times*
JBL	*Journal of Biblical Literature and Exegesis*
KuD	*Kerygma und Dogma*
KRS	*Kirchenblatt für die reformierte Schweiz*
RGG	*Die Religion in Geschichte und Gegenwart,* 3rd ed., 1957f.
RHPhR	*Revue d'histoire et de philosophie religieuses*
RThPh	*Revue de théologie et de philosophie*
SJTh	*Scottish Journal of Theology*
ThLZ	*Theologische Literaturzeitung*
ThW	*Theologisches Wörterbuch zum Neuen Testament*
ThZ	*Theologische Zeitschrift*
VC	*Verbum Caro*

WORKS BY OSCAR CULLMANN

"Les récentes études sur la formation de la tradition évangélique," *RHPhR,* 5 (1925), 459-477; 564-579.

"Les problèmes posés par la méthode exégétique de Karl Barth," *RHPhR,* 8 (1928), 70-83.

Le problème littéraire et historique du roman pseudo-clémentin. Étude sur le rapport entre le gnosticisme et le judéochristianisme, Études d'histoire et de philosophie religieuses, 23. Paris, 1930.

198

Oscar Cullmann

"La signification de la Sainte Cène dans le christianisme primitif," *RHPhR,* 16 (1936), 1-22 ("The Meaning of the Lord's Supper in Primitive Christianity," *Essays on the Lord's Supper,* Ecumenical Studies in Worship, I. Richmond, 1958).

"Les traces d'une vieille formule baptismale danes le Nouveau Testament," *RHPhR,* 17 (1937), 424-434.

"Königsherrschaft Christi und Kirche im Neuen Testament," *Theologische Studien* 10. Zollikon-Zürich, 1941 ("The Kingship of Christ and the Church in the New Testament," trans. by S. Godman, in: *The Early Church.* Philadelphia, 1956).

"Eschatologie und Mission im Neuen Testament," *EMM,* 85 (1941), 98-108. ("Eschatology and Missions in the New Testament," trans. by O. Wyon in: *The Background of the New Testament and its Eschatology,* Studies in honour of C. H. Dodd. Cambridge, 1956).

"Les origines des premières confessions de foi," *RHPhR,* 21 (1941), 77-110.

"La signification du baptême dans le Nouveau Testament," *RThPh,* 30 (1942), pp. 121-134.

Les premières confessions de foi chrétiennes, Cahiers de la *RHPhR,* 30 (1943). Paris, 1948. (*The Earliest Christian Confessions,* trans. by J. K. S. Reid. London, 1949).

"Le retour du Christ, espérance de l'Église selon le Nouveau Testament" (1943), trans. by A. Dumas, Cahiers théologiques, I. Paris-Neuchatel, 1944, 1945, 1948 ("The Return of Christ," trans. by S. Godman, in: *The Early Church.* Philadelphia, 1956).

"The Plurality of the Gospels as a Theological Problem in Antiquity" (1945), trans. by S. Godman, in: *The Early Church.* Philadelphia, 1956.

"The Proleptic Deliverance of the Body According to the New Testament" (1946), trans. by A. J. B. Higgins, in: *The Early Church.* Philadelphia, 1956.

Christ and Time, The Primitive Christian Conception of Time and History (1946), trans. by F. V. Filson. London, Philadelphia, 1951, 1942.

Weihnachten in der alten Kirche. Basel, 1947 ("The Origin of Christmas," trans. by A. J. B. Higgins, in: *The Early Church.* Philadelphia, 1956).

"Zur Diskussion des Problems der ausgebliebenen Parusie" — (Replik von Fr. Buri). Duplik von O. Cullmann, *ThZ,* 3 (1947), 428-432.

Baptism in the New Testament (1948), trans. by J. K. S. Reid, Studies in Biblical Theology, I. London, 1950, 1951, 1952, 1954, 1956.

"HYPER (ANTI) POLLON. Neutestamentliche Wortforschung," *ThZ,* 4 (1948), 471-473.

"Das Schweigen über Ernst Lohmeyer," *KRS,* 104 (1948), 376.
"HO OPISO MOU ERCHOMENOS" (1948), trans. by A. J. B. Higgins, in: *The Early Church.* Philadelphia, 1956.
"Jésus, serviteur de Dieu" (1948), *Dieu vivant,* 16 (1950), 17-34.
"La nécessité et la fonction de l'exégèse philologique et historique de la Bible," *VC,* 3 (1949), 2-13 ("The Necessity and Function of Higher Criticism," in: *The Early Church.* Philadelphia, 1956).
Early Christian Worship (1950), trans. by A. S. Todd and J. B. Torrance, *Studies in Biblical Theology,* 10. London, 1953, 1954, 1956.
"Zum Falle E. Lohmeyer," *KRS,* 106 (1950), 46.
"Paradosis et Kyrios, Le problème de la Tradition dans le Paulinisme," *RHPhR,* 30 (1950), 16-30.
" 'Kyrios' as Designation for the Oral Tradition concerning Jesus," *SJTh,* 3 (1950), 180-197.
"Early Christianity and Civilisation" (1951), trans. by S. Godman, in: *The Early Church.* Philadelphia, 1956.
"Sabbat und Sonntag nach dem Johannesevangelium," *HEOS ARTI* (Joh. 5, 17), in: *In memoriam Ernst Lohmeyer.* Stuttgart, 1951.
Peter — Disciple, Apostle, Martyr. A Historical and Theological Study (1952), trans. by F. V. Filson. London, Philadelphia, 1953, 1958.
"The Tradition. The Exegetical, Historical, and Theological Problem" (1953), trans. by A. J. B. Higgins, in: *The Early Church.* Philadelphia, 1956.
"Samaria and the Origins of the Christian Mission. Who are the *ALLOI* of John 4:38?" (1953), trans. by A. J. B. Higgins, in: *The Early Church.* Philadelphia, 1956.
"Die neuentdeckten Qumrantexte und das Judenchristentum der Pseudo-klementinen," in: *Neutestamentliche Studien für R. Bultmann, BZNW,* 21. Berlin, 1954.
"Rudolf Bultmann's Concept of Myth and the New Testament" (1954), *Concordia Theological Monthly,* 27 (1956), 13-24.
"Zur neuesten Diskussion über die *EXOUSIAI* in Rom. 13, I, *ThZ,* 10 (1954), 321-336.
PETRA, PETROS, KEPHAS, in *ThW,* VI. Stuttgart, 1955, pp. 94-112.
"Maurice Goguel (1880-1955)," in: *Annuaire 1955-1956 de l'École pratique des Hautes Études.* Paris, 1955.
"Zur Frage der Erforschung der neutestamentlichen Christologie," *KuD,* I (1955), 133-141.
"The Significance of the Qumran Texts for Research into the Beginnings of Christianity," *JBL,* 74 (1955), 133-141.
The State in the New Testament (1956), trans. by F. V. Filson. New York, 1962.

"Unsterblichkeit der Seele und Auferstehung der Toten. Das Zeugnis des Neuen Testaments," *ThZ*, 12 (1956), Festschrift zum 70. Geburtstag v. Karl Barth, pp. 126-156.

"Immortality of the Soul or Resurrection of the Dead? The Witness of the New Testament" (Ingersoll Lectures 1955), *Harvard Divinity School Bulletin*, 53 (1955-1956), 19; 5-36.

"Aegypterevangelium," in *RGG*, I (1956), Sp. 126-127.

"The Early Church and the Ecumenical Problem" (1957), *Anglican Theological Review*, 40 (1958), 181-188; 294-300.

The Christology of the New Testament (1957), trans. by S. C. Guthrie and A. M. Hall. Philadelphia, 1959.

"Secte de Qumran, Hellenistes des Actes et Quatrieme Évangile," in: *Les Mauscrits de la mer Morte. Colloque de Strasbourg 25-27 mai 1955*. Paris, 1957.

"La nécessité de la Théologie pour l'Église selon le Nouveau Testament," in: *Bulletin de la Faculté libre de Théologie protestante de Paris*, 58 (1957), 11-23.

"Cattolici e Protestanti. Un proposito d'ecumenismo," *Il Popolo*, Roma, 325 (23 Nov., 1957), 4.

"Ebioniten, Ebioniterevangelium, Geschichtsschreibung (im Neuen Testament)," Goguel, *RGG*, II, 1958, Sp. 297-298; 298; 1501-1503; 1687.

"Parusieverzogerung und Urchristentum, Der gegenwartige Stand der Diskussion." *ThLZ*, 83 (1958), Sp. 1-12.

A Message to Catholics and Protestants (1958), trans. by J. Burgess. Grand Rapids, 1959.

"A new Approach to the Interpretation of the Fourth Gospel" (1958), *ET*, 71 (1959), 8-11 (Oct.); 39-42 (Nov.).

"L'apôtre Pierre instrument du diable et instrument de Dieu: la place de Matt. 16.16-19 dans la tradition primitive," in: *New Testament Essays, Studies in Memory of T. W. Manson (1893-1958)*. Manchester, 1959.

"New Sayings of Jesus" (with H.-Ch. Puech), *Sunday Times*, London, 15 Nov., 1959.

"Overbeck, K. L. Schmidt," in: *Professoren der Universität Basel aus fünf Jahrhunderten*, ed. by A. Staehelin. Basel, 1960.

"An autobiographical sketch by Prof. Oscar Cullmann" (1960), trans. by T. N. Tyce, *SJTh*, 14 (1961), 228-233.

"Das Thomasevangelium und die Frage nach dem Alter der in ihm enthaltenen Tradition," *ThLZ*, 85 (1960), Sp. 321-334.

"Out of Season Remarks on the 'Historical Jesus' of the Bultmann School" (1960), trans. by J. L. Martyn, *Union Seminary Quarterly Review*, 16 (1961), 131-148.

"Petrus," "Urgemeinde," *Weltkirchenlexikon. Handbuch der Oeku-mene.* Stuttgart, 1960, pp. 1131-32, 1520-21.

"Petrusevangelium, Petruskerygma," *RGG,* V (1961), pp. 260-261.

"Tutti quelli che invocano il nome del Signor Gesu Cristo," *Protestan-tesimo,* 16 (1961), 65-80.

"Ecumenical Collection and Community of Goods in the Primitive Church," *Pax Romana Journal,* 6 (1961), 6, 7.

"The Gospel according to St. Thomas and its significance for Re-search into the Canonical Gospels," *The Hibbert Journal,* 60 (Jan. 1962).

"Le douzième Apôtre," *RHPhR,* 2-3 (1962), 133-140.

"The Reply of Professor Cullmann to Roman Catholic Critics," trans. by R. P. Meye, *SJTh,* 15, 1 (Mar. 1962), 36-43.

Cattolici e Protestanti. Un progretto di solidarieta cristiana. Bologna, 1962.

"The Gospel of Thomas and the Problem of the Age of the Tra-dition Contained Therein," *Interpretation,* 16, 4 (Oct. 1962), 418-438.

Salvation in History (1965), trans. by S. G. Sowers. New York, 1967.

WORKS ON OSCAR CULLMANN

Ambrosiano, A. *L'Eucaristia nell'esegesi di Oscar Cullmann,* 1956.

Arrieta, J. S. *La Iglesia del Intervalo: Aspecto Escatologico Del Tiempo De La Iglesia En Oscar Cullmann,* 1959.

Bini, L. *L'intervento di Oscar Cullmann nella discussione Bultmanniana,* 1961.

Bouttier, M., "L'oeuvre d'Oscar Cullmann," *Foi et Vie,* 44 (1946), 819-831.

Frisque, J. *Oscar Cullmann. Une theologie de l'histoire du salut.* 1960.

Harsveld, E. *The Theology of Oscar Cullmann* (unpublished thesis, Union Theological Seminary, New York), 1950.

Steck, K. G., "Die Idee der Heilsgeschichte. Hofmann-Schlatter-Cull-mann," *Theologische Studien,* 56 (1959).

Szabo, A. *Oscar Cullmann theologiai Munkassaga (1925-1955).* Dis-sertation, 1955.

I. HOWARD MARSHALL

James Denney

I. BIOGRAPHY

James Denney lived during an era of rich religious and intellectual life in Scotland. The tenaciousness and spirituality of Scottish religion is illustrated, perhaps paradoxically, by the fissiparousness of the Scottish Kirk. In 1843 there took place the Disruption of the church from the state when over 400 ministers and a third of the membership walked out of the Church of Scotland, the Established Kirk, to set up the Free Kirk — a church free from state control. It was the church led by Thomas Chalmers, that doughty evangelical, and the church in whose service Denney was to find his vocation. The period was also one of considerable intellectual activity. These were the days when Scots were to be found occupying the highest positions in the business and educational life of the world; Sir James Barrie could comment aptly, "There are few more impressive sights in the world than a Scotsman on the make." The Free Kirk played a great part in the theological scholarship of this time. Ideas from abroad, especially from Germany, were powerful both in theology and biblical study, and it was a professor in the Free Church College in Aberdeen, William Robertson Smith, who popularized the new views of the higher critics of the Old Testament to such an extent that he underwent a "heresy" trial in 1881.

Denney was born in Paisley on February 5, 1856 — the year of

Dr. Ian Howard Marshall is Lecturer in New Testament Exegesis, University of Aberdeen, and the author of *Christian Beliefs* and *Eschatology and the Parables*.

203

the publication of J. McLeod Campbell's famous book *The Nature of the Atonement*. His boyhood was spent in Greenock, where he received his education àt the Highlanders' Academy. In 1874 he entered Glasgow University, where he spent five years studying Classics and Philosophy under such teachers as R. C. Jebb and Edward Caird.[1] He graduated in 1879 with the rare distinction of a "double first."

Denney's earliest years had been spent in the Reformed Presbyterian Church, in which his father was a deacon. This small group, which had its beginnings in the seventeenth century Covenanting movement, united with the Free Church in 1876, and it was therefore the Free Church College in Glasgow (now Trinity College) which Denney entered to study for the ministry. We are not told anything of the motives which led Denny to take this step; it is probable that the life of the church in which he was brought up displayed that sturdy evangelicalism which was characteristic of the Scottish "free" churches, but it was only later, after the completion of his college course, that his wife Mary Brown (whom he married in 1886) led him to more definite evangelical convictions and encouraged him to read the works of C. H. Spurgeon.[2]

Denney spent four years (1879-83) in college under such teachers as A. B. Bruce, J. S. Candlish, and T. M. Lindsay, and then three years in a mission attached to Free St. John's Church in Glasgow. In 1886 he became minister of the East Free Church in Broughty Ferry, a small but select township just outside Dundee. He was one of a succession of scholarly ministers which included A. B. Bruce and James Moffatt, and he fully maintained the high quality of preaching which was traditional there. It is some indication of what an educated Scottish congregation of those days expected that Denney's two series of expositions, *The Epistles to the Thessalonians* (1892) and *The Second Epistle to the Corinthians* (1894), had their origin in his sermons at this time. It may be worth mentioning that he also conducted a church prayer meeting.

In 1897 Denney accepted the Chair of Systematic and Pastoral Theology in the Glasgow College. His fitness for the post — and some indication of his spreading fame — may be seen from his *Studies in Theology* based on lectures given in Chicago in 1894. But his real field was New Testament, and in 1899 he was transferred to the chair previously filled by A. B. Bruce. He occupied this position until his death in 1917, the last two years of his life also being oc-

[1] Denney had little sympathy with the philosophical position of Caird: *Letters of Principal James Denney to his Family and Friends* (1921), p. 49.
[2] W. Robertson Nicoll, in *Letters of Principal James Denney to W. Robertson Nicoll* (1920), p. xvi.

cupied with the duties of Principal of the College. Among his colleagues were James Orr, the most able advocate of orthodox evangelical Christianity of his day, and George Adam Smith, the superb expositor of the prophets.

As a scholar Denney produced a number of notable works: a commentary on the Greek text of *Romans* (1900), *The Death of Christ* (1902), with its supplement, *The Atonement and the Modern Mind* (1903), *Jesus and the Gospel* (1908), and *The Christian Doctrine of Reconciliation* (1917). But this list of main titles represents only part of a very considerable output which also included several important articles in encyclopedias, many learned articles in *The Expositor,* and a long series of articles and reviews in *The British Weekly* and elsewhere.

Denney had a great breadth of interests and was a very keen student of English literature.[3] Although his main interest was the training of students — it is acknowledged that he was a superb teacher in the lecture room — he also took a prominent part in the administration of his church as convener of the Central Fund Committee and was one of the leaders in the movement toward reunion within Presbyterianism. He also preached frequently, usually twice a Sunday. The greatest thing which could be said about him was inscribed on his memorial plaque: he was a "man of God, to whom many owed their souls."[4]

II. EXPOSITION

Two months after the death of Denney there appeared an article in *The Expository Times* by Professor H. R. Mackintosh with the title *Principal Denney as a Theologian.* The description may appear strange, since Denney was pre-eminently a New Testament scholar, but it is certainly justifiable. For it may well be argued that the only person who is qualified to be a Christian theologian is a biblical scholar, and that too much theology has been written by men whose speculations were not governed by knowledge of the basic document of Christianity. Further, Denney's writings show that he had the breadth of knowledge and interest in theology to warrant his being ranked as a theologian. His theological work is characterized both by a profound knowledge of and fidelity to the New Testament and by the ability to discuss broader issues with penetrating insight. To discuss the Christian thought of centuries on reconciliation and to make

---

[3] In a brief note on "Hate" in *The Expository Times,* XXI (1909), 41f., Denney was able to illustrate a point by quotations from Tyrtaeus, Epictetus, Shakespeare, and Ibsen.

[4] Quoted by J. Randolph Taylor, *God Loves Like That* (1962), p. 189.

pointed comments on the spiritual plight of modern man were matters equally within the province of this careful exegete of the New Testament.

Denney wrote no textbook on theology other than the brief survey given in his Chicago lectures, but in his last book he embarked upon what was according to his own conviction the central doctrine of the Christian faith. It is by his exposition of the fundamental theme of religion that his designation as a great theologian is justified. Our attention, therefore, will be concentrated upon Denney's contribution to this doctrine.

THE NATURE OF THEOLOGY

Shortly before he went to Chicago to deliver his series of lectures there, Denney commented whimsically to W. Robertson Nicoll on his aim: "What I mean to do, though the subject is systematic theology, is not anything very systematic: rather a review of the chief *loci communes theologici* with reference to current ideas, especially those of Ritschl, and also ideas not so current as they should be, especially those of the Epistles in the N. T."[5] When he defined his subject matter in his first lecture, he maintained that theology is the doctrine of God, a subject which is naturally related to all that enters into our knowledge.[6] The basis of theology, therefore, is to be found in the totality of our knowledge and experience of the world and God.

This may seem a somewhat surprising beginning for a theologian who proposed to reinstate "ideas not so current as they should be" and requires further investigation. What Denney claimed repeatedly is that theology must be based on "experience": "No doctrine has any value except it is based on experience . . . . All sound and legitimate doctrinal construction must be based on experience."[7] These words are echoed in the General Introduction of that well-known series of theological works *The Library of Constructive Theology:* "They [the authors] desire to lay stress upon the value and validity of religious experience and to develop their theology on the basis of the religious consciousness. In so doing they claim to be in harmony with modern thought."[8] We are tempted to ask, "Is Denney also among the modernists?"

Three points must be made by way of explanation. First, by his

---

[5] *Letters to Nicoll* (1920), p. 3.

[6] *Studies in Theology* (1894), p. 1.

[7] *The Christian Doctrine of Reconciliation* (1917), pp. 7, 26; see also p. 199.

[8] W. R. Matthews and H. W. Robinson, in H. R. Mackintosh, *The Christian Experience of Forgiveness* (1934) p. ix.

appeal to "experience" Denney was undoubtedly seeking to avoid the danger of theologizing on the basis of speculative *a priori* principles which would be classified as false by the experience of the Christian believer. He was opposed to such a system of thought as Hegelianism which attempted to interpret the Christian faith by its own philosophical categories in defiance of the realities of Christian experience. And by Christian experience Denney meant the evangelical experience of the reconciliation of sinners to God through the death of Christ.

Second, Denney was opposed to the idea that religion and theology form a separate compartment of human experience and thought with no relation to other aspects of experience and thought. Religious and scientific thought, for example, cannot be treated in isolation from each other as if they dealt with two entirely separate entities. When commenting on Kirsopp Lake's book *The Historical Evidence for the Resurrection of Jesus Christ,* he complained, "We have enough and to spare of the kind of man who splits the world into two unrelated sections called historical and spiritual."[9] The religious, metaphysical, and physical must be brought into mutual harmony. It follows that *"all* our knowledge must have something of revelation in it, and must contribute to our theology."[10]

Third, despite what has been said so far, Denney did work as a biblical theologian and derived his theological ideas from the revelation contained in the Bible. He was contemptuous of scholars who treated the New Testament books simply as repositories of ancient religious ideas which they might accept or reject according to their fancy, and stated firmly that "the chief business of the commentator is to elucidate their significance as vehicles of revelation."[11] In an important passage he insisted that the theologian must not work back from Christian experience to what Christ must have been like but must begin with the historical Christ and let his thoughts be completely inspired and controlled by Him.[12]

Why, then, did Denney place so much emphasis on experience — to the extent of placing Scripture and experience alongside each other as the sources of doctrine?[13] The answer is that Denney regarded Scripture as authenticating itself to the Christian consciousness; its authority depends upon the fact that it is recognized by the Christian consciousness as true and therefore as authoritative, and the fact that

---

9 *Letters to Nicoll* (1920), pp. 100f.
10 *Studies* (1894), p. 7. Denney was fully prepared to say that there is revelation outside of Christ and to find expressions of it in the traditional arguments for the existence of God (*ibid.,* pp. 5-7).
11 *Letters to Nicoll* (1920), p. 171.
12 *Studies* (1894), pp. 44-46.
13 *Reconciliation* (1917), p. 73.

it does so is due to the inward witness of the Spirit. The Scripture is self-authenticating to the believer, and it must be known and experienced in its character as a divine revelation before a doctrine of Scripture can be formulated.[14]

Denney never gave a fully developed statement of his doctrine of revelation, and it seems probable that he had not reached a clear and consistent position. In his earlier writings he seems to place more emphasis on revelation, while in his last work the emphasis on Christian experience is more noticeable. This latter emphasis is exposed to obvious objections. When, for example, he has to concede that "there is much about reconciliation which experience does not demonstrate, because experience is never complete,"[15] he is in fact admitting that Christian experience is not the final authority in theology. The truth is that Christian experience is itself determined by the revelation given in Christ and the Scripture and must let itself be moulded by these normative authorities: "all that is creative and normative in the Christian consciousness depends upon Him; and with Him, therefore, we must start."[16] The fact that Denney let his thinking be continually guided by the revelation given in the Scriptures is evidence that his practice in theology was sounder than his theory.

THE BIBLE AND ITS AUTHORITY

We must now glance at the estimate which Denney gave of the place and value of Scripture. He wrote: "No Christian questions such a proposition as this, that God actually speaks to man through the Scriptures, and that man hears the voice and knows it to be God's."[17] The vital question is how this doctrine is related to the findings of biblical criticism; must we, for example, be able to establish the scientific accuracy of the Gospel narrative before we can accept its claim to give us a revelation of God? Is faith continually in suspense while it waits for criticism to complete its work? Denney's answer was that the person who read the Gospels without presuppositions of any kind would be persuaded that Jesus was a real character whom he could accept as authoritative.[18] Further, this impression would be

---

[14] *Studies* (1894), pp. 202-204, 207.   In support of his view that the doctrine of inspiration is "not in the first instance a principle fundamental to the truth of the Christian religion" but part of the doctrine of the means of grace, Denney could appeal to the writings of Professors B. B. Warfield and A. A. Hodge.

[15] *Reconciliation* (1917), p. 24.

[16] *Studies* (1894), p. 45.

[17] *Ibid*, p. 204.

[18] *Ibid.*, pp. 205-209. The words of Christ are the final authority for all Christians, *The Epistles to the Thessalonians* (1892), p. 174.

unaltered by the results of Gospel criticism, a position which Denney justified by his belief that the spiritual revelation which we receive through the inward work of the Spirit as we read the Gospels acts as a guarantee for their historical truth in broad outline[19] and by his conviction that historical criticism in any case has not destroyed this broad outline.[20]

Having shown that the authority of Christ is real, Denney invoked its aid to guarantee the truth of the Old Testament as a whole. Here again, of course, criticism must be allowed to pursue its course, but Denney was persuaded that its results would not contradict the basic message which is authenticated to us by the witness of the Spirit.[21]

Finally, he turned to the apostolic writings, bearing in mind particularly those scholars of his day for whom the earthly Jesus alone was of significance and who made the variety within the apostolic writings an argument against their authority as a revelation binding upon us. Denney held that here also we find an authority which imposes itself upon us: "God by means of them [the apostolic Scriptures] interprets to us His love in Christ, and enables us to grasp it with heart and mind."[22]

From this survey it will be clear that Denney attributed a very real authority to the Scripture. In a sense this was as far as he was prepared to go in defining the nature of Scripture. He tended to fight shy of the word "inspiration." Although in one of his earliest works he could write with feeling of Paul's "consciousness of his own inspiration" and state that "the Bible is verbally inspired at least in the sense that nothing in it is otiose; every word is meant,"[23] he later argued that the inspiration of the Bible is to be seen simply in its unity as a testimony to God's sin-bearing love. "It is only as a whole that we can attach any meaning to its being inspired. There is no sense in saying that every separate sentence is inspired; we know that every separate sentence is not. There are utterances of bad men in the Bible and suggestions of the devil."[24] But Denney was uncertain about the implications of this statement. At one time he could commit him-

---

[19] *Ibid.,* p. 207. Denney developed a similar argument concerning the *moral* evidence for the resurrection of Jesus, *Jesus and the Gospel* (1908), pp. 122-131.

[20] Denney held that such criticism must accept in principle the possibility of the supernatural, *Studies* (1894), pp. 8-13, 207f.

[21] *Ibid.,* pp. 209-219. Here again Denney believed that our conviction that God revealed Himself in the history of Israel "guarantees the presence of a supernatural element in the history" (p. 216).

[22] *Ibid.,* p. 224.

[23] *The Epistles to the Thessalonians* (1892), pp. 84f., 109.

[24] *Death* (1902), p. 315.

self to saying that we are "not bound to the letter of what Jesus taught .... Nothing in them [the Apostolic writings] has legal or statutory authority, and spiritual authority must be trusted to win for itself the recognition which is its due."[25] At another time he wrote: "Neither is there any sense in going through the Bible with a blue pencil, and striking out what is not inspired that we may stand by the rest. This . . . is precarious and presumptuous in the highest degree."[26] On the whole, he accepted the authority of the actual words of Scripture, but also maintained the liberty of the critic.

Similarly, he was critical of the concepts of infallibility and inerrancy. "For verbal inerrancy I care not one straw, for it would be worth nothing if it were there, and it is not."[27] He felt that in view of the findings of criticism it was impossible to hold to infallibility in the sense that everything in the Bible is true according to the appropriate criteria of truth in each individual case. Yet he was prepared to describe the biblical doctrine of the Atonement as infallibly true,[28] and he stated: "The Word of God infallibly carries God's power to save men's souls. That is the only kind of infallibility I believe in. Authority is not authorship. God attests what is in this book as His own, but God is not the author of it, in the sense in which a man is the author of the book he writes. To say so is meaningless."[29]

In his practice as a biblical critic Denney was slow to use the blue pencil. Nobody can read his works without being impressed by the strength of the case which he makes for the trustworthiness of the New Testament and by his firm refusal to follow critical speculations. He had no sympathy with the kind of criticism which is based on refusal to admit the possibility of the miraculous (although he admitted that individual narratives were susceptible to criticism), but he followed the methods of literary criticism. He admits, for example, that the words "unto remission of sins" in Matthew 26:28 *may* be an addition by the evangelist, but, assuming this to be so, "if it were a case of calculating chances, the chances would be a thousand to one that Matthew was right in his rendering of the mind of Jesus, and that

---

[25] *The Authority of Christ*, in *A Dictionary of Christ and the Gospels*, I (1906), 147f., 152. "With all his reverence for the Old Testament Paul accepted nothing from it that did not speak to his conscience, and waken echoes there; and what so spoke to him from the third chapter of Genesis was not a mythical story of how death invaded Paradise, but the profound experience of the human race . . . in which sin and death interpenetrate, interpret, and in a sense constitute each other" (*The Atonement and the Modern Mind* [1903], pp. 68f.).

[26] *Death* (1902), p. 315.

[27] Quoted by J. R. Taylor, *op. cit.*, p. 140.

[28] *Studies* (1894), p. 223.

[29] *Letters to his Family* (1921), p. 23.

210

those who dissent from him at a distance of two thousand years are wrong."[30] He was prepared to ascribe a high historical value to the Gospel of John, although he recognized that it contained much interpretation of the history;[31] and he defended the unity of II Corinthians.[32] Attention has often been drawn to his denial of the Pauline authorship of the Pastoral Epistles, but it does not appear to be so well known that he adopted this view only in his later writings and with some hesitation.[33]

We may sum up Denney's attitude by saying that for him the authority of Scripture was the decisive factor in theology. This authority lay not in any theory of authorship or inspiration but in the truth of the Gospel contained in the Bible: "We find this truth in the Christian Scriptures undoubtedly, and therefore we prize them; but the truth does not derive its authority from the Scriptures, or from those who penned them."[34] It is the appeal which the Gospel makes to the believer by the Spirit which convinces him of the truth and authority of the Scriptures.

THE PERSON OF CHRIST

Denney is best remembered today for his discussion of the work of Christ, but he also devoted considerable attention to the person of Christ. He was convinced that the first task of the theologian "is to answer His own question, 'Whom say ye that I am?' "[35] In dealing with this question he made two excursions into Christology which must be summarized here.

In his *Studies in Theology* Denney asked two questions. The first concerned Christ's own estimate of Himself. Here Denney drew out

---

[30] *Reconciliation* (1917), p. 141.

[31] *Studies* (1894), pp. 58f. In *Death* (1902), p. 270, he wrote: "The contrast with the epistle on this very point is one of the evidences that the gospel is truer to its assumed historical position than many would admit; it is not his own mind the writer wishes to impart, but the mind of Christ; and though it is certainly by the same hand as the epistle, he does not feel at liberty to say everything in it that the epistle allows him to say." Nevertheless, Denney did not feel able to use the Fourth Gospel as a source for the mind of Jesus in *Jesus and the Gospel* (1908), p. 174.

[32] *The Second Epistle to the Corinthians* (1894), pp. 5f., 237-240, 289f.

[33] In *Thessalonians* (1902), pp. 15, 395-398, he defended Pauline authorship. Later, in *Death* (1902), p. 203, he wrote: "It is the combination of fulness and of something not unlike formalism that raises doubts as to the authorship. St. Paul was inspired, but the writer of these epistles is sometimes only orthodox." Concerning this last sentence V. Taylor has written: "Denney's sally . . . is more brilliant than just" (*The Atonement in New Testament Teaching* [1945], p. 47n.).

[34] *Atonement* (1903), p. 9. Cf. J. R. Taylor, *op. cit.*, pp. 138-140.

[35] *Studies* (1894), p. 17.

in broad terms His teaching about His own authority, His unique knowledge of God as His Son, His unique position as a man untainted by sin, and His claim to be the judge of men. The second question which then arises concerns the explanation of this remarkable person. It is not enough to be convinced of "His solitary greatness," or even that He has the religious value of God (to use the terminology of Ritschl). One must turn to the New Testament interpretation of Jesus, and there one finds a constant stress on the exaltation of the living Lord. His earthly life was seen as the incarnation of One who bears an essential and transcendent relation to God.

These views were elaborated in *Jesus and the Gospel* where Denney handled his subject from a somewhat different point of view. Already in his previous study he had drawn attention to various theologians of his day who seemed to regard Christ as little more than a person distinct from us in degree but not in kind, and asked pertinently, "Why should Christ have a place in theology at all, if all you can say of Him is, Look where you will among religious men, and you will not find one anywhere who is even approximately as good as He?"[36] He now proceeded to deal with this kind of attitude by answering two vital questions: "Is it the case that from the very beginning Christianity has existed only in the form of a faith which has Christ as its object, and not at all in the form of a faith which has had Christ simply as its living pattern?"[37] When this question has been answered in the affirmative by a detailed study of the evidence of the apostolic writers, including the evangelists, Denney then poses the second question: "Can the Christian religion, as the New Testament exhibits it, justify itself by appeal to Jesus? . . . Is the mind of Christians about Christ supported by the mind of Christ about Himself?"[38]

This second question is of considerable relevance for theology today. It is the question whether "from the Resurrection onward the Jesus of history was practically displaced by an ideal Christ of faith"[39] — a question posed in this form, be it noted, by Denney himself. Can we recover the Jesus of history, and does He correspond to the Church's conception of Him?

Denney began his answer in the right place with a cool and dispassionate survey of the evidence that the Jesus of history rose from the dead. He held that the main evidence to be considered was not the Gospel narratives but the fact that the resurrection was believed and preached from the beginning of the Church. From this Easter faith

---

[36] *Ibid.,* p. 266.
[37] *Jesus and the Gospel* (1908), p. 2.
[38] *Ibid.,* pp. 2f.
[39] *Ibid.,* p. 15.

one can work back to the certainty of the Easter event, especially
because of what Denney called the moral qualifications of the evidence
— the facts that it was the resurrection of Jesus and not of, say, Herod,
that it has meaning as a gospel, and that it exercised a moral power
upon men, are evidence which must be weighed against any *a priori*
objections to the supernatural and which, in Denney's opinion, more
than counterbalances them. Whatever be the minor difficulties involved in giving a coherent explanation of the resurrection narratives,
the fact of the resurrection is certainly to be accepted.

It is in the light of this conclusion that Denney felt able to examine
the self-consciousness of Jesus: "In particular, what place — in His
own apprehension — did Jesus fill in the relations of men to God?"[40]
He did so on the basis of the teaching recorded in the two earliest
sources (Q and Mark) commonly accepted by the critical scholars of
his day, and found them quite sufficient to prove his point. Various
scholars of course denied the authenticity or the implications of many
passages in these two sources, but Denney was able to show that an
immense amount of such criticism was dogmatic in its presuppositions,
arbitrary in its method, and unbridled in its speculations. In effect he
gives us a striking defense of the historicity of the two earliest Gospel
sources, and he shows that the Jesus depicted in them is one who knew
Himself to be related in a unique sense to God and claimed a unique
place in the faith of men. The position which Jesus assumed is entirely
consistent with the position which He was assigned in early Christianity and yet does not depend upon an interpretation or revaluation of
His earthly ministry and teaching on the basis of ideas held about Him
after His resurrection.

We may make one or two comments on this critical argument. It is
worth observing that throughout this exposition Denney was facing up
to and wrestling with the main representatives of gospel criticism in
his day; there are constant references to such scholars as Harnack,
Klostermann, Loisy, B. Weiss, J. Weiss, Wellhausen, and Wrede. He
was successful in his opposition to these representatives of radical and
liberal criticism. It may well be felt, however, that the modern scholar
who is persuaded that Denney's general position is to be adopted has
to face a greater challenge than he did; for it can be argued that Denney lived before the era of form criticism (the works of K. L. Schmidt
and M. Dibelius appeared two years after his death), and that the results of this science show that the period of oral tradition in the Church
sufficed to alter the words of Jesus beyond recognition. But while
Denney could not foresee the course of criticism and reply to it in advance, it is true that some of the basic things said by the form critics

[40] *Ibid.*, p. 159.

are simply a repetition of arguments used by scholars like Schmiedel and Wellhausen, and Denney did have his reply ready for them.[41]

On the basis of this exegetical study Denney suggested that the Christian Church could adopt as its creed some such words as: "I believe in God through Jesus Christ His only Son, our Lord and Saviour."[42] This statement safeguards the unique place of Christ in relation to God and men, while the Church is left with the right to work out freely the implications and expression of this faith. In other words, what joins men together in the Church is their faith in Christ rather than the doctrines which they hold. Denney pushes the implications of this unexceptionable statement to the point of strongly criticizing the need for adherence to creeds such as the Westminster Confession, although the creeds themselves are allowed to have a positive value.

Denney is certainly right in what he affirms: we are saved by Christ, not by doctrines about Him. But this does not free us from the need for doctrine, for he himself goes on to show what doctrines are implied by his brief creedal statement. It is only when some explanation of the doctrinal significance of his statement accompanies it that it has real value. This is a point of some importance, particularly when the question of the teaching (and teachers) of the Church arises. A Roman Catholic, for example, could doubtless subscribe to Denney's creed, but he would understand it in such a way and add such other matter to it that his conception of what belief in Christ is would be quite different from Denney's evangelical understanding of it. While Denney's creed may be adequate for the ordinary Christian brought up in an evangelical tradition, it is inadequate as a basis for church unity (the purpose for which Denney intended it) or for church teaching.[43] What is of value is his insistence that the creeds and confessions of the Church are not infallible and that it is wrong to demand total allegiance to them: there must plainly be some liberty of interpretation, such as was given by the Declaratory Acts of 1879 and later in Scotland.[44] But one cannot help feeling that Denney's view here tends to be one-sided.[45]

[41] See, for example, *Ibid.*, pp. 159-174, 179-188; cf. the estimate by A. M. Hunter, *Interpreting the New Testament*, 1900-1950 (1951), pp. 50f.

[42] *Ibid.*, p. 398.

[43] *Letters to Nicoll* (1920), p. 122.

[44] To agree with Denney on this point is not of course to deny the need for some confession of the supreme authority of Holy Scripture such as is found in the ordination services of the Reformed churches.

[45] See the discussion of this point by J. K. Mozley, *Some Tendencies in British Theology* (1952), pp. 134f., who thinks that the position outlined in the last chapter of *Jesus and the Gospel* (1908) is not wholly in line with

ATONEMENT AND RECONCILIATION IN CHRIST

There is no doubt that in the mind of Denney the doctrine of the atonement and reconciliation wrought by the death of Christ was the very center of Christian faith and theology. The knowledge of Christ in His redeeming love is the beginning and the end of the Christian life, and the whole of Christian faith and theology revolves around this doctrine. It was the theme which occupied Denney more than any other, and it is his work on this doctrine which merits him his reputation as a great theologian.

Human Sin and Divine Wrath

The doctrine of reconciliation is necessitated by the sin of man. Denney begins his exposition by declaring that man is more than a merely material being;[46] he is a creature made in the image of God. Nevertheless his actual state contradicts his essential nature. This is a conclusion which does not depend upon the historicity of Genesis 3, for "no one who knows what science or history is can imagine that either science or history is to be found in the first three chapters of Genesis; and it will be plain . . . that to seek for them is quite unnecessary to the Christian position."[47] Nor is it dependent upon the theory of evolution; even if there be an upward evolutionary process the fact remains that "we ourselves have fallen, not once but a thousand times."

Both human self-consciousness and the teaching of Jesus testify that man is a sinner — that is, he is conscious of the divine will and of his own will which seeks to resist it. Denney protested against the view of Ritschl that the only sin which can properly be called sin is the definitive rejection of Christ, all other sins being merely sins of ignorance; rather, all opposition to the will of God is sin.[48] Moreover, we suffer not merely from sinful acts but also from a sinful character. This is the doctrine of "total depravity," which means not that man is absolutely wicked but that his depravity extends to every part of his nature; "however deeply our nature may be identified with sin, it is not finally one with it."[49] Denney's doctrine of sin thus "makes it evident that we cannot save ourselves," but does not go so far as to imply "that not even God can save us."[50]

Denney's earlier thought; see, however, the earlier expression of Denney's position in *Studies* (1894), pp. 192-195.

[46] Otherwise there could be no such thing as materialism (*Studies* [1894], pp. 76-78).

[47] *Ibid.*, p. 78.

[48] *Ibid.*, p. 80; *Reconciliation* (1917), pp. 222-224.

[49] *Reconciliation* (1917.), p. 198.

[50] *Ibid.*, p. 199. Denney felt that the Westminster Confession came perilously near to excluding the very possibility of redemption (*ibid.*).

Is man responsible for his sin? Is sin due to the *physical* factor of heredity over which the individual has no control? In Denney's opinion physical heredity is not an exhaustive explanation of human nature. "The inherited bias may be strong, but it is not everything that is in any man's nature, and it is only when he ignores or renounces the relation to God, and freely makes the evil inheritance his own, that he makes it into a condemnation, and puts it between himself and life. What we inherit, strictly speaking, may be said to fix our trial, but not our fate."[51] Nor does the idea of divine election affect our responsibility. Indeed, "to introduce election or predestination into the course of a moral argument is to dismiss argument altogether."[52]

The assumption made by Denney in this teaching is that sin is not merely an imperfection on the human level but an act of rebellion against God. He strongly insisted that there are divine-human relationships and that these are governed by "law." It is easy to misunderstand this word, and to conceive of some mysterious legal authority standing "behind" God which prevents Him from acting freely as a loving Father. Denney, therefore, was at pains to deny that God's relationships with men were on a statutory or legal basis, so that we are like criminals before a judge. But neither is our relationship like that of "a naughty child before a parent whose own weakness or affinity to evil introduces an incalculable element into his dealing with his child's fault."[53] The essential point is that God's relationships with men take place on the moral plane, and there is nothing capricious about them. "Those relations are personal, but they must be determined on universal principles; in other words, they must be determined by law."[54] It is this sense, that God's principles of dealing with men are moral and that they must be universal in their necessity, that justified Denney's use of the word "law" in this connection.

Since this universal moral law exists, man must feel a sense of guilt before God, knowing that he is answerable to God for his sin. This is not simply a subjective feeling on the part of man. It is the guilt of sin which constitutes its power. "How can anyone be good who distrusts God the one spring of goodness, who is afraid of God, who is hiding from God, who hates God?"[55] More than that, man's feeling of guilt is fully justified because there is a real condemnation of sin by God. Denney felt that this was a truth which particularly needed to be emphasized in his day. It is no illusion that we have to answer

[51] *Studies* (1894), p. 91.
[52] *Reconciliation* (1917), p. 217.
[53] *Atonement* (1903), p. 47.
[54] *Reconciliation* (1917), p. 187.
[55] *Ibid.,* pp. 190f.

to God for what we have done.[56] The apostles do not prove this fact; "they declare it. The proof of it is left to conscience, and to the Spirit of God reinforcing and quickening conscience; if anything can be added to this, it is the Gospel itself; for if there were no such thing as the wrath of God, the Gospel would be gratuitous."[57] What Denney thus said in his earliest work of exposition he repeated in his last: "It is idle to speak of the wrath of God as unreal. It is as real as any revelation of what God is, or how He is affected in relation to man. Nothing that treats it as unreal can have any relevance as gospel to the situation of sinners."[58]

Denney believed that the human conscience testifies to this fact of divine wrath, and he regarded the pains of conscience as an important part of the punishment of sin.[59] But the punishment is not exhausted in the pains of conscience. Ultimately it finds expression in death, which Denney insisted was no purely physical phenomenon but is the wages of sin. Physical death and the "second death" are not to be separated from each other; together they constitute God's ultimate reaction to sin. Sin and death are inevitably bound up with each other. Death represents God's final retribution upon sin: "The reaction against evil is persistent, inexorable, absolute; when it goes on to the end, this is the end. Sin is something which is finally repelled by God . . . against which an annihilating sentence of God lies."[60]

The New Testament Teaching

From what has already been said it will be apparent that what has to be dealt with in the Atonement is "not man's distrust of God, but God's condemnation of man."[61] It is only when the latter is dealt with that man can find peace with God. According to Denney, Christ put away this condemnation by bearing it. "He takes it upon Himself, in the sense of the New Testament, by submitting to that death in which God's condemnation of sin is expressed. In the Bible, to bear sin . . . means to underlie its responsibility and to receive its consequences."[62] Again, "His death is conceived as putting away sin, because in that death our condemnation came upon Him. . . . It is a death in which the divine condemnation of sin comes upon Christ,

---

[56] *Studies* (1894), pp. 93f.
[57] *Thessalonians* (1892), p. 62.
[58] *Reconciliation* (1917), p. 147.
[59] *Studies* (1894), p. 103.
[60] *Reconciliation* (1917), pp. 209f.
[61] *Studies* (1894), p. 103.
[62] *Ibid.*, p. 104.

and is exhausted there, so that there is henceforth no more condemnation for those that are in Him."[63]

Denney believed that this understanding of the death of Christ as penal and substitutionary was the fundamental aspect of New Testament teaching about it. He held that "the death of Christ was what it was to him [Paul] only because it was capable of a certain interpretation,"[64] and strongly insisted that the New Testament does not merely state that there is a connection between His death and our forgiveness, but provides the theory which explains the connection: "God forgives our sins because Christ died for them."[65]

On no less than three occasions Denney reviewed the New Testament evidence; his work on *The Death of Christ* remains one of the standard treatments of the subject, giving as it does a detailed exegesis of all the relevant passages. It would be impossible in the brief space available to summarize the wealth of material in this work. It may suffice to note that in his earlier treatment in *Studies in Theology* Denney developed his argument by reference to I Corinthians 15:3ff.; II Corinthians 5:14, 21; Galatians 3:13; and Romans 3:21ff. He believed that this Pauline interpretation of the Cross was basic but also found it substantiated by the teaching of I Peter, John, Hebrews, Revelation, and I John; it is also substantiated by the teaching of Jesus in the Synoptic Gospels, although it is naturally not so prominent there: "Christ could not say much of the meaning of His death, when He could not get His disciples even to believe that He was going to die."[66]

The objection has been raised that in *The Death of Christ* "the living variety of interpretation is obscured."[67] It may be worth pointing out that the general trend of thought when Denney wrote was toward fragmentation of the New Testament teaching, and Denney was concerned to emphasize amid all the variety the fact of unity concerning the basic meaning of the Cross; he explicitly forestalled the criticism that the doctrine contained in such passages as those quoted above was all that the New Testament taught, but at the same time he believed that he had isolated what was fundamental in New Testament teaching.[68] His conclusion was: "The Cross is the place at which the sinless One dies the death of the sinful; the place at which God's condemnation is borne by the Innocent, that for those who commit themselves to Him there may be condemnation no more. I cannot read the New Testament in any other sense. I cannot see at the very heart of it

[63] *Ibid.,* p. 108.
[64] *II Corinthians* (1894), p. 226.
[65] *Studies* (1894), p. 104.
[66] *Ibid.,* p. 120.
[67] H. R. Mackintosh, *Expository Times,* Vol. XXVIII (1917), p. 492.
[68] *Studies* (1894), p. 118.

anything but this — grace establishing the law, not in a 'forensic' sense, but in a spiritual sense; mercy revealed, not over judgment, but through it; justification disclosing not only the goodness but the severity of God; the Cross inscribed, God is love, only because it is inscribed also, The wages of sin is death."[69]

These words, although taken from *Studies in Theology,* would adequately sum up the more detailed evidence provided in *The Death of Christ,* a work which curiously enough makes no attempt to construct a unified doctrine on the basis of the evidence collected. The general ethos of these two books is the same. But the question arises whether the same impression is given by the summary treatment of the New Testament teaching which forms the third chapter of *The Christian Doctrine of Reconciliation.* We should probably not attach any significance to the fact that the discussion here is placed in an apparently secondary position after a survey of the history of the doctrine; it is no doubt meant to act as a corrective to the mistakes of the theologians. It must also be borne in mind that the theme here is the wider one of reconciliation and that, having covered the ground at least once before, the author would naturally seek out new aspects of the subject for treatment. There is, however, a certain reticence in the later work to enter into the *modus operandi* of the Atonement — the idea of Christ bearing the condemnation of sin in place of the sinner — although the idea is by no means absent. We find instead a growing emphasis on the fact that in the death of Christ we see God Himself bearing sin in all its dreadful reality, thus doing justice to the divine moral order, and convincing us that the ultimate reality in the universe is sin-bearing love. It is this fact, that it is God Himself who bears our sin and assures us of His love, which receives a new prominence.

The Theology of the Cross

We must now consider the doctrine which Denney formulated on the basis of the New Testament evidence. The essential problem which Denney found to be solved in the doctrine of the Atonement is that expressed by Paul in Romans 3: how is God to be both just and the justifier of sinful men? There are of course those who deny that there is any such problem, but Denney claimed that the problem cannot be evaded. "Paul felt that the sin of the world made a difference to God; it was a sin against His righteousness, and His righteousness had to be vindicated against it."[70] Basic to Denney's position is the fact that God, no matter how great the extent of His love, cannot

---

[69] *Ibid.,* p. 124.
[70] *Death* (1902), p. 99.

forgive sin without doing justice to the moral necessities of His own nature. It will not do to call God's righteousness simply the moral aspect of His love or to say that His wrath is the obverse side of His love. Denney was prepared to go so far as to say that we must even think of God "taking part with us against Himself."[71] Such language may sound dangerous, but Denney was careful to safeguard himself against any suggestion that a loving Son propitiated an angry Father or that God suffers from an internal contradiction between His love and His righteousness. What Denney maintained was that the Atonement springs from the loving heart of God and at the same time does justice to the moral necessities of His nature which are expressed in wrath against sinners.

A second point is that the Atonement is related ultimately and finally to the death of Christ. In the last analysis it is of course Christ Himself who is the Atonement, but "if Christ had done less than die for us, . . . there would have been no atonement."[72] Even His life must be seen as a part of His death. Forgiveness is costly, and without the death of Christ God could not forgive us.[73]

We now ask, as our third point, what exactly took place on the Cross. The result of the death of Christ is clear: we are saved from the condemnation and penalty of our sins, which find their ultimate expression in death. It is equally clear that Christ did something for us which we could never have done for ourselves.[74] Denney took the view that on the Cross Christ bore the condemnation of our sins and died the death which was our due, so that the claims of divine holiness might be fully satisfied and we might know that God's nature is sin-bearing love.

Denney employed the word "substitute" to describe the role of Christ in this act of Atonement. He felt that the term "representative" was inadequate and misleading. It simply means that Christ acts "in our name, and in our interest," and implies that we put Him forward on our behalf and, so to speak, act in Him; but in fact it was God who put Christ forward while we were yet sinners, and He accomplished an act outside of us which we must make our own if it is to be efficacious for our sin.[75] Another word often used in discussions of the Atonement is "vicarious," but this is rarely found in Denney, possibly because he thought it to be vague in meaning. He preferred to use "substitute." It is important to understand what is

[71] *Reconciliation* (1917), p. 142.
[72] *Death* (1902), p. 200.
[73] *Death* (1902), pp. 38f., 78f.
[74] *Studies* (1894), p. 126.
[75] *Death* (1902), pp. 132f., 195f.

220

conveyed by this term. In the strictest sense of the term it means that a person does a certain *thing* instead of another *person* and for that person. There is, in other words, not only an exchange of *actor* but also an identity of the *act* performed. Denney's belief was that Christ bore our sins and died the death which is the divine sentence upon sin, thus making a propitiatory sacrifice for sin, and releasing us from its condemnation. "The sin is laid by God on the Sinless One; its doom is laid on Him; His death is the execution of the divine sentence upon it. When He dies, He has put away sin; it no longer stands, as it once stood, between God and the world."[76] "Christ died for our sins. *That death* we do not die."[77] There is no other word than substitute which expresses the role of Christ in bearing our sin. But to say this does not mean that the Father was angry with the Son,[78] nor that the Son suffered eternal death and the pains of hell (as taught by Luther, Calvin, and John Owen),[79] nor again that He suffered all the punishment which would otherwise fall on the human race.[80] Denney vigorously repudiated such notions which suggest "the idea of a transfer of merit and demerit, the sin of the world being carried over to Christ's account, and the merit of Christ to the world's account, as if the reconciliation of God and man . . . could be explained without the use of higher categories than are employed in book-keeping."[81] But he still maintained that nothing less than the idea of substitution could convey the truth of what Christ did on the Cross. *A propos* of II Corinthians 5:14f., he wrote: "His death was equivalent to the death of all. In other words, it was the death of all men which was died by Him."[82] And if substitutionary is the only word adequate to describe the role of Christ, penal is the only word which properly indicates the character of His act. Denney's final words on the matter were: "Can we say anything else than this: That while the agony and the Passion were not penal in the sense of coming upon Jesus through a bad conscience, or making Him the personal object of divine wrath, they were penal in the sense that in that dark hour He had to realize to the full the divine reaction against sin in the race in which He was incorporated, and that without doing so to the uttermost He could not have been the Redeemer of that race from sin, or the Reconciler of sinful men to God?"[83]

[76] *II Corinthians* (1894), p. 220.
[77] *Studies* (1894), p. 126.
[78] *Reconciliation* (1917), p. 262.
[79] *Ibid.*, pp. 48, 262-265.
[80] *Ibid.*
[81] *Death* (1902), p. 194; cf. p. 196.
[82] *Ibid.*, p. 84.
[83] *Reconciliation* (1917), p. 273.

Closely linked with this third point is the fourth one. We have seen that on the Cross Christ suffers in the place of men. But Denney also emphasized that the person who thus suffers is the Son of God. The Atonement is not achieved by the innocent suffering on behalf of the guilty, but by God bearing in His own person the sin of man and showing His essence to be sin-bearing love. In the Cross there is demonstrated for all time the love of God which bears the sin of mankind and thus appeals to them to return to Him.[84]

What must be made clear is that this is not an alternative doctrine of the Atonement to that comprehended under the title of substitution. We are not reconciled to God simply because He is love, but only because His love provides a propitiation for sin in the person of His Son who fully satisfies the divine moral order. In order to deal with sin, God has to provide the propitiation. Otherwise, we should fall into the error of minimizing the holiness of God and letting it be overruled by the fact of divine love. Denney's view is that because God bears sin to the uttermost and accepts judgment upon it, His attitude toward sinners is different from what it would otherwise have been.

Fifth, we must ask how the Atonement achieved upon the Cross becomes a reality in the reconciliation of men to God. The Atonement itself is regarded by Denney as an objective act affecting God Himself in the first place; it is the "finished work" of Christ, and because of it God is reconciled to sinners. While he admitted that in the New Testament God is not regarded as the object of reconciliation, he nevertheless believed that there is a sense in which we must say precisely this in order to convey the truth that but for the Cross God's attitude toward sinners would not be what it is.[85]

It is, therefore, on the basis of this finished work that sinners can be reconciled to God. And they are reconciled to God simply by putting their faith in the Savior who bore their sins. All that men are called to do is to commit themselves unreservedly and absolutely and forever to the redeeming love of God displayed in the Cross. Faith is self-abandonment to the love of God; faith accepts the reconciliation which He offers. It is man's "absolute committal of himself for ever to the sin-bearing love of God for salvation. It is not simply the act of an instant, it is the attitude of a life; it is the one right thing at the moment when a man abandons himself to Christ, and it is the one thing which keeps him right with God for ever."[86]

Such self-abandonment is the basic attitude of the sinner toward

---

[84] *Death* (1902), pp. 89, 116, 174, 181f., 189, 199.
[85] *Reconciliation* (1917), pp. 236-239.
[86] *Ibid.,* p. 291.

James Denney

God, and by it he is justified. "To trust it [the love of God] wholly and solely is the only right thing a man can do when confronted with it. And when he does so trust it he is completely, finally and divinely right."[87] This is central and crucial. But Denney also saw that such an attitude of faith must include and bear as its fruit a repentance which is in essence a reproduction of the mind of Christ concerning sin as revealed on the Cross. To have faith in Christ means that we come to share His mind and admit the justice of the divine condemnation of our sin. Faith in Christ has incapsulated within it the death to sin of which Paul speaks in Romans 6, and Denney strongly opposed any attempt to find two different and unrelated strands of Pauline teaching in Romans 3 and 6.[88] He believed that the whole Christian life could be summed up in terms of response to the death of Christ. "The propitiatory death of Christ, as an all-transcending demonstration of love, evokes in sinful souls a response which is *the whole of Christianity*."[89] The doctrine of substitutionary Atonement makes no room for antinomian abuses. "To accept the forgiveness so won [by the death of Christ] is to accept forgiveness which has in it God's judgment upon sin, as well as His mercy to the sinful; it is to have the conscience awed, subdued, made tender and sensitive to the holy will of God, and the heart bowed in infinite gratitude to His love."[90]

These five points sum up Denney's teaching about the Atonement in his *Studies in Theology, The Death of Christ,* and *The Atonement and the Modern Mind.* It was the opinion of G. B. Stevens that the last-mentioned of these works showed a change from Denney's earlier conceptions,[91] but it is generally agreed that Stevens has not made out his case. [92] The truth of the matter seems to be that Denney was careful to deny a legalistic interpretation of his doctrine in this book; he certainly did not abandon his essential teaching. There is, however, more plausibility in the suggestion, already mentioned, that there are changes in his last work, *The Christian Doctrine of Reconciliation,* consideration of which has therefore been deferred to this point.

There appear to be two points which receive a new emphasis in this work. In 1915 Denney wrote in a letter: "I have often wondered whether we might not say that the Christian doctrine of the Atonement just meant that in Christ God took the responsibility of evil upon

---

87 *Death* (1902), p. 89.
88 *Death* (1902), pp. 104-113; *Reconciliation* (1917) pp. 165f.
89 *Death* (1902), p. 104.
90 *Studies* (1894), p. 149.
91 *The Christian Doctrine of Salvation* (1905), pp. 194-197.
92 J. K. Mozley, *Some Tendencies in British Theology* (1952), p. 132.

Himself and somehow subsumed evil under good."[93] In His love God took upon Himself the sin of the world and so proved that the ultimate reality in the universe is sin-bearing love. This is a thought which Denney does not tire of repeating. Might it not then simply be said that in the Atonement God is accepting the worst that evil can do and showing that He can absorb it all and still love the sinner?

In fact what Denney says is something more than this. On the Cross Christ did not simply suffer the wickedness of men and show that God still loves them, true though this is; He demonstrated a love "which owns the reality of sin by submitting humbly and without rebellion to the divine reaction against it."[94] It is the word "divine" which must be underlined in this sentence. The claims of holiness in its wrath against sin had to be satisfied, and to the end Denney maintained that "Christ bowed His head in solemn submission to God's sentence upon [sin], and tasted death for every man";[95] and he used the word "substitutionary" to explain what he meant.[96]

The second new point is that Denney showed in his last work a considerable sympathy for the writing of J. McLeod Campbell. According to this view, the essence of the Atonement lies in the fact that Christ on behalf of mankind and in human nature acknowledges the justice of God's condemnation of sin. "He sees it as something from which, in the divine order, there is but one way of escape, that of an adequate repentance; and seeing, further, that for man left to himself there is no hope, because the very sin which calls for repentance has disabled him spiritually and made him incapable of a repentance really answering to his guilt, in a very agony of love He takes this responsibility of man to God upon Himself, and makes in the place of sinful men that deeply felt acknowledgment of human sin which is the repentance due from the race but beyond its power to render."[97] There are really two ideas here. One is that the decisive element in the death of Christ is that it represents "a perfect Amen in humanity to the judgment of God on the sin of man" — in other words, divine justice receives its due. The second idea present in this conception is that men are saved by making to God in Christ that response of repentance

---

[93] *Letters to his Family* (1921), p. 187. The letter was written to Professor P. Carnegie Simpson and dealt with the idea of a "struggling God."

[94] *Reconciliation* (1917), p. 234.

[95] *Ibid.,* p. 274.

[96] *Ibid.,* p. 282. Here the death of Jesus is described as "in some sense substitutionary," but Denney's exposition shows that he has not withdrawn anything of what he earlier said about substitution. The words "in some sense" are obviously designed to guard against crude ideas which Denney himself had never accepted; cf. *Studies* (1894), p. 126.

[97] *Reconciliation* (1917), p. 258.

and penitence which is the condition of forgiveness. Denney agreed with the first of these two ideas, although he thought that the word "repentance" was the wrong one to use for the attitude of Jesus. But he emphasized that this view was in danger of making Christ's attitude of love and obedience more important than His death. Christ did not merely acknowledge the justice of God's condemnation of sin; He actually bore that condemnation to the full, as Campbell himself admitted. As regards the second idea, we have already seen that Denney taught that faith included repentance, in the sense that we share Christ's mind about sin and admit the justice of the condemnation that would otherwise have fallen upon us. The purpose of the Cross certainly includes that we receive the mind of Christ. But what saves a man is not the reproduction in us of the moral qualities displayed by Christ on the Cross: "The Christian attitude to [the Cross] is not that of repeating it; it is that of depending upon it, believing in it, trusting it to the uttermost.[98] We are saved ultimately by what happened on the Cross as we trust the Savior who bore our sins in His own body on the tree. The theory that we are saved by penitence (as expounded by R. C. Moberly in *Atonement and Personality*) is irrevocably shattered by the simple fact "that in the New Testament μετανοεῖν and μετάνοια occur in all 55 times, but πίστις and πιστεύειν 470 times."[99]

In view of these considerations it is plain that Denney's basic teaching remained consistent to the end of his life, although it inevitably underwent rich and deep development.

SOME OTHER ASPECTS OF CHRISTIAN DOCTRINE

The teaching of Denney on the Atonement undoubtedly represents his major contribution as a theologian, a contribution by which his reputation must stand or fall. But before we proceed to an evaluation of his teaching it will not be inappropriate to indicate the general lines of his approach to other aspects of Christian doctrine so that we may the better appraise his understanding of the Christian faith.

The Resurrection

Denney, as we have already seen, attached great importance to the resurrection in his understanding of the person of Jesus. He also considered it to be of great importance in relation to the Atonement. He would certainly have regarded any attempt to subordinate the events of Good Friday to Easter Sunday as completely untrue to

[98] *Ibid.,* p. 284.
[99] *Ibid.,* p. 285n.

the genius of Christianity, but he was equally sure that a doctrine of the Cross which ignored the resurrection was faulty. "To preach the atonement means not only to preach One who bore our sins in death, but One who by rising again from the dead demonstrated the final defeat of sin, and One who comes in the power of His risen life — which means, in the power of the atonement accepted by God — to make all who commit themselves to Him in faith partakers in His victory. It is not His death, as an incident in the remote past, however significant it may be; it is the Lord Himself, appealing to us in the virtue of His death, who assures us of pardon and restores our souls."[100]

The Holy Spirit

Denney believed that in the theology of his day — for example, in Ritschlianism — the Holy Spirit occupied a position that did less than justice to His prominence in the New Testament. What he himself was concerned to stress was that the Spirit is active throughout the whole of Christian experience. He expressed this in two ways. First, he repeatedly affirmed that faith and the gift of the Spirit are but two sides of the same coin. "There is no Christian experience whatever of which it cannot be said in the same instant that it is the Spirit of God and the faith of man."[101] To put it more explicitly, "faith and the Spirit are correlative terms. The Spirit describes the Christian life as divinely determined, or as the gift of God; faith describes the very same life as humanly conditioned, a life which from first to last is one of trust in Christ."[102] Second, this means that possession of the Spirit is identical in experience with possession of assurance of salvation. The key to Denney's doctrine of the Spirit is Romans 5:5: "In experience, the Spirit is indistinguishable from the assurance that God is sin-bearing love; and to have that assurance in overpowering strength — as the apostle had it through faith in Christ — is to be full of the Holy Spirit."[103]

This means that the doctrine of the Spirit must be invoked to account for the whole of Christian experience. "Just because the action of the Spirit is implied as the correlative of faith at every point, it is illegitimate to call it in to explain one Christian experience more than another. For instance, we must not derive regeneration from it, or the new life, and then leave out justification."[104] It is

[100] *Death* (1902), pp. 202f.
[101] *Reconciliation* (1917), p. 169; cf. pp. 307-313; *Death* (1951), pp. 111-113; "Holy Spirit," in *A Dictionary of Christ and the Gospels,* I (1906), 738.
[102] *Reconciliation* (1917), p. 169.
[103] *Ibid.,* p. 166.
[104] *Death* (1902), p. 112.

thus through the Spirit that the living Christ who bore our sins makes His appeal to us in the Gospel; apart from the Spirit the Gospel would make no impression on men. But at the same time it is only through the Gospel that the Spirit brings men to faith: "The faith of which we are speaking is faith in Christ as He is proclaimed in the Gospel, and the divine causality is one which operates solely through this Christ and the appeal He makes to the sinful soul."[105]

One further point which must be mentioned here is that Denney expressed doubts concerning the fully developed church doctrine of the personality of the Spirit. While he certainly accepted the doctrine of the Trinity,[106] he was not happy with the orthodox formulations of it and held that, as far as the New Testament is concerned, "there is no justification . . . for representing the Spirit as a third person in the same sense as God and Christ."[107]

III. EVALUATION

In his survey of modern theories of the Atonement Dr. T. H. Hughes said of the work of Denney that "it has elements of real value."[108] The foregoing exposition of the thought of Denney should have shown that there are no grounds for the tinge of disparagement which seems to be present in this judgment. There is good reason to hope that the thought of Denney will receive fresh attention and that its true worth is now beginning to be seen.

THE ENVIRONMENT OF DENNEY'S THEOLOGY

Our understanding of the place of Denney in theology must begin with some indication of his relationship to currents of thought in his own day. Denney was thoroughly acquainted with the theological trends of his own time, and it is by his relation to these that he must in the first instance be assessed.

1. The dominant school of theology in Denney's lifetime was Ritschlianism, and Denney followed the example of his colleague, James Orr, in rejecting its basic principles. According to H. R. Mackintosh, Ritschl was attempting to avoid basing theology on a ready-made framework of philosophical conceptions; his purpose was to base it on the revelation of God in Christ. On the one hand, this meant that Ritschl deeply distrusted speculative metaphysics, and he

---

105 *Reconciliation* (1917), p. 312; cf. *Thessalonians*, pp. 344-346; "Regeneration," in *A Dictionary of Christ and the Gospels*, II (1907), 485-489.
106 *Studies* (1894), pp. 71-73.
107 *Reconciliation* (1917), p. 311.
108 T. H. Hughes, *The Atonement* (1949), p. 91.

gave the impression at least of divorcing the physical and moral worlds from each other. On the other hand, he was also opposed to mysticism in religion, that is, mysticism of the kind which was prepared ultimately to dispense with Christ. Mackintosh holds that what Ritschl was really opposed to was the type of theology, associated broadly with the name of Schleiermacher, which based theology on the "Christian consciousness" rather than on the revelation given in Christ,[109] although it is of course a fair question whether Ritschl had really emancipated himself from this subjective tendency.

Studies in Theology was very much a polemic against Ritschlianism. Denney's attacks have been criticized, probably with some justice, and it has been held that in many ways he stood close to the position of Ritschl.[110] Thus there were certain areas, such as the precise definition of the nature of Christ and the Trinity, where he refused to adopt speculative explanations, and he was firmly opposed to all kinds of mysticism which were not firmly related to the experience of reconciliation through the Cross, although it is doubtful whether his views on these questions were specifically due to the influence of Ritschl. Where Denney did differ decisively from Ritschl was in his doctrine of God and the Atonement. Here Ritschl simply abandoned vital features of the biblical revelation of God in Christ, in particular the wrath of God, and produced a doctrine totally at variance with that of Denney.[111] We may agree with the words of Mackintosh: "Latterly one felt disposed to call him one of the most Ritschlian theologians in the country, in the broad sense that he too based all belief on the felt value of the revelation of God in Christ. But he applied this general principle differently from Ritschl, and, one may take leave to think, occasionally to the much greater benefit of those who wish to understand the religion of the New Testament."[112] But "occasionally" is far too weak in this connection.

2. Denney was an opponent of the type of theology generally termed "liberal" or "radical" which felt free to pick and choose among the elements of the biblical revelation. While he himself insisted that "we do not lift our theology unreflectingly and indiscriminately from every word which the apostles wrote,"[113] he was a stalwart critic of

---

[109] For this summary, see H. R. Mackintosh, *Types of Modern Theology* (1937), pp. 138-180; cf. A. R. Vidler, *The Church in an Age of Revolution* (1961), pp. 106-111.

[110] A. E. Garvie, *The Ritschlian Theology* (1902²), held that Denney misunderstood Ritschl. See also H. R. Mackintosh, *op. cit.,* p. 491.

[111] *Studies* (1894), pp. 136-147.

[112] *Ibid.* Denney, however, remained critical of Ritschl, *pace* Mackintosh: cf. *The Expository Times,* XII (1900), pp. 135-139.

[113] *Reconciliation* (1917), p. 180.

all those who preferred their own speculations to the teaching of the New Testament and re-interpreted it according to their fancy.

In particular, he was opposed to the popular liberalism of the pulpit which was frequently heard in his day. One book which represented this approach and aroused a great deal of notice (or rather, notoriety) was *The New Theology* by R. J. Campbell, a book which freely surrendered many of the central truths of historic Christianity and replaced them by a vague doctrine of divine immanence. Incidental remarks in the letters of Denney indicate that he stood poles apart from such a position.[114]

3. Denney's own standpoint was that of orthodox Reformed theology, despite his deviations from some of its teachings. Basically he was an evangelist who presented the Gospel of the Cross with all his power. In an often quoted sentence he said that he had no use for a theology which does not help men to evangelize,[115] and he believed in the reality of a judgment from which men can be saved only through faith in Christ.[116] He used the Shorter Catechism as a basis for his Bible class and found it excellent "for evangelizing,"[117] he quoted the hymns associated with Ira D. Sankey, and he had a high regard for D. L. Moody.[118] The structure and content of his theology was essentially that of orthodoxy.

Nevertheless, he did not really care to be classified as "orthodox." While he was extremely conservative in his biblical criticism, his doctrine of Scripture was not that of traditional orthodoxy. He would probably not have called himself a Calvinist and certainly rejected the doctrine of predestination as a key factor in theology.[119] While he apparently believed in the existence of the devil,[120] he was somewhat unhappy about the second advent of Christ.[121] His position was that "there is room for a tremendous lot of agnosticism in theology."[122]

---

[114] *Letters to Nicoll* (1920), pp. 79-82, 85-87; *The British Weekly* (March 21, 1907).

[115] In *Letters to his Family* (1921), pp. xiif. Cf. P. E. Hughes, "Evangelist-Theologian: Appreciation of James Denney," *Christianity Today*, Vol. I, No. 4 (Nov. 1956), pp. 3ff.

[116] *Thessalonians* (1892), pp. 295-302. It is doubtful what force is to be allowed to his casual remarks on universalism in *Letters to his Family* (1921), p. 107.

[117] *Letters to his Family* (1921), p. 62.

[118] *Studies* (1894), p. 127.

[119] *Letters to his Family* (1921), pp. 105-107, 110.

[120] *Thessalonians* (1892), p. 103.

[121] *Letters to Nicoll* (1920), pp. 102f.; but see also *Thessalonians* (1892), pp. 59f.

[122] *Letters to his Family* (1921), p. 74.

We may say, therefore, of Denney that he represented an orthodox Reformed theology which recognized the force of the criticisms made against it, particularly by modern study of the Bible, and sought to achieve a more satisfactory formulation of traditional positions.

THE CONTROLLING CONCEPT IN DENNEY'S THEOLOGY

Although Denney never set out to outline a system of theology "in which the atonement made in the death of Christ should be the determinative principle," he made it clear that he did regard the Atonement as the key to the whole of Christianity: "In the experience of reconciliation to God through Christ is to be found the principle and the touchstone of all genuine Christian doctrine: whatever can be derived from this experience and is consistent with it is true and necessary: whatever is incompatible with it lacks the essential Christian character."[123]

This statement suggests that Denney had his own measuring stick by which to test the doctrines of Christianity, and that this measuring stick was not simply Holy Scripture taken by itself. Does this mean that Denney ultimately surrendered the authority of Scripture and replaced it by the authority of Christian experience, and does it not land him in a dangerous subjectivism? This is a criticism which can no doubt be made, especially when it is remembered that Denney's doctrine of the authority of Scripture was not crystal-clear. Yet two points must be noted which go far to mitigate the force of this criticism.

The first point is that this standard is essentially an evangelical one. It is fair to say that in adopting this as his touchstone Denney took what Reformed theologians have always considered to be the central theme of Scripture. Denney was convinced that the unity of the Bible is found in its witness to God's sin-bearing love, and therefore his standard of judgment is essentially that of Scripture itself.

The second point is that Denney did not use this principle to criticize certain parts of the content of Scripture, although he did insist that we accept from Scripture only what speaks to our consciences; his purpose in adopting it was that he might criticize other systems of theology which failed to do justice to the biblical teaching.

It is, therefore, not going too far to say that by this form of words Denney was attempting to express the familiar principle that the teaching of the Scriptures is the supreme authority for the theologian. Nevertheless, it remains doubtful whether any attempt to replace the

[123] *Reconciliation* (1917), p. 7; *Death* (1951), pp. 173-184.

authority of Scripture by the authority of some part of the message of Scripture — no matter how central that part may be and no matter how important it is to insist that it is the *central* message of Scripture — ultimately does justice to the fullness of God's revelation to men. We have already seen that Denney attributes slight importance to the question of the nature of revelation and inspiration, and there is no doubt that he thus fails to do justice to the very large and important place occupied in Scripture by this aspect of doctrine.[124]

A second point of the same kind is that Denney appears to have been in danger of regarding the doctrine of the person of Christ as a derivative from the doctrine of the Atonement. This was perhaps only a tendency in his thinking, but it is certainly present in such statements as: "The doctrine of the atonement . . . is the proper evangelical foundation for a doctrine of the person of Christ. To put it in the shortest possible form, Christ is the person who can do this work for us."[125] Now it is certainly true that this principle corresponds to the historical development of christological thought, and is of great importance in guarding against both unitarianism and the type of incarnationalism which separates the life and death of Jesus. But it remains true that the person of Christ can be distinguished in theory from His work as Redeemer, and that, while the New Testament teaching about the cosmic significance of Christ and His work in creation may have been investigated in the first place because of a desire to know more about the Redeemer, this teaching expresses truths about the person of Christ which are true independent of His work on the Cross.[126]

A third point which is worthy of consideration is that for all his insistence on the importance of the Spirit, Denney's concentration on the death of Christ as the central theme of Scripture may have led him to under-emphasize the place of the Spirit in Christian experience. He was certainly conscious that this accusation could be leveled against him,[127] but it is doubtful whether he was altogether successful in rebutting it. On the other hand, his insistence that the Spirit is not a vague supernatural power working independently of the Gospel needs careful pondering by those who tend to exalt the Spirit above Christ in their Christian theology and experience.

---

124 See, for example, the wealth of material in such a book as H. W. Robinson, *Inspiration and Revelation in the Old Testament* (1946).

125 *Death* (1902), p. 175.

126 A view similar to Denney's is adopted by O. Cullmann, *The Christology of the New Testament* (1959), and is open to the same criticisms.

127 *Death* (1902), p. 111; *Reconciliation* (1917), p. 310.

THE THEOLOGY OF THE CROSS

Sufficient comment has already been offered in the course of our exposition of Denney's teaching on the person of Christ to justify us in concentrating here on his understanding of the Cross.

There is no doubt that Denney would have wished his teaching to stand or fall by its faithfulness as an exposition of New Testament teaching. It is not proposed to argue at this point for or against the adoption of this criterion. This is a broader question. It is enough to say that the acceptance of the authority of Scripture as decisive is sufficient to empty of their force all criticisms of Denney's teaching which rest on the assumption that the teaching of Scripture can be ignored. Consequently, we do not need to discuss here criticisms which begin by denying that a doctrine of the Atonement has to deal with the question of God's holiness and His consequent wrath against sinners and conclude by affirming that an objective Atonement is unnecessary, as if the forgiveness of sinners posed no real problem for God Himself.[128] Denney's answer to such criticisms was quite simple: "The commentator on Romans, who does not write with the object of showing his superiority to his text, must be a virtuoso in exegetic evasion if he does not come on irreducible things in which Paul is rather Anselmic than Abälardian."[129]

Does Denney do justice to the teaching of the New Testament? Since his time the ground has been thoroughly canvassed more than once, but the general impression which one gains from the two most detailed and scientific studies of the evidence which have appeared in recent years, the trilogy by V. Taylor[130] and *Märtyrer und Gottesknecht* by E. Lohse (1955), is that Denney's work was basically sound.

This is not to deny the existence of disagreements at various points. For example, V. Taylor denies that in the New Testament forgiveness of sins is presented as the purpose — or, at least, the main purpose — of the death of Christ; the death was not necessary to enable God to remit sins, but is rather the means by which God evokes in us that penitence which is the human means of accepting the forgiveness that God freely offers.[131] It may fairly be argued that the existence of such texts as Matthew 26:28 and the undoubted fact that justifi-

---

[128] See the recent essay by G. W. H. Lampe, "The Atonement: Law and Love," *Soundings,* ed. A. R. Vidler (1962), for a denial that we should ascribe retributive justice to God.

[129] *Reconciliation* (1917), p. 80.

[130] *Jesus and His Sacrifice* (1937); *The Atonement in New Testament Teaching* (1940, 1945²); *Forgiveness and Reconciliation* (1941, 1946²).

[131] *Forgiveness and Reconciliation* (1941, 1946²), pp. 1-28, 195-199.

cation is dependent upon the death of Christ tip the scale in favor of Denney's interpretation.[132] Denney's interpretation of certain of the New Testament texts in the light of the Suffering Servant passages has also been implicitly criticized by more than one scholar,[133] but it is by no means certain that the criticisms are convincing, and the general trend of scholarship still upholds his view.[134]

More weight must be allowed to criticisms of Denney's discovery of substitution in New Testament teaching. We may draw attention to two writers in this connection. V. Taylor admits that the New Testament teaching comes within a hairsbreadth of substitution. Christ submitted to the judgment of God and voluntarily endured the consequences of human sin, but His obedience was not rendered instead of ours and our punishment was not transferred to Him. Rather, He provides a perfect sacrifice with which we can identify ourselves as we penitently approach God. Christ's work is not external to men, and it does not create a change in God's attitude to sinners, except insofar as God treats differently sinners whose attitude to Him has changed.[135]

More recently, D. E. H. Whiteley has stated that Christ's suffering was not a bearing of the penalty of sin instead of us (that is, substitution) but "vicarious suffering endured to save another from the penal consequences of his own sin"; "Christ . . . shared all that is human, sin alone excepted, in order that we might be united with him by baptism and thereby share his life as he had shared our life and death."[136] Whiteley urges that Paul's teaching is thus not substitution but participation; it is through incorporation in Christ who died for us that we enter into a relationship with God within which sin can be done away.

To the present writer it appears that Denney's interpretation of the evidence can be successfully defended against these other interpretations. The point which Denney would have emphasized is that the New Testament teaches that Christ was made sin for us and died our death, with the result that we do not have to die the death which is the wages of sin. We are confronted by the incontrovertible

132 *Ibid.*, pp. 38-40; cf. *Death* (1902), pp. 50f.
133 M. D. Hooker, *Jesus and the Servant* (1959); C. K. Barrett, "The Background of Mark 10:45," *Studies in the Gospels*, ed. A. J. B. Higgins (1959), pp. 1-18; Barrett, *Jesus and the Gospel Tradition* (1967), pp. 39-45.
134 O. Cullmann, *op. cit., passim;* J. Jeremias (with W. Zimmerli), *The Servant of God* (1957); also in *Journal of Theological Studies*, n.s., XI (1960), 140-144; E. Lohse, *op. cit.*
135 *The Atonement in New Testament Teaching* (1945), pp. 190-209.
136 "St. Paul's Thought on the Atonement," *Journal of Theological Studies*, n.s., VIII (1957), 240-255, esp. pp. 241, 243, 255. Cf. *The Theology of St. Paul* (1964), ch. 6.

facts that death is the wages of sin, that because of our faith in Christ we shall never suffer that death, and that Christ died for our sins. The conclusion seems equally incontrovertible, that Christ bore the death for sins which would otherwise have been our death and saved us from its agony, and there is no other word which adequately describes this than substitution. Whiteley is correct in stating that we participate in Christ: "We undergo eternal death in a 'harmless' form, since, through baptism, our potential sharing in the death died by Christ is made actual," but the force of his statement is surely that for us death is "harmless" while for Christ it was, if the word is permitted, "harmful," and that it is harmless for us *because* it was harmful for him. The truth is that both substitution of Christ for the sinner and participation by the sinner in Christ are necessary categories of interpretation. It is because Christ endured the Cross in our stead and exhausted the deadly power of sin that our death in Him does not carry the sting of death which is sin.

Further, it must be emphasized that Christ's work is in a certain sense complete "outside" of us. There is a finished work accomplished on Calvary which has made it possible for us to come to God and be forgiven. V. Taylor would hold rather that the Cross shows us the pardoning love of God freely available for us when we come and make the sacrifice of Christ our vehicle of approach to Him. But the truth is surely again on both sides. What Denney insisted is that we are forgiven by union with Christ in His death: God accepts "as righteous those who by faith unite themselves to Christ upon the Cross and identify themselves with Him in His death; for in doing so they submit in Him to the divine sentence upon sin and at bottom become right with God."[137] But it is equally true that this divine sentence is one that has already been carried out.

Again, it is doubtful whether Taylor's sacrificial theory is fully supported by the evidence. He is forced to admit that his theory of sacrifice is not explicitly taught in the New Testament, and that there is a gap in the teaching of Paul who nowhere teaches that Christ voices the sorrow and contrition of men in the presence of the Father. And while Taylor states rightly that the obedience of Christ does not render ours unnecessary, it is going too far to say that our obedience is immeasurably enriched by becoming one with that of Christ.[138] At such points as these the limitations of Taylor's interpretation are seen. But the question which Taylor forces us to answer is whether reconciliation with God is on the basis of Christ bearing the doom of our sin and thus doing full justice to the claims

[137] *St. Paul's Epistle to the Romans* (1900), p. 613.
[138] *The Atonement in New Testament Teaching* (1945), pp. 199, 203.

of the divine moral order or on the basis of perfect penitence expressed in the sacrifice of Christ. The fact that Taylor himself cannot avoid speaking of Christ's submission to the judgment of God and His sharing with men of sin's awful weight and penalty[139] suggests that the former idea cannot be excluded.

These considerations show that Denney's doctrine of substitution is firmly grounded in New Testament teaching. But, as we have already indicated, it is not a crude theory of transfer of punishment from the guilty to the innocent. Denney guards against this misconception in two ways. First, he insists that in the Cross we see God Himself in Christ bearing the burden of human sin and suffering for it. This does not mean that Christ simply bore the hatred of men for God and showed that God loves them through it all, true though this is. It means rather that He bore the reaction of divine wrath to sin and acknowledged the sanctity of the divine order which connects death and sin. As T. C. Hammond has expressed it: "The scriptural view is not satisfied by mere descriptions of the 'innocent suffering for the guilty' and similar half-truths . . . . It is nearer to Scripture . . . to say that, in view of the nearness to God of the Beloved Son, the Atonement was *God accepting in His own Person* the result of man's wrongdoing."[140] Denney was careful to insist that this does not mean that God's mercy and justice needed to be reconciled to each other.[141]

The second way in which Denney guards against misconception is by His insistence that the attitude of faith includes our repentance and acknowledgement of the justice of the divine judgment which Christ bore on our behalf. This is a point which was already been elaborated above.

When these criticisms are fairly evaluated, it will be seen that Denney's doctrine is powerful enough to absorb them. These are not the only objections which have been made,[142] and it is probable that the doctrine will continue to meet with objections. Nevertheless the growing trend of opinion in favor of the type of theory espoused by Denney shows that the future may well be on his side. A catalogue of supporters which includes P. Althaus, K. Barth, E. Brunner, F. W. Camfield, R. W. Dale, P. T. Forsyth, A. M. Hunter, L. Morris, H. M. Relton, H. W. Robinson, A. Schlatter, and T. F. Torrance

[139] *Ibid.*, pp. 87-90, 175, 203.
[140] *In Understanding Be Men* (1938[3]), p. 154.
[141] *Reconciliation* (1917), pp. 21f., 233.
[142] T. H. Hughes (*The Atonement* [1949], p. 91) held that Christ could not endure to the full the terror of death since He did not die under the shadow of a bad conscience, but here again Denney had already forestalled criticism (*Death* [1902], p. 77; *Reconciliation* [1917], p. 279).

in modern times and has a substantial following in earlier centuries is not lightly to be dismissed.[143] Naturally, the doctrine of penal substitution does not exhaust the meaning of the Cross — Denney recognized, for example, elements of the "Christus Victor" concept in John and elsewhere[144] — but it contains the heart of the matter. By his recognition of this essential aspect of the teaching of the New Testament, and by the evangelistic passion and moral fervor, coupled with the beautiful clarity of style and exactness of exegesis, with which he expounded it, Denney has laid claim to a place among "Creative Minds in Contemporary Theology," and Christian history will recognize the justice of his inclusion among their number.

[143] Cf. L. Morris, *The Apostolic Preaching of the Cross* (1955), pp. 273f. *The Cross in the New Testament* (1965), pp. 404-419.
[144] *Death* (1902), pp. 154f.

IV. BIBLIOGRAPHY

WORKS BY JAMES DENNEY

(A full bibliography of Denney's works is given by J. R. Taylor, *God Loves Like That,* London, 1962.)

The Epistles to the Thessalonians. ("The Expositor's Bible.") London, 1892.

The Second Epistle to the Corinthians. ("The Expositor's Bible.") London, 1894.

St. Paul's Epistle to the Romans. ("The Expositor's Greek Testament.") London, 1900.

Studies in Theology. London, 1894.

The Death of Christ. London, 1902. (Republished under the editorship of R. V. G. Tasker, London, 1951.)

The Atonement and the Modern Mind. London, 1903.

Jesus and the Gospel. London, 1908.

"Hate," *The Expository Times,* XXI (1909), 41f.

The Way Everlasting. London, 1911.

The Christian Doctrine of Reconciliation. London, 1917.

Letters of Principal James Denney to W. Robertson Nicoll, 1893-1917. London, 1920.

Letters of Principal James Denney to His Family and Friends. London, 1921.

Articles in *A Dictionary of the Bible* (1898-1904), *A Dictionary of Christ and the Gospels* (1906-1908), and *Encyclopedia of Religion and Ethics* (1908-1921) — edited by J. Hastings, and in *A Standard Bible Dictionary,* edited by M. W. Jacobus.

Articles in *The Expositor, The Expository Times,* and *The British Weekly.*

WORKS ON JAMES DENNEY

Hughes, P. E., "Evangelist-Theologian: Appreciation of James Denney," *Christianity Today,* Vol. I, No. 4 (Nov. 1956), pp.3ff.

Hughes, T. H. *The Atonement: Modern Theories of the Doctrine.* London, 1949.

Hunter, A. M. *Interpreting the New Testament, 1900-1950.* London
1951.
———— "The Theological Wisdom of James Denney," *The Expository
Times,* LX (1949), 238-240.
Mackintosh, H. R., "Principal Denney as a Theologian," *The Ex-
pository Times,* XXVIII (1917), 488-494.
Mozley, J. K. *Some Tendencies in British Theology.* London, 1952.
Mikolaski, S. J., "The Theology of Principal James Denney," *The
Evangelical Quarterly,* XXXV (1963), 89-96, 144-168, 209-
222.
Peake, A. S., *Dictionary of National Biography,* 1912-1921. Oxford,
1927.
Taylor, J. R. *God Loves Like That.* London, 1962.

8 F. F. BRUCE

C. H. Dodd

I. BIOGRAPHY

CHARLES HAROLD DODD was born on April 7, 1884, at Wrexham, Denbighshire, North Wales. He entered University College, Oxford, as a classical scholar in 1902, and achieved a first class in Classical Moderations (1904) and in the Final School of Literae Humaniores (1906). His earliest post-graduate activities were in the field of classical archeology. During a short period as classical lecturer in the University of Leeds he took part in excavations on the site of Corbridge (the Roman Corstopitum) in Northumberland. In 1907 he undertook research in Roman imperial numismatics at the University of Berlin, and continued his research in early Christian epigraphy as Senior Demy of Magdalen College, Oxford, from 1907 to 1911. During these years he also studied theology in Mansfield College, Oxford. The teaching faculty at Mansfield at that time was a distinguished one: it included Andrew Martin Fairbairn, who was succeeded as Principal in 1909 by William Boothby Selbie; there were also James Vernon Bartlet (in Church History), George Buchanan Gray (in Hebrew and Old Testament), and Alexander Souter (in Greek New Testament).

In 1912 Dodd was ordained to the Congregational ministry, and served until 1915 as minister of the Congregational Church in Warwick (to which he returned for a short time in 1918-19). In 1915 he was appointed Yates Lecturer in New Testament in Mansfield College, in

Dr. Frederick Fyvie Bruce is Rylands Professor of Biblical Criticism and Exegesis, University of Manchester, England. He is the author of *The Spreading Flame, Second Thoughts on the Dead Sea Scrolls, Israel and the Nations, The Letters of Paul,* and many other works.

succession to James Moffatt (who had taken Alexander Souter's place in 1911 when Souter became Regius Professor of Humanity in Aberdeen University). He remained in this post (latterly with the title Professor) until 1930. During the later years of his Mansfield appointment he also served the University of Oxford as Lecturer in New Testament Studies (1927-30) and Grinfield Lecturer in the Septuagint (1927-31).

In 1930 he was appointed to the Rylands Chair of Biblical Criticism and Exegesis in the University of Manchester in succession to Arthur Samuel Peake, who had died the previous year. His years at Manchester, though few, were fruitful.

From Manchester he was called in 1935 to succeed Francis Crawford Burkitt as Norris-Hulse Professor of Divinity in the University of Cambridge. He thus became the first Free Churchman to hold a university chair of divinity at Cambridge since 1660. He remained in the Norris-Hulse Chair until his retirement from active academic teaching in 1949. Both during these years and subsequently he held many special lectureships. He was Speaker's Lecturer in Biblical Studies at Oxford (1933-37), Shaffer Lecturer at Yale (1935), Ingersoll Lecturer at Harvard (1935 and 1950), Hewett Lecturer in the Episcopal Theological Seminary, Cambridge, Massachusetts, Union Theological Seminary, New York, and Andover-Newton Seminary (1938), Olaus Petri Lecturer at Uppsala (1949), Visiting Professor of Biblical Theology, Union Theological Seminary, New York (1950), Bampton Lecturer at Columbia University, New York (1950), Stone Lecturer at Princeton Theological Seminary (1950), Syr D. Owen Evans Lecturer, Aberystwyth (1954), and Sarum Lecturer, Oxford (1954-55).

Since his retirement from the Norris-Hulse Chair at Cambridge his best-known responsibilities have been those associated with his General Directorship of the New English Bible, from 1950 onwards. He was Convener of the Translators' Panel for the New Testament. The appearance of his name as a Companion of Honour in the Queen's Birthday Honours List of June 1961, three months after the publication of the New Testament in the New English Bible, was a well-merited recognition of his work in this respect, over and above his many other contributions to biblical scholarship.

II. EXPOSITION

BIBLICAL THEOLOGY

Professor Dodd has been distinguished throughout his long career as a biblical theologian. It is relevant therefore to say something about his attitude to biblical authority. In an earlier work, *The Authority of the Bible* (1928), he shows signs of the liberalism which dominated British theology during his formative years, as, for example, in his conclusion that "the religious authority of the Bible comes home to us primarily in inducing in us a religious attitude and outlook"[1] — in comparison with which the use of the Bible as a source of doctrine, while not unimportant, is secondary. At the same time there are more positive features, such as his insistence that the prophetic portrayal of God is "a revelation of truth itself to the seeking mind of man."[2] A fuller recognition of the objective character of the biblical revelation appears in *The Bible Today* (1946), where, for instance, the New Testament writings are described as "the authoritative record of that act of God by which He established relations between Himself and the Church; . . . the charter defining the status of the Church as the people of God, the terms upon which that status is granted, and the obligations it entails."[3] It might be said that this later work reflects the influence of the "biblical theology" of the 1930s and 1940s; but one would have to bear in mind, of course, that Dodd himself was one of the leading standard-bearers of this biblical-theology movement.

Probably his finest contribution to a comprehensive biblical theology is to be found in his Princeton Stone Lectures for 1950, *According to the Scriptures* (published in 1952). This study of the use of the Old Testament in the New establishes that there was nothing haphazard about the apostolic citation of the Old Testament writings. The *testimonia* adduced by the New Testament writers are drawn from fairly well-defined areas of the Old Testament; they display a few clearly recognizable patterns of promise and fulfillment; they exhibit "the rudiments of an original, coherent and flexible method of biblical exegesis"[4] which paid attention to the original context and was based on the historical intention of the passages quoted. This exegesis expresses a view of history as subject to the Lordship of God, whose "impact upon human society reveals itself negatively as judgment upon human action, positively as power of renewal, or redemption. This twofold rhythm of the pattern of history finds characteristic expression in terms of death and resurrection."[5] Since this exegetical principle — this "most original and fruitful process of rethinking the Old Testament"[6] — is common to Paul, John, and the writer to the Hebrews, none of them originated it; they all "received" it. The evidence points clearly to the mind of Jesus as its source.

1 *The Authority of the Bible* (1928), p. 297.
2 *Ibid.*, p. 117.
3 *The Bible Today* (1946), p. 8.
4 *According to the Scriptures* (1952), pp. 108f.
5 *Ibid.*, p. 129.
6 *Ibid.*, p. 110.

THE KINGDOM OF GOD

Realized Eschatology

All serious students of the New Testament are compelled to come to terms with the eschatological emphasis which pervades it — an emphasis which sometimes takes the form of an insistence that what the prophets of Old Testament times foretold has been fulfilled by the act of God in Christ, and at other times takes the form of an insistence that the end of all things is at hand. This eschatological emphasis may be expressed in apocalyptic categories (as in parts of the discourse in Mark 13 and parallels, in II Thess. 2:1-12, and in Revelation), but it is the eschatological note itself, and not its expression, that is important.

In the history of twentieth-century interpretation of New Testament eschatology, Dodd has established an undisputed reputation for himself as the chief exponent of what is called "realized eschatology," a viewpoint which has been profoundly influential on theological thinking, especially in Britain, for nearly a generation now. "Realized eschatology" was in fact Dodd's own phrase to describe this viewpoint,[7] according to which the burden of Jesus' ministry is that the Kingdom of God has come. In Jesus' preaching "the 'eschatological' Kingdom of God is proclaimed as a present fact, which men must recognize, whether by their actions they accept or reject it."[8] "This declaration that the Kingdom of God has already come necessarily dislocates the whole eschatological scheme in which its expected coming closes the long vista of the future. The *eschaton* has moved from the future to the present, from the sphere of expectation into that of realized experience."[9] The very meaning of eschatology is thus transformed; *eschaton* no longer means "last in point of time" but "ultimate in point of value."

> Judgment and unending bliss, the establishment of righteousness, the perfecting of human nature, and the renovation of the universe, are *religious* ideas only so far as they depend on the conviction that the Lord is King, and that His will is the ultimate good which the whole created universe is destined to realize. . . . Jesus declares that this ultimate, the Kingdom of God, has come into history, and He takes upon Himself the "eschatological" role of "Son of Man." The absolute, the "wholly other," has entered into time and space. And as the Kingdom of God has come and the Son of Man has come, so also judgment and blessedness have come into human experience.[10]

[7] *Parables of the Kingdom* (1935), p. 198.
[8] *Ibid.*, p. 44.
[9] *Ibid.*, p. 50.
[10] *Ibid.*, pp. 106f.

The teaching of Jesus does indeed include apocalyptic elements, taken over from the imagery of the book of Daniel and so forth, but in His teaching these elements acquire a new meaning; they symbolize the realization of the *eschaton* which He proclaims. The Little Apocalypse in Mark 13, if considered as an independent composition, belongs to a line of development which had no real future. But by incorporating it in the passion narrative, the evangelist gives it a significance in keeping with the whole tenor of Jesus' ministry, assuring the reader "that the story of suffering and defeat to which it is the immediate prelude has for its other side that eternal weight of glory which Christ attained through His passion."[11] But in the early Church these apocalyptic elements were widely reinterpreted along the old literal Jewish lines. The result was that, whereas Jesus had spoken of one triumph of the Son of Man, "they made a distinction between two events, one past, His resurrection from the dead, and one future, His coming on the clouds."[12]

Dodd acknowledges, indeed, that in some important aspects of this interpretation he was anticipated by Rudolf Otto.[13] In *The Kingdom of God and the Son of Man,* Otto speaks freely of the "inbreaking kingdom" in the teaching of Jesus, although he does not exclude a futurist element from the eschatology of the Gospels; the situation, as he interprets the Kingdom of God in the teaching of Jesus, is that "from its futurity it already extends its operation into the present."[14] But Otto laid stress on some of the parables in Mark 4 (especially the parables of the four soils and of the seed growing secretly) as embodying Jesus' distinctive teaching about the present inbreaking of the Kingdom of God.

The Parables of Jesus

To this parabolic element in the Gospel tradition Dodd paid special attention in his *Parables of the Kingdom,* which was published in 1935, his first full-scale exposition of "realized eschatology."[15] In his introductory chapter he agrees wholeheartedly with Adolf Jülicher's thesis that the Gospel parables do not admit of an allegorical interpretation, even when such an interpretation is supplied in the Gospel tradition itself. But, whereas Jülicher held that the single point which

---

11 *The Apostolic Preaching and Its Developments* (1944 ed.), p. 51.

12 *Parables of the Kingdom* (1935), p. 101.

13 *Ibid.,* p. 49, n. 1.

14 R. Otto, *The Kingdom of God and the Son of Man* (1943), p. 59.

15 Adumbrations had already appeared in his article "Das innerweltliche Reich Gottes in der Verkündigung Jesu," *Theologische Blätter,* vi (1927), 120ff., translated as "The This-Worldly Kingdom of God in our Lord's Teaching," *Theology,* xvii (1928), 258ff., and in his chapter on "Jesus as Teacher and Prophet," in *Mysterium Christi,* edited by G. K. A. Bell and A. Deissmann (1930), pp. 53ff.

each parable was designed to drive home was some ethical principle of broad general application, Dodd rightly looks for a point directly relevant to the situation to which Jesus' ministry was addressed.

One group of parables may be called "parables of crisis."[16] The crisis of which they speak will come unexpectedly, and it is necessary that the "sons of the kingdom" should be vigilant, lest it come upon them unawares, and they fail to meet its demands. In the formation of the Gospel tradition these parables were increasingly interpreted — or reinterpreted, as Dodd would prefer to say — of the parousia of Christ; but originally they referred to a crisis within the period of Jesus' ministry. The critical day will break in like a thief, or it will spring like a trap, and those who are asleep will be caught. Let the hearers of Jesus stay awake, like servants sitting up for their master to return home. This simile has been progressively robbed of its parabolic character and given the form of an allegory, in which Christ *is* the returning master and the parousia his homecoming.

But what was the original emergency for which the disciples were urged in these parables to be prepared? Since Jesus viewed His own ministry as *the* crisis of world history, His words to the general public who listened to Him might mean: Be prepared for any development in this critical situation. But for the inner group of His disciples the reference would be more specific, quite possibly to the occasion regarding which He warned them: "Keep awake and pray that you may not enter into temptation" (Mark 14:38) — the time of testing being His impending arrest in Gethsemane. Otherwise, like the people of Noah's day, they would be found unprepared for the disaster and be overwhelmed by it.

There are, however, other parables which on a *prima facie* reading might well be described as parables of growth, because in them some part is played by an on-going process.[17] Do they not indicate a rather prolonged development in connection with the Kingdom of God? Not really, says Dodd.

Three of these parables have to do with the growing and ripening of grain — the seed growing secretly (Mark 4:26-29), the parable of the Four Soils (Mark 4:3-9 and parallels), and the parable of the Tares (Matt. 13:24-30). According to Dodd, however, the point of the first is that the crop is now ripe. The seed has been sown already; it has passed through the various stages of growth. The ministry of John the Baptist has indicated clearly enough that no further growth need be expected; with the ministry of Jesus harvest-

16 *Parables of the Kingdom* (1935), pp. 154ff.
17 *Ibid.*, pp. 175ff.

time has come, and all that remains is to set to with the sickle and reap the crop.

The parable of the Four Soils is provided with an interpretation in Mark 4:14-20 (reproduced with variations by Matthew and Luke). This interpretation reflects later conditions; it "assumes a long period" during which Christian faith is tested by worldly cares and persecution. But the original meaning of the parable is closely in line with that of the seed growing secretly. It might have been objected to that parable that, in spite of the activity of the Baptist, the situation was not yet ripe: before the day of the Lord came a "restoration of all things" was expected and this had not yet come to pass. To this the parable of the Four Soils says No. When harvest time comes, no farmer delays because some of his seed has been wasted and has not produced fruit. That is one of the normal hazards of farming. Where in good ground there is a plentiful crop waiting to be reaped, there the farmer proceeds to reap it. To this same situation Dodd applies the words of Matthew 9:37f.: "The harvest is plentiful, but the labourers are few; pray therefore the Lord of the harvest to send out labourers into his harvest."

If the Markan interpretation of the parable of the Four Soils is to be set aside, the Matthaean interpretation of the parable of the Tares, which presents "the developed eschatology of the Church," is to be rejected outright: "we shall do well to forget this interpretation as completely as possible."[18] On the other hand, however, Dodd does not agree with those who look upon the parable itself as nothing more than a Matthaean recasting and elaboration of the seed growing secretly; it is a realistic and vivid incident from country life. What is its point? When Jesus proclaimed that the Kingdom of God had come, some might have objected: "That cannot be, for there are still too many sinners in Israel." The parable answers this objection with a reminder that a farmer does not hold up the harvest until he has weeded out all the tares among the wheat; so neither will the Kingdom of God be deferred because there are sinners in Israel. The Kingdom of God, by its very act of coming, itself carries out a process of "weeding" — separating the wheat from the tares.

The teaching of all three of these gospel parables Dodd finds expressed in the words of John 4:35-38, where Jesus speaks of the fields as being "already white for harvest" and sends His disciples out to reap, not to sow — for the sowing has already been done by others.

Along the lines of these "agricultural" parables some others which are not drawn from this area of life are also to be interpreted. For

---

[18] *Ibid.,* p. 184.

example, the parable of the Drag-net (Matt. 13:47-50) is accompanied by an interpretation which, like that of the parable of the Tares, points on to the consummation of the age and the last judgment. But, if we recall Jesus' close association with Galilean fishermen, we may suppose that the harvest of the sea presents analogies with the harvest of the land; the point of the drag-net would then be that fishers of men must cast their net widely. Similarly, in the parable of the great supper (Luke 14:16-24), guests are gathered in from the streets and lanes, from the highways and hedges. After all and sundry are collected, there is an inevitable sifting. But, in the situation to which these parables refer, the sifting takes place by the reaction of men to the demands of Jesus; such a sifting actually took place during His ministry.

So, again, the parable of the Mustard Tree (Mark 4:31f.) does not teach the lesson of great results from small beginnings (the description of the mustard seed as "smallest of all the seeds on earth" is regarded as the evangelist's gloss on the words of Jesus); it teaches rather that the time has now come when the blessings of the Kingdom of God are made available to all men, just as the mustard tree harbors the birds of the air. The parable of the Leaven (Matt. 13:33; Luke 13:20f.) was intended to show how in the ministry of Jesus the Kingdom of God was permeating and transforming the Judaism of his day.

In so far as any importance attaches to the element of growth in these parables, it refers to the period of preparation before the ministry of Jesus; but the main emphasis is on the crisis which His ministry has precipitated. The parables may indeed be reapplied to all kinds of new situations, but their original meaning cannot be grasped apart from their life-setting in Jesus' ministry.

The Coming of the Kingdom

The words in which Jesus' Galilean preaching is summarized in Mark 1:15 — "The time is fulfilled, and the kingdom of God is at hand; repent, and believe in the gospel" (RSV) — are interpreted by Dodd as an explicit announcement that the Kingdom of God has *arrived*. The Greek verb translated "is at hand" is ἤγγικεν, the perfect tense of ἐγγίζω; a literal translation would be "has approached" or "has drawn near." (It is interesting to observe that, despite Dodd's position of influence as General Director of the New English Bible, that version does not make Jesus say in Mark 1:15 "the kingdom of God has arrived" but "the kingdom of God is upon you.") One of Dodd's arguments for translating Mark 1:15 in this manner is that in the parallel statement of Jesus in Matt. 12:28 and Luke 11:20 — "the kingdom of God has come upon you" — the Greek verb is ἔφθασεν, the aorist tense of φθάνω, which does most probably imply that it has already arrived. He points out two passages in the Old Testament (Dan. 4:11, 22)[19] where one and the same Aramaic verb is translated by the Septuagint with ἐγγίζω and by Theodotion with φθάνω.[20] It follows that Jesus proclaimed from the beginning of His Galilean ministry onward that the long-expected Kingdom of God, had now come, and pointed to His own activity in expelling demons as evidence of this fact. Even when He said to His disciples, "there are some standing here who will not taste death before they see the kingdom of God come with power" (Mark 9:1), He meant that some of His hearers would realize before their death that the kingdom had come effectively in His own ministry. The word here translated "come" is ἐληλυθυῖαν, perfect participle of the common verb meaning "come." In Greek the verb in a clause dependent on a verb of seeing is regularly expressed in a participial form, and it is perfectly consonant with Greek grammatical usage to render our Lord's words: "there are some standing here who will not taste death before they see that the kingdom of God has come with power."[21] But grammatical considerations alone will not decide for us whether this coming with power preceded or followed our Lord's utterance.

Dodd's thesis has been attacked on both theological and linguistic grounds. An example of the theological attack is Professor R. H. Fuller's argument that "to place the decisive event in the past or present in this way not only does violence to the texts in which Jesus speaks of the Kingdom of God, not only fails to do justice to the way in which our Lord's earthly ministry is keyed up to a future event, to the tension which manifests itself on every page of the gospels, but, above all, *it destroys . . . the cruciality of the cross.*"[22] It may be that the treatment of the subject in *Parables of the Kingdom* gave some color to this last charge,[23] which Fuller emphasizes by italics; but the later and fuller statements of Dodd are framed in such a way as not to detract from the cruciality of the Cross, as we shall see.

[19] Daniel 4:8, 19, in Masoretic Text and LXX.

[20] The Aramaic verb is מטא; it is doubtful, however, whether this verb could be used without any object, direct or indirect, as ἐγγίζω is used in Mark 1:15. Professor Dodd also points out that LXX uses both ἐγγίζω and φθάνω as equivalents of the Hebrew verb נגע. See *Parables of the Kingdom* (1935), p. 44; *Expository Times,* xlviii (1936-37), 92, 140f.

[21] Cf. NEB: "before they have seen the kingdom of God already come in power" ("already" is supplied with this same force in Matt. 12:28 and Luke 11:20, NEB: "be sure the kingdom of God has already come upon you").

[22] R. H. Fuller, *The Mission and Achievement of Jesus* (1954), pp. 48f.

[23] Cf. *Parables of the Kingdom* (1935), p. 75: "In view of this declaration ['the kingdom of God has come'] it is not permissible, for example, to represent the death of Jesus as in any sense the condition precedent to the coming of the Kingdom of God."

An example of the linguistic attack is an article by Professor J. Y. Campbell in *The Expository Times* for November, 1936, in which he argues that the Septuagint and New Testament provide no evidence that the perfect ἤγγικεν ever means "has come" or "has arrived"; and that they do give evidence that φθάνω is capable of bearing other meanings in Hellenistic Greek than "arrive at" or "reach (already)." He questions further whether in Mark 9:1 "the perfect participle here indicates an action already complete from the standpoint of the subject of the main verb."[24] Dodd published a reply to this article in the December, 1936 issue of the same journal, expressing his satisfaction that Professor Campbell and he were agreed that ἤγγικεν in Mark 1:15 and ἔφθασεν in Matthew 12:28 and Luke 11:20 were substantially synonymous. "The difference between us," he said, "may be expressed thus: Mr. Campbell takes ἤγγικεν at its face value, and tries to make ἔφθασεν conform, while I take ἔφθασεν at its face value, and try to make ἤγγικεν conform. I believe his task is the harder." There is no need to pursue the linguistic debate farther, as in itself it is not conclusive. Much more important is the final paragraph of Dodd's reply:

> I concede certainly that if Mark meant " . . . till they shall see that the kingdom of God has come with power," it is not *necessarily* implied that the Kingdom had come at the moment of speaking. The prediction would be fulfilled if it came at any time between the utterance of the saying and the moment of perception, whenever that might be. But it is *consistent* with the view that the Kingdom of God actually came in the complex of events ending with the resurrection of Christ, and that the disciples shortly afterwards perceived that this was the case. The story of Pentecost may, in my view, be taken to represent the moment of perception.[25]

This is indeed an important concession; if the Kingdom of God came in the complex of events ending with our Lord's resurrection, then it had not come in its fullness at any earlier point in His ministry. But in that case the eschatology of His message before His death was not a completely "realized" eschatology. We are not surprised therefore to find Dodd later[26] speaking of "realized eschatology" as a "not altogether felicitous term," and expressing a liking for Professor Joachim Jeremias's "sich realisierende Eschatologie" (a phrase for which Professor Jeremias acknowledges his indebtedness to Professor Ernst Haenchen[27]), while pleading that he cannot translate

[24] J. Y. Campbell, "The Kingdom of God Has Come," *Expository Times*, xlviii (1936-37), 91ff.

[25] *Ibid.,* pp. 138ff.

[26] *The Interpretation of the Fourth Gospel* (1953), p. 447, n. 1.

[27] J. Jeremias, *The Parables of Jesus* (1954), p. 159.

it into English. What Professor Dodd felt unable to do has been done by Professor S. H. Hooke, who, in his English translation of Professor Jeremias's book on *The Parables of Jesus,* renders this phrase by "an eschatology that is in process of realization."[28] This phrase, whether in English or in German, is perfectly acceptable, and certainly more consonant with the total Gospel data than "realized eschatology."

It is no longer possible to say, then, that Dodd "destroys the cruciality of the cross," since he regards the crucifixion and resurrection of Jesus as the climax of the coming of the Kingdom of God announced in the Gospel. "The Kingdom of God is conceived as coming in the events of the life, death, and resurrection of Jesus, and to proclaim these facts, in their proper setting, is to preach the Gospel of the Kingdom of God."[29]

Reinterpreted Eschatology

To begin with, indeed, the resurrection of Jesus was expected to be followed, without delay, by His parousia. A long-deferred parousia, such as appears in the creeds of the later Church, cannot play the same part as an immediate parousia did in the first three or four years after the resurrection. The postponement of the parousia caused a break in what was originally felt as an indivisible experience, and necessitated a readjustment of the original perspective.

One form of readjustment involved a reversion to a futurist eschatology, which once again envisaged the coming of the Son of Man in power and glory as an event in the indefinite future. But there were some, more in tune with the mind of Jesus, who attained a profounder and more fruitful readjustment. One of these was Paul. In two important articles on "The Mind of Paul," first published in 1933 and 1934,[30] Dodd argued for a critical experience in the Apostle's career, *after* the writing of II Corinthians 10-13 and *before* the writing of II Corinthians 1-9 (on the view that our II Corinthians comprises at least two originally distinct documents), worthy to be described as a second conversion. One of the effects of this experience was that the futurist eschatology of Paul's earlier phase was replaced by his "Christ-mysticism," his insight that the eschatology realized in the earthly life of Christ continued to be realized by the power of His Spirit in the life of the Church. "The hope of glory yet to come remains as a background of thought, but the foreground is more and more occupied by the con-

---

[28] *Ibid.*

[29] *The Apostolic Preaching and Its Developments* (1944 ed.), p. 24.

[30] In *Bulletin of the John Rylands Library,* xvii (1933), 91ff.; xviii (1934), 69ff.; reprinted in *New Testament Studies,* pp. 67ff., 83ff.

templation of all the riches of divine grace enjoyed here and now by those who are in Christ Jesus."[31]

Another reinterpretation of eschatology appears in Hebrews, according to Dodd — namely, its reinterpretation in terms of a Platonic scheme, in which "the age to come" is identified with "that order of eternal reality whose shadows or reflections form the world of phenomena." The death of Christ, by which He passed into this eternal order, is thus "the point at which history becomes fully real, exhibiting no longer mere shadows, but 'the very image of realities.' "[32]

But it is in the Fourth Gospel that the cruder eschatology is completely refined away.[33] Even if it does retain references to a "last day" when those who are in the tombs will experience a resurrection of life or of judgment, John makes it clear that the Gospel is not concerned with this literal resurrection of the future so much as with eternal life as the present and permanent possession of believers in Christ. That eternal life which was manifested in the earthly life of the incarnate Word is manifested in the lives of His people by the gift of the Spirit. The decisive judgment is here and now; those who believe already possess the life that is life indeed, while those who refuse to believe are "judged already" and the wrath of God rests on them here and now.

Wrath and Propitiation

The "wrath of God," as Dodd understands it,[34] is not an attribute or activity of God as His love is. It is rather the impersonal process of retribution which can be seen working itself out on the plane of history; as the New English Bible puts it, "we see divine retribution revealed from heaven and falling upon all the godless wickedness of men" (Rom. 1:18).

In line with this interpretation of divine retribution as the working out of Nemesis in human life and history is Dodd's treatment of the group of Greek words traditionally translated "propitiate" and "propitiation."[35] These words (the verb ἱλάσκομαι and its cognates) are examined in the light of their Septuagint usage, where they represent a group of Hebrew words with the root כפר, denoting "an act whereby guilt or defilement is removed."[36] The appeasing of divine wrath does not enter into the biblical meaning of these words. We may see the

---

[31] *The Apostolic Preaching and Its Developments* (1944 ed.), p. 63.
[32] *Ibid.*, p. 45.
[33] *Ibid.*, p. 65.
[34] *The Epistle to the Romans* (1932), pp. 20ff.
[35] *The Bible and the Greeks* (1935), pp. 82ff.; *The Epistle to the Romans* (1932), pp. 54f.; *The Johannine Epistles* (1946), pp. 25ff.
[36] *The Epistle to the Romans* (1932), p. 54.

influence of these arguments in the RSV and New English Bible, where the "propitiation" of the older versions is replaced by terms like "expiate" and "expiation" or even (as in I John 2:2; 4:10, NEB) "the remedy for the defilement of our sins."

The Christian Hope

If the whole element of futurist eschatology must thus be removed from the essential apostolic Gospel, what place is there for Christian hope? "When each individual person reaches the frontier-post of death, he steps into the presence of the Eternal. And when in due course history ends, and the human race perishes from this planet, it will encounter God."[37] But the Christian knows that the God to be encountered is God in Christ. The historical revelation of God in Christ "does assure us what the final meaning of it all is."[38] For it is from the story of Jesus and its sequel that we learn "the true nature of the last frontier-post, and who it is that awaits us there. More than that we do not need to know."[39]

GOSPEL STUDIES

History and Form Criticism

Like his British contemporaries T. W. Manson and Vincent Taylor, and unlike a great many of his Continental contemporaries, Dodd has set a rather high estimate on the historical content of the Gospel tradition, finding in it more of the life-setting of Jesus' ministry and less of the life-setting of the early Church. In his younger days as a teacher of New Testament, he tells us, he felt the gap of thirty-five years or so between the Gospel events and their earliest surviving record to be a very serious matter. As he grew older, he realized that thirty-five years was not such a long time after all — for example, a man who (like himself) was thirty years old at the outbreak of World War I in 1914 remembered the circumstances vividly thirty-five years later. So, when Mark's Gospel appeared, there must have been many middle-aged or elderly people about who remembered quite distinctly what happened under Pontius Pilate, and if they had been presented with an imaginary or fictitious account of the events of A.D. 30 they would have said: "You are wasting your breath: I remember it as if it were yesterday!"[40]

This healthy appreciation of the role of surviving eyewitnesses is

[37] *The Coming of Christ* (1951), p. 26.
[38] *Ibid.*, p. 31.
[39] *Ibid.*, p. 32.
[40] *About the Gospels* (1950), p. 14.

a corrective to the radicalism of much Continental form criticism —
not that form criticism in itself necessarily leads to radical conclusions,
but so many form critics have combined with their form criticism other
attitudes which make such conclusions inevitable. In the hands of
a scholar who does not adopt these attitudes, form criticism can have
quite a different tendency.

In a lecture on "The Dialogue Form in the Gospels," delivered in
Manchester University in connection with the jubilee of the Faculty
of Theology in 1954,[41] Dodd advanced the view that among the various
"forms" which had been recognized in the Gospels it was necessary
to distinguish the dialogue or colloquy. The controversial dialogue,
as he pointed out, had long since been recognized as an important
"form," but what had been done for it (for example, by M. Albertz)
could be applied to other dialogues, whose purpose was didactic rather
than controversial. Some of these are not merely formal dialogues;
they develop a theme spontaneously in the course of conversational
interchange. They may be short and simple like the discussion about
tribute in Mark 12:14-17 or the question about authority in Mark
11:27-33; they may be longer and more elaborate like the conversation
with the rich man and its sequel in Mark 10:17-27 or the response
to the request of the sons of Zebedee in Mark 10:35-45; they may
even incorporate a parable like the dialogue with the lawyer in Luke
10:25-37 or the discussion with Simon the Pharisee in Luke 7:40-50.
But even when most allowance has to be made for the literary skill
of the evangelist, these conversations all exhibit this common feature,
that the interlocutor is made to co-operate in the solution of the
particular problem propounded. In the much longer and more elaborate
conversations in the Fourth Gospel, however (such as, for example,
those with Nicodemus or with the Samaritan Woman), where Dodd
discerns more evidence of the evangelist's artistry than in the Synoptic
examples, a different feature is visible. Now it is regularly Jesus who
initiates the discussion, and not (as in the Synoptic tradition) the
interlocutors. Now the interlocutors, far from helping forward the
unfolding of the theme, play a more passive part; they fail to understand some leading utterance of Jesus, and their obtuseness is made
the occasion for a more detailed exposition of the subject of the
utterance — the new birth in John 3, the living water in John 4. In
other words, the dialogue form in John is different from the characteristic dialogue form of the Synoptic evangelists, and presents closer
affinities (according to Dodd's judgment) to current Hellenistic usage.

[41] *Bulletin of the John Rylands Library,* xxxvii (1954-55), 54ff.; reprinted in
Theological Essays in Commemoration of the Jubilee (Manchester University:
Faculty of Theology, 1954), pp. 51ff.

But beneath the diversity of form there is at times a community of theme which suggests that the Synoptic and Johannine traditions alike go back to an earlier "unformed" tradition. Not only so, but the probability is envisaged that more of this unformed tradition of Jesus' teaching lies behind dialogues in the Fourth Gospel which have no such parallel in the Synoptic tradition, although they can be integrated with it. Dodd agrees, indeed, that the recognition of such material must call for very delicate judgment; but the quest, as he sees it, is far from hopeless.

Another essay in form criticism, which was contributed by Dodd to the R. H. Lightfoot memorial volume in 1955,[42] examines the appearances of the risen Christ narrated in the Gospels of Matthew, Luke, and John. He distinguishes two types of resurrection narrative — a concise narrative, containing only the indispensable facts, and a more elaborate and circumstantial narrative. The former type (exemplified by the appearances to the women in Matt. 28:8-10, to the disciples in Galilee in Matt. 28:16-20, and to the disciples in Jerusalem in John 20:19-21) exhibits a common pattern of five elements: (*a*) the disciples bereft of their Lord; (*b*) the appearance; (*c*) the greeting; (*d*) the recognition; (*e*) the word of command. The latter type (exemplified by the walk to Emmaus in Luke 24:13-35 and the appearance by the sea of Galilee in John 21:1-14) includes most of the elements of the former type (the recognition theme is specially prominent), but represents a freer and more individual treatment of the "unformed" tradition which lies behind the "form" in which the more concise type has been recorded. The remaining resurrection appearances in the Gospels are intermediate between these two types, some having more affinity with the one and some with the other. Other Gospel narratives which present a superficial resemblance to the resurrection narratives are studied; in particular, critical attention is paid to the view which has acquired the status of a dogma in one school of thought, that the transfiguration narrative is really an ante-dated resurrection appearance. Dodd carefully examines the transfiguration narrative point by point in comparison with the resurrection narratives, finding five salient points of difference offset by no single point of resemblance. His conclusion is that this interpretation of the transfiguration narrative cannot be substantiated by form criticism. And his conclusion on the application of form-critical methods to the resurrection narratives in general (the summary of resurrection appearances in I Corinthians 15:5ff. being also taken into the reckoning)

[42] "The Appearances of the Risen Christ," *Studies in the Gospels,* edited by D. E. Nineham (1955), pp. 9ff.

is that the description of these narratives in terms of "myth" is unjustified. If the more circumstantial narratives include traits which are properly described as legendary (a description which, in its formal sense, implies no judgment on their factual truth), form criticism can make no distinction between the main types of resurrection narrative and the types of narrative found elsewhere in the Gospels. The resurrection narratives stand on the same footing as those others not only as witnesses to what the early Church believed but also "as ostensible records of things that happened."[43]

Further examples of Dodd's study of Gospel form criticism will be found in his Hewett Lectures delivered in 1938, *History and the Gospel*. The chief value of form criticism for reaching conclusions about the historical value of the Gospels he there finds to lie in its enabling us "to study our material in fresh groupings, which point to distinct strains of tradition, preserved from various motives, and in some measure through different channels, and to compare these strains of tradition . . . in search of convergences and cross-correspondences."[44] When these groupings are studied separately, a remarkable fact emerges. Each of them gives a picture of the ministry of Jesus from a particular standpoint, but it is the same picture throughout. Whether it is different types of sayings ascribed to Jesus that we study, or different types of stories about Him, "it is not doubtful that from the beginning the tradition affirmed that He lived, taught, worked, suffered, and died as Messiah. We can find no alternative tradition, excavate as we will in the successive strata of the Gospels."[45] To some theologians (and others) this can only mean that the whole picture is historically suspect, that the objective and factual content of the Gospel story is minimal. Dodd, on the other hand, is of the opinion that those who stood under the immediate impact of the facts were not less likely to form a just estimate of their significance than "a supercilious and somewhat cynical Roman aristocrat"[46] like Tacitus, or modern writers whose view is essentially similar to his. "The assumption that the whole great course of Christian history is a massive pyramid balanced upon the apex of some trivial occurrence, is surely a less probable one than that the whole event, the occurrence *plus* the meaning inherent in it, did actually occupy a place in history at least comparable with that which the New Testament assigns to it."[47]

[43] *Ibid.,* p. 35.
[44] *History and the Gospel*, p. 91.
[45] *Ibid.,* p. 103.
[46] *Ibid.,* p. 108.
[47] *Ibid.,* p. 109.

C. H. Dodd

The Kerygma

The development of Gospel form criticism at the end of World War I was accompanied by a new emphasis on the life-setting of the individual items of material brought together in the Gospels. The revolution which these two emphases between them brought about may be appreciated if (confining ourselves for the moment to works produced in Britain) we compare a book like F. C. Burkitt's *The Gospel History and Its Transmission,* first published in 1906, with A. E. J. Rawlinson's volume on *The Gospel According to St. Mark* in the Westminster Commentaries series, first published in 1925. In the former the Markan narrative is regarded as so consecutive and watertight an account of the ministry of Jesus that any item of non-Markan tradition which cannot easily be fitted into the Markan narrative is historically suspect for that reason. In the latter work emphasis is laid on the "intrinsic improbability" of the preservation in the early Church of anything like a consecutive outline of the ministry, and the conviction is expressed that Mark's Gospel provides no evidence for tracing a chronological development of Jesus' public career from His baptism to His death. In this insistence Rawlinson had been anticipated by Karl Ludwig Schmidt who, in *Der Rahmen der Geschichte Jesu* (1919), propounded the thesis that Mark's Gospel is a compilation of separate units or *pericopae,* each of which was transmitted independently in the popular tradition of the early Church, and that their present arrangement is the work of the evangelist himself. The evangelist arranged them in accordance with similarity of subject matter or the like, but anything in the nature of chronological sequence is absent before we come to the passion narrative. The separate units, in Schmidt's view, had a high degree of historical worth, but no historical worth at all was to be attached to the short generalizing summaries (*Sammelberichte*) by which the evangelist joined them together.

In an article entitled "The Framework of the Gospel Narrative," contributed to *The Expository Times* in June, 1932 (Vol. xliii, pp. 396ff.) and reprinted twenty years later in *New Testament Studies,* Dodd specifically examined the generalizing summaries by themselves and found that when they were put together they made up something approaching a continuous narrative, "a perspicuous outline of the Galilean ministry, forming a framework into which the separate pictures are set."[48] Into this outline Mark fitted the rest of his material, consisting not only of isolated units but also of units which were already grouped together in the form in which he received them. Dodd offers the suggestion that he arranged this material by a cross between a chronological and a topical order. Thus, while the old view of the

[48] *New Testament Studies* (1952), p. 8.

Markan narrative as chronologically watertight has gone beyond recall, it is still possible to recognize in it "a genuine succession of events, within which movement and development can be traced."[49]

The thesis of the article just mentioned was elaborated a few years later in *The Apostolic Preaching and Its Developments*. What was the message which the apostles preached, their *kerygma*, to use Paul's Greek word for his preaching which has long since passed into contemporary theological jargon? So far as Paul's *kerygma* is concerned, it can be reconstructed in outline from references in his epistles, notably from I Corinthians 15:1-11, where he reminds the Corinthian Christians of the message which he brought them when first he visited their city. The Pauline outline may be restored somewhat as follows:

> The prophecies are fulfilled, and the new Age is
> inaugurated by the coming of Christ.
> He was born of the seed of David.
> He died according to the Scriptures, to deliver us out
> of the present evil age.
> He was buried.
> He rose on the third day according to the Scriptures.
> He is exalted at the right hand of God, as Son of God
> and Lord of quick and dead.
> He will come again as Judge and Saviour of men.[50]

A similar outline is yielded by an examination of the principal speeches recorded in the Acts of the Apostles, especially those assigned to Peter — and here Dodd finds it necessary to argue that these speeches are not the free invention of the author of Acts and do not show signs of Pauline influence. Indeed, in one respect he finds a marked difference between these speeches and the Pauline outline, in that the latter (in its earlier form, at least) stresses the expectation of the parousia of Christ, while the speeches in Acts (apart from Acts 3:20f. and 10:42) do not emphasize it (although they may imply it), insisting rather that the unprecedented has already happened: God has visited and redeemed His people.

The same outline is presupposed in Hebrews and I Peter; in the latter epistle particularly:

> the reader is aware of an atmosphere which seems in some respects
> nearer to that of the primitive Church, as we divine it behind the
> early chapters of Acts, than anything else in the New Testament.
> That in general its thought follows the apostolic preaching is clear,

---

[49] *Ibid.*, p. 11. See D. E. Nineham's critique of this argument in "The Order of Events in St. Mark's Gospel: An Examination of Dr. Dodd's Hypothesis," *Studies in the Gospels*, edited by D. E. Nineham (1955), pp. 223ff.

[50] *The Apostolic Preaching and Its Developments* (1944 ed.), p. 17.

and we could easily believe that in places its very language is echoed. . . . We shall not be so ready as some critics have been to put all this down to "Pauline influence." It is a clear echo of the apostolic preaching which lies behind Paul and the whole New Testament.[51]

This, of course, chimes in with Paul's own insistence that the message which he proclaimed was the same as that proclaimed by the other apostles (I Cor. 15:11).

Further, the outline of the *kerygma* which can be reconstructed from the epistles and the speeches in Acts is substantially the same as the framework which resulted from putting together in a continuous form the "generalizing summaries" of Mark's Gospel. Mark's Gospel is, in other words, an expanded form of the *kerygma,* in which the ministry of Jesus is narrated as a preface to the passion story, and the passion story itself is set within a frame of glory. In Matthew's and Luke's accounts (largely because of their combination of *didachē,* "teaching," with the *kerygma* or "preaching") the original perspective, emphasis, and balance of the *kerygma* are changed; in the Fourth Gospel, however, the fixed outline of the historical section of the *kerygma* can be discerned "no less clearly than in Mark, and even more clearly than in Matthew and Luke,"[52] and it is this Gospel which provides "the most penetrating exposition"[53] of the central meaning of the *kerygma.*

In all his discussion of the apostolic *kerygma* Dodd does not make the sharp distinction between it and the historic facts of the ministry of Jesus that many other theologians do; the *kerygma* does indeed combine event and interpretation, but in Dodd's judgment the interpretation is the true interpretation, apart from which the event must remain unintelligible.

The Law of Christ

Alongside its proclamation about Jesus, the primitive Church, as Dodd expresses it with characteristic understatement, "is likely to have preserved some memory of what He taught."[54] One way in which the memory of His teaching might have been preserved was in the practical catechesis of the early Church. In an article contributed to the memorial volume for T. W. Manson, Dodd takes samples from the catechetical material in the Epistles, compares them with parallel material in the Gospels, and concludes that this primitive catechetical instruction, while it was not the main channel through which the tradition of the sayings of Jesus came down, did supply a convenient frame-

---

[51] *Ibid.,* p. 44.
[52] *Ibid.,* p. 69.
[53] *Ibid.,* p. 75.
[54] "The Primitive Catechism and the Sayings of Jesus," *New Testament Essays,* edited by A. J. B. Higgins (1959), pp. 106ff.

work in which His teaching on various phases of Christian faith and life could be organized and preserved.

A fuller treatment of New Testament *didachē* was given in his American Bampton Lectures, *Gospel and Law*. There he points out the obvious resemblances between the ethical sections of the epistles on the one hand (especially the household codes) and the ethical teaching of contemporary Hellenistic Judaism and Stoicism on the other. But there are distinctively Christian features in New Testament ethics — the social implications of the body of Christ, the motif of the imitation of Christ, the place of *agapē* as the foundation of all Christian conduct, and (most important) the impact of the new thing which had appeared on earth with the ministry of Jesus, the in-breaking of the Kingdom of God. The relation between the kerygmatic summaries and fragments found here and there throughout the epistles and the framework of the Gospels has its counterpart in the relation between the ethical teaching of the epistles and the teaching of Jesus in the Gospels. Not only is the historicity of this teaching confirmed by Dodd's investigation, but its abiding validity for Christian ethics as "the law of Christ" — not in the sense of a new legalism but an authoritative law "written in the heart." Just as the Ten Commandments took their significance from the introductory declaration by the God who had delivered Israel from Egypt, so the law of Christ takes its significance from his redemptive act; "it is an obligation to reproduce in human action the *quality* and the *direction* of the act of God by which we are saved."[55]

The Fourth Gospel

It may well be that Dodd's most significant work will yet be adjudged to be his contributions to Gospel study, whatever may be thought of his eschatological interpretation. But none of the Gospels has received so much attention from him over the years as the Fourth Gospel. In his inaugural lecture at Cambridge in 1936 he described the interpretation of this Gospel as not only one of the outstanding tasks of our time, but the crucial test of our success or failure in solving the problem of the New Testament as a whole, and compared the Fourth Gospel to the keystone of an arch which at present fails to hold together. In the years that followed he gave himself unstintingly to this task, and when he sent *The Interpretation of the Fourth Gospel* to the publishers he kept back sufficient material on the same subject to make another book of the same size. After the publication of *The Interpretation of the Fourth Gospel* in 1953, he continued to work on this further material. Those who knew about it looked forward eagerly to its appearance in book form, and their expectations were exceeded

[55] *Gospel and Law* (1951), p. 71.

when, ten years later, they greeted *Historical Tradition in the Fourth Gospel*. In this volume the thesis is cogently sustained that behind the Fourth Gospel lies an ancient body of tradition, independent of the Synoptic records and worthy of high respect in its own right as a contribution to our knowledge of the historical facts about the life and ministry of Jesus.

We have already drawn attention to Dodd's treatment of the eschatology of this Gospel, and need not go back to that. But John wrote his whole record, he believes, for a Hellenistic public far removed in time and place from the time and place of the Gospel events. The background of thought which John presupposed in his readers he finds most clearly indicated by the literature of Rabbinic Judaism, Philo, and the *Hermetica;* and "the distinctive character of Johannine Christianity is brought out by observing the transformation it wrought in ideas which it holds in common with other forms of religion."[56] But Dodd leaves us in no doubt that he believes John's interpretation of the significance of Jesus' ministry to be the true and permanent one.

> He makes use of the strongest expressions for union with God that contemporary religious language provided, in order to assure his readers that he does seriously mean what he says: that through faith in Christ we may enter into a personal community of life with the eternal God, which has the character of ἀγάπη, which is essentially supernatural and not of this world, and yet plants its feet firmly in this world, not only because real ἀγάπη cannot but express itself in practical conduct, but also because the crucial act of ἀγάπη was actually performed in history, on an April day about A.D. 30, at a supper-table in Jerusalem, in a garden across the Kidron valley, in the head-quarters of Pontius Pilate, and on a Roman cross at Golgotha. So concrete, so actual, is the nature of the divine ἀγάπη; yet none the less for that, by entering into the relation of ἀγάπη thus opened up for men, we may dwell in God and He in us.[57]

III. EVALUATION

BIBLICAL THEOLOGY

The Bible, in Professor Dodd's words, is offered to us by the Church "as a 'revelation' of God,"[58] or more precisely "as the authoritative record of a divine revelation in history."[59] The history includes both event and interpretation, and according to the biblical interpretation "events in their actuality depend upon a supra-historical factor, the

---

[56] *The Interpretation of the Fourth Gospel* (1953), p. 133.
[57] *Ibid.,* pp. 199f.
[58] *The Bible Today* (1946), p. 12.
[59] *Ibid.,* p. 15.

Word of God."[60] That God does actually reveal himself in the course of human history is questioned or denied by other theologians; for example, in a contribution to the Dodd *Festschrift* Rudolf Bultmann took issue with a number of statements in *The Bible Today,* albeit in the friendliest and most modest fashion, suggesting that Dodd had confused the theological approach with that of the philosophy of history and turned the plan of God into an idea of the philosophy of history by representing the eschatological fulfillment as the high point of historical development and so as a phenomenon of history itself.[61] What Bultmann's own understanding of eschatological fulfillment is we know, and Dodd's representation is much more in line with the witness of the Bible itself.

When Dodd insists on the importance of the subjective factor in appreciating the authority of the Bible, he relates it closely to the inward witness of the Spirit;[62] but one sometimes feels that, just as Luther insisted on the criterion *was Christum treibt* in his assessment of the biblical writings, so (as regards the New Testament) Dodd's criterion is "realized eschatology."

THE KINGDOM OF GOD

Realized Eschatology

Dodd's eschatological interpretation must of course be appreciated in its twentieth-century context. That there is an unavoidable element of eschatology in the teaching of Jesus is certain; indeed, it is not only a question of an unavoidable element, for His teaching is essentially eschatological. Dodd refers to the tendency of the liberal criticism of his younger days to say that the eschatological, and especially the apocalyptic, material in the Gospels was foisted upon Jesus by His reporters, who were influenced by current thought. "With some relief we concluded that when Jesus spoke of the Kingdom of God He was talking about something we understood very well — progress towards a social ideal."[63] This misinterpretation received its quietus from the consistent eschatologists, pre-eminently from Albert Schweitzer.[64] According to the consistent eschatologists, Jesus expected the speedy advent of the apocalyptic Kingdom, Daniel's fifth monarchy; the most urgent business of men was to make ready for this dénouement, and

---

[60] *The Authority of the Bible* (1928), p. xi.

[61] " 'The Bible Today' und die Eschatologie," *The Background of the New Testament and Its Eschatology* (1956), pp. 402-408.

[62] *The Authority of the Bible* (1928), pp. 296f.

[63] *Ibid.,* p. 238.

[64] Cf. A. Schweitzer, *The Quest of the Historical Jesus* (1910); *The Mystery of the Kingdom of God* (1925); also J. Weiss, *Die Predigt Jesu vom Reiche Gottes* (1892).

His practical teaching was an interim ethic intended for the very brief interval before the end. The fact that the dénouement did not come as Jesus had expected and proclaimed necessitated for His followers a radical reappraisal of eschatology. Yet they continued to look for the advent of the Kingdom of God in the near future; its advent would now coincide with the return of Jesus in glory as the Son of Man. But Paul in particular represents this coming deliverance, which the return of Jesus is to accomplish for His people, as having already begun to operate. Paul's eschatology is thus a partially realized eschatology — one might almost say "an eschatology that is in process of realization" — and this is the essential setting of Paul's "being-in-Christ" mysticism. The fact that Paul expressed this mysticism largely in Hellenistic, non-eschatological terms, has blinded most of his interpreters to its eschatological motivation. The continued non-occurrence of the parousia, however, involved a further radical reappraisal of eschatology, with the result that a realistic eschatology disappeared for the most part from post-apostolic Christian theology.[65]

When once the consistent eschatologists had stated their thesis, it could not be ignored. To go back to the older liberalism seemed no longer possible; if consistent eschatology was unacceptable, a more persuasive account of the data must be brought forward. It is against this background that we must seek to understand Dodd's thesis. In his eyes, the reappraisal of eschatology which, according to Schweitzer, had to be made more than once by early Christians, had already taken place in the mind of Jesus himself. When Jesus proclaimed that the appointed time was fulfilled and the Kingdom of God had drawn near, He did so in language which could have left his hearers in little doubt that the Kingdom of which He spoke was the eternal and indestructible Kingdom which, according to the book of Daniel, the God of heaven would set up;[66] yet, if His proclamation meant that it had already arrived, its arrival had patently been marked by none of the apocalyptic concomitants which had passed from Daniel's visions into much popular expectation.

The Parables of Jesus

Jülicher's protest against the allegorization of the Gospel parables was necessary and salutary. Yet to deny that there is any allegorical element in any of them may be going to the opposite extreme from that

---

[65] Cf. A. Schweitzer, *Paul and His Interpreters* (1912); *The Mysticism of Paul the Apostle* (1931).

[66] Cf. the remark of Millar Burrows (quoted in *Parables of the Kingdom*, pp. 43, n. 1, 92, n. 1) that Daniel 7:22 is echoed in Matthew 12:28 and in Luke 11: 20 (and also, we might add, in Mark 1:15).

which Jülicher exposed as untenable. When, for example, in the parable of the Four Soils (quite apart from the interpretation which follows it), there seems to be some emphasis on the four kinds of soil on which the seed falls, we may not be mistaken in thinking that Jesus did have in mind the different kinds of reception that the message of the Kingdom experienced. And the statement that the seed which was sown in good soil produced thirty, sixty, and a hundredfold is one which must have struck any Palestinian peasant with amazement; tenfold or twelvefold would be a very good harvest. What Jesus is doing here is to import into the story He is telling features of the spiritual situation which the story is intended to illustrate — and that is of the essence of allegory.[67] Moreover, to interpret this parable in the sense that the sowing is already past and the reaping here and now, is easier if one comes to the parable with the principle of realized eschatology already established in one's mind than if one looks at the parable in the context of the ministry. This is still more evident in the parables of the Leaven and the Mustard Seed; they do not *prima facie* teach realized eschatology. Now, in the ministry, the seed is being sown; now the leaven is being put into the meal. "Now let it work!" And as surely as reaping follows sowing, as surely as the whole tub of meal will be leavened, so surely will the proclamation of the Kingdom accomplish God's purpose in the world.

It is probable, too, that the proclamation of the Kingdom in Jesus' ministry, in His parables and elsewhere, has more reference to the contemporary political situation than is allowed for by Dodd's thesis. If the Kingdom which Jesus proclaimed was Daniel's fifth monarchy, then what of the preceding monarchies (and especially the fourth) which it was to supersede? Most Jews at the beginning of the first century A.D. probably thought of the Roman Empire as Daniel's fourth monarchy; and many of them had rather definite ideas of the way in which it would be replaced by the coming Kingdom — ideas which Jesus repeatedly discouraged. But the situation was critical, and events were building up for the catastrophe which Jesus so plainly foresaw. A good deal of the apocalyptic language in His recorded teaching is to be interpreted with reference to the current crisis: the signs of the times were ominous, and only by a deep-rooted change of heart could His hearers avert the disaster to which otherwise they were hastening on.[68]

---

[67] Cf. M. Black, "The Parables as Allegory," *Bulletin of the John Rylands Library,* xlii (1959-60), 273ff.

[68] Cf. H. G. Wood, *Jesus in the Twentieth Century* (1960), pp. 152-158 ("Interpreting This Time").

C. H. Dodd

The Coming of the Kingdom

Without canvassing anew the linguistic arguments about Jesus' pronouncements regarding the coming of the Kingdom, it may be admitted that Dodd has done well to insist that Jesus did say that the Kingdom had arrived. If at the outset of His ministry He proclaimed simply that it had drawn near, later He was able to point to His mighty works as evidence that it had come. I see no compelling reason for taking ἤγγικεν in Mark 1:15 as precisely synonymous with ἔφθασεν in Matthew 12:28 and Luke 11:20, but it is most probable that the latter saying does mean that the Kingdom has already arrived. The Old Testament prophets had foretold for the messianic age just such works as Jesus was now performing; this is the point of His reassuring message to John the Baptist (Matt. 11:4-6; Luke 7:22f.). As He told the Pharisees, it was not necessary to look around for signs of the coming Kingdom: the Kingdom was there for their acceptance.[69]

Yet it is equally plain, from various things that Jesus said, that during His ministry the Kingdom was not unleashed in full power. He Himself had a baptism to undergo, and He felt restricted until the ordeal was over.[70] But the restrictions would shortly be removed; the Kingdom of God would be unleashed in power, and some of His hearers would live to see the day (Mark 9:1). First, however, the Son of Man "must suffer many things and be treated with contempt" (Mark 9:12). The Kingdom of God is both here and not yet here; eschatology is both realized and not yet realized. Both these strands are present in the teaching of Jesus, and it is for the interpreter to do justice to both, and not emphasize the one at the expense of the other. The Kingdom was present now in the sowing of the seed, with all the hazards to which the seed was exposed; it would be present in a form that none could fail to recognize when from the good soil the seed sprang up thirty and sixty and a hundredfold. The transition from the Kingdom in present weakness to the Kingdom in future power is marked by the suffering of the Son of Man. Hence the cruciality of the Cross in the Kingdom of God.

A close parallel to these two aspects of the Kingdom is presented by the two stages of the Spirit's ministry in the New Testament. The Spirit came upon Jesus at His baptism, anointing Him for His works of mercy and power. But when the same Spirit came upon the followers of Jesus, after His baptism of suffering and death, His power was manifested on a scale unexampled in His earlier ministry.

---

69 Luke 17:21. I do not stay to discuss the precise meaning of ἐντός in ἐντός ὑμῶν, save to say that ἐντός followed by the plural pronoun may mean "within you as a community" as readily as "within you as individuals." NEB renders "among you" and gives three further alternative renderings in a footnote.

70 Luke 12:50.

Reinterpreted Eschatology

By the suffering of the Son of Man the Kingdom of God triumphed. The old categories of biblical prophecy were transformed in their fulfillment. Even when the old symbols are retained, they are filled henceforth with a new significance, drawn from the act of God in Christ. It is plain enough that Dodd finds the apocalyptic imagery of the New Testament, and especially of the book of Revelation, uncongenial;[71] nevertheless, we must recognize that in the book of Revelation the imagery is used in a new way. Christ may indeed be portrayed as a victorious warrior, in terms borrowed from the portrayal of the divine conqueror over Edom in Isaiah 63:1-6,[72] but when we inquire how He has won His victory, we learn that He has done so by the shedding of His *own* blood. The triumphant Lion of the tribe of Judah is the sacrificed Lamb,[73] and His way of victory forms a pattern for His followers, who in their turn overcome "by the blood of the Lamb and by the word of their testimony" (Rev. 12:11). In Revelation, as in the Fourth Gospel, we hear one whose name is The Word of God[74] saying to His followers: "In the world you have tribulation; but be of good cheer, I have overcome the world" (John 16:33).

That a progression in eschatological thought can be discerned as we read the Pauline epistles in chronological order is clear; it is also clear that in his later epistles Paul sheds the apocalyptic terminology of his earlier writings. But a revolution midway in his apostolic career, such as Dodd envisages, is very difficult to establish. "Paul's revision of eschatology," says Dodd, "involved a transcending of the absolute dualism which relegated the whole natural order to the realm of evil."[75] Whether this dualism is so absolute as all that in Paul's earlier epistles may be questioned, but one of the clearest statements of "dualism" in all his writings appears in II Corinthians 4:3f., written *after* his "second conversion": "And even if our gospel is veiled, it is veiled in those who are perishing. In their case the god of this age has blinded the minds of the unbelievers, to keep them from seeing the light of the gospel of the glory of Christ."[76] There are other examples of the contrast between this age and the age to come in Paul's later epistles, but nothing quite so uncompromising as this. Certainly as Paul grew older the prospect of his surviving to see the parousia be-

---

[71] Cf., e.g., *The Apostolic Preaching and Its Developments* (1944 ed.), pp. 41, 64.

[72] Rev. 19:11ff.

[73] Rev. 5:5f.

[74] Rev. 19:13.

[75] *New Testament Studies* (1952), p. 122.

[76] Cf. G. E. Ladd, "The Place of Apocalyptic in Biblical Religion," *Evangelical Quarterly*, xxx (1958), 75ff., esp. 81-83.

came less probable in his eyes; but the parousia itself was as certain as ever: "For salvation is nearer to us now than when we first believed; the night is far gone, the day is at hand" (Rom. 13:11f.).[77] A similar perspective characterizes the writer to the Hebrews when he encourages his readers with the assurance that the Coming One will come without delay in a very short time and reminds them that they can actually see the Day approaching.[78] As for the Johannine writings, the First Epistle "holds out the prospect of a near Advent of Christ and end of the world, quite in the primitive way, taking no account of the profound reinterpretation of eschatology which is one of the distinguishing marks of the thought of the Fourth Gospel"[79] — and this is one of the arguments Dodd advances against ascribing the authorship of the Epistle to the evangelist himself (while at the same time "the Hellenistic element, which in the Fourth Gospel is fused with the Hebraic after a unique fashion, has in some respects freer play in the First Epistle"[80]). But even in the Fourth Gospel, with all its realized eschatology, there are repeated references to a last day when the resurrection life which believers enjoy now and the judgment which unbelievers have incurred already will be consummated by the action of one who is both Son of God and Son of Man.[81]

Wrath and Propitiation

That the wrath of God can be spoken of impersonally and absolutely in the Pauline letters is true; the *will* of God is also spoken of in the same way.[82] But just as "the will" is God's will, so "the wrath" is God's wrath — retribution indeed, but *divine* retribution. It is not at all easy to think that Paul conceived of retribution as being in some sense a force operating in the world independently of the will of God. "If our wickedness serves to show the justice of God, what shall we say? That God is unjust to inflict wrath on us? (I speak in a human way.) By no means! For then how could God judge the world?" (Rom. 3:5f.).[83] On the other hand, retribution does not operate mechanically;

[77] See the chapter on "C. H. Dodd's Realised Eschatology," in N. Q. Hamilton, *The Holy Spirit and Eschatology in Paul* (1957), pp. 53ff.

[78] Cf. C. K. Barrett, "The Eschatology of the Epistle to the Hebrews," *The Background of the New Testament and Its Eschatology* (1956), pp. 363-393, where it is allowed that the writer to the Hebrews may have known and used Platonic (or Philonic) categories, but maintained that his parables are eschatological parables, and that "the eschatological imagery is primary."

[79] C. H. Dodd, *The Johannine Epistles* (1946), pp. liiif.

[80] *Ibid.,* p. lii.

[81] John 5:21-29. Cf. W. F. Howard, *The Fourth Gospel in Recent Criticism and Interpretation* (4th ed., 1955), pp. 276-296.

[82] E.g., Rom. 2:18.

[83] Cf., for a view similar to Dodd's, G. H. C. MacGregor, "The Concept of the Wrath of God in the New Testament," *New Testament Studies,* vii (1960-61),

its course can be checked by the grace of God, who has set Jesus forth as a *hilastērion* for the removal of the sins which incurred His wrath. Whether "propitiation" or (as Dodd, for one, maintains) "expiation" is the better rendering of ἱλαστήριον may be argued indefinitely; if "propitiation" be retained, it will take its meaning from the context as truly as in the Septuagint the various words of this group acquired a new meaning in their Hebraic context, different from that which they had had in pagan Greek. If, as Romans 1:18 says, "we see divine retribution revealed from heaven and falling upon all the godless wickedness of men" (NEB), then how (we ask) is this retribution to be averted? The answer comes in Romans 3:25 where Jesus, by virtue of His sacrificial death, is presented as our *hilastērion* — our mercy-seat (which is the meaning borne by the word in the Septuagint), for the removal of sin from the divine presence (where it inevitably incurs wrath) as well as from the human conscience. The important point is that God takes the initiative and provides the *hilastērion;* it is not an offering that the sinner makes to appease God. When this is kept in mind, the word may quite happily be rendered "propitiation"; a pro-pitiation that God provides is quite different from something that the sinner might try to do to propitiate God.[84]

The Christian Hope

It is true that theology is compelled to operate with "boundary sym-bols" that lie outside our experience and are difficult to imagine, like the "prior" of creation and the "beyondness" of ultimate destiny.[85] Hence it is not easy to put the Christian hope into non-symbolical words. Dodd certainly expresses the essential truth when he says that God in Christ waits to greet His people at the last frontier-post. Paul expresses it by saying that Christ, by indwelling His people now through his Spirit, is already their hope of coming glory — a glory not only for them but for all creation. The reconciled fellowship which the people of Christ enjoy under His headship is a foretaste of that cosmic recon-

---

101ff.; for a contrary view, R. V. G. Tasker, *The Biblical Doctrine of the Wrath of God* (1951); L. Morris, *The Apostolic Doctrine of the Cross* (1955), pp. 161-166.

[84] Dodd's account of the ἱλάσκομαι group of words in biblical Greek has been widely accepted by other scholars; see, however, L. Morris, *op. cit.,* pp. 125ff.; R. R. Nicole, "C. H. Dodd and the Doctrine of Propitiation," *Westminster Theological Journal,* xvii (1954-55), 117ff. Dodd gives a concise statement of "The Doctrine of the Death of Christ" in *According to the Scriptures* (1952), pp. 123-125.

[85] Cf. J. Dillenberger, *Protestant Thought and Natural Science* (1961), pp. 294f.

ciliation of the future when the universe will be liberated from frustration and decay and find its true head in Christ.[86]

Gospel Studies

In reviewing, some time ago, a book on Jesus by a Continental theologian, I remarked that one had only to compare it with the work of Professor Dodd and certain other British scholars to realize how conservative our own fellow countrymen are. This remark — a truism to readers conversant with modern theological trends — called forth some incredulous questioning. Various quotations were produced from Dodd's commentary on Romans and *The Authority of the Bible* to prove that he could by no means be described as conservative. The word, of course, is inexact and relative in its meaning; but the fact is that quite a number of modern theologians do actually regard Dodd's outlook as excessively conservative. We have already seen Bultmann's remarks on what he has said about the relation between revelation and history; similar criticisms have been made more particularly about his position with regard to history and the Gospel, in the light of what has been called the "Collingwoodian" revolution in historical studies.[87] The view taken in this chapter is that Professor Dodd's work in Gospel studies has done much during the past generation to establish the validity of the New Testament record of Jesus, and that his work will stand. His pioneer activity in the study of realized eschatology has been such that no one can ever read the Gospels now without recognizing the large element of realized eschatology present in them. He has, no doubt, exaggerated that element to the point where much less than justice is done to counterbalancing elements; but that is the defect of the pioneer's qualities. He has not laid down his pen, and we look forward to further contributions made by him to the study of Christ and the Gospels. In his eighty-fifth year he enjoys a secure place in the esteem of his colleagues and disciples as the *doyen* of British New Testament scholars.

[86] Cf. Col. 1:19f., 27; Rom. 8:19-25; Eph. 1:9f.; 3:9f.
[87] Cf. D. E. Nineham, "Eye-witness Testimony and the Gospel Tradition," *Journal of Theological Studies,* n.s., xi (1960), 253ff.; T. A. Roberts, *History and Christian Apologetic* (1960).

IV. BIBLIOGRAPHY

WORKS BY C. H. DODD

(A fuller bibliography up to the year 1954 is provided in *The Background of the New Testament and Its Eschatology,* edited by W. D. Davies and D. Daube in honour of C. H. Dodd [Cambridge: University Press, 1956], pp. xiii-xviii.)

The Meaning of Paul for Today. London, 1920.

The Gospel in the New Testament. London, 1926.

The Authority of the Bible. London, 1928.

"The This-Worldly Kingdom of God in our Lord's Teaching," *Theology,* xvii (1928), 258ff.

"Ephesians," "Colossians," "Philemon," *The Abingdon Bible Commentary.* New York, 1929.

"Jesus as Teacher and Prophet," *Mysterium Christi* (edited by G. K. A. Bell and A. Deissmann). London, 1930.

The Bible and Its Background. London, 1931.

The Epistle to the Romans. London, 1932.

There and Back Again. London, 1932.

The Bible and the Greeks. London, 1935.

Parables of the Kingdom. London, 1935.

The Present Task in New Testament Studies. Cambridge, 1936.

The Apostolic Preaching and Its Developments. London, 1936.

"The First Epistle of John and the Fourth Gospel," *Bulletin of the John Rylands Library,* Manchester, Vol. xxi, No. 1, 1937.

The Johannine Epistles. London, 1946.

The Bible Today. Cambridge, 1946.

Benefits of His Passion. London, 1947.

The Gospel and the Law of Christ. London, 1947.

Christian Beginnings: A Reply to Dr. Barnes's "The Rise of Christianity." London, 1947.

"The Fall of Jerusalem and the 'Abomination of Desolation,'" *Journal of Roman Studies,* Vol. xxxvii, 1947.

About the Gospels. Cambridge, 1950.

The Coming of Christ. Cambridge, 1951.

C. H. Dodd

Gospel and Law. New York, 1951.
According to the Scriptures. London, 1952.
The Old Testament in the New. London, 1952.
Christianity and the Reconciliation of the Nations. London, 1952.
Man in God's Design According to the New Testament (with P. I. Bratsiotis, R. Bultmann, H. Clavier). Valence (Drôme), 1952.
New Testament Studies. Manchester, 1952.
The Interpretation of the Fourth Gospel. Cambridge, 1953.
"Ἔννομος Χριστοῦ," *Studia Paulina in honorem Johannis de Zwaan.* Haarlem, 1953.
"The Dialogue Form in the Gospels," *Bulletin of the John Rylands Library,* Manchester, Vol. xxxvii, No. 1, 1954.
Three Sermons. London, 1954.
"The Appearances of the Risen Christ: An Essay in Form-Criticism of the Gospels," *Studies in the Gospels: Essays in Memory of R. H. Lightfoot* (edited by D. E. Nineham). Oxford, 1955.
"The Primitive Catechism and the Sayings of Jesus," *New Testament Essays: Studies in Memory of T. W. Manson* (edited by A. J. B. Higgins). Manchester, 1959.
"Une parabole cachée dans le quatrième Évangile," *Revue d'Histoire et de Philosophie Religieuses,* Vol. xlii, Nos. 2-3, 1962.
Historical Tradition in the Fourth Gospel. Cambridge, 1963.
More New Testament Studies. Grand Rapids, 1968.

WORKS ON C. H. DODD

Hamilton, N. Q. "C. H. Dodd's Realised Eschatology," *The Holy Spirit and Eschatology in Paul.* Edinburgh, 1957.
Nicole, R. R. "C. H. Dodd and the Doctrine of Propitiation," *Westminster Theological Journal,* xvii (1954-55), 117ff.
Robinson, J. A. T. "Theologians of our Time: XII. C. H. Dodd," *The Expository Times,* lxxv (1963-64), 100ff. Reprinted in *Theologians of Our Time* (edited by A. W. Hastings and E. Hastings). Edinburgh, 1966, pp. 40ff.

9 WILLIAM YOUNG

Herman Dooyeweerd

I. BIOGRAPHY

Herman Dooyeweerd, born in the Netherlands at Amsterdam on October 7, 1894, is professor of the Philosophy of Law at the Free University of Amsterdam. His home background blended two strains of the Reformed tradition; his father was a follower of Dr. Abraham Kuyper, the eminent theologian-statesman and founder of the Free University, while his mother was rooted in the searching school of Puritan-like piety associated with the separation movement (*afscheiding*) and with the independent theologian and pastor of Elberfeld Dr. H. F. Kohlbrügge. The Kuyperian strain is most prominent in Dooyeweerd's work, though his emphasis on self-knowledge is akin to one of the aspects of Kohlbrügge's teaching.

During his undergraduate days at the Free University, Dooyeweerd's interests were largely directed to the aesthetic aspect of life, although he also felt the attraction exerted by the lectures of Professors D. P. D. Fabius, Anema, and Herman Bavinck. In 1917, under the supervision of Fabius, he defended a doctoral dissertation on the cabinet in Dutch Law.

In 1922, Dooyeweerd accepted the post of Adjunct Director to the recently established Abraham Kuyper Foundation with the intention of devoting himself to systematic study of the foundations of the Neo-Calvinist life-and-world view in its application to law, ecnomics, and politics. In this capacity he was the editor of *Nederland*

Dr. William Young is Assistant Professor of Philosophy at the University of Rhode Island. He is the author of *Towards a Reformed Philosophy,* and cotranslator of Vol. I of Dooyeweerd's *New Critique of Theoretical Thought.*

en Oranje, a popular organ of the Anti-Revolutionary Party and the founder of a new organ with the title *Anti-Revolutionaire Staatkunde,* in which he published an important series of articles on the conflict over Christian politics (1924-27). The subtitle of this series contains the term *wetsidee* ("idea of law"), which was to become the keyword of his later philosophy.

In 1926, Dooyeweerd published an article on Calvinism versus Neo-Kantianism in the *Tijdschrift voor Wijsbegeerte,* in which he issued a warning not only against those who accepted Neo-Kantianism as the definitive result of the entire development of philosophical thought, but also against those Calvinists who were attempting to adapt Neo-Kantianism to a Christian life-and-world view.

The year 1926 also marks Dooyeweerd's appointment as professor of the Philosophy of Law, Encyclopedia of Jurisprudence, and Old Fatherland Law at the Free University. His inaugural address dealt with the significance of the idea of law, in the sense of the universal structures of order in the cosmos, for the science and philosophy of jurisprudence. Together with his brother-in-law, Dr. D. H. Th. Vollenhoven, professor of Philosophy at the Free University, Dooyeweerd continued the development of his philosophical system until his major work on The Philosophy of The Cosmonomic Idea in three volumes was ripe for publication (1935-36).

Dooyeweerd's thought develops themes stressed by Abraham Kuyper, especially those of sphere-sovereignty and the heart of man, while it is severely negative toward Scholastic elements in Kuyper's theology. The fundamental significance of the characteristic structures of the aspects of experience occurred to Dooyeweerd during a walk in the dunes along the Dutch coast and is the central conception of his inaugural address. Later he included in his vision of knowledge and reality the important transcendental critique of theoretical thought, the idea of cosmic time, the theory of structures of individuality and their interlacements, and the distinction between naive experience and the theoretical attitude, as well as other themes. Modern philosophy is subjected to the transcendental critique in the first volume of the systematic trilogy (published in a four-volume revised translation as *A New Critique of Theoretical Thought,* 1953-1958), while Greek philosophy through Plato is dealt with in the first volume, the only published one, of another trilogy on Reformation and Scholasticism in Philosophy (1949). Portions of the unpublished volume on Scholasticism have appeared as articles in the quarterly *Philosophia Reformata,* organ of the Society for Calvinistic Philosophy, of which Dooyeweerd is the chief editor. In addition to numerous articles, lectures, and shorter books, Dooyeweerd has published his extensive lectures on the Encyclopedia of Jurisprudence (1946) and an excellently written series of addresses delivered during his North American tour in 1959, entitled *In the Twilight of Western Thought.*

The philosophy of the cosmonomic idea met with supporters and opponents both within and outside of Reformed circles. The original editorial board of *Philosophia Reformata* included Dr. J. Bohatec, the eminent Calvin scholar in Vienna, and Dr. H. G. Stoker of Potchefstroom, South Africa. The name of Dr. C. Van Til of Westminster Theological Seminary, Philadelphia, was added to the list in the second issue. Opposition to the views of Dooyeweerd and Vollenhoven was voiced by Dr. Valentinus Hepp, professor of Dogmatics at the Free University, who in a series of brochures entitled *Dreigende Deformatie* (Threatening Deformation — 1936-37) dealt with the theological issues relating to the soul, the two natures of Christ, and common grace. Hepp's diagnosis charged the new philosophy and related trends in theology with biblicism and a misguided progressivism issuing in positions conflicting with Reformed doctrine. Dooyeweerd's antipathy to "Scholasticism" in historic Reformed as well as Roman Catholic theology must be understood in relation to this unhappy controversy within his own church and university.

From outside of Reformed circles the charge has commonly been brought that what Dooyeweerd and Vollenhoven were doing was not philosophy but theology. On the other hand, Dooyeweerd's work has received sympathetic recognition in some Roman Catholic and non-Christian circles. Dr. Michael J. Marlet, S. J., published his *Grundlinien der Kalvinistischen "Philosophie der Gesetzidee" als Christlicher Transzendentalphilosophie* in 1954 with an accompanying preface by Dooyeweerd, in which he speaks of his original intention to give an "ecumenical Christian" foundation to the philosophy of the cosmonomic idea and of his explicit removal of the term "Calvinistic" philosophy from the English edition of his first trilogy, although he still regards his work as a fruit of the Calvinistic Reformation. The volume of essays, *Perspectief,* celebrating the twenty-fifth year of the Society for Calvinistic Philosophy, contains an article by Dr. C. E. Langemeijer on the significance of Dooyeweerd for the philosophy of non-ecclesiastical quarters, one by Dr. J. J. Louet Feisser on the contribution of the philosophy of the cosmonomic idea to the renewal of philosophical insight, and one by Professor Marlet on philosophy of the cosmonomic idea and Thomistic thought. Louet Feisser's contribution includes a discussion of the agreement of Dooyeweerd with the Dutch personalist philosopher Ph. Kohnstamm as well as with Professor A. J. de Sopper, both of whom, although non-Calvinists, came to express their sympathy with his philosophy. Another striking instance of recognition of Dooyeweerd's work may be mentioned. Dr. J. P. van Mullen, a modernist and Neo-Kantian philosopher, had sharply disqualified Dooyeweerd's line of thought, but in the course of time revised this judgment drastically and acknowledged the influence exercised by this Reformed philosophy on his later thought.

Since 1948 Dooyeweerd has been a member of the Royal Dutch Academy of the Sciences. He has extended his influence beyond the Netherlands by lecturing in South Africa, France, and North America.

II. EXPOSITION

The philosophical structure erected by Dooyeweerd in his systematic trilogy and numerous other writings is extremely complex and consequently does not lend itself to concise exposition. The system may be divided into five parts as follows: (1) the transcendental critique of theoretical thought, in which the foundations of philosophy are laid; (2) the general theory of the spheres of law, in which the outlines of a cosmology or account of the coherence of the aspects of creation are sketched; (3) epistemology, developed in the light of the cosmonomic idea; (4) the theory of structures of individuality and human society; and (5) the basic theme of philosophical anthropology, discussing the place of man in the cosmos. The concluding theme is reserved for exhaustive treatment in the unpublished final volume of the trilogy on Reformation and Scholasticism. Dooyeweerd has given some indications of the lines along which he has been thinking on this important topic.[1]

The present discussion is restricted to a consideration of topics having particular interest for theology and of the theological implications that have been drawn, especially those drawn by Dooyeweerd himself. Since the transcendental critique of theoretical thought has come to occupy an increasingly prominent place in Dooyeweerd's thought,[2] consideration will be given to relevant aspects of this critique, especially the doctrine of the antithetic *Gegenstand*-relation as characterizing the attitude of theoretical thought, and the theory of the basic religious motives of theoretical and particularly of philosophical thought. Then topics will be selected from the general theory of the

---

[1] See in particular the lecture "What Is Man?" in *In the Twilight of Western Thought* (1960), and the discussion in Vol. III, pp. 781ff. of *A New Critique of Theoretical Thought* (1953), but especially the anthropological theses *Correspondentie-Bladen* (Dec., 1942) and the article on the task of a philosophical anthropology in *Philosophia Reformata*, 1961.

[2] Cf. the space devoted to the sharpened version of the critique in the English translation of Vol. I of the systematic trilogy and in *In the Twilight of Western Thought*, the subtitle of which is "Studies in the Pretended Autonomy of Philosophical Thought."

spheres of law, which provide the background required for an understanding of Dooyeweerd's views as to the nature of theology and its relation to philosophy and the other sciences. Epistemology will receive some attention in connection with the *Gegenstand*-relation, while the theory of individuality, and in particular Dooyeweerd's denial of the metaphysical conception of substance, will be found to have not only anthropological but also far-reaching theological consequences. Our choice of the limited topic of the theological aspects of Dooyeweerd's philosophy should thus not prove a hindrance to an understanding of his system as a coherent whole, but rather provide a thread like that of Ariadne for direction through the labyrinth to its very heart.

The Transcendental Critique of Theoretical Thought

The term "transcendental critique" is initially forbidding to the reader who prefers ordinary language to an artificially technical terminology. Americans may also associate the word "transcendental" with the Transcendentalist movement in nineteenth-century New England. Notwithstanding the danger of misunderstanding, the term does perform a useful function, although perhaps an unintended one. It points unmistakably to Kant's critical or transcendental philosophy as the background of Dooyeweerd's analysis. No doubt Dooyeweerd would insist on the differences between his transcendental critique and that of Kant. Kant raised only such questions as: "How is Pure Mathematics possible?" "How is Natural Science possible?" "How is Metaphysics possible?" But Dooyeweerd asks "How is Theoretical Thought as such possible?" Even if Dooyeweerd is justified in making this distinction between the problem of his transcendental critique and that of Kant's, the distinction itself implies a fundamental agreement, namely, both Kant and Dooyeweerd raise a transcendental question, in the sense of a question having the form "Under what conditions is X possible?" where "X" may stand for some branch of inquiry, for knowledge in general or for Dooyeweerd's "theoretical thought." In the transcendental critique, then, Dooyeweerd does raise questions of the sort that Kant had previously asked, even though Dooyeweerd's question has a characteristic twist which is absent from those raised by the sage of Königsberg.

The twist just mentioned consists in Dooyeweerd's intention to call into question the "pretended autonomy of philosophical thought." By "autonomy," Dooyeweerd may be taken to mean a form of self-sufficiency or independence, expressing itself in relation to religion and divine revelation. "Autonomy" in the sense of independence of

274

experience in general, the *a priori* in a Rationalist or Kantian sense, is not referred to expressly, although this type of autonomy is no doubt included in Dooyeweerd's view along with that shared by empiricist philosophies that approach human experience without reference to divine revelation. Dooyeweerd recognizes distinct forms of the assumption of the autonomy of human reason in ancient, medieval, and modern philosophy. "As soon as we seek to penetrate to the root of these fundamentally different conceptions, we are confronted with a fundamental difference in presuppositions which surpasses the boundaries of theoretical thought."[3]

The fact that some form of the postulate of autonomy has been uncritically adopted by the greater number of philosophers in the present as well as in the past accounts for the break-down of communication among conflicting philosophical movements. "A debate between philosophical trends, which are fundamentally opposed to each other, usually results in a reasoning at cross-purposes, because they are not able to find a way to penetrate to each other's true starting-points. The latter seem to be masked by the dogma concerning the autonomy of philosophical thought."[4] The attempt of logical positivism to provide criteria of meaning, as by the verification principle, has not helped.

The Attitude of Theoretical Thought and the Antithetic Gegenstand-Relation

The transcendental critique for Dooyeweerd is a transcendental critique of theoretical thought. What does "theoretical thought" signify? Theoretical thought, for Dooyeweerd, is distinguished sharply from naive everyday experience, and thus from the functioning of thought on that pre-scientific level. Theoretical thought is scientific thought in a Continental rather than Anglo-American usage of "scientific." Mathematics, the natural sciences, the so-called social sciences, the normative disciplines, theology, and philosophy are alike considered as sciences, and the attitude of thought as it functions in these disciplines is termed "theoretical." How is this attitude of thought characterized as distinguished from that of naive experience? This question is answered in terms of the antithetic *Gegenstand*-relation.

In naive experience, the ordinary man has an integral, immediate contact with reality in its structures of individual things and concrete events. The formation of concepts on the naive level is not directed toward the distinguishable aspects of things and events, but to the things and events themselves. The logical aspect of the given is

3 *In the Twilight of Western Thought* (1960), pp. 2f.
4 *Ibid.*, p. 3.

experienced as an implicit component of that reality. Naive experience is characterized by "the subject-object relation," in which *"objective* functions and qualities are unreflectingly ascribed to things . . . within modal aspects in which it is not possible for them to appear as *subjects."*[5] Thus water is experienced as necessary for life, a bird's nest is a typical object of life, and a rose, which neither feels, thinks nor appreciates beauty, has objective qualities of sensory color and odor, objective logical characteristics, and objective beauty.

Sharply contrasted with the subject-object relation of naive experience is the antithetic *Gegenstand*-relation of theoretical thought. Although the German word *Gegenstand* is commonly translated "object" in philosophical literature, Dooyeweerd detects a confusion running through much modern epistemology in the identification of the object of naive experience with the *Gegenstand* of theoretical inquiry. Discussions of "naive realism" are commonly based on the mistaken supposition that the attitude of naive experience is a crude theory of reality, sometimes confused with a "copy theory." By a *Gegenstand* Dooyeweerd means a field of inquiry for theoretical thought, obtained by abstraction from the concrete given reality of naive experience. This *Gegenstand* is viewed as standing in a relation of opposition to the logical aspect of the act of thought. The act of thought has a concrete character, while the logical aspect and the opposed non-logical aspect or *Gegenstand* are abstract. Thus the *Gegenstand* is formed by a mental operation of abstraction from the data provided by immediate experience. Logical objectivity, however, is denied to be a being that is merely intended in the logical aspect of a subjective concept. "Temporal reality itself has a logical object-side."[6]

The antithetic structure of the theoretical attitude of thought is asserted to have a purely intentional character. This gives the impression of being a doctrine of a nominalistic tenor. (The *Gegenstand* may be roughly identified with the universals of Scholastic philosophy, although represented as a theoretical abstraction to which nothing corresponds in reality.) In a rather obscure manner, the *Gegenstand* is said to offer resistance to the attempt to grasp it in a logical concept. From this resistance the theoretical problem originates. Theoretical problems include such notoriously difficult questions as: What is a number? What is space? What is motion? What is life? What is feeling? What is thought? and What is faith? Number, space, motion, life, feeling, thought and faith are examples of what Dooyeweerd calls "modal aspects" and represent the type of *Gegenstand* (with the puzzling exception of thought itself, which is referred to in a footnote

[5] *A New Critique of Theoretical Thought,* I (1935), p. 42.
[6] *Ibid.,* II, 389.

276

to a statement on page 40 of Volume I of the *New Critique*) in terms of which theoretical thought is defined.

The notion of the *Gegenstand*-relation, introduced in the first part of the transcendental critique, is clarified by the fuller exposition in the second chapter of the *New Critique* devoted to the epistemological problem. Brief introductory comments are made as to the *Gegenstand* as viewed by phenomenologists and also by Kant. Then in discussing the question, "Is it possible to speak of the *Gegenstand* of knowledge?", Dooyeweerd denies that the *Gegenstand* is opposed to the subject of knowledge, even if this subject is reduced to the "I think" of the "transcendental consciousness." Nor could the *Gegenstand* be opposed to our cognitive selfhood without making epistemology impossible. The correlate to the *Gegenstand* must be found within the diversity of modal aspects, not in the I-ness which is the heart of man. Dooyeweerd attempts to explain the difficult notion of "resistance" as follows: "The resistance as such is due to an antithetical opposing act, which is essentially a theoretical act of setting apart the several aspects of the cosmic meaning-systasis. This setting apart is only possible by means of analysis. For this reason the analytical modality must show a very special and indissoluble correlation with the '*Gegenstand*.' "[7] The term "systasis" is used to distinguish the natural coherence of the modal aspects of reality from the theoretical attitude implied in the word "synthesis." Likewise the analytical subject-object relation is said to have a merely enstatic character, since naive thought has no "opposite" to its logical function and does not perform any synthesis of logical and non-logical aspects.

The notion of the *Gegenstand* may be interpreted in the light of the history of the rationalist tradition in Western philosophy. Parmenides was the first to insist that to think must be to think *of* something. The discovery of the intentionality of thought by Parmenides was of epoch-making significance. Plato developed this conception in speaking of the Idea that is apprehended by pure theoretical thought. Aristotle and the medieval Scholastics have continued this tradition in their discussion of the problem of universals. In Kant, a twist was given by the "Copernican revolution" in epistemology, which makes the *Gegenstand* revolve about the thinker rather than the thinking mind about the *Gegenstand*. For Kant the *Gegenstand* or object of thought is produced by the mind, formed by the application of its own categories to the material of experience. Dooyeweerd is addressing himself to the perennial problem of the metaphysical status of universal concepts, in the peculiarly acute form it has assumed as a result of the influence of Kant. The problem of

[7] *Ibid.*, pp. 467f.

interpretation, to which our assessment will address itself, can be formulated thus: does Dooyeweerd view the *Gegenstand*-relation fundamentally in realistic or in nominalistic terms? Is the *Gegenstand* already implicitly given in the structure of the world and simply abstracted from it? Or is it the product of abstraction in such a way as to be actually a construction of the human mind?

The Conditions of the Possibility of Theoretical Thought

What makes theoretical thought possible? This question, characteristically transcendental in its form, receives a threefold answer in the *New Critique*. First, the antithetic-relation is the issue of an abstraction from the continuity of the coherence of the modal aspects in cosmic time. In the second place, theoretical thought requires a synthesis of the logical and the non-logical aspects, which presupposes a unified selfhood that transcends these aspects and thus transcends time itself. Finally, the concentric direction of the selfhood is itself possible only by reason of its relation to its Origin, the Origin of all meaning, which a Christian philosophy will recognize in God, the Sovereign Creator of the Cosmos. Every philosophical system is based on the answers given to these three basic transcendental questions relating to the world, the self, and God respectively. The questions relate to non-theoretical factors in the nature of things. The philosopher's choice of a position in relation to these factors determines the cosmonomic idea, or idea of law (*wetsidee*), in which the theoretical answer to the basic transcendental questions is formulated. This idea gives direction to further systematic constructions. The decisive factors for the foundation of philosophical theories are thus non-theoretical. Since the self and its relation to the Origin are presupposed in any philosophical theory, the non-theoretical foundations of philosophy are determined by factors that may be spoken of as religious in character. The word "religious" is employed not in a restricted sense associated with specific acts of worship, creedal formulation, or ecclesiastical organization, but in a wide sense referring to the relation of man, and through him of the cosmos, to God, the Origin of meaning. The selfhood of man, understood in biblical terms as the heart out of which proceed all the issues of life (Prov. 4:23), is viewed as the religious root of human existence, in which an attitude of apostasy from God or of renewal in Christ prevails. Among the issues proceeding from this apostate or renewed heart is theoretical thought and, in particular, philosophy.

The Basic Religious Motives in the History of Philosophy

Dooyeweerd represents the development of philosophy in Western civilization as the expression of four basic religious motives. For a

278

religious motive to influence philosophy "it must give rise to a common belief within the faith-aspect of our experience" and "it must gain a socio-cultural power within the historical aspect of human society."[8] Religious motives thus have a central communal character and often exercise their influence unconsciously. Ancient philosophy was dominated by the form-matter motive. Christianity expresses the radical biblical motive of creation, fall, and redemption. Scholasticism combines the Greek and Christian motives in the synthesis motive of nature and grace. Modern humanistic philosophy exhibits the motive of nature and freedom.

The Greek, Scholastic, and Humanistic motives possess a dialectical character in that each of these is composed of two central motive powers in polar opposition to one another. In ancient and modern philosophy, the religious absolutization of particular aspects of experience inevitably calls forth their correlates. "In other words, any idol that has been created by the absolutization of a modal aspect evokes its counter-idol."[9] While theoretical antitheses can be resolved by theoretical synthesis, there is no synthesis that can solve the antitheses resident in basic religious motives. Dooyeweerd may be said to be prescribing a dissolution rather than a solution of the problems arising from the tensions between form and matter, nature and grace, nature and freedom in ancient, medieval and modern philosophy respectively.

The contrast between form and matter which was explicitly formulated by Aristotle as the theme of his predecessors as well as of his own philosophy is traced by Dooyeweerd to its religious origins in the opposition between the pre-Homeric religion of life and death and the later cultural religion of the Olympian gods, the religion of form, measure, and harmony. The form-matter motive determined the Greek view of nature, which from the outset ruled out the biblical idea of creation. The dominant metaphysical opposition between being and becoming in Greek philosophy must be understood as the expression of this religious motive.

The radical central biblical motive is the "theme of creation, fall into sin, and redemption by Jesus Christ as the incarnate Word of God, in the communion of the Holy Spirit."[10] This basic motive is distinguished from ecclesiastical creeds that refer to it and from human theological formulation in general. Psalm 139:1-12 is quoted by Dooyeweerd as a striking instance of the integral character of the scriptural creation motive. Biblical revelation reveals man to himself,

8 *In the Twilight of Western Thought* (1960), p. 34.
9 *Ibid.*, p. 37.
10 *Ibid.*, p. 42.

279

as bearing the image of God in his heart as the integral radical unity of all structures and functions of temporal reality. The revelation of the fall is indissolubly associated with that of the creation. Sin in its radical scriptural sense can play no role in the dialectical basic motives, because it can be apprehended only in the genuine self-knowledge that issues from the Word-revelation. The fall concerns the integral center, the heart or soul, of man. Sin, however, is not an independent principle of origin, as opposed to God the Creator. There is no ultimate dualism in the created cosmos. The Divine Word by which all things were created became flesh in Christ Jesus, and has accomplished a radical redemption, the regeneration of man and in him of all the created temporal cosmos, which was concentrated religiously in man. In the same creative Word, God upholds the fallen cosmos by common grace, until in the last judgment redeemed creation will be freed from sin and will shine in perfection, while even in Satan and his kingdom the justice of God will shine as the affirmation of the Creator's absolute sovereignty.

This scriptural motive was threatened on all sides in the Hellenistic world. The battle against Gnosticism was waged and the Nicene dogma established. The apologists and the Alexandrian School, however, adapted from Philo's Jewish synthesis-philosophy the logos-speculation. Among the orthodox Church Fathers, philosophical thought reached its high point in the thought of Augustine. The insight that the Word of God is the only firm ground of truth led Augustine to reject the autonomy of theoretical thought. Yet this gain proved to be slight, when philosophy was restricted to a theological framework as the handmaid of theology. Neo-Platonic and Stoic influences in Augustine's thought mark the beginning of Scholastic accommodation of Greek thought to Christian doctrine. Biblical emphases in Augustinian theology are seen in his anti-Manichean insistence on the creative sovereignty of God and his anti-Pelagian accentuation of the radical character of the fall, as well as his interpretation of history in the *De Civitate Dei* as the conflict between the earthly city and the City of God.

The attempt to bridge the gap between Greek, and in particular Aristotelian, philosophy and the biblical religious motive gave rise to the Scholastic synthesis-motive of nature and grace, attaining its most perfect expression in the philosophical and theological achievement of Thomas Aquinas. Philosophy is distinguished sharply from theology by being regarded as the work of the autonomous natural reason. Dogmatic theology is assigned to the supernatural sphere of grace and is derived from revelation, though not contrary to reason. The Thomistic synthesis of the motives of nature and grace found clear expression in the adage: *Gratia naturam non tollit, sed perficit* ("Grace does not cancel nature, but perfects it").

Nominalism in late medieval thought represented an antithetic form of the nature-grace motive, in which any point of connection between the natural and the supernatural sphere was denied. Thus the process of the secularization of philosophy began.

The fourth basic religious motive is that of modern humanism, the theme of which is nature and freedom. The religious character of this motive has been disguised under the influence of the dogma of autonomy. Dooyeweerd gives the following account of the origin of the modern freedom motive: "The freedom-motive originates in a religion of humanity into which the biblical basic-motive had been completely transformed. The *renascimento* device of the Italian Renaissance meant a real rebirth of man into a new, creative and entirely new, personality. This personality was thought of as absolute in itself and was considered to be the only ruler of its own destiny and that of the world."[11] The new view of nature conceived it as the macrocosmic counterpart of the new, religious personality-ideal. In nature reside infinite possibilities for the creative power of man. The dialectical tension between the motives of nature and freedom in modern philosophy receives its sharpest formulation in the philosophy of Kant, in which nature is viewed as reality in the grip of the deterministic ideal of science while freedom prevails in the sphere of practical reason to which the primacy is ascribed. On the contemporary scene, logical positivism and existentialism represent the opposed poles of the nature-freedom motive and testify to a fundamental crisis of humanistic philosophy.

Metaphysical Foundations

Dooyeweerd does not use the term "metaphysics" with approval. He carries on a sustained attack against what he labels "speculative metaphysics" in all of the forms it has exhibited in the history of philosophy. The transcendental critique, for Dooyeweerd no less than for Kant, has the effect, if not the intention as well, of cutting off at the root every theory that professes to transcend the limit of time and to unfold the mysteries of a realm beyond possible human experience in this world.

Despite the avowed opposition to traditional metaphysics, the philosophy of the cosmonomic idea has what may be called a pronounced metaphysical character in the sense of fundamental principles as to the nature of reality, the order of the world, the nature of the human self, and the relation of world and self to the ultimate origin of all

[11] *Ibid.*, p. 46.

created reality. In a more specific sense, it is a metaphysical system, since cosmology is developed as a prerequisite for epistemology. The transcendental critique, which is the gate to all further divisions of this philosophy, is not identified with epistemology, although the kinship of these two branches of the system is unmistakable.

Meaning and Law

Philosophy is defined as theoretical thought directed to the totality of the meaning of our cosmos. Meaning is said to be the mode of being of created reality. No created thing is self-sufficient; each one points beyond itself to others and above to the Origin of all. Dooyeweerd has evidently resolved to use the word "meaning" (*zin*) in an unusual and even novel sense. Yet the use of this term appears to suggest that he is attempting to resolve problems that have bothered other philosophers who have engaged in the analysis of meaning, especially Husserl and other phenomenologists. Dooyeweerd has not devoted much attention to the analytic philosophy that predominates in the English-speaking world. Occasional references to logical positivism, however, do occur in his work.

Dooyeweerd's paradoxical statements about meaning do not appear to resemble propositions of semantics, although some of them do lend themselves to translation into statements about the use of language. Among other things, the thesis that linguistic expressions have reference only in a context would be understood as a basic tenet of a linguistic version of this doctrine. A difficulty would arise, however, in the attempt to discover a semantic counterpart to the irreducibly ontological assertion that reality does not have meaning, but *is* meaning.[12] The doctrine of meaning in the philosophy of the cosmonomic idea must be admitted to be metaphysical in a sense in which traditional doctrines of substance are called metaphysical. It involves general propositions about everything that can be said to be. "Meaning" for this philosophical perspective is the all-encompassing category of reality. God alone as the Origin of meaning does not fall under it.

A second basic category is that of law. By law (*wet*) is meant a principle of order or structure to which individually existing things are subjected. "Law" and "subject" are indissolubly correlated with each other. Law is said metaphorically to be the boundary between God, the sovereign Lawgiver, and the Cosmos. God is not subject to the law. "Meaning" and "subject to law" thus appear to be equivalent expressions. Dooyeweerd insists on the subject-law correlation as necessary, if the dialectical tension between rationalistic and irrationalistic views of reality is to be avoided. Rationalism attempts to reduce the subject

---

[12] *A New Critique of Theoretical Thought*, I (1935), 96f.

side of reality to the law-side and leaves no room for individuality, while irrationalism seeks to derive from the subject the rule of its behavior, which thereby loses its general character and becomes a reflection of the individuality of the subjects.[13]

Dooyeweerd's emphasis on an order of law in the universe indicates an affinity between his view and that of classical doctrines of natural law. Reflections on the theme of natural law played a significant role in the formative stages of Dooyeweerd's philosophical development.[14] Dooyeweerd, although critical of the Augustinian doctrine of the eternal law and the Thomist theory of natural law, is no less insistent than the classical tradition that the norms of human behavior are integrated in a total order of the world which is independent of the mind and will of man.

Cosmic Time and the Modal Aspects

Time might also be regarded as a universal category of empirical reality in the philosophy of the cosmonomic idea. Cosmic time is defined as an indissoluble correlation of order and duration in distinction from all its special modal aspects. Man transcends cosmic time only in the religious center of his existence. The cosmonomic (law) side of time is the order of succession or simultaneity, while the factual (subject) side is the duration which differs with various individualities. Modal and individuality structures of temporal reality are alike structures of cosmic time. In naive experience "we have an immediate integral experience of cosmic time in the uninterrupted coherence of all its modal aspects, inclusive of the normative ones, and in concentric relatedness to the selfhood."[15] In the experience of looking at one's watch and discovering that one is "too late," the integral character of the naive consciousness of time is exemplified.

Dooyeweerd employs the symbol of refraction of light through a prism in his elucidation of the relationship between cosmic time and the modal aspects. Cosmic time is a prism through which the supratemporal totality of meaning of our cosmos is broken up into its temporal modal aspects of meaning. The modal aspects are not derived from one another, even as the colors of the spectrum do not owe their origin to one another. "Each modal aspect is sovereign in

---

[13] See Dooyeweerd's reply to Professor Van Peursen in *Philosophia Reformata,* 1960, especially pp. 107ff.

[14] See Albers' *Het Natuurrecht volgens de Wijsbegeerte der Wetsidee* (1955), especially chapter 1, on the development of Dooyeweerd's conception of natural law.

[15] *A New Critique of Theoretical Thought,* I (1953), 33.

its own sphere, and each aspect in its modal structure reflects the fullness of meaning in its own modality."[16]

In the theoretical attitude the modal aspects of time are explicitly distinguished. In Dooyeweerd's most mature formulation, there are fifteen of these aspects, arranged in the following serial order: number, space, motion, energy, organic life, psychical feeling, logical analysis, history, language, social intercourse, economic saving, aesthetic harmony, legal retribution, moral love, and religious faith. The aspects are modal in the sense of reference to the universal "how" of the aspects of reality, not the concrete "what" of things and events. Dooyeweerd refuses to infer from his doctrine of the theoretical antithesis in the *Gegenstand*-relation that the modal aspects are products of theoretical abstraction. They are rather transcendental conditions of every concrete subjective human experience. We cannot along a theoretical way abstract from time what is not according to its nature contained in time. The modal aspects are not theoretical abstractions, but the setting of them apart is the result of a theoretical analysis necessary for philosophy from a critical point of view.[17]

A startling consequence of the theory of cosmic time is that the logical aspect of thought is temporal in character. By this Dooyeweerd does not mean to assert simply that it takes time, sometimes at least, to arrive at a logical conclusion. He flatly asserts: "The logical order of simultaneity and of prius and posterius is as much a modal aspect of the integral order of time as the physical. It has meaning only within the cosmic time-order in the coherence of *all* its modal aspects. Therefore it is meaningless to set the *logical* prius and posterius in opposition to the *temporal* before and after, as if the former had no authentic meaning as time-aspect."[18] Dooyeweerd appears to be maintaining two theses in asserting the temporality of logic in this paragraph: (1) the logical aspect occupies a place in the sequence of the modal aspects of reality, and this sequence is a temporal one; (2) logical order is itself a mode of temporal sequence or simultaneity. The "therefore" of the concluding sentence indicates that the second thesis is grounded in the first. How this is the case is not indicated, although it would appear that the first thesis presupposes the truth of the second, in that it treats a serial order of a logical or mathematical type as a temporal order. At this juncture a curious feature of the philosophical system exhibits itself. The transcendental critique is represented as the only entrance to the other subdivisions of the philosophy. Yet the explanation of the antithetic *Gegenstand*-relation

---

[16] *Ibid.,* p. 102.
[17] *Philosophia Reformata,* 1960, pp. 136, 138.
[18] *A New Critique of Theoretical Thought,* I (1953), 30.

presupposes the truth of the cosmological doctrine that the logical aspect is one aspect among others in a temporal series of modal aspects of reality. Dooyeweerd may have recognized this phenomenon in his insertion of a preliminary discussion of cosmic time in the prolegomena of the *New Critique* prior to the development of the sharpened transcendental critique of theoretical thought.

A few words may be in order at this point as to the place of analogy in Dooyeweerd's thought. Analogy is a technical term for a moment or element in a modal aspect that points back to an earlier aspect in the series. Thus, logical space is an analogical moment in the logical aspect, by which reference is made to the original meaning of space. Analogy is not to be dismissed as metaphor, nor is it to be interpreted in terms of the metaphysical tradition and its doctrine of *analogia entis* (analogy of being). One could label Dooyeweerd's doctrine as that of *analogia temporis* (analogy of time). A full discussion may be found in Dooyeweerd's article on the doctrine of analogy in Thomistic philosophy and in the philosophy of the cosmonomic idea.[19] In the next section, some examples of analogy in theological concepts will be given.

THEOLOGICAL CONSEQUENCES OF THE REFORMED PHILOSOPHY

Dooyeweerd is not a professional theologian, and he emphatically denies that he is engaged in theology in the construction of a Christian philosophy. His philosophical method and doctrines, however, have important consequences for theology, to which our attention must now be directed. In *The Twilight of Western Thought,* he states: "Theology is above all in need of a radical critique of theoretical thought which, because of its biblical starting-point, is able to show the intrinsic influence of the religious basic motives both upon philosophy and theology. This is the first service which the new Reformed philosophy can render its theological sister.[20] We may consider, then, the place assigned to theology in the system of the cosmonomic idea and the relationship between philosophy and theology in the new Reformed philosophy. Consideration of special theological issues will follow this general discussion.

The Place of Theology in the System of the Sciences

Theology is included among the special sciences (*vakwetenschappen*). Each special science has as its *Gegenstand,* or field of inquiry, one of the abstracted modal aspects of temporal reality. The field of

---

[19] *Philosophia Reformata*, 1942, pp. 47-55; cf. also 1948, pp. 26-31, 49-58, and 1952, pp. 151-184.
[20] *In the Twilight of Western Thought* (1960), p. 156.

inquiry for theology is the aspect of faith, the boundary aspect of cosmic time. Revelation as such, even Word-revelation as such in its concreteness, is denied to be the theoretical object of theological thought. The central basic motive of Holy Scripture is non-theoretical in character. Of it Dooyeweerd asserts: "So long as this central meaning of the Word-revelation is at issue we are beyond the scientific problems both of theology and of philosophy. Its acceptance or rejection is a matter of life and death to us, and not a question of theoretical reflection. In this sense the central motive of Holy Scripture is the common supra-scientific starting point of a really biblical theology and of a really Christian philosophy. It is the key of knowledge of which Jesus spoke in His discussion with the scribes and lawyers. It is the religious presupposition of any theoretical thought which may rightly claim a biblical foundation. But, as such, it can never become the theoretical object of theology; no more than God and the human I can become such an object."[21]

It seems strange that the central biblical themes of creation, fall, and redemption should be denied to be the field of inquiry of systematic theology. What other subject matter is there for this venerable discipline? Dooyeweerd's answer is that the object of dogmatic theology is nothing but the Divine Word-revelation as it presents itself within the modal aspect of faith.[22] The Word of God in its full and actual reality is distinguished from its restricted sense as the object of theological thought. Dogmatic theology engages in theoretical reflection on creation, fall into sin, and redemption only so far as their revelation is related to the faith aspect of our temporal experience and forms the content of creedal formulas. The distinction made here is not perfectly clear. It is undoubtedly true that Christians need not be scholarly theologians to experience the work of saving grace in their hearts. But what sense does it make to say that "there must be a difference in principle between creation, fall, and redemption in their central sense as the key to knowledge, and in their sense as articles of faith, which may be made into the object of theological thought"?[23] Dooyeweerd states the sound principle that orthodox theology is no guarantee of central spiritual knowledge. From this he concludes, without indicating the missing premise of the enthymeme: "Therefore, the scholastic term *sacra theologia* testifies to an unbiblical over-estimation of theology."[24] Another consequence is in the direction of minimizing the importance of theological controversy and of providing an ecumen-

21 *Ibid.,* p. 125.
22 *Ibid.,* p. 143.
23 *Ibid.,* p. 145.
24 *Ibid.,* p. 146.

286

ical basis of the Church. The spiritual basic motive is depicted as the judge of every ecclesiastical doctrine and the central basic principle of a continual reformation of the Church's doctrine.

Theology as a special science has philosophical foundations, which are in turn dependent on the central religious motive of theoretical thought. The faith-aspect which delimits the theoretical object of theology displays an intrinsic coherence with all the other modal aspects. The faith-aspect presents a certain central moment of meaning as its irreducible kernel as well as a series of analogical moments the meaning of which is determined by the modal kernel of the faith-aspect. This analogical structure of the faith-aspect obliges theology to employ analogical concepts. "That is to say, these concepts are also used by the other special sciences, but in a different modal sense; nevertheless, there is an inner coherence between these different modal meanings. Such theological concepts of an analogical character are, for instance, those of time, number, space, movement, force and causality, life, emotion, distinction, power, symbol, signification and interpretation, justice, guilt, imputation and punishment, love, etc."[25] If by the isolation of the analogy of punitive justice, the latter is opposed to the love of God, the theological conception of justice passes over into a pseudo-juridical view and the truth of faith is falsified. An economic analogy occurs in the expression "redeeming the time." The symbolic analogy is evident in the fact that the interpretation of Scripture is not purely philological, or even merely historical, but is essentially pistical, that is, characterized by the faith-aspect, because in Scripture the Holy Spirit signifies symbolically the divine truth in faith.

Not only the first fourteen modal aspects, but time also is qualified by its relation to the faith-aspect. In the faith-aspect time exhibits a pistical meaning which is immediately related to the central religious meaning of the divine revelation. Sacred history can be understood only in the order and duration of the faith-aspect in which it has an eschatological perspective. The days of creation are also to be understood only in faith-time. By conceiving of them in the physical aspect of time, theology involved itself in the dilemma of conceiving them astronomically as 24-hour days or as geological periods. Application of this alternative to God's resting on the seventh day results in blasphemy. The Decalogue exegetes the days of creation as signifying God's will that the believing Jew should refer his six workdays to the six divine creative works and the Sabbath day to the eternal sabbatic rest of God the Creator. The exegetical dilemma, so branded by Dooyeweerd as Scholastic, originated from a fundamental disregard of the faith-aspect of the temporal order. Dooyeweerd dissociates him-

[25] *Ibid.*, p. 149.

self also from the allegorical interpretation originating in Philo of Alexandria and accepted by Origen and Augustine, as well as from its revival in the framework hypothesis of N. H. Ridderbos. He denies that the temporal meaning of the creation account may be reduced to a merely literary mode of representation, although he finds this view far preferable to the astronomical or geological interpretation.

Philosophy and Theology

Dooyeweerd aims at a Christian philosophy of a non-theological character. He opposes this aim to the two principal types of classical Christian thought, the Augustinian and the Thomist. While Augustine rightly denied the autonomy of human reason and refused to accept pagan philosophy as an autonomous science, he identified Christian theology with true Christian philosophy. By thus allowing a discussion of philosophical questions only within a theological context, he opened the way for a penetration of Christian theology by Greek philosophical ideas. On this view theology is understood both in the non-theoretical sense of the true knowledge of God and ourselves (*Deum et animam scire*) and as the "theoretical explanation of the articles of faith in their scientific confrontation with the texts of Holy Writ and with heretical views."[26] Dooyeweerd ascribes the whole conception of theology as the queen of the sciences and philosophy as its handmaid to a Greek origin, interpreting a passage of Aristotle's *Metaphysics B* as meaning that the metaphysical doctrine of God has the control and guidance over all other sciences, which, as its slaves, may not contradict its truths. This identification of dogmatic theology with Christian philosophy on the one hand and with the holy doctrine of the Church on the other remained characteristic of the Augustinian tradition in Scholasticism.

A new view was introduced in the *Summa Theologiae* of Thomas Aquinas. The same fundamental ambiguity remains in the use of the terms "theology" and *"sacra doctrina."* But, in opposition to Augustianism, Thomism sharply distinguishes dogmatic theology (*sacra doctrina*) from philosophy, even from philosophical or natural theology which depends on the light of reason alone. Dooyeweerd describes the Thomistic philosophy as "the Aristotelian system at some points elaborated in an original way and mixed with Augustinian, Neo-Platonic, and Stoic ideas."[27] Christian theology, on the other hand, has a supernatural character, deriving its knowledge from divine revelation, and not needing the aid of philosophy, although, according to the Encycli-

---

[26] *Ibid.*, p. 115.
[27] *Ibid.*, p. 118.

cal *Aeterni Patris* of Pope Leo XIII, requiring philosophy to give it the character and spirit of a science.

Dooyeweerd accepts the Augustinian denial of the autonomy of human reason and the Thomist insistence on the distinction between philosophy and theology, thus proposing the idea of a Christian philosophy distinct from theology. His solution of the historic problem of the relationship between philosophy and theology proceeds from the principle that true knowledge of God and self-knowledge are fundamentally non-theoretical, derived from the operation of God's Word and Spirit in the heart. Thus the central principle of knowledge is the same for dogmatic theology and for Christian philosophy.

Special Theological Consequences

If theology requires a philosophical foundation and that not in a merely formal sense of the instrumental use of logic in theology, the question arises: what changes will be required of classical Reformed theology if it is subjected to the transcendental critique proposed by Dooyeweerd? Although Dooyeweerd disclaims theology as his field of work, he has from time to time indicated certain theological consequences of his philosophical principles. Aside from *obiter dicta* on creation, predestination, Christology, and other topics of theological importance, four major lines of modification of historic Christian theology as required by the new Reformed philosophy may be mentioned: (a) the repudiation of natural theology; (b) the reinterpretation of the doctrine of common grace; (c) the reformulation of the conception of the human soul; and (d) the implications of the rejection of the metaphysical concept of substance. Some questions may also be raised concerning Dooyeweerd's view of Holy Scripture.

The Repudiation of Natural Theology

The attack upon the nature-grace motive applies to classical "Reformed" scholasticism as well as to Roman Catholic theology. An immediate consequence of this polemic is the repudiation of natural theology in general and of the proofs of the existence of God in particular. Since metaphysics as a rational science with a subject matter transcending time is eliminated by the transcendental critique, natural theology as a branch of metaphysics is rendered impossible. The five ways developed by Aquinas for the demonstration of the existence of God are rejected as tacitly presupposing an idea of the Origin instead of providing a genuine proof. The entire enterprise of natural theology is condemned as resting upon the assumption of the autonomy of human reason in the natural sphere. The two-level theory of nature as the preamble of grace by which it is perfected is thus rejected, as

289

is also the parallel construction of the doctrine of common grace to be mentioned in the next section.

Dooyeweerd does not deny the plain teaching of Romans I that there is a revelation of God in nature, sufficient to render the heathen without excuse. In his reply to Van Peursen, he even refers to it as "general Word-revelation," but explains it, not as meaning that God's voice resounds in apostate religion, but rather that the truth of the general Word-revelation is in these religions held down in unrighteousness and perverted. In general revelation Dooyeweerd finds no grounds for a natural religion or a natural theology. In this matter he is in agreement with many contemporary theologians, but not with the overwhelming majority of Reformed divines from the seventeenth up to the early twentieth century.

The Reinterpretation of the Doctrine of Common Grace

Closely related to the question of natural knowledge of God is that of common grace, a divine restraining of the operations and effects of sin that comes short of regeneration. This doctrine, intimated by Calvin and discussed by the Puritans in relation to the experience of conversion, was reinterpreted by Dr. Abraham Kuyper as a cultural concept by which, in relative independence of the work of saving grace, the commendable elements of secular culture received a relative justification. Dooyeweerd adopts the Kuyperian view of common grace in its essential character as an explanation of the conservation of the fallen cosmos, but seeks to guard against the interpretation that common grace provides an autonomous territory for human thought and action.

In his reply to Van Peursen,[28] Dooyeweerd denies that his statements about common grace amount to a theological conception. He professes to have spoken only "from the central biblical basic motive and so far as philosophical investigation was concerned in it." "I was thereby compelled," he writes, "to choose a position against a dualistic conception which seeks to avoid the radical and integral grasp of the central motive of the divine Word-revelation by conceiving the relation between special and common grace in the sense of the scholastic basic motive of nature and grace." This choice of a position, he insists, is of a central religious character and may not be called a "theological conception." The assertion that common grace is to be understood only in terms of the divine grace in Christ Jesus is nothing but the central witness of Scripture that only in Christ Jesus can God look on fallen mankind in grace.

[28] *Philosophia Reformata,* 1960, pp. 147f.

The Reformulation of the Conception of the Human Soul

The crux of Dooyeweerd's attack on Scholasticism is to be found in his critique of the commonly accepted distinction of body and soul, and especially of the creationist view of the origin of the soul.[29] Dooyeweerd sets his view of the heart of man as the religious root of human nature in sharp opposition to the doctrine of the rational soul formulated in the philosophy of Plato and Aristotle and baptized by Augustine and Aquinas, defended by Voetius against Cartesian innovations, and incorporated in the terminology of the Westminster Confession of Faith and Catechisms.

There are several converging sources for Dooyeweerd's view of the heart and for his rejection of the classical doctrine of the soul. For his positive doctrine he appeals both to the central biblical motive and to special texts, such as Eccles. 3:11, which he exegetes as meaning that in the heart man transcends time. The doctrine appears to have been developed in confrontation with the views of Kant and Husserl on the transcendental ego. Against the classical realist doctrine, whether Platonic or Aristotelian, he argues that the view of the soul as a substance distinct from the body is the result of the hypostatization of the logical and ethical functions or modal aspects, which is the consequence of erroneously supposing that there is something in the structure of reality answering to the *Gegenstand*-relation. Against traditional dichotomy the argument is also repeatedly insisted on that this view originated from the form-matter motive and is an integral part of the nature-grace motive. A special argument against creationism is that it leads to an antinomy in theology, in that it cannot explain the transmission of Original Sin without making God the author of sin or resorting to untenable dodges. An underlying necessity for the rejection of dichotomy is the rejection of the metaphysical concept of substance.

The Implications of the Rejection of the Metaphysical Concept of Substance.

Reinterpretation of the idea of the human selfhood is by no means the only or potentially the most serious consequence of the rejection by Dooyeweerd of the metaphysical concept of substance. The concept enters not only into classical theological formulation as to the nature of man, but also into the orthodox doctrine of the Trinity and the person of Christ. Dooyeweerd has not drawn any explicit consequen-

---

[29] Brevity in the present account of so cardinal a topic may be justified by reference to fuller discussions in my book *Towards a Reformed Philosophy* (1952), pp. 107-112, 141-144, and my article "The Doctrine of Man in the Amsterdam Philosophy" (see bibliography).

ces in this area, although Vollenhoven published an article on the question of the impersonal (ἀνυπόστατος) human nature of Christ[30] which gave rise to controversy.[31] Consequences of a drastic nature would appear to follow from the rejection of the concept of substance incorporated not only in the Westminster standards but in the Nicene and Chalcedonian Creeds. The controversy as to whether the Son is of the same substance as the Father would appear to be meaningless, if the concept of substance is unacceptable for Christian thought. The same would apply to discussions concerning the divine and human natures of Christ, for "nature" is in this context synonymous with "substance." Dooyeweerd would no doubt emphatically deny any intention to overthrow the foundations of historic Christian dogma and such an intention is not to be suggested as any part of his motivation. But the question of the consequences of his denial of substance cannot be avoided in even a brief survey of his importance for theology. It would seem that the anti-metaphysical doctrine — one is tempted to say "metaphysics" — of the new philosophy requires at the least a radical reformulation, if not reformation, of the trinitarian and christological dogma accepted by all branches of historic Christianity.

Some misgivings have been expressed by conservative American theologians as to Dooyeweerd's attitude toward biblical authority and the doctrine of inspiration. Dooyeweerd's publications provide insufficient evidence for a judgment as to his view of the inspiration of Scripture. He does speak of the "infallibility of God's Word"[32] and elsewhere contrasts the Word of God with the confession of the Church into which errors may enter. Yet it is not to be inferred that Dooyeweerd identifies the Word of God with the language of the Bible. His extremely vague way of speaking about the divine Word-revelation is calculated to raise doubts as to his acceptance of the doctrine of plenary and verbal inspiration as formulated by the scholastic Reformed divines of the seventeenth century. Even if this suspicion should prove to be well founded, it would not warrant the charge that Dooyeweerd denies that the Scriptures are inspired of God. On p. 144 of *In the Twilight of Western Thought,* Dooyeweerd approaches an explicit statement of his view of biblical inspiration. He uses the expression "incarnation of the Word-revelation in the Holy Scriptures" and speaks of the Scriptures as "a collection of books written by different men in the course of ages, be it through divine inspiration, yet related to all the modal aspects of our temporal horizon

[30] *Philosophia Reformata,* 1940, pp. 65-79.
[31] See V. Hepp, *Dreigende Deformatie,* III, and H. Steen, *Philosophia Deformata,* chapter 16.
[32] *In the Twilight of Western Thought* (1960), p. 115.

of experience." He then adds: "It is, however, only under the modal aspect of faith that we can experience that this Word-revelation in the Scriptures has been inspired by the Holy Spirit." Dooyeweerd has avoided any detailed pronouncements as to the nature and extent of the inspiration of Scripture, a subject he would no doubt assign to the province of dogmatic theology. His interest, as we have seen, lies in the basic religious motive of Holy Scripture in its relevance to the foundations of theoretical thought.

III. EVALUATION

The importance of Dooyeweerd's contribution to Christian thought can scarcely be overestimated. He has forged a powerful weapon in his transcendental critique of theoretical thought, by which the strongholds of unbelief may be assailed at their very foundations. He has given a penetrating detailed analysis of the development of Western philosophy in which the methods of the *New Critique* demonstrate their fruitfulness. He has provided a *de facto* refutation of the allegation that there has never been a Christian philosophy by producing a full-scale specimen. The massiveness of the systematic construction is matched by the relentless insistence that every thought must be brought into captivity to the obedience of Christ. One should not on this account conclude that Dooyeweerd regards himself as having attained perfection in the realm of Christian philosophy. He is aware of the working of sin even in thought that is oriented to the religious motive of Holy Scripture. His reply to Van Peursen's criticisms concludes with an admission of awareness that the radical transcendental critique of philosophical thought, necessary as it is, is in the full sense of the word a risky undertaking, subject to human fallibility in the attempt to probe a philosophical line of thought to its central driving force. The following critical discussion, therefore, is not calculated to weaken the distinctive Christian witness of the new Reformed philosophy, but rather to indicate a lack of clarity in that witness in certain of its teachings and the necessity of maintaining the continuity of historic Christian teaching, especially in the form of the classical Reformed confessions.

PHILOSOPHICAL FOUNDATIONS

The Transcendental Critique of Theoretical Thought

The transcendental critique is not only the gate by which access is gained to the remaining divisions of the new philosophy. It may justly lay claim to the position of the most valuable contribution made by Dooyeweerd to philosophical thought as such as well as to the Christian cause. Although Dooyeweerd does not speak of apologetics in connection with his thought and would no doubt repudiate most of what is usually counted as belonging to this discipline, it remains true that the transcendental critique is an extremely powerful weapon for the defence of the Christian faith. To the charge that Christians are irrational and prejudiced in giving faith to an alleged revelation, it replies in a way that puts the infidel critic on the defensive. The autonomy of human reason has been assumed in a dogmatic manner and the hidden religious motives of non-Christian thinkers are unmasked. New lines for the development of apologetic argument are thus indicated by the transcendental critique.

The transcendental critique is not only an apologetic weapon but also a contribution to philosophy. In fact, its value as a weapon is entirely dependent on its validity as an argument. Its contribution consists in raising certain penetrating questions and in proposing provocative answers to them. The question of the distinguishing character of theoretical thought is one that strikes at the very heart of vital philosophical issues. In the stress on the fundamental role of self-knowledge in its inseparable association with knowledge of God, the reverberation of the opening words of Calvin's *Institutio* is heard in generalized tones resounding to the furthest precincts of science.

Yet the transcendental critique as proposed and formulated by Dooyeweerd should be considered as a program to be undertaken rather than as an achievement to be accepted in its finality. There are unclear formulations, gaps in the reasoning, and at least the appearance of vicious circularity in the procedure. These defects in the logic of the transcendental critique concern, first of all, the obscure notion of the antithetic *Gegenstand*-relation, secondly, the steps of argument by which the conditions of the possibility of theoretical thought are demonstrated, and, finally, the notion of a basic religious motive and the way it functions in the foundations of theoretical thought.

The Obscurity of the Gegenstand-*relation*

An initial difficulty concerns the choice of the German word *Gegenstand* to refer to a theoretical object. The word is, as Van Peursen has remarked, "loaded" with connotations derived from neo-Kantianism, although Dooyeweerd is insistent and emphatic in his disavowal of association with Kantian or neo-Kantian doctrines. Dooyeweerd undoubtedly denies the neo-Kantian view of a relation between the transcendental logical subject of thought and "objective reality." But the language in which he expresses this denial uses terms such as *Gegenstand*, which are practically unintelligible apart from reference to their use in German philosophy. Can such language be used to refute a doctrine that is formulated in it, without the risk of accepting, no doubt unconsciously, some of the assumptions made by the doctrine in question?

Aside from initial difficulties, which may last over a period of several years, in the effort to understand just what Dooyeweerd means by a *Gegenstand* and the antithetic relation which holds between the *Gegenstand* and the logical aspect of thought, a central ambiguity remains relating to the perennial antithesis of nominalism and realism. Does Dooyeweerd view the theoretical object as a human construction or as an integral factor in the real world? Some statements suggest the first, while others seem to point to the latter answer. On the one hand, Dooyeweerd speaks of the purely intentional, that is, mental character of the antithetic structure of theoretical thought and denies the existence of anything in reality that corresponds to the *Gegenstand*-relation. This denial of any correspondence between the *Gegenstand*-relation and a state of affairs in the real world provides a ground for the rejection of the classical doctrines of the soul as a substance distinct from the material body. On the other hand, Dooyeweerd speaks of the *Gegenstand* as an abstracted modal aspect and categorically denies that the modal aspects are produced by abstraction. His fundamental conception of the cosmic order of law likewise militates strongly against the nominalistic interpretation of the *Gegenstand*-relation.

The obscurity in question could be pointed up in the form of an inconsistent triad of propositions, apparently asserted in the transcendental critique. These propositions are easily shown to imply a formal contradiction.

1. No modal aspect is the product of theoretical abstraction.

2. Every *Gegenstand* is a product of theoretical abstraction.

3. Some modal aspect is a *Gegenstand*.

If the first proposition is rejected, nominalism is accepted. If the second is rejected, realism, including the metaphysics of substance, cannot be rejected. The third proposition appears to be an obvious consequence of the statement that the *Gegenstand* of theoretical thought is an abstracted modal aspect. Unless some misunderstanding of the basis of the transcendental critique is involved, the doctrine of the *Gegenstand*-relation must be rejected as self-contradictory. The difficulty of the supposition that as acute a philosopher as Dooyeweerd has based his system on a self-contradiction of so simple a character leads to the conclusion that some clarification of the notion of the *Gegenstand*-relation is imperative. If the notion is not self-contradictory, at least it is extremely unclear and can hardly bear the weight of the far-reaching consequences for logic, metaphysics, anthropology, and theology that Dooyeweerd derives from it. This conclusion is confirmed by the fact that difficulties in the notion of the *Gegenstand*-relation have been pointed out not only by Prof. Van Peursen, but also by Prof. Van Riessen, himself a fellow worker in the Reformed philosophy, and by F. Kuyper in the 1962 issue of *Philosophia Reformata.*

Gaps in the Transcendental Critique

Only a few hints can be given in this article as to lacunae in the transcendental arguments relating to the order of cosmic time, the supra-temporal concentration point in the selfhood of man, and the ultimate Origin in terms of which the religious concentration in the selfhood must be understood. If the antithetic *Gegenstand*-relation is found unacceptable, the problem of theoretical synthesis may be dismissed as a pseudo-problem. At least the notion of synthesis no less than that of antithesis requires clarification. How does Dooyeweerd's doctrine of synthesis differ from the Kantian critique? The gaping abyss in the argument, however, concerns the step to the selfhood, the transcendent heart of man as the starting point that is required for theoretical synthesis to be possible. Dooyeweerd's observations about the "isms" in philosophy arising from the attempt to find the Archimedean point of theoretical thought in a modal aspect and his cogent critique of the Kantian and phenomenological theories of the transcendental ego do not necessitate the truth of his own doctrine as to the human self, even in a formal sense without the specific Christian content of the doctrine in the Reformed philosophy. Finally, if proofs of the existence of God are disqualified, the introduction of references to the Origin of meaning must be a pure assumption or act of faith, and not the conclusion of a transcendental deduction. Perhaps the method adopted by Dooyeweerd in the *Critique* is hypothetical rather than purely deductive. As a strictly deductive argument, it involves a series of fallacies, namely, affirmations of the consequent. If, however, all that is said is: "Suppose the order of cosmic time, suppose a transcendent selfhood directed to the Origin of meaning; then theoretical thought can be understood in terms of the *Gegenstand*-relation, of theoretical synthesis of the logical and non-logical aspects, and of a basic religious motive," then the brilliance of this hypothesis must be admired, but its acceptance or modification must rest on further considerations to be brought to light by its consequences.

296

Circularity of the Critique and the Notion of a Religious Motive

In two respects a charge of circularity may be brought against the *New Critique*. First, its formulation requires reference to cosmological and anthropological as well as epistemological doctrines developed in later sections of the philosophy which are represented as dependent on the transcendental critique. The theory of cosmic time, a doctrine of the relation of the logical to non-logical aspects, the distinction between the heart of man and the bodily functions are required by the critique and at the same time justified by it. Possibly a careful reformulation of the philosophy of the cosmonomic idea would eliminate this formal circularity that mars its method. Such a restatement would certainly provide a clarity which is greatly to be desired.

A more basic issue as to circularity enters the critique with the introduction of the notion of a religious motive. The transcendental critique is presented for acceptance by all philosophers who are willing to examine the foundations on which theoretical thought rests. Yet the failure to develop a transcendental critique or to accept it when it has been developed is ascribed to the influence of the dogma of the autonomy of theoretical thought. This dogma is seen to be an expression of an apostate religious motive. Must one then accept the biblical motive in order to be capable of accepting the transcendental critique which issues in the exhibition of the religious motives that dominate theoretical thought? Dooyeweerd's explicit answer[33] is that "what is stringently proved . . . is the thesis, that the concentric direction of thought in its self-reflection cannot originate from the theoretical attitude of thought itself, and that it can issue only from the ego as a supra-theoretic individual centre of human existence." The transcendental critique up to this point remains strictly within the theoretical sphere and lays bare structural states of affairs which no critical thinker can ignore. Yet this does not mean that the transcendental critique is unprejudiced. If it were, this fact would refute its own conclusions. Dooyeweerd breaks through the vicious circle by three considerations: (1) the supratheoretical presuppositions of the critique free theoretical thought from dogmatic "axioms"; (2) the contents of the supra-theoretical presuppositions, not the very necessity of them, can be questionable; and (3) the supra-theoretical character of the starting-point of theoretical thought is demonstrable, but its central religious character cannot be proved theoretically, because this insight belongs to self-knowledge which transcends the theoretical attitude.

Even if the transcendental critique has been vindicated from the

33 In *A New Critique of Theoretical Thought,* I (1953), 56.

charge of circularity, problems remain as to the nature of a basic religious motive and its influence on theoretical thought. Possibly "motif" would be preferable to "motive," but "ground-motive" was used as a translation of "grondmotief" in the *New Critique* and Dooyeweerd himself has used "basic motive" in his *In the Twilight of Western Thought*. A basic religious motive is described, if not defined, as "the central spiritual motive power of our thinking and acting" and is asserted to be "operative in the ego as the center of our temporal horizon of experience." As a communal motive it lies at the foundation of a community of thought. The last statement indicates that a religious motive is not simply an individual psychological factor, not even one deeply rooted in the unconscious levels of the psyche. The notion of a communal motive, transcending but expressed in the motivation of individual minds, is not free from obscurity. An attempt might be made to elucidate it as a disposition widespread in a certain community or culture to think in terms of a certain framework of categories and concepts. An element of mysticism cleaving to Dooyeweerd's way of speaking about religious motives is eliminated by this dispositional formulation. One can no longer speak of a mysterious influence exerted by such a motive, but simply of a pervasive tendency in the philosophical systems of certain groups of thinkers. Understood in these reduced proportions, the basic religious motives in the history of Western thought prove to be illuminating, though subject to criticism in terms of their accuracy and adequacy in providing a unified view of masses of intellectual cultural phenomena.

One general criticism can be suggested: is it possible to do justice to such enormous masses of material as are exhibited in ancient medieval, and modern philosophy by applying such simple formulations as the form-matter, nature-grace, and nature-freedom motives? And is it possible to do justice to the full content of Christianity by reference to Creation, Fall, and Redemption? Why not refer to the "self-contained ontological Trinity" as Dr. Cornelius Van Til does, or as a Calvinistic thinker to "the whole counsel of God" with accentuation on eternal predestination and divine providence? How is the motive to be extracted from the full system in which it expresses itself? Dooyeweerd argues frequently from the basic motives to particular philosophical and, in spite of his protestations, even theological consequences. Are such inferences conclusive, or do they merely present an appearance of argument to support positions held on other grounds? To condemn a philosophical thesis by alleging it to be an expression of an apostate religious motive is hardly an adequate procedure of immanent criticism, nor is an appeal to the basic motive of Scripture a convincing method of establishing what looks like a theological view, say, on the topic of common grace. Dooyeweerd's difficult distinction between the non-theoretical motive of Holy Scripture and the theoretical object of scientific theology has been set forth in the exposition above.

Dooyeweerd himself has avoided superficiality in the application of his thesis as to the dualistic motives by insisting on the "royal road of immanent criticism" and by pursuing this road with great care in his elaborate discussions of ancient and modern philosophies in both of his trilogies.

Metaphysical Foundations: Meaning, Law, Time, Modal Aspects, Analogy

A critique of the metaphysical constructions of the new philosophy is impossible within the limits of the present paper. A few brief observations will have to suffice.

1. The word "meaning" is used in a peculiar sense by Dooyeweerd to formulate a metaphysical doctrine as to the nature of reality.

2. The doctrine of law as the boundary between God and the cosmos is intended to cut off metaphysical speculation about that which transcends time. This suggests the question, how there can be states of affairs independent of human subjectivity, if absolute truths transcending time are denied.

3. The theory of cosmic time is a large-scale metaphysical construction worthy of detailed analysis. Here the only question to be raised is that of the justification of the claim that logic is temporal. Is this a consequence or is it a presupposition of the *Gegenstand*-relation? Whichever it is, it appears to be a critical dogma that stands or falls with that of the *Gegenstand*-relation.

4. Is the theory of the modal aspects a faithful account of states of affairs in reality? Or is it a speculative construction that misconstrues reality by confusion of types of categories? Do history and language belong to the same type of category? Does either of these fall under a common proximate genus with number or space? Man speaks, but there is no verb usable in a parallel way with "speaks" for man's functioning in spheres of number, space, or history. Such simple linguistic observations suggest that the notion of a "modal aspect" or "temporal function" conceals a set of category mistakes. If so, much of the theory of the law-spheres collapses, and with it the doctrine of analogy based on this theory.

THEOLOGICAL CONSEQUENCES

An evaluation of Dooyeweerd's views about theology in its relation to philosophy ought not to forget that these views were forged in the heated fires of controversy. Professor Hepp had accused the new philosophy of deviating from time-honored theological views on the soul, the natures of Christ, common grace, and other themes and thus of threatening deformation within the Reformed camp. Dooyeweerd has retorted by developing a theory that sets narrow limits to the scope of theological investigation and that brands traditional positions in theology and even in philosophy as "scholasticism." Scholasticism for Dooyeweerd is not exclusively a Roman Catholic phenomenon, but is found in much traditional Reformed thought. Scholasticism is represented as rooted in the nature-grace motive, as uncritically accepting the dogma of autonomy for the natural reason while elevating theology to a queenly status as a supernatural discipline, and as corrupting Christian theology by introducing the anthropological doctrine of dichotomy of material body and rational, immortal soul.

Is Dooyeweerd's indictment of classical Reformed theology, from which neither Calvin nor the Reformed confessions are exempt, warranted in the light of Holy Scripture, of reason, and of history?

Theological doctrines and creedal formulations can be shown to be erroneous only by an appeal to Holy Scripture, even as their truth can be exhibited only by pleading the warrant of Scripture. Vague assertions as to the basic religious motive expressed in theological and even in creedal statements prove nothing. In particular, a theological anthropology must be accepted or rejected only after a thorough and critical examination of the mass of biblical texts has been completed. There is no central biblical witness about the soul or heart that can be isolated from the many texts in which mention is made of the soul, spirit, heart, or mind of man. Many of these texts accentuate the intellectual function of the soul and thus lend support to a view of the primacy of the intellect alien to Dooyeweerd's theory. The doctrine of the soul as a real entity, for which the philosophical term "substance" has commonly been employed, distinct from the material body, endued with reason and capable of separate subsistence, though incomplete in the period between death and resurrection, cannot be refuted by a deduction from the problematic theory of the *Gegenstand*-relation. Nor can deductions from religious motives take the place of painstaking exegetical analysis. The well-known difficulty for creationism posed by the transmission of Original Sin has not been recently discovered, and "scholastic" solutions in terms of careful distinctions applied judiciously to the scriptural data ought not to be peremptorily dismissed, even though they require careful examination.

Dogmatic theology uses logic as an instrument and metaphysics as establishing certain principles as well as concepts employed in theology as a science. Yet the distinctive principle of theology is not derived

300

from philosophy, not even from Christian philosophy. Theology is directly related to revelation as its norm and the source of its content in a way in which neither philosophy nor the special sciences are. This fact or state of affairs provides a ground for denying that theology may be considered as one of the special sciences, even if to it is assigned the faith-aspect as defining the scope of its theoretical object. Theology is concerned with the entire Word of God, with the "whole counsel of God," not simply with a faith-aspect. Ultimately, by its faithful account of the teaching of the Word of God, theology aims at the knowledge of God Himself. To call theology thus conceived the "queen of the sciences" is not to reduce other sciences to the position of slaves, nor even philosophy to that of a handmaid. With Scripture as an infallible constitution in no need of amendment or of extraneous interpretation, theology may reign securely with philosophy as a wise counsellor and the other sciences as freely functioning in their allotted positions.

Sharp as the above criticism of Dooyeweerd's theological views may sound, it is offered in appreciation of his concern that theology ought to be purified from contamination by alien philosophical conceptions. Dooyeweerd is fully justified in insisting that theology must work in co-operation with a Christian rather than a secular philosophy and in claiming for philosophy a status independent of theology as a science. His combination of the Augustinian conception of a Christian philosophy with the Thomist insistence on the distinction between philosophy and theology is admirable, even though his own view of the place of theology in the order of the sciences tends unduly to limit its scope and underestimate its value. Theology does have much to profit from a new critique of theoretical thought, but such a critique must be executed in a rigorous philosophical manner and purified from formal and material defects that mar the appearance of a Reformed Christian philosophy. From such a philosophical critique Reformed theology can only benefit. Dooyeweerd is to be honored as having pointed the way to this goal and as having made considerable advances in its accomplishment.

IV. BIBLIOGRAPHY

Works by Herman Dooyeweerd

De Ministerraad in het Nederlandsche staatsrecht (*The Cabinet in Dutch Law*). Amsterdam, 1917.

"In den strijd om een Christelijke Staatkunde. Proeve van een fundeering der Calvinistische levens- en wereldbeschouwing in hare wetsidee" ("In the Conflict about Christian Politics. Attempt at Founding a Calvinistic Life- and World-View in its Cosmonomic Idea"), *Antirevolutionaire Staatkunde* (1924-27).

Calvinisme en Natuurrecht (*Calvinism and Natural Law*). Amersfoort, 1925.

"Calvinisme contra Neo-Kantianisme" ("Calvinism vs. Neo-Kantianism"), *Tijdschrift voor Wijsbegeerte* (1926)

De beteekenis der Wetsidee voor Rechtswetenschap en Rechtsphilosophie (*The Meaning of the Cosmonomic Idea for the Science and Philosophy of Law*). Kampen, 1926.

De crisis de Humanistische staatsleer in het licht eener Calvinistische kosmologie en kennistheorie (*The Crisis of the Humanistic View of the State in the light of a Calvinistic Cosmology and Epistemology*). Amsterdam, 1931.

"Norm en Feit" ("Norm and Fact"), *Themis* (1932).

"Het tijdsprobleem en zijn antinomieen op het immanentiestandpunt" ("The Problem of Time and Its Antinomies on the Immanence standpoint"), *Philosophia Reformata* (1936, 1939).

De Christelijke Staatsidee (*The Christian Idea of the State*). Rotterdam-Utrecht, 1936.

Recht en Historie (*Law and History*). Assen, 1938.

"Geloof en Wetenschap" ("Faith and Science"), *Geloof en wetenschap* (1938).

"De niet-theoretische voor-oordeelen in de wetenschap" ("Non-Theoretical Prejudices in Science"), *Philosophia Reformata* (1938).

"Kuyper's Wetenschapsleer" ("Kuyper's Theory of Science"), *Philosophia Reformata* (1939).

"Het tijdsprobleem in de Wijsbegeerte der Wetsidee" ("The Problem of

Time in the Philosophy of the Cosmonomic Idea"), *Philosophia Reformata* (1940).

"De leer der analogie in de Thomistische wijsbegeerte en in de Wijsbegeerte der Wetsidee" ("The Doctrine of Analogy in Thomistic Philosophy and in the Philosophy of the Cosmonomic Idea"), *Philosophia Reformata* (1942).

"De leer van de mens in de wijsbegeerte der wetsidee" ("The Doctrine of Man in the Philosophy of the Cosmonomic Idea") *Correspondentie Bladen* (1942).

Encyclopaedie der Rechtswetenschap (Encyclopedia of Jurisprudence) Amsterdam, 1946.

"Introduction to a Transcendental Criticism of Philosophic Thought," *The Evangelical Quarterly* (1947).

"Het wijsgeerig tweegesprek tusschen de Thomistische philosophie en de Wijsbegeerte der Wetsidee" ("The Philosophical Dialogue between Thomistic Philosophy and the Philosophy of the Cosmonomic Idea"), *Philosophia Reformata* (1948).

Transcendental Problems of Philosophic Thought. An Inquiry into the Transcendental Conditions of Philosophy. Grand Rapids, 1948.

Reformatie en Scholastiek in de wijsbegeerte. I: Het Grieksche Voorspel (*Reformation and Scholasticism in Philosophy. I: The Greek Prelude*). Franeker, 1949.

"The Contest about the Concept of Sovereignty in Modern Jurisprudence and Political Science," *Free University Quarterly* (1951), pp. 85-106.

"De transcendentale critiek van het theoretisch denken en de theologia naturalis" ("The Transcendental Critique of Theoretical Thought and Natural Theology"), *Philosophia Reformata* (1952).

A New Critique of Theoretical Thought (4 vols.). Vol. I. *The Necessary Presuppositions of Philosophy* (translated by David H. Freeman and William Young). Amsterdam and Philadelphia, 1953.

A New Critique of Theoretical Thought (4 vols.). Vol. II. *The General Theory of the Modal Spheres* (translated by David H. Freeman and H. de Jongste). Amsterdam and Philadelphia, 1954.

A New Critique of Theoretical Thought (4 vols.). Vol. III. *The Structures of Individuality of Temporal Reality* (translated by David H. Freeman and H. de Jongste). Amsterdam and Philadelphia, 1957.

"Del Vecchio's Idealistic Philosophy of Law Viewed in the Light of a Transcendental Critique of Philosophic Thought," I - II, *Philosophia Reformata* (1957).

A New Critique of Theoretical Thought (4 vols.). Vol. IV (Index of Subjects and Authors by H. de Jongste). Amsterdam and Philadelphia, 1958.

"De verhouding tussen wijsbegeerte en theologie en de strijd der facul-
teiten" ("The Relationship between Philosophy and Theology
and the Conflict of the Faculties"), *Philosophia Reformata*
(1958).

*In the Twilight of Western Thought. Studies in the Pretended Autono-
my of Philosophic Thought.* Philadelphia, 1960.

"Van Peursen's critische vragen bij *A New Critique of Theoretical
Thought*" ("Van Peursen's Critical Questions on *A New Critique
of Theoretical Thought*"), *Philosophia Reformata* (1960).

"What is man?" *International Reformed Bulletin* (1960).

"De Taak ener wijsgerige anthropologie en de doodlopende wegen tot
wijsgerige zelfkennis" ("The Task of a Philosophical Anthropology and the Blind Alleys in Philosophical Self-knowledge"),
Philosophia Reformata (1961).

WORKS ON HERMAN DOOYEWEERD

Albers, O. J. L. *Het Natuurrecht volgens de Wijsbegeerte der Wetsidee
(Natural Law According to the Philosophy of the Cosmonomic
Idea).* Nijmegen, 1955.

Brummer, Vincent. *Transcendental Criticism and Christian Philosophy.*
Franeker, 1961.

Clark, Gordon H. "Cosmic Time," *The Gordon Review* (February,
1956), pp. 94-99.

Conradie, A. C. *The Neo-Calvinistic Concept of Philosophy.* Natal,
1960.

Freeman, David H. "A New School of Christian Philosophy," *Journal
of Religion,* XXXVIII (1958), 46-53.

———————— *Recent Studies in Philosophy and Theology* (Chap. II).
Philadelphia, 1962.

Holmes, Arthur F. "Dooyeweerd: Some Questions and an Alternative,"
The Reformed Journal (January, 1964), pp. 11-14.

Jager, Ronald, "Dooyeweerd and the Irony of Rationalism," *The Reformed Journal* (September and October, 1964), pp. 9-13 and
pp. 16-21.

Jellema, Dirk. "The Philosophy of Vollenhoven and Dooyeweerd," *Calvin Forum,* XIX (1954), 169-172, 192-194.

———————— "New Synthesis Philosophy," *Calvin Forum,* XX (1954),
31-33.

Kroner, Richard. "New Critique of Theoretical Thought," *Review of
Metaphysics,* VIII (1954), 321-324.

Marlet, M. Fr. J. *Grundlinien der kalvinistischen "Philosophie der
Gesetzidee" als Christlicher Transzendental philosophie (Main*

Lines of the Calvinistic "Philosophy of the Cosmonomic Idea" as a Christian Transcendental Philosophy). Munich, 1954.

Mekkes, J. P. A. "The Philosophy of Vollenhoven and Dooyeweerd (A Reply to Mr. D. Jellema, Ph.D.)," *Calvin Forum,* XX (1955), 219-222.

Nash, Ronald H. *Dooyeweerd and the Amsterdam Philosophy.* Grand Rapids, 1962.

Plantinga, Alvin, "Dooyeweerd on Meaning and Being," *The Reformed Journal* (October, 1958), pp. 10-15.

Puchinger, G. "Dr. Herman Dooyeweerd," *Perspectief (Perspective,* the anniversary volume of the 25th year of the Society for Reformed Philosophy). Kampen, 1961. (*Perspectief* also contains an exhaustive bibliography of Dooyeweerd's publications, prepared by C. Groen).

Spier, J. M. *Introduction to Christian Philosophy.* Philadelphia, 1954.

——————— *What Is Calvinistic Philosophy?* Grand Rapids, 1953.

Young, William. *Towards a Reformed Philosophy.* Franeker and Grand Rapids, 1952.

——————— "The Doctrine of Man in the Amsterdam Philosophy," *Westminister Theological Journal* (November, 1959), pp. 1-12.

10 SAMUEL J. MIKOLASKI

P. T. Forsyth

I. BIOGRAPHY

PETER TAYLOR FORSYTH was born in Aberdeen, Scotland, on May 12, 1848, the first of five children to Isaac Forsyth and Elspet Mac-Pherson. It is unlikely that Isaac ever earned more than thirteen shillings per week, but by hard work and thrift the couple planned for the education of their son. To supplement their meager income, Elspet filled the house with university students to whom she was as much mother and benevolent creditor as landlady. Following parish and grammar schooling, Peter competed for the Aberdeen University scholarships in Latin translation, was placed twenty-first among 244 competitors, and won the Cargill Bursary of twenty pounds sterling for four years. His academic record was outstanding in Greek, Latin, and English; at the end he took a first in Classics and tied for first in Moral Philosophy. He was tutor in Latin during the academic year 1871-72; then, at the suggestion of W. Robertson Smith, he traveled to Germany for a term under Ritschl at Göttingen. Already set on a path by F. D. Maurice, Forsyth's interest in the moral constitution of things was strengthened.

In September of that year he began study at Hackney College but withdrew after two years, and there followed many months of uncertainty brightened only by his engagement to Miss Mina Magness, whom he married in 1877, the year following his settlement in the Congregational Church at Shipley, a suburb of Bradford. Neither he

Dr. Samuel J. Mikolaski is Professor of Systematic Theology at the International Baptist Theological Seminary, Rüschlikon-Zürich, Switzerland. He is the author of several articles and of the forthcoming book, *The Grace of God*.

nor the church was recognized by the Yorkshire Union, probably due to his theological opinions and unsophisticated ways. He shared in the abortive Leicester Conference of 1877-78, an unofficial meeting of Congregationalists mostly, convened to discuss the extent to which theological agreement should condition religious communion. Forsyth favored a broader base of intercommunion, but the Conference failed because some feared that Unitarian views might gain a foothold in the Union. Subsequently Forsyth agreed with R. W. Dale, who opposed him at Leicester, that freedom must be within the truth of the Gospel. Only later is the vital evangelical thrust of Forsyth's theology evident; at this stage he fought social injustice, the heavy hand of tradition, and the prevalent pessimism of Schopenhauer.

In 1878 he moved to St. Thomas' Square Congregational Church, Hackney, in London, where, confronted by problems of biblical criticism, he experienced a deepening of faith. Here too, he began his children's sermons, and developed an interest in religious art forms. Next, in 1885, he went to Cheetham Hill Congregational Church, Manchester, where he grappled forcefully with some of the social questions created by life in an industrial area. He wrote a column on current affairs for *The Manchester Guardian* (1885-1889) under a pseudonym, his political and social interests being at their highest at this time; also, he gave a series of lectures on religious art to the common people which were published later as *Religion in Recent Art*.

For six years, from 1888, he ministered to the Clarendon Park Congregational Church, Leicester. In 1889 he vigorously supported the famous Dock Strike, and eleven years after he was rejected by the Yorkshire Union he preached their annual sermon in Bradford. During Spring Term of 1893 he served with distinction as College Pastor at Mansfield College, Oxford. By this time he was on intimate terms with R. W. Dale, and when Dale died in 1893 it was a great grief to Forsyth.

Yielding to pressure put upon him, Forsyth reluctantly left Leicester in 1894 for the Emmanuel Congregational Church, Cambridge, where he became the spokesman for the nonconformist cause. Grief beset him in the sudden illness, then the death, of his wife and in his own crumbling health, though the Church loyally sustained him. Providentially, in 1897, he married Bertha Ison, a person of unflagging energy who devoted herself to his well-being. It was she who made his last twenty-four years so serene and theologically productive. During this period, while holding to the legitimacy of critical textual study, he began to inveigh against the attenuation of the Gospel and its reduction to concern with purely social and political questions. Without doubt "The Holy Father and the Living Christ," his sermon preached before the Leicester Meeting of the Union in 1897, marks a pivotal point in his theology. It also earned him the adulation and praise of the religious world. Here his evangelical faith, born of the reality to him of the crucified and risen Christ, fairly bursts out with explosive force. Honors poured in on him from this time forward. In 1899, with others, he visited the International Congregational Council convened in the Tremont Temple, Boston, and the reaction to his address "The Evangelical Principle of Authority" was wildly enthusiastic.

In 1901 he was elected Principal of Hackney College (later New College), London, and he began over twenty years of fruitful theological writing. He fought for free education, charging that the Anglican bishops were using the Education Act to foster Anglican sentiments in the schools. In the first specially called assembly of the Union in 1906 the resolution condemning the attempt by the House of Lords to revise the Bill, allegedly in favor of the Establishment, was moved by John Massie, member of parliament, and P. T. Forsyth, freechurchman. He publically attacked the Chinese Labor Bill designed to import cheap far-eastern labor into the Transvaal under conditions, he charged, that amounted to slavery. He was most upset by the controversy with R. J. Campbell over the New Theology. Campbell charged that Forsyth had abandoned the principles of freedom that he espoused at the Leicester Conference. Forsyth replied that then it was a question of freedom to intercommune; now it was a question of preserving the evangelical Gospel that makes us free. He charged that Campbell's views were really Hegelian and that they could not be reconciled with the biblical doctrine of the Holy Father acting in the incarnate, crucified, and risen Son. In 1907 he delivered the famous Lyman Beecher lectures on preaching at Yale University, later published as *Positive Preaching and the Modern Mind.*

The sheer intellectual vigor of the man so frail of body is astounding. He visited numerous conferences, immersed himself in denominational work, prepared lectures, wrote books, raised funds, met students, administered the college, and led in the work of the co-operating University of London theological faculties. The long hours spent at his desk late at night seemed to squeeze his very life into the words that flowed from his pen. Controversy will continue about his style as a writer, but those who take the trouble to probe his meaning will be rewarded richly. On the fourth Armistice Day, November 11, 1921, P. T. Forsyth, aged seventy-three, died in his sleep. Of himself he had once written:

> There was a time when I was interested in the first degree with purely scientific criticism. Bred among academic scholarship of the classics and philosophy, I carried these habits to the Bible, and I

found in the subject a new fascination, in proportion as the stakes were so much higher. But fortunately for me, I was not condemned to the mere scholar's cloistered life. I could not treat the matter as an academic quest. I was kept close to practical conditions . . . . It also pleased God by the revelation of His holiness and grace, which the great theologians taught me to find in the Bible, to bring home to me my sin in a way that submerged all the school questions in weight, urgency, and poignancy, I was turned from a Christian to a believer, from a lover of love to an object of grace. And so, whereas I first thought that what the churches needed was enlightened instruction and liberal theology, I came to be sure that what they needed was evangelization, in something more than the conventional sense of that word . . . . I withdrew my prime attention from much of the scholar's work and gave it to those theological interests, imbibed first from Maurice, and then more mightily through Ritschl, which come nearer to life than science, sentiment, or ethic ever can do. I immersed myself in the logic of Hegel, and corrected it by the theology of Paul, and its continuity in the Reformation, because I was all the time being corrected and humiliated by the Holy Spirit. To me John Newton's hymn which I spoke of is almost holy writ. My faith in critical methods is unchanged. My acceptance of many of the new results is as it was. This applies to the criticism of traditional dogma no less than of Scripture. But the need of the hour, among the only circles I can reach, is not that. The time for it will come, but not yet. It is a slow matter. For what is needed is not mere change of view, but a change and a deepening in the type of personal religion, amounting in some cases to a new conversion . . . . I am sure no new theology can really be theology, whatever its novelty, unless it express and develop the old faith which made those theologies that are now old the mightiest things of the age when they were new.[1]

II. EXPOSITION

The range and depth of Forsyth's theology cannot be grasped by reading one or two of his books, for he was never a systematic theologian. But this is not to say that his views are not systematic in character. By patient analysis they emerge as a reasoned whole organized around certain essential theological ideas. He consciously rejected Hegel's monism, Schopenhauer's pessimism, and Lessing's historiographical skepticism. Positively, his faith is marked by the experiential motif of a Wesley, the theological vigor and earthiness of a Luther, the moral passion of a Maurice, and the world-embracing kingdom concept of a Ritschl. History and experience, criticism and

[1] *Positive Preaching and the Modern Mind* (1909), pp. 281, 282, 283, 285, 287.

faith, process and morality were not for him mutually exclusive ideas but realities properly belonging together in evangelical faith and witness.

He saw the new science and textual criticism more as stepping stones to confirmation of the Gospel's truth than as rocks to crush faith. With these and other tools he felt that evangelical theology (to him the only legitimate claimant to the mantle of the apostles) could be reset upon the biblical base, soundly reasoned, experientially originated, and witnessing to the Holy God acting redemptively in Jesus Christ. The truth needs both apostolic missionary faith and new evidence continually addressing our categories of thought, he said.[2] To conserve all the phenomena, evangelical faith is essential to the view of the whole case. The essential nature of the world is of persons, intelligence, and morality; without these we cannot even begin to think as we do of the world we live in or of the kind of people that we are.

THE WORLD: NATURAL AND MORAL

The concept of evolution appealed to Forsyth because it afforded a more plastic view of the world and a more subtle working of the Spirit, provided that persons are not sacrificed to system, Incarnation to immanence, and that categories like sin, judgment, and redemption are not displaced by process. German idealism, he charged, "pre-occupies us with the physical notion of monistic process, instead of the moral notion of personality and freedom of action and crisis, sin and sanctity."[3] Evolution can supplement the doctrine of creation but it cannot be a substitute for redemption.[4] Hegel, he said, had turned action into a succession of principles that devoured personal life and the moral value of history.[5] God the absolute Person is the norm that makes process progress: all process must serve personality and freedom in grace.[6]

Primal reality is persons in action: "morality is the nature of things"; it is a moral order and a moral movement of personal relations.[7] The moral is the bedrock of the relations between God and the world in both creation and redemption. The last great reality is a supreme will — a person not in repose but in action;[8] the key to history is

---

2 *Holy Christian Empire* (1902), p. 16.
3 *The Old Faith and the New Theology* (1907), p. 48.
4 *Positive Preaching and the Modern Mind* (1909), p. 269.
5 *The Justification of God* (1916), p. 192
6 *Positive Preaching and the Modern Mind* (1909), p. 214.
7 *The Principle of Authority* (1913), pp. 179-180; note p. 4 also.
8 *Positive Preaching and the Modern Mind* (1909), p. 49; note also pp. 175-176, 302, 333, 346.

311

not puppet ideas but the will as free,[9] and this is exhibited concretely in Jesus Christ.[10] Man's spirit reflects the constitution of the divine spirit:

> The created soul is created by soul. Its life is in some form God's life. And if that be so, the real meaning of creation is the output of something which reflects the creator's freedom, and is therefore not a thing but a will.[11]

Soul is neither a static entity nor a section of human nature but its unity expressed in space and time as personality that is developing under the discipline of faith.[12] Soul is both a stage and a growth — it is a "close," that is, a point in the history of an entity's development: "nature evolves to a close, which is none the less a real close because it has within itself an evolving history."[13] Also, he says: "You only *are* because of your power to *become* what you are, to *grow*. Incessant growth is a condition of perfect living personality."[14] The purpose of life is the spiritualizing of finite existence, and in this the grace of God is prevenient; God invades us but he does not assault us; "we are mastered but not concussed."[15]

THE HOLY FATHER AND THE LIVING CHRIST

Forsyth's conception of the divine holiness turned a searchlight upon the theology of his time when the father-image of God degenerated to the genial and amoral. The climax of revelation is not to think of God simply as Father but Holy Father, "He is *Holy* Father and Redeemer, and it is His holiness of fatherhood that is the source of our redemption and sonship."[16] The God-created world must reflect His own holiness, which is its purpose, and which He secures in the Cross where that holiness is smitten by our sin.[17] Holiness is of the personal God, public and universal; but, if the latter, it does not absorb persons, nor is it bare power.[18] Rather it is the moral absolute, the public righteousness of God, the ideal good not in abstraction but translated

---

[9] *The Justification of God* (1916), pp. 51-52.
[10] *The Person and Place of Jesus Christ* (1909), p. 197.
[11] *The Principle of Authority* (1913), p. 158. Note also *Christ on Parnassus* (n.d.), p. 227; *The Holy Father and the Living Christ* (1897), pp. 138-139; *London Theological Studies* (1911). p. 149.
[12] *Religion in Recent Art* (1889), p. 55; *Positive Preaching and the Modern Mind* (1909), p. 139.
[13] *The Person and Place of Jesus Christ* (1909), p. 146.
[14] *Christian Perfection* (1899), p. 119 (italics his).
[15] *Positive Preaching and the Modern Mind* (1909), p. 64.
[16] *The Holy Father and the Living Christ* (1897), p. 4.
[17] *The Person and Place of Jesus Christ* (1909), p. 228.
[18] *London Theological Studies* (1911), p. 155.

by our religious consciousness to the transcendent, personal God.[19] "God's holy law is his own holy nature."[20] The New Testament for this reason, he argued, speaks not of love alone, which is morally impossible, but of holy love that did not spare the only Son.

In polar relation to holiness is Forsyth's doctrine of the living Christ as the concrete manifestation of it. A threefold answer is given by him to the question: What is this faith in this Christ? It is faith in an historic Christ, a living Christ, and a Christ personal to each of us.[21] Faith in Christ is tied to the historical realities, yet we do not view Him at arm's length as One who lived admirably and died nobly, but as One who having lived through the events comes through them to us as Victor, Redeemer, and King[22]: "realize a living Christ, and He will produce in you a living faith." Of this vital faith he writes:

> He must be personal to us. He must be *our* Saviour, in *our* situation, *our* needs, loves, shames, sins. He must charge Himself with *our* souls. We believe in the Holy Ghost.[23]

INCARNATION AND TRINITY

Like Athanasius, Forsyth was concerned with the evangelical presentation of the Gospel. Therefore he too expressed Christology in terms of what the Savior must be to accomplish redemption. By the Cross we understand the Incarnation as God with us, God acting to save:

> Indeed, God is in Christ in such a way that Christ's express statement of unity with the Father is of less moment for us than the total impression produced by His whole life and person. This experience teaches us that His presence is God's presence, His action on us God's action, His forgiveness of us God's forgiveness.[24]

Rejecting the Arian doctrine, Forsyth upheld the creed that in Christ we have God's real presence.[25] Christ experienced growth,[26] but He is not the self-realization of the divine Spirit in the world, nor does He acquire divine personality in the world; His life is the redinte-

---

19 *Positive Preaching and the Modern Mind* (1909), pp. 149, 293-294; *The Christian Ethic of War* (1916), p. 147; *The Principle of Authority* (1913), p. 6.

20 *The Work of Christ* (1910), p. 113.

21 *The Holy Father and the Living Christ* (1897), p. 101.

22 *Ibid.*, pp. 116, 119.

23 *Ibid.*, p. 146.

24 *Faith and Criticism* (1893), p. 119; note *The Cruciality of the Cross* (1909), p. 18.

25 *The Person and Place of Jesus Christ* (1909), p. 83.

26 "Not even God could create a character full blown," *Religion in Recent Art* (1889), p. 221.

gration in history of the divine life through a moral process.[27] Forsyth adopted a kenotic Christology: the divine attributes were not parted with but retracted in a different mode of being, becoming potential not actual. Already pledged to the personal and the moral, he believed that the modern concepts of corporate personality and the interpenetration of selves in what is a complex notion of unity could mark significant gains in our understanding of the Trinity. Trinity, Incarnation, and the Cross join in the following:

> The Father who *spoke* by His prophets must *come* to save in the Son and must *occupy* in the Spirit. He offers, gives, Himself in the Son and conveys Himself in the Spirit . . . . It is all one holy love and grace, in this Eternal threefold action, both within God and upon man. Only on this Trinitarian conception of God can we think of such a salvation as ours.[28]

HOLY SCRIPTURE AND REVELATION

Though he did not bring the results of exegetical study into his published work, the biblical categories strongly undergird the theology of Forsyth. He used the canons of biblical criticism without becoming a judge of Holy Writ. Because the Church gave us the canon but not the books (which were written by inspired men), the true successor of the apostles is the Gospel, he said.[29] The final Word was God-given in history and the free Spirit fills the Word and mediates it to the soul; therefore orthodoxy dare not degenerate into intellectualism.[30] He held faith essential to sound criticism and agreed with James Denney that we require a dynamic statement of the Gospel commensurate with the scale of divine grace.[31] Forsyth reserved the term inspiration for the use God made of the human instruments and the term revelation for the content of the divine message. Concerning the former he says:

> I do not believe in verbal inspiration. I am with the critics in principle. But the true minister ought to find the words and phrases of the Bible so full of spiritual food and felicity that he has some difficulty in not believing in verbal inspiration.[32]

[27] *The Person and Place of Jesus Christ* (1909), p. 261.
[28] *Ibid.*, p. 327; note *The Cruciality of the Cross* (1909), p. 101; *The Work of Christ* (1910), p. 152.
[29] *Rome, Reform, and Reaction* (1899), p. 224.
[30] *Faith, Freedom, and the Future* (1912), p. 1; *The Principle of Authority* (1913), p. 397.
[31] *Positive Preaching and the Modern Mind* (1909), pp. 19-21, 133, 279; *Holy Christian Empire* (1902), pp. 12-14.
[32] *Positive Preaching and the Modern Mind* (1909), p. 38; cf. pp. 125-126.

In the apostles' message, he said, word and event join, interpreted to them and us by the Holy Spirit through a psychological process which, if a-logical, was not irrational.[33] The Word of God is neither the letter nor the doctrines of the Bible but the *long act of revelation and redemption* which it records, namely Jesus Christ. The testimony of Christ is the spirit of Scripture.[34] Through Scripture we face revelation not *about* but *in* Christ;[35] three stages in fact are discernible, he said: the incarnate fact, then the apostolic word interpreting it, finally the fact again but enshrined in the soul of the believing Church.[36]

What then is revelation? It is not, for Forsyth, a thing of creeds or truths, but a knowledge ethicized, a thing of persons and acts.[37] It is not something to hold but to obey, not a mystery of the Church but the moral key to history, not process but act — act, that is, as historical, particular, discrete, and personal.[38] He accounts for this idea historically as follows: English Independency is made up of the Calvinist stress on the Word, the Anabaptist freedom of the Spirit, and the English love of democratic constitutional government. A balance of Word and Spirit is maintained, he said, when we confess the fontal Word together with the Spirit's presence in the Church filling and mediating it.[39]

Nevertheless, he argues that experience is not revelation nor the test of it; what is given to experience is revelation, and this is the historical events, namely Christ and His Cross, apostolically interpreted.[40] Revelation is an act prolonged into an infinite series of acts in the human soul. Revelation happens when the Spirit acts *directly* through the *medium* of the Word. He writes:

> Revelation then may be defined as the free, final and effective act of God's self-communication in Jesus Christ for man's redemption . . . . real revelation is always Christ revealed in us, and revealed as Redeemer.[41]

33 *The Person and Place of Jesus Christ* (1909), pp. 152, 160-161, 165-167.

34 *Ibid.*, p. 179; *Rome, Reform, and Reaction* (1899), pp. 134-135.

35 *Faith and Criticism* (1893), pp. 98-99.

36 *The Person and Place of Jesus Christ* (1909), p. 159.

37 *Positive Preaching and the Modern Mind* (1909), p. 266; *The Person and Place of Jesus Christ* (1909), ch. VII; *Rome, Reform, and Reaction* (1899), p. 125.

38 *The Church and the Sacraments* (1917), pp. 101-102; *Positive Preaching and the Modern Mind* (1909), pp. 214, 279, 346-347, 349.

39 *The Atonement in Modern Religious Thought* (1900), p. 73; *Faith, Freedom, and the Future* (1912), pp. 296-304.

40 *Positive Preaching and the Modern Mind* (1909), p. 211; *The Atonement in Modern Religious Thought* (1900), p. 71. Note especially *The Principle of Authority* (1913), p. 75.

41 *Faith and Criticism* (1893), pp. 116, 121; note p. 104 and *Faith, Freedom, and the Future* (1912), pp. 33-34.

Humanity, Sin, and Judgment

For Forsyth, personality, as a theological concept, has to be rescued from individualism. He says that the racial life is solidaric organically, socially, and ethically. While an individual is a discrete entity, individual persons are created only within interdependent social life. A living soul is a life-giving spirit. So then, in Hegelian language, he rejects the atomism of individual souls for the conception of society where individual souls find their unity in a higher super-individual personality.[42] "Personality is created by social influences and finds itself only in these,"[43] he says; even our personal response to Christ is mediated by history. But the climax of racial solidarity is moral:

> The unity of the race is a moral unity . . . . It is in the conscience where man is a member of a vast moral world. It is the one changeless order of the moral world, emerging in conscience, that makes man universal . . . . What makes the world God's world is the action and unity of God's moral order of which our conscience speaks.[44]

Forsyth admired the older Reformed doctrines of the Atonement for their sense of the moral order of things, even if he criticized them at other points. They saw sin as individual and racial, he says, and adds: "the more we realize the solidarity of man the more his moral condition becomes a collectivism of guilt."[45] As such it must have a central, collective treatment — the objective atonement. Sin is rebellion against God and the meanness of a world of tragedy and death that turns upon its guilt,[46] which cannot be cured by verbal explanations but by divine action. Forsyth's best illustration of solidaric life is that of marriage; man and wife, he says, are more than one flesh, they are one personality "by the harmony of an indelible psychic difference."[47] Rather than diminishing responsibilty for sin, the concept heightens it:

> It was I who, at my will's centre, did that thing. It was my will and self that was put into it. My act was not the freak of some point on my circumference. It came from my centre. It was my unitary, indivisible self that was involved and is infected.[48]

[42] *Theology in Church and State* (1915), pp. 156, 157, 184.

[43] *Positive Preaching and the Modern Mind* (1909), p. 262.

[44] *The Work of Christ* (1910), p. 122-123.

[45] *Positive Preaching and the Modern Mind* (1909), p. 58.

[46] *Faith and Criticism* (1893), p. 141; *Positive Preaching and the Modern Mind* (1909), pp. 56, 333; *The Taste of Death and the Life of Grace* (1901), p. 26.

[47] *Marriage, Its Ethic and Religion* (n.d.), p. 34.

[48] *Christian Perfection* (1899), p. 6.

The sin that leaves man helplessly infected, though not totally corrupted, calls forth judgment from the divine holy love that can be assuaged only by an objective, efficacious atonement that is of world dimensions.[49] Wrath, curse, and hell are terms, he said, that denote the divine wrath upon the sinner as well as his sin.[50] If some judgment appears to work as a part of the world order, we cannot think the less that it is God acting: the wrath of God is God judging sin; He attaches to sin and executes against it due penal consequences.[51] Actually this is a ground for optimism for, said Forsyth in a word by which he is now well known, "if He cares enough for us to be angry He cares enough to redeem."[52] Law and judgment are the conditions of freedom and redemption; it is love that yields satisfaction to them:

> Every remission imperils the sanctity of law unless he who remits suffers something in the penalty forgone, and such atoning suffering is essential to the revelation of love which is to remain great, high, and holy.[53]

THE ATONEMENT

Forsyth devoted most of his interest to the Work of Christ. While volumes like *The Work of Christ and The Cruciality of the Cross* seem small in comparison with the bulk of his published work, it should be remembered that the objective Atonement is the controlling idea of his theological perspective.

Approaches to the Doctrine

Of names in the history of the doctrine, Forsyth felt that the Reformers, McLeod Campbell, F. D. Maurice, and Albrecht Ritschl were especially significant. The following are some things he either rejected or questioned seriously: the method of cataloguing texts;[54] that the Cross procured grace not issued from grace; that God is reconciled by any means exterior to Himself;[55] that in the Atonement the divine attributes conflict;[56] that God is mollified by a third party;[57] that the Atonement cost the Father nothing;[58] that Christ suffered the equiva-

---

[49] *The Taste of Death and the Life of Grace* (1901), p. 75; *The Cruciality of the Cross* (1909), p. 22.

[50] *The Holy Father and the Living Christ* (1897), p. 22.

[51] *The Work of Christ* (1910), p. 240.

[52] *Holy Christian Empire* (1902), p. 11.

[53] *The Atonement in Modern Religious Thought* (1900), p. 88.

[54] *Ibid.*, pp. 72-73.

[55] *Ibid.*, p. 64.

[56] *The Work of Christ* (1910), p. 117.

[57] *The Cruciality of the Cross* (1909), pp. 40-41.

[58] *The Atonement in Modern Religious Thought* (1900), p. 64.

lent punishment for sin;[59] that the sufferings of Christ *per se* atone;[60] that Christ bore arbitrary punishment for sin;[61] that there occurred a ledger transfer of our guilt to Christ or that God punished Christ;[62] that mercy was released by appeasement of justice;[63] and that love can forgive without regard to holiness.[64] Positively stated, the satisfaction of Christ lies, Forsyth said, in His obedience, though not to the wounded honor or punitive justice of God.[65] Paul does use forensic language,[66] expiation and forgiveness do go together,[67] sin was judged in the Cross and holiness was confessed by Christ's obedience.[68] Christ is God saving in God's way; therefore the Atonement is central to the very nature of God.[69] The breached communion between God and man requires redemption, he said;[70] the Cross therefore marks the revelation of the divine dealing with sin.[71]

Forsyth uses at least four principles to interpret the Cross. He says that it should be viewed: (a) as self-interpreting, because it carries its own meaning to the conscience in the light of the conditions of divine and human life;[72] (b) teleologically, in terms of ends rather than antecedents, for "all great interpretation is teleological;[73] (c) ethically, as God dealing with sin because forgiveness comes only at great cost where love deals with sin according to holiness;[74] (d) relevantly, for its due effects on man need to be grasped, though full value must go to the Cross as the cause.[75] What God does *for* us is the ground of His doing anything *with* us.[76]

[59] *Ibid.,* p. 65.
[60] *The Cruciality of the Cross* (1909), p. 41.
[61] *The Atonement in Modern Religious Thought* (1900), pp. 66-68.
[62] *The Cruciality of the Cross* (1909), p. 41.
[63] *The Atonement in Modern Religious Thought* (1900), p. 67.
[64] *Ibid.,* p. 66.
[65] *Ibid.,* p. 67.
[66] *Ibid.,* pp. 69-70.
[67] *Ibid.,* p. 72.
[68] *The Work of Christ* (1910), p. 181.
[69] *Faith and Criticism* (1893), p. 131; *Postitive Preaching and the Modern Mind* (1909), p. 178.
[70] *Positive Preaching and the Modern Mind* (1909), p. 56.
[71] *The Atonement in Modern Religious Thought* (1900), p. 63.
[72] *Ibid.*
[73] *Positive Preaching and the Modern Mind* (1909), pp. 321-322.
[74] *Ibid.,* p. 255; *The Atonement in Modern Religious Thought* (1900), pp. 74-75.
[75] *The Work of Christ* (1910), pp. 185-186: *Nihil in effectu quod non prius in causa.*
[76] *The Holy Father and the Living Christ* (1897), pp. 64-65.

Christ and the Holiness of God

The significance for Forsyth of the objective, or Godward, side of the Atonement can be summarized under four headings, as follows:

1. *The Righteous divine law was fulfilled in the judgment Christ bore.* This is expressed in at least four ways. First, Christ's death has prime regard to the holiness of God[77] or to hallowing the divine name,[78] not in historically dispersed redemptive power, but in a climactic personal act that transforms history.[79] He says:

> I have sought to construe the satisfaction to a holy God as consisting only in a counterpart and equal holiness rendered under the conditions of sin and judgment.[80]

Second, there is the moral necessity of upholding the divine law in an act that manifests *both* love and righteousness,[81] because "the enforcement of God's holiness by judgment is as essential to a *universal and eternal* Fatherhood as is the outflow of His love."[82] Third, the judgment was penal not to Christ's conscience but to His personality; the consequence was attached *by God* to sin, and this Christ took upon Himself, thereby dooming its evil principle; "you can therefore say that although Christ was not punished by God, He bore God's penalty upon sin."[83] Fourth, when Christ died our death, He knew the horror and meanness of it as no one but He could: "Alone He fulfilled the condition of feeling a moral death utterly universal, and therefore dreary, cold, loathsome, to such a soul as His."[84]

2. *On the Cross Christ confessed holiness perfectly.* The moral value of Christ's act stands in the mode of His submission to the divine judgment; this is the perfect confession of holiness. Here, as McLeod Campbell and Maurice before him, Forsyth tries to avoid pitfalls of older views. Christ's submission, His obedience, is God doing in man what man could not do; the first point therefore is not equivalence of penalty but holy obedience owning the righteousness of God revealed

---

77 *The Cruciality of the Cross* (1909), p. viii; note p. 39.
78 *The Justification of God* (1916), p. 11.
79 *Positive Preaching and the Modern Mind* (1909), pp. 335f.
80 *Ibid.*, p. 368.
81 *Ibid.*, p. 332; *The Church and the Sacraments* (1917), p. 5.
82 *The Holy Father and the Living Christ* (1897), pp. 29f. (the italics are his); note *The Atonement in Modern Religious Thought* (1900), p. 86.
83 *The Work of Christ* (1910), p. 147; note *The Holy Father and the Living Christ* (1897), pp. 35f.; *Missions in State and Church* (1908), p. 17.
84 *The Taste of Death and the Life of Grace* (1901), pp. 30f.; note pp. 17, 22f.; *The Cruciality of the Cross* (1909), p. 29.

in the law.[85] The obedient sanctity is the satisfying thing before God.[86] Second, this submission was in fact in the midst of penalty, under all the conditions of sin, death, and judgment as realities of the moral life of God and man.[87]

3. *The Atonement was primarily an act within God and therefore objective.* In the Cross, punisher and punished, judge and victim, priest and sacrifice are one, he maintained. This truth emerges in a variety of forms. First, the Cross is the self-donation of God to which sacrifice all man's sacrifices are but response.[88] Second, redemption is not delegated; it is God acting in the Son: "The old theologians were right when they insisted that the work of redemption was the work of the whole Trinity — Father, Son, and Holy Spirit."[89] Third, only God could fulfill the law He never broke: "The agent of judgment becomes the object of judgment, and so becomes the agent of salvation."[90] Fourth, the Atonement is the self-reconciliation of God and thus the ground of individual conversions.[91] Fifth, the Cross is the self-satisfaction of God in the constitution of man, that is, God meeting in man the conditions of his own life.[92] Sixth, the Cross is the self-justification of God, for "God was in Christ expiating sin to His own holiness."[93] We note the following:

> A holy God self-atoned in Christ is the moral centre of the sinful world. Our justification by God has its key in God's justification of Himself.[94]

4. *By the Cross Christ wins the moral victory of the world.* God triumphs in Christ over the forces of evil:

[85] *Faith and Criticism* (1893), p. 141; *The Atonement in Modern Religious Thought* (1900), p. 68.

[86] *Positive Preaching and the Modern Mind* (1909), p. 294; *The Cruciality of The Cross* (1909), pp. 92-95.

[87] *The Holy Father and the Living Christ* (1897), pp. 36, 73-74; *The Work of Christ* (1910), pp. 83, 133, 146-174, 201.

[88] *The Cruciality of the Cross* (1909), p. 94; *The Principle of Authority* (1913), p. 372.

[89] *The Work of Christ* (1910), p. 152; note *The Taste of Death and the Life of Grace* (1901), p. 47.

[90] *The Atonement in Modern Religious Thought* (1900), p. 81; note *The Work of Christ* (1910), pp. 82f., 169; *The Principle of Authority* (1913), p. 190.

[91] *The Work of Christ* (1910), pp. 93f.

[92] *The Atonement in Modern Religious Thought* (1900), p. 85; *The Work of Christ* (1910), p. 204.

[93] *Faith and Criticism* (1893), p. 141.

[94] *The Justification of God* (1916), p. 94; note pp. 40, 109, 124, 174.

> To see sin, sorrow, and death continually under the Cross, to see the grace of God triumphing over them in it, is the very soul and victory of faith.[95]

The Cross bears first upon the state of the moral world so that Christ revolutionizes it, changes the relations between God and the world, and thus establishes the ground of justification.[96] Christ acted upon the power of gathered and personalized evil when it failed to destroy the perfection of His holiness in His death.[97]

Christ and the Race

It concerns us here to show answers to two questions from Forsyth: (a) How is Christ related to the race? and (b) How does His work bear upon human need?

On the first, Forsyth says that the life of humanity stands in Christ so that He can therefore satisfy the conditions of the holy nature, and fulfill the demands of the redemptive passion, of God.[98] Christ's life and the racial life interpenetrate, and this generic relation that he sustains to it has always been the case: His life is the root of ours.[99] At this point Forsyth held the doctrine of the two natures to be too atomistic. The relation of Christ to us is not static, as of identity, but dynamic, as of self-identification.[100] This is not a matter of ideas and poor copies of them but of the conscience and interpenetration of moral life. The prime category is not ontic as a continuity of substance, but moral in Christ's "assumption of man's *conditions* of personality, and his renunciation of God's."[101] Whether a phrase like "corporate personality" used by Forsyth is felicitous may be questioned, but the relationship of Christ to humanity as generic, dynamic, and moral, where human life is taken up into Christ's, and in virtue of which what Christ is and does becomes ours, seems important. Christ thus becomes the universal person; salvation is individual because it is corporate; Christ is the mediator on the universal scale.[102] Primary

95 *The Taste of Death and the Life of Grace* (1901), p. 68.

96 *Positive Preaching and the Modern Mind* (1909), p. 333; *The Cruciality of the Cross* (1909), p. 101; *The Justification of God* (1916), p. 133; *The Holy Father and the Living Christ* (1897), pp. 31, 69; *The Work of Christ* (1910), pp. 56f., 129.

97 *Missions in State and Church* (1908), p. 60; note pp. 17f.

98 *The Atonement in Modern Religious Thought* (1900), pp. 81f., 86.

99 *The Holy Father and the Living Christ* (1897), p. 136.

100 *The Person and Place of Jesus Christ* (1909), pp. 333f.; *The Work of Christ* (1910), p. 158.

101 *The Person and Place of Jesus Christ* (1909), p. 352.

102 *Theology in Church and State* (1915), pp. 157, 184; *The Christian Ethic of War* (1916), p. 118; *The Work of Christ* (1910), p. 87; *Faith and Criticism* (1893), p. 113.

to this universality is Christ's holiness; His relation to the race is extensive because of the primary, intensive character of His holiness. Christ's moral excellence, His exclusiveness, is His universality.[103]

Christ and Human Need

We turn now to the second question, How does Christ's work bear upon human need? The answer will be discussed in six points.

1. *By His obedience Christ made a perfect racial confession of holiness.* When Christ bore our judgment He did not confess sin but holy judgment. The holiness of God was perfectly understood, owned, and praised as obedience to the moral requirements of holy grace on the universal scale.[104] Forsyth defines this in contrast to the confession of sin by men as

> the confession of holiness from sin's side amid the experience of judgment on the scale of the race, until the confessing race was thus put in right relation to God's holiness. Then judgment had done its perfect work. The race's sin was covered and atoned by it, i.e., by the God who bore it.[105]

Christ, said Forsyth, met wounded holiness by personal holiness on the eternal scale of the holy God, to the joy and satisfaction of God. This obedience makes ours possible and guarantees the satisfactoriness of it. Our repentance is latent in the quality of Christ's obedient response:

> It was the obedience which makes ours possible; it was inimitable, but reproducible. It cannot be emulated, it can but be repeated by Himself in the members whose life and whole it is.[106]

2. *By reason of this obedient perfect confession Christ was made sin for us.* Conscience, Forsyth said, can rest only if the judgment was borne, not as sin imputed to Christ but of Christ made sin for us; not as judgment borne by man, for that would have meant his end; not as judgment borne by God, for that would have missed the mark; but of judgment borne by God in man. We are judged not only by Him, but in Him, and so are judged to salvation.[107]

---

[103] *The Work of Christ* (1910), p. 184; *Missions in State and Church* (1908), p. 204.

[104] Note Ch. V, "The Cross the Great Confessional," in *The Work of Christ* (1910); *Religion in Recent Art* (1889), p. 208; *The Cruciality of the Cross* (1909), pp. 97-99.

[105] *The Work of Christ* (1910), p. 133.

[106] *Faith and Criticism* (1893), p. 128; note *The Principle of Authority* (1913), p. 390.

[107] *The Cruciality of the Cross* (1909), pp. 101, 298; *Positive Preaching and the Modern Mind* (1909), p. 312.

3. *Christ bore the evil consequences of sin for us.* Commenting on Holman Hunt's painting "The Scapegoat," Forsyth said that Christ is really the object of pity in the picture because He groaned under the spiritual burden of the world's condition. The physical death showed the hideous spiritual death — our death — that He died.[108]

4. *Christ accomplished an eternal mediation.* The Redeemer's mediatorial work, Forsyth said, is simply the prolongation of the energy of His redeeming act: "It is the intercession of Christ that is the moving force within all the spiritual evolution of history."[109] Christ's mediation belongs to the nature of our continuing communion with God; it is the soul of our continuing state of reconciliation and forgiveness.[110]

5. *Christ's work carries forward power to generate our response.* As well as bearing our sin, Christ by His Cross transfers the act of grace into our own personal experience. By the Cross the holy love of God is brought home to us under the actual conditions of sin, judgment, and grace, creating in us the power of responding to Him:

> . . . Christ had to make the soul which should respond to Him and understand Him. He had to create the very capacity for response. And that is where we are compelled to recognize the doctrine of the Holy Spirit as well as the doctrine of the Saviour. We are always told that faith is the gift of God and the work of the Holy Spirit . . . . the death of Christ had not simply to touch like heroism, but it had to redeem us into power of feeling its own worth. Christ had to save us from what we were too far gone to feel.[111]

6. *Christ created a new humanity.* A new moral reality, a new conscience of the race, was created by the Cross, says Forsyth. So final and universal was this that Christ became the center of the divine providence; in other words, the course of history unfolds in the train of His triumph:

> Human history, the history of peoples, transpires within Redemption. It is slowly bent into the history and evolution of God's forgiveness of man by judgment which makes it a new creature. The New Humanity comes by the loving and saving judgments of God in the world.[112]

---

108 *Religion in Recent Art* (1889), pp. 209f.; *The Work of Christ* (1910), p. 189; *The Taste of Death and the Life of Grace* (1901), pp. 15, 27f., 44.
109 *The Holy Father and the Living Christ* (1897), p. 141; note pp. 143f.
110 *Positive Preaching and the Modern Mind* (1909), p. 254.
111 *The Work of Christ* (1910), p. 18; note p. 192.
112 *The Christian Ethic of War* (1916), p. 189.

THE CHURCH IN THE WORLD

What Forsyth said in a little-known series of lectures on the Church[113] in 1896 pretty well sums up his views, for by that time he had achieved his theological maturity. He held that two great medieval principles, the organic unity of the Church and its spiritual independence from the State, are properly the heritage of Independency. The Reformers and Puritans rightly believed in "the autonomy of faith, the independence of the Church, its duty to obey Christ speaking by His spirit among Christian people."[114] Since he and other citizens were called upon to support the Establishment, he felt free to criticize it as well as to appreciate it. On the relation of Church to State he preferred the dictum "trust the grace of God" (in its action on the people) rather than "trust the people." This means the Gospel in the hands of evangelical people; it means the principles of free faith, free action, and free giving as the response of free men to the gift of free grace in Jesus Christ.

The Individual Christian as the Real Christian

On the ground of the objective Atonement, Forsyth said that Christians ought to regard all men as savable, that God could make armies of the wrecks of men. The starting point of Christianity is that men be converted individually to Christ. This personal faith is

> personal trust in a personal Saviour, the soul's direct, experiential, and priestless answer to God's grace as the forgiveness of sin, the destruction of guilt, and reconciliation by the blood of Christ alone.[115]

To Forsyth, three characteristics of the faith that justifies are: (a) a man's worth is measured not by what he is to a church but to God's Word and presence in Christ; (b) faith inevitably issues in practical justice, goodness, help, and blessing; (c) the value of our highest work depends not on results but on the faith that inspires it. It is the Church that is the priest in the Kingdom; every believer executes the office of priesthood.[116] Thus, while Roman Catholics stress the subjective side of religious experience, Protestants stress the moral side.

Church Life as Interdependent Life

The double thrust of discrete persons in vital interdependent relations is pivotal in Forsyth's theology of redemption and the Church.

[113] *The Charter of the Church* (1896).
[114] *Ibid.*, p. 12.
[115] *Rome, Reform, and Reaction* (1899), p. 50.
[116] *Ibid.*, pp. 170, 209.

"Individualism kills individuality and liberty,"[117] he says, applying this principle as much to persons as churches. An empire follows the Cross inevitably, he says; thus the Kingdom of God, larger than any individual or church, is the only universal society. The last great battle will be won by spiritual power which will be the genius of the new empire.[118] Nevertheless, the evangelical character of this life, rooted in the Bible and the Gospel, attests both the vitality of independence and its difference from episcopacy:

> We are evangelical; we find Christianity not in the Church but in the Gospel. We are Churchmen; and we find in the Gospel alone the true charter and freedom of the Church. We are evangelical Free Churchmen. If we follow the Reformers by going to the Bible before the Church, we have no room for the priest because the New Testament has none.[119]

Like every true society, the Christian community is not formed by simple addition. Something new and special is created that has the nature of corporate life. Each soul is not attached to but enters Christ, who carries the Church within His corporate person.[120] How can Independency get freedom in England yet acknowledge the corporateness of the Church, Forsyth asked? Only if Independents can convince the State that they are churches and members of that great federation of Christians which is now the only possible form in which the Church can be universal,[121] that is, a United States of the Church which, in fact, bears out New Testament unity, and which is fatal to both granular Independency and monarchical Episcopacy.[122]

Only the Gospel can be the foundation of the Church, he said; only the Gospel secures freedom of thought and action within the Church.[123]

> No church could exist for the mere and sole purpose of religious liberty. Such an organized company would be a netful of gas . . . . a church cannot live without a theology . . . . for this purpose the church must have its summaries with a dogmatic base which makes them distinct from the science of religion pursued in a university.[124]

---

117 *The Principle of Authority* (1913), p. 280.
118 *Holy Christian Empire* (1902), pp. 32, 37.
119 *Rome, Reform, and Reaction* (1899), p. 67.
120 *The Church and the Sacraments* (1917), p. 43.
121 Note the analogous views on the complex nature of unity that Leonard Hodgson has advocated, which have had a significant impact upon Faith and Order discussions (e.g., *For Faith and Freedom* [1957], Vol. II, Ch. vi).
122 *The Church and The Sacraments* (1917), p. 107.
123 *Faith, Freedom, and the Future* (1912), pp. 137-148.
124 *Theology in Church and State* (1915), pp. 110, 113.

Our faith answers achieving grace; the Cross and the Gospel stand in the center of the Kingdom. To belong to Christ is therefore to belong to the one Church; regeneration achieves the communion of God with man, and of man with nature.[125] The final stage will be the Kingdom of God that reflects in itself the righteousness the Cross honored. We look for world-righteousness among the people of the Kingdom of God.[126]

The Sacraments as Act

For Forsyth, the significance and power of the sacraments lay in the event happening, in the act performed in faith, not in the episcopacy, nor in the elements. Here are the spiritual and moral realities of God's self-giving to man and of man's to God:

> . . . the cardinal thing in the Sacraments is the reality of the Church's act (and of Christ's act in it), and the comparative indifference of the elements. In the elements we have but a symbol, but morally in our act, we unite with reality.[127]

Baptism is the corporate act of the Church attesting anew the meaning of redemption to the consciences of all; the act confesses openly the Word of regeneration. The power of Word and Sacrament is the same; the difference is material not formal. Forsyth held the effect of baptism to be psychological; it "opens up the understanding of the Word in a never-to-be-forgotten experience."[128] He justifies infant baptism on grounds of sovereign grace; the adult looks back to an experience of Christ; we with the child look to a future experience expected and provided for within the Church.[129] The Church can administer baptism to both confessors and infants, he said, but in the case of the child the effect is not immediate and subliminal but prospective and psychological.[130]

The Communion act creates a moral effect by the response of the participant to Christ.[131] The action of institution by our Lord is symbolized; thus, what the letters and words are to the Word, the elements are to the Supper. The work of Christ forever done is given to us anew:

[125] *The Church and the Sacraments* (1917), pp. 67, 92.
[126] *The Roots of a World-Commonwealth* (1918), p. 9.
[127] "Church, Ministry, and Sacraments," p. 50; note *The Church and the Sacraments* (1917), p. xv.
[128] *The Church and the Sacraments* (1917), p. 199.
[129] *Ibid.*, p. 213.
[130] *Ibid.*, pp. 224-226.
[131] *Ibid.*, p. 232.

> We are invited to eat the bread. So they were invited to assimilate Christ, not as ideal but as crucified, not as hopeful but as final. As life is action it feeds on the divinest Act . . . . It is not that the finished sacrifice is offered to God afresh, even by Christ (far less by a priest), but the sacrifice made once for all functions afresh.[132]

The table is the real center of the Church's common and social life; there the sin of humanity is conquered by the grace of God in a holy Kingdom.[133]

Prayer

Forsyth believed that the greatest and truest thoughts about God are generated in prayer, but that right thought has its essential condition in a right will. His finest comments on prayer are found in a little book written during the dark days of World War I. Here he says that our prayer is an answer to God's praying, that is, to Christ's confession of holiness in the Cross. Christ's act of self-giving was an act of prayer in the Spirit, and is the analogue of our praying. We turn our will to God either by way of resignation or impetration; we yield to His will or He to ours.[134] Yet Forsyth appears hesitant about petitionary prayer. Assuredly for him prayer is more than speech — it is action and achievement, and one may share his anxiety where some expect the arbitrary thing that is contrary to nature to happen. His conclusion is that by prayer we rise in Christ the Redeemer to be integrated into the true universality of the universe. Few will contest this as the final divine purpose, though others will contest the idea that the universe now expresses this universality, therefore leaving a larger place for divine action in the world in response to prayer.

Immortality

The ground of man's immortality, Forsyth said, is that the Lord has need of him. While rejecting double predestination, Forsyth found comfort in the doctrine of election in two ways: election is not to prerogative but to God's service and to sacrifice, and election is to a moral process that will continue after death. Forsyth held that the state of the soul is not fixed irretrievably at death; therefore, the election is to stages and methods of endless growth.[135] Curiously, he felt that Christians had thrown out too much by rejecting the doctrine of purgatory. Positing a doctrine of value that not one good will fail, he applies it to lives in this way: "There are more conversions on

---

[132] *Ibid.*, pp. 242f.
[133] *Ibid.*, p. 260.
[134] *The Soul of Prayer* (1916), p. 16.
[135] *This Life and the Next* (1918), p. 13.

the other side than this, if the crisis of death opens the eyes as I have said."[136] In the same context he urges a return to prayer for the dead.

With his conception of eternity bound up in time, Forsyth interpreted immortality also as a present judgment upon life. We should view life *sub specie aeternitatis*. In the following beautiful passage he gives his faith in the afterlife:

> There are those who can quietly say, as their faith follows their love into the unseen, "I know that land. Some of my people live there. Some have gone there on secret foreign service, which does not admit of communications. But I meet from time to time the Commanding Officer. And when I mention them to Him He assures me all is well."[137]

III. EVALUATION

It is puzzling to some that Forsyth, so widely read in classics, philosophy, and theology, with such broad interests including art and social ethics, should be apparently so conventional in his theological perspective. Ever after the renewal of his own faith he remained the warm-hearted evangelical spirit who encompassed life and theology in his own conversion experience and continuing devotion to Jesus Christ. His writings are voluminous and impressive showing the vigor and freshness of an original mind that could not be contained in commonplaces. Forsyth wrote painstakingly. His cutting phrases were born of an inner agony that measured words to ideas meticulously. From the Reformers he grasped the concept of the historically given Word of God and from the Pietists the vitality of the Spirit making that Word vital in life, but always on solid philosophical, theological, and experiential grounds. Forsyth planted the Cross of Christ at the center of what is Christian.

The Nature of Reality

Persons and Reality

Process alone cannot account for reality as we know it, he says; act also is involved in the meaning of creation. The plasticity we discern must serve purposive intention. God has in view the creation of persons; they, in interpersonal relations, are the highest order of reality. Involved as they are in one another's lives for the perfecting of personhood, they not only respond to but are creative of values. The nature of grace as relation and grace as act that intrigues some today interested Forsyth also, but he tried to penetrate the nature of

---

[136] *Ibid.,* pp. 42f.
[137] *Ibid.,* p. 47.

the life where the grace of God confronts it. He advanced the idea of the developing person, still discrete, still a moral being, but come to a certain stage. These stages he calls "closes," a spiritual and psychological conception aimed to yield a more dynamic view of reality. A "close" is a medial terminus in the moral and spiritual development of a man, just as it might be organically in the biological development of the organism. The reality of life is the successive "closes" or character achievements at those points. Christ is the final "close" actualized in the Incarnation and acting redemptively in the Cross.

God's purpose, Forsyth says, is to fashion us, by Creation and Redemption through the Spirit, according to Jesus Christ. Christ is not the classic instance of the unworthy binding of the ideal to mortality, but is the liberty of the true Son of God actualized in history. The freedom He exhibits is not the purposeless escape of gas from a main, nor the inexorable drive of blind forces, nor the invincible attraction of a magnet ahead, but the intelligent, beneficent, and creative use of the events and conditions of life for the divine glory. In the true use of freedom the self-limitation of God ceases; it ceases in the perfect use of freedom by the spiritual beings to whom He gave it. At that time our acts, which are so opaque to us now, will be transparent to the understanding and God will be All in all.

Forsyth and A. N. Whitehead

A similarity between the metaphysical ideas of Forsyth and those of A. N. Whitehead is apparent. Forsyth died at about the time Whitehead was turning serious attention to writing philosophy. It is likely that the thought of the two men goes back to common elements in the thought of the time, probably to a revised scientific Platonism.

Reality, for Whitehead, consists of an organized system of what he designates "actual entities" or "actual occasions," which, he says, are subjects or selves. They are the "final real things of which the world is made up"[138] and appear to be very much like the "closes" of which Forsyth speaks. There are also what he calls "eternal objects" which are the ideals, values, or abstract ideas of objects which are realized by the actual entities. He defines an eternal object as "any entity whose conceptual recognition does not involve a necessary reference to any definite actual entities of the temporal world."[139] As subjects or selves, actual entities experience data or materials drawn from other actual entities at their demise by means of a process of prehension or feeling.[140] The being of actual entities is constituted by their becoming.

---

138 A. N. Whitehead, *Process and Reality* (1941), p. 27.
139 *Ibid.*, p. 70.
140 *Ibid.*, p. 35.

The prehension of an eternal object he calls a conceptual prehension which constitutes the mental pole of an actual entity; whereas, the prehension of the concrete data of another actual entity is known as a physical prehension and constitutes the physical pole of the actual entity. The eternal objects as guiding ideals govern the selection and absorption of a datum. Thus guided by certain ideals, the actual entity may prehend a datum positively or negatively (reject it) in accordance with a subjective aim that it has fashioned for itself from its prehension of particular eternal objects. This subjective aim is the ideal which the actual entity has selected for itself from the world of eternal objects, for it is a *causa sui* in this process, and its choice will determine its own nature, development, and character at the point of satisfaction. All actual entities endure for a definite period and at their death they "give out" concrete data for ingression into other actual entities.

What is important for our use here is: (1) the concept of teleological, free, valuing, actual entities; (2) the eternal objects as objects of value to actual entities; (3) the fact that God conserves the eternal objects in the arrangement of ideal possibilities for actual entities in Himself; and (4) that God acts not coercively but persuasively. Whitehead says the following about Christ with which Forsyth, with his doctrine of the Plerosis, could agree:

> The life of Christ is not an exhibition of over-ruling power. Its glory is for those who can discern it, and not for the world. Its power lies in its absence of force. It has the decisiveness of a supreme ideal, and that is why the history of the world divides at this point of time.[141]

Reality and the Moral

If ultimate reality is of persons and interpersonal relations then we are concerned with life and action; in short, with morality. This pervades Forsyth's theology on the relations between God and man. He insisted that a purely intellectual act does not exist for us; if personal, an act is moral also. The world is on a moral footing; the Cross bears upon the moral issue of the world's life. We cannot rest reconciliation and forgiveness on any verbal solution to the problem of sin. Atonement is inescapable. Acts of persons to moral issues are involved because fundamentally the universe is moral. Subjective theories of the Atonement fail because they cannot take account of the evil outside the sinner's soul.

The divine law, therefore, is not a human social accretion, nor a mythological formula of pagan vintage reflecting ungodlike anger. We do not make God subject to law, rather, the divine law is the

---

[141] A. N. Whitehead, *Religion in the Making* (1926), pp. 56-57.

manifestation of God in the moral constitution of the universe. It is the ground of God's relations to the world and of our dealings with one another. The law of God is the possibility and condition of freedom. One-sided conceptions of the divine love cannot grapple with the reality of sin, guilt, and judgment.

THE CROSS AND THE GOSPEL

The work of Christ has two sides, Forsyth says: what God does for us is the ground of what he does in us, and this double reality, preached, is the Christian Gospel. Given the conditions of divine and human life, the two sides — objective and subjective — are inevitable, like the two sides of a coin. Sin is expiated by the blood of Christ and, far from the conception of transaction, the vindication of righteousness stands in God Himself. Conversely, Forsyth's concept of solidarity bears equally well upon the relevance of Christ's work to the race as it does upon racial guilt. Christ not only achieves redemption; His life and response, conceived as generic to the racial life, is the response actually made under the righteous judgment. Forsyth's experiential theology is no glib believism, nor nebulous knowledge of God, but the full-orbed Gospel of redeeming grace in Jesus Christ. The Gospel was given apostolically; it is to be proclaimed and received. Faith reaches out on the ground of the apostolic word, mediated by the Holy Spirit, to its true home in the God and Father of our Lord Jesus Christ.

REVELATION, HISTORY, AND THE BIBLE

Some question may be raised whether Forsyth satisfactorily bridged the concepts of the objective Word given in history and the personal confrontation of men by God in experience, though it is easier to criticize on this thorny issue than to show the right path. Forsyth's stress on experience is important; nevertheless, did he, and have *we,* probed sufficiently well the question of the finite modalities that God may use in his self-revelation? Forsyth's emphasis upon the Word given in history sets him apart from some tendencies toward the irrational in contemporary theology. A popular non-theistic stance in philosophy today is not to deny God, but to deny the possibility of saying anything about Him. This is to deny the revelational function of language, and some theologians seem willing to reinforce the secularist's argument. It would be helpful to know the answer to this question: Why cannot language be the vehicle of revealed truth as alleged? If this is so, What is Scripture? and, Can we then say anything at all about God?

While he was on the side of critical science, which every student of Holy Scripture must take seriously, Forsyth aimed to conserve, not destroy, the Gospel. He was very conscious in his own experience of the mothering role the Bible must have for faith, yet only later in life did he combat forces unleashed in his time that undercut faith. The fact is that when the Bible was lost to the people in one way of its use, its place in their lives was never recovered by what was to be the new way which the new scholarship was supposed to yield. This problem is still a central one for Christianity. At issue is the spirit of a man, the conviction of faith that Holy Scripture is indispensable and normative, and, that its contents stand properly under the umbrella of the term *revelation*. Quite appropriately, evangelical theology can claim the heritage of two giants like Forsyth and Spurgeon; it can also contrast them, as only the evangelical spirit properly can, from within. Dr. Helmut Thielicke is discovering the vitality and contemporary relevance of C. H. Spurgeon to German readers today.

The theological question can be stated simply: Can we divide the knowledge of God from the knowledge about God? and, Is not Holy Scripture normative of both? When we are done restricting revelation to the knowledge of God, we may be asked, as H. D. Lewis has asked,[142] whether we have displaced one cliché by another, more modern perhaps, but probably less vital. Where Holy Scripture is vitally related to faith, there faith is vital. Nothing is autonomous here save God who has given us the knowledge of Himself in Jesus Christ, prophetically and apostolically in Holy Scripture. Today confrontationists universally veer away from projecting their own experience or any other non-biblical experience as normative of faith. Why are the experiences of Moses, David, Jeremiah, Paul, or John used instead? The answer is not far to see: our experiences are vital to ourselves but not normative for one another; but what Holy Scripture conveys is normative for us all.

THE FORSYTH HERITAGE

There are obvious parallels between Forsyth and other evangelical theologians of his time like R. W. Dale and James Denney. Surprisingly, the parallels extend to more recent writers, sometimes of diverse denominational connection, like Leonard Hodgson, formerly Regius Professor of Divinity in the University of Oxford. What Forsyth and Hodgson say about revelation, the concept of reality as ultimately of persons, and the objective Atonement are large areas of congruity, though Hodgson developed his thought independently and carried

[142] *Our Experience of God* (1959).

forward his concepts of law, freedom, Incarnation, and Trinity to points beyond those of Forsyth.

Forsyth and J. K. Mozley

In the English-speaking community, the theologian probably most influenced by Forsyth has been the Anglican J. K. Mozley. He acknowledges his indebtedness to Forsyth on the objective Atonement, though he feels in Forsyth a lack of the aesthetic appeal of the Cross.[143] Mozley also notes that in Christology Forsyth tended to accommodate the classical two-natures doctrine to the dynamic concept of two personal movements, of God to man and of man to God. Mozley feels that this concept of the mutual involution of personal movements tends to overcome the problem of the relative impersonality of our Lord's human nature, especially when the doctrine is oriented, as Forsyth does it, to a kenotic Christology. In this way Forsyth conceived of the Incarnation as process as well as act; as the plerosis or the self-fulfillment of Christ in humanity where the infinite God consented not to know. Mozley is eager to retain the vitality of the Nicene and Chalcedonian formulae and is, I think properly, critical of Forsyth's evasiveness on questions of being; nevertheless he feels that Forsyth does mitigate the force of apparently static conceptions of the divine and human natures.[144] It may be noted, however, that where the ancient Fathers speak of substance they do not mean materiality but reality, so that on whatever ground writers like Forsyth change categories it is not at all clear that part of that ground should be the alleged static conceptions of the ancients.

Forsyth and Emil Brunner

In recent years some have called Forsyth the "Barth before Barth." While the similarities between Forsyth and the crisis theologians are obvious, that there is a close connection between Forsyth and Barth is improbable. However, that there may be such a connection between the work of Forsyth and Emil Brunner appears worthy of mention.

It is a striking fact that in a recent study of Dr. Brunner's theology,[145] no mention of Forsyth occurs. Neither in Dr. Brunner's autobiographical notes nor in the comments he makes on the essays evaluating his theology does Forsyth's name appear. Some other facts, however, need to be drawn into the discussion now.

143 J. K. Mozley, *The Doctrine of the Atonement* (1915), pp. 220f. Note also Canon Mozley's Preface to the 1947 and later printings of *The Church and the Sacraments.*
144 J. K. Mozley, *The Doctrine of the Incarnation* (1949).
145 C. W. Kegley, *The Theology of Emil Brunner* (1962).

Following his doctoral study in theology at Zurich, the young Dr. Brunner, seriously engrossed in questions of Christian social action, yet increasingly absorbed by a question more fundamental than ethics — the doctrine of God, went to England for two years. To learn English, he taught French for a living and became deeply interested in some aspects of British life and theology. He was interested in the Christian Labor Movement and developed a friendship with Ramsey MacDonald and others. On the religious front, he made the acquaintance of Dr. William Temple, later Archbishop of Canterbury. At this time, not surprisingly because of the social, ethical, and theological character of his preaching and writing, the work of P. T. Forsyth came to the young Dr. Brunner's attention. Brunner mentioned his interest in Forsyth during an interview on the B.B.C.[146] In *The Christian Doctrine of Creation and Redemption* Brunner expresses appreciation for the extensive British school of theologians of the Cross, especially mentioning McLeod Campbell, P. T. Forsyth's *The Work of Christ,* and Donald Baillie.[147] In *The Christian Doctrine of God* he places Forsyth in the main line of creative writers who shook off the spirit of the Enlightenment.[148] Finally, it is at least of interest to note that J. K. Mozley, whose theology was significantly shaped by Forsyth's ideas, wrote one of the Foreword notices to the English edition of *Der Mittler*,[149] drawing attention to the work of Forsyth.

If there was an influence of Forsyth on Brunner's theology, it occurred probably at a formative stage of the young Swiss theologian's thought, perhaps during the time when he was moving from a prime interest in Christian social ethics to dogmatics. This is a movement, incidentally, that parallels the earlier development of Forsyth's own life. Brunner's stay in England (1913-14) was just prior to his first published work (1914). There followed military duty and then his first and only settlement in the pastorate (1916-1925). In 1925 he was elected to the Chair of Theology at Zurich. During the intervening years he had published some work. For his inaugural lecture he chose the theme "Philosophy and Revelation."[150] This address seems to reflect the influence of Forsyth, at this early crucial stage, if such influence is to be found at all. Yet one must be cautious and generous.

[146] *The Listener,* February 16, 1961, p. 307.

[147] Emil Brunner, *The Christian Doctrine of Creation and Redemption* (1952), p. 315.

[148] Brunner, *The Christian Doctrine of God* (1952), p. 92.

[149] Brunner, *The Mediator* (1952), p. 9 (first published in English in 1934).

[150] The inaugural address is entitled "Die Offenbarung als Grund und Gegenstand der Theologie" and appears along with "Gnosis und Glaube" and "Auf das Buchzeichnen des Lesers" in *Philosophie und Offenbarung* (1925). It was delivered on January 17, 1925.

A comparison of this kind must be sensitive to the breadth and depth of an intellectual giant like Brunner. Who can sort out the influences in the life of a man? Then too, there is the sheer individualism of the man himself who makes certain ideas distinctively his own — indeed, he fashions them in the press of his own soul and intellect. Also, the coincidental appearances of similar ideas in various places are known to have occurred.

In his address Brunner made a difference between science and theology based on revelation. In science one senses the autonomy of reason in its question-putting techniques. The kind of answer one gets seems prejudged by the demand that they be questions man can ask, and answer. Forsyth, too, rejects the autonomy of reason, though he was more favorably disposed to its role in revelation. Brunner contends that what is given is neither true nor false, but the understanding of it — that is, the judgment we make of it.[151] The last ground of objective truth can never become object itself. This circularity has been noted often before, and the answer has been that the mind knows that it knows more than itself. Brunner's point is that the certitude of revelation is given in the immediacy of confrontation, not in a discursive fashion. Here he and Forsyth would agree substantially. Forsyth maintained the subjective certitude *in* but not *of* experience, though he would handle differently the historical data comprising the intelligible core of the faith.

Of greater importance is the stress both place upon *action*. This is one of the most dominant of Forsythian motifs and, as a part of it, there is also the enormously important concept of the moral. We have to do with action, not static being, Forsyth said, and if with action then with morality, because every intellectual act is in that right a moral act also. The truth we see depends upon the men we are. The truth confronting us makes its demand for commitment. Brunner advanced a concept that is identical. Thinking, he said, is an action that happens as a part of the action of life. There is, therefore, not such a thing as pure thinking, or abstraction, but thinking-acting. All scientific questions (theoretical) are also life-questions.[152] This meant that for Forsyth as for Brunner and others, the break with the Idealism of the nineteenth century was complete. For both, the God with whom we have to do is personal and moral from the start; the drama of life

---

151 "Nur im Zusammenhang ist Wahrheit erkennbar," *ibid.*, p. 8.
152 *Ibid.*, p. 8: "Denn alles Denken ist ja ein Handeln und findet Statt in einem Zusammenhang des Handelns, des Lebens . . . . So wird die theoretische Fragestellung zur sittlichen, die erkenntnistheoretische Problematik wird zur ethischen, die wissenschaftliche zur Lebensfrage."

is moral at bottom. The highest reality we know is not of the nature of abstraction, but of persons in interpersonal relations.[153]

As a result, the issue of sin and grace (as against the concepts of process and ideas) is forced to the fore immediately. The primacy of the moral and the personal means simply that such realities cannot be dealt with in non-moral and impersonal ways. Readers of Forsyth will sense the force of this in his theology, bearing, as it does, upon the nature of reality, the reality of guilt, and the necessity of Atonement. The outline of the thought of the two men is remarkably congruent at this point. We cannot, Brunner said, solve moral problems by ontology (the continuity of the divine and human beings), reason (the rational telescoping of the divine and human as in Idealism) or feeling (the absorption of the human into the divine; mysticism cannot deal with guilt).[154] To suppose that God can abrogate his law in forgiveness is a mental aberration. The dealing with sin must be by *action,* not words; no verbal solution to the problem of evil and sin is possible.[155] The moral issue is that God *acts* to give forgiveness in a manner consistent with His own righteousness. The concept fundamental to the Church's faith that God was in Christ[156] accomplishing redemption therefore stands out sharply in both writers.

A further similarity occurs in their doctrines of revelation. Both, as noted, turned away from the theology of the Enlightenment. The views of Forsyth have been sufficiently well stated in this essay already. Brunner said that Idealism, with the stress on process, immanence, and abstraction, pictured revelation as the glimmering-through of the appearances of the divine in the cosmic process;[157] everywhere in the human consciousness the door opens to the divine being. Human spirit becomes the divine spirit; we feel ourselves part of the divine order. In sharpest contrast — indeed, contradicting this — Brunner, like Forsyth, calls revelation act, not process; therefore it is unique. Revelation is unique, a "here" and only "here," an "at-that-time" and only "at-that-time," a "He" and only "He."[158] God is God and the world is the world; they cannot be telescoped; there is no continual, automatic passage of God to the world that can be called revelation. The force of *Einmaliges,* unrepeatableness, seems to carry Brunner's

---

[153] *Ibid.,* p. 9. On p. 10 he wrote: "So kann die Frage bei jenem abstrakten Ergebnis nicht stehen bleiben."

[154] *Ibid.,* p. 12.

[155] *Ibid.,* p. 14.

[156] *Ibid.,* p. 15.

[157] P. 17, "Offenbarung ist . . . das Durchschimmern des göttlichen Urgrundes aller Erscheinungen in den Erscheinungen."

[158] P. 19, "Offenbarung ist ein Einmaliges, ein Hier und nur hier, ein Damals und nur damals, ein Er und nur er."

concept beyond Forsyth's not at the point of the personal confrontation, but where Forsyth involves more of the historical element.
Brunner lays a greater stress upon the unheard of (non-rational)
turning point of revelation, upon the breach, the discontinuity of revelation with all that is known discursively, than does Forsyth; though
they share the idea of the self-movement of God to man and the characterization of revelation as act.[159] Brunner's earlier formulation of it
can be illustrated by his understanding of the Logos concept, not as
theoria, a beholding, a seeing of the divine, but as the deed-word
where God discloses himself in action; where He gives Himself.[160] The
revelation-deed is concerned with one primary fact: expiation of guilt.[161]
Such development as this in what appears to be Forsythian language,
if a coincidence, is quite remarkable.

[159] *Ibid.,* p. 20.
[160] *Ibid.,* pp. 20, 25. On p. 32 he describes the logos as "Das Tatwort, darin
Gott sich selbst ausspricht, mehr noch: worin er sich selbst gibt."
[161] *Ibid.,* p. 22: "Denn die Tat der Offenbarung ist hier immer die Sühnetat."

IV. BIBLIOGRAPHY

SELECTED WORKS BY P. T. FORSYTH

Religion in Recent Art. Manchester, 1889.
"Revelation and the Person of Christ," *Faith and Criticism.* London, 1893.
The Charter of the Church. London, 1896.
The Holy Father and the Living Christ. London, 1897.
Christian Perfection. London, 1899.
Rome, Reform, and Reaction. London, 1899.
Essay No. III (no title) in *The Atonement in Modern Religious Thought. A Theological Symposium.* London, 1900.
The Taste of Death and the Life of Grace. London, 1901.
Holy Christian Empire. London, 1902
"The Evangelical Churches and the Higher Criticism," *Contemporary Review,* Vol. lxxxviii, 1905.
"Christian Aspects of Evolution," *The London Quarterly Review,* October, 1905 (later published separately, London, 1950).
"Revelation and the Bible," *Hibbert Journal,* Vol. IV, 1906.
Positive Preaching and the Modern Mind. London, 1909 (second ed.); Grand Rapids, 1964 (pb.).
"Immanence and Incarnation," *The Old Faith and the New Theology* (edited by Charles H. Vine). London, 1907.
Socialism, the Church and the Poor. London, 1908.
Missions in State and Church. London, 1908.
"The Insufficiency of Social Righteousness as a Moral Ideal," *Hibbert Journal,* Vol. VII, 1909.
The Cruciality of the Cross. London, 1948 (reprint of 1909 ed.); Grand Rapids, 1965 (pb.).
The Person and Place of Jesus Christ. London, 1955 (reprint of 1909 ed.); Grand Rapids, 1965 (pb.).
The Work of Christ. London, 1952 (reprint of 1910 ed.).
The Power of Prayer (with Dora Greenwell). London, 1910.
"Orthodoxy, Heterodoxy, Heresy, and Freedom," *Hibbert Journal,* Vol. VIII, 1910.
Christ on Parnassus. London, 1911, reissued 1959.
"Christ and the Christian Principle," *London Theological Studies.* London, 1911.

P. T. Forsyth

Faith, Freedom, and the Future. London, 1912, reissued 1952.
The Principle of Authority. First published in 1913; reset and republished London, 1952, with the addition of some footnotes and an index.
Marriage: Its Ethic and Religion. London, n.d.
Theology in Church and State. London, 1915.
The Justification of God. First published in 1916; reset and republished London, 1948, with the omission of the author's preface and the addition of a foreword by D. R. Davies.
The Christian Ethic of War. London, 1916.
"Church, Ministry, and Sacraments," The Validity of the Congregational Ministry (with J. V. Bartlet and J. D. Jones). London, 1916.
The Soul of Prayer. London, 1916, reissued 1949; Grand Rapids, 1965 (pb.).
The Church and the Sacraments. First published in 1917; reset and republished London, 1947, reprinted 1953, with the addition of a Note by Mrs. Jessie Forsyth Andrews and a Preface by Canon J. K. Mozley.
Congregationalism and Reunion (two lectures delivered in 1917). London, 1952.
The Roots of a World-Commonwealth. London, 1918.
This Life and the Next. London, 1918.
God the Holy Father. London, 1957.
Revelation Old and New (edited by John Huxtable). London, 1962.
The Church, the Gospel and Society. London, 1962.

WORKS ON P. T. FORSYTH

Andrews, Jessie Forsyth, "Memoir," published in the 1952 ed. of Forsyth's The Work of Christ.
Barth, Markus. "P. T. Forsyth: The Theologian for the Practical Man," The Congregational Quarterly, October, 1939.
Bradley, W. R. P. T. Forsyth, The Man and His Work. London, 1952.
Brown, R. A. P. T. Forsyth, Prophet for Today. Philadelphia, 1952.
Escott, Harry. Peter Taylor Forsyth. London, 1948.
Glover, W. B. Evangelical Non-Conformists and Higher Criticism in the Nineteenth Century. London, 1954
Griffith, G. O. The Theology of P. T. Forsyth. London, 1948.
Gummer, S. "Peter Taylor Forsyth: A Contemporary Theologian," London Quarterly Review and Holborn Review, October, 1948.
Hughes, P. E. "Forsyth: Theologian of the Cross," Christianity Today, 23 December, 1957.
Hughes, T. H. "A Barthian Before Barth?" Congregational Quarterly, July, 1934.

————— "Dr. Forsyth's View of the Atonement," *The Congregational Quarterly,* Vol. XVIII, No. 1, January, 1940.

Leembruggen, W. H. "P. T. Forsyth: A Theologian of the Cross," *Reformed Theological Review,* Melbourne, 1945.

Rodgers, John H. *The Theology of P. T. Forsyth.* London, 1965.

11 COLIN BROWN

Charles Gore

I. BIOGRAPHY

CHARLES GORE belonged to the second generation of the Anglo-Catholic movement in the Church of England. When he was born in 1853, its first leader, John Henry Newman (1801-80), had been a Roman Catholic nearly eight years. When Gore went up to Oxford in 1871 the movement was nearly forty years old. To the minds of many, including some of the bishops, Anglo-Catholicism had become identified with authentic Anglicanism.

The movement had begun as a protest against the rising tide of secularism and state interference in the affairs of the church. On July 14, 1833, John Keble (1792-1866) preached at Oxford the celebrated Assize Sermon which Newman regarded as the start of the movement.[1] Keble's text was I Samuel 12:23. His theme was

Colin Brown is Vice-Principal of Tyndale Hall and teaches theology at the University of Bristol. He is the author of several articles and reviews, and of a recent book.

[1] J. H. Newman, *Apologia Pro Vita Sua* (1864), Pt. iii. *Anglo-Catholicism* is the term generally used to describe the High Church movement in the Church of England which began with the *Oxford Movement*. This latter term, which draws attention to the movement's place of origin, is usually restricted to the period between 1833 (Keble's sermon and the beginning of the Tracts) and 1845 (Newman's conversion). *Tractarianism* is a synonym drawing attention to the movement's principles which were expressed in the *Tracts for the Times*. From the vast literature on the subject special mention may be made of the following: S. C. Carpenter, *Church and People, 1789-1889* (1933); Y. Brilioth, *The Anglican Revival* (1925); O. Chadwick (ed.), *The Mind of the Oxford Movement* (1960); R. W. Church, *The Oxford Movement* (1891); G. Faber, *Oxford Apostles*, 2nd ed. (1936); S. L. Oilard, *A Short History of the Oxford Movement*, new ed. (1963); E. R. Fairweather (ed.), *The Oxford Movement* (1964).

National Apostasy. The same year Newman began the *Tracts for the Times*.

The Tractarian antidote to the irreligion of the times consisted at first in a revival of the High Church ideals of the seventeenth century. The movement's devotion was drawn from the Book of Common Prayer. On the doctrines of the creeds and in its view of the Bible it was traditionally orthodox. But from the first its mood was determined by the notion of Apostolic Succession. The mark of a true church was a valid ministry, and the mark of a valid ministry was episcopal ordination in the Apostolic Succession.[2] As time wore on, the movement became increasingly "Catholic." In 1840 E. B. Pusey (1800-82) summed up Tractarianism (or Puseyism, as it was also commonly called) as follows:

(1) High thoughts of the two Sacraments.

(2) High estimate of Episcopacy, as God's ordinance.

(3) High estimate of the visible Church as the Body wherein we are made and continue to be members of Christ.

(4) Regard for ordinances, as directing our devotions and disciplining us, such as daily public prayers, fasts, and feasts, &c.

(5) Regard for the visible part of devotion, such as the decoration of the house of God, which acts insensibly on the mind.

(6) Reverence for and deference to the ancient Church, of which our own Church is looked upon as the representative to us, and by whose views and doctrines we interpret our own Church when her meaning is questioned or doubtful; in a word reference to the ancient Church, instead of the Reformers, as the ultimate expounder of the meaning of our Church.[3]

But even this was too mild for the more wayward spirits. W. G. Ward's *Ideal of a Christian Church* (1844) did not shrink from recognizing that ideal in the Church of Rome. It had long been apparent that Newman's thoughts were drifting in that direction. In 1841 he wrote the notorious *Tract XC* which endeavored to show that, "while our Prayer Book is acknowledged on all hands to be of Catholic origin, our Articles also, the offspring of an un-Catholic age, are, through God's good providence, to say the least, not un-Catholic, and may be subscribed by those who aim at being Catholic in heart and doctrine." It was a forlorn hope. Public outcry against the novelty of the doctrine and the speciousness of the argument soon forced the hand of Newman's bishop. Oxford appealed to Canterbury, and the

---

[2] *Tracts for the Times* (1833ff.), Nos. 1, 4, 7, 10, 17, 24, 33, 35, 42, 44, 46.

[3] H. P. Liddon, *Life of Edward Bouverie Pusey,* 3rd ed. (1893), II, 140.

Tracts were brought to an abrupt end.[4] Newman lingered on in the Church of England another four years in semi-monastic retirement. In 1845 he took the inevitable step and made his submission to Rome.

The conversion to Rome of Newman, Ward, and numerous others did little to halt the progress of the movement. It merely marked the end of its first phase. The next few years saw an unprecedented revival of Catholic devotion and practices in the Church of England. The 1850's saw the advent of ritualism and the first of many court cases over eucharistic doctrine and practice.[5] By the end of the century some seventy religious communities had been founded.[6] It was against this background that Gore grew up.

Charles Gore was a convert to ritualism from about the age of eight. In old age he recalled how he had come across an anti-Catholic book entitled *Father Clement*. Until then he had known nothing but Low Church services. "But the book described confession and absolution, fasting, the Real Presence, the devotion of the Three Hours, the use of incense, etc., and I felt instinctively and at once that this sort of sacramental religion was the religion for me."[7] *Father Clement* had had the opposite of its intended effect.

No less permanent was the effect exerted upon Gore's youthful mind at Harrow by one of the younger masters, Brooke Foss Westcott (1825-1901), the biblical scholar and future Bishop of Durham. It was from Westcott, says Gore's biographer G. L. Prestige, that Gore learned "the moral value of exact scholarship; the insight to be gained from a religious study of history; the spiritual glories of simple living; love of the poor."[8] It was Westcott who introduced him to the ideal of disciplined asceticism which was to find a permanent memorial in the Community of the Resurrection which Gore founded while still in his thirties.[9] In later life the two men shared a common concern over social questions,[10] and for a time at least Gore shared Westcott's view of Christ as the consummator of creation.[11]

Charles Gore enjoyed the sort of academic career which has marked out many a man for a bishopric or a seat in the cabinet. From

[4] M. Trevor, *Newman: The Pillar of the Cloud* (1962), p. 245.
[5] Cf. S. C. Carpenter, *op. cit.,* pp. 212-250.
[6] P. F. Anson, *The Call of the Cloister* (1955), pp. 590ff.
[7] *The Reconstruction of Belief* (1926), pp. viif.
[8] *The Life of Charles Gore* (1935), p. 9.
[9] *Ibid.,* pp. 10ff., 137-151; cf. Anson, *op. cit.,* pp. 122-139.
[10] See below, pp. 362-64. Cf. J. Carpenter, *Gore: A Study in Liberal Catholic Thought* (1960), pp. 243-268.
[11] See below, pp. 356f. Cf. B. F. Westcott, *Christus Consummator* (1886); L. B. Smedes, *The Incarnation: Trends in Modern Anglican Thought* (1953), pp. 52ff.; but see also J. Carpenter, *op. cit.,* pp. 174f., 184ff.

Harrow he won a scholarship to Balliol College, Oxford. A first in Classical Moderations and a first in Greats were followed by a Fellowship at Trinity in 1875. But Gore's path was already plain. Ordination (deacon 1876, priest 1878) led to his appointment as Vice-Principal of Cuddesdon (1880), the Anglo-Catholic theological college near Oxford. This was followed in 1884 by his appointment as the first Principal of Pusey House, Oxford. The house was intended as a memorial to Dr. Pusey, the most learned of the Tractarians. It contained the Doctor's library. But more than that, it was to be (to quote the scheme's prime mover, H. P. Liddon) "a home of sacred learning, and a rallying-point for the Christian faith."[12] It was here that Gore emerged as the remodeler of Anglo-Catholicism.

The Oxford of those days was still in the throes of a prolonged series of intellectual convulsions. The Oxford Movement of the 1830s had given birth to Anglo-Catholicism. In 1859 Charles Darwin published *The Origin of Species*. Within a decade evolution had established itself as scientific orthodoxy.

The year 1860 had seen the publication of a symposium, *Essays and Reviews*. All but one of the symposiasts had Oxford connections. Today their pleas for free inquiry, liberal ideas, and caution about the supernatural may well strike the reader as dull, long-winded, and commonplace. But in 1860 they provoked a storm of controversy which lasted a decade and brought two of the authors before the Judicial Committee of the Privy Council. But the real scandal of the book was not that such views should be entertained, but that they should be entertained by men of authority in the Church. As it was, the unorthodoxy of 1860 became the orthodoxy of 1900.

Hard on the heels of *Essays and Reviews* came the Colenso controversy. John William Colenso (1814-83) had been appointed the first Bishop of Natal in 1853. Controversy over his liberal views was brought to a head with the publication of his *Commentary on the Epistle to the Romans* (1861) and his papers on *The Pentateuch and the Book of Joshua Critically Examined* (1862-79). In the former he questioned eternal punishment and current sacramental teaching; in the latter he challenged the authorship and accuracy of the books in question. Colenso was excommunicated by Bishop Gray of Cape Town, but retained his see over a technicality. The dispute dragged on well into the twentieth century. But the closing decades of the nineteenth saw the triumph of the critical ideas Colenso had pioneered. Old Testament studies were dominated by S. R. Driver (1846-1914) and W. Robertson Smith (1846-94). In New Testament studies the quest of the historical Jesus, initiated in England by George Eliot's

---

[12] G. Crosse, *Charles Gore* (1932), p. 20; cf. Prestige, *op. cit.*, pp. 48ff.

translation of D. F. Strauss's *Life of Jesus* (1846) and J. R. Seeley's *Ecce Homo* (1865), was now in full flight. In the recovery of the Jesus of history, the miraculous was to be treated with caution and critical techniques applied to the full.

The rising star in the philosophical firmament was T. H. Green (1836-82) whose influence at Oxford (and over British philosophy generally) lasted well into the present century. Green's anglicized brand of Hegelian idealism viewed reality as an organic, personal whole. There was no hint in Green that behind the universe there was a transcendent, personal God, but his stress on personality was sufficient to make theologians believe that his ideas could be utilized to bridge the gap between orthodox Christianity and the modern mind. And this was the task which occupied Gore's mind throughout his life.

From the mid-1870s Gore had been associating with a group of younger Oxford dons. Though Catholic in outlook, they felt unable to share the conservatism of Liddon, Pusey, and the older Tractarians.[13] The upshot was a new (and more Catholic) version of *Essays and Reviews*. Its title was *Lux Mundi* (1889), and Charles Gore was its editor. Evolution, Green's idealism, and the critical approach to Scripture all found a place. Doctrines like the verbal inspiration of Scripture, once regarded as essential, were now discarded as an embarrassing encumbrance, but at least the incarnation remained as the bedrock of faith and the key to all doctrine. Yet even here the more discerning critics were far from convinced that *Lux Mundi* was not a theological Trojan horse. The Tractarian old guard felt that they had been stabbed in the back. Newman, now in the last year of his long life, commented: "It is the end of Tractarianism. They are giving up everything."[14] It was said that Liddon died of a broken heart. But the die was cast, and the book went through ten editions in a year. Within a couple of decades most of the symposiasts became professors or bishops or both. Gore himself was soon honored by being made the Bampton Lecturer at Oxford for 1891. His lectures, *The Incarnation of the Son of God,* and also his *Dissertations on Subjects Connected with the Incarnation* (1895) amplified his position. The *Lux Mundi* synthesis of liberalism and Catholicism set the trend which was to dominate Anglican thinking for more than half a century.

Gore did not remain long at Pusey House. Now in his forties, he became for a short while Vicar of Radley (1893), a village some miles from Oxford. He brought with him the newly established Community of the Resurrection of which he himself was the Superior. But Radley

---

13 *Lux Mundi* (1889), pp. vii-x.
14 M. Trevor, *Newman: Light in Winter* (1962), p. 640.

did not keep either Gore or the Community for long. In 1899 the Community migrated to its present home at Mirfield in Yorkshire. By that time Gore had already been five years a canon of Westminster. Two years later he became a bishop.

Gore's appointment to the see of Worcester (1901) was by no means popular. Many were alarmed at his combination of Catholicism and rationalism, and others were fearful of his socialism. For the year of the publication of *Lux Mundi* had also seen the formation of the Christian Social Union. To some extent it was the same group that was behind both enterprises. But their socialism was very mild, Gore himself claiming that it was no more than a repudiation of *laissez-faire* individualism. Anyone of any shade of theological and political opinion might join. What mattered was that the Church should repent and live out the implications of its faith. This, however, did not prevent the *Church Times* from reminding Gore and his colleagues "that the spiritual and the material are distinct spheres . . . . Nor is the Church the Church of the poor only, but of the rich also."[15] But Gore was not the man to be deterred by verbal brickbats. He followed Westcott as president of the Christian Social Union in 1901, and retained a life-long concern for social issues.

Between 1902 and 1919 Gore occupied three bishoprics. His first see, Worcester, was largely rural, but it was made unwieldy by the presence of the great industrial city of Birmingham to the north. From the first, Gore pressed for the creation of a new diocese of Birmingham. To that end he spared neither effort nor money (including much of his own). It was almost a foregone conclusion that Gore would be its first bishop.

The six years at Birmingham, from 1905 to 1911, saw Gore at the height of his powers. The diocese was efficiently run. A theological duel with R. J. Campbell, the nonconformist divine, over the latter's "new theology" ended with Campbell's reception into the Church of England.[16] A steady stream of books, articles, reviews, and sermons over the years had built up a considerable and ready public. Even when he could not win agreement, Gore's generous high-minded-

[15] *Church Times,* July 27, 1894; cf. K. S. Inglis, *Churches and the Working Classes in Victorian England* (1963), p. 278.

[16] Campbell, the minister of the City Temple and an old acquaintance of Gore, taught a popular version of Hegelian immanentism. He asserted that there was no dividing line between the being of God and that of man. Gore's refutation took the form of a series of Lenten addresses, delivered in Birmingham Cathedral in 1907 and published under the title *The New Theology and the Old Religion* (1908). J. Carpenter, *op. cit.,* p. 77, observes that the debate marked a turning point in Gore's thinking. Henceforth, Gore turned increasingly to biblical prophecy as the source of his thought.

ness and awareness of vital issues commanded the respect of churchman and nonconformist alike. In the House of Lords he was not afraid to raise his voice on matters of Church and State.[17] Gore was not only the acknowledged leader of the Anglo-Catholic party; he was a national figure. He was, wrote W. R. Inge, "the strongest man in the English Church," enjoying "an influence in the Anglican Church which is probably far greater than that of any other man."[18]

As a bishop Charles Gore combined the Tractarian ideal of a father in God and the Victorian ideal of a paternal disciplinarian. Lax clergy found him a menace. Extreme Anglo-Catholics found him a disappointment. For although Gore made no secret of his Catholic leanings, he was not the man to wave party flags. It is true that Gore allowed prayers for the dead, but those who looked to him to sanction the Roman practices of Exposition, Benediction, and veneration of the Reserved Sacrament looked in vain. For public worship Gore insisted on the Book of Common Prayer until such a time as it might be changed officially in a Catholic direction.[19]

In matters of doctrine also Gore strove to maintain what he considered a moderate, reasonable Anglicanism. While criticism had thrown much into the melting pot, there was a limit to criticism, and that limit was marked by the creeds. As that of a liberal, Gore's ideal is expressed in the Erasmian dictum: "Let the essentials of the faith be limited to the fewest articles possible."[20] As a Catholic, Gore could say of the creeds: "It is the whole question of what is really true, and claims to be permanent in Christianity." [21]

Gore believed he had no option but to condemn those who withheld subscription to the creeds. At Worcester he had caused the resignation of one of his clergy, the Rev. C. E. Beeby, because he denied the miracles of the creeds. In 1914 when the debate on the subject was at its height, Gore pressed the bishops of the Convocation of Canterbury for an affirmation of their belief in the historical truth of the creeds. In 1917 when Herbert Hensley Henson (1863-1947) was nominated

17 G. Crosse, *Charles Gore* (1932), p. 80.

18 *Outspoken Essays (First Series)*, new imp. (1927), p. 114.

19 Cf. Gore's memorandum in the *Report of the Royal Commission on Ecclesiastical Discipline* (1906), items 14877-15106 in Vol. II, pp. 494-508; C. Gore, *The Body of Christ* (1901), pp. 269-288; *Reservation Addresses* (1917); G. L. Prestige, *The Life of Charles Gore* (1935), pp. 293-303, 379ff., 390ff. See also below, p. 360.

20 *The Reconstruction of Belief* (1926), p. 844.

21 *The Basis of Anglican Fellowship* (1914), p. 7. On Gore's approach to the creeds, see also below, pp. 352f., and A. M. Ramsey, *From Gore to Temple* (1960), pp. 77-91; J. Carpenter, *Gore: A Study in Liberal Catholic Thought* (1960), pp. 105-110; G. L. Prestige, *The Life of Charles Gore* (1935), pp. 243-247, 357-363, 394-403.

to the see of Hereford, Gore was foremost among those who pressed the Archbishop of Canterbury not to consecrate in view of Henson's ambiguous attitude on this score.

At a time when other churchmen seemed more agnostic than the agnostics, Gore became something of a rallying-point for those who, without being evangelicals, nevertheless wanted to hold on to the central truths of Christianity. Gore bore witness to a Christianity which stood for something, a Church which had a mission, a Bible which was substantially dependable, and a Savior who was God incarnate. The leader of the *avant-garde* Liberal Catholicism of 1889 had become the guardian of orthodoxy. It was not that Gore's views had changed. It was the times that had.

The years as Bishop of Oxford, from 1911 to 1919, were perhaps something of an anticlimax. Gore still remained a national figure. Work amongst the country folk and the students of Oxford and Cuddesdon had its consolations, but he missed the pulsating life of a great city. He was oppressed by problems of diocesan reorganization, theological strife, and above all the war. Even his friends noticed a certain irritability. His health was strained, and at times he found difficulty in speaking. Never an optimist, Gore became increasingly pessimistic about the future. The bishops seemed to be wanting in Catholic principle.[22] At times Gore seemed to be standing alone in the defense of his faith.

Gore resigned from Oxford in 1919. "I have a passion to write," he told a friend. "As a diocesan bishop, I can keep level with my business, but I have only time to write little books. I must write something bigger before I die."[23] His hope was more than amply fulfilled.

On being made a bishop, Gore had withdrawn from the Community of the Resurrection. On resignation, he took the honorary title of Prelate Brother, but did not return. Instead, he took quarters in London and plunged into writing. Book followed book in rapid succession. Among them was his massive trilogy *Belief in God* (1921), *Belief in Christ* (1922), and *The Holy Spirit and the Church* (1924), which were published together in 1926 under the title *The Reconstruction of Belief*. Critics of the trilogy were answered in a further

[22] For a full account of these years, see Prestige, *op. cit.,* pp. 320-426. The last straw for Gore was the decision to throw open the Church Assembly franchise to the unconfirmed (*ibid.,* p. 422). Though the Church of England was still subject to Parliament, the creation of the Church Assembly in 1919 was intended to make it more democratic. Gore regarded confirmation as a necessary qualification of Church membership (see below, pp. 359f.). The decision not to insist on confirmation as a qualification for the franchise was the immediate occasion of Gore's resignation from office.

[23] G. Crosse, *Charles Gore* (1932), p. 98.

volume *Can We then Believe?* (1926). *Christ and Society* (1928) summarized his social teaching. Now past his seventy-fifth year, Gore saw the publication in 1928 of *A New Commentary on Holy Scripture.* The following year he published *Jesus of Nazareth,* and in 1930 he brought out his Gifford Lectures on *The Philosophy of the Good Life.*

In the midst of all this, Gore found time to travel abroad. Despite his misgivings, he took part in the Malines Conversations (1921-5), sponsored by Lord Halifax and Cardinal Mercier in the hope of further-ing the reunion of the Church of England with the Church of Rome.[24] For the first time in his life Gore became a licensed curate, and preached and ministered in various London churches. He joined the staff of King's College, London, and both lectured and tutored in theology. Almost to the end, Gore remained intensely active. He died January 17, 1932, five days short of his seventy-ninth birthday.

II. EXPOSITION

When Gore wanted to describe his theology the term which most readily suggested itself was *Liberal Catholicism.* To Gore it was synony-mous with Anglicanism, which in turn was synonymous with God's answer to the plight of modern man. What he meant appears outlined in a statement as early as 1889.

> I believe with a conviction, the intensity of which I can hardly ex-press, that it is . . . the God-given vocation of the Church of Eng-land to realize and offer men a Catholicism which goes behind the Reformation in real and unimpaired connection with the Catholicism of the past . . . which is Scriptural and represents the whole of Scrip-ture; which is rational and can court the light of all genuine enquiry; which is free to deal with the new problems and wants of a new time while it does the old work of conversion and sanctification; which acknowledges the authority of its ministry, but an authority consti-tutional, not absolute; scriptural, not arbitrary.[25]

Such was the pattern of Gore's thinking in 1889. It remained the same to the day of his death. The marks of Catholicism were three: apostolic succession, high sacramentalism, and a common rule of faith.[26] Gore's liberalism consisted in a steadfast refusal "to ignore the claims of reason in the largest sense, whether as shown in philoso-

---

[24] Prestige, *op. cit.,* pp. 478-489; cf. G. K. A. Bell, *Randall Davidson* (1935), II, 1254-1303; Lord Halifax, *The Conversations at Malines, 1921-5* (1930); W. H. Frere, *Recollections of Malines* (1935).

[25] *Report of the Church Congress of 1889,* p. 302; cf. J. Carpenter, *op. cit.,* pp. 42-61.

[26] *The Reconstruction of Belief* (1926), p. 903.

phy or science or historical criticism, or in the spiritual experience of mankind."[27] In the pages that follow we shall examine how Gore worked out this conception of Liberal Catholicism.

AUTHORITY, APOLOGETICS, AND METHOD

Gore's particular contribution to *Lux Mundi* was an essay on "The Holy Spirit and Inspiration." Later works amplified Gore's teaching on salvation, the Church, and the sacraments, but nothing he ever afterwards wrote substantially modified the general outlook presented here.[28]

The essay opened on a characteristically Catholic note. All life is the operation of the Spirit, but the Church is "in a preeminent sense . . . the Spirit-bearing body." The theme (like the whole essay) was elaborated by means of ample references to the Greek Fathers and occasional references to Scripture. It soon led to an exposition of authority as the Spirit-guided Church.[29]

In analyzing this concept Gore noted four characteristics of the Spirit's working.[30] On the one hand, it is *social*. The very notion of the Church is enough to make the point obvious. On the other hand, (to use Gore's phrase) the Spirit *nourishes individuality*. Individual illumination acts as "a purifying force upon the common mind of the Christian society," In the third place, (again using Gore's own words) the Spirit *consecrates the whole of nature*. There can be no dichotomy between God's truth in the realm of grace and God's truth in the realm of nature. Finally, Gore spoke of *the gradualness of the Spirit's method*. As in the sciences, so in religion; human knowledge is gradual and progressive.

The central section of the essay consisted in a brief reaffirmation

---

[27] *Ibid.*

[28] Cf. *The Reconstruction of Belief*, pp. 771-901; "The Bible in the Church," in *A New Commentary on Holy Scripture* (1928), pp. 1-18; *The Doctrine of the Infallible Book* (1924).

[29] *Lux Mundi*, p. 317; cf. "Once more, the belief in the Holy Scriptures as inspired requires to be held in context by belief in the general action of the Holy Spirit upon the Christian society and the individual soul. It is, we may perhaps say, becoming more and more difficult to believe in the Bible without believing in the Church" (p. 338); "Most rational surely is the attitude of the early Church towards Scripture. The Scripture was regarded as the highest utterance of the Spirit, the unique and constant test of the Church's life and teaching. But the Spirit in the Church interpreted the meaning of Scripture. Thus the Church taught and the Scripture tested and verified or corrected her teaching: and this because all was of one piece, the life of the Church including the Scriptures, the inspired writers themselves appealing to the Spirit in the Churches" (p. 340).

[30] *Ibid.*, pp. 322-333.

of the orthodox doctrines of the divinity and personality of the Spirit and His procession from the Father and the Son.[31] But all this was merely by way of preparation for the novel conclusion. All that Gore had so far said was familiar enough in Catholic writers. His master-stroke lay in contending that there was nothing incompatible between this and the acceptance of biblical criticism. As a matter of fact, Gore was saying nothing new. The French Oratorian Richard Simon (1638-1712) had made the same point over two hundred years earlier.[32] But it was new to Anglo-Catholicism. Previously it had been imagined that Scripture, reason, and tradition were all saying the same thing. In Gore's opinion they were not. But his view of the working of the Spirit enabled him to salvage the Catholic concept of authority as the Spirit-guided Church. Henceforth, Scripture, reason, and tradition must be allowed to correct or (as Gore would have said) *interpret* each other. The way was open to accept the latest scientific and critical theories and still keep a Catholic view of the Church as the arbiter of truth.

Toward the end of the essay Gore sketched his idea of a reverent yet critical approach to Scripture. Inspiration must not be thought of as something belonging to the written word but rather as the insight of the writer.[33] Not all the Psalms were written by David,[34] but the imprecatory Psalms must not be dismissed as "utterances of selfish spite: they are the claim which righteous Israel makes upon God that He should vindicate Himself."[35] On the other hand, modern criticism teaches us that we can no longer regard all parts of Scripture as equally historically accurate. The Pentateuch was not written by Moses, but consists of various strata written at different times in Israel's history.[36] Although "the record from Abraham downward is in substance in the strict sense historical,"[37] we must recognize "a considerable idealizing element in the Old Testament history."[38]

Gore was not insensitive to what, to many, was the Achilles' heel of his argument — the discrepancy between Christ's view of Scripture and that of the critics. His reply was two-pronged.[39] Christ's reference to Jonah's resurrection as a type of his own (Matt. 12:40), to the

---

[31] *Ibid.*, pp. 333-336.
[32] *Histoire Critique du vieux Testament* (1678); cf. Karl Barth, *Church Dogmatics*, I, 2 (1956), 559.
[33] *Lux Mundi*, p. 351.
[34] *Ibid.*, p. 353.
[35] *Ibid.*, p. 350.
[36] *Ibid.*, pp. 352f.
[37] *Ibid.*, p. 351.
[38] *Ibid.*, p. 354.
[39] *Ibid.*, pp. 358-360.

flood as a historical event (Matt. 24:37f.), and his ascription to David of Psalm 110 (Matt. 22:41-6) were simply arguments *ad hominem.* To reason with men on their own premises (regardless of whether they were true or not) was part and parcel of our Lord's method. But it was the second prong of the argument that was really barbed. It was Gore's almost incidental appeal to *kenosis.* In becoming a man, Christ had laid aside such divine attributes as omniscience, omnipotence, and omnipresence. Christ's knowledge was in a sense no different from that of any other man of his time. In other words (though Gore did not care to say so plainly), Christ could make mistakes.

In later writings Gore sharply distinguished his view of authority from that of Rome. In the first place, in contrast with the labyrinth of Roman *de fide* definitions, it was Gore's view that articles of faith should be kept to a minimum.[40] In the second place, he rejected as absolutist the Roman claim to define irreformable dogmas.[41] In the third place, he repudiated such Roman additions to the deposit of faith as transubstantiation, the immaculate conception, papal infallibility, and the invocation of the saints.[42] In each case Rome had violated the Vincentian maxim which limited the function of tradition to interpreting Scripture.[43] Authentic doctrine is that which has been held *ubique, semper, ab omnibus,* which for Gore meant the teaching of Scripture as understood by the early Church.[44]

Behind the first two of these objections stood Gore's liberalism. Underlying the third was his conviction that Christianity was a historical religion centering around a normative point in time. The past supplied not only the fundamental doctrines of the faith; it contained

[40] See above, p. 347; cf. *The Reconstruction of Belief,* pp. 844, 904-6.

[41] *Ibid.,* pp. 805-816.

[42] *Ibid.,* pp. 811ff., 931f.

[43] "But the function of the Church tradition was to interpret, not to add to, 'what was written', and tradition meant the tradition as patent from the beginning. This ancient idea of Church authority was admirably explained in the little work of Vincent of Lerins written A. D. 434 — *Adversus profanas omnium novitates haereticorum commonitorium* — which became the classic on the subject" (*ibid.,* p. 817; cf. *Roman Catholic Claims,* 10th ed. [1909], pp. 37-59).

[44] Gore regarded the first three centuries as "the pure centuries." The fusion of Church and State in later centuries had a polluting effect on Christian teaching. Moreover, Gore assigned a particular significance to the first four ecumenical councils: Nicea (325), Constantinople (381), Ephesus (431), and Chalcedon (451). "The authority of the ecumenical councils has a pre-eminence, because there a particular doctrine, which had already agitated the Church and been very fully discussed, was brought into distinct light, and the collective mind of the Church was brought to bear upon it, in a sense which gives their decisions an importance and precision which uncontested tradition cannot quite reach" (*The Reconstruction of Belief,* p. 935).

their very foundation. Indeed, the doctrines were fundamental precisely because they stood in such close historical proximity to the central event of the faith. For the Incarnation of the Son of God is the primary fact of Christianity. Moreover, when judged by sound historical canons, the New Testament writers were sound witnesses to that fact. There is an authentic ring of truth in the story they relate.[45] The textual evidence is good.[46] Although as ordinary human beings the writers were prone to make mistakes,[47] their witness was factual and unadorned almost to the point of naïveté.[48] Of Mark and Luke (the earliest written Gospel witnesses, in his opinion[49]) Gore could claim that they "had the freest access to original witnesses of the events which they describe. Their intentions were conspicuously simple and honest. They appear to have no design except to record things as they happened."[50] Of the New Testament generally he insisted that we could use its documents "as a whole with confidence in their authenticity and trustworthiness."[51] Indeed, Gore was not afraid to claim that it was simply prejudice against the miraculous and supernatural which led to the negative results of scholars like Renan and Harnack.[52] In view of all this it was inadmissible to treat the miracles of the creeds as merely symbolical.[53] The truths of Christianity had no basis apart from their historical foundation. But Christianity had nothing to fear from the impartial historian. The appeal to history was the sheet-anchor of Gore's faith and the spearhead of his apologetic.

If Gore grounded his defense of the faith upon history, he could also appeal to philosophy and experience. In *The Reconstruction of Belief* he argued that reflection on the natural world led to a sense of unity and purpose which was in no way diminished by the doctrine of evolutionary development.[54] More important, our moral sense conveys "irresistibly" the conviction of value, purpose, and duty.[55] In *The Philosophy of the Good Life* Gore turned to comparative religion. From a survey of the world's great religious teachers — Zarathustra, Confucius, Mohammed, Socrates, Plato, the Hebrew prophets,

---

[45] *Jesus of Nazareth* (1929), 1946 edn., pp. 143f.; *The Reconstruction of Belief*, pp. 252-282.
[46] *The Reconstruction of Belief*, pp. 184-214.
[47] *Jesus of Nazareth*, pp. 123ff.
[48] *The Reconstruction of Belief*, pp. 490f. *Jesus of Nazareth*, pp. 132ff.
[49] *The Reconstruction of Belief*, pp. 186-206; *Jesus of Nazareth*, pp. 135-142.
[50] *The Reconstruction of Belief*, p. 215.
[51] *Ibid.*, p. 212.
[53] See above, pp. 347f., and *The Reconstruction of Belief*, pp. 262-282.
[54] *Ibid.*, pp. 52ff.
[55] *Ibid.*, pp. 55ff.

and Jesus — he built up an impressive testimony to the supremacy of the good, which finds its highest expression in Christianity.

But in the last analysis the value of such arguments is limited. By itself philosophy can only offer a pantheism in which spiritual values are immersed in the material world.[56] For personal, intelligible encounter with the living God we must turn to the historical revelation, mediated first by the Hebrew prophets and then by Christ.[57] Reflection on the moral experience of mankind and the natural world can show that faith is not an absurd postulate. The very idea of "absolute values on which the good life is based is an ultimate act of faith, to refuse which is to repudiate both religion and humanism. It is this faith alone that can make life worth living."[58] And a similar act of faith is basic to science, for the scientist cannot proceed at all without the belief that nature will prove "reasonable."[59] But none of these arguments can create faith.

In the reconstruction of belief in the twentieth century philosophy and science may prepare the way for historical evidence. But in the end the truth of Christianity is a moral issue demanding self-commitment.

> The sum of our answer is this: historical evidence never is, nor can be, demonstrative evidence, such as can put an absolute constraint upon the wills of men or their reasons. There always remains room for faith or, on the other hand, the opportunity to escape conviction. The final determination between faith and unfaith in the case of Jesus, certainly rests upon the consideration — Do I or do I not find room in my mind for the idea of God as the Creator and Redeemer of men in general and of myself in particular, who comes near to mankind and to me at last in a human character — in Jesus of Nazareth? If we can find in our mind no room for this divine Saviour, we shall find means no doubt to dispose of the evidence. But if we find room for the idea, we shall also find the evidence very cogent — enough, or more than enough, to make the self-committal of faith the reasonable reaction.[60]

THE INCARNATION

In *Lux Mundi* the doctrine of *kenosis* appeared as a device for explaining how Christ could make mistakes. In the Bampton Lectures on *The Incarnation of the Son of God* (1891), the *Dissertations*

[56] *The Reconstruction of Belief*, pp. 57ff.

[57] *Ibid.*, pp. 61-132.

[58] *The Philosophy of the Good Life* (1930), Everyman's Library ed. (1935), p. 288.

[59] *Ibid.*, pp. 288-291.

[60] *Jesus of Nazareth*, p. 144; cf. *The Reconstruction of Belief*, pp. 288-292.

354

on Subjects Connected with the Incarnation (1895), and other later writings it became the key to the incarnation. The term itself derives from a Greek noun meaning *emptying, depletion*. Gore applied it to the alleged laying aside of Christ's divine attributes at the Incarnation.

> The Incarnation of the Son of God was no mere addition of a manhood to His Godhead: it was no mere wrapping around the divine glory of a human nature to veil it and make it tolerable to mortal eyes. It was more than this. The Son of God, without ceasing to be God, the Son of the Father, and without ceasing to be conscious of His divine relation as Son to the Father, yet, in assuming human nature, so truly entered into it as really to grow and live as Son of Man under properly human conditions, that is to say also under properly human limitations. Thus, if we are to express this in human language, we are forced to assert that within the *sphere* and *period* of His incarnate and mortal life, He did, and as it would appear did habitually — doubtless by the voluntary action of His own self-limiting and self-restraining love — cease from the exercise of those divine functions and powers, including the divine omniscience, which would have been incompatible with a truly human experience.[61]

In support of this view, Gore appealed to the biblical account of Christ's human experiences,[62] which, he claimed, showed that there was "no single certain passage of the New Testament against it."[63] On the other hand, Paul positively taught it in II Corinthians 8:9 and Philippians 2:5-11.[64] The former describes the Incarnation as "self-beggary," and the latter actually contains the word *kenosis* in its verbal form: Christ "did not count equality with God a thing to be grasped, but emptied himself (ἑαυτὸν ἐκένωσεν), taking the form of a servant, being born in the likeness of men" (Phil. 2:6f. RSV).

To Gore, *kenosis* was not only a means of reconciling Christ and the critics. It was also the expression of the bishop's psychological interest in trying to understand Jesus as a living, integrated personality. Neither the creeds nor the Fathers went far enough in portraying Christ's psychological unity. The orthodox definition of His two natures with its stress on "two natures, without confusion, without change, without division, without separation"[65] was adequate as far as it went. But it gave the impression of an abstract dualism.[66] Even the older Tractar-

[61] *Dissertations on Subjects Connected with the Incarnation,* 2nd ed. (1896), pp. 94f.
[62] *Ibid.,* pp. 76-88.
[63] *Ibid.,* p. 88.
[64] *Ibid.,* pp. 88-90; cf. *The Reconstruction of Belief,* pp. 521f.
[65] The Definition of the Council of Chalcedon, A.D. 451; cf. H. Bettenson, *Documents of the Christian Church* (1943), p. 73.
[66] *The Reconstruction of Belief,* pp. 513-524. *Dissertations,* pp. 162ff.

ians had erred in this direction. For when Colenso had anticipated Gore's teaching, Liddon had resorted to the two-natures teaching as proof of Christ's infallibility without considering what effect the Incarnation might have on Christ's divinty.[67] Traditional Christology was too abstract and dualistic. *Kenosis* safeguarded the unity of Christ's person,[68] by showing what it meant for divinity to become united with humanity.

If *kenosis* was a liberalizing of Catholicism, it was also a catholicizing of liberalism in so far as it was Gore's expression of the Tractarian teaching on the divine humility.

> From this point of view the Incarnation might seem to be the supreme and intensified example of that general divine sympathy, by which God lives not only in His own life but also in the life of His creatures and (in a sense) might fall in with a general doctrine of the divine immanence. [69]

These words draw attention to two strands in Liberal Catholic teaching which Gore in part reproduced and in part transcended. The first (to which we shall return to under the heading of Redemption) was a tendency to shift the focus of the Atonement from the Cross to the whole drama of the Incarnation. The second was a propensity to connect Incarnation and immanence by viewing Christ as the supreme example of divine indwelling in the world.

The theme of Gore's Bampton Lectures was the unity of nature and grace: "the Son of God who redeems is also the creator, and . . . His mediation in grace is strictly on the lines of His earlier mediation in nature."[70] There is a progressive evolution in which the Incarnation is "the crown of natural development."[71] It is, however, possible to overemphasize this aspect of Gore's thought. In his later writings Gore reacted sharply against it.[72] Even in the Bampton Lectures he insisted that Christ is *Christus Redemptor* no less than *Christus Consummator*.[73] And in *Belief in Christ* Gore contended that it was irrational pride which understood the Incarnation as only the foremost example of God in all men.[74]

[67] H. P. Liddon, *The Divinity of our Lord and Saviour Jesus Christ*, 4th ed. (1869), pp. 454f. Gore did not openly attack Liddon and the Tractarians, but his views made it sufficiently plain that he was rejecting their teaching at this point. Cf. J. Carpenter, *op. cit.*, pp. 157ff.

[68] *Dissertations*, pp. 202-207.

[69] *Ibid.*, p. 172; cf. J. Carpenter, *op. cit.*, pp. 171f.

[70] *The Incarnation of the Son of God* (1891), p. 40.

[71] *Ibid.*, p. 43.

[72] *The New Theology and the Old Religion* (1907), pp. 88, 129, 222f.

[73] *Ibid.* p. 36.

[74] *The Reconstruction of Belief*, p. 475.

REDEMPTION, SIN, AND THE TRINITY

Some corrective is also needed to the widespread view that for Gore the Incarnation is the Atonement.[75] In fact, the Atonement figures much more prominently in Gore's thought than is often supposed. Gore could even claim that "everything in the New Testament appears to depend on this initial sacrifice of atonement, reconciliation, and propitiation."[76]

Generally, Gore treated Christ's redemptive work under three heads: Example, Sacrifice, and New Life.

> There is *Christ in front of us,* who sets before us the standard of the new life — in whom we see the true meaning of manhood. That is to kindle our desire. Then there is *Christ for us* — our propitiation or atonement — winning for us, at the price of His blood-shedding, freedom from all the guilt and bondage of the past, the assurance of free forgiveness, and the fresh start. Then there is *Christ in us* — our new life by the Spirit, moulding us inwardly into His likeness, and conforming us to His character. And the three are one. Each is un-intelligible without the others. The redeeming work of Christ lies in all together.[77]

We shall postpone detailed consideration of Gore's understanding of the Atonement to our final assessment of his views.[78] But it is worthwhile pausing to examine two important corollaries of his teaching on redemption. The first concerns his concept of sin; the second involves his doctrine of the Trinity.

Gore's view of redemption corresponded to his view of sin as power and guilt. His liberalism prevented him from construing in a literal fashion the story of the Fall in Genesis 3. But though Adam might not be a historical person, the doctrine of original sin contained deep truths. In the light of experience and psychology no purely individual account of sin is possible. Sin was in the race as a malignant power before it is in the individual. Every human being is born to an inheritance of sin. Moreover, sin involves guilt. It is more than animal instinct. It is that lawlessness and rejection of God for which man is morally accountable. This is the testimony of the Christian revelation which finds ample corroboration in human experience.[79]

The orthodox doctrine of the Trinity was no mere philosophical abstraction to Gore. "It emerged simply in the process of believing in

---

[75] Cf. L. B. Smedes, *The Incarnation,* p. 50, with J. Carpenter, *op. cit.,* pp. 183-189.

[76] *The Reconstruction of Belief,* p. 589.

[77] *Ibid.,* p. 596.

[78] See below, pp. 369f.

[79] *The Reconstruction of Belief,* pp. 552-575.

Christ as the Son of God Incarnate and in the realized activity of the Holy Spirit — the Spirit. of God received from the ascended Christ."[80] Although mysterious, it is not irrational. The ultimate principles of biology and physics are equally mysterious, but are nonetheless rational. For what makes a belief rational is not our capacity to demonstrate it *a priori,* but that it should be grounded in experience and be capable of interpreting experience.[81]

To appreciate the doctrine of the Trinity we need to relive the experience of the first disciples. On the other hand, the doctrine is more than a value judgment placed on experience. If it were so, we might be disposed to regard the Spirit as no more than the general influence of God in the souls of men. As a corrective we must interpret experience in the light of the New Testament which, as always, is normative for theological truth.[82]

Gore's doctrine of the Trinity epitomized his liberal reconstruction of Catholicism. Though above reason, the doctrine was not contrary to reason, and indeed it illuminated reason. It was grounded in redemption and therefore ultimately in the Incarnation attested by Scripture and the early Church. The orthodox doctrine of the creeds was made relevant to contemporary experience. And, finally, the Trinity was the ground of personal existence in mutual society.

> Is it not a delight to believe that the ultimate reality is not monotonous unity, but a unity which contains in itself a fellowship of persons — one with a unity which can never be realized among human persons, but which at the same time assures us that personality and personal life essentially involves fellowship?[83]

That fellowship, the goal of creation and the fruit of redemption, was realized in the Catholic Church.

CHURCH, SACRAMENTS, AND MINISTRY

In *Lux Mundi* Gore expounded the idea of the Spirit-guided Church as the arbiter of truth. But this was in fact only one aspect of the larger Catholic idea of the Church as the extension of the Incarnation.

> The Church embodies the same principle as the "Word made flesh," that is, the expression and communication of the spiritual and the divine through what is material and human. It is a human and material society. Its sacraments are visible instruments: its unity is that of a visible organization bound into one at least by the link of an

80 *Ibid.,* p. 544.
81 *Ibid.,* p. 545.
82 *Ibid.*
83 *Ibid.,* pp. 548f.

358

apostolic succession and an historical continuity. But this visible, material, human society exists to receive, to embody, and to communicate a spiritual life. And this life is none other than the life of the Incarnate. The Church exists to perpetuate in every age the life of Jesus, the union of manhood with Godhead.[84]

The thought of the Church as the extension of the Incarnation represents a whole complex of ideas. On the one hand, it means that through the material sacraments of the Church, the spiritual grace of Christ is communicated. On the other hand, the Church presents an analogy of the Incarnation by being both material and spiritual. Gore can also say that the Church extends the Incarnation as a child carries the characteristics of its parent.[85] But underlying all these ideas is the belief that the Church is in a literal sense "Christopher," since she is the bearer of the Spirit of Christ.[86]

The principal means by which the Spirit imparts the life of Christ to the Church are the sacraments, notably baptism (which includes confirmation), the eucharist, and orders.[87]

Baptism effects "the great transition from the world of sin to the world of righteousness."[88] Reviewing the New Testament language about baptism, Gore claims:

> Incorporation into Christ or His body, the being invested in a new spiritual nature which is Christ, "cleansing" from defilement mediated by washing, a new birth into a new spiritual status — all these phrases convey the same idea, and the process thus variously described is assigned to the same agent, the Holy Spirit, with the same external rite as its instrument. There is then in baptism an outward and visible sign and an inward and spiritual gift, and the two appear to be inseparably connected.[89]

He goes on to say that, like the other New Testament writers, Paul "believed in baptism as acting *ex opere operato,* if by that is meant simply that he believed a real change of spiritual status to be wrought in all cases through the visible rite."[90] But it is not an *opus operatum* that secures salvation apart from a life of faith.[91]

84 *The Incarnation of the Son of God*, p. 219.
85 *Ibid.*, p. 224.
86 *The Body of Christ*, p. 30; *Roman Catholic Claims*, pp. 26ff.; cf. above p. 350.
87 *The Reconstruction of Belief*, pp. 744-770. Gore disallowed penance, extreme unction, and marriage as sacraments in the strict sense. The first lacked an outward sign and the two latter were not of dominical institution. Nevertheless, they were sacramental (*ibid.*, p. 769).
88 *Ibid.*, p. 747.
89 *Ibid.*, p. 746.
90 *Ibid.*, p. 747.
91 *Ibid.*, pp. 748ff.

On the subject of confirmation Gore departed from the traditional view of the Catholic Church in the West by refusing to regard it as a separate sacrament. Rather, it is the completion of baptism. From Acts 2:38; 8:17f.; 19:6, Gore deduced that "baptism prepared for the gift of the Holy Spirit, but the laying on of the hands of the apostles was the normal instrument of its bestowal."[92] This is not to say that today the Spirit is not given in baptism; confirmation is the renewal of the baptismal promises and the means of conferring the gift of the Spirit for the full responsibilities of adult Church membership.[93]

In several ways Gore's eucharistic teaching anticipated ideas now strenuously advocated in the Liturgical Movement. Whereas most successors of the Tractarians spared no effort to import into the Church of England the theology and practices of medieval Rome, Gore tried to get behind Western Catholic tradition. The primitive Church was his ideal. "I rejoice," he said, "in the patristic recognition of mystery and absence of precise formula, much more than in medieval logic."[94] It was this logic which had produced the dogma of transubstantiation, and which in turn had given rise to a whole gamut of extra liturgical devotions which had ended by shifting the focal point of the eucharist from communion with Christ to the adoration of an external presence. To Gore, Reservation of the Blessed Sacrament was legitimate only for the communion of the sick.[95] For the whole purpose of Communion is nothing less than "the communication of Christ to each receiver."[96] Moreover, the communion is horizontal as well as vertical. It is the communion of Christ's people with each other no less than with God.

> Thus the body of Christ renews the body which is His Church, and the blood, which is the life of Christ, reinvigorates its common life.[97]

On the crucial questions of the Real Presence and Eucharistic Sacrifice which have traditionally divided Catholics and Protestants, Gore again reformulated Catholic thought. The result was an impressive, if not altogether successful, attempt to steer a middle course between the Scylla of Rome and the Charybdis of what is often imagined to be Zwinglianism.[98]

[92] *Ibid.,* p. 751.
[93] *The Religion of the Church* (1916), p. 52.
[94] *Reservation, A Report of a Conference Held at Farnham Castle* (1926), p. 5.
[95] See above p. 347, n. 19.
[96] *The Religion of the Church,* p. 54.
[97] *Ibid.,* p. 56.
[98] See below, n. 102. On Zwingli, see G. W. Bromiley, ed., *Zwingli and Bullinger* (The Library of Christian Classics, Vol. 24, 1953), pp. 176-238.

360

According to Gore,

> . . . the spiritual presence of Christ in His body and His blood (and all that goes with it) rests not on the precarious faith of any individual, but is so relative to the faith of the Church as a whole — that common faculty which rests at bottom on the activity of the Holy Ghost — as that apart from faith, or for one who in no way shares it, it can no more in any intelligible sense be said to exist than the beauty of nature can be said to exist for what is quite without reason. For here again existence proves to mean a relation to a consciousness — only now it is not mere rational sensibility, but spiritual faith.[99]

E. L. Mascall[100] and James Carpenter[101] are among those who have drawn attention to the intellectual gymnastics performed by Gore in order to reach this position. Despite his fulminations against logical explanations, Gore has not eliminated philosophy. In fact, he has merely substituted one form (Idealism) for another (Aristotelian Thomism). For as in Idealism the mind (in differing degrees) constitutes the objects of the external world, in Gore faith constitutes the reality of Christ's presence in the Eucharist.

Gore's view of Eucharistic Sacrifice again attempts to steer a middle course. On the one hand, it neither repeats nor renews the sacrifice of the Cross. On the other hand, it is no mere mental recollection of a past event.[102] In the Eucharist, the *whole* Christ is objectively present.[103]

Gore gives three reasons for this. In first place, the consecration of the Church's earthly offering is accepted at a heavenly altar and is united with Christ's heavenly offering.[104] In second place, the elements on the altar become the body and blood of the "Lamb as it had been slain" in virtue of their consecration by the Holy Spirit.[105] Both views are drawn from the Fathers, though the former is more Latin and the latter more Greek in its emphasis. But common to both is Gore's third and fundamental reason. The sacrifice of Christ *for* us is only finally consummated *in* us through communion.[106]

> What He does first for us, He must ultimately do in us. . . . Thus only by communion can we in any effective sense share the eucharistic sacrifice, so far as that sacrifice is not merely human effort, but is identified with Christ's offering, and attains thereby its spiritual valid-

99 *The Body of Christ* (1901), pp. 152f.
100 *Corpus Christi* (1953), pp. 138-156.
101 *Op. cit.*, pp. 233ff.
102 *The Body of Christ*, pp. 174f., 182f.
103 *Ibid.*, p. 182.
104 *Ibid.*, pp. 185-192.
105 *Ibid.*, pp. 192-199.
106 *Ibid.*, pp. 199-209.

ity. Only in Christ can we offer and plead Christ. We have an altar whereof we are to eat.[107]

From the very first Tractarian *Tract,* the doctrine of Apostolic Succession had been the linchpin of Anglo-Catholicism.[108] It was both a call to arms to the clergy and the *sine qua non* of the valid administration of the sacramental life of the Church. Gore's liberalism never permitted him to modify this view.

> The Church's doctrine of succession is thus of a piece with the whole idea of the Gospel revelation, as being the communication of a divine gift which must be received and cannot be originated — received, moreover, through the channels of a visible and organic society.[109]

Conversely, violation of Apostolic Succession is tantamount to heresy.[110] Any nonconformist ministry which lacks episcopal ordination in the Apostolic Succession is both "irregular" and "invalid." By this, Gore did not mean that its fruits must all be discounted. God might bless men through such a ministry, but they had no right to expect Him to do so. Such a ministry "falls outside the conditions of covenanted security and cannot justify its existence in terms of the covenant."[111] This was the motive behind Gore's opposition to the South India scheme.[112] In all plans for reunion among Protestant churches, episcopal reordination must be regarded as an essential condition.

THE CHURCH'S MISSION IN SOCIETY

The original Tractarians had not been original social thinkers. Pusey had given away a fortune, but like his evangelical counterpart, Lord Shaftesbury, the foremost social worker of the century, his actions were prompted by sheer compassion and simple obedience to biblical precepts. Social work, as Shaftesbury saw it, consisted of legislation against excesses and the organization of private charity. But as the nineteenth century wore on, a twofold development took place in the minds of Christian Socialists like F. D. Maurice and

[107] *Ibid.,* pp. 199ff.

[108] See above, p. 342.

[109] *The Church and the Ministry* (1889), p. 75; revised by C. H. Turner, 1919, 3rd imp. (1949), p. 63.

[110] *Ibid.*

[111] *Ibid.,* 1st ed., p. 345; 1949 imp., p. 305.

[112] G. L. Prestige, *op. cit.,* pp. 518-522. The South India scheme for reunion among Protestant churches provided for mutual recognition of ministries regardless of the mode of ordination; cf. R. Rouse and S. C. Neill, eds., *A History of the Ecumenical Movements, 1517-1948* (1954), pp. 473-476.

thinkers like B. F. Wescott and the *Lux Mundi* group.[113] On the one hand, an attempt was made to relate sociology with the idea of the brotherhood of all men in Christ. It was no longer enough to translate the precepts of Scripture into action. Disregarding the biblical teaching on regeneration to life in Christ, Maurice and Westcott canvassed the idea that all men are in Christ already and that sociology is the outworking of this life. On the other hand, the same group of thinkers tended to encourage attempts to unite manual labor, to press for economic reforms, and even to identify the Church's mission with some form of socialism.

Although the *Lux Mundi* group was involved in these developments and Gore himself played a prominent part in the Christian Social Union, Gore tended to stand to one side. Although socialist in sympathies, he refused to treat economic socialism as a panacea.[114] His view of sin did not permit him to share the widespread belief in the inevitability of human progress.[115] Moreover, the Church must not align itself too closely either with the State or any other particular body.[116] Finally, although he believed in brotherhood, he did not endorse Maurice's view of the brotherhood of all men in Christ.

Nevertheless, Gore was passionately concerned with social issues. Perhaps two quotations from his own writings sum his attitude best.

> The principle of brotherhood must act as a constant counterpoise to the instinct of competition. The principle of labour shows that the idle and selfish are "out of place" in a Christian community. The principle of justice forces us to recognize that the true interest of each member of the body politic must be consulted. The principle of public responsibility reminds us that each one is his brother's keeper. . . . What we want is not more Christians, but, much rather, better Christians — that is to say, Christians who have more perception of what the moral effort required for membership in the catholic brotherhood really is.[117]

> Thus I believe the most pressing call upon the Church today is to remember that its authority and mission rest simply upon the Word of God, and that this is first of all the challenge to a new life —

---

[113] On the churches and social work in this period, see S. C. Carpenter, *Church and People, 1789-1889* (1933); E. Hodder, *The Life and Work of the Seventh Earl of Shaftesbury K.G.*, one vol. ed. (1887); J. W. Bready, *Lord Shaftesbury and Social Industrial Progress*, 4th imp. (1933); A. R. Vidler, *The Theology of F. D. Maurice* (1948); A. Westcott, *Life and Letters of Brooke Foss Westcott*, 2 vols. (1903); K. S. Inglis, *Churches and the Working Classes in Victorian England* (1963); G. F. A. Best, *Shaftesbury* (1964); K. Heasman, *Evangelicals in Action* (1962).

[114] J. Carpenter, *op. cit.*, p. 249.

[115] *Ibid.*

[116] *Ibid.*

[117] *St. Paul's Epistle to the Ephesians*, 6th imp. (1905), p. 190.

a difficult but glorious life. It is called to direct its chief attention to making the Christian doctrine of the Kingdom of God again understood and summoning men with a fresh understanding to live the life. It will be a very difficult task. But only so can we hope to get men to understand the truth about the authority of the Church; for this doctrinal and sacramental authority is strictly relative to its moral and social mission. And only by giving this the first place in importance does there seem to me to be much hope for restoring the understanding of what the Church is for.[118]

The first of these quotations draws attention to Gore's .method. What is needed is a renewal of the Church's life. The second draws attention to the place of social thinking in his thought. It is the Church's mission to realize the life of Christ in each generation. It was in preaching these themes that Gore made his chief contribution to sociology. This was the motive which lay behind his sociology and concern for Church work overseas. This was the motive which lay behind his attempt to construct a Liberal Catholicism. It is this motive — regardless of its success or lack of it — which gives the key to the life and work of Charles Gore.

III. EVALUATION

AUTHORITY, APOLOGETICS, AND METHOD

In some ways Gore's approach to Scripture exhibited a reverent sanity which was notably absent from many writers at the turn of the century. Gore was certainly swimming against the stream in his conservative estimate of the New Testament. He was bold enough to assert its historicity when many were only too ready to jettison the miraculous. And he was not afraid to speak his mind about the prejudices of those who did so. Gore was, of course, unaware of the complications raised by form criticism on the Continent. But many of the arguments of *Jesus of Nazareth* and *The Reconstruction of Belief* are fundamentally sound and will still be standing when many more fashionable theories have long been forgotten.

To some, Gore's sorties into the realms of philosophy were misguided; to others they were not nearly so long or bold as they might have been. At best, they may be said to be Gore's attempt to do justice to that general revelation spoken of in Psalm 19, Acts 14:16f., 17:22-31, and Romans 1:19-21. For Gore's philosophy was never a piece of *a priori* speculation; it was always an attempt to evaluate religious experience.[119] But although Gore made use of philosophical

---

[118] *The Reconstruction of Belief*, pp. 780f.
[119] Cf. J. Carpenter, *op. cit.*, pp. 62-93.

arguments, his theology did not rely on them. In the last analysis, Gore's thought stands or falls as a piece of biblical theology. It is here that Gore is at his most disappointing.

As an Old Testament scholar, Gore laid no claims to originality. In *Lux Mundi* he accepted as certain the conclusions arrived at by Professor Driver.[120] After that he does not appear to have given serious thought to the other side of the question. Pusey's arguments had been swept aside. Gore did not grapple with critical problems as his contemporaries James Orr in *The Problem of the Old Testament* (1906) and A. H. Finn in *The Unity of the Pentateuch* (1918). And yet Gore was not aware of the far-reaching implications of the problem or of his position as the leading advocate of Old Testament criticism in the Anglo-Catholic party.[121]

Gore's failure to think through his conclusions at certain crucial points is most apparent in his treatment of Christ's use of the Old Testament. In *Lux Mundi* he showed himself aware of the problem.[122] But in view of his vague appeal to *kenosis* he felt free to return an open verdict as to the conclusions that might be drawn from this.[123] It was a patent evasion of the problem. Even Gore's later essays are hardly more satisfactory at this point.[124] The uniform testimony of all four Gospels shows that Christ regarded the Old Testament as the Word of God which He came to endorse and fulfill.[125] Close examination of His teaching indicates that the word *infallible* is by no means an unwarrantable epithet for His verdict on the Old Testament.[126] Moreover, in expounding this view, Jesus also expounded a view of authority which flatly contradicted *kenosis*: Jesus Himself

---

[120] *Lux Mundi*, p. 352; cf. G. L. Prestige, *op. cit.*, p. 118.

[121] G. L. Prestige, *op. cit.*, pp. 103f, 113f.

[122] See above, pp. 351f.

[123] *Lux Mundi*, p. 360.

[124] *The Reconstruction of Belief*, ch. 9; *A New Commentary on Holy Scripture*, pp. 1-18; *The Doctrine of the Infallible Book* (1924).

[125] Matt. 4:4, 7, 10; 5:17-19; 9:13; 12:3, 5; 19:4f.; 21:16, 42; 26:54, 56; Mark 7:8, 13; 12:24; Luke 4:17-21; 16:17; 18:31; 24:46f.; see further J. W. Wenham, *Our Lord's View of the Old Testament* (1953); J. I. Packer, 'Fundamentalism' and the Word of God (1958); B. B. Warfield, *The Inspiration and Authority of the Bible* (1951).

[126] The term itself simply means free from error — that what is said is consistent, coherent, and corresponds with the facts. As such, infallibility is the presupposition of all language. For unless language corresponds with reality it is pointless and meaningless. Much of our everyday language fulfills these requirements and is therefore infallible. Where it is not, it is not due to an inherent defect in the structure of language, but to a mistake on the part of the speaker. When the claim of infallibility is applied to Scripture it means that, in virtue of its divine inspiration, Scripture says accurately what it purports to say.

has received supreme authority from the Father as the revealer of truth; His own words have eternal significance.[127]

Gore failed to see that his appeal to *kenosis* was double-edged. He himself wanted to restrict its use to explaining away Christ's attitude to the Old Testament. On occasion he could say that Jesus "affirmed as one who had a right to affirm infallibly."[128] What Gore failed to perceive was that once the principle of *kenosis* was admitted it could be applied to any aspect of Christ's teaching. It was all too understandable that the next generation of Anglo-Catholics found themselves unable to accept Gore's ambiguous conservatism. At its center, Gore's view of the authority of Christ contained a remarkable piece of intellectual double-think: he wanted to affirm and to deny Christ's authority at once.

Gore's alternative to the authority of Scripture — that of the Spirit-guided Church — has won a large following among Anglo-Catholics, but it is hardly convincing. In this concept Scripture, reason, and tradition each has its part to play. But at any given moment it is never quite clear which of the three has the casting vote. Nor is it possible on Gore's principles to show why one view is superior to another. In the last analysis the amount of weight given to any one of the three elements depends upon one's private disposition.[129] In other words, the concept of the Spirit-guided Church is just a disguised form of subjectivism. Moreover, this concept drives a wedge between the authority of Christ and that of the Spirit. It enables a man to deny by the Spirit what Christ affirmed by His words. In fact, by elevating the role of reason and tradition it appears to be doing what Jesus expressly forbade the rabbis to do. It makes void the Word of God by appealing to the tradition of men.[130]

This ambiguous attitude toward Scripture left its mark on Gore's work as a dogmatic theologian and expository preacher. His theological works have a definite biblical bias. But there is an absence of insight into the finer points of exegesis. All too often (as we shall see below) they fall short of what Scripture has to say on any given point. There is a lack of depth. Gore also wrote a number of commentaries and devotional works. But today they are of more value to the student of Gore's thought than to the expository preacher or the private reader in search of devotional reading.

Gore's thinking on Scripture was in fact the result of a collision.

---

[127] Matt. 5:18; 7:24ff.; 11:27; 28:18; Mark 1:22; 13:31; Luke 16:17; John 3:34f.; 5:20, 24; 7:16, 29; 8:12; 10:15; 13:3; 14:6; 17:25.
[128] *The Reconstruction of Belief,* pp. 777f.
[129] J. I. Packer, *op. cit.,* pp. 50f., 170ff.
[130] Mark 7:8, 13.

Conservatism, Tractarianism, and liberal criticism clashed head-on. The result was a compromise, which tried to please all but which in fact can be satisfying to few. It was ingenious, but remains unconvincing.

THE INCARNATION

Gore's failure to think through plausible but superficial solutions to great theological problems is no less apparent in his doctrine of *kenosis*.[131] On the one hand, it does less than justice to the biblical evidence. On the other hand, it raises insuperable difficulties for anyone who like Gore wants to retain orthodox doctrines of God, Christ, Providence, and Redemption.

Gore appealed to Philippians 2:5-11 and II Corinthians 8:9 as clinching proof of the biblical character of the doctrine. But although *kenosis* might well be read into these passages, neither posits that laying-aside of Christ's divine attributes at the Incarnation which is the essence of the doctrine. Both passages suggest abasement and humiliation. Neither demands *kenosis*.[132] Much more convincing is the view that relates the verb κενοῦν (= to empty) in Philippians 2:7 with Isaiah 53:12 ("he poured out his soul to death").[133]

The attributes of omniscience, omnipotence, and omnipresence are in fact essential aspects of divinity. Without them God would be less than God. If Christ were divested of them, he would no longer be God. In other words, if the kenotic view of the Incarnation is valid, it is difficult to see how Christ can be regarded as both God and man. He would be, as the Arians held, something less than God and something more than man.

But if this is so, what becomes of the Trinity for the thirty years of the incarnation? An important strand of New Testament teaching insists that the Second Person of the Trinity is the agent of Provi-

---

131 On *kenosis*, see D. M. Baillie, *God Was in Christ* (1948), pp. 94-98; E. L. Mascall, *Christ, The Christian, and the Church* (1946), pp. 12, 25-28, 49ff.; J. Carpenter, *op. cit.,* pp. 156-182; L. B. Smedes, *The Incarnation: Trends in Modern Anglican Thought* (1953), pp. 1-15.

132 Most scholars regard the kenotic interpretation of Phil. 2:7 as highly improbable; cf. M. R. Vincent, *The Epistles to the Philippians and to Philemon* (I.C.C.), 4th imp. (1950), p. 59; M. Jones, *The Epistle to the Philippians* (Westminster, 1918), pp. 31f.; J. H. Michael, *The Epistle of Paul to the Philippians* (Moffatt, 1928), pp. 90ff.; F. W. Beare, *A Commentary on the Epistle to the Philippians* (Black, 1959), pp. 81f. and 159-174 (appended note by E. R. Fairweather on the 'Kenotic' Christology); R. P. Martin, *The Epistle of Paul to the Philippians* (Tyndale, 1959), pp. 99ff.

133 J. Jeremias, *The Servant of God* (1957), p. 97; R. P. Martin, *An Early Christian Confession* (1960), pp. 26f.; H. W. Robinson, *The Cross of the Servant* (1926), p. 5.

dence.[134] What happens to the cosmic functions of the Word, if he is divested of omniscience, omnipotence, and omnipresence? Those who reject *kenosis* are not unaware of the great problems here. They are, however, aware that there is a great mystery at the heart of the Incarnation. It is a mystery that *kenosis* turns into a pseudo-dilemma.

E. L. Mascall is not far wrong when he claims that kenoticism is a kind of inverted monophysitism: "Whereas the monophysitism of the Eutychians absorbed the human nature into the divine, that of the kenoticists absorbs the divine nature into the human."[135] From the start the whole undertaking was vitiated by a false assumption and a pseudo-question. The assumption took it for granted that Godhead and manhood cannot exist together without in some way canceling each other out.[136] The question asked what must happen to the Godhead when it becomes compressed into manhood.[137] The answer that came out was inevitably false.

James Carpenter has pointed out that Gore's thought was further vitiated by an indiscriminate use of terminology.[138] At times Gore spoke of the *abandonment* and *surrender* of the divine attributes. But he could also speak of their *restraint*. In so far as he used the former concepts, he moved increasingly away from the biblical core of his thought. In so far as he used the latter, he came closer to the New Testament pattern of thought.[139] The New Testament insists on Christ's full divinity[140] as well as his full humanity.[141] It makes no secret of Jesus' human limitations.[142] But it also offers an alternative solution to *kenosis*. Christ's knowledge and activity are bounded by the Father's will. What He does, He does in voluntary obedience to the Father. The limitations of His earthly ministry are not determined by the mode of the Incarnation; they are determined by the eternal

---

[134] Matt. 11:27; Luke 10:22; John 1:1ff.; 3:35; Col. 1:17; Heb. 1:3.

[135] *Christ, the Christian, and the Church*, p. 12.

[136] *Ibid.*, p. 49.

[137] *Ibid.*, p. 15.

[138] *Op. cit.*, p. 167.

[139] Gore himself was not unaware of the problems created by *kenosis*; cf. *The Reconstruction of Belief*, p. 522.

[140] See, for example, the implications of such passages as Matt. 11:27f.; 16:16f.; 22:34-46; 28:18ff.; Mark 2:1-12; 8:35-38; 10:40; Luke 10:16; John 1:1-18; John 5:23f.; 10:30; 14:6ff.; 20:28; Rom. 1:4, 7; 9:5 (?); I Cor. 2:8; II Cor. 13:14; Heb. 1:1ff.; I John 2:23; 4:2, 14f. On the titles and claims of Jesus see B. B. Warfield, *The Lord of Glory* (n.d.); L. Morris, *The Lord from Heaven* (1958); O. Cullmann, *The Christology of the New Testament* (1959, 1963²); A. Richardson, *An Introduction to the Theology of the New Testament* (1958).

[141] Matt. 4:2; 8:24; Luke 2:40, 52, 26:39ff.; John 4:6; 11:35; 12:27; 19:28, 34; Acts 2:22; Rom. 5:15; Heb. 2:9; 4:15; 5:7; I John 4:2.

[142] Mark 13:32 and passages noted above.

relationship between the Father and the Son within the Trinity.[143] In other words, it is not a matter of the temporary loss or reduction of the divine attributes but of the Son's obedience in His use of them.

Broadly speaking Gore's teaching on redemption stands out as an important return to biblical perspectives. If his emphasis fell on the patristic theme of the re-creation of the new humanity in Christ, the same could be said of Scripture.[144] Gore rightly rejected Moberly's doctrine of vicarious penitence.[145] The idea is absent from Scripture, and it is impossible to see how anyone could repent of someone else's sin or how this could affect the relationship between God and sinful man. If the theme of Christ's victory over the powers of evil, stressed in recent years by Gustaf Aulén in *Christus Victor* (1931), remains in the background, it is nonetheless present.[146] Moreover, Gore rightly perceived that Christ's redemptive work has both an objective and a subjective reference.

It is when we examine his teaching more closely that we see how Gore's emphases fall short of the biblical ones. In the last analysis, Gore wanted to distinguish *vicarious sacrifice* from *vicarious punishment*. The former he accepted; the latter he denied.[147] His thoughts at this point appear to have been sidetracked by the false assumption that the latter involves a variance of will between the Father and the Son whereas the former does not[148] The point Gore wanted to make — that Christ's sacrifice was voluntary — was true, but irrelevant to his dismissal of vicarious punishment. There is no *a priori* reason why a man might not out of sheer love voluntarily take upon himself the deserts of another. And the New Testament amply attests that this was so in the case of Christ.[149]

---

143 Matt. 3:15; 5:17f.; John 5:19; 7:16; 12:49f.; 15:10; 17:4; Gal. 4:4; Phil. 2:6ff.

144 *The Reconstruction of Belief*, p. 595; cf. Matt. 7:13-27; 19-28; 25:34; Mark 10:17; John 3:16; 15:1-27; Rom. 8:21ff., 29f.; I Cor. 1:2; 6:9; 15:50; II Cor. 5: 16-21; 6:16ff.; Gal. 3:26-4:7; 5:21; Eph. 2:1-22; Col. 3:1-11; I Pet. 2:9-12; Rev. 21:1-22:5.

145 *Ibid.*, p. 593; cf. R. C. Moberly, *Atonement and Personality* (1901).

146 *The Epistles of St. John* (1920), p. 135; cf. John 12:31; 16:11; II Cor. 4:4; Eph. 4:8ff.; Col. 2:13ff.; I John 3:1-12; Rev. 12:7-12.

147 *The Reconstruction of Belief*, pp. 591ff.

148 *Ibid.*, p. 593.

149 Matt. 26:28; Mark 10:45; Luke 22:37 = Isa. 53:12; John 3:16; 10:11, 18; 15:13; Rom. 5:6-21; I Pet. 2:21-4; I John 4:10. On redemption generally see L. Morris, *The Apostolic Preaching of the Cross* (1955); J. Murray, *Redemption Accomplished and Applied* (1955).

As a matter of fact, Gore's doctrine of redemption is guilty of a double omission at this point. On the one hand, it fails to pay adequate attention to those passages of Scripture which regard Christ's death as a propitiation of divine wrath.[150] On the other hand, it fails to place redemption in the wider context of divine wrath against sin as exhibited in the law.[151]

As a consequence, Gore found himself involved in a double derangement of two other vital aspects of biblical thought. On the one hand, he was forced to invert the biblical order of redemption. The New Testament teaches that Christ's obedience was necessary in order to make His death perfect.[152] Gore held that the death of Christ was necessary to make His obedience perfect.[153] For Gore believed that God granted redemption in view of Christ's complete obedience. The New Testament is more precise. Christ's loving obedience is that which led Him so to identify himself with sinners that He bore the wrath of God against sin. In the last analysis, it is the death of Christ, not His obedience, which propitiates divine wrath. On the other hand, these gaps in Gore's thinking created a vacuum which in the New Testament is filled by the doctrine of justification by faith.[154] It is true that Gore could speak of receiving the benefits of Christ's sacrifice "solely by faith."[155] But, in general, Gore's thought was divorced from that forensic element in justification which in the New Testament is the foundation of the Christian life. This omission had its inevitable effect on Gore's teaching of the Church, ministry, and sacraments.

Gore's use of biblical concepts often suggests a closer proximity to biblical thought than his intentions appear to allow. Nevertheless, he came far nearer to biblical thinking on redemption than many of his contemporaries. What is lacking is what sometimes today is called failure of theological nerve. It was a failure to follow through to the end the teaching that he found in Scripture. It was a failure that was inevitable in view of Gore's determination to construct a Liberal Catholicism instead of a genuinely biblical theology.

[150] John 1:29; Rom. 3:25; II Cor. 5:21; Gal. 2:20f.; 3:13; Heb. 9:28; I John 2:2; 4:10; I Pet. 1:18ff.
[151] Exod. 20:5, 7; Ps. 7:11; Ezek. 18:4, 20; Rom. 1:18-2:11; 3:19f.; 6:23; Gal. 3:10ff.; Col. 2:13f.; Heb. 12:18-29.
[152] Matt. 3:15; Rom. 5:6-21; Gal. 3:13; Heb. 5:8f.; 10:8ff. Cf. notes 148-150.
[153] *The Reconstruction of Belief,* p. 597.
[154] Gen. 15:6; Luke 18:14; Rom. 1:16f.; 3:21-31; 4:1-25; 5:1f., 17ff.; 8:1, 33f.; 10:4; Gal. 2:16; 3:1-21; Eph. 2:8; Phil. 3:9; Jas. 2:14-26.
[155] *The Reconstruction of Belief,* p. 597.

CHURCH, SACRAMENTS, AND MINISTRY

It must be admitted that, unlike the Anglican Reformers, more recent evangelical Anglicans have had little positive to say about order and ministry. In reaction against formalism they have tended to stress evangelism and cultivate personal piety. To this extent Gore's teaching on the Church, ministry, and sacraments was a notable attempt to recover a lost balance in Anglican thinking. Moreover, in some respects, his views were remarkably free from defects which have vitiated Anglo-Catholic thinking. Gore repeatedly urged that the point of Holy Communion was *communion*. On the question of orders he was more concerned with principles than with trying to read back into the New Testament later particular forms.[156] Nevertheless certain defects in his teaching cannot be passed over.

Gore's doctrine of baptism suffered from his failure to relate it to the wider context of justification by faith. It is true that Gore could speak of the "supremely important place" of faith "which opens our hearts to the promises of God and commits our whole life to His will." But in the same sentence he could also speak of "baptism, which actually and spiritually introduces us into the covenant of grace and the fellowship of the Spirit."[157] In expounding this he fails to note that what is said about the effects of baptism in the New Testament is also said of the Word and faith.[158] And he fails to see the parallelism between baptism and circumcision as the covenant sign of justification by faith.[159] Although the covenant is mentioned, Gore's theology failed to do justice to the covenant framework of biblical theology.

Gore's teaching on the Real Presence and Eucharistic Sacrifice fails to do justice to his intention of retaining communion with Christ as the focal point of the rite. His interpretation of both points leaves far more room for an external, sacrificed presence than either the New Testament or the Anglican Articles and Prayer Book would allow. Gore's philosophical explanation of the real presence has al-

---

[156] *The Church and the Ministry*, p. 241.

[157] *The Reconstruction of Belief*, pp. 748f.

[158] Cf. John 3:5; Acts 2:38, 22:16; Rom. 6:3-11; I Cor. 12:13; Gal. 3:27; Eph. 5:26; Col. 2:12f.; Tit. 3:5; I Pet. 3:21, with Acts 13:38f.; 15:9; 19:4f.; Gal. 3:26; Eph. 1:13; 2:8; Col. 2:12; I Pet. 1:21ff. See further P. Ch. Marcel, *The Biblical Doctrine of Infant Baptism* (1953); J. Murray, *Christian Baptism* (1952); G. R. Beasley-Murray, *Baptism in the New Testament* (1962). On confirmation, see G. W. H. Lampe, *The Seal of the Spirit* (1951); and *The Churchman*, Vol. 77, No. 2 (June, 1963).

[159] Rom. 4:1-12; Col. 2:11f. See Murray, *op. cit.*

ready been examined.[160] His exposition of eucharistic sacrifice breaks down through its failure (despite protests to the contrary) to do justice to the finished work of Christ. The uniqueness of the cross, the resurrection, ascension, and heavenly session of Christ preclude all views of a heavenly altar or need of a sacrificed presence in the Lord's supper.[161]

It remains to be said that even those passages in Gore which stress communion in the Eucharist tend to tie grace too exclusively to the sacrament. Gore's failure to bring out the importance of the New Testament teaching on faith has already been noted. Again Gore tended to invert the biblical order. His stress fell on placing communion with Christ in the context of the Lord's supper. In the New Testament the Lord's Supper is placed in the context of communion with Christ.[162]

The motive behind Gore's doctrine of Apostolic Succession was high. It was no less than the vindication of the divine origin of the Church and its ordinances. Unfortunately, it was harnessed to a "pipeline" theory of ministerial succession, akin to that of Rome but rejected by Rome,[163] and devoid of basis in both Scripture and history.[164] The idea of a hierarchical ministry stemming alone from the apostles and perpetuating itself by laying-on-of-hands is foreign to the New Testament and to the Anglican formularies. As Gore realized, it unchurched millions of professing Christians by claiming to be of the *esse* of the Church and denying the credentials of churches which lacked it. But in fact from the Reformation onwards the Church of England consistently recognized the validity of non-episcopal Reformed ministries. And indeed it would be impossible for Gore or anyone else to furnish proof of his apostolic pedigree back through the ages to the time of the apostles.

---

[160] See above, pp. 360ff.

[161] Acts 2:27-36; 13:34ff.; Rom. 1:4; 4:25; I Cor. 15:17; Heb. 1:3, 13; 7:26ff.; 9:23-9. Cf. A. M. Stibbs, *The Finished Work of Christ* (1954).

[162] Cf. Matt. 26:26ff.; Mark 14:22ff.; Luke 22:14-20; I Cor. 10:16ff.; 11:23-23, with John 6:32-65 and the passages on faith cited in notes 153 and 157.

[163] The Bull of Leo XIII, *Apostolicae Curae* (1896; reprinted in *Anglican Orders,* 1962).

[164] A. Ehrhardt, *The Apostolic Succession in the First Two Centuries of the Church* (1953); N. Sykes, *Old Priest and New Presbyter* (1956); and "Ecumenical Movements in Great Britain in the Seventeenth and Eighteenth Centuries," in R. Rouse and S. C. Neill, *A History of the Ecumenical Movement* (1954); C. O. Buchanan, "The Church of England and Apostolic Succession," in *The Churchman,* Vol. 75, No. 1 (March, 1961); T. W. Manson, *The Church's Ministry,* London (1948).

CONCLUSION

Some six months after Gore's death a close friend wrote this of him:

> It is sometimes said that Gore's mind did not develop after the crisis in his thought represented by *Lux Mundi*. If by this is meant that he was not aware of, or had not tried to come to terms with, most of the best that had been said and written in the relevant fields since then, it seems to me clearly untrue. He was a systematic and astonishingly rapid reader, carefully annotating all the more important books. . . . On the other hand, if the statement means that by the time *Lux Mundi* came to be published he had adopted principles which he retained substantially unaltered for the rest of his life, it seems to me to contain much truth. I sometimes felt that to explain certain characteristic positions it was necessary to go back behind the immediate arguments to earlier mental habits. It was as if the intense conflict of those early days in Oxford had left its mark on a sensitive and highly strung nature so that his mind latterly tended to run into fixed gladiatorial attitudes suitable, let us say, to a battle with a Traditionalist, an encounter with a Darwinian, a deadly grappling with a Papist, and so on. He had been fighting so intensely and on so many different fronts that the alignments almost became established frontiers.[165]

This verdict is neither cavilling nor censorious. Gore's thought was massive. It was also fixed. There was scarcely a department of Christian theology in which Gore had not something to say. And what he said, he said often. In literary output Gore is the nearest English rival to Karl Barth. But in content the utterances of the later years differ little from those of the early.

There is a sense in which Charles Gore has no place in a volume devoted to creative thinkers. This is not to say that Gore was not influential. Still less is it an attempt to deny Gore's position as the leading exponent of Liberal Catholicism. But the very concept of Liberal Catholicism is not that of something *creative* but of something *created*. It was a compromise theology created by a clash of conflicting theologies. It was Tractarianism seeking to come to terms with liberalism and still retain a fidelity to Scripture.

The way Gore sought to fuse together these heterogeneous elements was often ingenious. His ideas have become the stock-in-trade of many a lesser man who has found himself in the same position. But time and time again they fail to stand up to close scrutiny. The finished product contains a series of cracks which run from top to

---

[165] J. Conway Davies, "Charles Gore," *Theology*, Vol. 25, No. 149 (November, 1932), pp. 259f.

bottom. It could hardly be otherwise. For Liberal Catholicism attempted to reconcile the irreconcilable. The result was an arbitrary collection of views. Some were true; some were half-truths; others were false. But the greatest weakness of Liberal Catholicism was not this or that particular doctrine. It was a failure to give that unqualified loyalty to Christ and Scripture which alone gives cohesion and truth to a body of doctrines.

Long before Gore's death the Anglo-Catholic party had picked up and discarded other versions of Liberal Catholicism. Despite his loose attitude toward the Reformed theology of the Thirty-Nine Articles, there was much that Gore valued in the Church of England's Protestant heritage. Despite the accretions encrusted in his teaching, Gore retained a love of the Bible and a sense of its importance which has to be seen at first hand to be appreciated. His Christian instincts were truer than the system he expounded. For all his learned writings, Gore's heart was better than his head.

IV. BIBLIOGRAPHY

(The following is only a selection of major works. For an exhaustive bibliography, see J. Carpenter, *Gore: A Study in Liberal Catholic Thought* [1960], pp. 271-301.)

WORKS BY CHARLES GORE

Lux Mundi: A Series of Studies in the Religion of the Incarnation (Charles Gore, ed.). London, 1889.

The Church and the Ministry. London, 1886. Revised by C. H. Turner (1919).

The Incarnation of the Son of God. Being the Bampton Lectures for the Year 1891. London, 1891.

Dissertations on Subjects Connected with the Incarnation. London, 1895.

The Creed of the Christian. London, 1896.

The Sermon on the Mount. A Practical Exposition. London, 1896.

St. Paul's Epistle to the Ephesians. A Practical Exposition. London, 1898.

St. Paul's Epistle to the Romans. A Practical Exposition. London, Vol. I, 1899; Vol. II, 1900.

The Body of Christ. An Inquiry into the Institution and Doctrine of Holy Communion. London 1901.

The New Theology and the Old Religion. London, 1907.

Orders and Unity. London, 1909.

The Question of Divorce. London, 1911.

The Basis of Anglican Fellowship in Faith and Organization. London, 1914.

The Religion of the Church as Presented in the Church of England, a Manual of Membership. London, 1916.

The Epistles of St. John. London, 1920.

Belief in God. London, 1921.

Belief in Christ. London, 1922.

The Doctrine of the Infallible Book. London, 1924.

The Holy Spirit and the Church. London, 1924.

Can We Then Believe? London, 1926.

The Reconstruction of Belief (a one volume edition of *Belief in God, Belief in Christ,* and *The Holy Spirit and the Church*). London, 1926.

Christ and Society. London, 1927.

A New Commentary on Holy Scripture including the Apocrypha (Gore general editor). London, 1928.

Jesus of Nazareth. London, 1929.

The Philosophy of the Good Life (Gifford Lectures for 1929-30). London, 1930.

WORKS ON CHARLES GORE AND HIS TIMES

Carpenter, James. *Gore: A Study in Liberal Catholic Thought.* London 1960.

Carpenter S. C. *Church and People, 1789-1889.* London (1933), 1959.

Crosse, G. *Charles Gore: A Biographical Sketch.* London, 1932.

Davies, J. Conway. "Charles Gore," *Theology,* Vol. 25, No. 149 (November, 1932), pp. 259ff.

Latourette, K. S. *Christianity in a Revolutionary Age.* London, 1960 (II), 1962 (IV).

Mozley, J. K. *Some Tendencies in British Theology from the Publication of Lux Mundi to the Present Day.* London, 1951.

Prestige, G. L. *The Life of Charles Gore.* London, 1935.

Ramsey, A. M. *From Gore to Temple: The Development of Anglican Theology between Lux Mundi and the Second World War, 1889-1939.* London, 1960.

Smedes, L. B. *The Incarnation: Trends in Modern Anglican Thought.* Kampen, 1953.

Vidler, A. R. *The Church in an Age of Revolution, 1789 to the Present Day.* London, 1961.

12 THEODORE MINNEMA

Reinhold Niebuhr

I. BIOGRAPHY

REINHOLD NIEBUHR was born an American citizen in Wright, Missouri, on June 21, 1896. This placed him within the American setting of the late nineteenth and early twentieth centuries. His father, Gustav Niebuhr, was a German immigrant who served as pastor to a German immigrant church. Through his father and the immigrant community within which he grew up Niebuhr became exposed to German traditions and culture.

A significant factor in the early life of Niebuhr is his religious background and training. His father was a minister in the Lutheran Church.[1] Primarily through the influence of his father, Niebuhr chose to enter the ministry. He studied at Elmhurst College and Eden Theological Seminary, denominational institutions of the Lutheran Church. After graduating from Eden Seminary he engaged in graduate study at the Divinity School of Yale University. He concentrated his study in problems of epistemology, and after two years he received a Master of Arts degree. At this point he discontinued his formal education because of family needs and because "epistemology bored me . . .

Dr. Theodore Minnema is Associate Professor of Religion and Theology at Calvin College, and author of *The Social Ethics of Reinhold Niebuhr*.

[1] This particular Lutheran denomination was an offshoot of the Prussian Church Union in Germany. In 1934 this Lutheran group united with a Calvinistic group to form the Evangelical and Reformed Church. This latter union in 1956 merged with the Congregational Church which is known as the United Church of Christ. Neibuhr has remained affiliated with these mergers.

and frankly the other side of me came out: I desired relevance rather than scholarship."[2]

In 1915 Niebuhr entered the ministry of the Lutheran Church. His first and only pastorate was the Bethel Evangelical Church in Detroit, Michigan, which he served from 1915 to 1928. His experience in Detroit proved to be one of the most formative influences in the development of his thought and interest. Here the problems of social ethics came into sharp focus. It was a time when the injustices of capitalism were growing acute. Labor was fighting its way into a position of recognition. The social tension between management and labor was being intensified.

Niebuhr deeply involved himself in the struggle between management and labor. The conditions which he observed among the working class committed him to their cause. Their times of poverty were acute. Working conditions were frequently hazardous, and the pressures of mass production were having debilitating effects on the bodies and minds of the workers. These cruel realities tended to be obscured by the many loud claims of economic growth and progress. While these claims were being widely accepted and defended, Niebuhr began seriously to question them. The whole system of capitalism he regarded with increasing suspicion and criticism as its detrimental consequences became apparent.

The policies of Henry Ford, whose automobile industry was centered in Detroit, became for Niebuhr representative of the capitalistic system. While many in America were hailing Ford as the great humanitarian of industry, Niebuhr was severely attacking the policies of Ford.[3] He saw that technical efficiency in producing Ford automobiles was reducing workers to mere cogs in an impersonal assembly line. The "five dollars a day" which Ford established as a minimum appeared at the time to be a very adequate wage. But Niebuhr attacked it as being grossly inadequate because workers had long lay-off periods during times of retooling. Though the workers received five dollars a day, there was no assurance about the number of days that they would work. Niebuhr was particularly sceptical of the humanitarian motives to which Ford appealed in defending his economic policies. Supposedly, his policies were producing great profits for workers, but, as Niebuhr observed, these very same policies were producing even greater profits for Ford himself.

> What a civilization this is! Naive gentlemen with a genius for mechanics suddenly become arbiters over the lives and fortunes of hundreds of thousands. Their moral pretensions are credulously accepted at

[2] June Bingham, *Courage to Change* (1961), p. 83.
[3] *Ibid.*, pp. 129ff.

full value. No one asks whether an industry which can maintain a reserve of a quarter of a billion ought not make some provision for its unemployed.[4]

As a pastor Niebuhr was very sensitive to personal and individual problems. He had the capacity to share meaningfully in and learn from the experiences of his parishioners. For example, he records this visit to an elderly lady nearing death:

> I relearned the essentials of the Christian faith at the bedside of the nice old soul. . . . I was conscious of the nobility which was the fruit of the simple faith of a simple woman; and that was not the only time in parish duties in which I learned the meaning of Christ's prayer: "I thank Thee, Father, that Thou hast withheld these things from the wise and prudent and revealed them unto babes." . . . We in the churches ought to admit more humbly than is our wont that there is a mystery of grace which no one can fathom.[5]

Though a successful pastor, Niebuhr never limited his interests to his immediate pastorate. He participated in social and political affairs, and wrote in various secular and religious journals. He lectured on many college and university campuses. International affairs concerned him deeply, and he increased his knowledge of them through travel abroad.

Through all these varied and broad experiences the theology of Niebuhr underwent a significant development. When he entered the ministry he concurred in the optimistic liberalism of the day, but became increasingly disillusioned with it through his experience of contemporary events. The moralistic creed of liberalism uncritically assumed the goodness of man and the inevitability of human progress. Niebuhr discerned that both assumptions were contradicted when modern man and society were subjected to a thorough analysis. The corrupting element of self-interest in both man and society was too persistent and pervading to be excluded from one's basic assumptions or dismissed as a defect that could be eradicated by human effort and reason. Moral self-deception remained mixed with man's best intentions. The social injustices which accompanied the developments in history made human progress ambiguous. For example, modern science was harnessing the forces of nature in order to preserve and enrich life. Modern technology was making available an economy of abundance promising prosperity and welfare for all. But men were using the instruments of science and technology not only to help man-

---

[4] *Ibid.*, p. 133. Quoting from Niebuhr's book, *Leaves from the Notebook of a Tamed Cynic.*

[5] Charles W. Kegley and Robert W. Bretall (eds.), *Reinhold Niebuhr, His Religious, Social, and Political Thought* (1956), p. 36.

kind but also to exploit it. Science and technology increased the potential of man not only to save life, but also to destroy it. The latter reality was starkly demonstrated by the First World War and its aftermath of social unrest and disorder.

The perplexing and troubling moral situation in both man and society became for Niebuhr the great challenge to which he has never stopped responding. His theological response was a rejection and subsequent ceaseless criticism of one of the basic claims of liberalism, namely, that man has resources within himself for his own perfectibility. Niebuhr shifted his emphasis to the imperfection of man and the incompleteness of human history. He underscored how moral predicaments and evil are inextricably involved in the human situation. Through this negative criticism of man and history he introduced in America a theological perspective that developed into a theological movement variously known as Neo-Orthodoxy, Dialectical Theology, and Christian Realism. In America, Niebuhr has remained the outstanding leader of this theological movement.

In 1928 Niebuhr became Professor of Applied Christianity at Union Theological Seminary in New York City. By this time he had already published one book, *Does Civilization Need Religion?* The academic environment and the opportunities of research in teaching stimulated Niebuhr to even greater theological productivity. For more than three decades he continued to lecture and to publish writings of theological consequence. His work has had a notable impact both nationally and internationally. In 1939 he was honored with the invitation to deliver the 1939-40 Gifford Lectures at the University of Edinburgh, Scotland. These Lectures form the contents of Niebuhr's most systematic and comprehensive work, *The Nature and Destiny of Man.*

The academic environment never caused Niebuhr to withdraw from immediate issues and problems of the day. His life is an exemplary demonstration of working with ultimate and immediate issues at the same time. Theoretical reflection never abstracted him out of the practical affairs of the day. His prodigious activity in social and political affairs cannot be recounted in this brief sketch. Let it be said that Niebuhr never hesitated to associate or join a group or movement which to him promoted social justice and gave aid to men in their moral predicament. "During the thirties and forties there were many permanent or ad hoc organizations doing 'one good thing,' and Niebuhr lent his name to more than a hundred of them."[6]

Two movements which played a particularly important role in Niebuhr's thinking were pacifism and socialism. Shortly after World War I he joined the pacifists and, subsequently, became chairman of the

---

[6] Bingham, *op. cit.*, p. 205.

380

Pacifist Fellowship of Reconciliation. Though an active promoter of pacifism for more than ten years, he eventually rejected the pacifist position on the grounds that it led to moral irresponsibility. For more than a decade he politically identified himself with the Socialist Party. In 1930, though nominated against his will, he was the Socialist Party candidate for Congress on the upper west side of New York City. He resigned from the party in 1940 because of its policies of pacifism and isolation. After this he became active in the Liberal Party, a party limited mainly to the City of New York.

Niebuhr retired in 1960 as the Charles A. Briggs Graduate Professor Emeritus of Ethics and Theology at Union Theological Seminary. He is still active both as lecturer and writer. He continues to reside in New York City.

II. EXPOSITION

DOCTRINE OF MAN

The doctrine of man is fundamental to Niebuhr's system of thought. Early in his career he underwent certain profound disillusionments about man, but never did he lose interest in or concern for man. His disillusionments resulted, however, as we have seen, in a fundamental reinterpretation and reconstruction for the doctrine of man.

A basic source for the study of man is human experience. Niebuhr is well aware that as one interprets human experience certain assumptions and presuppositions are implied. In his approach he chooses to keep assumptions and presuppositions implicit and provisional so as to avoid making experience a mere mirror in which one sees only what his assumptions and presuppositions permit him to see. In this sense he seeks to be a realist by confronting openly the total contents of experience whether they are encouraging or despairing, harmonious or contradictory. In his method he wants to avert the illusions which he believes have befallen many systems of thought. Only after the realities in experience have been thoroughly studied should assumptions and presuppositions be affirmed and where necessary modified. Niebuhr believes that if one remains true to the facts of experience, the Christian faith will be confirmed or at least present the most acceptable answer to the inescapable problems disclosed in human experience.[7]

To Niebuhr one of the most obvious facts of human experience is its contradictoriness. On this note he begins his great work on anthropology,

[7] *Human Destiny* (1946), p. 6; *Christian Realism and Political Problems* (1953), p. 185.

The Nature and Destiny of Man

> Man has always been his most vexing problem. How shall he think
> of himself? Every affirmation which he may make about his stature,
> virtue, or place in the cosmos becomes involved in contradictions when
> fully analysed.[8]

The contradictions which are involved in man's "stature, virtue, or
place in the cosmos" are known and clarified through self-analysis.
The self discovers that what it affirms on one level of its existence it is
forced to deny, at least partially, on another level. For example, the
self through analysis concludes on the one hand that it is a "child of
nature." It obviously participates in the vitalities and processes of nature. On the other hand the affirmation "child of nature" is the conclusion of an analysis and to analyze implies a vantage point above the
object of analysis, implying also that man is more than or "outside" of
nature. But if man attempts to deny consistently his being classified
as a creature of nature with the animals, more contradictions are disclosed. The consistent claim that man is not a "child of nature" is contradicted by man's being unable to disassociate himself completely from
nature. The natural drives, impulses, and processes which remain an
inseparable part of man refute all attempts to abstract man from nature. Furthermore, if man attempts to escape his involvement in nature by identifying himself with reason or his rational capacities, this
again results in a contradiction. To claim reason as a level unique to
man is to imply that man is no more than reason. In order to recognize
and affirm the uniqueness of reason, one must assume a point outside
reason from which recognition and affirmation can be made. In short,
man implies in all his affirmations about himself some point outside or
above that which he affirms.

The foregoing examples expressing the contradictory and dialectical
character of self-analysis set the framework for anthropology. The
framework is constructed around two disharmonious or paradoxical
facts.

> The obvious fact is that man is a child of nature, subject to its
> vicissitudes, compelled by its necessities, driven by its impulses, and
> confined within the brevity of the years which nature permits its
> varied organic forms, allowing them some, but not too much, lati-
> tude. The other less obvious fact is that man is a spirit who stands
> outside of nature, life, himself, his reason, and the world.[9]

[8] *Human Nature* (1946), p. 1.
[9] *Ibid.*, p. 3.

Man or the self exists in an environment of dialectical tension. The tension extends between two paradoxical facts or levels of experience. These levels warrant separate clarification.

Nature is that dimension of existence which stands under laws of necessity and causality. There is movement and process, but it all transpires within given forms and boundaries, such as species and genus. In this realm there are no free decisions and, as a consequence, there is no real history but an "endless repetition within the limits of each given form."[10] These natural forms and vitalities within which man participates give to human existence a creaturely quality. Creatureliness is that aspect of human existence which involves man in the dynamics of nature's vitality and form.

Spirit is a dimension of freedom. It accounts for man's having a vantage point above the facts of nature. Freedom is demonstrated through man's being able to question and challenge not only the forms of nature, but also all rational and conceptual formulations. Man, as Niebuhr emphasizes, has the freedom to "stand outside of" nature and reason. Man can transcend within the activity of consciousness all natural forms and rational formulations. The self has the capacity to project itself to a pinnacle of consciousness where it experiences freedom from the structures of nature and reason.

Something implicit in the above approach must now be made explicit. So far the approach has been the method of self-analysis or self-knowledge. The self knows that it is involved in a dialectical tension between the different levels of nature and spirit. But what exactly is the "self"? Niebuhr writes, quoting Pascal, that the self is one of those "mysteries without which man remains a mystery to himself."[11] Here is a mystery with which thinking begins. The self is an assumption in this context with which one must begin and is not reducible to further antecedent causes. Included in this assumption are certain qualities about the self. It is a power center. It is dynamic and has the capacity to explore and transform its environment. It is involved in nature, but it also can dynamically rise above or transcend the natural level. It can reorder the stuff of nature through rational reconstruction. The rational level of consciousness the self can also transcend, meaning that what the self forms through reason, it can stand above as judge and dispose of as it sees fit. The dynamic capacity of the self becomes most mysterious when it transcends not only nature and reason, but itself by making itself its own object through self-consciousness. Self-consciousness is a phenomenon that demonstrates in experience the dimension of the eternal, a final type of freedom. It is the point at which

[10] *Ibid.,* p. 26.
[11] *Christian Realism and Political Problems* (1953), p. 179.

the self expresses the "capacity of standing continually outside itself in terms of indefinite regression,"[12] or "infinite regression."[13] This peak of transcendence is where "the self makes itself its own object in such a way that the ego is finally always subject and not object."[14] Here the self, as subject, confronts no object or temporal limitations, but the dimension of absolute freedom, the eternal and the infinite.

A summary definition of the self in terms of consciousness is as follows:

> The fact is that there is no escape from the "rational absurdity" of the real self because it is at once in time and beyond time. It is spatial and yet non-spatial. And there is no sharp distinction between its spatial and non-spatial dimensions. Yet this double fact, which outrages the sense of rational coherence, is a fact of daily experience.[15]

Basic ingredients for Niebuhr's doctrine of man are existential phenomena or the phenomena of self-consciousness. Consequently, in Niebuhr's thought the terms man and self are used interchangeably. Man is approached in terms of his vertical structure and not first of all in terms of chronological history. The vertical levels of consciousness, rather than the historical sequence of facts (such as, Creator, creation, fall, and redemption), are the immediate framework for interpreting the doctrine of man. The doctrine of man is reconstructed through the existential principle of self-transcendence. It is within this anthropological framework that other basic Christian doctrines are reinterpreted and reconstructed.

Doctrine of Sin

The doctrine of sin holds a prominent place in the theology of Niebuhr. In his writings the evils of society receive the major emphasis. He has rendered a great service through his profound analysis of the ethical tension between different power centers in human history. Though social tensions are of primary concern, they are interpreted as reverberations of deeper tensions in individual man. Evil is rooted in human nature and is not just a social problem. Conflicts in society arise out of inner conflicts in man.

The source of the inner conflicts in man is the duality of his nature. On the one hand the human self is conscious of its involvement in nature and finiteness with their threats of change, decay, and death. On the other hand the self through the dimension of spirit and freedom consciously transcends the limits of nature. This dimension is the

12 *Human Nature* (1946), p. 13.
13 *Ibid.*, p. 277.
14 *Ibid.*, p. 14.
15 *Ibid.*, p. 24.

higher level of consciousness, such as the imagination, from which the self can anticipate the perils of nature and seek to escape them. This double awareness of nature and spirit, of being threatened by forces of nature and of being able to gain a perspective of escape from them, creates in man an inner tension, which Niebuhr terms anxiety. Anxiety is the full consciousness of the existential dimensions of life.[16]

The self needs an answer to the problem of its anxiety. It wants a security that overcomes the dangers and threats of nature and makes permanent the perfections envisioned from the perspective of spirit and freedom. This pursuit for an ultimate security is involved in all the human achievements of history and culture. History and culture result from man's expanding power or transcendence over his dualistic environment. Man through his power seeks to increase his security. For example, science and technology are forms of human power that are used to increase human security within the forces and processes of nature. Reason as an instrument for re-ordering life and society into various forms of community is another form of power that can be employed for the promotion of greater security.

Security through power instead of solving man's problem eventually intensifies it. Power in history leads to contradictory results for man. It both increases and decreases his security. For example, science is a historical force that has increased human security through its preserving of life as demonstrated in modern medicine. But science also increases insecurity by producing great threats to life such as the possibility of a thermonuclear war. The historical process appears to refute the assumption that more power means more security.

In human relations the same power-insecurity dilemma exists. Man resorts to power over others to make himself secure. Man assumes that the more supremacy he has, the greater will be his security. Self-interest is made the road to security. The consequence is conflict. Supremacy is maintained only by forcing others to submit who in turn have power to oppose. The more a man extends his position by domination, the more he increases the insecurity of his position, because domination aggravates the power potential in others. An example is the tyrant who, though in a position of extreme power, is also extremely insecure because of the inevitable resistance that tyranny provokes.

The power-insecurity dilemma is found also in collective man. Social groups seek security through power even as individual man.

> The most important similarity between the life of individuals and collective organisms is that the latter, like the former, have the same

[16] *Ibid.*, p. 182.

sense of the contingent and insecure character of human existence and they seek by the same pride and lust for power to hide or to overcome that insecurity.[17]

Groups are organized and competing centers of power.[18] A measure of harmony between social centers of power is possible through a balance of power. Whatever social center holds the preponderance of power will be temporarily most secure, but its very preponderance will also increase its insecurity through increased tension with other competing social centers. The domineering self-interest impulse in social groups accounts for injustice in group relations.

The root of evil is man's misinterpretation and misuse of power. In his insecurity man individually and collectively infects his power with a force destructive of others. Human power in itself is not evil; history does witness to its creative and constructive use, and man does through his power preserve life and promote harmony in human relations. Life is not complete anarchy. However, in all the human achievements which preserve and promote life, a contradiction emerges. The power that produces human accomplishments and order produces destruction and disorder.

> The same action may reveal a creative effort to transcend natural limitations, and a sinful effort to give an unconditioned value to contingent and limited factors in human existence.[19]

At this point one may ask the question, why is man so insecure that he falls into the evil of both misinterpreting and misusing his power? The fact that he does is for Niebuhr amply demonstrated through history and experience. But could man develop into a virtuous being who perfectly interprets and uses his power so as to avoid destruction and disorder? It is in answer to this latter question that certain biblical perspectives in the thought of Niebuhr become explicit. For he believes that not only does experience now testify to the universality of evil, but in history evil remains "inevitable."[20]

The inevitability of evil, which underscores Niebuhr's divergence from theological liberalism, is explicated by means of the doctrine of original sin. Original sin is defined within the structure of self-consciousness. There is a level of self-consciousness which is free from original sin. It is the level of anxiety in which there is an awareness of insecurity within the existential dimensions of nature and spirit, finite-

---

[17] *Faith and History* (1949), p. 218.
[18] Niebuhr thoroughly explores this theme in *Moral Man and Immoral Society* (1932).
[19] *Human Nature* (1946), pp. 183f.
[20] *Ibid.*, pp. 251ff.

386

ness and freedom. "Anxiety alone is neither actual nor original sin."[21]

The inevitability of sin arises on the level of the human will. The human will produces concrete actions. These actions never fulfill the demands of anxiety. Anxiety is created by the infinite demands of spirit and freedom in relation to nature. Human and historical actions always have within them natural qualities of finiteness and temporality. Sin occurs inevitably because the paradoxical dimensions of nature and spirit, finiteness and freedom, can never be harmonized in human action. Therefore, sin is to a degree the result of human finiteness.

> This weakness is partly due to finiteness. The propulsive powers of the self, with its natural survival impulse, do not suffice to fulfill the obligations which the self as free spirit discerned.[22]

But the weakness is not merely one of finiteness, because the consciousness of man has within it a sense of guilt or responsibility for the evil in its actions. "The fact of responsibility is attested by the feeling of remorse or repentance which follows the sinful action."[23] The facts of guilt and remorse disclose that evil is a consequence of freedom and not mere necessity. The self through its inner capacity of transcendence and freedom contemplates its actions and "discovers that some degree of conscious dishonesty accompanied the act, which means that the self was not deterministically and blindly involved in it."[24] By "conscious dishonesty" is meant that the self or man perversely interprets his power of will and its achievements as possessing the perfections of pure spirit, such as absoluteness, infinity, and ultimacy. The anxiety of man has within it the demands which only God has the qualities to fulfill, but man abortively seeks fulfillment of such transcendent demands in himself, his history, and the culture which he produces.[25] Man creates false finite gods to relieve an anxiety which only the transcendent God can relieve.

The interpreting of original sin with respect to the complexities of the moral consciousness of man substantially alters the traditional and evangelical doctrine of original sin. By original sin Niebuhr does not mean evil in its entire sweep of history beginning with the fall of Adam. Original sin is a perverse inclination which is presupposed in each individual human act. It is not a biblical-historical category, but "a dialectical truth which does justice to the fact that man's self-love and self-centeredness are inevitable, but not in such a way as to fit into the

---

21 *Ibid.*, p. 250.
22 *Human Destiny* (1946), p. 108.
23 *Human Nature* (1946), p. 255.
24 *Ibid.*
25 *The Self and the Dramas of History* (1955), pp. 20-22.

category of natural necessity."[26] It is a presupposition which must be affirmed to prevent "natural necessity" in man from becoming sheer moral determinism or fatalism. Original sin explains evil as being inevitable, yet man remains responsible because he has an inner freedom, a moment or level of transcendence over his action which contradicts the inevitability of original sin. In his consciousness man keeps returning after each guilty action back to the sinless moment of anxiety with all its existential ingredients of nature and spirit, finiteness and freedom. Original sin is disclosed in that moment of guilt in the consciousness of man subsequent to imperfect human action.

DOCTRINE OF CHRIST

The power-insecurity predicament finds an answer in Christ. Christology in the thought of Niebuhr is an inseparable counterpart to anthropology. In Christology there is a clarification and answer to the problem of "inevitable" evil as found in anthropology.

Niebuhr does not construct Christology independent of the human situation. Christology for him is not a doctrine defined by itself and then related to human affairs. He does not first establish the truth of Christ and then proceed to the application of this truth to history. The truth of Christ is explicated in terms of the relevance of Christ. Relevance is achieved through the uncovering in Christ of elements which are common to the human situation, uniquely different from it, and complementary to it.

Niebuhr made fundamental to his anthropology the dimension of spirit. By virtue of spirit, man in his self-consciousness has the capacity to stand continually "outside" himself in terms of "indefinite regression." This concept "outside" takes on an explicit Christian meaning in relation to Christ. The "outside" dimension, disclosed through the analysis of self-consciousness, in Jesus Christ corresponds to "otherworldliness." Jesus taught the dimension of spirit and the freedom of the self to transcend nature and reason by emphasizing values that were impossible of realization in human history. The ethical values which Jesus taught in the Sermon on the Mount are outside the natural order as it is now experienced. They are spiritual ideals of another world which contradict the existential world of the here and now. Concerning the Gospel ethic Niebuhr writes:

> The ultimate moral demands upon man can never be affirmed in terms of the actual facts of human existence. They can be affirmed

[26] *Human Nature* (1946), p. 263.

388

only in terms of a unity and a possibility, a divine reality which transcends human existence.[27]

The tension between ethics of Jesus and the moral achievements of this world was primarily a tool of critical analysis in the earlier writings of Niebuhr. He criticized liberalism for obscuring the ethical tension between the Gospel and society.[28] The Gospel as found in the Sermon on the Mount was not a morally and socially attainable goal as claimed among liberals, but an "impossible possibility."[29] Liberalism had removed the existential tension from the teachings of Jesus. In contrast Niebuhr stressed the tension of contradiction between the ethical demands of Jesus and the ethical possibilities of history, this contradiction being analogous to the one between spirit and nature, freedom and finiteness.

Orthodoxy comes under Niebuhr's criticism for pessimistically dismissing the ethics of Jesus as being irrelevant to sinful human society. Orthodoxy severed the ethical tension between the Sermon on the Mount and the realities of history by simply emphasizing the impossibility of it all. It failed to recognize that even though Jesus constructed an ethic impossible of fulfillment, yet it had relevance. It was an ethic which gave meaning and urgency to all moral striving when it was properly related to history.

The relation between the ethics of Jesus and history Niebuhr explains as being paradoxical rather than just contradictory.[30] The term paradox which includes the tension of contradiction also implies for Niebuhr a relation of concurrence. Gospel and history must eventually be comprehended within a unity if the relation between them is to remain meaningful. On the one hand, such a unity must take seriously the discontinuity between the Gospel ethic and all historical attempts to realize this ethic in the forms of human love and justice. On the other hand, this unity must give relevance to the Gospel ethic. It must avoid reducing the Gospel ethic to a norm which simply places all forms of historical justice and love under condemnation without offering moral growth and progress.

The problem of unity between Gospel and history corresponds to the human predicament of the self existing in the paradoxical dimensions of spirit and nature. The Gospel-history relation is the common human predicament stated in biblical terms. "The real fact is that

---

27 *An Interpretation of Christian Ethics* (1935), p. 50.
28 *Does Civilization Need Religion* (1927), pp. 171, 172.
29 *An Interpretation of Christian Ethics* (1935), pp. 58-60.
30 *Ibid.*, p. 57.

the absolute character of the ethic of Jesus conforms to the actual con-stitution of man and history."[31]

The uniqueness of Christ is found particularly in the Cross. The Cross symbolizes the perfection which gives the final clarification and answer to the evil in the human situation.

> In apprehending the Cross as the symbol of the ultimate perfection Christian faith has always been profounder than the theologies which sought to rationalize it. For faith has consistently regarded the Cross as the point in history where the sinful rivalries of ego with ego are transcended; and it has not tried with too much consistency to fit every action of the historical Jesus into the symbol of per-fection.[32]

The Cross is like a lighted prism standing at the intersection of time and eternity, history and the trans-historical. It refracts beams of light into human history and also into eternity. It reveals some-thing about man and also about God. The one Cross discloses dif-ferent things according to the direction of approach.

When approached from the side of human history, the Cross dis-closes "The Possibilities and Limits of History."[33] It makes known the ethical norm of perfection in history. Imperfection and evil are not normative for history as one might be tempted to conclude from human experience. The Cross is where Christ witnessed to what man and history ought to be. It reveals the possibility of perfection to history.

The specific content of the perfection in the Cross is "sacrificial love." This "sacrificial love" from the point of view of history has all the aspects of "impossibility" or "foolishness." It was an act in which the self gave up all its historical claims. In terms of history it was a complete self-sacrifice. On the Cross the self did not exercise power to preserve itself. In the insecurity of the moment, the self (Christ) did not yield to the temptation of exercising its power to maintain itself. Hence on the Cross something "impossible" was transacted. There was power present without the sin of self-interest which according to Niebuhr is inevitable when the self exercises its power in history. The Cross as perfect power cannot be harmoniously embodied in a historical form. Therefore, its historical form is a symbol embodying the paradox of power as "powerlessness."

> It is impossible to symbolize the divine goodness in history in any other way than by complete powerlessness, or rather by a consistent refusal to use power in the rivalries of history. For there is no self

[31] *Human Destiny* (1946), p. 50.
[32] *Ibid.*, pp. 72, 73.
[33] *Ibid.*, Chapter III.

in history or society, no matter how impartial its perspective upon the competitions of life, which can rise to the position of a disinterested participation in those rivalries and competitions. It can symbolize disinterested love only by a refusal to participate in the rivalries. Any participation in them means the assertion of one ego interest against another.[34]

"Sacrificial love" as norm corresponds to the dimension of freedom in human nature. It assumes a freedom to transcend or stand "outside" all natural impulses and necessities.

The Cross as norm can only be meaningful in the total context of time and eternity. Though the Cross stands in history it needs more than history for its interpretation. Niebuhr writes: "It is an act in history; but it cannot justify itself in history."[35]

To say that the Cross "cannot justify itself in history" means that it is an action which does not involve itself in corresponding historical benefits. From the point of view of history the Cross appears very unjust and "foolish." "Sacrificial love" on the Cross is the giving up of everything in history and the receiving of nothing in history in return. But to faith the Cross is more than history. It is a disclosure from God, and in this disclosure God "justifies" the Cross. He does this by bestowing very meaningful benefits upon history through the Cross.

In the Cross, God makes clear his relations to history. He has a dual relation of wrath and of mercy or forgiveness. Divine wrath is manifested in the suffering of Christ. In the suffering of Christ, God reveals his opposition to human evil. But the Cross also discloses mercy and forgiveness because the suffering of Christ represents God taking upon Himself the consequences of sin through His Son. God transcends his wrath by fulfilling the demands of perfection Himself. This fulfillment means forgiveness for man and history. It means that God's final relation to history is one of sovereign love in which God overcomes the evil disorders of history by voluntarily suffering their effects Himself.

The revelation of God in Christ is known through its relevance. This relevance is discerned by faith, but it is further validated by experience. The relevance of Christ is demonstrated in that He fits the structural needs of man. He is a necessary counterpart of history with its incompleteness and ethical corruptions. The judgment or wrath of God makes man conscious of his having corrupted life through self-interest and false claims of perfection. It creates contrition or despair which opens man to the truth of his situation that he is finite

---

[34] *Ibid.*, p. 72.
[35] *Ibid.*, p. 68.

and guilty of denying his finiteness. But judgment is only part of the truth. The complete truth is that God is merciful. To the contrite He extends forgiveness by perfecting all the imperfect strivings of man and offers power for renewed ethical effort.[36]

Christ as the counterpart to history answers man's moral problem, but does not annul the problem.[37] The self remains involved in the paradoxical dimensions of nature and spirit. The self remains in all its actions guilty for not realizing its true norm. Within the limits of history, condemnation of evil remains valid in relation to God. But man is offered a perspective of faith in which he apprehends, in Christ, that even though God condemns evil within the limits of history, God has a freedom which transcends history. Through this power of transcendence God perfects and meaningfully completes the moral efforts of man in history.[38] However, God's transcending fulfillment of history and history itself do not coalesce, but remain in dialectical relation even as spirit and nature in man.

In Christ there are both "wisdom" and "power." The "wisdom" aspect has been dealt with in some detail in the discussion of Christ as the norm of history. The "power" of Christ, though in experience inseparable from the "wisdom" of Christ, receives further explication in Niebuhr's doctrine of grace.

DOCTRINE OF GRACE OR SALVATION

Grace has two aspects, "the conquest of sin in the heart of man on the one hand, and the merciful power of God over the sin which is never entirely overcome in any human heart, on the other."[39] The power of God in man is the sanctifying grace of God which makes the believer into a new creature. The power of God over man is justifying grace which renders to man forgiveness and righteousness. A factor to be reckoned with in addition to these two aspects of grace is sin. Grace in the believer gives a new source and center to life, but sin remains present.

The two aspects of grace Niebuhr clarifies by relating them to the moral experience of man. A good example of how Niebuhr relates grace to the believer is his explanation of Galatians 2:20.[40] In this passage Niebuhr sees the recipient of grace as the existential self dy-

---

[36] *Ibid.*, p. 57.
[37] *Ibid.*, p. 97.
[38] *Ibid.*, pp. 54, 55.
[39] *Ibid.*, p. 100.
[40] "I am crucified with Christ: nevertheless I live; yet not I, but Christ liveth in me: and the life which I now live in the flesh I live by the faith of the Son of God, who loved me, and gave himself for me."

namically involved on various levels of existence ranging from the
limitations of nature to the freedom of spirit. He interprets this passage as "an application of a very comprehensive and profound Pauline
text to the moral and spiritual experience of man."[41] The application
is divided into a series of existential moments or levels in the moral
and spiritual life of man.

1. "I am crucified with Christ." This phrase describes the initial
working of grace. Grace is an experience which originates as an intervention in the human consciousness. It is sensed by the "I" as a
deeper inner disruption. "The first assertion of his (Paul's) interpretation is that the old, the sinful self, the self which is centered in itself,
must be 'crucified.' It must be shattered and destroyed."[42] The "I" or
self here presupposed is the "I" on the level of "original sin." It is
the self which cannot escape preoccupation with itself and the sin of
self-interest. Grace, which in this context is identified with the words
"crucified with Christ," is the holiness and wrath of God disintegrating
the self into despair and repentance.

2. "Nevertheless I live." The negative character of this phrase is
interpreted as underscoring the identity of the self after its renewal.
To be "crucified with Christ" does not destroy selfhood but restores
it. The "I live" is the self set free from its premature and abortive
attempts to perfect itself according to its partial and limited perspectives. It is set free as a consequence of a "power" or "grace" from
beyond itself. This freedom is a level of experience in the act of self-
transcendence. "This new self is the real self; for the self is infinitely
self-transcendent; and any premature centering of itself around its own
interests, individually or collectively, destroys and corrupts its freedom."[43]

3. "Yet not I, but Christ liveth in me." Up to this point grace has
been described primarily as the power which shatters the old sinful self
and renews the self to the level of existential freedom. The further
significant problem is how grace functions as sanctification and justification. The third phrase in the passage indicates the distinction between grace as sanctification and as justification.

The negative assertion, "Yet not I," Niebuhr terms the "negation of
the negation."[44] The preceding phrase, "Nevertheless I live," was interpreted as a denial that the self had been destroyed through the experience of being "crucified with Christ." Now this denial is made

[41] *Human Destiny* (1946), p. 107.
[42] *Ibid.*, p. 108.
[43] *Ibid.*, p. 110.
[44] *Ibid.*, p. 114.

subject to another denial, "Yet not I; but Christ liveth in me." This final denial, or the "negation of the negation" is regarded, even as the foregoing assertions in the text, as an existential moment and level of moral experience. This final level concurs with the foregoing levels in asserting the transcendent source of grace and the preserved identity of the human self. However, on this level grace reveals a double meaning or inner distinction. It reveals that the "new self" is not only a fruit of a "power not our own," but its newness is in a certain sense incomplete. It contains the affirmation that the "new self is never an accomplished reality."[45] Grace on this final level is experienced not only as a sanctifying "power not our own," but also as a justifying action in which divine mercy completes and perfects the self insofar as it "is never an accomplished reality."

The fact that "the new self is never an accomplished reality" does not of itself posit the necessity of continued forgiving grace. It may mean that the new self is merely in process toward perfection and not in contradiction to what perfection demands. To assert the continued necessity of forgiving and justifying grace one must also assume that in the new life generated by grace a contradiction "between human self-will and the divine purpose remains."[46] The presence of such a contradiction in the believer Niebuhr finds taught in "Yet not I, but Christ liveth in me." The new self, though it accepts Christ as norm, experiences fulfillment of the norm "by faith." The existential self, though renewed in Christ, conforms to perfection never actually but only through intention. It never fully realizes what it intends. Consequently, it sins and remains in continued need of forgiveness and justification. This conclusion Niebuhr finds further supported in the final words of the text, "And the life which I now live in the flesh I live by the faith of the Son of God, who loved me, and gave himself for me."

Niebuhr's explanation of Galatians 2:20 in terms of existential levels of experience is certainly debatable on the basis of careful exegesis. But exegesis is not in this instance Niebuhr's concern. His concern is "with the relevance of the biblical doctrine of grace to the experiences of life."[47] The experiences of life disclose a persistent contradiction between perfection and concrete historical action. According to logic grace as sanctification would seem to eliminate the necessity of continued justification, but "the experience of the Christian ages refutes those who follow this logic without qualification."[48] There is an exis-

---

[45] *Ibid.*
[46] *Ibid.,* p. 121.
[47] *Ibid.,* p. 119.
[48] *Ibid.,* p. 122.

tential level where the self experiences renewal and another level where the self remains guilty. "It happens to be true to the facts of experience that in one sense the converted man is righteous and that in another sense he is not."[49]

In the experience of grace a certain hiatus remains between the initial work of grace and its completion. Initially grace gives rise to new selfhood. The new self receives Christ as norm. But in experience the new self and its norm remain in partial tension and discontinuity. The hiatus and discontinuity between the new self and its norm underscores the necessity of historically complementing sanctifying grace with justifying grace.

Justification forms the capstone to the victory of grace. It is victory to which experience and history point, but which they never embrace. Grace in experience and history, that is, sanctifying grace, looks beyond itself for its own fulfillment. It continues to confess imperfection both in the profession of truth and virtue. The very fruit of grace is that historical truth and virtue remain problematical.

> This is the paradox of grace applied to the truth. The truth, as it is contained in the Christian revelation, includes the recognition that it is neither possible for man to know the truth fully nor to avoid the error of pretending that he does.[50]

Grace in history lives by the admission that all perfection and fulfillment is beyond history. What Niebuhr means by final fulfillment beyond history is found in his teachings of eschatology.

DOCTRINE OF ESCHATOLOGY

When explaining the completion and fulfillment of history, Niebuhr assumes, even as he does in all the different aspects of his theology, the paradoxical nature of human existence. In human existence there are two forms of termination corresponding to the two dimensions in human nature. There is physical death, a point in time when man ceases to be, corresponding to his nature-finiteness dimension, and there is also a termination of life which connotes the attainment of a purpose. "By reason of man's rational freedom the 'end' has another meaning. It is the purpose and goal of his life and work. It is *telos*."[51] The end as *telos* corresponds to the freedom-spirit dimension in man by virtue of which he projects the moral and spiritual goal of ever-widening unity and harmony. This goal, as sacrificial love or perfect unity with God and man, is above nature and history.

---

[49] *Ibid.*, p. 125.
[50] *Ibid.*, p. 217.
[51] *Ibid.*, p. 287; also *Faith and History* (1949), p. 235.

The end of life as *telos* is the form of termination to which the various eschatological symbols of the New Testament apply. The *finis* of man as a natural-finite creature threatens all the trans-natural goals and unities for which man as a free spirit strives. To this threat and peril of meaninglessness the doctrine of eschatology gives an answer. It is a revelation which illumines the *telos* of history which man as a "child of nature" cannot realize.

The dialectical framework out of which Niebuhr interprets the contents of Christian revelation gives to eschatological symbols a double character. They are relevant to history, but they themselves are trans-historical. They have meaning for history, but they themselves are not a point in history. Their double and dialectical character accounts for the position that these symbols must be taken "seriously" but not "literally."[52]

The "serious" character of the eschatological symbols is validated by their correspondence to the whole ethical and historical problem of man. They clarify and keep meaningful the whole dialectical relation between eternity and time, God and man. The "parousia," the "last judgment," and the "resurrection" all in a peculiar way keep the ethical problem of history clearly defined, and they constitute the fulfillment and perfecting of history which the "first" coming of Christ and the grace of God in history anticipate.

The "parousia" symbolizes the triumphant return of Christ. The Christ, who entered history and witnessed to the sovereignty of God through "suffering love," comes again as Victor. His victorious return indicates that the norm of history will not always be fulfilled in the tensional and paradoxical form of "suffering love." For if the norm of existence is interpreted as being eternally in tension with an opposing force, a dualism results in which the sovereignty of God and His love is imperiled. The Christian in history accepts the norm of life as being "suffering love," but through faith apprehends that beyond history love is triumphant.[53]

The interpreting of the triumphant return of Christ as a trans-historical event clarifies the false extremes at which man tends to arrive when judging the historical process. It refutes the false optimism of utopianism which projects a complete ethical and moral triumph in the temporal-historical order. "Against utopianism the Christian faith insists that the final consummation of history lies beyond the conditions of the temporal process." At the same time it rejects other-worldliness by interpreting the "end" as the fulfilling of history rather than as a simple negation. The trans-historical form of the triumphant

[52] *Ibid.*, pp. 236, 237.
[53] *Human Destiny* (1946), p. 290.

return of Christ holds the opposite extremes of utopianism and other-worldliness in a dialectical unity.[54]

The "last judgment," a symbol subordinate to the parousia, clarifies subordinate ethical tensions in the dialectical structure of history. Even though in history a certain contradiction is experienced between time and eternity, between nature and spirit, the last judgment by Christ means that man is finally judged by a norm which corresponds to true manhood. Man is judged according to his sin and not his finiteness. "Christ as judge means that when the historical confronts the eternal it is judged by its own ideal possibility, and not by the contrast between the finite and the eternal character of God."[55]

Judgment further signifies the seriousness of good and evil in history. Though in history the ambiguity of good and evil remains inescapable, God does not accept this situation with indifference. The last judgment underscores the gravity of historical decision. "The very rigour with which all judgments in history culminate in a final judgment is thus an expression of meaningfulness of all historic conflicts between good and evil."[56]

The final significance of the last judgment lies in its emphasis upon the double character of all historical striving. In history good and evil are always inseparably involved in human action. There is no complete fulfillment and perfection in any human achievement. The last judgment, insofar as it is a *last* judgment, accentuates this ethical hiatus in all historical efforts. As a final judgment, in which time and history culminate, it means that ultimately all human works are called into question. And that all works are questioned and judged rules out the idea that any historical accomplishment is perfect enough to stand beyond ethical scrutiny and criticism.[57]

The "resurrection" is the eschatological symbol which points to the harmonious culmination of the whole human enterprise, and yet consistently maintains the dialectical tension of history. The spirit-freedom and the nature-finite dimensions of human life exclude the possibility of a final unity and harmony in history. For this reason a false unity is often reached by dissolving the tension between these dimensions. A purely spiritual conception of fulfillment as a non-corporeal existence falsifies the significance of the natural-finite dimension. A literalistic conception of fulfillment annuls the permanently transcending character of the spirit-freedom dimension over natural and rational categories.[58]

[54] *Ibid.,* p. 291; also *Faith and History* (1949), p. 291.
[55] *Human Destiny* (1946), p. 292.
[56] *Ibid.,* pp. 292, 293.
[57] *Ibid.,* p. 293.
[58] *Ibid.,* pp. 295, 297.

The resurrection, as an eschatological symbol, properly recognizes the twofold character of life with its unavoidable conflicts, and makes clear that ultimately the two dimensions of existence will be harmonized. The permanent tension in history between spirit and nature is upheld in that the resurrection is accomplished by a power outside of history, that is, God. Only a power outside of history can overcome the conflict of power in history. The ultimate harmony of spirit and nature, eternity and time is witnessed in the resurrection of the body. The bodily resurrection testifies to the final unity governing the present historical tensions of spirit and nature. The new "spiritual body" represents a transfiguring of the spirit-nature dialectic into a unity of fulfillment.[59]

The *telos* of history, as comprehended in the eschatological symbols of the Bible, conforms to and fulfills the whole existential situation of man. It forms a trans-historical counterpart to the tensions of power and grace in history without annulling these tensions. Some of the various interrelations between grace in man and the eschatological grace beyond man should be traced in order to gain a more comprehensive view of Niebuhr's conception of fulfillment.

Grace in man was an experience of new selfhood and victory over sin. This victory, which in experience and history remains problematical or "a having and not having of the final virtue and truth,"[60] in the symbol of Christ's return is revealed as actually accomplished. Grace in man, which gives rise to new and ever-widening obligations, in the symbol of the last judgment is enforced. The struggle to improve self and history through ethical decision finds corresponding support in a last judgment which will examine all ethical efforts. Finally, the grace in history, which prompts man to take history seriously as a sanctifying process, is vouchsafed in the symbol of the resurrection. In the resurrection all the meaningful struggles to sanctify life and history are preserved and transfigured into a final harmony.

Eschatology forms the final acts of God to justify and fulfill history.

DOCTRINE OF REVELATION

In the preceding material the term "symbol" was used in reference to revelation. Another term which Niebuhr uses synonymously with "symbol" is "myth." The meaning of these terms is significant to an understanding of Niebuhr's conception of revelation.

---

[59] *Ibid.*, p. 298; also *The Self and the Dramas of History* (1955), pp. 237, 238.

[60] *Faith and History* (1949), p. 240.

Revelation presupposes a relation between God and man, eternity and history. This relation Niebuhr believes to be dialectical. A good summary of what Niebuhr means by a dialectical relation between God and history is the following statement:

> The relation between the temporal and the eternal is dialectical. The eternal is revealed and expressed in the temporal but not exhausted in it. God is not the sum total of finite occasions and relationships. He is their ground and they are the creation of His will.[61]

By means of the dialectical relation Niebuhr holds in tension two apparently contradictory claims concerning God. On the one hand, God as the ground and fulfillment of existence lies "outside of existence," "separate and distinct from the temporal world." On the other hand, God is "revealed and expressed in the temporal" and finiteness is the "creation of his will." God is transcendent to history and yet involved in history.

At this point a theological problem emerges that is common to the history of Christian doctrine. Does the transcendence of God rule out the direct identification of God in history through conceptual categories? Does the transcendence of God exclude a relation of continuity between God and history?

In answering the theological problem involved in the foregoing questions Niebuhr places the emphasis on God's transcendence over and discontinuity with history. God cannot be defined positively in conceptual and temporal categories. "From the standpoint of human thought this unconditioned ground of existence, this God, can be defined only negatively."[62] Man confronts God but he can never identify God with human and historical concepts. "He contemplates the eternal but he cannot name it. When he names it he gives it a name which introduces, again, his own finite perspectives."[63]

A negation must be applied to all the revelation of God in history. God reveals himself in history, but what God reveals of Himself must not be identified with the form in which revelation comes. The form of revelation is "symbol" or "myth," while its content consists of a meaningful disclosure of God. The "symbol" itself may be a product of the primitive mind and imagination, but its content is a profound revelation of the meaning of life and of ultimate truth. For example the fall of man is "myth" or "symbol." "The fall is not historical. It does not take place in any concrete human act."[64] But it does significantly contribute to the meaning of life. It gives a

---

[61] *Beyond Tragedy* (1937), p. 4.
[62] *Human Destiny* (1946), p. 14.
[63] *Beyond Tragedy* (1937), p. 61.
[64] *Ibid.*, p. 11.

framework of meaning to the guilt factor in human consciousness. Man is guilty before God because evil is not a defect in creation, but arises in the freedom of man to transcend nature and creation. The "myth" of the fall clarifies the inward experience of guilt in relation to human freedom.[65]

The dichotomy between meaning and historical form accounts for the use of "symbol" and "myth" in reference to revelation. These terms represent a historical and immanent formulation of that which is transcendent. A "symbol" or "myth" in itself is never to be directly identified with the divine or God. Through the "symbol" the divine becomes transparent and meaningful to man in history even though historical categories can never embody the divine.

To avoid misunderstanding, it should be made clear that revelation as "symbol" does not mean that revelation is fiction or a product of the imagination. The reality of God and His revelation Niebuhr maintains. But since the reality of God has been defined as a dialectical relation of transcendence to all that is immanent and human, no immanent or human form can be directly identified with God. The "symbol" does represent a negation of continuity between God and man, but at the same time it points to God as a reality in relation to man.

The "symbol" in a certain sense qualifies the radical discontinuity between man and God. To insist, as Niebuhr does, that the "symbol" is meaningful and representative of the divine is to posit a form of organic unity between God and the historical process. Between God and man there is an analogy which functions in and through the "symbol."

Furthermore, Niebuhr's respect for and continual reference to the biblical "symbols" indicate a certain trust in Scripture as that place where the unity between God and history transpires in a distinctive way.[66] His conception of "symbol" rules out an absolute dualism between God and man, the transcendent and the historical. However, it does provide him with a provisional dualism which keeps all the contents of history, biblical "symbols" included, in a dialectical tension.

Niebuhr's conception of divine transcendence rests upon the assumption that divine transcendence and self-transcendence are continuous. Transcendence is not a realm unique to God, but a depth in human reality.[67] Consequently, it is in the human consciousness that God is directly accessible, particularly, in the act of self-tran-

[65] *Ibid.,* p. 12.
[66] *Christian Realism and Political Problems* (1953), pp. 197-199.
[67] *Human Nature* (1946), pp. 126, 127; also *Human Destiny* (1946), p. 299.

scendence in which a man's self stands "outside of nature, life, himself, his reason, and the world."[68]

The direct continuity between transcendence and self-consciousness is the basis upon which the problematic character of "symbols" rests. The "symbols" represent the transcendent, while the human consciousness is the point where transcendence is immediately apprehended. Therefore, in the religious consciousness the symbolic representations of the transcendent can be simultaneously set up and negated.

III. EVALUATION

Niebuhr offers a challenging reconstruction of Christian doctrine. He has formulated doctrine in the crucible of contemporary experience and history. Between the contemporary world and the Christian Gospel Niebuhr has promoted a mutual confrontation and exposure.

His perceptive analyses of the modern world in many ways are very convincing. It is not that Niebuhr analyzes all the major problems of modern man, though he does analyze an unusually large number throughout his writings, but he has given an approach and method which remain useful in the continuing analysis of human culture.

The defining of man in dynamic terms fits well the concrete human situation. Man at the level of common self-reflection regards himself in a number of changing ways. He is, as Niebuhr underscores, a self who is aware of various levels of existence ranging from the lower impulses of appetite to the higher ideal levels of spirit and destiny. That these levels in man cause inner conflicts and contradictions is a fact most people know painfully well.

The reducing of the problem in man to the problem of power is a profound simplification that throws much light on the complexity of human evil. That the ego as a center of power is inclined to over-extend itself in terms of reason and act of will is a neat way of getting at a root common to evil. Individually it makes clear an indictment that too often lies submerged in the obscurity of the subconscious. The power of self-interest, the power of pride to dominate others, and the power of the appetites that tempt to self-indulgence Niebuhr has made inescapably evident in man by means of a simple but incisive diagnosis.

The same formula of approaching life in dynamic terms and making power the central issue lends clarity to the complicated disorders of society. History is replete with evidence of social groups, from the size of the family to the larger bodies of people such as nations and empires, who live in the tension of power. Wars, exploitation, unjust

[68] *Ibid.,* p. 3.

discrimination, and other forms of social disorder all prove upon analysis to have roots in the abuse of power.

The fundamental position that power holds in Niebuhr's system of thought gives it an affinity with the mentality of modern man. A cursory look at modern culture indicates that power is the center of human interest. This interest for many is a sign of their faith. Power in its scientific form, social form, or material form is interpreted as a way to salvation. It is at this point that Niebuhr, I believe, has made one of his greatest contributions.

Niebuhr has underscored the dilemma in human power. Well can he appeal to the power of atomic energy as a symbol of the fact that power in the hands of man is ambiguously productive of good and evil. This symbol is but one instance of how Niebuhr seeks to place all of power and life in human culture under a critical judgment.

In the early twentieth century, human resources were being considered adequate to meet all human needs. Science held forth the promise of some sort of final deliverance from physical suffering. In the sphere of human relations the reason of man combined with his assumed innate goodness offered progress over social injustice and its eventual eradication. The perfectibility of man was regarded as possible by man himself. The perfection of history was considered possible through the power in history.

Niebuhr has persistently and methodically attacked modern man's conscious and unconscious claims to perfection or the possibility of perfection in history. In his earlier writings Niebuhr refutes the basic assumption of liberalism, namely, the moral soundness of human nature. His refutation has a two-pronged attack. The reliability of reason as an instrument of truth is disproved by demonstrating how self-interest infects rational analysis. Liberalism betrayed its own self-interest in that its claims, such as its emphasis on individual freedom, were in part a defense of its own comfortable status in society. In addition to indicating reason, Niebuhr indicated the human will as being impotent in the realization of perfection. The will never would or could achieve the perfection that it intended.

The Social Gospel, a theological movement within the broader historical movement of liberalism, Niebuhr rightly controverted in showing how the Gospel ethic cannot be fulfilled by man through his natural capacities. He rightly brought under criticism all human efforts to achieve the perfection of love as given in the Gospel. The Gospel does not offer a simple ethical ideal to man on the assumption that he can fulfill it if only he will try hard. Niebuhr has rendered a service in showing how the Gospel has the function of criticism. The Gospel places man under judgment and uncovers what he should be.

Niebuhr in a certain sense has carried on a tradition found in the Protestant Reformers. The Reformers subjected society to criticism. For example, Calvin placed the medieval culture built around the Roman Catholic Church under the criticism of the Word of God. What could not meet the test of God's Word Calvin, at least theoretically, rejected.

Niebuhr also has engaged in comprehensive criticism. He has placed much of culture under the "Word" of God. But he has in his criticism developed an approach that goes far beyond the Reformers. Niebuhr believes that it is necessary to force criticism over the totality of history, including the Bible and its contents.

At this juncture one raises the question: from what final ground does Niebuhr make his criticism and its subsequent reconstruction? To criticize and judge implies a norm, standard, or higher authority in terms of which criticism and judgment are made.

Niebuhr repeatedly indicates that his criticism presupposes a Christian norm or answer. He could not diagnose the moral abnormalities of modern man without knowing or assuming in some sense the norm of the Gospel in Christ. Granting this, we can pose the question of authority more exactly and precisely by asking: how does one know the norm of the Gospel in Christ? Put more briefly: how does one know Christ?

In response to this question Niebuhr, I believe, diverges to a significant degree from the Protestant Reformers and evangelical Christianity. Historically, Christianity has underscored an unbreakable bond between Christ and Scripture. The norm for stating who Christ is was the Scripture which revealed Him. Christ is defined by the facts disclosed about Him in Scripture. Consequently, all facts, including the virgin birth, are necessary for arriving at an authentic construction of Christ. Christ cannot be abstracted from Scripture and defined apart from it or in contradiction to it.

Niebuhr reconstructs Christ and the Gospel in terms of relevance. Concern for relevance is necessary for communication. But relevance has implicit within it a problem that has troubled the Christian Church for many ages. Relevance always demands a degree of adjustment. Facts must be given forms which fit the minds of the recipients. This may begin with translation into another language. The Septuagint made the Old Testament relevant to Greek-speaking people. But relevance may demand more. It may require the recasting of facts into new concepts and categories to fit the mentality of the recipients. The early Christian creeds were in part efforts to make the Gospel relevant by using concepts and categories that fitted minds formed by

Greek culture. In this whole enterprise of relevance there remains the problem of adjusting without losing that which is essential to the Gospel.

Niebuhr, in order to gain relevance, has been too uncritical in his acceptance of the concepts and thought patterns of our modern world. His reconstruction of man as a duality of spirit and nature is an accommodation to existentialism which obscures and annuls some of the essentials in the anthropology of the Bible. For example, in Scripture evil is not something which to a degree is inevitable because of the finiteness of man. It is the result of man's abuse of moral freedom and not a result of his paradoxical nature.

This accommodation to existentialism also demands a whole new pattern of thought as to the loci of human creation, fall, and redemption. Certainly in Scripture these are primarily historical moments revealed through historical events rather than vertical levels of consciousness. To reconstruct what the Bible represents as history into levels of consciousness is to recast the message of the Bible into such a different form that the question is bound to be asked: is this still the message of Scripture?

The most serious accommodation which Niebuhr undertakes in order to make the Gospel relevant is his reconstruction of Jesus Christ. In his reconstruction there is an emphasis which is in keeping with the New Testament. The Cross of Christ does hold a central position in New Testament thought, even as it does in Niebuhr's theology. But the interpretation of the Cross as a dialectical structure corresponding to the dialectical structure of man is subject to question from several points of view. It reduces the perfection of Christ to a locus that is foreign to historic Christianity. Furthermore, it is an interpretation which abstracts the Cross out of the Levitical economy, which in Scripture forms an inseparable background to the sacrificial work of Christ. Christ was fulfilling law as concretely given in the Old Testament and not law as the "possible impossible" norm of existence.

A final question, and perhaps the most crucial one that Niebuhr's reconstruction of Christ and His Cross raises, is one of validity. What makes the Cross of Christ and finally Christ Himself a valid and authentic disclosure of truth and grace? To this question Niebuhr gives an answer that threatens the message of the Gospel. The finality of Christ rests on a dialectical experience of simultaneously denying and laying claim to final truth and virtue, "a having and not having of final truth and virtue."

Niebuhr starts out by placing all of human knowledge in a proble-

---

[69] *Faith and History* (1949), p. 240.

matic context. Man's concepts and his rational ordering of facts are always less absolute and final than the freedom he perceives above them through self-transcendence. This is also true for Christ as historical fact. In confrontation with Christ it is disclosed to the self that all facts including the historical facts of Christ Himself are problematical and subject to ambiguity.[70]

The dialectical method which Niebuhr has employed to great advantage as an instrument for analyzing social and ethical problems is incompatible with the contents of the Gospel. The Gospel according to Niebuhr consistently affirms a dialectical structure around all historical facts and in so doing renders its own contents problematical. Such a conclusion is unacceptable according to the simple thrust of the Gospel message. Christ was unambiguous in His claim to being the Truth, so unambiguous that for this the Jews crucified Him. Christ made absolute claims in conceptual form and historical categories — for example, that He was the "Son of Man," "the resurrection and the life," "and that no man cometh unto the Father but by me," etc. The listeners to Christ well understood the absolute claims in these statements, and as a result they responded with the intensity that absoluteness evokes. They were unconditionally for Him or against Him. Likewise the apostles militated against uncertainty concerning certain facts. Paul wrote that any uncertainty about the resurrection of Christ makes "faith vain; ye are yet in your sins" (I Cor. 15:17). Paul insisted that in his message he possessed a truth that at best is exceedingly problematical in other traditions (Acts 17:22-30), but in Christ is revealed with finality. ". . . God shall judge the secrets of men, according to my gospel by Jesus Christ" (Rom. 2:16). The thrust of the Gospel is a call to be liberated from the world in which truth is uncertain and ambiguous, and to live in Christ in whom truth and life are secure. Christ does not support the dialectical approach, but renders it invalid as a means of testifying to Him.

Niebuhr has put forth a great effort to make the Gospel relevant to modern man. In doing so he has accommodated the Gospel to fit the framework of existentialism. Such an accommodation, though well motivated, can result in the very opposite of what it intends to accomplish. Accommodation of the Gospel to the modern mind in order to make it relevant may result in reducing too much of the Gospel to irrelevancy.

[70] *Beyond Tragedy* (1937), p. 61.

IV. BIBLIOGRAPHY

WORKS BY REINHOLD NIEBUHR

Does Civilization Need Religion? New York, 1927.
Leaves from the Notebook of a Tamed Cynic. New York, 1929.
Moral Man and Immoral Society: A Study in Ethics and Politics.
New York, 1932.
The Contributions of Religion to Social Work. New York, 1932.
An Interpretation of Christian Ethics. New York, 1935.
Beyond Tragedy: Essays on the Christian Interpretation of History.
New York, 1937.
Christianity and Power Politics. New York, 1940.
Reflections on the End of an Era. New York, 1940.
*The Children of Light and the Children of Darkness: A Vindication
of Democracy and Critique of Its Traditional Defense.* New
York, 1944.
Discerning the Signs of the Times: Sermons for Today and Tomorrow.
New York, 1946.
The Nature and Destiny of Man: A Christian Interpretation (I. *Human
Nature,* II. *Human Destiny*: Gifford Lectures). New York, 1946.
*Faith and History, A Comparison of Christian and Modern Views of
History.* New York, 1949.
The Irony of American History. New York, 1952.
Christian Realism and Political Problems. New York, 1953.
The Self and the Dramas of History. New York, 1955.
*The Structure of Nations and Empires: A Study of the Recurring
Patterns and Problems of the Political Order in Relation to
the Unique Problems of the Nuclear Age.* New York, 1959.
A Nation So Conceived (coauthor A. E. Heimert). New York, 1963.

WORKS ON REINHOLD NIEBUHR

Bingham, June. *Courage to Change.* New York, 1961.
Kegley, Charles W. and Robert W. Bretall (editors). *Reinhold Niebuhr, His Religious, Social, and Political Thought.* New York,
1956.

13 RICHARD ACWORTH

Pierre Teilhard de Chardin

I. BIOGRAPHY

MARIE-JOSEPH-PIERRE TEILHARD DE CHARDIN was born on May 1, 1881, at Sarcenat, a few miles west of Clermont-Ferrand, in Auvergne, France. Pierre was the fourth child in a family of eleven, his father being a country gentleman respected in the neighborhood, whose hobby was natural history. The original name of the family was Teilhard, the addition *de Chardin* being derived from a paternal grandmother. Teilhard was brought up in a devoutly Catholic home, and educated, from 1892 onwards, at the Jesuit college of Mongré, Villefranche-sur-Saône. He entered the Jesuit noviciate at Aix-en-Provence in 1899. In 1901 he had to leave France as a result of the expulsion of the religious orders; his community moved to the Channel Island of Jersey, where he studied philosophy from 1902 till 1905, a period followed by three years teaching chemistry and physics at Cairo. In 1908 Teilhard went to England for four years of theological studies at Ore Place, Hastings, during which he was ordained priest in August 1911. Both in Jersey and at Hastings, Teilhard studied in houses of the exiled French Jesuits; in both places he was taught the traditional Scholasticism current at the time; the revival of interest in biblical and patristic studies within the Roman Catholic Church had not yet begun. Scholasticism certainly had some influence on Teilhard's thought, but his primary inspiration was to come from a very different quarter.

Richard Acworth, formerly a Jesuit priest, is now a clergyman of the Church of England. A graduate of the University of Oxford, he is currently preparing a doctoral thesis for the University of Paris (Sorbonne).

From childhood on, Teilhard had been interested in geology and natural history. He seems to have acquired this interest from his father; and though he thought for a moment of abandoning it as contrary to his religious vocation, he was encouraged by his superiors to keep it up. In Jersey and Egypt he spent much of his spare time collecting fossils. Up till the period of his theological studies at Hastings, however, his primary interest was in geology rather than in paleontology; and he shared the belief, generally held around him, in the fixity of biological species. It is interesting to observe that Teilhard's conversion to evolutionism was a result, not of any scientific investigation on his part, but of his reading Bergson's *Évolution Créatrice*. But according to Teilhard himself, his reading of Bergson did no more than stir up a fire that was already burning within him;[1] he already had a quasi-mystical love of the material universe and a strong feeling for its unity. Even in childhood, he tells us, his attitude toward nature had been religious rather than scientific.[2] Now he found that the theory of evolution offered an explanation that satisfied his instinctive attitude toward the world, and he embraced it with an enthusiasm that never faltered.

It was also during his years at Hastings that Teilhard's interest first became specially directed toward the problem of human origins. His interest in fossil hunting brought him into contact, in 1909 or 1911, with Charles Dawson, the "discoverer" of the Piltdown Man. Through Dawson, Teilhard also met Sir Arthur Smith Woodward, and in 1912 accompanied the two of them in their investigations of the Piltdown site. Later that year Teilhard left Sussex for Paris to begin the scientific study of paleontology under Marcellin Boule at the Paris Natural History Museum. On a return visit to England in the summer of 1913, however, Teilhard was again digging at Piltdown, where he found a left canine tooth which seemed to fit a jaw previously discovered at the same spot. From the start, some paleontologists doubted whether the various remains found at Piltdown all belonged to the same individual, or even species; but the *Eoanthropus* of Piltdown was destined for a long career as one of man's ancestors until it was exposed as a fraud in 1953, consisting of a human skull and an orangutang's jaw, the whole suitably stained and the teeth doctored. By the time of the discovery of this forgery, both Dawson and Woodward were dead. Teilhard fully accepted the evidence of the fraud, though he always refused to believe that his old friend Dawson could have been its author. There is no reason to suppose that Teilhard himself had anything to do with the fraud, but the incident shows his gullibility when working with respected "experts." The excitement of working with Dawson and Smith Woodward, and of

---

[1] *Le coeur de la matière* (1950), unpublished essay quoted in N. Corte, *Pierre Teilhard de Chardin, His Life and Spirit* (London, 1960), p. 10.

[2] *Mon Univers* (1918), unpublished essay quoted in Claude Cuénot, *Teilhard de Chardin* (Écrivains de Toujours), pp. 25-26.

being personally involved in the "discovery" of some of man's earliest origins, had a decisive effect in directing his interest toward the study of human fossil remains.[3]

In December 1914, Teilhard was mobilized in the French army, serving with great distinction as a stretcher bearer with a regiment of Moroccan skirmishers. He was twice mentioned in dispatches, was decorated with the Médaille Militaire, and made a Chevalier of the Legion of Honour. His years at the front were decisive ones in the formation of his thought. Teilhard's attitude to the war was almost that of a detached observer; he likened its struggles to those which had marked the progress of evolution in the past. At the front, he felt, the soldiers were lifted above their own individuality and lived a higher, quasi-collective life.[4] But Teilhard also collected fossils in the trenches, preparing the thesis he was to defend at the Sorbonne in 1922 on *The Mammals of the Lower Eocene Period in France.*

After demobilization in March 1919, Teilhard returned to Paris to finish his paleontological studies. Once he had obtained his doctorate, he was appointed to a chair of geology at the Institut Catholique of Paris, paying a first visit to China in 1923-24 to inspect the fossil remains on which a fellow Jesuit, Père Licent, had long been working. After his return to France, Teilhard had several years of intense activity, lecturing and working out the details of his vision of the world, in correspondence with Maurice Blondel and in close contact with the theistic-evolutionist philosopher Edouard Le Roy. Teilhard's talks to students and others were highly popular, but his evolutionism and his resultant ideas on original sin brought him into disrepute with his ecclesiastical superiors. He was forbidden to publish his first major work, *Le Milieu Divin,* completed in 1927, and the same year was compelled to give up his post at the Institut Catholique. By this time he was back in China, and Peking remained the center of his activities from then until 1945, though his stay there was interrupted by five visits to France and three to the United States, as well as by expeditions to Java, India, and other parts of Asia. At Peking, Teilhard was associated with the American and Chinese scientists who excavated the site at Chou-kou-tien, some forty miles away, where the skulls of the so-called Peking Man (*Sinanthropus*) were discovered. Teilhard and the scientists with whom he worked considered that the owners of these ape-like skulls were responsible for the remains of fire and tools found on the site, and were therefore human, but other authorities, including Boule, thought that *Sinanthropus,* whose

---

[3] On Teilhard's connection with Piltdown, see C. E. Raven, *Teilhard de Chardin, Scientist and Seer,* pp. 53-60. But Raven's suggestion that the Piltdown "remains" were forged as a patriotic religious fraud is a piece of special pleading; it seems obvious that the aim of the forger was to help establish the theory of evolution, an aim in which he succeeded for forty years.

[4] *The Making of a Mind,* pp. 203-205.

remains showed signs of having been eaten, was more probably the game hunted by true men, a conclusion that seems more likely in view of the fact that ancient remains of true men were also found on the site.[5]

It was while he was in China that Teilhard wrote *Le Phénomène Humain* (*The Phenomenon of Man*), perhaps his principal work; it was this period too that saw the shifting of his center of interest from the past to the future of human evolution, a future he saw in terms of the growth of a collective human super-consciousness. After the war, Teilhard returned to France. He became friendly with Sir Julian Huxley, and took a great interest in UNESCO and in all forms of international planning. He was still unable to obtain permission from Rome to publish either *The Phenomenon of Man* or *Le Groupe Zoologique Humain* (*Man's Place in Nature*), the shorter work which he composed in 1949 and which forms the clearest summary of his mature thought; but Teilhard's influence was now growing fast, and he was elected to the French Institute in 1951. A year later, he accepted an appointment in New York with the Wenner-Gren Foundation for Anthropological Research, under whose auspices he also made two visits to South Africa to study sites where apparently man-like fossils had been found. He revisited France for the last time in 1954, dying quite suddenly at New York on April 10, 1955.

From this account of his life, it might appear that Teilhard was a lonely and isolated figure, at least within the Roman Catholic Church. It is true that his superiors preferred in general to keep him away from France, and forbade the publication of his more speculative writings. But Teilhard had many sympathizers within as well as outside the Jesuit Order, and he built up through his travels a worldwide circle of friends. Teilhard was never a professional theologian, and in a sense he does not fit naturally into a book on Creative Minds in Contemporary Theology. But he was a deeply religious man as well as a passionate believer in evolution, and his writings mark the most radical and complete attempt that has yet been made to elaborate an evolutionary version of Christianity. These writings have been made the object of intensive publicity ever since his death, and their influence at the present time can hardly be over-estimated. That is why it is important to examine his views in some detail.

II. EXPOSITION

By far the greater part of Teilhard's writings is not concerned with directly theological topics. His thought centers round his vision of the

---

[5] On Chou-kou-tien, see M. Boule, *Les hommes fossiles* (3rd ed., 1946), esp. pp. 126 and 409. For an anti-evolutionist view, see P. O'Connor, *Science of Today and the Problems of Genesis*, ch. 5. Teilhard's articles on the subject may be found in *The Appearance of Man*.

world in evolution. Teilhard saw the world as an evolutionary process from unorganized multiplicity to organized unity, but the unity he envisaged was a unity in Christ, and Christ was seen as the motive force of the whole process. It is thus impossible to consider his theological ideas in isolation from the rest of his system. We shall attempt to summarize Teilhard's view of the world under three main headings: The Origin of Man; Human Progress and the Future; Christ and Evolution.

THE ORIGIN OF MAN

Teilhard begins his book *Man's Place in Nature* with an outline of some of the basic principles that underlie his interpretation of the evolutionary process. In his view, which in this respect is fundamentally Aristotelian,[6] the nature of any being is fully displayed only in its most developed form; for this reason, the understanding of man is the key to the understanding of the universe. Teilhard regards man as an integral part of the physical universe, the highest point to which evolution has yet attained; the nature of matter, accordingly, is most fully displayed in its "hominized" form, in man. Armed with this insight, Teilhard is able to say that thought and physical matter are two sides of one essential reality. Life manifests the real nature of matter, and the reflective self-conscious thought of man manifests the real nature of life. Life is in germ in all matter, and thought in all life.[7]

Viewed "from outside," so to speak, matter may be described in terms of plurality, unity, and energy; but all beings have an "inside" as well as an outside, and their inner face is life or consciousness. It is only when consciousness reaches a certain level that it can be perceived by the outside observer, and the inner face of what is normally regarded as non-living matter is therefore described by Teilhard as "pre-life" or pre-consciousness. In Teilhard's view, the level of consciousness is precisely correlative with the complexity of organization of a unified being: elementary material particles have only a rudimentary form of pre-consciousness; but as they unite into successively higher and more complex unities, such as atoms, molecules, and living cells, the level of consciousness rises in proportion. The gradual organization of matter into ascending forms of complexity and consciousness is called by Teilhard "cosmogenesis."[8]

Since cosmogenesis or evolution proceeds, in Teilhard's opinion,

---

[6] *The Basis and Foundations of the Idea of Evolution* (1926), published in *The Vision of the Past*, p. 129 (note). In this note, Teilhard declares that Aristotelian hylomorphism is the equivalent, in a static view of the world, of modern evolutionism.

[7] *Man's Place in Nature*, pp. 17-19.

[8] *The Phenomenon of Man*, chs. 1 and 2; *Man's Place in Nature*, pp. 19-25.

from unorganized multiplicity to organized unity, the starting point of the process would be a pure and undifferentiated multiplicity; such a multiplicity, however, could never have existed as such, and is for Teilhard no more than a limiting concept.[9] The most primitive form of being actually known is that of the sub-atomic particles, which already have a rudimentary organization. These particles form themselves into unified systems which we call atoms, and these again combine to form molecules. In each case, the lower beings are subsumed into the higher, more organized whole; they do not lose their individual existence but they acquire a higher significance as part of a fuller, more developed and more conscious Whole. According to Teilhard, an organic Whole is always of a higher nature and value than are its constituent parts.[10]

In Teilhard's view, the gradual organization of particles into atoms and atoms into molecules is already a manifestation of the same evolutionary force which has since led to the emergence of life and of man himself, and which is still the motive force of human progress. Apart from what Teilhard calls "tangential energy," the energy which has long been recognized by physicists and on which the laws of thermodynamics are based, matter also manifests another form of energy; this energy, which he names "radial," is always active in drawing matter into organized unity. Radial energy is the motive power of evolution; as will be seen in due course, it is ultimately, in Teilhard's view, a manifestation of the incarnate Christ.[11]

Some of the molecules formed under the influence of radial energy are of an amazing complexity. This is particularly true of those which are known as proteins. These occur today, as Teilhard recognizes, only within living organisms; but in his view they must formerly have formed independently through the effects of radiation on the earth's surface. The complex "pre-living" protein molecules are often hardly distinguishable from the simplest living cells, such as viruses; and Teilhard considers that the threshold of life must have been crossed when some of these complex molecules acquired an organization that enabled them to assimilate other matter and to reproduce their kind.[12] Though the change that took place at this moment of "vitalization" does not look large, it marked a decisive step forward in the evolution of the universe, for it opened the way for the development of organisms of ever increasing complexity and specialization. Teilhard does not claim to know whether

[9] *Mon Univers* (1924). This important essay, which is not to be confused with the earlier one of the same title to which Note 2 refers, is published in *Science et Christ*, p. 74.

[10] *Ibid.*

[11] *The Phenomenon of Man*, pp. 62-66; *Mon Univers*, in *Science et Christ*, p. 85.

[12] *Man's Place in Nature*, pp. 28-32.

"vitalization" took place only once or on a number of occasions, or how many protein molecules were affected; the origin of life is hidden from our eyes. In any case, he declares, living matter spread quickly over the earth's surface, where it can be regarded as forming a new layer, the "biosphere."[13] Despite its special properties, however, there is nothing in the biosphere that was not already present in inorganic matter, except a more complex organization with its corollary of increased consciousness.

Once life had emerged from pre-living matter, it began to develop in diverse directions. Teilhard does not propose any particular theory to explain the evolution of living things. Radial energy, it is true, is always working toward an increase of complexity and consciousness, but its movement is a "groping" one, and Teilhard leaves much room for the operation of natural selection. Life gropes forward in all possible directions, most of which turn into blind alleys where no further progress is possible; but certain lines of advance appear. As a result, certain groups or phyla of living things tend to form the spearhead of evolutionary progress, while the remaining forms quickly become stabilized. When it first emerged, the biosphere consisted of practically undifferentiated monocellular beings; but these soon began to divide into two groups, the proto-plants and the proto-animals, the latter being parasitic on the former. Multicellular beings divided into plants and animals, and the latter in their turn divided into two main groups which had an evolutionary future—the arthropods (of which the most important are the insects) and the vertebrates—as well as into many lower forms of life, most of which were destined to remain stationary. However, the details of the evolutionary process hardly interested Teilhard. To criticisms of the explanations suggested by Darwin, Lamarck, and other evolutionary theorists, he always replied that the certainty of transformist evolution, which he considered absolute, was independent of any particular explanation of its mechanism. For his faith in evolution was not based on biology or even, primarily, on paleontology; it flowed rather from the imperative need he felt to grasp the world as a unified process.[14]

As has been seen, Teilhard regarded complexity of organization, with its corollary of higher consciousness, as the criterion of the place that should be allotted to a species in the evolutionary scale. But while it is easy to see that a molecule is more highly organized than an atom, it is not so easy to compare the relative complexity of, say, a tree, an insect,

13 *Ibid.,* pp. 37-41.
14 "To be a transformist, as I have often said, is not to be a Darwinian or a Lamarckian or the disciple of any particular school. It is quite simply to admit that the appearance of living creatures on earth obeys an ascertainable law, whatever that law may be" (*The Transformist Paradox* [1925], in *The Vision of the Past,* p. 98).

a reptile, and a mammal. With what type of complex organization is consciousness particularly associated? Teilhard has no difficulty in deciding that what matters is the degree of organization of the nervous system, and its concentration in the head and ultimately in the brain. The degree of "cephalization" and "cerebralization" thus becomes the criterion of what he calls the "psychic temperature" of a living being, the criterion, that is to say, of its level of consciousness. This criterion enables Teilhard to exclude plants from any possibility of being regarded as the axis or spearhead of evolutionary progress; insects, whose perfect activity shows no sign of further development, can also be excluded, since their ganglions do not form true brains. The vertebrates form the spearhead of evolution, and as they too spread out into different phyla, the lead is taken by the mammals, then by the primates, and finally by the anthropoids.[15]

In the pliocene period, a dense population of anthropoid apes covered the sub-tropical parts of Africa and Asia. These anthropoids, Teilhard tells us, were of varied types, and were in a state of active mutation. They were the most highly cerebralized of all animals, and their psychic temperature was reaching a critical point. At this period, the climate, flora, and fauna of the earth were not widely different from those which prevail today. Life was approaching the threshold of "hominization," the emergence of Man.[16] The crucial step, according to Teilhard, was made when certain anthropoids acquired the power of reflective thought, when they acquired self-consciousness and not only knew like other animals, but knew that they knew.

Man, Teilhard tells us, entered the world noiselessly;[17] it is impossible for us to pin down the moment or manner of his appearance. The first origins of every species are lost to our view, for it is only when a population has become numerous and relatively stable that it can be expected to leave any fossil remains. There is thus no point in searching for traces of "the first man." What we actually find are the remains of primitive man-like beings in different parts of the world: the "pithecanthropoids" of Java and South Africa, the "sinanthropes" of Chou-kou-tien. It is difficult to say, in particular cases, whether or not these ape-men had crossed the threshold of thought, whether or not they were men. The only certain criterion of "hominization" is the use of fire or tools. Teilhard was inclined to think that the South African "ape-men" were not yet human, while Peking Man, in view of the fire and tools found near his remains, was. None of these groups, in Teilhard's view, probably represents the ancestors of modern man; but the same sort of

15 *Man's Place in Nature*, pp. 47-57.
16 *Ibid.*, pp. 57-62.
17 *The Phenomenon of Man*, p. 184; *Man's Place in Nature*, pp. 64-65.

mutation was in progress in parallel groups of anthropoid apes, and from one of these modern men are descended.[18] In view of the impossibility of pinning down the exact moment of hominization, Teilhard leaves open the question of whether this took place in a single pair of anthropoids, who could thus be identified with the biblical Adam and Eve, or whether it took place independently in several groups; but the logic of his theory suggests that the latter is the more probable alternative. But though the question of monogenism (descent from a single pair) is thus an open one from the scientific point of view, there is no doubt that all men belong to a single biological phylum.[19]

Though the first appearance of man, like that of life, was hardly noticeable, hominization marked a second decisive turning-point in the evolutionary process. The complexity of organization of certain material beings had now reached the point where thought had become conscious of itself. During the first period of mankind, physical cerebralization continued rapidly, for the brain of the "sinanthrope" is closer to that of an ape than to that of modern man (*homo sapiens*). With the appearance of *homo sapiens,* however, between twenty and thirty thousand years ago, this physical evolution seems to have reached a platform or come to a halt;[20] in any case, in Teilhard's opinion, the forward movement of evolution is no longer primarily physical. In Man, the earth has become conscious of itself; in Teilhard's phrase, it has found its soul.[21]

HUMAN PROGRESS AND THE FUTURE

If evolution is a movement from unorganized multiplicity to organized unity, from rudimentary consciousness to reflective thought, it is evident that Man represents the highest point which it has yet attained. But the question arises whether the evolutionary process is still active. The human brain seems to have ceased developing, and contemporary men do not seem to be, as individuals, more intelligent than their forbears. The originality of Teilhard's evolutionary doctrine consists in his answer to this question: in his view, it is not so much the individual man who is now evolving, but Humanity. Teilhard sees technical progress and the advance of science and civilization as biological phenomena which prolong the whole process of cosmogenesis. Although mankind has continued, like every other biological phylum, to branch out into different

---

[18] *Man's Place in Nature,* pp. 64-73.

[19] *The Phenomenon of Man,* pp. 186-189; *Man's Place in Nature,* pp. 64-65.

[20] *The Phenomenon of Man,* pp. 199-202; *Man's Place in Nature,* pp. 72-78; *Some Reflections on Progress* (1941), published in *The Future of Man,* pp. 68-69; *Le coeur de la matière* (1950), unpublished essay quoted in E. Rideau, *Teilhard de Chardin: A Guide to His Thought,* p. 361.

[21] *The Phenomenon of Man,* p. 182.

varieties (races) and incipient species, this tendency to divergence has been counterbalanced by the emergence of a network of human thought and work which links all men together, and which enables each generation to pass on to its successors, by means of education, the progress it has made. In this way, human conscious activity adds another "layer" to the earth's surface, the "noosphere."[22] It was to the development of the noosphere, and in particular to the tendency toward convergence and "socialization" which he discerned in it, that Teilhard devoted most of his attention in the latter part of his life.

In Teilhard's opinion, two phases must be distinguished in the development of the noosphere. The first phase, which lasted until the beginning of the present century, was primarily one of simple expansion. Mankind went forth to subdue the earth. With the development of consciousness in the higher species of animals, the individuals become more independent of the group than is the case with more primitive beings, and in mankind this tendency is particularly accentuated. Having attained self-consciousness, the human individual is free, and mankind thus seems to split up into a multitude of autonomous individuals. It is true that this tendency has always been counterbalanced by certain convergent forces, such as those which lead to the formation of families, nations and civilizations; nevertheless, in Teilhard's view, the divergent, individualist tendency predominated throughout the "expansive" phase of human progress, culminating in the individualistic Liberalism of the eighteenth and nineteenth centuries. If one's study of mankind stopped short at the beginning of the present century, one might imagine that the autonomous human individual was destined to be the end product of the evolutionary process.[23]

Teilhard was convinced, however, that in recent years the development of the noosphere has entered a new phase, in which "compression" has taken the place of expansion. The whole surface of the earth is occupied, and its population is approaching saturation point. Civilization has become universal, science and conscious economic and political organization are becoming worldwide; the general acceptance of the theory of evolution has given to mankind a belief in progress and the sense of belonging to a single species. All these factors, in Teilhard's opinion, go to show that mankind is in the process of being unified or "socialized" into a single, higher, organic super-consciousness. Teilhard recognizes that the first reaction to the realization that the individual is in the process of being incorporated into an organism larger than himself is likely to be one of fear and resistance; the individual is afraid of losing his own personality and freedom. But Teilhard thought that this fear

---

22 *Man's Place in Nature*, pp. 79-82; *Le coeur de la matière, loc. cit.*
23 *Man's Place in Nature*, pp. 93-95.

was misplaced. Just as the individual molecule or cell is not suppressed but perfected by its incorporation into a living organism of a higher order, so the human individual becomes more, not less human, through his integration into the Super-Humanity that is being born. In Teilhard's view, the unification of mankind is a biological phenomenon, the culmination of the evolutionary process.[24]

A vision of this kind has, of course, political connotations; and although Teilhard never advanced a political program as such, he gave much attention to problems of a broadly political nature.[25] Holding as he did that organic unification was the path of progress, he followed the totalitarian movements of the 1930's with sympathetic interest. Both Fascism and Communism, however, fell short of his ideal. Teilhard welcomed the internationalism of the Communists, their faith in matter, in progress, and in a planned society, but he reproached them for their exclusion of a spiritual ideal. In Fascism and Nazism, he welcomed the sense of the organic national community, the ability to make a whole people vibrate with a common enthusiasm; their shortcoming consisted in their failure to realize that a single race is too small a unit to satisfy a Humanity that has become conscious of its unity as a species with a common destiny. Nationalism, in Teilhard's view, is a kind of magnified individualism. Teilhard recognized defects in the current totalitarian ideologies, but he considered that their ideal of a fully self-conscious and unified organic society was right. They had tried to achieve this ideal society in an inadequate and premature way. The true Total Society must be worldwide, and must be based on a genuine unanimity of desire, a common enthusiasm.[26] Teilhard's judgment of Fascism and Communism was more favorable than his judgment of Liberalism. For classical Liberalism considers that the state exists only for the sake of the individual citizens; its belief in individual freedom and its consequent opposition to coercive government planning represent the antithesis of Teilhard's ideal of an organic Super-Humanity.[27] In Teilhard's view, the fundamental division amongst men was not between "right" and "left," but between those who believed in progress and in an organized Super-Humanity and those who did not; if they were true to their deepest insights, progressive Democrats, Fascists and Communists would find

[24] *Ibid.*, ch. 5, esp. pp. 100-104.
[25] On Teilhard's political thought, see C. Soucy, *Pensée logique et pensée politique chez Teilhard de Chardin*, pp. 101-220.
[26] *Sauvons l'humanité* (1936), published in *Science et Christ*, pp. 180-182; *Esquisse d'un univers personnel* (1936), published in *L'Énergie humaine*, pp. 98-99; *The Grand Option* (1939), published in *The Future of Man*, p. 39; *Life and the Planets*, in *The Future of Man*, pp. 118-119.
[27] *Sauvons l'humanité, loc. cit.; Some Reflections on Progress*, in *The Future of Man*, p. 72. Teilhard invariably equates individualism with egoism.

themselves on the same side, opposed only by the forces of selfish individualism and of inertia; and such a division would, for the first time in history, clearly divide the "good" from the "bad." For the latter, Teilhard had no sympathy.[28]

Although Teilhard held that the future of mankind must lie in organized unity, he did not imagine that all sorts of unity were beneficial. It is only an organic unity, not a mere artificial aggregate, that comports an intensification of consciousness; and at the human level organic unity can only come about by means of a unanimous desire for the end that is to be obtained. However, in contemporary man evolution has become conscious of itself, and by this very fact has become responsible for its own future.[29] It is therefore essential, Teilhard held, that research and planning should be directed, on a worldwide scale, to the conditions for the emergence of a Super-Humanity. The eugenic control of heredity must be developed so as to ensure the emergence and dominance of the most progressive characters; the use of economic resources must be carefully planned, and a universal control of production and exchange instituted.[30] The most important factors, however, are of a psychological nature: Teilhard urges psychologists to aid men to achieve a sense of belonging to the human race and of having a share in its collective future; but in the last resort the force of love alone can unite mankind. Economic and demographic factors are forcing mankind to become an organized unity; but if this unification is to liberate men, they must become conscious of their place in the evolutionary process; then, filled with a love that approaches adoration for the movement carrying them forward, they will freely choose to play their part in the construction of the coming Super-Humanity.[31]

This brings us to a crucial point in the interpretation of Teilhard's thought. The welding of mankind into an organic super-consciousness is,

---

[28] *Sauvons l'humanité*, in *Science et Christ*, pp. 185-186: if it came to a war between the two groups, Teilhard declares, no one would need to fear that he was firing on a brother.

[29] *The Phenomenon of Man*, pp. 216-221; *L'évolution de la responsabilité dans le monde* (1950), published in *L'Activation de l'énergie*, pp. 213-221; *Du cosmos à la cosmogenèse* (1951), in *L'Activation de l'énergie*, pp. 264-265. According to Teilhard, it is precisely a man's realization of evolution and of its consequences that entitles him to be regarded as "modern."

[30] *L'énergie humaine* (1937), published in *L'Énergie humaine*, pp. 157-171; *The Directions and Conditions of the Future* (1948), published in *The Future of Man*, pp. 293-305. Teilhard specifically envisages the planned breeding of races on a world scale.

[31] *Some Reflections on Progress*, in *The Future of Man*, pp. 72-74; *The Planetization of Mankind* (1946), *ibid.*, pp. 134-136; *How may we conceive and hope that human unanimization will be realised on earth?* (1950), *ibid.*, pp. 281-284; *Les conditions psychologiques de l'unification humaine* (1949), published in *L'Activation de l'énergie*, pp. 182-184.

418

in his view, the culmination of the whole evolutionary process; but the achievement of this Super-Humanity finally depends on love. It would seem, however, that love is free. Can it be said, in this case, that the final success of evolution is assured, or does this success depend on human co-operation? And a second question arises too: Is it possible to love and adore a collective unity? Teilhard's reply to the first of these questions is somewhat hesitant; as has been seen, he thought it vital that social planners should take all possible steps to favor the development of an evolutionary world-consciousness. His final judgment, however, is that the success of evolution *both* depends on human freedom *and* will inevitably be attained. Till now, evolution has always been successful in the end, and one cannot believe that it will fail at its highest point. Moreover, since all men have an inner attraction toward the final end of Humanity, this end is bound to be attained on the whole, even though each individual, considered in isolation, is capable of refusing it, and some do so. At times one has the impression that Teilhard's confidence is simply due to his innate optimism, that it is really less an inability than a refusal to envisage the possible failure of Humanity. But this is not the whole explanation, for it is at this point that his religious faith comes into play. In his view, behind the apparent dominance of chance and freedom, evolution is moved by a divine power; the "radial energy" which makes for unity and organization is ultimately to be identified with the charity of the Incarnate Christ, and a divine power cannot finally fail to attain its objective.[32]

It is this same religious faith that also provides the answer to the second question formulated above. If the Super-Humanity that mankind is destined to form were nothing more than a collective unity of men, it would not be possible to give oneself to it in wholehearted love. Man reaches out for an Absolute, and he can only love a person. But in fact, Teilhard held, *Omega,* the final point of convergence of mankind, is not just the unification of Humanity in itself; it is also its unity with God in Christ. The Super-Humanity now in process of formation will be an organic Whole grouped around and animated by Christ. It is for this reason that it marks the definitive end of the whole process of evolution.

[32] *The Phenomenon of Man,* Part 4, and esp. pp. 308-310; *Man's Place in Nature,* ch. 5. *Man's Place in Nature* leaves open a bare possibility of failure, and Teilhard's final certainty is expressed in the essays published in *L'Activation de l'énergie* and in *Science et Christ,* and in the unpublished essays *Christianisme et évolution* (1944), *Le coeur de la matière* (1950), and *Le Christique* (1955). Extracts from these essays are contained in C. Cuénot, *Teilhard de Chardin* (Écrivains de Toujours). Cf. also C. Soucy, *op. cit.,* pp. 183-189. In *The Planetization of Mankind,* published in *The Future of Man,* pp. 124-125, Teilhard declares that human unification will be free because men will come to love the determinism that is drawing them together.

CHRIST AND EVOLUTION

The account of Teilhard's system that has been given up to this point has been based on his two chief speculative works—*The Phenomenon of Man* and *Man's Place in Nature*—and on his sociological and political essays. These books were intended by their author to form a descriptive analysis of the world and of mankind as they appear to us; they were phenomenological, not metaphysical or theological works.[33] Teilhard's religious thought is closely integrated with his theory of the evolutionary process. It is not yet possible to give a definitive picture of it, as several of his most important essays on this subject have not yet been published in their entirety. Nevertheless, no doubt attaches to the main lines of his theological position, which will here be briefly examined under the following headings: The Role of Christ in the Evolutionary Process; The Problem of Evil and the Value of the World; The Christian Church and Evolution; The Sources and Affinities of Teilhard's Thought.[34]

The Role of Christ in the Evolutionary Process

When he adopts a scientific or phenomenological point of view, Teilhard, as has been seen, is not prepared to speak of the origin of the world; in his theological writings, however, he has no hesitation in declaring that it was created by God. In his view, however, to create is to unite, to draw into unity, for pure multiplicity is nothingness. What God primarily designed in creating the world was the Whole Christ, the union of all things, and particularly of mankind, in the Body of Christ; and the whole history of evolution is that of the building up, by slow and painful stages, of this Body.[35] The Whole Christ, however, could not be the end product of evolution if Christ had not been present in matter from the start. It was Christ's influence, which could be described as "grace" in a broad sense, which, from the beginning of time, has been drawing matter upwards into organized unity and consciousness. Christ is therefore described by Teilhard as the *"Évoluteur,"* and the Incarnation,

---

[33] Cf. the Introductions to *The Phenomenon of Man* and *Man's Place in Nature.*

[34] Apart from *Le Milieu divin,* Teilhard's theological views are scattered through a series of essays, some of which are published in *Science et Christ,* but many of which still await publication. Important extracts from these unpublished works are contained in E. Rideau, *Teilhard de Chardin: A Guide to his Thought,* and in the books of Claude Cuénot.

[35] *Super-Humanité—Super-Christ—Super-Charité* (1943), published in *Science et Christ,* p. 213.

which is "the visible face of creation," is coextensive with the duration of the universe.[36]

But in addition to being "born" in matter from the beginning, drawing it upward in a groping and pre-conscious way, Christ was also born in due time of the Virgin Mary; He became a human being in order to draw mankind consciously into the unity of His Body, and to share and consecrate their joys and sorrows. His death and resurrection taught men no longer to fear death as a return to nothingness, but to accept it with humility and confidence as the necessary passage to God. Teilhard held firmly to the historical reality of the Incarnation, for in his view Christ could not unite mankind into a Super-Humanity centered on Himself unless He were present within it. By His resurrection, Christ took conscious and full possession of His role as the universal Center. Since His ascension, He transmits His influence to us particularly through the Eucharist; through transubstantiation He is physically present in the consecrated Host, and from this center His personal energy radiates so that, having transformed this little piece of matter into Himself, He may gradually unite the whole earth into His Body.[37]

But although Teilhard accepted the reality of the historical Incarnation, his religion was centered on the Whole Christ, whose fullness lies ahead of us, the final point of convergence of the whole evolutionary process.[38] Everything that contributes to the progress of mankind, and thus to the final success of evolution, contributes directly to the building up of the Body of Christ. Not only the good intentions of men, or their specifically "religious" activity, but also their achievements—in technical progress, scientific research, and social progress, for instance—contribute directly to the construction of the *pleroma*. But men do not achieve this by their own independent power; they do it by virtue of that grace which is the moving force of evolution. In the measure that he is integrated in the whole forward movement of mankind, each man can truly say that he is more truly Christ than he is himself,[39] and his work will bear fruit for eternity. The individual, it is true, can cut himself off from the common movement of mankind; but if he does so, he cuts himself off from Christ.

[36] *Mon Univers* (1924), in *Science et Christ*, pp. 88-89 and 92; *Christianisme et évolution* (1944) quoted in Cuénot, *Teilhard de Chardin* (Écrivains de Toujours), pp. 139-144.

[37] *Mon Univers*, in *Science et Christ*, pp. 92-94.

[38] "Christ is becoming more and more indispensable to me. . . . But at the same time the figure of the historical Christ is becoming less and less substantial and distinct to me" (Letter of January 8, 1936); "In fact, my pan-Christism is in some way 'trans-Christic'" (Letter of April 20, 1948). Both letters are quoted in Rideau, *op. cit.*, p. 622.

[39] *Mon Univers* (1924), in *Science et Christ*, p. 86.

Salvation, in Teilhard's view, is collective; the individual is perfected only in the perfection of humanity. God is present to the individual elements that make up the world only in and through that Body of Christ which is the Whole.[40]

In some of his writings, Teilhard speaks of a "final option," a choice for or against God to be made by mankind as a whole once it has attained its unity in a single super-consciousness.[41] He became, however, more and more certain that, since the soul or moving force of evolution is Christ, this choice will be for God. Once Humanity has reached the highest possible degree of organized unity, civilization, common consciousness, and love, then Christ will be made manifest, and mankind will be caught up, in a sort of paroxysm, into a timeless and perfect unity with Him. The *parousia* will mark the term of the whole evolutionary process of Christogenesis, a term, however, that is outside the process itself, since it marks the final unity of mankind with its transcendent Center, Christ.

The Problem of Evil and the Value of the World

Since evolution is the process by which Christ gradually welds an unorganized multiple into an organic unity centered on Himself, it is clear that goodness can be fully realized only when this process is completed. Teilhard is compelled, therefore, to regard multiplicity as in some sense evil. The process of evolution is a slow and difficult one, which in its lower stages can only grope its way forward; and Christ's "incarnation" in matter has from the first been painful and laborious. The multiple resists the upward movement of evolution, and in this sense all creation, all gathering into unity, can, in Teilhard's view, be regarded as redemptive.[42]

In his essay *Mon Univers* (1924), Teilhard speculates on the origin of evil in the universe; did this recalcitrant multiple originate, perhaps, through the culpable disintegration of a previously unified Whole which could be called, in biblical terms, the First Adam? In this case, the world's history would not be that of a simple rise toward unity, but rather of a return to it, in Christ the Second Adam.[43] In his later works, Teilhard does not repeat this strange suggestion, which would place a sort of original sin before the beginning of the present universe; instead,

[40] *Ibid.,* pp. 105-106.
[41] *Ibid.,* p. 112.
[42] *Ibid.,* pp. 88-89.
[43] *Ibid.,* p. 109.

he affirms that multiplicity, disorder, suffering, and evil are necessary characteristics of a world that is not yet fully organized.[44]

The evil that is necessarily associated with unorganized multiplicity is of course, in the first instance, a natural imperfection rather than a moral evil. But when the evolutionary process reaches the level of reflective thought, it manifests itself also in moral evil.[45] It is clear that the traditional Christian doctrine of original sin cannot be fitted without modification into Teilhard's system, for it is hard to see how primitive beings who had only just crossed the threshold of thought could be capable of committing a sin of absolute gravity, which would have serious effects for their posterity. But Teilhard held in fact that evil presented a much less serious problem in an evolutionary view of the world than in a static one: an evolving universe is necessarily a universe which travails, which suffers, and which sins. Teilhard did not see suffering, war, and sin as scandals in themselves; he saw them rather as the necessary price of progress. However, he admitted that there was more sin and suffering in the world than one would expect from the mere fact that evolution has not yet reached its term; and he attributed this excess of evil to original sin, which he interpreted in terms less of hereditary transmission than of human solidarity: since the first sins of men, there has been a kind of atmosphere of sin in the world. But sin, in his view,

---

[44] *Christologie et évolution* (1933); *Le Christ évoluteur* (1942); *Introduction au Christianisme* (1944). The text of these unpublished works is quoted in Rideau, *op. cit.,* pp. 538-541. Cf. also *Le Milieu divin,* pp. 64-65.

[45] "There is *only a single evil*: disunity. We call it 'moral' when it affects the free regions of the soul. But . . . even then, it remains of a *physical* essence" (*Mon Univers,* in *Science et Christ,* p. 109). Evil is "the very expression of a still incompletely organized plurality. . . . In a world that is still in process of formation, this transitory state of imperfection is manifested, in detail, in the form of a certain number of culpable actions: the very first instances of these, and the most decisive (although the least conscious in human history) could well be taken separately and described as a 'primitive fault'. But what constitutes the original weakness for the creature, is in reality the radical condition that causes it to be born from the multiple, so that it continually retains in its fibres . . . a tendency to sink back into the dust. In such conditions, evil is not an unforeseen accident in the universe. It is an enemy, a shadow that God inevitably raises up simply by the fact that he decides on the creation" (*Christologie et évolution* [1933], quoted in Rideau, *op. cit.,* pp. 540-541).

"The origin of evil does not present the same difficulties . . . in a universe whose structure is evolutionary as it does in an initially perfect static universe. . . . Physical and moral disorders arise spontaneously in a self-organising system, *so long as* that system is not completely organised. *Necesse est ut eveniant scandala*" (*Note sur le péché originel,* added to *Le Christ évoluteur* [1942], quoted in Rideau, *op. cit.,* p. 539).

has its root in the very nature of a world created imperfect; it is like a shadow raised by God's act of creation out of the multiple.[46]

If the march of evolution is necessarily a path of suffering and sin, the Cross cannot be regarded primarily as an act of atonement for human sin. To regard the passion and death of Christ as a mere act of expiation would be to take too low a view of its significance, Teilhard tells us; Christ did indeed bear the sins of men, but He also bore the whole suffering and effort of evolutionary progress.[47] The Cross represents that fight against disunity, suffering, sin, and death which will not be finally won until the *pleroma* is attained. Faced with an evil such as that of disease, therefore, man's first reaction must be to fight it; in so doing, the doctor and the research worker are joining with God in His struggle against evil. But since their short lives bear no proportion to the slow evolution of the Whole Christ, they cannot expect to live to see His final victory over death; but humbly accepting death as He Himself did, they have confidence that, through it, they will be more closely united to Him. [48]

As has been seen, however, though all men are called to join in the communal task of building up the Body of Christ, the individual remains free to refuse his cooperation. Sin consists precisely in this refusal. The man who, out of avarice, laziness, or selfishness, refuses to play his part in the unification of mankind in Christ, cuts himself off from the unity in which alone is salvation; persisted in, this path leads to damnation. It has been suggested that hell has no real place in Teilhard's system, and that he introduced it only to satisfy the demands of orthodoxy,[49] but this does not seem to be true. On the contrary, throughout his political essays Teilhard always supposes that some individuals will refuse to join in the progress of the world toward a collective Super-Humanity, but will choose instead an egoistic self-sufficiency. Since Teilhard held that mankind is a biological super-organism whose progress and unification are animated by Christ, he is only logical in supposing that those who refuse their co-operation will be damned. Salvation, for Teilhard, as has been seen, is collective, but damnation is individual.

Teilhard recognized that his view of sin and suffering as necessary elements of an evolutionary creation raised certain difficulties. According

[46] *Note sur le péché originel, loc. cit.*
[47] *La signification et la valeur constructrice de la souffrance* (1933), published in *L'Énergie humaine,* pp. 65-66; *The New Spirit* (1942), in *The Future of Man,* pp. 94-95; *Christianisme et évolution* (1945), quoted by Cuénot, *Teilhard de Chardin* (Écrivains de Toujours), p. 142.
[48] *Le Milieu divin,* pp. 62-65; *Mon Univers,* in *Science et Christ,* p. 100.
[49] C. E. Raven, *op. cit.,* p. 179.

to the traditional Christian view, God, being infinite and therefore self-sufficient, has no need of the world; He created it out of pure generosity. But if God could not create without unleashing so much evil and suffering, is pure benevolence a sufficient explanation of the creation? Moreover Teilhard also had a second objection to the traditional doctrine: it seemed to him to involve the denial that the world has any ultimate value in itself. If man is to face up to the labours and sufferings involved in perfecting the world, he must be convinced that the *pleroma* he is helping to construct has an absolute worth. If the whole created universe can add nothing to God, then both man and Christ Himself are finally valueless. The role of a guest invited to the divine banquet might satisfy someone who looked only for individual happiness as the end of his existence; but once man has woken up to his responsibility for carrying evolution to its successful conclusion, he refuses to regard himself as a mere recipient of divine charity, and demands that his efforts should be valuable in themselves.[50]

Teilhard's solution to this problem was only tentative. He admitted that God is in some sense self-sufficient, but held that, if creation was to be worthwhile for God and life worthwhile for men, the *pleroma* must be supposed to add something to God's perfection. The Scholastic notion of God as *Ens a Se,* he suggested, needed re-thinking. If one admitted that being is unification and that the unification of a wider multiple involves an enhancement of being, then one could conceive that, beyond the independent and eternal unification of the three divine persons in the Trinity, God could still acquire an additional perfection by drawing a created multiple into union with Himself.[51] Teilhard believed that the creation of the world was a free act on God's part, but he was inclined to identify freedom, at its highest level, with necessity;[52] the world, he thought, is too serious a matter to depend on the arbitrary generosity of God.

---

[50] "What have we to do with the selfish happiness of *sharing* the joy of the Supreme Being when we can dream of the infinitely greater happiness of completing it?" (*Action et activation* [1945], in *Science et Christ*, p. 228). " 'God creates out of love' is a fine scholastic phrase: but what is this love, then, inexplicable in its subject and degrading for its object, that is *based on no need* (unless it be the pleasure of giving for the sake of giving)?" (*Contingence de l'univers et goût humain de survivre* [1943], quoted by Rideau, *op. cit.,* p. 509). Cf. also *Christianisme et évolution* (1945).

[51] *La Centrologie* (1944), published in *L'Activation de l'énergie*, pp. 103-134; *Comment je vois* (1948); *Le coeur de la matière* (1950); *Contingence de l'univers. . .* (1953). Quotations from the last three (unpublished) works may be found in Rideau, *op. cit.,* pp. 511-513.

[52] *Comment je crois* (1934), unpublished essay quoted in Soucy, *op. cit.,* p. 202; and see Note 32 *supra*.

425

The Christian Church and Evolution

In Teilhard's view, as has been seen, evolution is basically a process of Christogenesis; as *"Évoluteur,"* at once its motive force and its final consummation, Christ is the essential figure in the evolution of the universe. It remains for us to examine the role Teilhard attributed to Christianity and to the Church in building up the *pleroma.*

In a series of essays spread over many years, Teilhard examined the religious state of mankind. He could not help observing that Christianity seemed to be losing its power to attract mankind. Teilhard was convinced, however, that this decline of Christianity was not due to any growth of skepticism or irreligion; on the contrary, contemporary man was full of idealism, and his complaint against Christianity was that it failed to measure up to or to express his highest ideals. For a new religion was rising amongst men, the religion of Progress, with a boundless faith in man and in the world. Far from encouraging materialistic self-indulgence, this new religion involved a passionate desire to give oneself unselfishly to the task of building the collective future of mankind. Teilhard believed that this new faith was rooted in the discovery of the evolutionary process and that it represented an irreversible mutation of man's religious consciousness; but he also held that, in its present form, it had serious weaknesses. In particular, lacking the idea of a personal Absolute as the term of evolution, it could offer no adequate object for the devotion it excited, and its aspirations were in consequence dangerously vague. In fact, it needed to be completed by Christianity.[53]

For Teilhard held that the essential message of Christianity is true: God has entered the world to draw all things to Himself.[54] The contemporary eclipse of Christianity is due, in Teilhard's opinion, to the fact that the churches have allowed themselves to become fixed in a pre-evolutionary and individualistic view of the world, and in an otherworldly conception of God and of salvation; as a result, they are unable to satisfy the highest aspirations of modern man. Christians have sometimes tried to reconcile themselves to the new vision of the world, but

[53] Cf. *Le Christianisme dans le monde* (1933); *L'Incroyance moderne* (1933); and *Réflexions sur la conversion du monde* (1936), all published in *Science et Christ*; and the extracts from *Christianisme et évolution* (1944) and *Le Christique* (1955) contained in Cuénot, *Teilhard de Chardin* (Écrivains de Toujours), pp. 66-67 and 139-144.

[54] "By the incarnation, God has descended into nature to super-animate it (*pour la suranimer*) and to bring it back to Himself: that is the substance of Christian dogma" (*La Mystique de la science* [1939], published in *L'Énergie humaine,* p. 220).

they have not yet accepted the modern faith in progress in a genuine and wholehearted way. Teilhard realized that a full acceptance of the evolutionary view of the world would involve a radical transformation of Christian doctrine, to such an extent that he spoke on occasion of the resulting religion as a "Neo-Christianity";[55] but he felt certain that this would not only conserve all that was essential in the traditional teaching, but would make its truth and beauty appear more clearly than ever. Only since the discovery of evolution, he held, could the full significance of St. Paul's texts on the *pleroma* be realized, and the cosmic Christ appear in His full grandeur.[56] As St. John baptized the Alexandrian concept of the Logos, so contemporary Christians must baptize the modern "Neo-Logos," the moving spirit of a developing universe. Teilhard thought that this integration of Christianity and evolutionism was already present in germ in his own life and work; once it was generally accepted, Christianity, fused with the new religious energies rising in mankind, would sweep through the world. The modern religion of progress, whether Marxist or Humanist, is in Teilhard's view an expression of Christ's spirit, and is only waiting to be baptized. Then faith in God and faith in the world will be joined in a consistently evolutionist Christianity, destined to be the universal religion of the future and the inspiration of mankind in the final stage of its progress toward *Omega.*[57]

In view of Teilhard's difficulties with his religious superiors, and the fact that Rome did not allow him to publish most of his writings, it is not surprising that his many humanist friends wondered why he did not leave the Roman Catholic Church. But Teilhard was convinced, not only that Christianity was destined to burst into new life, but also that the Roman Church as an organized body represented, in a special sense, the life of Christ in the world. Teilhard saw Christianity, like every other reality, on the analogy of a biological organism. During his earthly life, Christ, he held, had introduced a "phylum" of Christianity into the world, and this embryo could grow and progress only inside a

---

[55] In *Le coeur du problème*, a letter sent to the French Assistant to the General of the Jesuits in 1949, Teilhard spoke of "the urgent necessity for Christian faith in the 'Above' to incorporate the human neo-faith in a 'still to come'. This latter is born (and this is something that has happened and nothing can change) of the objective emergence of the ultra-human (releasing a neo-humanism, and automatically entailing a neo-Christianity)" (quoted in Cuénot, *Teilhard de Chardin, a Biographical Study*, pp. 270-271). Cf. also *L'Étoffe de l'univers* (1953), published in *L'Activation de l'énergie*, p. 405.

[56] *Super-Humanité—Super-Christ—Super-Charité* (1943), in *Science et Christ*, pp. 208-212; *Du cosmos à la cosmogenèse* (1951), in *L'Activation de l'énergie*, pp. 271-272; *La Parole attendue* (1940), quoted in Rideau, *op. cit.*, pp. 377-378.

[57] See references in Note 53 *supra*.

developing, collective tradition and within an organized body. Regarding evolution as a slow and painful process, he was less shocked by the reticence of ecclesiastical authorities toward his ideas than other men would be; he was confident that, in time, his outlook would be adopted by the Church. Convinced of the necessarily social nature of reality, and holding that the path of progress was that of organized unity, Teilhard was entirely sincere when he wrote to the General of the Society of Jesus that the whole structure of his thought bound him to the hierarchical Church.[58] The Roman Catholic Church represented, in his view, that portion of humanity which had become explicitly conscious of its unity with Christ; it was destined to be the center around which mankind would gather. "The ascending axis of hominization," he wrote in a letter, "runs through Rome."[59]

Since Teilhard believed that Christ was the source of all evolution, in the religious as in other spheres, it might be expected that he would be an advocate of a broad ecumenism embracing all religions. In fact, however, this was not altogether the case. For Teilhard held that the Eastern religions were fundamentally unprogressive; Buddhism had no faith in the world, while Islam, with its emphasis on the divine transcendence, set no value on human effort. Alone of the great world religions, Christianity, with its Pauline belief in the gradual building up of the Body of Christ, was capable of inspiring human progress. Accordingly, Teilhard suggested that ecumenical effort should be concentrated in two directions: the elaboration among Christians of all denominations of a Christianity that would be at once orthodox and open to all the values of an evolving world, and, on the other hand, the development among all men of a common faith in the world and in humanity. If these two faiths were fully developed, he thought, they would be found to converge. The essential division, in his view, was between those who did and those who did not believe in the communal future of mankind; and the most important ecumenism was that which would bring together Christians and all believers in Progress.[60]

---

[58] Letter quoted in Rideau, *op. cit.,* p. 598. Teilhard also suggested, in *Introduction au Christianisme* (1944), quoted by Rideau, p. 599, that the concentration of the Church's spiritual government in the Pope and Councils was analogous to the "cephalization" of the higher animals, i.e. to the concentration of the central organs of their nervous systems in their heads.

[59] Quoted in Rideau, *op. cit.,* p. 597.

[60] *L'Oecuménisme* (1946), in *Science et Christ,* pp. 251-254; cf. also the texts quoted by Rideau, *op. cit.,* pp. 631-635. Teilhard did not entirely despair of the Eastern religions, in the measure that they seemed to be being modified by the modern belief in progress (Rideau, p. 640). In *Le Christianisme dans le monde* (1933), he wrote: "The first great event to happen . . . will be the schism between believers and non-believers in the future of the world" (*Science et Christ,* pp. 144-145).

The Sources and Affinities of Teilhard's Thought

It is not possible, in the space here available, to attempt any exhaustive analysis of the relationship of Teilhard's doctrine with that of other thinkers. The influence of Aristotle and Bergson on his thought has already been mentioned, as has Teilhard's contact with his contemporaries Maurice Blondel and Edouard Le Roy, and, in later life, Sir Julian Huxley.[61] Teilhard's pan-psychism has an obvious affinity with that of Leibnitz, as his political and social theories, and especially his conception of freedom, have with those of Hegel and Marx; but it seems probable that these similarities are due more to a convergence of thought than to the direct influence of these philosophers. The ideas of progress and of socialization are the dominant myths of our time, and Teilhard seems to have absorbed them more through personal contacts and random conversations than from any explicit study of their philosophical sources.

In its essence, however, Teilhard's system is very much his own, and the basic sources of its inspiration can be identified through his own testimony. Teilhard was brought up as a Roman Catholic, and the devotion to the Sacred Heart of Jesus, which he learned from his mother, colored much of his early writing. On the other hand, as he tells us himself, his natural tendency had always been toward pantheism, seeking an Absolute in the world of nature.[62] In his youth, he did not dare to give free rein to his instinctive pantheism, because he did not see how it could be reconciled with his Christian faith. His soul was divided between these two conflicting tendencies until he descried, in the theory of evolution, the means of reconciling them.[63] A static pantheism, such as that of Spinoza, cannot be reconciled with Christianity, since its Absolute is an impersonal Whole. Teilhard's essential belief was always in the Whole, in the goodness, the organic unity, and the infallibility of the world;[64] but he also believed in Christ, in personal immortality, and in the value of human effort. The theory of evolution, he thought, enabled him to combine these beliefs into a consistent view

[61] Teilhard's Aristotelianism is probably derived from Aquinas and other Scholastic philosophers. Teilhard's supporters frequently claim that he has done for evolutionism what Aquinas did for Aristotelianism; saying this, they forget that Aquinas's incorporation of Aristotle was the weakest aspect of his thought.

[62] *Mon Univers* (1918), quoted in Cuénot, *Teilhard de Chardin* (Écrivains de Toujours), pp. 25-26; *Le Christ dans la matière* (1916), quoted *ibid.*, pp. 148-150.

[63] *Le coeur de la matière* (1950), quoted in H. de Lubac, *The Religion of Teilhard de Chardin*, p. 336 (note 56 to ch. 14).

[64] *Mon Univers* (1924), in *Science et Christ*, pp. 67-72; *Comment je crois* (1934), quoted in Rideau, *op. cit.*, p. 376.

of the world; in an evolving world, the Absolute could be seen as being ahead. Teilhard amended Bergson's evolutionism in the light of St. Paul's teaching on the Body of Christ. This enabled him to see the Absolute (*Omega*) as an organic Whole which, on the analogy of a living body, would not suppress its constituent parts, but perfect them. Hence Teilhard was able to deny that he was a pantheist in the sense condemned by the Church, for he did not believe that the Whole suppressed its parts; but he also held that his view of Christ as the heart or center of all things and as the moving force of the evolutionary process enabled Christianity to appropriate the element of truth pantheism contained, for it enabled the world and evolution itself to become the objects of love and adoration.[65] Teilhard's doctrine thus represents an attempted synthesis of Christianity and pantheism, supposedly made possible by a theory of convergent evolution.

III. EVALUATION

Unlike the majority of Roman Catholic evolutionists till recently, Teilhard saw that evolution cannot be regarded simply as an alternative means of accounting for the origin of the human body, while leaving the central doctrines of Christianity unaffected. Moreover, if his theory is compared with the somewhat similar one proposed by the Anglo-Catholic theologian L. S. Thornton, it will be seen that Teilhard is more consistent in that, where Thornton introduced the Incarnation from outside, although it was meant to be the climax of the evolutionary process, Teilhard insists that Christ has been present in the universe from the beginning, drawing matter upward into unity with Himself.[66] Teilhard takes evolution seriously, and at the same time he avoids many of the pitfalls into which modernist theologians often fall; accepting the historical Incarnation and putting Christ at the center of his explanation of the world, he avoids a relativism that would make all religions of equal value. Furthermore, in contrast to a purely materialist evolutionism, Teilhard's system restores man to a key place in the universe, while his view of *Omega* as the unity of mankind with God in Christ provides a genuine reason for envisaging a satisfying and final end of the evolutionary process. Teilhard's thought represents an exceptionally coherent transposition of Christianity into evolutionary terms, and it thus raises in an acute form the question of whether this transposition is justified and whether the resulting religion is genuinely Christian.

---

[65] *The Phenomenon of Man*, pp. 327 and 309-310; *Esquisse d'un univers personnel* (1936), in *L'Énergie humaine*, pp. 103-104 and 113; *L'énergie humaine* (1937), *ibid.*, p. 163. Cf. also C. Soucy, *op. cit.*, pp. 204-207.

[66] On Thornton, see C. E. Raven, *op. cit.*, and P. E. Hughes, *Christianity and the Problem of Origins*, pp. 28-30.

THE VISION OF THE PAST

One cannot help being struck, when reading Teilhard, by the vigor, not to say arrogance, of his affirmation of the truth of the theory of evolution. The distinguishing mark of a modern man, he tells us, is that he can see nothing save in evolutionary terms; and to question the truth of evolutionism is a sure sign of backwardness.[67] Yet the critical reader cannot help observing, at the same time, that Teilhard advances no solid proof of the evolutionary theory and that, in fact, many of his arguments tend to show that such a proof cannot be given.

Teilhard declares, it will be remembered, that all or most species quickly become static, except for those which represent the axis or spearhead of evolution. He also thinks that man stopped evolving physically, in any observable way, at least twenty thousand years ago. He thus equivalently admits that it is impossible for us to observe any transformation of species actually taking place. Teilhard also declares that, from a paleontological point of view, the origins of every species necessarily disappear; it is only when a phylum or species has become numerous and well established that it can be expected to leave any fossil remains. He thus admits that no fossils have been or are likely to be found that could bridge the gaps between the biological phyla, each of which makes its appearance in a fully recognizable form. His attempt to explain away this awkward state of affairs is ingenious; but, as Louis Bounoure has written, one would have to be touched by an evolutionary grace to find it convincing.[68] In any case it is clear that Teilhard thus admits that paleontology provides no direct evidence that phyla arise by evolutionary transformation.

As has been seen, Teilhard also held that the theory of evolution did not require any particular explanation of the transformation of species; the disproof of the theories of Lamarck, Darwin, or the neo-Darwinians would not endanger the certainty of the basic evolutionary doctrine. In other words, the truth of evolutionism does not depend, in Teilhard's view, on any particular biological evidence. Now all this is very convenient, it might be thought, for the theory of evolution. By this very fact, however, Teilhard admits that the theory is proved neither by ordinary observation nor by paleontology nor by biology, and that it is really, in his view, an *a priori* certitude, independent of particular evidence. The only positive argument for evolution on which Teilhard insists is that this theory alone enables the successive appearance of the biological phyla in the course of geological time to be

[67] *The New Spirit* (1942), in *The Future of Man,* p. 85; and see the texts quoted in Note 29 *supra*.

[68] L. Bounoure, *Déterminisme et finalité,* p. 65.

rationally explained; living beings can be classified, and the only rational form of classification is in terms of common descent. In the absence of any direct evidence of either the fact or the manner of evolution, however, the theory can provide no more than a pseudo-explanation of the origin of phyla and species, similar to the *virtus dormitiva* and other imaginary forces which excited the ridicule of seventeenth- and eighteenth-century philosophers and scientists. This is particularly true of Teilhard's "radial energy," which is simply a hypostatization of the process of unification which he imagines, without any evidence, to have taken place. The statement that the possibility of rational classification presupposes a genealogical relationship among the forms to be classified is entirely gratuitous, since classification both can be and actually is made primarily in terms of comparative anatomy.

That no scientific evidence yet discovered proves the truth of the theory of evolution is the explicit opinion of many eminent biologists. After examining the various suppositions necessarily made by evolutionists, and finding that none of them has been strictly proved, Professor Kerkut (of Southampton University) rightly condemns the dogmatic tone in which the theory is commonly propounded.[69] In his lucid and often witty book *Déterminisme et finalité,* Louis Bounoure (Professor of General Biology at Strasbourg University) calls for a return to the humility and critical skepticism that should characterize the true scientist, and for the abandonment of the circular arguments and unverifiable speculations of the evolutionists. Bounoure rightly points out the fallacy of the argument, brought by Teilhard as by other evolutionists, which declares that evolution must be true because no alternative theory can be suggested; on the contrary, he declares, it is better to have no theory and to admit one's ignorance than to cling to a misleading theory. Considered even from a pragmatic point of view, moreover, evolution is an unfruitful hypothesis; none of the great advances made by biology in the course of this century—in the fields of embryology, genetics, and biochemistry, for example—owes anything to the theory of evolution; and even paleontology owes its essential classification to Cuvier, a resolute *fixiste.* Science, in Bounoure's view, cannot solve the problem of origins, but biology can and does disprove the evolutionary theory, since it shows that living organisms can vary only within limits which in some cases are wide but which are fixed for each species. New varieties and races can be developed, but even in laboratory conditions new species of animals cannot.[70]

[69] G. A. Kerkut, *Implications of Evolution.*
[70] L. Bounoure, *op. cit.* Among other important scientific criticisms of evolutionism may be mentioned: Prof. Paul Lemoine, *Conclusions générales* in Vol. 5 of the *Encyclopédie Française*; Prof. W. R. Thompson's Introduction to

To conclude this short discussion of the scientific evidence for and against the theory of evolution, it may be said that there is certainly no conclusive proof of its truth, but that there is, on the contrary, strong evidence for its falsehood. On the one hand there is the complete absence of positive evidence where one would expect to find it, an absence Teilhard admits by the very fact that he tries to explain it away; on the other hand there is the fact of the stability of species. Every living creature, moreover, is perfect of its kind, a unified and highly complicated organism perfectly adapted to its conditions of life. No merely groping or rudimentary consciousness can account for the perfection of the bodily mechanism even of a monocellular being, let alone of an insect or a mammal, or the perfection of the instinctive behavior which results from that mechanism; this behavior presupposes the highest intelligence, which, however, cannot be in the creatures themselves, since they show no sign of it in other circumstances.[71] Science cannot prove creationism any more than it can prove evolutionism, but an unprejudiced consideration of the organization and behavior of living things shows that the traditional Christian belief in special creation is a more reasonable one than is faith in a mythical evolutionary process.

Teilhard's faith in evolution, as has been seen, was not dependent on empirical evidence. In this sense it could be described as a metaphysical belief. His evolutionism has, however, no more claim to be regarded as genuinely philosophical than as scientific. For the primary canon of sound philosophical method insists on the same critical skepticism that is required of the scientist; indeed the philosopher has even more need to be critical than has the scientist, since his conclusions are not susceptible of empirical verification. The genuine philosopher must take the greatest care to overcome his emotional preferences; he must be wary of accepting the popular catch-phrases and myths of the moment for genuine insights; he must weigh all theories in the balance of truth, affirming as true nothing that is open to doubt. In all these respects Teilhard falls short, for it is clear that his wholehearted acceptance of evolutionism was primarily due to his innate leaning toward pantheism, his pre-rational craving to see the world as a unified system, and to his desire to identify himself with the enthusiasms of his contemporaries. He had not learned that distrust of emotional impressions and of popular opinion which is the particular legacy of the great philosophers of his own country. It is only fair to add, however, that Teilhard never claimed to be a philosopher. He saw the modern faith

---

the "Everyman" Centenary Edition of Darwin's *Origin of Species*; Dr. M. Vernet, *La grande illusion de Teilhard de Chardin;* Dr. R. E. D. Clark, *Darwin: Before and After.*

71 Bernard Acworth, *Bird and Butterfly Mysteries*; L. Bounoure, *op. cit.*

in progress as a new religion rising on earth, and it seems true to say that his own belief in convergent evolution was essentially a religious faith. Teilhard was pre-eminently a believer, but the question remains whether his religion was Christian.[72]

It is evident that the text of the Old Testament absolutely excludes the theory of evolution. It is, of course, now fashionable to say that the Bible has no teaching on the *how* of creation, and to write off the first chapter of Genesis as a mythical account whose only positive teaching is that God is the ultimate source of all things. The more conservative Catholics cling to monogenism, but rather on the basis of St. Paul's teaching than on that of Genesis. But if one is willing to take the Book of Genesis at its word, the ten-times-repeated "according to its kind," "according to their kinds," could hardly be clearer than it is, teaching a truth that is fully confirmed by the observations of naturalists. Equally clear is the incompatibility of evolutionism with the biblical account of the Fall, an incompatibility that is admitted by Teilhard and by the many theologians who are at present seeking a new interpretation of original sin to harmonize with the supposed fact of evolution. One can of course reconcile evolutionism with the first two chapters of Genesis if one is willing to "demythologize" these to a sufficient extent, and this is what is increasingly being done by contemporary biblical critics; but it would be disingenuous to claim that "the progress of biblical scholarship" shows that Genesis can be reconciled with evolutionism, since in reality the supposed truth of evolutionism is what generally prompts the critics to interpret Genesis in the way they do.

But it would be wrong to suppose that the incompatibility of evolutionism with Christianity depends only on a strict interpretation of the first chapters of Genesis and of parallel texts. For it cannot seriously be denied that the whole biblical view of the world, expressed in the New Testament as well as in the Old, supposes that the world and man were created perfect, and that the disorder into which man's world has fallen is due to his own fault. There is no biblical ground, any more than there is an empirical one, for describing the world of matter and of animals as imperfect or disordered; it is only man who, by the misuse of his free-will in refusing to be subject to God, has introduced disharmony into the universe. The biblical doctrine is thus the reverse of the evolutionary perspective, and in particular of Teilhard's theory of creation by gradual unification. For Teilhard holds that the world was created imperfect, and that disorder is the very nature of a creation that is not yet fully

---

[72] Evolution is often accepted on the ground of human progress in knowledge and in control over nature; this progress was regarded by Teilhard as a real continuation of biological evolution. This argument will be considered below.

organized. Holding this view, he cannot avoid attributing the primary responsibility for evil to God, though he tries to mitigate the immorality of this view by representing multiplicity as a quasi-real principle of evil and dispersion which God can overcome only gradually, and which thus limits His omnipotence. Teilhard thought of himself as an optimist, and criticized Puritans and Jansenists for allegedly regarding the world as evil; but paradoxically it was he, not they, who denied the goodness of creation. Teilhard's God could not have looked at His creation in the beginning and pronounced it good; He could only have seen it as starting its painful ascent from disorder toward goodness.

As has been seen, Teilhard's sense of the suffering and effort involved in evolution was so strong that it led him to deny that God could have created the world out of pure generosity. The world, he held, must add something to God's perfection; otherwise it would not have been worthwhile for Him to create it. In this way, however, he undermines the divine transcendence, and directly contradicts the biblical doctrine of the gratuity both of creation and of redemption. Only this inadequate view of God can explain Teilhard's objectively blasphemous assertion that it would be humiliating for man to be merely the recipient of God's favor, and his demand that human effort should be able to contribute to the divine perfection.

But Teilhard's theory also has another consequence: it blurs the distinction between physical imperfection and moral evil. For if evil is the necessary price of progress, then sin cannot be taken seriously. As a result, Teilhard fails to see that man's heart is estranged from God, and does not appreciate his need of redemption. He thus sees the incarnation and death of Christ primarily in cosmic terms, as the means of overcoming disunity, rather than as God's merciful intervention to pay the debt of human sin. Even those who are generally favorable to Teilhard usually admit the inadequacy of his view of sin, but they fail to recognize that this view is inseparable from his whole evolutionist position. Denying the radical nature of sin, Teilhard in effect denies the holiness of God and the absolute nature of the moral law. But at the same time, by denying man's responsibility for evil, he deprives him of his essential dignity and value as a moral being. Not to take sin seriously is a sign that one does not take man seriously either.[73]

[73] The low value Teilhard set on man is also seen from the fact that he thought the "cosmic" rôle that he attributed to Christ a higher and more dignified one than that of redeeming mankind; cf. *Christianisme et évolution* (1945), quoted in Cuénot, *Teilhard de Chardin* (Écrivains de Toujours), p. 142.

HUMAN PROGRESS AND CHRIST

Though Teilhard's whole doctrine is dependent on the theory of evolution, his own more particular contribution to this theory consists in his view that human progress represents the continuation of the evolutionary process, which is destined to reach its culmination in a unified and organized Super-Humanity. Now there is no doubt that the evident fact of technical progress is one of the chief factors that dispose people to believe in evolution, but it is not difficult to see that there is no real connection between the two processes. It is because man, unlike God, does not possess the initial knowledge necessary to make, for instance, a perfect machine at his first attempt, that he has perforce to be an "evolver"; it is only by degrees that he learns to know and master natural forces, and thus to make the material world subservient to his purposes. To suppose that God acts in the same way, bringing His works to perfection only by gradual stages, is to suppose that He too lacks either the knowledge or the power to do otherwise.[74] But the changes brought about by man's gradually extending control over nature are changes not in man himself, but in his environment and in the outward conditions of his life. Not only does every child have to start again from scratch, but material progress is not accompanied by any change in human nature or by any necessary advance in the fields that give intrinsic value to human life. The well-to-do dweller in a modern industrial society is not necessarily more sensitive to beauty, sounder in his judgment, more unselfish and honest in his behavior, or more devoted to his family, than is the "backward" and illiterate peasant whom he perhaps despises; still less, of course, is he necessarily more closely united to God by adoption and grace. Technical progress and the acquirement of wealth or comfort are legitimate and natural objects of human enterprise, but it is a mistake to suppose that they bring about any change in human nature itself.[75]

Teilhard is able to represent technical and scientific progress as a real evolution of mankind only because he regards humanity as a single super-organism. It is important to realize that this theory, which is an essential part of Teilhard's whole conception of convergent evolution, is derived entirely from evolutionary speculation. In his book *The Phenomenon of Man*, which purports to give a descriptive analysis of man, Teilhard devotes only ten pages (206-215) to the whole history of mankind from the neolithic age till the nineteenth century, while devoting

[74] Cf. Bernard Acworth, *op. cit.*, pp. 110-112, and the same author's *This Progress*, pp. 210-213.
[75] Cf. Jacques Ellul, *Exégèse des nouveaux lieux communs*, pp. 178-194, 251-259.

the rest of the book, which has 284 pages, to the (mythical) pre-history of man and to his equally mythical future. The true sources of knowledge about man—revelation and history—are entirely neglected, and Teilhard passes almost directly, in the words of the title of one of his essays, from the pre-human to the ultra-human.[76] In consequence it is not surprising that his view of the merely human is defective.

As a result of his view of mankind as an organic unity inspired by Christ, Teilhard considers that humanity as a whole is better and more valuable than any individual, and regards the ideas and aspirations that are dominant in the world—and in particular its faith in progress—as necessarily true. Regarding evolution as a movement toward organized unity, he makes this movement itself the criterion of morality and demands a "pre-adherence" to all that it may involve.[77] He thus suppresses the duty, and indeed the possibility, for each individual human being to form his own independent judgment in matters either of belief or of conduct. In Teilhard's view, the individual has no direct access either to a stable truth or to God Himself, who is present only in the Whole; the supremacy of conscience is thus overthrown, and nonconformity with the world becomes the basic sin.

Teilhard's view on these matters is both false and dangerous. Common observation shows that men are usually more reasonable when acting as individuals than when submerged in a larger group. Sound philosophy insists on the importance of each man's judging for himself, since popular opinions are usually the expression, in part at least, of sentiment or prejudice. It is true that, in science, numbers of observers are needed to multiply experiments and to correlate results, but the interpretation of these data remains the prerogative of the individual. Above all, morality demands that each individual person be recognized as a responsible moral agent. Though regarding himself as a humanist, Teilhard thus denies the true value and dignity of the individual human being. This dignity, on the other hand, has a firm basis in both the Old and New Testaments, which teach that every human being is made in the image of God and is directly responsible for his actions to Him alone.[78]

The low value Teilhard set on human beings, considered individually, is also seen in his depreciation of the juridical conception of men's relationships with God and with one another, and in his preference for

---

[76] *From the Pre-Human to the Ultra-Human* (1950), published in *The Future of Man*, pp. 289-297.

[77] "Only one way remains open for us: to trust ourselves to the infallibility and the finally beatifying value of the operation which is drawing us together" (*L'énergie humaine* [1937], in *L'Énergie humaine*, p. 156). Cf. also *Mon Univers* (1924), in *Science et Christ*, p. 94.

[78] Cf. Gen. 1:26-27; Rom. 2:15; Jer. 17:7-10; Ezek. 18:1-32; Rom. 14:10-12; I Cor. 4:1-5; I Cor. 10:1-5.

seeing these relations on a physical or organic model. To be subject to law is the condition of a free creature, having absolute rights and duties, whereas the parts of an organism are not free and have value only within the whole to which they belong. Teilhard did not recognize man's true position as a free and responsible, but sinful, creature; as a result his view of man, despite his contrary intention, is not more but less than human.

Teilhard's view of mankind as a single super-organism is at the root of his political ideas, which show a serious lack of concern for human freedom.[79] Though Teilhard was doubtless right in seeing Communism, Fascism, and the "democratic" upholders of a centrally planned society as being fundamentally on the same side, opposed only by individualist Liberalism, he was entirely wrong in his evaluation of this phenomenon. Individualism, in the sense in which it is opposed to collectivist ideologies, so far from being identified with selfishness, consists in respect for the rights and freedom of other people, and in a refusal to seek unfair advantages for oneself at their expense. Teilhard favored a world government and the worldwide planning and control of commerce and industry, thus depriving individuals of the power to manage their own affairs and leaving them at the mercy of a central authority which could control every aspect of their lives. He also favored a world eugenic program, designed to eliminate "backward" races and to promote "progressive" strains. In every department of life, the human individual was, in Teilhard's eyes, subordinated to the supposed good of humanity as a whole.

It is possible that this description of Teilhard's program for mankind could be regarded as unduly somber, since he thought that the individual attained his true perfection within an organic unity and that socialization must be brought about by the force of love and of a common enthusiasm for progress. In itself this objection is true, though Teilhard's call for psychologists to aid men to attain unanimity has a certain aura of brainwashing, and his conception of freedom is inadequate. There is no reason to doubt his sincerity in thinking that mankind would freely choose organized unity and would be perfected by it; his idealism is as evident as is his naivete, but there is no one so dangerous as a misguided idealist, and no tyranny so absolute as one that demands not only to be obeyed, but also to be loved.

The fundamental objection to Teilhard's view of mankind as an organic whole inspired by Christ is, however, that this view is directly opposed to the teaching of the Bible. As has been seen, Teilhard's evolutionism resulted in his neglect of the Fall and in his failure to take

[79] Teilhard's attitude toward totalitarianism forms an instructive contrast with that adopted (for instance) by Barth, Bonhoeffer, and Brunner.

sin seriously; in consequence, he failed to see that man's heart is turned away from God. The Old Testament is a record of human apostasy, in which even the Chosen People are seen continually slipping back into idolatry. God chose and sanctified individuals—patriarchs, judges, and prophets, for instance—to be His witnesses; and the Old Testament frequently makes mention of just men who were God's friends; but its picture of mankind as a whole leaves no doubt of its corruption. The New Testament records the merciful entry of Christ into the world to save sinners, but it also represents Him as rejected by "the world" and as foretelling the persecutions His followers would have to undergo. "To as many as received Him, He gave power to become the sons of God," but His Kingdom was not to be of this world. Far from suggesting, as does Teilhard, that mankind would welcome Christ's second coming as the culmination of its progress, the New Testament speaks constantly in terms of widespread apostasy before the End.[80] Christ's return will bring deliverance to His elect and will establish the reign of justice and righteousness, but it will be a day of judgment for the world.

Teilhard himself realized that his outlook differed widely from the biblical view of the world. In a letter written a year before his death, he declared that he had no sympathy with biblical creationism, which he found childish and anthropomorphic;[81] elsewhere he affirmed that not even the profoundest respect for the words of Jesus could prevent one from seeing that the Gospel was expressed in "neolithic" terms,[82] and he commented unfavorably on the "rabbinical and cavilling" side of St. Paul's writings.[83] Teilhard considered that the historical Christ was merely the germ from which the Christian religion was to grow,[84] and this view obviously leaves no room for any claim to finality on behalf of the historical revelation, such as that made by St. Paul in Galatians 1:8. In spite of this, however, Teilhard thought that his vision of mankind as an organic unity centered on Christ coincided with the doctrine expressed by St. Paul, especially in Ephesians, Philippians, and Colossians; and shortly before his death he summed up his view of the world in terms of I Corinthians 15:26-28. This interpretation of St. Paul has been strongly

[80] Cf. John 1:12; John 18:36; Luke 18:8. A view similar to that of Teilhard on this matter is, however, widespread among contemporary Catholic theologians.

[81] "I do not recognize in myself any sympathy for biblical creationism (save in the measure that it grounds the possibility of union). Otherwise, I find the biblical idea of creation rather childish and anthropomorphic" (Letter of January 14, 1954, quoted in Philippe de la Trinité, *Rome et Teilhard de Chardin*, p. 168).

[82] *Le Phénomène chrétien* (1950), unpublished essay quoted in Rideau, *op. cit.*, p. 319.

[83] *Christologie et évolution* (1933), unpublished essay quoted *ibid.*, pp. 319-320.

[84] This expression is taken from a conversation reported by Cuénot, *Teilhard de Chardin* (Écrivains de Toujours), pp. 147-148.

defended by Raven,[85] among others; but the New Testament clearly shows that the Body of Christ of which the Apostle speaks, so far from being identical with mankind as a whole, is made up of those men and women whom the Father has called out of the world and given to Christ, and who are saved by grace working itself out in repentance and faith.[86] It is absolutely true, in the biblical perspective, that the individual can be saved only in and through Christ, but Teilhard's fundamental mistake, which vitiates the whole of his moral, political, and religious teaching, consists in identifying the Body of Christ with what is really unregenerate humanity. Teilhard's view that mankind as a whole is united to Christ, and that only the individual who dares to separate himself from it can be lost, is thus the exact reverse of the biblical doctrine. Even apart from the explicit teaching of the New Testament, however, it would seem that no one whose moral vision was not dimmed by evolutionary "biologism" could mistake the spirit of the world for the Spirit of Christ, or imagine that a worldwide eugenic program, for instance, could prepare the way for the *parousia*.

At first sight, Teilhard's theology, with its emphasis on the Incarnation and on the central role of Christ in the evolutionary process, seems preferable, from the orthodox Christian point of view, to the "secularizing" and "demythologizing" theories of existentialist and Liberal theologians. But this appearance is deceptive, for Teilhard's view reverses the whole biblical perspective of the relations of God, man, and the world, and thus falsifies all moral and religious values. Identifying mankind with the Body of Christ, Teilhard in effect calls on us to adore unregenerate humanity and to accept its values. Such a view is more dangerous than any skepticism, in the measure that it is worse to worship a false God than not to worship any God at all. Teilhard tells us that "mankind has reached the biological point where it must either lose all confidence in the universe or else resolutely worship it. . . . The time is past when God could impose Himself on us simply from outside, like a master or a proprietor. The world will not kneel down henceforth except before the organic center of its evolution."[87]

In identifying this mythical "center of the world's evolution" with Christ, Teilhard's intention was to baptize the modern cult of progress; in reality, however, he was laying the foundation for the religion of antichrist. II Thessalonians 2 and Revelation 13 make it clear that the kingdom of antichrist will be a totalitarian world-state, controlling every aspect of the lives of men; the antichrist will identify himself with Christ

---

[85] *Op. cit.,* ch. 8.
[86] Cf. Eph. 2; John 17, etc.
[87] *Le Phénomène spirituel* (1937), published in *L'Énergie humaine,* p. 136. Part of this text is quoted in Rideau, *op. cit.,* pp. 318-319.

and will demand the worship due to God. Deceiving all but the elect, he will be adored by the rest of mankind and will persecute all who refuse to admit his pretensions.[88]

Teilhard's teaching on the coming Super-Humanity involves just this false identification of Christ with the "center" or moving spirit of mankind organized into a totalitarian world community. If one's God is a false one, one does not become a Christian by identifying him or it with Christ.

This judgment of Teilhard's system may seem harsh. It is not in any way suggested, however, that he himself was aware of the real significance of what he was doing. On the contrary, it is clear that he was so completely under the influence of "progressive" mythology, and of the theory of evolution on which it is based, that he sincerely believed that he was translating the basic message of Christianity into modern terms. For while many other aspects of his theology are open to detailed objection, all Teilhard's errors can be traced back to the two fundamental ones we have examined: his acceptance of the theory of evolution, and his identification of mankind as a whole—and indeed of the universe—with the Body of Christ. And these two theories are closely linked together, for it is Teilhard's evolutionism that leads him to identify Christ with the moving force of the world. Hence no criticism of Teilhard can be adequate which does not go to the root of his thought: evolutionism. This is unfortunately the case with most Roman Catholic critics of Teilhard, and in particular of the *Monitum* in which the Roman Holy Office warned against the uncritical acceptance of his ideas.[89] These critics presumed that evolution was a scientific theory without direct religious significance, but in this they were mistaken. As has been seen, evolutionism has no firm scientific or philosophical basis, but is a religious—fundamentally pantheistic—view of the world; it was his consistent adoption of this view that led Teilhard away from historic Christianity.

Teilhard's often poetical and visionary style can easily lead one not to take his writings seriously. But it would be a mistake to underestimate the appeal that his thought makes to those who have been taught to accept evolution as proved and who have no firm belief in the authority of the Bible. Teilhard gives an apparently Christian expression to beliefs taken for granted by many, perhaps most, of our contemporaries. The societies

---

[88] On antichrist and the end of history, see the excellent study by the German Catholic philosopher, Josef Pieper, *The End of Time*.

[89] The *Monitum* was dated June 30, 1962, and published in *Acta Apostolicae Sedis* 54 (August 6, 1962), p. 526. Those Catholic critics of Teilhard who take their stand on Thomist philosophy fail to see that Aquinas's attempted synthesis of Aristotelianism with Christianity presents a certain analogy with Teilhard's transposition of Christianity into evolutionary terms.

that have been formed to study and propagate his ideas[90] bring together Roman Catholics and Marxists, Anglicans and atheistic Humanists, in a common sympathy which Teilhard would have welcomed as the beginning of that fusion of Christianity with the modern religion of progress which he foresaw. Teilhard's Neo-Christianity puts Christians before a crucial choice, which will have a decisive effect on the future both of the Roman Catholic *aggiornamento* and of the ecumenical movement. These movements have, till now, been marked both by a revival of concern for the Bible and by a desire to adapt Christianity to the evolutionary view of the world; but Teilhard's thought shows that these two tendencies are mutually incompatible: one cannot combine evolutionism with fidelity to the biblical revelation. It may be conjectured that the choice between these two alternatives will cut across all existing denominational boundaries; but once it has taken place Christians will not be divided in terms of secondary issues, but in terms of their fundamental loyalty to the Word of God, to that truth which makes men free.

[90] E.g. *The Pierre Teilhard de Chardin Association of Great Britain and Ireland,* of London. Similar societies exist in Paris and Brussels.

IV. BIBLIOGRAPHY

(The following bibliography is far from complete. A full list of works by and about Teilhard de Chardin has been published by Ladislaus Polgár, *Internationale Teilhard-Bibliographie, 1955-1965,* Freiburg-Munich, 1965).

PRINCIPAL WORKS BY TEILHARD DE CHARDIN

Genèse d'une pensée. Lettres 1914-1919. Paris, 1961 (*The Making of a Mind. Letters from a Soldier Priest, 1914-1919.* London, 1965).

Lettres de voyage (1923-1955). Paris, 1961 (*Letters from a Traveller, 1923-1955.* London, 1967).

Le Groupe zoologique humain. Paris, 1956 (*Man's Place in Nature.* London, 1966).

Le Phénomène humain. Paris, 1955 (*The Phenomenon of Man.* London, 1959).

L'Apparition de l'homme. Paris, 1956 (*The Appearance of Man.* London, 1965).

La Vision du passé. Paris, 1957 (*The Vision of the Past.* London, 1966).

Le Milieu divin. Paris, 1957 (*Le Milieu Divin.* London, 1960).

L'Avenir de l'homme. Paris, 1959 (*The Future of Man.* London, 1964).

L'Énergie humaine. Paris, 1962.

L'Activation de l'énergie. Paris, 1963.

Science et Christ. Paris, 1965.

Hymne de l'univers. Paris, 1963 (*The Hymn of the Universe.* London, 1965).

(Of the above books, all save *Le Groupe zoologique humain, Le Phénomène humain,* and *Le Milieu divin* are collections of essays and other shorter works. *Le Groupe zoologique humain* has also been published in French under the title *La Place de l'homme dans la nature.*)

WORKS ON TEILHARD DE CHARDIN

Corte, N. *La Vie et l'âme de Teilhard de Chardin.* Paris, 1957 (*Pierre Teilhard de Chardin, his Life and Spirit.* London, 1960).

Cuénot, Claude. *Pierre Teilhard de Chardin; Les grandes étapes de son évolution*. Paris, 1958 (*Pierre Teilhard de Chardin, his Life and Spirit*. London, 1960).

———. *Teilhard de Chardin* (Écrivains de Toujours). Paris, 1962.

———. *Lexique Teilhard de Chardin*. Paris, 1963.

Francoeur, Robert T. (ed.). *The World of Teilhard de Chardin*. Baltimore, 1961.

de Lubac, Henri (S.J.). *La Pensée religieuse du Père Teilhard de Chardin*. Paris, 1962 (*The Religion of Teilhard de Chardin*. London, 1967).

Rabut, Olivier (O.P.). *Dialogue avec Teilhard de Chardin*. Paris, 1958 (*Dialogue with Teilhard de Chardin*. London, 1961).

Raven, C. E. *Teilhard de Chardin, Scientist and Seer*. London, 1962.

Rideau, Emile (S.J.). *La Pensée du Père Teilhard de Chardin*. Paris, 1965 (*Teilhard de Chardin: A Guide to his Thought*. London, 1967).

Soucy, Claude. *Pensée logique et pensée politique chez Teilhard de Chardin*. Paris, 1967.

Towers, Bernard. *Teilhard de Chardin* (Makers of Contemporary Theology). London and Richmond, Va., 1966.

de la Trinité, Philippe (O.C.D.). *Rome et Teilhard de Chardin*. Paris, 1964.

Vernet, Maurice. *La grande illusion de Teilhard de Chardin*. Paris, 1964.

(Cuénot was a friend of Teilhard and is a warm admirer of his ideas; his books give perhaps the most authentic picture of Teilhard's thought. Rideau is particularly valuable for the quotations he gives from Teilhard's unpublished works. Soucy's book is essential for any study of Teilhard's political and social ideas. Raven expresses the welcome given by an Anglican evolutionist to Teilhard's thought, while Vernet effectively criticizes Teilhard from a biological point of view.)

OTHER WORKS REFERRED TO IN TEXT

Acworth, Bernard. *This Progress*. London, 1934.

———. *Bird and Butterfly Mysteries*. London, 1955.

Boule, Marcellin. *Les Hommes fossiles*. Paris, 3rd ed. 1946.

Bounoure, Louis. *Déterminisme et finalité*. Paris, 1957.

Clark, Robert E. D. *Darwin: Before and After*. Exeter, 1966.

Darwin, Charles. *The Origin of Species* ("Everyman" Centenary Edition, with Introduction by W. R. Thompson). London, 1956.

Ellul, Jacques. *Exégèse des nouveaux lieux communs*. Paris, 1966.

Hughes, Philip Edgcumbe. *Christianity and the Problem of Origins*. Philadelphia, 1964.

Kerkut, G. A. *Implications of Evolution*. Oxford, 1960.

Pierre Teilhard de Chardin

O'Connor, Patrick. *Science of Today and the Problems of Genesis.* St. Paul, Minn., 1960.

Pieper, Josef. *Über das Ende der Zeit.* Munich, 1950 (*The End of Time.* London, 1954).

Encyclopédie Française, Vol. 5 (Les Êtres Vivants). Paris, 1938.

14 KENNETH HAMILTON

Paul Tillich

I. BIOGRAPHY

T HE THOUGHT of Paul Johannes Tillich is intimately connected with the events of his life, events which provide many dramatic contrasts and illustrate the transition from the self-confidence of the nineteenth century to the anxiousness of the twentieth. Born August 20, 1886, in Starzeddel-bei-Guben, a village in the province of Brandenburg near the Silesian border, where his father was a minister of the Prussian Territorial Church, Tillich grew up in the medieval towns of Schönfliess-Neumark and Königsberg-Neumark. This environment fostered both a sense of the past and a delight in nature that, reinforced by a life-long devotion to German poetry, remained with him in the romantic and mystical stamp of his mind. In 1900 his family moved to Berlin, where the cultural riches of the great city awakened intellectual excitement. Even before graduating from the *gymnasium* he had received a good grounding in philosophy. Through philosophical argument he found means of combatting the conservative theology of his father. He has said that this early experience gave him understanding of the tension between the religious and the humanistic streams of European culture.

From 1904 to 1909 he studied at the universities of Berlin, Tübingen, and Halle. In 1911 he presented his thesis for the degree of Doctor of Philosophy at Breslau, and in 1912 his thesis for the Licentiate of

Dr. Kenneth Hamilton is Assistant Professor of Systematic Theology at United College, Winnipeg, Manitoba. His published works include *The System and the Gospel: A Critique of Paul Tillich* (1963).

Theology at Halle — both theses on aspects of Schelling's later thought. At Halle he studied under Martin Kähler, whose "mediating theology" became the inspiration of his own theological outlook. In 1912 he was ordained into the Evangelical Lutheran Church of the province of Brandenburg, and engaged in parish work until the outbreak of the First World War. Four years as an army chaplain were followed by five years as a *Privatdozent* of theology at the University of Berlin. The war years stimulated in him two very different yet allied preoccupations: a love of art and engagement with radical social ideals. The first led to his making a theology of culture the focus of his teaching at Berlin, while the second resulted in his active participation in the German Religious Socialist movement. Modern painting, Marxism, and psychoanalysis were for him different aspects of twentieth-century culture with which a theologian, as a man of his times, must grapple if he is to speak relevantly to his generation.

In 1924 he went to occupy the chair of theology at Marburg. Here he came into contact with existentialism through the teaching of Martin Heidegger, who was professor of philosophy at Marburg from 1923 to 1929. Here also he began work on his system of systematic theology, a work which was not to reach a definite form until his years in America. From 1926-1929 he was professor of religion and social philosophy at Dresden and at Leipzig, and in 1929 was called to the chair of philosophy at Frankfurt-am-Main. When Hitler became German Chancellor in 1933 he was dismissed from his position. At the invitation of Reinhold Niebuhr, who was then visiting Germany, he went to the United States in November 1933 to become Charles Briggs Graduate Professor of Philosophical Theology at Union Seminary, New York.

At the age of forty-seven, Tillich began a new career in the New World. He was already known in the land of his adoption through H. Richard Niebuhr's translation of his *Die religiöse Lage der Gegenwart* (*The Religious Situation,* 1932). At first in translation, but soon in English, his articles and contributions to books began to appear, although only one book of his authorship (*The Interpretation of History,* 1936) was published between 1933 and 1948. (The latter year saw the publication of both *The Protestant Era* and *The Shaking of the Foundations.*) When the first volume of the *Systematic Theology* came out in 1951 he had long been recognized as one of the leading figures in American Protestantism. And in 1952 his position was recognized by his being made the subject of the first volume of the Macmillan Company's series The Library of Living Theology. A dozen volumes since have come from his pen, including the second and the third (concluding) volumes of the *Systematic Theology.* He remained at Union Seminary until his retirement in 1954, after which he went to Harvard as University Professor and Professor of Theology.   Subsequently, he transferred to Chicago in 1962, where he served as John Nuveen Professor of Theology in the Divinity School in the University of Chicago. Tillich died on October 23, 1965.

For very many years Tillich was widely regarded, together with Reinhold Niebuhr, as the foremost champion in North America of European "neo-orthodoxy."   It was assumed that he belonged to the Barthian camp — and this in spite of the fact that already in 1935 he had declared his opposition to Barthian theology in an article, "What Is Wrong with the 'Dialectic' Theology?" His *Systematic Theology,* however, showed his independence as a philosophical theologian.   In fact, there was no radical alteration in his general outlook after his departure from Germany, but only a continuous development along the lines indicated by his earliest writings.   Some changes in emphasis there indeed were. While still convinced that his work for the religious socialist cause was right and necessary, he no longer engaged in political activity. And a visit to Japan in 1960 brought home to him the importance of the dialogue between Christianity and other religions.

Although Tillich founded no "school," his teachings have been debated — by Roman Catholics as well as by Protestants — more keenly than those of any other theologian in North America.   European interest, too, has been rekindled by his presence in his homeland for periods since the Second World War. (A German "Complete Works" is now being published.) Britain has recently "discovered" him.   So he has a truly international reputation. Probably only Rudolf Bultmann has exerted a comparable influence upon present-day theology.

II. EXPOSITION

Theological Perspective

Tillich's pilgrimage through life convinced him that the fitting symbol of his personal and intellectual development is the border line. What he has learned has been the result of fruitful tension between opposing values, attitudes, and opinions.[1] In particular, he has felt the tension between the tenets of religious faith and the demands of the intellect.   His career, in fact, has been one where he has been called upon to serve both theology and philosophy, and he has never tried to keep the two concerns in separate compartments.   "As a theologian I tried to remain a philosopher, and conversely so."[2]

---

[1] *The Interpretation of History* (1936), p. 3. Part One of this book is headed "On the Boundary: An Autobiographical Sketch." The dates given in footnote references to Tillich's books are those of the English publication.

[2] *Ibid.,* pp. 40f.

His *Systematic Theology* represents the summation of his life's work. It is conceived as an *apologetic* theology in conscious opposition to the kerygmatic theology which Karl Barth holds to be the true type of Christian theology. Apologetic theology is philosophical theology, or a discipline which answers questions asked by man because he is man, whether he is inside or outside the Christian Church.[3] The Christian believes that God has spoken in revelation. Yet the Christian is also a human being, subject to the universal conditions of life. So, if he is to receive the truth, he cannot receive it (as Barth believes) as a stone thrown from heaven. He must receive it in his human situation. Apologetic theology starts with the human situation as this is found in one particular cultural milieu. It uses the intellectual resources available at the time, and it speaks to man where he happens to be. Therefore, no theology is final or authoritative, but represents one stage in the ongoing human quest for God, and illustrates one way of approaching the divine revelation.

Nevertheless, theology is not philosophy. In his earlier writings Tillich differentiated between the two by calling theology "theonomous metaphysics." This label indicated that theology was the recognition of a reality going beyond a purely rational interpretation of experience by becoming aware of the revelation of the divine in the "depths" of experience. Later, under the stimulus of Heidegger's "existential" philosophy, he took his analysis further.[4] He began to define philosophy as asking the question of the nature of reality as a whole. Theology he defined as asking the question of the meaning of reality for us.[5] The crucial difference between the two disciplines was that the former sought reality for its own sake, while the latter sought reality for the sake of the individual. Tillich explains this distinction by saying that the philosopher wishes to serve the "universal *logos,*" while the theologian is committed to "a particular *logos*" within a special community.[6] Thus, abstractly viewed, philosophy and theology can never meet. But actually philosophers are existing beings, and they cannot help being theologians as well as philosophers. Also, because theologians seek to understand and to state in objective terms the particular *logos* to which they are committed, they show a philosophical loyalty that makes them suspect in the eyes of the religious community which they represent.

The fact that theologians have made a commitment to a particular

---

[3] *Systematic Theology,* I (1951), pp. viii, 6.

[4] *The Interpretation of History* (1936), pp. 38ff. Here Tillich points out that his concept of "theonomous metaphysics" made its appearance in his *Das System der Wissenschaften nach Gegenständen und Methoden* (1923).

[5] *Systematic Theology,* I (1951), pp. 18, 20, 22.

[6] *Ibid.,* pp. 25f.

logos — that they confess a particular faith — means that they have entered "the theological circle." They have an "ultimate concern." This truth provides us with a formal criterion of theology, applicable to any religious system of belief. *The object of theology is what concerns us ultimately.*[7] A religious believer will probably say that his ultimate concern is God, but the confession is too restricted an answer to embrace all possible theologies. Tillich suggests that an analysis of the concept "ultimate concern" will give us a universally valid statement of the content of every ultimate concern, thus suggesting a second formal criterion of theology. *Our ultimate concern is that which determines our being or not-being.*[8] When, for example, the Christian quotes the commandment of Jesus that we are to know that the Lord our God is one and is to be loved with heart, soul, and mind (Mark 12:29), he gives expression to his ultimate concern and declares the total character of this concern.[9] The two criteria of all theologies provide an abstract translation of the Christian conviction.

Christian theology is one type of theology, arising out of one particular complex of religious convictions. The word "theology" conveys the meaning of *logos* (reasoning) about *theos* (God and divine things).[10] Theology takes many forms, according to its foundation in particular religious myths and cults. Christianity is built upon the belief that the Logos (universal Reason) has become manifest in the man Jesus, who is therefore worshipped as the Christ. Although the claims of Christian belief are not proved by the mere fact that this claim has been made, Christian theology is provided with a good case for urging its right to be termed a *final* theology on the basis of such a claim. For, if the Logos has appeared in an individual life, the ultimate concern of Christians is centered in the union of the absolutely universal with the absolutely concrete.[11] The myths and rites of all other religions must then be seen as partial and inadequate in face of the Christian confession that the event "Jesus the Christ" has universal meaning.

Christian theology has the task of presenting the content of Christian faith in a systematic form. A purely kerygmatic theology bases theology on revelation, isolating theology from the rest of knowledge. Catholicism and Protestant Orthodoxy tie revelation to a traditional natural theology, ignoring philosophical criticism of natural theology. Post-Schleiermacherian Protestantism has based theology on an independent philosophy of religion. Tillich tries to overcome the weaknesses of these theological approaches by using a "method of correlation." The

[7] *Ibid.*, p. 12. Cf. *The Protestant Era* (1948), pp. 87, 92.
[8] *Systematic Theology*, I (1951), p. 14.
[9] *Ibid.*, pp. 11f.
[10] *Ibid.*, p. 15; cf. *The Protestant Era* (1948), p. 84.
[11] *Systematic Theology*, I (1951), pp. 15-18.

method of correlation unites philosophy and theology by taking the questions asked by philosophy about the universal human situation and answering them out of the resources of the Christian revelation.[12] So he describes his apologetic theology as an "answering theology." Such a theology completes kerygmatic theology by taking into account the human situation. "It answers the questions implied in the 'situation' in the power of the eternal message and with the means provided by the situation whose questions it answers."[13] The method of correlation used in apologetic theology does not distort the Christian message, because the answers received derive their content from the revelatory events of the Christian faith. But the form of the answers is dependent upon the structure of the questions asked, and thus there is a mutual dependence between question and answer.[14]

Tillich sees his method as a valid alternative to three inadequate methods: the *supranaturalistic,* the *naturalistic,* and the *dualistic.*[15] Supranaturalism presents the Christian message in the form of revealed truths owing nothing to human receptivity. But man cannot receive answers to questions which he has never asked; and he does ask questions of a spiritual order relevant to the Christian message. Naturalistic or "humanistic" theology assumes the truth of Christianity to be contained in man's progressive religious evolution — man supplies the answers to his own questions. The dualistic method attempts to bridge the distance between God and man by means of "natural theology." But the method of correlation alone permits a philosophical analysis of the human situation to be related to the contents of the Christian faith. By using this method "existential questions" and "theological answers" can be developed in a systematic form, taking into account the whole of reality as it presents itself to us, and exhibiting the Christian answers to the questions of existence.

REVELATION

For theology the doctrine of God is primary. Tillich recognizes this, but he feels that it is necessary at the outset to justify his apologetic stance. Therefore, the heading of the first of the five Parts of his *Systematic Theology* is "Reason and Revelation." "Being and God" occupies second place.[16]

---

[12] *Ibid.,* pp. viif., 30, 59ff.

[13] *Ibid.,* p. 6.

[14] *Ibid.,* p. 64.

[15] *Ibid,* pp. 64-66. Cf. *Systematic Theology,* II (1957), p. 10; *The Protestant Era* (1948), pp. 82f.

[16] The headings of the Parts in the *Systematic Theology* are all double, each showing the philosophical concepts and the theological symbols to be correlated in that particular Part.

Tillich was raised in an era dominated by the philosophical tradition of German nineteenth-century idealism. But in the early years of this century a reaction set in; metaphysics "in the high *a priori* style" became discredited; and various brands of realism were proposed. Tillich, nevertheless, looked for a reconstruction of metaphysical thinking.[17] In *The Religious Situation* he adopted a program intended to usher in a new metaphysics under the banner of "belief-ful realism." Belief-ful realism, unlike other kinds of current realistic philosophies, broke through what Tillich termed "the closed circle of finite existence" in order to recognize the presence of the eternal in time and history. It proceeded "by way of the intuition of the Unconditioned in the symbols of the conditioned."[18] It required faith; for it had to do with religion in the widest sense of the word, that is, with the relation of man to the eternal in the present. In the "unconditioned depth" of all cultural activities of man, however secular they might seem to be on the surface, lay a religious element.[19] As he wrote at a later date: "Religion is the substance, the ground, and the depth of man's spiritual life."[20] And again: "In abbreviation: religion is the substance of culture, and culture is the form of religion."[21]

Belief-ful realism — afterwards renamed "self-transcending (ecstatic) realism" or "self-transcending (ecstatic) naturalism" — is the clue to Tillich's doctrine of revelation. Wherever that which is unconditional breaks into the conditioned, there is revelation of the divine mystery. This is why theology may be called "theonomous metaphysics," for it is thought acknowledging an ultimate concern and, on this account, open to the divine. But revelation can be received only in a "revelatory situation" and cannot communicate general information about the world, and so theology must be correlated with philosophy: the particular *logos* must be brought into relation with the universal *logos*. When this is done, revelation is seen to be the "depth" of reason or "ecstatic" reason.[22]

Now, if revelation can be defined in terms of reason, it might appear that theology can be absorbed into philosophy. Tillich's whole system, nevertheless, is built upon the assumption that this is not possible.

---

[17] He tells us that the idealism of Schelling remained an abiding influence. Other influences were neo-Kantianism, the Philosophy of Values, and Husserl's Phenomenology. See *The Interpretation of History* (1936), pp. 35ff., 60.

[18] *The Religious Situation* (1932), p. 83. Cf. *The Interpretation of History* (1936), p. 16.

[19] *The Religious Situation* (1932), p. 35. Cf. *The Shaking of the Foundations* (1948), pp. 52-63.

[20] *Theology of Culture* (1959), p. 8.

[21] *Ibid.*, p. 42.

[22] *Systematic Theology* (1951), pp. 79, 111ff.

Reason (which he terms "ontological" reason in order to distinguish it from "technical" reason or mere reasoning) essentially establishes truth because it is the *logos* structure of the mind which corresponds to the *logos* structure of reality.[23] Actual reason, however, is not essential reason, because it is involved in the contradictions of finite existence. In existence actual reason is "split" reason. It is parted from its depths. The philosopher's concern with the universal *logos* brings him face to face with the conflicts in actual reason, forcing him to the quest for revelation. The theologian (who may be a philosopher too) encounters revelation. Yet he encounters it in the finite, conditioned world of existence only where the conditioned becomes "transparent" to its unconditioned ground. He cannot prove revelation to be rational, because revelation manifests itself through myth and cult, which seem to have no part in the realm of reason. It is necessary, then, to understand that the seeming conflict between reason and revelation is not real, being simply the result of our situation in existence. "Essentially reason is transparent toward its depth in each of its acts and processes. In existence this transparency is opaque and is replaced by myth and cult. Therefore, both are utterly ambiguous from the point of view of existential reason."[24] The validity of any revelation is rejected by the "rationalist," who identifies essential reason with existential reason. He fails to see that myth and cult represent the depth of reason in symbolic form. That which is unconditional cannot be represented directly in the conditioned; and therefore it must be represented symbolically.

It follows that philosophy cannot absorb theology into itself, since reason is parted from its own depths. Without theology, with its turning toward the particular *logos,* philosophy must become shallow and inhuman. At the same time, theology needs philosophy and the universal *logos* so that it may not forget the claims of reason or imagine that it possesses the truth entirely and not merely in symbolic guise. Theology must not become narrow and superstitious.

God

By describing the way in which revelation discloses truth symbolically, yet not in such a form that it may be grasped intellectually (in "the cognitive act"), Tillich has set the stage for his doctrine of God. "God" is a religious symbol, born of myth and cult. Yet the philosopher as well as the theologian is concerned with God, for the philosopher seeks to analyze the structure of reality. He is bound to ask what the word "is" means, thus embarking upon the study of being (ontology), the basic philosophic task. In asking why anything *is* he contemplates possi-

---

[23] *Ibid.,* p. 75.
[24] *Ibid.,* p. 80.

ble non-being; and he discovers that on the human level all being is finite being, or being mixed with non-being. He is then driven to ask what that power of being may be which preserves finite being from disruption by non-being. He is driven to ask about the ground of the ontological structure of being, an absolute which determines the structure of everything which has being without itself being subject to structure. This Ground is indicated in the concept of being-itself, or in the symbol "God." If we say that God is being-itself we have arrived at the point where philosophy and theology meet.[25]

An often quoted sentence by Tillich runs: "It is as atheistic to affirm the existence of God as it is to deny it." The explanation of this sentence is given in the one following it: "God is being-itself, not *a* being."[26] For God to be being-itself (or the "ground" and "power" of being) means that He is above everything belonging to finite being, and it is to the finite level that Tillich assigns existence. All finite beings exist. But God simply *is*. In describing the transcendence of God, Tillich speaks of His abysmal nature. God transcends every finite being infinitely, so that each being is swallowed, as it were, by an abyss (*Abgrund*). In describing the immanence of God, Tillich speaks of His creative nature. Everything finite participates in the infinite power of being, or it could have no being. God is the creative ground of being.

This latter aspect of God's relation to the world explains how it happens that the knowledge of revelation is symbolic knowledge. For Tillich religious language is always symbolic language. Through symbols we can express indirectly that which cannot be expressed directly. The characteristic of a symbol is that it participates in the reality of that to which it points.[27] And all things participate in God, and so can point to Him.

Religious believers refer to God by many names. They address Him as the Living God, the Creator, God Almighty, the Eternal, the Holy

---

[25] In *Systematic Theology,* I (1951), Tillich says that the statement that God is being-itself is the sole non-symbolic statement that can be made about God (p. 239). But in *Systematic Theology,* II (1957), he corrects himself, saying that this is where the symbolic and the non-symbolic coincide. In saying that God is being-itself we are speaking rationally and "ecstatically" at one and the same time (p. 10).

The little work *Biblical Religion and the Search for Ultimate Reality* (1955) deals directly with the problem of the relation between ontology and religious faith. Tillich there argues that ontology must clarify for faith the meaning of the religious assertion that God *is* (p. 82).

[26] *Systematic Theology,* I (1951), p. 237. Cf. *The Protestant Era* (1948), pp. 63f.

[27] *Systematic Theology,* I (1951), pp. 131, 239. Cf. *Dynamics of Faith* (1957), p. 42; "The Meaning and Justification of Religious Symbols," *Religious Experience and Truth; A Symposius,* ed. Sidney Hook (1961), p. 4.

Father, the Supreme Spirit. They call Him personal and loving. Words taken from experience of the world are applied to that which is beyond the world. Tillich comments that the ontological structure of being supplies the material for the symbols which point to the divine life.[28] Applied to God, of course, "life" itself is a symbol. There is no change in God, so that when He is called the Living God what is meant is that He is the unchanging yet creative ground of all living beings. Because the power of being-itself is in all finite being, anything that exists may be used as a symbol for the divine life. This truth serves to explain why, in the history of religion, innumerable natural objects have been worshipped as forms of the divine. In highly developed religions, such as the Judeo-Christian faith, personalistic symbols predominate. God is named Lord and Father, since these names belong to the I-Thou relationship. When the New Testament states that God is love it probes deeply into the character of the divine life. Love, before it is an emotion, is an ontological concept. It is the unity of two trends in every life-process, trends toward separation, on the one hand, and toward reunion, on the other. That God is love means that He is the fulfillment of life — "the ultimate unity of being with being within the divine ground."[29]

God could not be the Living God unless the power of being-itself affirmed itself as *being* over against *non-being*. God's being must embrace non-being and, through non-being, reveal itself.[30] This brings us to the question of how God, according to Christian theology, reveals Himself in finite being, manifesting Himself in the sphere of human existence. This is the question of mankind's salvation, or of *the Christ*.

MAN AND CHRIST

The realm of the actual is the realm of finitude. "Being is finite, existence is self-contradictory, and life is ambiguous."[31] It is in this realm that the Christian message is proclaimed. But the Christian message is not only teaching adapted to the conditions of human life in general; for it must be proclaimed to men in the special situation existing at a particular time in history. The Christian theologian, too, is involved in the collective experience of the church of his day. He necessarily views the Gospel from the place where he happens to be standing. On this account he requires a norm of systematic theology which is as par-

[28] *Systematic Theology,* I (1951), p. 243.
[29] *Ibid.,* pp. 280f. Cf. *Love, Power, and Justice* (1954), pp. 24ff; *Dynamics of Faith* (1957), pp. 112ff.
[30] *Systematic Theology,* I (1951), 252, 270. Cf. *The Courage to Be* (1952), pp. 178-81.
[31] *Systematic Theology,* I (1951), p. 81.

ticular and concrete as the formal criterion for all theology is general
and abstract, a norm adapted to the spiritual horizons of the age. Believing the characteristic experience of our day to be one of disruption
and meaninglessness, Tillich suggests that a relevant norm is to be found
in the reality of the "New Being" — a concept derived from Paul's concept of the "new creation" in Christ.[32] Christians today will see that
it is meaningful to express their faith by saying that the New Being
manifest in Jesus as the Christ is their ultimate concern. In this way
theology will have a material norm according to which Scripture can
be interpreted, just as Luther's norm of justification by faith served as
the criterion for evaluating Scripture at the time of the Reformation.

The New Being is asked for because of man's present experience of
the meaninglessness of life, which is the result of a particular historical
experience of the universal human predicament; and the universal human
predicament arises out of man's involvement in the self-contradictions
of existence. Theologically speaking, this means that the doctrine of
Christ is tied to the doctrine of man. The Christ, who brings the New
Being, is the answer to the question raised by human existence. The
Christ cannot be known apart from man. Conversely, man cannot be
truly known apart from the Christ who reveals the meaning of man's
existence.

God *is* and does not exist, being beyond essence and existence. But
in the whole of reality (as distinct from its eternal Ground) there is
a split between essence and existence. Man experiences himself as
being other than God, because he finds himself (in Heidegger's phrase)
"thrown" into existence. He does not have the "aseity" of God, the
power of being in, of, and by one's self.[33] His being is finite, and his
consciousness of his finitude results in anxiety.[34] This anxiety cannot
be removed. It is a universal human state, for it is the existential awareness of non-being. It is the penalty of existing in a "split" universe.

While the being of God eternally embraces and conquers non-being,
man as finite is continually threatened by non-being. This is why anxiety accompanies existence. Tillich remarks that the etymology of
the word "existence" indicates that man in existence is "standing out"
of non-being, while remaining in it.[35] This is why existence is self-
contradictory. Yet the existing individual, although anxious and be-
sieged by the forces of disruption and meaninglessness, participates
in the power of being, though always in a finite way. He feels himself
and his world to be estranged from God, nevertheless he is able to

[32] *Ibid.*, pp. 49f. Cf. *The New Being* (1955), pp. 15-24.
[33] *Systematic Theology*, I (1951), p. 196.
[34] *Ibid.*, p. 191. Cf. *Systematic Theology*, II (1957), pp. 25, 34-36; *The Courage to Be* (1952), pp. 34ff.
[35] *Systematic Theology*, II (1957), pp. 20f.

hope for the coming of a new reality in which existential estrangement is overcome. He can look forward to the reign of the Messiah, the Christ who can rescue him from the evil structures apparent in the human predicament. In other words, he understands his present situation as the consequence of a "fall" from his essential being, and he is engaged in the quest for "salvation."

The Fall is not an event taking place at the beginning of history. It is a non-temporal transition from essence to existence.[36] It is a "fall" and it is tragic, since it results in the situation where man is estranged from his essential being. At the same time, it is not simply evil. It contains creative possibilities; and it is possible only because man is "made in the image of God." The Fall stems from the truth that man is finite freedom. Man is free, because he is a self; and man is finite freedom because his freedom is exercised within a world which limits him, which is his "destiny." His being is mixed with non-being: he is finite. But he is also aware that he is finite. He possesses what Tillich calls "the power of infinite self-transcendence," a power evidenced in the fact that he is never satisfied with any stage of his finite development but longs for the infinite. "Being-itself manifests itself to finite being in the infinite drive of the finite beyond itself."[37] The biblical story connects the Fall directly with the sin of Adam, the first man. Theology, however, must recognize the Fall as a cosmic fact: the transition from essence to existence. It then will appear that the meaning of sin is *estrangement* from essential being. "The disruption of the essential unity with God is the inmost character of sin."[38] In existence man is estranged from the ground of his being, from other beings, and from himself.[39]

Tillich believes that the concept of estrangement declares the true character of sin, because it makes plain that, while estranged man has left the ground of his being, he still belongs essentially to it. Love, which is the striving for the union of the separated, is the opposite of estrangement.[40] If sin is termed "unbelief," unbelief means "un-love." It is man's turning away from God, and it leads to all the evils of man's existence: pride and selfishness, guilt and fear of death, loneliness and despair. In his estrangement man experiences love as a command which he cannot obey, while God appears as a destructive threat — He is known as wrath.[41] No act of man's can lead to the overcoming of existential estrangement, so long as it is formed within the context of

---

[36] *Ibid.*, pp. 29f.
[37] *Systematic Theology*, I (1951), p. 191.
[38] *Systematic Theology*, II (1957), p. 48.
[39] *Ibid.*, p. 44.
[40] *Ibid.*, p. 47.
[41] *Ibid.*, p. 77.

existential estrangement.[42]   Therefore, New Being must precede new acting. Salvation must come from the side of God. The human predicament must be overcome by a divine power discovered within the limits of finitude.

All religions are united in the quest for a New Being, or the expectation of a transformed reality.   Religions claim that this reality is made available through historical groups, which may be nations, families, or churches.[43] It is the claim of Christianity that the New Being has appeared in its final manifestation through the Christ expected in Israel, who has come in Jesus of Nazareth.

JESUS THE CHRIST

Jesus Christ is not a proper name, so Tillich insists, but the combination of a name and a title. Jesus is a historical person. And He is also the Christ for the historical group which receives Him as the Christ. The meaning of the believing reception of Jesus as the Christ is the conviction that there has appeared that which conquers existence under the conditions of existence.   The basic Christian theological assertion is that Essential God-Manhood has appeared within existence.[44]   Existence has been conquered within one personal life, and thus has been conquered in principle. (A personal life is the sole full actualization of the potentialities of being that is known to us.)   In Jesus the Christ the New Being defeats the old being.

Jesus as the Christ is the bearer of the New Being. The New Testament shows us how Jesus, while fully subject to all the conditions of existence, brought the New Being in the totality of His being, as His recorded words, deeds, suffering, and death proclaim. His death was the expression of a wholly sacrificial life; and the quality of this life makes us see that He has conquered existence, for He lived a wholly selfless life. "He proves and confirms his character as the Christ in the sacrifice of himself as Jesus to himself as the Christ."[45] Nevertheless, we may well ask how we can be sure that the record of the New Testament is trustworthy. Did Jesus actually live, and live so as to prove Himself to be the Christ? The answer to this question cannot be given in any historical examination of the biblical records themselves, because faith in that which is beyond existence is not to be based upon any accumulation of facts gathered out of existence. For an answer we must turn to the faith of the Christian Church. It is there that we can find the living proof that the New Being actually has appeared in ex-

[42] *Ibid.,* p. 79.
[43] *Ibid.,* p. 88.
[44] *Ibid.,* p. 98. Cf. *Systematic Theology,* I (1951), p. 57.
[45] *Systematic Theology,* II (1957), p. 123.

istence. If the power of the New Being is actual in the community called by the name of Jesus Christ, then the New Being *has* appeared. It is logically possible (though historically absurd) to believe that a personal life other than that of Jesus has brought the Christian Church into being. But, if that supposition is not entertained, the truth that the New Being has appeared in Jesus as the Christ must be believed.[46]

So Tillich argues that participation and not historical proof guarantees the reality of the event upon which Christianity is based. We may ask, then, how the power of the New Being has been communicated to the Christian community, if this communication cannot be proved on the basis of historical data. Tillich answers that the power which has created and preserved the community of the New Being is the "picture" of Him in whom it has appeared.[47] The reality of the power of the New Being was in the personal life of Jesus. The disciples of Jesus encountered this reality through the picture created by the reality. The picture, as a symbol of the reality to which it pointed, had power to transform the being of the disciples. The disciples were no longer in quest of the New Being. They had encountered the New Being in the picture of Jesus as the Christ.

Because the reality of the New Being in Jesus as the Christ is a reality to be accepted in faith, the events in the life of Jesus upon which the Christian message are founded must be symbols as well as events. This truth is illustrated in the interrelated events of the Cross and the Resurrection. Both Cross and Resurrection are events, for otherwise the New Being would not have entered existence to conquer it. But Cross and Resurrection are also symbols and parts of a myth. In order to clarify the symbolic aspect of these events Tillich puts forward a theory of the Resurrection, which he calls the "restitution" theory.[48] In the "ecstatic" experience of the disciples the picture of Jesus became indissolubly united with the reality of the New Being, being raised above transitoriness and taking on the character of an eternal spiritual presence. In this experience the negativity of existence was overcome, for the death of Jesus was not able to separate the New Being from the picture of its bearer. The restitution theory sees

---

[46] *Ibid.,* p. 114. For Tillich there are always two elements involved in faith. The first is the certainty that accompanies awareness of the unconditional. The second is the uncertainty that accompanies every manifestation of the unconditional in time and space, making faith in any particular symbol of the unconditional a risk to be taken with courage. ("The risk of faith is based on the fact that the unconditional element can become a matter of ultimate concern only if it appears in a concrete embodiment" — *Theology of Culture,* p. 28) Faith in Jesus as the Christ involves the risk, then, that the appearance of the New Being may not have been in Jesus of Nazareth.

[47] *Ibid.,* pp. 114-17.

[48] *Ibid.,* pp. 156-58.

the Resurrection as the restitution of Jesus to the dignity of the Christ (Jesus is one with God) in the minds of the disciples. In historical terms, the restitution of Jesus as the Christ may belong to a time prior to Peter's confession of Jesus as the Christ. It is not an isolated event belonging to the time after the death of Jesus.

The conquest of the negativity of existence establishes Jesus as the Christ in the experience of the Christian Church. Pointing out that the root meaning of "salvation" is "healing," Tillich says that theology should interpret salvation as the overcoming of the split introduced by existence.[49] In reuniting that which is estranged — God and man, man and his world, man and man — the New Being discloses the meaning of man's existence in a healing way. Participation in the New Being is regeneration, or (in Paul's phrase) being *in* Christ. It is the state of having been drawn into the new reality manifest in Jesus as the Christ.[50] Justification follows regeneration. It makes man that which he essentially is, and from which he is estranged. The justified man must accept that he is accepted.[51] This he can do when he is drawn into the power of the New Being in Christ that makes faith possible in spite of continuing estrangement. Faith that he is accepted is the channel through which grace is mediated to him, witnessing to the state of unity between God and man, however fragmentarily realized this state may be. Transformation by the New Being is sanctification, or the actual reunion of God and man. The power of the New Being transforms the whole of life through the sanctifying work of the Spirit, who is the actuality of the New Being.[52]

THE SPIRIT

Just as the Christ in Tillich's thought comes as the answer to the self-contradictions of existence, so the Spirit comes as the answer to the ambiguities of life.

Life is the "actuality" of being, and it is ambiguous because it is a mixture of essential and existential elements.[53] For example, if we say that something is living, we indicate in the same breath that it is dying. In any organism the process of self-integration is in continuous struggle with disintegration; and a diseased organism displays life in disintegration. Things that become actual subject themselves universally to the conditions of existence, for actualized creation and

49 *Ibid.*, p. 166. Cf. *Dynamics of Faith* (1957), pp. 108ff.
50 *Systematic Theology*, II (1957), p. 177.
51 *Ibid.*, pp. 178f. Cf. *The Courage to Be* (1952), pp. 163ff.
52 *Systematic Theology*, II (1957), pp. 179f.
53 *Systematic Theology*, III (1963), pp. 12, 30.

estranged existence are identical.[54] In a fallen world the split between essential and existential being is manifest in the ambiguity of all life.

In its essential nature life displays both unity and diversity. When analyzing the essential structure of life Tillich speaks of the *multidimensional unity of life*.[55] There are also sections (or "realms") of life in which one dimension or another predominates. In the psychological realm the dimension of "spirit" actualizes itself; and man is that organism in which the dimension of spirit is dominant.[56] Spirit is the unity of power and meaning, and, so far as human knowledge goes, is found in man alone.[57] Spirit in man has three interpenetrating functions: morality, culture, and religion.[58] All three are marked by life's ambiguity, and each of the three throw into relief the existential predicament of man. The ultimate norm of the moral law is *agape,* but *agape* transcends the moral law and at the same time leads man to despair of all human morality, since it confronts man with the gulf between willing and doing. Cultural aims break down in the division between theory and practice, the individual and society, and educational ideals and historical realities. Religion, which represents the self-transcendence of life,[59] leads to a reduplication of ambiguities. It claims to transcend the world and to transform the greatness of man's spirit into holiness, yet it is tied to the world and its absolute claims frequently distort the divine into the demonic. Thus religion may prove to be the greatest obstacle to true spirituality, and may indeed bring about the most complete profanization of the sacred. It is always inclined to the opposite evils of lording it over the world and of conforming to the world; and in both cases the transcendent is lost in the finite.

Wherever spirit is driven into a successful self-transcendence, this takes place because finite life is grasped by that which is ultimate and unconditional and the ground of its being. This experience — the experience of "ecstasy" — is symbolically described in terms of the revelatory experience of God as Spirit, or (as Tillich prefers to say) of "Spiritual Presence."[60] Spiritual Presence creates unambiguous life, for the essential relation of the human spirit to the divine Spirit is one of mutual immanence.[61] Where there is Spiritual Presence, or New Being, or *agape* (the love which characterizes the divine life),

---

[54] *Systematic Theology,* II (1957), p. 44.
[55] *Systematic Theology,* III (1963), pp. 12, 15-17.
[56] *Ibid.,* p. 26.
[57] *Ibid.,* pp. 22-25; Cf. *Systematic Theology,* I (1951), pp. 249f.
[58] *Systematic Theology,* III (1963), pp. 44ff.
[59] *Ibid.,* p. 95.
[60] *Ibid.,* p. 111. Cf. *The Eternal Now* (1963), pp. 81-91.
[61] *Systematic Theology,* III (1963), p. 114.

there is participation in the transcendent unity of unambiguous life.[62] But, although Spiritual Presence is perpetually manifested in the world, its manifestation in time and space is always fragmentary.

Jesus, as the Bearer of the New Being, is the keystone in the arch of spiritual manifestations in history.[63] So the event "Jesus as the Christ" is the center of history. The Spirit, which made Him the Christ, was the Spirit working in the world before the event of His life in history; and this same Spirit has been manifest in the Spiritual Community created by the impact of this event. The Spiritual Community is not the same as the Christian Church, which is involved in the ambiguities of religion. The Spiritual Community is either latent ("before Christ" in terms of time or in terms of existential encounter) or manifest.[64] In it is found unambiguous life, uniting — though in fragmentary fashion — the three dimensions of the spirit, namely, religion, culture, and morality. It is the community of the New Being, where Spiritual Presence creates unambiguous health in the individual, in spite of the fact that the conditions of existence still remain.

Tillich explains that in Spiritual Presence God is manifested under a definite aspect. That He can be manifested under other aspects is one reason for the symbols of the Trinity: Father, Son, and Spirit. But the symbols express primarily the dialectics of life in the movement of separation and reunion, which is a threefold movement.[65]

THE KINGDOM OF GOD

Even healing under the impact of the Spiritual Presence cannot liberate the individual from the necessity of death. So man is driven to ask the question of total healing through history and beyond history, the question of universal salvation which is answered in the biblical symbols of "Kingdom of God" and "Eternal Life." (The first symbol, indeed, embraces the second. It stands for unambiguous life both immanent in and transcending history.[66])

While there is a historical dimension to all life-processes, history proper is human history; for history belongs with spirit.[67] Spirit is the unity of power and meaning. History drives toward the universal

---

[62] *Ibid.,* p. 140. Cf. *Dynamics of Faith* (1957), pp. 112ff.

[63] *Systematic Theology,* III (1963), p. 147. Cf. *The Interpretation of History* (1936), pp. 251ff.

[64] *Systematic Theology,* III (1963), pp. 152-55. Cf. *Systematic Theology,* I (1951), pp. 132, 143.

[65] *Systematic Theology,* III (1963), pp. 284, 293. Cf. *Systematic Theology,* I (1951), pp. 228, 250f.

[66] *Systematic Theology* III (1963), pp. 108f, 356f.

[67] *Ibid.,* pp. 297, 300ff.

fulfillment of the potentiality of being (power); and it also is where events find significance, being the arena of human purposes (meaning). But history remains ambiguous, apart from the manifestation in it of the Kingdom of God. For Christian faith, the appearance of the Christ is the decisive manifestation of the Kingdom. It gives a definite center to the whole of history, thus illuminating history with unambiguous meaning.[68] Everything before and after this event is both preparation and reception. There is a rhythm to the history of salvation, since, according to the Bible, the Kingdom is manifested only at the moment of the "fulfillment of time" — *kairos,* in Greek.[69] If the manifestation of the Christ is the "great *kairos,*" there are also other *kairoi* when the Kingdom "breaks through" into history. The Spirit may be latent at times, and manifest with history-shaking power at special moments. However, at any time in history the Kingdom is at once present and not yet present.[70] Its victories within history are fragmentary.

ETERNAL LIFE

The end of history (doctrinally considered in "eschatology") is the inner aim or *telos* of history symbolized as Eternal Life.[71] Eschatological symbolism presents the relation of the temporal to the eternal in the mode of the future, as creational symbolism presents the same relation in the mode of the past. The latter indicates the dependence of creaturely existence upon the eternal, while the former indicates the fulfillment of creaturely existence in the eternal. Both modes are included in the eternal "now."[72] Eternal Life is the ultimate and ever-present end of life universal. The positive in life is freed "in the end" from its ambiguous mixture with the negative. This can be called "essentialization."[73] The new which has been actualized in time and space adds something to essential being, so that the New Being is realized within the Kingdom of God in its fulfillment "above" history. Essentialization is the elevation of the positive into Eternal Life. This is a matter of universal participation. All that is positive is thus elevated, so that individual lives, however stunted, find a vicarious fulfillment through the participation of their essences in the essences of others who have reached a high degree of fulfillment. The symbol of "resurrection of the body" expresses the truth of essentializa-

[68] *Ibid.,* pp. 364ff.
[69] *Ibid.,* pp. 369ff. Cf. *The Interpretation of History* (1936), pp. 129ff.; *The Protestant Era* (1948), pp. 32-51.
[70] *Systematic Theology,* III (1963), pp. 390ff.
[71] *Ibid.,* p. 394.
[72] *Ibid.,* pp. 395f. Cf. *The Eternal Now* (1963), pp. 77, 122-32.
[73] *Systematic Theology,* III (1963), pp. 400f., 406f.

tion, in that it speaks of the spiritually transformed total personality of man in Eternal Life.[74] "Beyond" death there is the New Being, which is the transformation of the old being, but not its replacement by another being altogether.

The symbols of "heaven" and "hell" represent the polar ultimates in the experience of the divine. They point to the reality constituting the states of blessedness and despair, that is, the amount of fulfillment or non-fulfillment which goes into the individual's essentialization.[75] For this reason they must be taken seriously, though not literally. Since everything that is created is rooted in the eternal Ground of being, "eternal death" is an impossibility — non-being cannot prevail against the power of being. Yet, if we take seriously religious and ethical decisions made by individuals, we must admit the possibility of death "away" from eternity or the failure to reach eternity through an inability to transcend temporality.[76]

Finally, we must conceive of Eternal Life as life "in" God. Everything that has being is present "in" God in the form of potentiality, in ontological dependence, and in ultimate fulfillment. (The biblical symbol of God being "all in all" could be called "eschatological pan-en-theism."[77]) But, because the temporal is in the Eternal, the world-process means something for God.

> . . . the eternal act of creation is driven by a love which finds fulfilment only through the other one who has the freedom to reject and to accept love. God, so to speak, drives toward the actualization and essentialization of everything that has being. For the eternal dimensions of what happens in the universe is the Divine Life itself. It is the content of the divine blessedness.[78]

By ending his system at the point where man is considered in his significance for the Divine Life, Tillich believes that his theology has given shape to a theocentric vision of the meaning of existence.

III. EVALUATION

Theological Perspective

Tillich's determination to be both a genuine philosopher and a genuine theologian is one which has had creative consequences for our age. Like Schleiermacher in his day, he has impressed "religion's cultured despisers" and has also forced Christian believers to realize the

---

[74] *Ibid.*, pp. 412f.
[75] *Ibid.*, p. 418.
[76] *Ibid.*, pp. 415f.
[77] *Ibid.*, p. 421.
[78] *Ibid.*, p. 422.

necessity for rethinking their faith in face of the challenge of contemporary thought-forms. He has reminded us that defending "the faith which God entrusted to His people once and for all" (Jude 3) is a task that has to be undertaken anew in each generation. And he has proved that theology can be excitingly alive and relevant to the whole of human existence.

Yet the attempt to serve two masters, respecting each equally, is obviously a perilous one. There is a large likelihood that theology will be lost in philosophy or *vice versa*. Tillich's claim is that there is a "basic identity" of the two, as well as a "qualitative difference."[79] However, we must ask how Tillich knows that this is so. His most direct answer is given in the relatively early work *The Interpretation of History*. Here he argues that a philosophy of meaning is the basis of his system, which attempts to relate philosophy and theology as sciences. He adds: "The presupposition of the success of this attempt is, of course, that the theonomous character of knowing be acknowledged; that is to say, that thinking is rooted in the absolute as the foundation and abyss of meaning."[80] In this work he still speaks of theology as "theonomous metaphysics," and he refers to his work as a philosophy of religion. In the *Systematic Theology* he stresses that theology and philosophy cannot meet, and he denies that theology can be based upon a philosophy of religion. But, since he grants that philosophy and theology both ask the same question (the question of being), it does not appear that his viewpoint has changed substantially.

Instead of presenting himself as a philosopher of religion, Tillich now comes forward as a philosophical theologian employing the method of correlation. In the method philosophy poses questions which theology answers. The difficulty which arises in connection with the method is that the answers seem to be dictated by the questions. For example, Tillich says that God is the answer to the question of human finitude, so, when the method of correlation is used, God must be called the infinite power of being which resists the threat of non-being.[81] Now Tillich's claim that God as the answer to human finitude cannot be derived from the analysis of existence is a claim that hardly stands; for his explanation of the meaning of finitude rests upon an ontological analysis relating the finite to the absolute. Here we learn that being-itself is the answer to the question of human

---

[79] "Reply to Interpretation and Criticism," *The Theology of Paul Tillich*, Charles W. Kegley & Robert W. Bretall, eds. (1952), pp. 336f.

[80] *The Interpretation of History* (1936), pp. 38f.

[81] *Systematic Theology*, I (1951), p. 64.

finitude. Being-itself is the infinite power of being resisting the threat of non-being. So, when Tillich says that it is the duty of theologians to insist that God must be called being-itself or the absolute,[82] we have a new word to insert in a previously known answer. This does not alter the answer. We still focus our attention upon the same concept (the infinite power of being . . .) as before, but now we attach to the concept the name "God." We have simply substituted the theological term *God* for the philosophical term *absolute*.

It would seem, then, that the method of correlation "correlates" theological terms with philosophical concepts much as the method of conscription "correlates" young men with the armed forces. While Tillich continued to speak of his work as a philosophy of religion, the fact that theology for him was philosophically contained was partly evident. Now that fact is hidden, because the method of correlation is called a *theological* method. But Tillich has never wavered in his belief that theological statements have meaning only after they have been conscripted into the service of philosophy and are regimented within a total system of thought. This process he describes as one of interpreting religious symbols according to theological principles and methods.[83] It is unavoidable, because for him the search for meaning and the search for being are indivisible. "If one starts to think about the meaning of biblical symbols, one is already in the midst of ontological problems."[84] Tillich's assumption is that the ontologist *knows,* and therefore is able to explain the way in which Christian theologians "must" interpret the biblical symbols. We should note that the method of correlation, as Tillich explains it, does not simply depend upon our agreeing that religious language is symbolical language but also upon our agreeing that the ontologist holds the key to the interpretation of all religious symbols. It is this second proposition which is vital to Tillich's theological perspective. The method of correlation falls apart if the ontologist is denied the right to establish, on his own terms, the meaning of religious language.

Thus the method results in a reduction of theology to ontology — although some philosophers might be inclined to think that the ontology proposed by Tillich resembles, more than anything else, a theosophy. An ontology containing terms ("power," "ground," "abyss," "threat") which are, to say the least, highly metaphorical can be called a philosophical enterprise only by straining the word "philosophical" so as to admit the Tillichian sense.

[82] *Ibid.,* p. 239.
[83] *Ibid.,* p. 240.
[84] *Biblical Religion and the Search for Ultimate Reality* (1955), p. 83.

REVELATION

The shape of Tillich's thinking stands out most clearly when he turns to look at revelation. He asserts that there is a basic identity of theology and philosophy. The particular *logos* cannot contradict the universal *logos,* and so theology is a rational discipline. Equally, philosophers may use "ecstatic" as well as "calculating" reason when they treat the subject matter of their philosophy as an ultimate concern. When reason is driven beyond itself to its "ground and abyss," the genuine mystery of being appears and we are in the presence of revelation.

Revelation, we must note, is not for Tillich in the first place *Christian* revelation. It is found in the context of the "mystical a priori," or immediate awareness of something that transcends the cleavage between subject and object.[85] It breaks forth in the intuition of the immediate presence of whole, undivided being which is the experience of being as over against non-being. In this experience the power of being to heal the "split" in actual reason is felt. The Christian theologian, standing in the "theological circle," *adds to* the "mystical a priori" the criterion of the Christian message.[86] Revelation for him is the final revelation of Jesus as the Christ, the Bearer of the New Being. This is because revelation can be received only in a revelatory situation.[87] Revelation has revelatory power only for those who participate in it; and the Christian theologian, within the "theological circle," has accepted the New Being in Jesus as the Christ as his ultimate concern. In his acceptance of the final revelation the theologian is grasped by a revelatory experience in which the mystery of being has manifested itself in a final and universal way. Jesus is the final revelation of God for those who accept Him as the Christ, because He is transparent to the divine mystery. As the Bearer of the New Being He does not claim anything for Himself.[88]

Here, as we see, the revelation of God in Christ is explained by being set within the structure of Tillich's ontology. The "symbols" of Christian faith are so interpreted that they conform to the picture of reality which Tillich has conceived. Described in terms of "belief-ful realism" this means that the Unconditioned is intuited in the symbols of the conditioned. When Peter said to Jesus, "Thou art the Christ," he accepted Him as the medium of final revelation.[89] That is, he accepted the Unconditioned to be seen "through" Jesus, of

[85] *Systematic Theology,* I (1951), p. 9.
[86] *Ibid.*
[87] *Ibid.*, p. 129.
[88] *Ibid.*, pp. 128, 132-35.
[89] *Ibid.*, p. 136.

468

which Jesus (a conditioned being) was the symbol. Any other interpretation of the biblical record is ruled out by Tillich's world view. Naturalism judges Jesus to be simply a good man. Supernaturalism asserts that He is the Man from Heaven, the only Son of God. But self-transcending naturalism knows that He is the Bearer of the New Being. It knows this because it knows that no finite being can have ultimate significance in itself, but only in so far as it becomes transparent to its divine Ground. A Divine Man is a contradiction in terms.

In short, self-transcending naturalism answers all the questions, as well as asks them. It does not invent the "symbols" of religious faith, of course; and to that extent it does not "provide the answers." But, having heard what is proclaimed in religious myth and cult (where Christianity is concerned, that is the Gospel — *kerygma* — set forth in creed and preaching and sacrament within the Christian Church), it pronounces its verdict upon the truth and error there contained. It effectively "demythologizes" religious faith. And, although it does not wish to abolish myth as such, this is because it believes that the symbol as well as the concept can be a medium for communicating truth. For Tillich's ontology is also a theosophy. It believes in "ecstatic" as well as in "calculating" reason. It presupposes the "mystical a priori." It thinks that the power of being can be experienced, as well as that the structure of being can be analyzed. It does not admit that the Christian revelation is authoritative, except in the sense that all revelation is authoritative, that is, to the extent to which it illustrates the power of the Unconditioned breaking into the conditioned, so that man is grasped by the ground and abyss of his being and meaning.

GOD

Since for Tillich God is being-itself, he declares that the analogy of being (*analogia entis*) between the finite and the infinite provides the sole means of speaking about God.[90] In practice this means that the doctrine of God is limited to the terms of his ontology. Biblical statements ("symbols") about God, therefore, must be trimmed to allow them to fit within Tillich's world view. Not only is it blasphemous to say that God exists (which would make Him subject to the "split" between essence and existence), but God may be called the Living God only because He is the Ground of all life.[91]

Tillich's doctrine of God is intended to set our conception of God

[90] *Ibid.*, pp. 131, 239f.
[91] *Ibid.*, p. 242.

469

free from theological oversimplification and distortion. Yet it would seem that the result is to imprison God within the bounds of his ontology by insisting that the biblical "symbols" must be interpreted in terms of his analysis of being-itself, non-being, and finite being. If God is the Ground of being, He is not the Creator, except in the sense that he eternally "creates Himself." Creation is identical with His life.[92] He is not responsible for man's existence, for man exists only when he has actualized his (finite) freedom so as to be outside the creative Ground of the divine life.[93] Thus "Creation" and "Fall" coincide. Actualized creation and estranged existence are identical.[94]

Such a God as Tillich portrays is the Absolute. He is the God who may be inferred from the view that finite being participates in being-itself, in spite of being estranged from it. To this extent He gives meaning to life. He is also — and this point must be stressed — more than a philosophical God, for He is discovered through religious experience as a "power" manifesting itself wherever individuals have an ultimate concern. To this extent He gives substance to faith. Yet He is not the Maker of heaven and earth who is proclaimed in the Christian creeds. He is not the God who spoke by the prophets and, in the final age, in His Son (Hebrews 1:1, 2). When Tillich has finished interpreting the creedal and biblical "symbols," we are left with an immanent power in the universe, driving us toward the infinite.[95] Religious faith, in its Christian form or in any other, amounts to awareness of this power; and Tillich's analysis assures us that our awareness comes from our participation in the Ground of our being.

God as the Ground of Being is thus the God in whom Tillich would have us place our trust. But this God belongs to the circle of pantheistic theory. Ultimately, Tillich's God absorbs everything into Himself. Although transcending infinitely all beings ("the whole of reality"), He is the Structure of being ("reality as a whole"). God is love, because He can love Himself through the separation within Himself. Tillich adds: "And through separation *from* himself (in creaturely freedom) God fulfils his love of himself — primarily because he loves that which is estranged from himself."[96] Yet we must remember that, according to Tillich, estrangement means that what is separated still belongs to that from which it is separated. Thus God loves man simply because essential humanity (in which man participates in spite of ex-

[92] *Ibid.,* p. 252.
[93] *Ibid.,* p. 255.
[94] *Systematic Theology,* II (1957), p. 44.
[95] "The infinite passion, as faith has been described, is the passion for the infinite" — *Dynamics of Faith* (1957), p. 9.
[96] *Systematic Theology,* I (1951), p. 282.

istential estrangement) includes the union of man and God. The corollary of the proposition that God does not exist is that God is not the God of existing individuals.

MAN AND CHRIST

Since his God is the Ground of Being and not the Creator, it is natural enough that Tillich should substitute for the Pauline "new creation" his own norm of the "New Being." For him, existence as such, and not merely sinful existence, is to be overcome. The Christian form of faith is that the New Being has appeared in its final manifestation through the medium of Jesus as the Christ. But the New Being is not tied to particular symbols. "It has the power to be free from every form in which it appears."[97] So today, when man is conscious especially of the meaninglessness of human life, the New Being may be experienced through the seriousness of despair about meaning.[98] For where the decision is made to accept meaninglessness without hope of discovering meaning, this decision becomes a meaningful act. In an ultimate situation, man is thrown back upon the power of being, even though there are no concrete religious symbols through which that power may be mediated. The religious nature of the experience comes from its ultimacy. God need not be named, so long as man is driven to the depth of life so as to be made aware of the Ground of his being. "He who knows about depth knows about God."[99]

Tillich thinks of the New Being as that which precedes and gives reality to each and every concrete manifestation of the power of being in symbolic form, including its "final" manifestation in the picture of Jesus as the Christ. Indeed, the Cross is interpreted by him as the symbol of the self-negation of the finite, and so of the non-ultimacy of every human religion, including Christianity.[100] We can see, therefore, why he believes that the Christian theologian adds the criterion of the Christian message to the "mystical a priori." The latter is basic, the former only a clarification (though the most complete) of the truth that in the depth of life the Unconditioned breaks into the conditioned. Jesus as the Christ can truly be the Christian's ultimate concern, but this comes about because the Christian participates in "the

[97] *Systematic Theology*, II (1957), p. 165.
[98] *Systematic Theology*, III (1963), pp. 227f. Cf. *The Courage to Be* (1952), pp. 172ff.
[99] *The Shaking of the Foundations* (1948), p. 57.
[100] *Systematic Theology*, III (1963), pp. 102, 154. Cf. *The Courage to Be* (1952), pp. 188f.; *Dynamics of Faith* (1957), pp. 122f.

historical continuum" which receives its meaning through him.[101] Similarly, the Christian's experience of deliverance from sin is a historically conditioned experience, the truth of which rests upon the inclusive truth that, while human existence is the state of estrangement from being and meaning, existence may be conquered by the power of being. For, although "structures of destruction" are the mark of existence, they "are counterbalanced by structures of healing and reunion of the estranged."[102] It seems that the answer to the question of estranged existence may be (or may not be) the Christ. But it is always the power of being discoverable — according to Tillich's analysis — in the depth of life.

JESUS THE CHRIST

The evidence that Tillich's theology is built upon the assumptions of his ontology and not upon the Christian message is forthcoming at the beginning of his theological system, when he outlines his doctrine of revelation. But the conflict between these assumptions and the content of the historic Christian faith first becomes unmistakably plain at the point where he turns to develop his Christology. For this reason some who were willing to accept *Systematic Theology* Volume I, containing the first two Parts of his system, found it impossible to accept Volume II, containing the third Part, "Existence and the Christ."[103] Before he relates the life, death, and resurrection of Jesus to his metaphysic of being, non-being, and finite being, the implications of Tillich's world view may not be recognized. These implications cannot be overlooked when we find Tillich dividing emphatically what Scripture has joined: the personal name "Jesus" and the title "Christ."

Self-transcending naturalism must deny the combination "Jesus Christ," because it holds that the power of being is revealed only in "ecstatic" experience of the depth of life. It must hold that it is absurd to believe without qualification that an existing individual, Jesus by name, can *be* the Christ. A spiritual reality can "appear" or "be manifest" in existence under the appropriate conditions, namely, when reason is driven to its transcendent Ground. Thus Jesus can be received as the Christ when the "picture" of Jesus is united in the minds of His followers with the reality of the New Being. The objective reality allowing Jesus to be received as the Christ is the disappearance of Jesus in the Christ. It is this reality which makes the

---

[101] *Systematic Theology,* II (1957), p. 101.

[102] *Systematic Theology,* II (1957), p. 75.

[103] See, for example, George H. Tavard's explanation in the Preface (vii) to *Paul Tillich and the Christian Message* of how he came to write this book on Tillich's Christology.

statement that Jesus *is* the Christ a possible statement.[104]   Two of Tillich's metaphors emphasize his fundamental viewpoint here.   The first is "transparency."   Jesus as the Christ reveals God by becoming transparent to the eternal Ground of His being.   The second is "bearer."   Jesus is the Bearer of the New Being.   He is not the Christ in Himself, but the vehicle in which the Christ is carried into existence.

The scriptural declaration that Jesus Christ has come in the flesh (1 John 4:2) is a misleading form of words for Tillich, and he specifically objects to the doctrinal term *Incarnation*.[105]   The message of self-transcending naturalism is that essential manhood has appeared under the conditions of existence, showing that man is ultimately at one with the Ground of his being.   The historical medium through which we become aware of this ultimate truth may be important for us, but only because of our historical situation.   So, to confess belief in Jesus — the vital demand of the New Testament (John 3:18; Acts 4:13) — is not vital, and may well be idolatrous.   In the Gospel story, the fact that Mary sat at the feet of Jesus, listening to *Him* was unimportant. *"But Mary was ultimately concerned.*   This is the one thing needed."[106]

The Spirit, the Kingdom of God, and Eternal Life

Tillich has compared himself with an architect.   He has labored to construct a theological system.   But we may ask on what foundation and with what materials he has built; and the answer is clearly that he has built on the Ground of Being with the materials of his ontology. *Jesus Christ and the biblical revelation have been fitted into a structure already complete without them.*   No use of the word "correlation" can get round the fact that Tillich makes completely universal claims for his presentation of God the Absolute as the Ground of Being discoverable in the depths of life.   Neither the Bible nor Christian doctrine can add one iota to the sum of knowledge there disclosed.   Each, in its own way, merely illustrates his ontological analysis.

By the time we come to the fourth and fifth Parts of the *Systematic Theology* we are quite familiar with the process which Tillich calls *de-literalizing the religious symbols,* but which might more prosaically be described as reading Christianity as an allegory of the ontological world view.   We could tabulate Tillich's basic argument concerning the Holy Spirit, the Church, and the Last Things in the following fashion.

---

[104] "What is particular in him is that he crucifies the particular in himself for the sake of the universal" — *Christianity and the Encounter of the World Religions* (1963), p. 81.

[105] *Systematic Theology*, II (1957), p. 95.

[106] *The New Being* (1955), p. 159. Italics in the original.

Allegory: The Holy Spirit bestows the gift of faith.

Reality: The Power of being is discovered in life as spiritual Presence. When we are grasped by Spiritual Presence we participate in the transcendent unity of unambiguous life. At present such participation is fragmentary.

Allegory: The Holy Spirit is God's gift to His Church.

Reality: The Spirit's invasion of the human spirit occurs in social groups, creating the Spiritual Community. All churches are both actualizations and distortions of the Spiritual Community.

Allegory: Christ will deliver up the Kingdom to the Father, and God will be all in all.

Reality: Universal participation in the Ground of Being can come only in essentialization, where the Absolute gathers into itself all that is positive in the movement from essence to existence, thus fulfilling itself through the world-process.

Tillich believes that his theology is theocentric. Although it starts with man's relation to God, it ends with God's relation to man and his world. But it must be said that, since Tillich bases his system upon the Ground of Being it is from the first Absolute-centered[107] in the manner of nineteenth-century idealism. Lacking a genuine doctrine of Creation, it knows man only in the Absolute — firstly in unity with the divine, in essential manhood, then in the contradiction of existence, both within and outside the divine Ground, and finally in essentialization, elevated into the divine. It is no accident that Tillich's key term "estrangement" is borrowed from Hegel. Self-transcending naturalism (belief-ful realism) as a philosophical stance assumes a Hegelian-style dialectic of thesis, antithesis, and synthesis; for there the basic structure of being manifests itself in polarities which are united in the Ground of Being. Within itself, the finite world points beyond itself. Tillich's idealism is modified in a "theosophical" direction by his indebtedness to Boehme, Schelling, and Heidegger. (He finds in Heidegger, despite his "atheism" a genuine "theonomous philosophy.") On this side he insists that reason is parted from its "depths" and requires to be supplemented by revelation. But revelation, as he conceives it, is rooted in the "mystical a priori" and is prior to any particular religious belief.

Nowhere is the fundamental character of Tillich's theology more evident than in his appeal to what he calls the "Protestant principle." Historically, the word "Protestant" indicates a positive "protestation"

[107] In his later writings Tillich avoids the term *Absolute*. But he makes clear that this is because the term seems to exclude the finite from the Ground of Being, and not because of any more basic objection. See "Reply to Interpretation and Criticism," *The Theology of Paul Tillich* (1952), p. 331.

or confession of faith in the salvation that comes in Jesus Christ. But Tillich's Protestant principle is a negative and abstract principle establishing "the attitude of protest against form."[108]   It indicates the belief that the Unconditional cannot be bound to any manifestation of itself in the conditioned.   Tillich would combine with the Protestant principle the "Catholic substance," in order to achieve a rounded theological outlook.   The Catholic substance, however, is *not* the Christian *kerygma* either.   It is "the concrete embodiment of the Spiritual Presence,"[109] or the actuality of the Ground of Being discovered in the Christian Church to the extent to which the Church is indeed the Spiritual Community.   Neither Protestant principle nor Catholic substance witnesses ultimately to Jesus Christ but to the power of the infinite within the finite.

Tillich's theology is an impressive accomplishment, the product of a supple, precise, encyclopedic, and immensely creative mind.   But it is not so much Christian theology as a translation of Christian theology into the language of theosophical-ontological speculation.   Sometimes the translation helps us to see the original in a clearer light.   But, more often, the translation does violence to both the spirit and the letter of that which it translates.   Faith is not knowledge, and Tillich claims to *know*.   His apologetic theology attempts to break down the New Testament distinction between *pistis* and *gnosis,* so that he appears in the light of a latter-day Gnostic.   Yet his theological enterprise is undertaken with the missionary purpose of bringing together the conviction of Christian faith and the hunger of the contemporary world for a gospel that is relevant to its needs.   We cannot do other than admire his combination of spiritual zeal with intellectual integrity and the humility of heart that shines through all he has written.

[108] *The Protestant Era* (1948), p. 206.
[109] Systematic Theology III (1963), pp. 6, 245.

IV. BIBLIOGRAPHY

Books by Paul Tillich in English

(a) Theological and Philosophical

The Religious Situation. New York, 1932.
The Interpretation of History. New York, 1936.
The Protestant Era (with essay by James Luther Adams). Chicago, 1948.
Systematic Theology, Vol. I. Chicago, 1951.
The Courage to Be. New Haven, 1952.
Love, Power, and Justice: Ontological Analyses and Ethical Applications. New York, 1954.
Biblical Religion and the Search for Ultimate Reality. Chicago, 1955.
Systematic Theology, Vol. II. Chicago, 1957.
Dynamics of Faith. New York, 1957.
Theology of Culture (edited by Robert C. Kimball). New York, 1959.
Christianity and the Encounter of the World Religions. New York, 1963.
Morality and Beyond. New York, 1963.
Systematic Theology, Vol. III. Chicago, 1963.
The World Situation. Philadelphia, 1965 (reprinted from the essay in *The Christian Answer,* ed. Henry P. Van Dusen, New York, 1945).
The Future of Religions. New York, 1966.
On the Boundary; An Autobiographical Sketch. New York, 1966 (reprinted from the essay in *The Interpretation of History*).
Perspectives on 19th and 20th Century Protestant Theology (edited and with an Introduction by Carl E. Braaten). New York, 1967.
My Search for Absolutes (with a Prologue by Ruth Nanda Ashen, and drawings by Saul Steinberg). New York, 1967.

(b) Sermons

The Shaking of the Foundations. New York, 1948.

Paul Tillich

The New Being. New York, 1955.
The Eternal Now. New York, 1963.

ARTICLES BY PAUL TILLICH IN ENGLISH

"Autobiographical Reflections," in *The Theology of Paul Tillich* (edited by C. W. Kegley and R. W. Bretall). New York, 1952.

"Being and Love," in *Moral Principles of Action* (edited by R. N. Anshen). New York, 1952.

"The Conception of Man in Existential Philosophy," *Journal of Religion,* XIX (July, 1939), 201-15.

"Depth," *Christendom,* IX (Summer, 1944), 317-25.

"Existential Analyses and Religious Symbols," in *Contemporary Problems in Religion* (edited by H. A. Basilius). Detroit, 1956.

"Existentialism, Psychotherapy, and the Nature of Man," in *The Nature of Man in Theological and Psychological Perspective* (edited by Simon Doniger). New York, 1962.

"Freedom and the Ultimate Concern," in *Religion in America* (edited by J. Cogley). New York, 1958.

"The Idea of a Personal God," *Union Review,* II (November, 1940), 8-10.

"The Kingdom of God and History," in *Oxford Conference Series,* New York, Willet-Clark, 1938.

"The Meaning and Justification of Religious Symbols," in *Religious Experience and Truth: A Symposium* (edited by Sidney Hook). New York, 1961.

"The Nature of Man," *Journal of Philosophy,* XLIII (December, 1946), 675-77.

"Philosophy and Theology," *Religion in Life,* X (Winter, 1941), 21-30.

"The Problem of the Theological Method," *Journal of Religion,* XXVII (April, 1947), 16-26.

"The Relation of Religion and Health," *Review of Religion,* X (May, 1946), 348-84.

"Religion and Secular Culture," *Journal of Religion,* XXVI (April, 1946), 79-86.

"The Religious Symbol," *Journal of Liberal Religion,* II (Summer, 1940), 13-33.

"Reply to Interpretation and Criticism," in *The Theology of Paul Tillich* (edited by C. W. Kegley and R. W. Bretall). New York, 1952.

"Theology and Symbolism," in *Religious Symbolism* (edited by F. E. Johnson). New York, 1955.

"What Is Divine Revelation?" *The Witness,* XXVI (April, 1943), 8f.

"What Is Wrong with the 'Dialectic' Theology," *Journal of Religion,* XV (April, 1935), 127-45.

Books on Paul Tillich

Adams, James Luther. *Paul Tillich's Philosophy of Culture, Science and Religion.* New York, 1965.

Armbruster, Carl L. *The Vision of Paul Tillich.* New York, 1967.

Brown, D. Mackenzie. *Ultimate Concern: Tillich in Dialogue.* New York, 1965.

Hamilton, Kenneth. *The System and the Gospel: A Critique of Paul Tillich.* New York, 1963.

Hopper, David. *Tillich: A Theological Portrait.* Philadelphia, 1967.

Kelsey, David H. *The Fabric of Paul Tillich's Theology.* New Haven, 1967.

Killen, R. *The Ontological Theology of Paul Tillich.* Kampen, Netherlands, 1956.

Martin, Bernard. *The Existentialist Theology of Paul Tillich.* New York, 1963.

McKelway, Alexander J. *The Systematic Theology of Paul Tillich: A Review and Analysis.* Richmond, 1964.

Paul Tillich in Catholic Thought (edited by T. A. O'Meara and C. D. Weisser). Dubuque, 1964.

Religion and Culture; Essays in Honor of Paul Tillich (edited by Walter Leibrecht). New York, 1959.

Tavard, George H. *Paul Tillich and the Christian Message.* New York, 1962.

The Theology of Paul Tillich (edited by C. W. Kegley and R. W. Bretall). Vol. I, "The Library of Living Theology." New York, 1952.

Thomas, J. Heywood. *Paul Tillich: An Appraisal.* Philadelphia, 1963.

———. *Paul Tillich.* London and Richmond, Va., 1965.

15 Kenneth Hamilton

Dietrich Bonhoeffer

I. BIOGRAPHY

IT IS THE LIFE fully as much as the thought of Dietrich Bonhoeffer that has caught the imagination of men of our age and made him so central a figure in the contemporary theological scene. The commemorative tablet erected in the church at Flossenbürg, the village where he was hanged by the SS at the age of thirty-eight, reads "Dietrich Bonhoeffer, a witness of Jesus Christ among his Brethren," and adds simply the place-names and dates of his birth and death. The designation "witness," *martyr,* is the highest title the Church of Jesus Christ can bestow on one of its members. And, although Bonhoeffer did not die directly on behalf of his faith, he died because of his refusal to compromise in taking a path he believed he must take as a follower of his Lord. His commitment to the way of self-sacrifice had been made long before his arrest and imprisonment. It is no wonder that, among the many voices claiming to be heard on account of some special insight their owners possess into the Christian Gospel, even our skeptical and sophisticated generation should pause to listen to one who has proved his right to be considered a servant of the Gospel.

Dietrich Bonhoeffer was born on February 4, 1906, in Breslau, Germany. His father Karl Ludwig Bonhoeffer was an eminent neurologist, and his mother Paula (née von Hase) came from a distinguished family. There were eight children in the Bonhoeffer household, Dietrich and his twin sister Sabine being the sixth and seventh. In 1912 the family moved to Berlin. Karl Bonhoeffer, appointed to the newly founded chair of psychiatry in the University of Berlin, set up house in a suburb favored by members of the university. So there was a maximum of cultural stimulation in the home. However, although there had been churchmen in the von Hase family, the atmosphere within the family circle was agnostic and dominated by scientific interests. Dietrich, indeed, had inherited from his mother a love of music, and at one time it was thought possible that he might make this his career. But when he was sixteen, Dietrich decided to enter the ministry of the Prussian Church.

In 1923 the seventeen-year-old student entered the University of Tübingen, taking classes in theology and philosophy there and also finding time for travel in Italy and North Africa. In 1925 he enrolled at the University of Berlin, and two years later, at twenty-one, obtained his Licentiate in Theology, having completed a dissertation entitled *Sanctorum Communio: A Dogmatic Inquiry into the Sociology of the Church.*[1] He next went to Spain for a year, serving as assistant in a German congregation in Barcelona, and returning to Berlin to finish in 1930 a second dissertation allowing him to qualify as a teacher of theology at the university: *Act and Being: Transcendental Philosophy and Ontology in Systematic Theology.*[2] September 1930 saw him a Sloane Fellow at Union Theological Seminary, New York, experiencing his first exposure to New World society and church life.

In his two dissertations Bonhoeffer can be seen leaving behind the preoccupations of his teachers at Berlin and moving forward to discuss the new issues that were being raised in the "dialectical" theology of Karl Barth and the "existential" and "anthropological" concerns of Rudolf Bultmann and Friedrich Gogarten. Berlin boasted at the time a galaxy of liberal scholars, including Adolf Deissmann, Adolf von Harnack, Karl Holl, Hans Lietzmann, and Reinhold Seeberg. The influence of Ernst Troeltsch, who retired in 1923, was still dominant. Troeltsch's religio-historical approach to Christianity explains the treatment of the "sociology" of the Church in *Sanctorum Communio*, although the dissertation was prepared under the direction of Seeberg and engages with Seeberg's viewpoint rather than with Troeltsch's. Bonhoeffer was to admire all his life the combination of scholarly zeal, broad cultural concern, and personal piety that characterized the liberal teachers under whom he was trained. Harnack, in particular, won his affection. A neighbor as well as a teacher, Harnack seemed to him to typify all that was best in the older generation of scholars. And, when the world-famous historian of dogma died, he read an address on behalf of the students of his generation at the memorial service held on

---

[1] Title as in London ed.; New York ed. *The Communion of Saints.* The dissertation first appeared in an abridged edition, subsidized by the author in 1930. A second edition came out in 1954. The English translation is from the third edition (1960); and the material omitted previously, and placed in the third German edition in an appendix, is restored to the body of the English text.

[2] First ed., 1931. English translation from second ed. (1956).

June 15, 1930. In prison thirteen years later, he could still turn back to his old teacher's books with amazement at their author's ability. But, at the same time, he knew that the cultural milieu that had shaped the outlook of nineteenth-century liberalism had disappeared and could not be formative for him and his contemporaries.

As a schoolboy during the First World War, with its bitter aftermath of blockade and the humiliation of the Treaty of Versailles, Bonhoeffer saw the dissolution of the securities of nineteenth-century middle-class life in the German Fatherland. During his stay in America, when he preached for the first time in English, he told how the war had come into his own family, his eldest brother (Karl Friedrich) having been seriously wounded at eighteen, and the next eldest (Walter) having died of wounds at seventeen. He went on to discuss the question of German "guilt" for the war. Though Germany was not alone guilty, he said, guilt there was, and also a lesson to be learned by every German who loved his country passionately, as he himself did. "It seems to me that this is the meaning of the war for Germany: we had to recognize the limits of man and by that means we discovered anew God in his glory and almightiness, in his wrath and his grace."[3] This was the theme that he discovered above all in Karl Barth's "theology of crisis," and he lectured on this theology in 1931 before he returned from America to his homeland.[4] But he had little hope of making his audience understand Barth's essential message. The New World was at that time still firmly wedded to the ideas of progress and the power of human will to remake society, too much so to understand the European who had seen a whole cultural age depart, never to return. Yet, while the lack of any sound theology in the American churches appalled him, their social involvement made a lasting impression on him.

When the summer of 1931 came around, he returned home. A projected voyage by way of India, where he had hoped to clarify his interest in pacifism by seeing something of the non-violence program of Gandhi, did not materialize. Instead, he spent three weeks at Bonn, attending a seminar of Karl Barth's. His one regret at this time was that he had not been able to have Barth for a teacher, and the first-hand encounter with him was no anti-climax. He found Barth as personally fascinating as he was powerful in print. While never one to follow another slavishly, either in thought or in life, Bonhoeffer acknowledged in Barth a unique source of theological inspiration, an anvil on which the metal of his own thinking must be hammered out. From then on, also, Barth became a personal guide, whose letters counted for much whenever difficult decisions were to be made.

3 *No Rusty Swords,* p. 80.
4 See *ibid.,* Appendix II, pp. 361-372, for the text of this lecture.

481

The autumn of 1931 brought him to his position as a teacher and involved him in the practical church work (both local and ecumenical) that was to become the focus of his life when, after Hitler came to power, formal academic life was closed to him. In September he attended meetings of the World Alliance for Promoting International Friendship through the Churches, of which he soon became a secretary. In November he was ordained. As well as attending to his academic duties, he served as chaplain to the Technical High School in Berlin and as leader of a boys' confirmation class in Wedding, a slum area. In this last task he showed his concern for preaching Christ beyond the conventional limits of the Church's life, finding not only that he must interpret the Christian message in terms his religiously disinterested pupils could understand, but also that he had to live alongside them to make his teaching effective.

During 1932 Bonhoeffer's work in connection with the ecumenical movement expanded, taking him to conferences in Britain (London, two conferences), Switzerland (Geneva and Gland), and Czechoslovakia (Westerburg), as well as at home in Berlin. He was busy at the same time with his lectures, including a theological exposition of Genesis 1–3, which was published next year as *Creation and Fall*.[5] His thinking at this period was brought to a focus in a series of lectures on Christology given during the summer semester of 1933.[6] But meanwhile the political situation in the nation had changed rapidly and fatefully. By 1931 the Nazi Party had grown from insignificance to become the strongest force in the German Parliament, and in January 1933 Hindenburg appointed Hitler Chancellor. Bonhoeffer responded immediately by attacking the Nazi "leadership principle" in a radio broadcast on the first of February. His talk was taken off the air part way through. The cutting short of this broadcast by the authorities was prophetic of the future. By being silenced, Bonhoeffer's voice was to carry to the ends of the earth.

However, Bonhoeffer's first concern in opposing the Nazi regime was not political but theological. For him practical Christian action could never be severed from theology. Thus at the 1932 Youth Peace Conference in Czechoslovakia, speaking on the theme of the need for the ecumenical movement to find an undergirding theology, he argued that the Anglo-Saxon view of peace as an intrinsic good could not be supported by Christians, since external peace is other than the peace of Christ's promise to His disciples.[7] So his energies at this time were

[5] English translation from 1937 ed.

[6] These lectures have been reconstructed from students' notes. Title of the New York ed. *Christ the Center*, London ed. *Christology*.

[7] "A Theological Basis for the World Alliance?" in *No Rusty Swords*, pp. 157-173, especially pp. 168-171.

channeled into a concrete task within his own church. Instead of opposing Nazi power in the secular sphere, he concentrated upon fighting the
pressure that Nazi ideology was exerting upon the Church, both ex-
ternally through state edicts and internally through the influence of the
"German Christians." For instance, he had no illusions about the
extent of Hitler's proposals to deal with "the Jewish question." His twin
sister Sabine had a Jewish husband. Yet when he spoke out—promptly
and fearlessly—against the notorious *Aryan Clauses* of April 1933 he
did not protest the government's action but declared the obligation of
the Church to refuse to implement it *in order to remain Christ's Church.*[8]
His first duty, as he saw it, was to expose and identify heresy within the
Christian community. In this task he found a powerful ally in Karl Barth.
The end-result was the Barmen *Declaration* of May 1934 and the
separation of the Confessional Church from the Reich Church.

In October 1933 Bonhoeffer, having applied for leave of absence from
the university, went to London to take charge of two German congrega-
tions. Barth strongly disapproved, accusing him of deserting at the
moment when his presence was most required to lead the faltering
anti-German Christians. But in England, especially through his contact
with the bishop of Chichester, G. K. A. Bell, he was able to explain
the situation at home and prepare the way for the recognition of the
Confessing Church in the ecumenical movement when, officially, the
German Christians held all the key positions. In the capacity of leader
of the German Youth delegation he attended the ecumenical conference
at Fäno, Denmark, July 1934, at which the churches were asked "to
refuse to recognize as Christian any church which renounces its universal
character."[9]

Once again, Bonhoeffer hoped to visit India. Dr. Bell supplied him
with introductions, but meanwhile a call came from home to lead a
seminary in Pomerania for the Confessing Church. Located on the Baltic,
first at Zingst and later at Finkenwalde near Stettin, the school was
intended for those who, their formal theological training completed, were
preparing for the pastorate. One of Bonhoeffer's students was Eberhard
Bethge, who became his assistant and, after his death, was to become
his biographer and editor of his writings. In 1936 Bonhoeffer's authority
to teach was withdrawn by German officials, and the seminary was
closed by order of Himmler in 1937; but it continued underground—
many of its students suffering arrest—until 1940. Bonhoeffer also
initiated a community within the school, the *Bruderhaus*, where he
experimented with a form of Protestant "monasticism," one not bound
by the rules of the cloister yet attempting to create a discipline of

[8] "The Church and the Jewish Question," *ibid.*, pp. 221-229.
[9] *Ibid.*, p. 294.

communal living. His experience during this period is contained in the two books *The Cost of Discipleship*[10] and *Life Together.*[11]

Early in 1936 he and some of his students were invited to visit Sweden and Denmark. At the end of August he and Bethge attended a meeting, held in Switzerland at Chamby, of the Universal Council for Life and Work. This was a preparatory meeting for the World Conference on Church, Community, and State planned for the summer of 1937 at Oxford, England. On leaving Chamby the two friends spent a brief, refreshing vacation in Italy. During February 1937 Bonhoeffer was again at a Life and Work meeting—this time in London. But there were to be no German delegates at all from the Reich Church or Confessing Church at the Conference in July. The year was a hard one for the Confessing Church, for the authorities were now systematically moving to destroy its life. Martin Niemöller, with whom Bonhoeffer had been in close touch since coming to Pomerania and to whom he dedicated *The Cost of Discipleship*, was arrested on the first of July. In September came the closing of the seminary, and in November, the arrest of twenty-seven of its students. Anti-Jewish measures were being stepped up too. In 1938 Bonhoeffer's sister Sabine and her husband fled as refugees to England. Meanwhile Hitler's annexation of Austria and fomenting of the Czechoslovakian crisis made all Europe afraid.

Anxious about the increasing isolation of the harassed Confessing Church, and foreseeing how it could damage the Church were he to be called to military service and refuse, Bonhoeffer was once more in London in March 1939, consulting with Dr. Bell. The final outcome was that, through the action of Reinhold Niebuhr (who was in Britain that year to give the Gifford Lectures), he was invited by Union Seminary to New York. He left for America in June, but returned before the end of July. With the outbreak of a European war seemingly inevitable, it became clear to him that he could not settle to work apart from those who were carrying on the church struggle at home. He had been invited by Dr. John Baillie to give the Croall Lectures in Edinburgh in October that year, and, though doubtful of being allowed to go, began to prepare material on the subject of "Death in the Christian Message." On September 3 the Second World War began.

Early in 1938 Bonhoeffer had made contact with the political underground seeking to overthrow Hitler. His sister Christine's husband Hans von Dohnanyi, who was in the intelligence service, now recruited him for the Resistance by enrolling him as a civilian agent. By this means he was able to travel throughout Germany and maintain his contacts abroad, while his activities in the Church were almost wholly proscribed. For-

[10] First published 1937. English translation abridged 1948, complete 1959.
[11] First published 1938. English translation 1954.

bidden to participate in church affairs since 1938, his license to preach was withdrawn in 1940 and he had to report to the police at regular intervals. The following year his books were condemned. Yet he was able to visit Switzerland in 1941, making contact with W. A. Visser 't Hooft. During a journey to Sweden in 1942 he met Dr. Bell and communicated to him the Resistance's terms for a German surrender.[12] The rejection by the British Government of this overture meant that there was no alternative for the underground except the assassination of Hitler —a course Bonhoeffer himself had urged—and the result was the unsuccessful bomb plot of July 20, 1944.

In April 1943 Bonhoeffer and his brother-in-law were arrested at his parents' house, though only on suspicion. Part of the manuscript of an ambitious work, his *Ethics*, which he had been writing during the previous three years, fell into the hands of the Gestapo; but the greater part was successfully hidden and was retrieved and pieced together after the war by Eberhard Bethge.[13] Bonhoeffer was first imprisoned in the Tegel Military Prison, near Berlin. He was treated with special consideration, largely because his mother's cousin was General von Hase, the City Commandant of Berlin. He was able to have books, to write, and to receive parcels from his family. However, the integrity of his character and his active concern for his fellow prisoners made an impression far beyond the accident of his connections, an impression that was acknowledged by all who were brought into contact with him right to his last days. This was the period to which we owe the *Letters and Papers from Prison*.[14] After the failure of the bomb plot, evidence of his complicity, as well as that of Hans von Dohnanyi, of his brother Klaus, and of his sister Ursula's husband Rudiger Schleicher, was unearthed. That October, he was transferred to the Gestapo prison in Berlin on Prinz Albrecht Strasse. Following the bombing of the prison during an air raid, he was sent to the concentration camp of Büchenwald, then to Schönberg, and finally to Flossenbürg. There he was hanged only a few days before the arrival of the Allies. His brother and his two brothers-in-law were executed around the same time, at the concentration camp of Sachsenhausen.

To the last he exhibited a marvelous courage and compassion. At Schönberg his final act was to conduct a service, preaching on the texts of the day, Isaiah 53:5 and I Peter 1:3. As he was led away to Flossen-

---

[12] Dr. Bell's account of the meeting is recorded in *The Contemporary Review,* No. 958 (1945), pp. 203ff.

[13] 1949. English translation, 1955.

[14] Edited by Eberhard Bethge, 1951 (expanded ed., 1955). Title as in London eds., 1953, 1956, 1967, and New York paperback ed., 1962. New York hardcover ed., 1953, entitled *Prisoner for God.*

bürg and execution, he said, "This is the end—for me the beginning of life."

II. EXPOSITION

The attempt to give any reliable account of Bonhoeffer's theological views presents peculiar difficulties. In the nature of things, some uncertainties must always arise when a writer's life is cut short while he is still feeling his way through current problems that are actively in his mind. There are those, indeed, who believe that Bonhoeffer's theological writings, more especially the fragments of the war years, are too slight to constitute a theology at all. For example, Paul Tillich has been reported as saying, "Everyone is always quoting 'Letters and Papers from Prison.' Bonhoeffer's martyrdom has given him authority—martyrdom always gives psychological authority—but in fact he didn't live long enough for us to know what he really thought."[15] On the other hand, it has been argued that we can clearly trace the course of Bonhoeffer's thinking and see where the earlier theological outlook leads into the last "prison letters" phase, the character of which is unmistakable even though incompletely realized. The debate, in this event, turns upon whether the last phase presages a radical break with the past[16] or is to be understood as an effort to move forward without repudiating the broad theological base on which previous work has been erected.[17]

In the judgment of the present writer continuity rather than discontinuity is the mark of Bonhoeffer's theology, the contrary impression being largely the result of the fact that, both in Germany and in the English-speaking world, interest in Bonhoeffer sprang initially from his reputation as a courageous opponent of the Nazi tyranny. Curiosity about the psychology of a martyr-hero therefore was a primary motive in turning our attention to the *Letters and Papers from Prison*, with the unfortunate result that not only was the study of his theology begun

[15] Quoted in Ved Mehta, *The New Theologian*, p. 139.

[16] Thus John A. Phillips, who in his *Christ for Us in the Theology of Dietrich Bonhoeffer* speaks (p. 142) of a "revolution in Bonhoeffer's thinking."

[17] Thus John D. Godsey, who in his *The Theology of Dietrich Bonhoeffer* raises the issue of continuity or discontinuity, and asserts his conviction (p. 264) "that the last development in Bonhoeffer's theology, while indeed unexpected, does in no sense represent a break with the theology of the former periods but rather a bold consummation of the same." He discusses the various proposals to find a unifying factor in Bonhoeffer's thought, proposed respectively by Eberhard Bethge, Karl Barth, and Gerhard Ebeling, and concludes for his part that continuity resides in Bonhoeffer's Christology. It is interesting to find that Phillips (*op. cit.,* Preface) dismisses Godsey's book as presenting "a descriptive, journalistic, and for the most part uncritical treatment of the subject."

486

from the wrong end[18] but also his prison letters themselves were used to justify a current "theology of secularity" having no essential connection with Bonhoeffer's own position and in many respects contradicting it.

There are two statements in the prison letters that are crucial for our understanding of Bonhoeffer's mind. The first is the opening of the letter to Bethge dated April 22, 1944 (pp. 158-159):[19]

> You say my time here will be very important for my work, and that you're looking forward to what I shall have to tell you later, and to read what I have produced so far.—Well, you mustn't expect too much: I have certainly learnt a great deal, but I don't think I have ever changed very much. There are some who change a lot, but many hardly change at all. I don't believe I have ever changed very much, except at two periods in my life, the first under the first conscious impact of Papa's personality, and the second when I was abroad. I think you are very much the same. Self-development is of course an entirely different matter. Neither of us has had any sudden break in our lives. Of course we have deliberately broken with a great deal, but that again is an entirely different matter. Our present experiences hardly represent a real break in the passive sense. In the old days I often used to long for such a break, but I think quite differently about it to-day. Continuity with the past is a wonderful gift. St. Paul wrote II Timothy 1.3a as well as I Timothy 1.13!

The second is from the letter of June 8, 1944 (p. 194):

> You have asked me so many important questions on the subjects that have been occupying me lately, that I should be happy if I could answer them all myself. But I'm afraid the whole thing is very much in the initial stages. As usual, I am led on more by an instinctive feeling for the questions which are bound to crop up than by any conclusions I have reached already.

These two statements must be taken together. The first indicates the base from which Bonhoeffer operated: a life lived in a faith that remains constant. The second has to do with his attitude of openness that is always ready to follow a question where it leads, because it does not fear that receiving fresh insights can possibly overthrow long-cherished truths, but rather believes that this will only allow them to be possessed more surely.

His attitude he learned from his liberal teachers, never ceasing to be

---

[18] This is the thesis of James Patrick Kelley's article "Bonhoeffer Studies in English: How Theologians Become Popular," *Lexington Theological Quarterly*, Vol. III, No. 1 (Jan. 1968), pp. 12-19.

[19] Quotations are from the New York paperback ed., 1962.

grateful for the example they set in the matter of respecting at all costs the available evidence and of refusing to trim unpalatable facts in order to make them fit preferred conclusions. But his basic orientation he found in the historic faith of the Christian Church, a faith which he believed nineteenth-century liberalism had turned away from and which was being rediscovered for his own generation—particularly through Karl Barth's theology of the Word of God.

If there is one key that opens the door to his theology more than any other, it is the recognition that at all stages of his career he consciously formed his own concepts with Barth in mind more than any other living theologian. The older thinker served him as admired model, as friendly antagonist (the long-standing opposition between Reformed and Lutheran traditions not being forgotten, though not being absolutized either), and as challenge to serve in his own fashion, for the use of the contemporary Church, what Barth himself calls the "happy science" of theology. While he gladly acknowledged to the end his debt to his teachers at Tübingen and Berlin, they could not help him to struggle with his central concern, namely, the faithful proclamation of the Gospel of Jesus Christ for our own day. Here Barth was his true teacher and guide, remembered from first to last in opposition just as much as in agreement. He did not wish ever to be a Barthian.[20] But equally he never ceased to wish to carry forward the theological renascence that he believed Barth to have begun.

GOD, GIVER OF REVELATION

In *Letters and Papers from Prison,* June 8, 1944, Bonhoeffer outlines (p. 197) the course of theology in this century, through the breakdown of liberal theology to the post-liberal attempt "at a completely fresh start" going back to the Bible and the Reformation. He mentions Heim, Althaus, and Tillich, and then adds (p. 198),

> Barth was the first to realize the mistake that all these efforts (which were all unintentionally sailing in the channel of liberal theology) were making in having as their objective the clearing of a space for religion in the world or against the world.
>
> He called the God of Jesus Christ in to the lists against religion, *"pneuma* against *sarx."* That was and is his greatest service (the second edition of his Epistle to the Romans, in spite of all its neo-Kantian shavings). Through his later dogmatics, he enabled the Church to effect this distinction all along the line.

[20] See his caustic remarks (*No Rusty Swords,* p. 120) about the "pundits" at Bonn during his visit to hear Barth lecture, their scent for "thoroughbreds" and their reluctance to welcome him because of his "bastard theological derivation." For Barth himself he expresses only admiration.

He goes on to give some pointed criticism of Barth—but not of this contribution. Here indeed is the place where his deepest convictions about theology begin.

The God of Jesus Christ against religion. Barth's understanding of the absolute contrast between revelation, as God's self-disclosure of Himself through His Word, and religion, as man's attempt to reach God through his own efforts,[21] is assumed by Bonhoeffer to be the necessary starting-place for true reflection about the Christian faith. The biblical categories of "spirit" *(pneuma),* the sphere of the divine, and "flesh" *(sarx),* the sphere of the human, are appealed to in order to show that there can be no way through from man to God. The action of God alone can connect the two spheres. He is known only through His self-revelation.

This theme is as prominent in Bonhoeffer's earliest writings as in his latest. In the two dissertations it is already assumed, and not argued except incidentally in the context of other discussions, since both productions are concerned with aspects of the reception of revelation in the human sphere. Here we come across such typical statements as: "Not religion but revelation, not a religious community but the church: that is what the reality of Jesus Christ means" (*Sanctorum Communio,* p. 112); and, "Revelation is its own donor, without preconditions, and alone has the power to place in reality. From God to reality, not from reality to God, goes the path of theology" (*Act and Being,* p. 89). However, for a direct statement concerning the basic importance of this approach to theology we have to turn to the lecture on the Theology of Crisis he gave in America in 1931, where he knew that his audience thought of theology in a very different way from his—namely, in terms of "religion and ethics." Explaining in his lecture that Barth is to be understood as a theologian and not as a philosopher, he turns aside to generalize in these terms (*No Rusty Swords,* p. 362):

> This at least must be clear, what we intend to be: Christian theologians or philosophers. To be unclear on this point means that we in any case are not Christian theologians. For the Christian theologian must know the proper and stable premise of his whole thinking, which the philosopher does not recognize: the premise of the revelation of God in Christ, or, on the subjective side, faith in this revelation.

For Bonhoeffer there can be no question of any natural theology by means of which, from the human side, the difference between the two spheres can be annulled at any point. During his period as a university teacher this is one issue to which he returns continually, taking issue with a variety of contemporary and historic philosophers and theologians

---

21 See *The Epistle to the Romans* (Oxford, 1933), pp. 49-53, 136-138; *Church Dogmatics* (Edinburgh, 1956), I/2, pp. 280-361.

who have believed that there must be a method of establishing the reality of God apart from faith. Against all such claims he insists that the transcendence of God is not to be identified with any idea of transcendence that man can conceive. *Act and Being,* for example, traces two streams of thought attempting to grasp the nature of God's transcendence from the perspective of the human mind: the transcendentalist tradition stemming from Kant, and the idealistic tradition stemming from Hegel's transformation of Kant's critical philosophy. The conclusion is that the two streams, though sharply diverging at the beginning, tend to converge in the end. The first makes God unknowable, a non-objective thing-in-itself. The second pulls God into the reflecting-self which can make God its object. But, in the last resort, both know only the thought that remains in itself and contemplates its own image.

Bonhoeffer's emphasis upon the transcendence of God as being *sui generis* and not to be confused with philosophical concepts of transcendence appears again in the prison letters.

The theological focus of the issue of God's transcendence that "shipwrecks" man's notions of transcendence is presented in the lectures on Christology of 1933. The force of these lectures is well indicated in the title given to the American edition of the English translation—*Christ the Center.* Bonhoeffer begins by asserting that Christ, the Word of God, can neither be approached as a conceivable idea nor be understood apart from worshipping acceptance. This Logos requires that we speak of Him first by remaining silent, so that we may accept Him by our belief.

> Because of its claim to be *the* discipline *par excellence* and the centre of its sphere, christology stands alone. There is no proof by which it can demonstrate the transcendence of its subject. Its statement that this transcendence, namely the Logos, is a person, a man, is a presupposition and not subject to proof.[22]

The Logos confronts our human logos, our intellect, which strives to grasp all subjects by asking the question "How?" and by proceeding to classify the subject before it. But this subject is an Anti-Logos refusing to be classified. In the presence of the Anti-Logos, then, there is only one question we may ask, namely, "Who are you? Speak!" This is the question of "deposed, distraught reason"—and, equally, the question of faith. Christ alone can give the answer, and He must indeed have already spoken before we ask. "Jesus' testimony to himself stands by itself, self-authenticating. It is the backbone of any theology" (p. 32).

Furthermore, the Incarnate Word questions *us* concerning our ability to stand before Him. He asks who we are that we address Him and yet

[22] *Christ the Center,* p. 28.

do not know Him. "The mere fact that man for his part can be questioned like this shows who it is that asks. Only God can ask like this" (p. 34).

Thus revelation creates faith. It cannot be validated by anything outside itself, or by anyone except the God who gives us His Living Word in Jesus Christ.

JESUS CHRIST, GOD REVEALED

It is in his christological teaching that Bonhoeffer most thoroughly reflects the Lutheran basis of his thinking. Luther used to insist that it was the part of Christian faith to "see God in the despised man Jesus," and in Bonhoeffer's lectures on Christology this motif is echoed. Bonhoeffer asserts (p. 94) that the heart of Lutheran Christology lies in the theological category of the *genus maiestaticatum,* according to which the predicates of the Godhead are received by the human nature of the man Jesus Christ. Beyond the speculative arguments of Luther himself and their developments by the Lutheran schoolmen, so he insists, is a commitment in faith to the scriptural witness to the Word made flesh. The intention of the intricate terminology, as distinct from its actual result in the church polemics of the time, was not to elaborate explanations of how incarnation is possible, but to proclaim the reality of the Incarnate One. "The question is no longer, *How* can God be humiliated man? but rather, *Who* is the humiliated God-Man?" (p. 111).

Again, we find that Bonhoeffer never varied throughout his life in his understanding of the significance of the reality and truth who is Jesus the Lord of Christians. In *Christ the Center* we are introduced to the title of Jesus "the man for others," which features in the prison letters. In the lectures the title is given more precisely in the formula "He is *pro me* as pioneer for the others" (p. 48). Lutheran in orientation, Bonhoeffer's Christology is founded specifically upon Chalcedonian orthodoxy, and expounded in conscious opposition to the ancient and modern "heresies" seeking to bend the biblical presentation of the God-man to serve the non-biblical interests of various theories of salvation.

Christ the Center, reconstructed by Bethge from students' notes, is in two parts: "The Present Christ" and "The Historical Christ." (A third part, "The Eternal Christ," was planned but never delivered.) In considering history Bonhoeffer, interestingly enough, takes no account of the distinction in the German language—so heavily insisted upon by Bultmann and others—between *Geschichte* and *Historie.* He is content to point out (pp. 74-76) that historical investigation, dealing in probabilities, by itself cannot establish or refute the claim that Jesus is the Christ. What is crucial for faith is to be able to make the assertion that

491

the Christ of preaching is identical with the Jesus of history; and this is attested in Scripture. After all, we should never feel constrained to raise the issue of the Historical One had we not already encountered the Risen One through the Word of the Bible. So the burden of doubt concerning the historicity of Jesus is bound up with recognizing the Bible to be a book that comes down to us through history. Faith in Jesus Christ as Lord reaches us only when we find God's Word speaking in Scripture. While we remain simply on the historical plane we can meet, at most, evidence of a Christ-cult. (The liberal-humanistic alternative of a "religion of Jesus," focussed on the faith *of* Jesus in the Father of all men, is no longer a view having any historical backing.) At the same time, the faith that says "Lord" is also a faith looking to the man who lived his life among men in history. We cannot separate the Exalted Christ from the Humiliated Christ.

On the theological level we seek the Lord who is present to us eternally. There have been from the beginning two distortions of the witness of Scripture to the Present Christ, one Greek and the other Hebrew, one seeing a spiritual presence that only touches history and the other seeing a good man elevated out of history to become the Son of God: the docetic and the Ebionite heresies (pp. 78-88). Bonhoeffer believed that the Ebionite heresy hardly survived beyond the Monarchians. Modern views seeming to assert the all-importance of the historical man Jesus are no more than superficially in this tradition. Docetism is the dominant heresy of the modern world, whether in the cult of the historical Jesus or in theories separating the man Jesus from the eternal Christ.

Bonhoeffer located the origin of docetic Christologies in a particular philosophical presupposition to which the saving work of Jesus is made to conform.

> The reason for the constant deflection of ancient christologies into docetism lies in its conception of redemption, in which the nature (essence) and personal character (individuality) of man are differentiated. The abstract doctrine of God and the idea of redemption have the same presupposition, the contrast of idea and phenomenon which we have already mentioned. The idea is substance, the phenomenon is accident; Christ the God is substance, Jesus the man is accident (p. 81).

The result of adopting this viewpoint is (pp. 43-45) that the Present Christ is found either in a supra-temporal influence persisting in the Christian community or else in an ideal character discovered in the picture of the man Jesus by our discernment. In both variants the result is a depersonalizing of the Present Christ. He is present as a power, *dynamis,* and not as a person. This is true, says Bonhoeffer (p. 44), even where the "personality" of Jesus is supposed to reveal His Christ-hood; for personality is fundamentally an apersonal concept, issuing in the "neuters" *power* and *value*. The Christhood is separated from the man Jesus and lives on as a historical energy or an intuited ideal.

The basic flaw of such Christologies stems, in Bonhoeffer's eyes, from the attempt to begin with an idea of redemption rather than with the person Jesus Christ. "Christology is not soteriology" (p. 37). (Once more, this theme is taken up in the prison letters.) The error of trying to know Christ only through His work began, in the modern period, with Melanchthon, and continued with Schleiermacher and Ritschl; whereas, for Luther, the person interprets the work (pp. 37-38). Doctrinally, there is a fatal omission—the Risen Christ is ignored. "Hidden in the background of this idea of Christ there lies the fact that it does not deal with the resurrection, but only with Jesus up to the cross, with the his-torical Jesus" (p. 44). This comes about because Jesus is taken simply as the temporal manifestation of an eternal power or value that persists eternally apart from Him. It is not the Risen One, but the historical influence or inspiring example of the dead Jesus that is real for us today. Christ can be thought of like Socrates or Goethe.

> Ritschl and Herrmann put the resurrection on one side, Schleiermacher symbolizes it; in so doing they destroy the church. Paul says: "If Christ has not been raised, your faith is futile and you are still in your sins" (I Cor. 15.17) (p. 45).

Luther, on the other hand, interpreted the presence of Christ in the light of the ascension.

How, then, is the Risen Christ present? Bonhoeffer answers this question in the first place by saying that Christ's is a concealed presence.

> This God-man Jesus Christ is present and contemporaneous in the form of the 'likeness', i.e. in veiled form, as a stumbling block *(scandalon)*. This is the central problem of christology. . . . The offence caused by Jesus Christ is not his incarnation—that indeed is revelation—but his humiliation (p. 46).

This declaration of the *scandalon* by Bonhoeffer points to the christolog-ical fact he has insisted upon: that we can never ask "How?" of Christ but must always ask "Who are you?" Christ's presence is concealed, that is, it is not available for inspection and validation. Just as, during His earthly life, Jesus was not seen to be the Messiah, so His presence on earth now is not seen except by faith. To His contemporaries at large the miracles of Jesus were not regarded as signs of His working His Father's work but as evidence of His contact with demonic powers (p.

115). "Even the sinlessness of Jesus is incognito, 'Blessed is he who is not offended in me' (Matt. 11.6)" (p. 113). If the Risen and Ascended Christ is now present in the Church, nevertheless the Church does not look like the community of the redeemed, for it resembles every other religious community.

This is where Bonhoeffer introduces the Lutheran *pro me* motif, quoting Luther, " 'So it is one thing if God is there, and another if he is there for you' (WA 23, 152)" (p. 48). It is not the individual's response to Christ that is here the concern of Bonhoeffer, who was always afraid of the pietistic development in Lutheranism (he often called it "Methodism"), with its concentration upon the awakening in the single soul of a consciousness of its need of redemption. Such an "existential," personal awareness is included, certainly. But for Bonhoeffer the individual is fully himself only when sharing the life of the community—and indeed of humanity. I know that Christ is "for me" when I stand as a Christian in the Church and as a human being with my brethren. Thus Christ's presence *pro me* is stated by him (pp. 48-49) as consisting in (1) being "pioneer, head and firstborn of the brethren who follow him"; (2) standing in their place as the Crucified, with the consequence that "mankind is crucified, dies, and is judged in him"; (3) acting as the new humanity, with the consequence that because "the new humanity is in him, God is gracious towards it in him."

Bonhoeffer's understanding of Christ's presence as being an actual entering into humanity on our behalf is a cosmic vision, and it does not stop with the idea of the salvation of individual souls but presses on to envisage the salvation of all created beings. He writes of the Humiliated One (pp. 112-113), "He entered man's sinful existence past recognition. . . . He was really made sin for us, and crucified as the *peccator pessimus* . . . . As the one who bears our sin, and no one else, he is sinless, holy, eternal, the Lord, the Son of the Father." As such, for him Jesus Christ really can be identified with His Body, the Church, and it too can be seen as the center of history (p. 65). Yet, since the form of Christ's presence in the Church is not yet what it will be when He comes again in glory, we see at present nothing but the Humiliated Christ.

> If Jesus Christ is to be described as God, then we may not speak of this divine essence, of his omnipotence and his omniscience, but we must speak of this weak man among sinners, of his cradle and of his cross. When we consider the Godhead of Jesus, then above all we must speak of his weakness (p. 108).

This is the voice that speaks also in the prison letters, in another context yet to the same purpose. But consideration of that must wait until we have looked at his view of man—selfish and sinning humanity in cor-

494

rupted community—and at his view of the Church, where man's sin has been taken up into the sinlessness of the Church's Lord.

MAN, THE RECIPIENT OF REVELATION

In his two dissertations Bonhoeffer is at pains to counter the liberal view that man knows what he is apart from God and outside the knowledge of God's revelation. *Communio Sanctorum* argues against idealism the reality of the concrete person existing in time and achieving personal being in the concrete situation of moral responsibility. Says Bonhoeffer (p. 31), "The Christian person arises solely from the absolute distinction between God and man; only from the experience of the barrier does the self-knowledge of the moral person arise." We meet other persons because the concrete person in his concrete life is willed by God. "God, or the Holy Spirit, comes to the concrete Thou, only by his action does the other become a Thou for me, from which my I arises. In other words, every human Thou is an image of the divine Thou" (p. 36).

This technical and abstruse language is continued in *Act and Being,* where it is used in the context of a polemical engagement with contemporary philosophers and theologians. But, if the style is complicated, the root of his argument is simple. A large part of the dissertation is taken up by argument directed to showing how a wide spectrum of contemporary, post-liberal thinkers—from Tillich, through Gogarten and Knittermeyer and Grisebach, to Bultmann—continues to try to find a "thoroughfare via 'ourselves' to knowledge of God" (p. 97). For faith there can be no such path. As Luther says (*Works,* XXIII, 135), God is nearer to me than my existence is; He it is who first discloses my existence to me. So Bonhoeffer comments (p. 96), "It is speaking of God which first enables us to speak truly of ourselves."[23] Revelation does not wait upon our reception of it, but places us in the truth.

But here a problem arises that is to engage Bonhoeffer, in one form or another, for the rest of his life. So long as he felt that his task was to stand with Barth and assert the primacy of revelation over against idealism's rationalistic imperialism, he could refer everything to God's will. In the *Sanctorum Communio* he could write (p. 31) that idealism had no understanding of the human person because it had "no voluntarist

---

[23] Bonhoeffer's inaugural lecture "Man in Contemporary Philosophy and Theology" (July 31, 1930) recapitulates many of the themes of *Act and Being.* In the lecture he opposes the beliefs that seek to find the reality of man in his possibilities (Scheler), in his self-questionings (Heidegger), or in his limitations (Tillich). He then develops the argument that "man understands himself not in reflection upon himself, but in the act of reference to God, i.e. only at the point where he really stands before God" (*No Rusty Swords,* p. 65).

concept of God." But now he faces the question of how interpreting God in terms of will inevitably leads to stating theology in terms of a transcendentalist philosophy, where God is seen wholly in terms of "act" and never enters the sphere of "being." This means that revelation cannot reveal to us anything about our "being" as persons.

Already in the first dissertation he had crossed swords with Barth in a lengthy footnote (pp. 226-227) on the nature of Christian love, arguing that Barth dissolves the neighbor by saying we love the Unknown One in him rather than loving the person he is in himself. Challenging Barth's statement in his *Romans* (p. 452) that the other man is significant simply as "a parable of the Wholly Other," and "in himself is trivial and temporal," he had asked (p. 227), "Am I ultimately alone in the world with God?" Now in *Act and Being* he takes up the criticism that afterwards was to appear in the *Letters and Papers from Prison* in the often quoted charge contained in the letter of June 8, 1944 (p. 198; my italics), " . . . *His theology of revelation* becomes positivist, a 'positivism of revelation,' as I put it." The present form of his criticism in *Act and Being* is that Barth's understanding of revelation as God's free act seems to demand a non-temporal movement which cannot involve the historical person, whose response in faith "becomes at most a pointer to God's activity" (pp. 82-83). The man to whom revelation comes is discontinuous with himself if, as Barth puts it, the man to whom God reveals Himself (*sich offenbart*) is the man to whom God cannot become manifest (*offenbar*) (p. 101). A timeless act cannot have continuity with our being in time. Consequently, Barth "can conceive revelation as non-revelation" (p. 102).

The alternative Bonhoeffer proposes is to accept Barth's argument that the Word of God cannot be bound and is not "objectively" available to us, but to revise the presentation of revelation in terms of "act" alone.

> In revelation it is a question less of God's freedom on the far side of us, i.e. his eternal isolation and aseity, than of his forth-proceeding, his *given* Word, his bond in which he had bound himself, of his freedom as it is most strongly attested in his having freely bound himself to historical man, having placed himself at man's disposal. God is not free *of* man but *for* man. Christ is the Word of his freedom. God is *there,* which is to say: not in eternal non-objectivity but (looking ahead for the moment) "haveable", graspable in his Word within the Church. Here a substantial comes to supplant the formal understanding of God's freedom. If it should prove itself, it will suggest a redirection of the act toward ontological ideas (pp. 90-91). .

Naturally, there is no thought in Bonhoeffer's mind of going back to some man-made ontological theory. Seeking what he calls a *genuine* and *theological* ontology, he finds it in revelation conceived as a mode of the being of man, which is also the being of the divine person—the reality of revelation "understood as 'being in Christ' i.e. 'being in the Church' " (p. 115).

Thus man and his existence are not entities we can know in themselves. Only in Christ and in the Church, the community of which Christ is the Living Head, does it become "permissible to speak theologically about the nature of man, his knowledge of God, God's knowledge of him" (p. 116).[24]

THE CHURCH, CHRIST PRESENT IN THE WORLD

The Church is the constant preoccupation of Bonhoeffer's thinking, because of his concern with the "concrete" in our existence. When he chose his career and became an academic, he was also strongly attracted to the pastoral ministry.[25] Events led him into the thick of church politics when the struggle with the German Christians became acute, but he was already deeply engaged in the practical side of the ecumenical movement. In his work at the seminary at Finkenwalde he was directly involved in planning a strategy for churchmen living under battle conditions within a hostile state. Only in his final imprisonment was he forced to live and think in isolation from the Christian community—and still his thoughts were about the future role of the Church in the world!

The *Sanctorum Communio* shows Bonhoeffer beginning his work as a thinker by engaging himself with the meaning of the Christian Gospel for community, anxious to be brought "close to the problem of reality, of the real barrier, and thus of basic social relations" (p. 31). His argument springs from the assumption that the mesage of Christianity is not about abstractions but about actual life, not about man in general but about men facing the practical problems of their existence—about *persons*. "Concrete personal being arises from the concrete situation" (*ibid.*). And personal being means persons in relation. This is the conviction leading him to attempt "a dogmatic inquiry into the sociology of the church" (the subtitle to his dissertation). "In the Christian concept of God, known to us from the revelation in Christ, but also from the church of Christ, the community of God and social community belong together" (p. 40). Thus he can assert, "The church is the presence of

[24] Cf. the inaugural lecture "Man in Contemporary Philosophy and Theology": "Therefore man can no longer understand himself from himself, but only from Christ, who exists as community, i.e. from his Word, which the community hears and without which the community does not exist" (*No Rusty Swords*, p. 68).

[25] Cf. his letter to Barth after his arrival in London in October, 1933. "I have always very much wanted to become a pastor; I've already told you that a couple of times before" (*No Rusty Swords*, p. 234).

Christ, as Christ is the presence of God" (p. 101). For that which makes the Church the Church, namely, the unity of the preached Word and the sacraments, is the visible restoration of community shattered by sin. Because God's will is always directed toward "actual historical man," and man has departed from God, " . . . now God himself must speak and act, and because his Word is always deed this means that he simultaneously accomplishes a new creation of men" (p. 103). Christ has come in history both as the revelation of God and as the fulfillment of His will for community.[26]

Bonhoeffer will have no playing with the notion of an ideal Church divorced from the empirically visible church. In *Act and Being* he argues, "The community in question is concretely visible, is the Christian Church which hears and believes the preaching of the Word" (p. 125). This Church is not the institutional "Catholic Church," which proves to be the "true" Church by pointing to its historical continuity and world-wide extension, but neither is it a spiritual company composed of individuals who have separately responded to the preaching of the Word and who, added together, compose an invisible fellowship of "true" believers. "It is outside 'me' that the gospel is proclaimed and heard, that Christ 'is' in his community" (p. 123). Consequently, Bonhoeffer says of the Church not only that it is created through the presence of Christ in Word and sacrament, but also that it *prays*. It lives and acts through the faith that it confesses. It is the Body that lives under the control of its Head.

But what then are we to make of the evident fact that the Church is not the conspicuous place where Christ is seen, that it is divided, permeated by godlessness, confused in its utterances, and appears more concerned with its institutional forms than with its obedience to its Lord? Bonhoeffer's reply in *Act and Being* is that the Church can be a "true" community of persons only because it is "Christ-founded." Apart from the Holy Spirit within it, it is a religious community founded by men, and therefore can be observed "hovering between entity and non-entity" (p. 25). In Christ it "is"; but, since it is a community of sinners, it also "is not"—it is a part of the old, disrupted order disobedient to God's will and serving the Old Adam rather than the New. In a paper "What Is the Church?" prepared in 1932 in connection with his Berlin lectures he addresses himself directly to this topic.

> The church is a bit of the world, a lost, godless world, under the curse, a complacent, evil world. And the church is the evil world to the highest degree because, in it, the name of God is misused, because in it God is made a plaything, man's idol. Indeed it is simply the eternally lost, anti-

[26] In *Christ the Center* Bonhoeffer asserts that, because Christ is the center of history, the Church too must be understood as the center of history (p. 65).

Christian world if it emerges from its ultimate solidarity with the evil world and sets itself up, boasting against the world. But the church is a bit of the qualified world, qualified by God's revealing, gracious Word, which, completely surrendered and handed over to the world, secures the world for God and does not give it up. Really in the world, really the presence of God. The church is not a consecrated sanctuary, but the world, the world called by God to God; therefore there is only *one* church in all the world.[27]

This is the Church in its duality, seen from the human side and from the divine side. He goes on to say that we miss the point if we think that there are two churches being spoken of here. "The church is one and the same with its visible form and its hidden godliness. Just as there is one and the same Lord, the carpenter's son from Nazareth and the Son of God" (p. 155).

Christology is Bonhoeffer's reference whenever he describes the Church. As Christ's messiahship was hidden during his earthly life, so the "godward" side of the Church is hidden except to those who are "within the communion" of the Humiliated One known by the Body as the Exalted One. Bonhoeffer ends *Christ the Center* with a meditation on how the Church can never strive for a visible confirmation of its way, since its way is to renounce all claims for itself. It is only good "if the church humbly acknowledges its sins, allows itself to be forgiven and acknowledges its Lord" (p. 118). Its visibility is always in duality. Yet this visibility is what makes it the Church. The *scandalon* cannot be removed, and nowhere else can we find Christ.

The Church is visible, a concrete community. It was this conviction that fired Bonhoeffer as he entered the "church-struggle" on behalf of the Confessing Church. Although it was a task he took up reluctantly, once committed he pursued it with energy and single-minded intensity. The firm conclusions he reached dismayed even many who were with him in principle. In a paper "The Question of the Boundaries of the Church and Church Union" printed in *Evangelische Theologie,* June 1936, we find the sharp statement,

> *Extra ecclesiam nulla salus.* The question of church membership is the question of salvation. The boundaries of the church are the boundaries of salvation. Whoever knowingly cuts himself off from the Confessing Church in Germany cuts himself off from salvation.[28]

A little later in the same paper he explains that saying that there is no salvation outside the Church is not a theoretical judgment about who is

---

27 *No Rusty Swords,* pp. 153-154.
28 *The Way to Freedom,* pp. 93-94.

saved and who is lost but a humble confession that the Church is the only place where the promise of God rests. There is, Bonhoeffer adds, an analogy here with Luther's words about God being everywhere, yet it is not His will that you should look for Him everywhere.[29]

The Confessing Church was to be a disappointment for Bonhoeffer, as he found it turning in upon itself rather than going forward to meet the challenge of the times. The evidence is to be seen in the *Letters and Papers from Prison.* Characteristically, we find him writing on Reformation Day, October 31, 1943, and commenting (p. 71) on how Luther's hopes for the Church and for Western Christendom were brought to nothing. The parallel with his own times is clear. Yet one of his last letters, dated August 10, 1944, concludes (p. 242), equally characteristically, "God does not give us everything we want, but he does fulfill his promises, i.e. he still remains Lord of the earth and still preserves his Church. . . ." Christ's presence in the Church may remain hidden, but the Church cannot cease to be the place where He chooses to be found.

ETHICS, THE CHRISTIAN IN THE WORLD

For one whose thought begins with the concrete person in the concrete situation, the problem of ethics must immediately present itself. And so it is with Bonhoeffer, whose interest in the subject runs through his life and comes to a peak in the fragments of the *Ethics,* the book he had hoped to make his *magnum opus.*

Already in 1929, in an address given to the congregation at Barcelona, Bonhoeffer lays down the general direction of his ethical thinking. "What Is a Christian Ethic?" begins by separating ethical codes, which are the product of history, from the Christian message, which stands beyond good and evil in its proclamation of the grace of God, since that grace is not bound by men's good or evil works. The Christian message brings no new commandment, in the sense of any moral principle—including the principle of love. Rather, it reminds us that we are not our own and must look continually to God to know His will for us. Led by the Holy Spirit, we find freedom in the decision that must be made in faithfulness to God, and not to rules. The Christian "acts because the will of God seems to bid him to, without a glance at others, at what is usually called morals, and no one but himself and God can know whether he has acted well or badly" (*No Rusty Swords,* p. 44). At the same time, the Christian cannot take ethical decision lightly, as though his conduct were guaranteed to be right because he is in the service of God. Ethics is a "matter of earth and blood," and the Christian remains earthbound, even when his

[29] Cf. the reference to Luther's explanation of the presence of Christ in the sacrament in *Christ the Center,* p. 57.

desire is towards God" (p. 47). Without entering into all the complexities of the earthly situation, and finding how the world never offers us more than the choice between one evil and another, we cannot know how God is always leading us through evil to Himself.

This early address gives us the abiding core of Bonhoeffer's ethical outlook. Just as he cannot think of anyone's faith as being real unless that faith acknowledges Christ concretely present in the Church, so he cannot think of anyone as having the right to call himself a Christian in the presence of others unless he is ethically involved as a Christian in his concrete situation among these others. This emphasis, during the period at Finkenwalde, produced the works outlining a strategy of dedicated Christian living: *The Cost of Discipleship* and *Life Together.* The first book, with its attack upon the prevalence in Lutheranism of "cheap grace" (justification by faith made into a theory to be accepted instead of the recognition that we belong to God), was one his Lutheran conscience afterwards disapproved of somewhat, because it tended to bend the Christian life too much in the direction of a cultivation of "holiness." Nevertheless, he would not go back on it.[30] The conviction remained firm that there can be no obedience without concrete action, and that when Christ calls a man He calls him to die: both in taking the way of suffering from which there is no turning back, and also in embracing the love of the other which is a dying to self.[31]

The *Ethics,* as we have it, is a pile of roughly cut stones. It confirms and develops the stance of the Barcelona address, insisting that Christian ethics must be neither abstract nor "practical" but concrete. Over against the slogan of "formation" used by the German Christians it sets the New Testament command to be *con*formed with the Incarnate One, to be a "new man" in Christ living "before God." Over against the traditional Lutheran appeal to "the orders of creation"—which had been used, e.g. by Gogarten, to support the German Christian position—it sets the four "mandates" of labor, marriage, government, and the Church. These last are not realities "given" in the order of creation, but are the means whereby God wills to preserve a fallen creation and remake it so that "the reality of Christ with us and in our world" (p. 77) may be fully manifest.

An urgent emphasis running through the *Ethics* is that of the importance of seeing the whole world as the place where the will of God is to

---

[30] See *Letters and Papers from Prison,* letter of July 21, 1944 (p. 226).

[31] Luther's description of the sinful self as the *cor curvatum in se* was always a favorite one with Bonhoeffer, and thus the destruction of the self-enclosed heart becomes for him the proof of the action of grace. For his description of the two deaths in Christian life see *The Way to Freedom,* pp. 254-255. The theme of action paving the way for death is finely stated in his poem "Stations of the Way to Freedom" prefixed to the *Ethics.*

be obeyed. This theme is developed in particular within two sections (pp. 55-72) headed "The Concept of Reality" and "Thinking in Two Spheres," leading into the section on "The Four Mandates." Bonhoeffer's thesis is that, since Jesus Christ is the good—reality itself— and through Him alone we know both God and the world, we cannot think that we can oppose God to the world or the sacred to the secular. The fallen world certainly has fallen under the sentence of God and struggles against the reconciling message of the Church. We must recognize the struggle for what it is, yet we must remember one thing more about the world in its rebellion. "In this way it is also, and indeed especially, the lost and sentenced world that is incessantly drawn into the event of Christ" (p. 71).

The *Letters and Papers from Prison,* from the point of view of Bonhoeffer's theological teaching, is significant in that it shows us the thinker wrestling with the way in which the "lost and sentenced world" is to be brought into touch with the reconciliation known in the Church. Much of the debate that has arisen around the interpretation of the new phrases appearing in the prison letters—"religionless Christianity," "man's coming of age," "worldly existence"—is beside the point; for it assumes that Bonhoeffer was trying to work out some philosophy of history requiring us to adapt the Christian Gospel to the self-understanding of the modern age, whereas he continued to reject strenuously this illusion of idealistic thinking (March 9, 1944, pp. 144-145). What he did believe is that we must accept "the facts and achievements of any given period" realistically as telling us where men are, since this is the place where they have to be reached with the Christian Gospel. Just now, he suggested (April 30, 1944, p. 162), we are "proceeding to a time of no religion at all" and our problem is to find how Christ can become the Lord even of those with no religion. So—

> . . . In what way are we in a religionless and secular sense Christians, in what way are we the *Ekklesia,* "those who are called forth," not conceiving of ourselves religiously as specially favoured, but as wholly belonging to the world (p. 164)?

One answer he suggests is located in the distinction (developed in the *Ethics*) between the penultimate and the ultimate, between the things before the last, which the world is conscious of, and the last things, which are gathered up in God's justification of sinners. To maintain a hold upon the last things will require a "secret discipline" where, in a world that has forgotten the meaning of "inwardness," the Christian must strengthen his hold upon the ultimate reality of faith.

But, by the very nature of his unnaturally isolated situation, Bonhoeffer mostly asks questions without giving answers.

One thing the *Letters and Papers from Prison* makes quite plain. There is no alteration in his basic theology, as there is none in his beliefs. He is as insistent as ever that revelation establishes reality, that the New Testament is not a mythological garbing of universal truth, and that the penultimate exists from and is supported by the ultimate. "How can men endure earthly tensions if they know nothing of the tension between earth and heaven?" (April 11, 1944, p. 157). Equally, he is confident that accepting without reservation the relative goodness of the world does not endanger our grasp upon the Gospel. ". . . God requires that we should love him eternally with our whole hearts, yet not so as to compromise or diminish our earthly affections, but as a kind of *cantus firmus* to which the other melodies of life provide the counterpoint" (May 20, 1944, p. 175). Thus he has no scruples about asking questions that seem to endanger the security of faith, or in suggesting that the religious "garment" in which the Christian message has been wrapped to date may be discarded without losing the substance of the message. In particular, he believes that tying the Gospel to any one apologetic is self-defeating. "Religionless" man is not necessarily more impervious to the call of Christ than "religious" man. "The world's coming of age is then no longer an occasion for polemics and apologetics, but it is really better understood than it understands itself, namely on the basis of the Gospel, and in the light of Christ" (June 8, 1944, p. 200).

Sending the outline of his proposed new book on Christianity in the modern age, Bonhoeffer writes to Bethge: "The Church must get out of her stagnation. We must move out again into the open air of intellectual discussion with the world, and risk shocking people if we are to cut any ice" (August 3, 1944, p. 235). He speaks of the excitement of intellectual discovery. Yet he knows that theological analysis is fallible and impermanent, while the Gospel is always the same. "The God of Jesus Christ has nothing to do with all that we, in our human way, think he can and ought to do. . . . One thing is certain: we must always live close to the presence of God. . . . We can claim nothing for ourselves, and yet we may pray for everything" (August 21, 1944, p. 243).

At the end of the letter where these words are written, another thought strikes him (about the sins of weakness). He makes some observations, and concludes, "I must ponder further on this" (p. 244). This is typical of his method—to strike out in thought and then to think it through in relation to the central point of the Gospel: Jesus Christ and the redemption that comes through Him. *Letters and Papers from Prison* gives us only dislocated theological jottings, requiring much pondering and restatement. But it is a true testament to Bonhoeffer the adventurous theologian, whose theology was always rooted in the concrete situation of a life lived in faith.

III. EVALUATION

GOD AND REVELATION

Bonhoeffer's conception of the nature and task of theology is outlined in the lecture "The Theology of Crisis" he gave in New York in 1931.

> The deepest antinomy seems to me to be the antinomy between pure act and reflection—as the old dogmatics said, *actus directus* and *reflexus*. God is known only in the pure act of referring to God. Theology and philosophy are executed in reflection, into which God does not enter. Philosophy essentially remains in reflection; man knows himself and God only in reflection. Theology at least knows of an act of God, which tears man out of this reflection in an *actus directus* towards God. Here man knows himself and God not by looking into himself, but by looking into the Word of God, which tells him he is a sinner and justified, which he never could understand before. So as Luther said: *pecca fortiter, sed crede fortius,* Barth could say: *reflecte fortiter, sed crede fortius.*[32]

Although this is an early statement, it remains in its essential affirmation true for the mature Bonhoeffer also. However strongly he might disagree with Barth in other places, he never departed from his theology of the Word of God, and, on this account, continued to call himself a "modern" theologian.[33] His decisive break with liberalism came through his rejection of his teacher Seeberg's notion of a "religious a priori,"[34] and from that time on he was to reject outright any kind of natural theology.[35] On the basis of Barth's setting "spirit" against "flesh," revelation against religion, he distinguished also "epistemological transcendence" from the transcendence of the Living God—a distinction found in his latest writings as in his earliest.[36]

[32] *No Rusty Swords,* p. 372. Cf. Bonhoeffer's inaugural lecture (1930) "Man in Contemporary Philosophy and Theology," where a very similar terminology is used (*No Rusty Swords,* pp. 50-69; especially pp. 64-66). In *Act and Being* (p. 175) he even finds in Barth himself the "danger" of locating the act of belief in "reflexion."

[33] See *Letters and Papers from Prison,* August 3, 1944, p. 235.

[34] See *Act and Being,* pp. 44-48.

[35] Cf. his criticism of American theology: "American theology and the American church as a whole have never been able to understand the meaning of 'criticism' by the Word of God and all that signifies. . . .A symptom of this is the general adherence to natural theology" (*No Rusty Swords,* p. 117). Referring to the *Christian Century* articles "How my mind has changed in the last decade," he remarked of the contributors, "And *all,* finally, are united in deliberate rejection of Barth's criticism of natural theology" (*ibid.,* p. 115).

[36] See *Communio Sanctorum,* p. 33; *Act and Being,* p. 69; *Letters and Papers from Prison,* April 30, 1944, pp. 165-166; "Outline for a Book," in *Letters,* pp. 237-238.

Our estimate of Bonhoeffer's teaching about God and revelation, therefore, will depend upon our estimate of the Barthian "revolution" in theology that cuts the link between human reason and divine revelation. Yet, on this ground, Bonhoeffer believed that Barth was no innovator, and he himself appealed here to the teaching of Luther.[37] Where he went on to criticize Barth, he attacked Barth at the point of his "Kantian trimmings," which seemed to make the Word of God so (epistemologically) transcendent that it could not be found concretely in time, where man lives. Bonhoeffer's solution, namely, that God's Word is the Incarnate Word that lives in the Church as community, is one that raises its own problems. At the moment, however, we may turn to two aspects of the doctrine of God and revelation that have not received extended treatment from Bonhoeffer: the Holy Spirit and the Scriptures.

The Holy Spirit is most fully discussed in the *Sanctorum Communio*. There it is stressed that God reveals Himself as the Holy Spirit in order to build up His Church (p. 104).[38] Christ and the Spirit are inseparably connected; for "the Holy Spirit has no other content than the fact of Christ," and Christ "participates in the actual building of the church in time . . . only in the action of the Holy Spirit" (p. 116). The Spirit, being for us "solely the Spirit of the church" (p. 115), makes all individualistic notions of faith impossible. Certainly, each individual is moved according to his own election in Christ, but already as a member of the communion of Christ. "God sees the church of Christ and the individual in one act" (p. 118), which is the act of the Spirit's gift of faith to the individual and His building up of the Church. Thus the doctrine of predestination is grounded in the doctrine of the Spirit, the Personal Spirit of the community of persons.

It is the Holy Spirit, too, who inspires the record of Scripture. "The Bible is the Word only in the church" (p. 161). Both preaching and the Scriptures remain the word of man so long as they are not inspired by the Spirit. "The Spirit has not united himself in substance with the word of the Bible" (*ibid.*).

On this basis, Bonhoeffer accepts without question the validity of a critical approach to the Bible. At the same time he insists that the Bible is the place where the self-attestation of Jesus is handed down to us. In *Christ the Center* he links the question of the exegesis of Scripture with

[37] *No Rusty Swords*, p. 362; *Act and Being*, p. 47.
[38] Cf. the entry in the catechism prepared by Bonhoeffer, in collaboration with Franz Hildebrandt, for the confirmation class at Wedding: *"Who is the Holy Spirit?* No spirit of the world, but the Spirit of God and Christ, who is present in the church. Without him we would know nothing of Christ, just as without Christ we would know nothing of God. In him the Godhead fulfils itself on earth, for 'if thou didst not have a church, thou wouldest not be God' (Luther)" (*No Rusty Swords*, p. 147).

the question of the recognition of Christ in the Jesus of history through faith in the Resurrection.

> . . . Verbal inspiration is a bad surrogate for the resurrection. It means the denial of the sole presence of the Risen One. It eternalizes history instead of seeing and recognizing history in the light of God's eternity. It fails in the attempt to level the difficult ground. The Bible also remains a book among books. We must be ready to admit the concealment in history and thus accept the course of historical criticism. But the Risen One encounters us right through the Bible with all its flaws. We must enter the straits of historical criticism. Its importance is not absolute, but at the same time it is not a matter of indifference. In fact it never leads to a weakening of faith but rather to its strengthening, as concealment in history is part of Christ's humiliation (p. 76).

However, in his own exegetical works (which were strongly influenced by his old teacher at Tübingen, Adolf Schlatter) he made practically no use of biblical criticism. In the Introduction to *Creation and Fall* (1933), based on his lectures of the previous winter semester on the first three chapters of Genesis, he insists that in the Church it is "theological interpretation" that matters. Historical considerations cannot control the exegesis, since the One God here is speaking to His Church.

In all these statements, there is a full consistency in Bonhoeffer's understanding of the "objectivity" of God's revelation of Himself. With Barth, he agrees that God's Word is never bound to man's vision, and cannot be tested by human standards of what is counted to be objectively given. Only faith *knows*. Yet he goes beyond Barth in believing that Christ "is" in the Church, and so he finds that the Holy Spirit speaks directly to us in the Church through the words of the Bible. Lecturing on "The Church Is Dead" in 1932 at the Conference at Gland, Switzerland, he said, ". . . Has it not become terrifyingly clear again and again . . . that we are no longer obedient to the Bible? We are more fond of our own thoughts than of the thoughts of the Bible. We no longer read the Bible seriously, we no longer read it against ourselves, but for ourselves" (*No Rusty Swords,* p. 185).

CHRIST AND THE CHURCH

Since Bonhoeffer puts the whole "concreteness" of the Gospel into the presence of the Risen Christ in His Church, our ability to know where the Church of Jesus Christ is becomes of central importance for our salvation—and the salvation of the world. Ruled out is the supposition that the Church as an institution can stand as the embodiment of Christ in the world, or that the world is to be brought to perfection under the guidance of the Church. In the lecture "The Church Is Dead" Bonhoeffer insists upon this truth.

> No visible city of God is erected in this world, it would not be even if there were international understanding everywhere; everything which the church does here is transitory, it is only intended to hold together the collapsing orders of the world, to preserve it from falling back into chaos. This action of the church is indispensable, but the new order, society, community is not the order of the kingdom. All orders and all communities of the world will have to perish when God creates his world anew and the Lord Christ comes again to judge the old world and build the new.[39]

In the same year as this lecture he wrote also "Thy Kingdom Come: The Prayer of the Church for God's Kingdom on Earth," in which he pointed out that Christians can cease to believe in God's Kingdom in two ways: by adopting an other-worldly stance, which places God's rule entirely in the hereafter, and by adopting a "pious secularism" by means of which we seek to build the Kingdom as an earthly Utopia. The prayer for the coming of the Kingdom upon earth cannot be prayed either by pious individualist or by fanatical utopianist.

> Rather, this prayer is prayed solely by the congregation of the children of the earth, who refuse to separate themselves from the world and who have no special proposals to offer for its improvement. . . . Here at the very center of this dying, disrupted, and desirous world something becomes evident to those who can believe—believe in the resurrection of Jesus Christ. Here the absolute miracle has occurred. . . . Here the kingdom of God itself comes to us on earth, comes to our world.[40]

We must notice how another element is now brought into the picture of Christ present in the Church. It is the element of Christ's presence in the believing Church publishing the news that God's Kingdom is already present in the world—Christ present as the first-fruits of the New Creation. This means that the "place" of the Church in the world remains no longer of first importance. Instead, the accent is laid upon the recognition by members of the Christian community of the witness to be made in the world to the "miracle" of God's act of redeeming His fallen creation. This seems to join together, in prospect, Bonhoeffer's early concern for the Church to understand itself as community, the concern of his "middle period" for costly Christian discipleship, and the final concern for "worldly" holiness.

[39] *No Rusty Swords,* p. 188.
[40] J. D. Godsey, *Preface to Bonhoeffer,* p. 36.

"Thy Kingdom Come" states that the Kingdom of God appears on earth in two forms, divided into Church and "the order we call the state." "The kingdom of God exists in our world exclusively in the duality of church and state. Each is necessarily related to the other; neither exists for itself. Every attempt of the one to take control of the other disregards this relationship of the kingdom of God on earth" (*ibid.,* p. 40). *Christ the Center* also speaks (p. 65) of Christ as being present to us in the double form of Church and state—the Church being the hidden center of the state. The discussion of "Thinking in Terms of Two Spheres" in the *Ethics,* with its strong condemnation of dualistic thinking of separated "spaces" comprising the Church and the world, might be imagined to show a shift in viewpoint. Yet, the *Ethics* simply underlines the earlier insistence upon the duality of forms under which the Kingdom "attests itself." Error enters into this way of thinking only where the "spaces" of world and Church are conceived statically and made to exclude each other, as though the "reality" of the world were outside the "reality" of Christ. Thus the *Ethics* asserts (p. 65),

> The unity of the reality of God and of the world, which has been accomplished in Christ, is repeated, or, more exactly, is realized, ever afresh in the life of men. And yet what is Christian is not identical with what is of the world. The natural is not identical with the supernatural or the revelational with the rational. But between the two spheres is in each case a unity which derives solely from the reality of Christ, that is to say from faith in this ultimate reality.

The conclusion is "that there is no real possibility of being a Christian outside the reality of the world and that there is no real worldly existence outside the reality of Jesus Christ" (p. 66).

Once again, we find a full continuity in Bonhoeffer's theology as he advances, spurred on by the personal experiences he had as a Christian and a churchman in the crises of the twentieth century, to find how the Christian faith must be lived *concretely,* here and now. The belief that God "is" for us in the community of the Church leads directly to the recognition that the Church as an institution cannot be walled around in order to contain the Living Christ there. Where the Church's faith was attacked by the forces of unfaith it was necessary to assert, "No salvation outside the Church!" But Bonhoeffer insisted that the Confessing Church was not then confessing against other church bodies in general— only "*in concretissimo* against the German Christian Church and against the neo-pagan divinization of the creature," where the will to destroy the Christian Church in Germany was at work (*No Rusty Swords,* pp. 337-338). A strategy of defense may be needful for us at a particular moment without our seeking thereby to limit God's work for His whole creation.

MAN AND THE WORLD

When Bonhoeffer speaks of "secular" life he usually is talking about our day-to-day involvement in the business of living—quite without any theory of the status of "the secular." While his references to "religionless Christianity" have been interpreted as an invitation to throw out the concept of the supernatural and to concentrate our energies on improving the present lot of mankind, there is absolutely no indication that he ever wavered in his declared belief that wishing to build "the secular city" is the way of faithlessness.[41] Nor can his proposal for a "non-religious" interpretation of biblical concepts be read as a desire to find the "secular meaning" of the Gospel by accommodating the Word of God to the horizons of a contemporary world view.[42] Although reading in prison Carl-Friedrich von Weizsäcker's book *The World View of Physics* influenced him to take up a positive attitude to the "world come of age," it is quite mistaken to imagine that he regarded "secularization" as having decidedly Christian roots, on the model (say) of Gogarten's theories. His own "world view" when he was in prison is expressed in the confession, "Never have we realized, as we do to-day, how the world lies under the wrath and grace of God. . . . If we can save our souls unscathed from the débris of civilization, let us be satisfied with that" ("Thoughts on the Baptism of D.W.R.," *Letters,* May, 1944, pp. 183-184).

The "world come of age" is reckoned by Bonhoeffer to be a hopeful beginning for "clearing the decks for the God of the Bible" because it means "an abandonment of a false conception of God" (July 16, 1944, p. 220). "Religion" has encouraged, first, a metaphysical notion of God, and next, a God called in to meet our needs in the "inner life"—a "God of the gaps," since science takes care of the external world and its needs. But, in Bonhoeffer's eyes, God has never been a metaphysical postulate for faith, and the idea of "inwardness" he connects with the Renaissance and not with the Bible. When Bonhoeffer speaks of a "worldly" interpretation of Christianity, he turns first of all to the Old Testament, a better understanding of which, he feels, helps us to rid ourselves of the view of Christianity as a religion of "salvation" in the style of pagan

---

[41] In the *Ethics* Bonhoeffer remarks (p. 87) how "Christian radicalism," in its world-improving quite as much as in its world-denying form, arises from "hatred of creation," and is an attempt to cast out devils through Beelzebub.

[42] "Meaning," says Bonhoeffer in the prison letters (August 21, 1944, p. 244) is only a translation of what the Bible means by "promise." This is in line with his continual insistence that reality is never encountered in abstract ideas but only in a concrete confrontation with the personal God.

salvation-cults.[43] God's allowing Himself to be "edged out of the world" allows us to stop pretending that He is available as, when, and where we may wish to make use of Him.

Bonhoeffer, then, has no intention of trimming the historic Christian faith to encourage "secular" man to declare it "relevant."[44] That would be as mistaken as has been the former accommodation of the Gospel to fit the mould of "religious" man. The "world" he wishes to bring to the forefront of the Christian's attention is the sphere of earthly existence into which Christ, the Word made flesh, has come. It is the sphere of the *penultimate* deriving its meaning from the *ultimate* of faith. It is the sphere Barth's "positivism of revelation" has left to one side, uncared for. So we exhibit little confidence in the Gospel so long as we wait for people to feel helpless and afraid and ready to turn to the offer of religious consolation in some "last secret place." A better way would be "that we should not speak ill of man in his worldliness, but confront him with God at his strongest point. . ." (July 8, 1944, p. 214).

The mission for Christians in the modern world is one Bonhoeffer feels he understands. How it is to be achieved is another matter, and this occasions all the unanswered questions that fill the prison letters. Is there still room for the Church (as an organization)? How do we interpret biblical terms for men with no religious background? What *is* Christianity, and indeed who *is* Christ for us today? (The last question does not mean Bonhoeffer doubts Christ's relevance for today, but it reflects his uncertainty about where today the "boundaries" between the Church and the world, the two spheres of Christ's presence, are to be drawn.) One thing he is certain of. In an age that has almost forgotten the language of traditional faith, the Christian speaks more clearly in deeds than in words. So he writes of the Church: "She must not underestimate the importance of human example, which has its origin in the humanity of Jesus, and which is so important in the teaching of St. Paul. It is not abstract argument, but concrete example which gives her word emphasis and power" ("Outline for a Book," *Letters,* p. 240).

Another thing he thinks he is certain of. "We are proceeding towards a time of no religion at all: men as they are now simply cannot be

---

[43] "I am thinking over the problem at present how we may reinterpret in the manner 'of the world'—in the sense of the Old Testament and of John 1.14—the concepts of repentance, faith, justification, rebirth, sanctification and so on" (May 5, 1944, p. 169). Earlier in the same letter (p. 167) he writes: "What do I mean by 'interpret in a religious sense'? In my view, that means to speak on the one hand metaphysically, and on the other individualistically. Neither of these is relevant to the Bible message or to the man of to-day."

[44] "The *relevant* is not where the present age announces its claim before Christ, but where the present age stands before the claims of Christ" ("Interpretation of the New Testament," *No Rusty Swords,* p. 311).

religious any more" (April 30, 1944, p. 162). Here, speaking with the wisdom of hindsight, we can say that he was quite mistaken. He did not reckon with the staying power of *homo religiosus,* religious man who is always thinking he has outgrown his ancestral religion—and always either turning back to it or else seeking some substitute. Today, more than twenty years after Bonhoeffer's death, the traditional churches are, though shaken, yet not "changed beyond recognition," as he forecast. "Religion" is a prestige subject at our universities. And increasing around us are religious creeds of all kinds, including various brands of New Christianity (many of them claiming Bonhoeffer as their inspiration), each busily turning Christian faith into a salvation-cult by confidently explaining "how" Christ rescues us from other-worldliness into secularity, from transcendence into immanence, from the service of Yesterday's God into the service of the God of the Future.

The major ambiguity present in Bonhoeffer's last phase of thought lies in his apparent implicit acceptance of a progressive view of history (a view he explicitly rejects) through his use of the term "man come of age."[45] Thus, while rightly condemning as futile an apologetic directed to calling back a past cultural situation, he seems to expect far too much from an apologetic directed to the present situation. On his own showing, changes in cultural patterns do not affect the continual evasion of the Word of God on the part of the *cor curvatum in se.*

If there is at present an opportunity, because of the decay of belief in a God who is merely a hypothesis, for a "clearing of the decks for the God of the Bible," there must be equally an empty house waiting for seven more dangerous man-made gods to take the place of the God-of-the-gaps-and-*deus-ex-machina* that has departed. There can be no possible correspondence between advance in human knowledge and maturity in Jesus Christ, so that present-day "religionless" man cannot be more open to an apologetic for faith than were his religious forefathers. Nor is this consideration chiefly one of an abstract analysis of the cultural world situation. It has important practical consequences for the life of the Church. If religionlessness is not absolute, then the Gospel has to be preached to men who are not only estranged from Christian piety but also vulnerable to neo-pagan superstition, not only strongly world-affirming but also despairingly world-weary. The institutional Church is required in the world, not because the Gospel is a religious message but precisely because it is the only power that can turn men away from man-made religion. Without the visible Church, the proclamation that God's Kingdom has been brought into the world by Jesus Christ, and

---

[45] Kornelis H. Miskotte says in his *When the Gods Are Silent* (New York: Harper and Row, 1967, p. 81) that Bonhoeffer left the concept of the world come of age "somewhat undefined and that in any case he very much overestimated it."

will come triumphantly when Christ comes again, will not be heard. Instead, men will fly to salvation-cults when they are fearful; or when they are confident they will deify their own schemes for raising Utopian Babel-towers, and sacrifice their brothers so that their will may be done on earth, even though the whole world must be laid waste in the process.

Bonhoeffer rightly condemned those who wish to be more "godly" than Christ, who did not scorn the human world, the manger in the stable and the cross of wood. He might also have gone on to doubt whether we can aspire to be more "religionless" than Christ, who, coming to supplant the teaching and the worship of synagogue and temple, nevertheless Himself taught and worshipped in synagogue and temple. Bonhoeffer was not granted time—or the freedom of testing his ideas in the community of believers—to bring his theological work to full fruition. The sweep of his thinking that presses on to seek the significance of the whole Christ for the whole world has so much to teach us, that we do his memory little service by stopping short with his tentative explorations. Our prayer now should be his: "May God in his mercy lead us through these times. But above all may he lead us to himself!" (July 21, 1944, p. 227).

IV. BIBLIOGRAPHY

Works by Bonhoeffer

Akt und Sein: Transzendentalphilosophie und Ontologie in der systematischen Theologie. Gütersloh, 1931. 2nd ed., Munich, 1956 (*Act and Being.* New York, 1961; London, 1962).

Christology. London, 1966. *Christ the Center.* New York, 1966 (Translated from *Gesämmelte Schriften,* Band III).

"Concerning the Christian Idea of God," *The Journal of Religion,* Vol. XII, No. 2 (April 1932), pp. 177-185.

Dein Reich, komme! Das Gebet der Gemeinde um Gottes Reich auf Erden. Berlin, 1933. Republished together with "Die erste Tafel: Eine Auslegung der ersten drei Gebote" (written in 1944), Hamburg, 1957 (Translated with an essay "Bonhoeffer the Man" by John D. Godsey, and a bibliography, under the title *Preface to Bonhoeffer.* Philadelphia, 1965).

Ethik. Munich, 1949 (*Ethics.* London and New York, 1955).

Das Gebetbuch der Bibel: Eine Einführung in die Psalmen. Salzuflen, 1940.

Gemeinsames Leben: Theologische Existenz heute. Munich, 1939. 8th ed., 1955 (*Life Together.* New York, 1954; London, 1955).

Gesämmelte Schriften, Bandes I-IV. Munich, 1958-61 (Selections arranged chronologically. *No Rusty Swords.* London and New York, 1965. *The Way to Freedom.* London and New York, 1966).

Nachfolge. Munich, 1937. 5th ed., 1955 (*The Cost of Discipleship.* London, 1948; New York, 1959).

Sanctorum Communio: Eine dogmatische Untersuchung zur Soziologie der Kirche. Berlin u. Frankfort/Oder, 1930. 2nd ed., Munich, 1955 (*Sanctorum Communio.* London, 1963. *The Communion of Saints.* New York, 1963).

Schöpfung und Fall: Theologische Auslegung von Genesis 1–3. Munich, 1933. 3rd ed., 1955 (*Creation and Fall.* London and New York, 1959).

Versuchung. Munich, 1953. 2nd ed., 1954 (*Temptation.* London and New York, 1955).

Widerstand und Ergebung: Briefe und Aufzeichnungen aus der Haft.
Munich, 1961. 6th expanded ed., 1955 (*Letters and Papers from
Prison.* London, 1953; *Prisoner for God.* New York, 1953; re-
published in 1962 with the title of the London ed.).

BIOGRAPHY

The definitive biography is Eberhard Bethge's *Dietrich Bonhoeffer:
Theologe—Christ—Zeitgenosse* (Munich, 1967). Useful short biographical sketches are included in several of the English-language translations
of his books; see especially: the "Memoir" by G. Leibholz in *The Cost
of Discipleship,* John D. Godsey's essay "Bonhoeffer the Man" in
Preface to Bonhoeffer, and the Foreword by Bethge in *Letters and
Papers from Prison.* While items in the *Gesämmelte Schriften* are
grouped according to subject matter, *No Rusty Swords* and *The Way to
Freedom* have arranged this material chronologically, providing notes
and tables of dates interspersed between the sections. Because Bonhoeffer's life is so intimately related to his thinking, most of the works
listed below contain biographical references. Ved Mehta's "Pastor
Bonhoeffer" is primarily biographical.

SELECTED WORKS ON BONHOEFFER

Bethge, Eberhard, *et al. Bonhoeffer in a World Come of Age.* Philadel-
phia, 1968.
Ebeling, Gerhard, "The 'Non-religious Interpretation of Biblical Con-
cepts' " and "Dietrich Bonhoeffer" in *Word and Faith.* Phila-
delphia, 1963.
Fuller, Reginald H., "The World Come of Age: A Second Look at
Bonhoeffer," pp. 133-163 in *Conflicting Images of Man,* edited
by William Nicholls. New York, 1966.
Gibbs, John, "Dietrich Bonhoeffer" in *The New Theologians: Bultmann,
Bonhoeffer, Tillich, Teilhard de Chardin,* by T. G. A. Baker *et al.*
London, 1964.
Godsey, John D. *The Theology of Dietrich Bonhoeffer.* London and New
York, 1960.
Gould, William Blair. *The Worldly Christian—Bonhoeffer on Disciple-
ship.* London, 1968.
Hamilton, Kenneth. *Revolt Against Heaven,* pt. 4, "A Voice Affirming
Heaven." Grand Rapids, 1965.
———. *What's New in Religion?* pt. 3: "About Bonhoeffer's 'Worldly'
Christianity." Grand Rapids, 1968.
Hamilton, William. *The New Essence of Christianity.* New York, 1961.
———. "Thursday's Child" and "Dietrich Bonhoeffer" in *Radical The-*

ology and the Death of God by Thomas J. J. Altizer and William Hamilton. Indianapolis, 1966.

Hordern, William E. *A Layman's Guide to Protestant Theology,* ch. 10, "Dietrich Bonhoeffer and Worldly Christianity." Rev. ed. New York, 1968.

Jenkins, Daniel. *Beyond Religion.* Philadelphia, 1962.

Jenkins, David. *Guide to the Debate About God,* ch. 7, "Bonhoeffer and the Mistake of Looking for Data About God." Philadelphia, 1966.

Macquarrie, John. *Twentieth-Century Religious Thought,* ch. 20, "A German Theologian (*D. Bonhoeffer*)." New York, 1963.

Marty, Martin E. (ed.). *The Place of Bonhoeffer: Problems and Possibilities in His Thought.* New York, 1962.

Mehta, Ved, "Pastor Bonhoeffer" in *The New Theologian.* New York, 1965.

Moltmann, Jürgen, and Jürgen Weissbach. *Two Studies in the Theology of Bonhoeffer.* New York, 1967.

Phillips, John A. *Christ for Us in the Theology of Dietrich Bonhoeffer.* London and New York, 1967 (London ed. entitled *The Form of Christ in the World*).

Porteous, Alvin C., "Dietrich Bonhoeffer: Worldliness as a Christian Stance" in *Prophetic Voices in Contemporary Theology.* Nashville, 1966.

Robertson, E. H. *Dietrich Bonhoeffer.* London and Richmond, Va., 1966.

Robinson, John A. T. *Honest To God.* Philadelphia, 1963.

Sherman, Franklin. "Dietrich Bonhoeffer" in *A Handbook of Christian Theologians,* ed. Dean G. Peerman and Martin E. Marty. Cleveland, 1965.

Smith, Ronald Gregor (ed.). *World Come of Age.* London and New York, 1966.

———. *Secular Christianity,* ch. 3, "Faith Not Religion." New York, 1966.

Zimmerman, Wolf-Dieter, and R. G. Smith (eds.). *I Knew Dietrich Bonhoeffer.* New York, 1966.

515

Index of Proper Names*

*Names of biblical persons are not included.

518